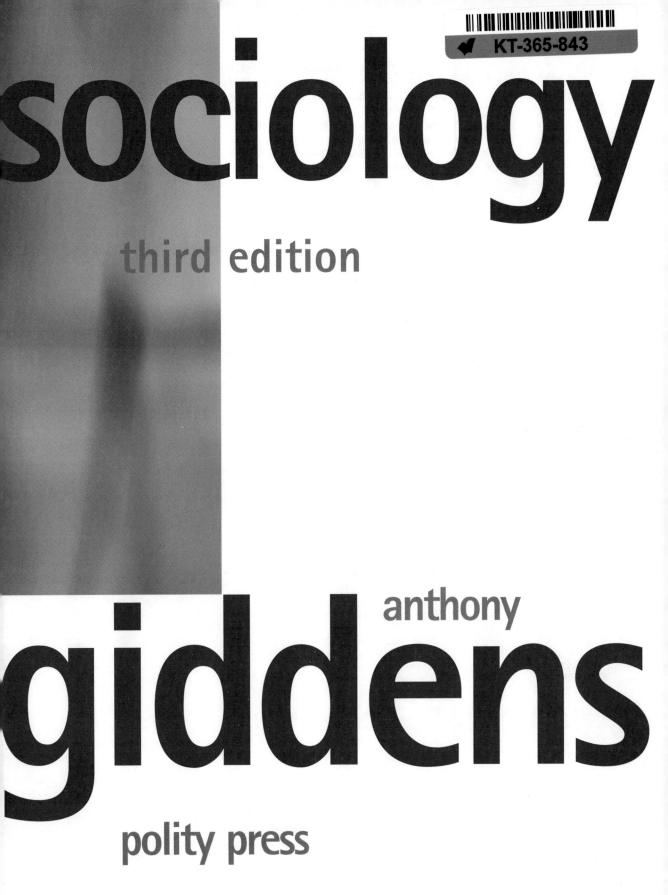

sociology

third edition

anthony

giddens

polity press

Copyright © Anthony Giddens, 1989, 1993, 1997
The right of Anthony Giddens to be identified as author of this work has been
asserted in accordance with the Copyright, Designs and Patents Act 1988.

First edition published 1989
Second edition published 1993
This edition published in 1997 by Polity Press
in association with Blackwell Publishers Ltd.
Reprinted 1998

Editorial office:
Polity Press
65 Bridge Street
Cambridge CB2 1UR, UK

Marketing and production:
Blackwell Publishers Ltd
108 Cowley Road
Oxford OX4 1JF, UK

ISBN 0–7456–1802–2
ISBN 0–7456–1803–0   (pbk)

A CIP catalogue record for this book is available from the British Library.

Desk editor: Sue Leigh
Production controller: Lin Lucas

Typeset in Palatino 10/12 pt
by Wearset, Boldon, Tyne and Wear
Printed in Great Britain by TJ International, Padstow, Cornwall

This book is printed on acid-free paper.

CONTENTS

PREFACE
TO THE THIRD EDITION

For this edition I have revised the text in a radical and thoroughgoing way. All the empirical data have been brought up to date. I have made use of the most recent research materials available, taken from a variety of sources: books and research journals, newspapers and periodicals as well as Internet search. Where necessary I have also revised the more theoretical sections so as to introduce students to the most pressing issues of the moment. By integrating these new materials with tried and tested parts of the text, I have aimed to produce a book that is a state-of-the-art introduction to sociology.

Among the changes made from the previous edition, there are completely new chapters dealing with the sociology of the body and with mass media and popular culture. The sociology of education now has a chapter of its own. Chapters which carry the same headings as in the previous edition have been extensively rewritten and in most cases reorganized. I have retained the strongly comparative outlook which I believe was a distinctive feature of previous editions.

I owe a great debt to the many readers of the book who have sent me suggestions for revision, or have drawn my attention to infelicities or errors. I also want to thank the following people in particular for the diverse forms of help they have given me. For their help with US materials, I owe a debt to Chris Allen, Mitch Duneier, Steve Dunn, Don Fusting, Susan Gaustad and Diane Wysocki. For the UK I want to thank the following individuals in particular: among academics, Ulrich Beck, Deirdre Boden, Claudius Gellert, Montserrat Guibernau, David Held, Michael MccGwire, John Thompson and Benno Werlen. Avril Symonds cheerfully and efficiently typed numerous drafts and redrafts of chapter sections. At Polity in Cambridge I owe thanks to Julia Harsant, Gill Motley, Sue Pope, Nicola Ross and Andy Winnard. At Blackwell in Oxford I am greatly indebted to Jane De Gay, Rebecca Harkin, Sue Leigh, Lin Lucas, Jane Rose and Pam Thomas. Don Hubert put much work into helping to prepare and edit the manuscript. Alena Ledeneva worked as my research assistant during the period of its final preparation. She provided invaluable suggestions for improving the book as a whole. Ann Bone copy-edited the book with great skill, insight and flair.

ABOUT THIS BOOK

This book was written in the belief that sociology has a key role to play in modern intellectual culture and a central place within the social sciences. After teaching at all levels of sociology for many years, I became convinced of the need to filter some of the discipline's current advances and developments into an elementary introduction to the field.

My aim has been to write a work that combines some originality with an analysis of all the basic issues of interest to sociologists today. The book does not try to introduce overly sophisticated notions; nevertheless, ideas and findings drawn from the cutting edge of the discipline are incorporated throughout. I hope it is not a partisan treatment; I endeavoured to cover the major perspectives in sociology in an even-handed, although not indiscriminate, way.

MAJOR THEMES

The book is constructed around a number of basic themes, each of which helps to give the work a distinctive character. One major theme is that of the *world in change*. Sociology was born of the transformations that wrenched the industrializing social order of the West away from the ways of life characteristic of preceding societies. The world that was created by these changes is the primary object of concern of sociological analysis. The pace of social change has continued to accelerate, and it is possible that we stand on the threshold of transitions as fundamental as those that occurred in the late eighteenth and nineteenth centuries. Sociology has prime responsibility for charting the transformations that have taken place in the past, and for grasping the major lines of development taking place today.

A second fundamental theme of the book is the *globalizing of social life*. For far too long, sociology has been dominated by the view that societies can be studied as independent unities. But, even in the past, societies have never really existed in isolation. In current times we can see a clear acceleration in processes of global integration. This is obvious, for example, in the expansion of international trade across the world. The emphasis on globalization in this book also connects closely with the weight given to the interdependence between First World and Third World today.

Third, the book takes a strongly *comparative* stance. Sociology cannot be taught solely by understanding the institutions of any one particular society. While I have of course slanted the discussion especially towards Britain, such discussion is always balanced by a rich variety of materials drawn from other societies or cultures. These include researches carried out in other Western countries, but I have also referred often to Russia and the East European societies, societies currently undergoing substantial changes. This book also includes more material on Third World countries than has been usual hitherto in introductions to sociology. In addition, I strongly emphasize the relationship between sociology and anthropology, whose concerns overlap comprehensively. Given the close connections that now mesh societies across the world with one another, and the virtual disappearance of many forms of traditional social system, sociology and anthropology increasingly become indistinguishable.

A fourth theme is the necessity of taking a *historical orientation* to sociology. This involves far more than just filling in the 'historical context' within which events occur. One of the most important developments in sociology over the past few years has been an increasing emphasis on historical analysis. This should not be understood solely as applying a sociological outlook to the past, but as a way of contributing to our understanding of institutions in the present. Recent work in historical sociology is used widely in the book, and provides a framework for the interpretations offered within most of the separate chapters.

Fifth, particular attention is given throughout the text to *issues of gender*. The study of gender is ordinarily regarded as a specific field within sociology as a whole – and this volume contains a chapter which explores thinking and research on the subject. However, questions about gender relations are so fundamental to sociological analysis that they cannot simply be relegated to a subdivision of the discipline.

A sixth theme is the relation between the *social* and the *personal*. Sociological thinking is a vital help to self-understanding, which in turn can be focused back on an improved understanding of the social world. Studying sociology should be a liberating experience: sociology enlarges our sympathies and imagination, opens up new perspectives on the sources of our own behaviour, and creates an awareness of cultural settings different from our own. In so far as sociological ideas challenge dogma, teach appreciation of cultural variety and allow us insight into the working of social institutions, the practice of sociology enhances the possibilities of human freedom.

ORGANIZATION OF THE BOOK

There is not much abstract discussion of basic sociological concepts at the beginning of this book. Instead, concepts are explained when they are introduced in the relevant chapters, and I have sought throughout to illustrate ideas, concepts and theories by means of concrete examples. While these are usually taken from sociological research, I have quite often used material from other sources (such as newspaper reports) for illustrative purposes. I have tried to keep the writing style as simple and direct as possible, while endeavouring to make the book lively and 'full of surprises'.

The chapters follow a sequence designed to help achieve a progressive mastery of the different fields of sociology, but I have taken care to ensure that the book can be used flexibly and is easy to adapt to the needs of individual courses. Chapters can be deleted, or studied in a different order, without much loss. Each chapter has been written as a fairly autonomous unit, with cross-referencing to other chapters at relevant points.

HOW TO MAKE USE OF THIS BOOK

BASIC CONCEPTS

● Each chapter opens with a box listing the BASIC CONCEPTS to be covered. These BASIC CONCEPTS are indicated in CAPITAL LETTERS where they first appear in the text. The BASIC CONCEPTS are the key concepts you need to grasp in each field covered.

➡ This symbol in the margin will signal where a BASIC CONCEPT first appears in the text. A glossary of all the BASIC CONCEPTS can be found at the end of the book.

IMPORTANT TERMS

● Each chapter ends with a box listing the **important terms** covered. **Important terms** are indicated in **bold letters** where they first appear in the text.

These **important terms** are less central than BASIC CONCEPTS, but are none the less worth trying to master.

A glossary of all the **important terms** can be found at the end of the book.

SUMMARY

1 Summary points can be found at the end of each chapter.

FURTHER READING

A list of books for further reading can also be found at the end of each chapter, and is indicated by

this symbol in the margin.

1

WHAT IS SOCIOLOGY?

> # BASIC CONCEPTS
>
> ● *sociology* ● *science*

W̶e live today – at the end of the twentieth century – in a world that is intensely worrying yet full of the most extraordinary promise for the future. It is a world awash with change, marked by deep conflicts, tensions and social divisions, as well as by the destructive onslaught of modern technology on the natural environment. Yet we have possibilities of controlling our destiny and shaping our lives for the better that would have been unimaginable to earlier generations.

How did this world come about? Why are our conditions of life so different from those of our parents and grandparents? What directions will change take in the future? These questions are the prime concern of sociology, a field of study that consequently has a fundamental role to play in modern intellectual culture.

SOCIOLOGY is the study of human social life, groups and societies. It is a dazzling and compelling enterprise, as its subject matter is our own behaviour as social beings. The scope of sociological study is extremely wide, ranging from the analysis of passing encounters between individuals in the street to the investigation of global social processes. A brief example will provide an initial taste of the nature and objectives of sociology.

THE SCOPE OF SOCIOLOGY: A FIRST EXAMPLE

Have you ever been in love? Almost certainly you have. Most people from their teens on know what being in love is like. Love and romance provide, for many of us, some of the most intense feelings we ever experience. Why do people fall in love? The answer at first sight seems obvious. Love expresses a mutual physical and personal attachment two individuals feel for one another. These days, we might be sceptical of the idea that love is 'for ever', but falling in love, we tend to think, is an experience arising from universal human emotions. It seems natural for a couple who fall in love to want personal and sexual fulfilment in their relationship, perhaps in the form of marriage.

Yet this situation, which seems so self-evident to us today, is in fact very unusual. Falling in love is *not* an experience most people across the world have – and where it does happen, it is rarely thought of as having any connection to marriage. The idea of romantic love did not become widespread until fairly recently in our society and has never even existed in most other cultures.

Only in modern times have love and sexuality come to be seen as closely connected. John Boswell, a historian of medieval Europe, has remarked on how unusual are our modern ideas about romantic love.

2

In Europe of the Middle Ages, virtually no one married for love. There was in fact a medieval saying: 'to love one's wife with one's emotions is adultery'. In those days and for centuries afterwards, men and women married mainly in order to keep property in the hands of family or to raise children to work the family farm. Once married, they may have become close companions; this happened after marriage, however, rather than before. People sometimes had sexual affairs outside marriage, but these inspired few of the emotions we associate with love. Romantic love was regarded as at best a weakness and at worst a kind of sickness.

Our attitudes today are almost completely opposite. Boswell quite rightly speaks of 'a virtual obsession of modern industrial culture' with romantic love:

> Those immersed in this 'sea of love' tend to take it for granted . . . Very few premodern or non-industrialized contemporary cultures would agree with the contention – uncontroversial in the West – that 'the purpose of a man is to love a woman, and the purpose of a woman is to love a man'. Most human beings in most times and places would find this a very meagre measure of human value! (Boswell 1995, p. xix)

Romantic love thus cannot be understood as merely a natural part of human life; rather, it has been shaped by broad social and historical influences. These are the influences sociologists study.

Most of us see the world in terms of the familiar features of our own lives. Sociology demonstrates the need to take a much broader view of why we are as we are, and why we act as we do. It teaches us that what we regard as natural, inevitable, good or true may not be such, and that the 'givens' of our life are strongly influenced by historical and social forces. Understanding the subtle yet complex and profound ways in which our individual lives reflect the contexts of our social experience is basic to the sociological outlook.

DEVELOPING A SOCIOLOGICAL OUTLOOK

Learning to think sociologically – looking, in other words, at the broader view – means cultivating the imagination. As sociologists, we need to imagine, for example, what the experience of sex and marriage is like for people – the majority of humankind until recently – to whom ideals of romantic love appear alien or even absurd. Studying sociology *cannot* be just a routine process of acquiring knowledge. A sociologist is someone who is able to break free from the immediacy of personal circumstances and put things in a wider context. Sociological work depends on what the American author C. Wright Mills, in a famous phrase, called **the sociological imagination** (Mills 1970).

The sociological imagination requires us, above all, to *'think ourselves away' from the familiar routines of our daily lives in order to look at them anew*. Consider the simple act of drinking a cup of coffee. What could we find to say, from a sociological point of view, about such an apparently uninteresting piece of behaviour? An enormous amount. We could point out first of all that coffee is not just a refreshment. It possesses *symbolic value* as part of our day-to-day social activities. Often the ritual associated with coffee drinking is much more important than the act of consuming the drink itself. Two people who arrange to meet for coffee are probably more interested in getting together and chatting than in what they actually drink. Drinking and eating in all societies, in fact, provide occasions for social interaction and the enactment of rituals – and these offer a rich subject matter for sociological study.

Second, coffee is a *drug*, containing caffeine, which has a stimulating effect on the brain. Coffee addicts are not regarded by most people in Western culture as drug users. Like alcohol, coffee is a socially acceptable drug, whereas marijuana, for instance, is not. Yet there are societies that tolerate the consumption of marijuana or even cocaine, but frown on both coffee and alcohol. Sociologists are interested in why these contrasts exist.

Third, an individual who drinks a cup of coffee is caught up in a complicated set of *social and economic relationships* stretching across the world. The production, transport and distribution of coffee require continuous transactions between people thousands of miles away from the coffee drinker. Studying such global transactions is an important task of sociology, since many aspects of our lives are now affected by worldwide social influences and communications.

Finally, the act of sipping a cup of coffee presumes a whole process of *past social and economic development*. Along with other now familiar

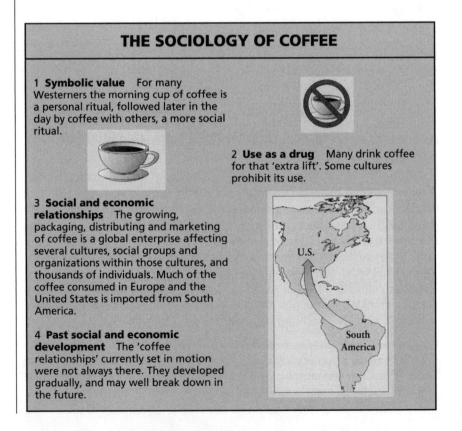

THE SOCIOLOGY OF COFFEE

1 Symbolic value   For many Westerners the morning cup of coffee is a personal ritual, followed later in the day by coffee with others, a more social ritual.

2 Use as a drug   Many drink coffee for that 'extra lift'. Some cultures prohibit its use.

3 Social and economic relationships   The growing, packaging, distributing and marketing of coffee is a global enterprise affecting several cultures, social groups and organizations within those cultures, and thousands of individuals. Much of the coffee consumed in Europe and the United States is imported from South America.

4 Past social and economic development   The 'coffee relationships' currently set in motion were not always there. They developed gradually, and may well break down in the future.

U.S.

South
America

items of Western diets – like tea, bananas, potatoes and white sugar – coffee became widely consumed only from the late 1800s. Although the drink originated in the Middle East, its mass consumption dates from the period of Western colonial expansion about a century and a half ago. Virtually all the coffee we drink in the Western countries today comes from areas (South America and Africa) that were colonized by Europeans; it is in no sense a 'natural' part of the Western diet.

Studying sociology

The sociological imagination allows us to see that many events that seem to concern only the individual actually reflect larger issues. Divorce, for instance, may be a very difficult process for someone who goes through it – what Mills calls a personal trouble. But divorce, he points out, is also a public issue in a society like present-day Britain, where over a third of all marriages break up within ten years. Unemployment, to take another example, may be a personal tragedy for someone thrown out of a job and unable to find another. Yet it goes far beyond a matter for private despair when millions of people in a society are in the same situation: it is a public issue expressing large social trends.

Try applying this sort of outlook to your own life. It isn't necessary to think only of troubling events. Consider, for instance, why you are turning the pages of this book at all – why you have decided to study sociology. You might be a reluctant sociology student, taking the course only to fulfil a degree requirement. Or you might be enthusiastic to find out more about the subject. Whatever your motivations, you are likely to have a good deal in common, without necessarily knowing it, with others studying sociology. Your private decision reflects your position in the wider society.

Do the following characteristics apply to you? Are you young? White? From a professional or white-collar background? Have you done, or do you still do, some part-time work to boost your income? Do you want to find a good job when you finish your education, but are you not especially dedicated to studying? Do you really not know what sociology is but think it has something to do with how people behave in groups? More than three-quarters of you will answer yes to all these questions. College students are not typical of the population as a whole but tend to be drawn from more privileged backgrounds. And their attitudes usually reflect those held by friends and acquaintances. The social backgrounds from which we come have a great deal to do with what kinds of decisions we think appropriate.

But suppose you answer no to one or more of these questions. You might come from a minority-group background or one of poverty. You may be someone in mid-life or older. All the same, however, further conclusions probably follow. You are likely to have had to struggle to get where you are; you might have had to overcome hostile reactions from friends and others when you told them you were intending to go to college; or you might be combining higher education with full-time parenthood.

Although we are all influenced by the social contexts in which we find ourselves, none of us are simply *determined* in our behaviour by those contexts. We possess, and create, our own individuality. It is the business of sociology to investigate the connections between *what society makes of us* and *what we make of ourselves*. Our activities both *structure* – give shape to – the social world around us and at the same time are structured *by* that social world.

The concept of *social structure* is an important one in sociology. It refers to the fact that the social contexts of our lives do not consist just of random assortments of events or actions; they are structured, or *patterned*, in distinct ways. There are regularities in the ways we behave and in the relationships we have with one another. But social structure is not like a physical structure, such as a building, which exists independently of human actions. It is reconstructed at every moment by the very 'building blocks' that compose it – human beings like you and me.

Intended and unintended consequences

This permanent process of the construction and reconstruction of social life is based on the meanings people attach to their actions. But our actions may bring about results different from those we desire. Sociologists draw an important distinction between the purposes of our behaviour – what we *intend* to bring about – and the **unintended consequences** of that behaviour. For instance, two parents might want to make their children conform to socially accepted ways of acting. To achieve their goal, the parents act in a strict and authoritarian way. The unintended consequences of their authoritarianism, however, might be to drive the children to rebel and break loose from orthodox standards of behaviour.

Sometimes actions undertaken with a particular aim in view have consequences that actually *prevent* the achievement of that aim. Some years ago, laws were introduced in New York City compelling the owners of deteriorating buildings in low-income areas to renovate them up to a minimum standard. The intention was to improve the basic level of housing available to poorer sections of the community. The result was that owners of run-down buildings abandoned them altogether or put them to other uses, so that there was a greater shortage of satisfactory accommodation than before.

What we do in our lives and the ways in which our actions affect others must be understood in terms of a mix of intended and unintended consequences. It is sociology's task to study the resulting balance between **social reproduction** and **social transformation**. Social reproduction refers to how societies 'keep going' over time; social transformation to the changes they undergo. Social reproduction occurs because there is continuity in what people do from day to day and year to year and in the social practices they follow. Changes occur partly because people intend them to occur, and partly because of consequences that no one either foresees or intends.

EARLY ORIGINS

We human beings have always been curious about the sources of our own behaviour, but for thousands of years our attempts to understand ourselves relied on ways of thinking passed down from generation to generation, often expressed in religious terms. (For example, before the rise of modern science, many people believed that natural events such as earthquakes were caused by gods or spirits.) The objective and systematic study of human behaviour and society is a relatively recent development, whose beginnings date from the early 1800s. The background to the origins of sociology was the series of sweeping changes ushered in by the French Revolution of 1789 and the emergence of the Industrial Revolution in Europe. The shattering of traditional ways of life wrought by these changes resulted in the attempts of thinkers to develop a new understanding of both the social and natural worlds.

A key development was the use of science instead of religion to understand the world. The types of questions these nineteenth-century thinkers sought to answer – what is human nature? why is society structured like it is? how and why do societies change? – are the same questions sociologists try to answer today. Our modern world is radically different from that of the past; it is sociology's task to help us understand this world and what the future is likely to hold.

Auguste Comte

No single individual, of course, can found a whole field of study, and there were many contributors to early sociological thinking. Particular prominence, however, is usually given to the French author Auguste Comte (1798–1857), if only because he actually invented the word 'sociology'. Comte originally used the term 'social physics', but some of his intellectual rivals at the time were also making use of that term.

Auguste Comte,
1798–1857

7

Comte wanted to distinguish his own views from theirs, so he coined the term 'sociology' to describe the subject he wished to establish.

Comte believed that this new field could produce knowledge of society based on scientific evidence. He regarded sociology as the last science to develop – following on from physics, chemistry and biology – but as the most significant and complex of all the sciences. Sociology, he argued, should contribute to the welfare of humanity by using science to understand and therefore to predict and control human behaviour. In the later part of his career, Comte drew up ambitious plans for the reconstruction of French society in particular and for human societies in general, based on his sociological viewpoint.

Émile Durkheim

The writings of another French writer, Émile Durkheim (1858–1917), have had a more lasting impact on modern sociology than those of Comte. Although he drew on aspects of Comte's work, Durkheim thought that many of his predecessor's ideas were too speculative and vague and that Comte had not successfully carried out his programme – to establish sociology on a scientific basis. To become scientific, according to Durkheim, sociology must study social facts, aspects of social life that shape our actions as individuals, such as the state of the economy or the influence of religion. Durkheim believed that we must study social life with the same objectivity as scientists study the natural world. His famous first principle of sociology was 'Study social facts as *things*!' By this he meant that social life can be analysed as rigorously as objects or events in nature.

Émile Durkheim, 1858–1917

Like the other major founders of sociology, Durkheim was preoccupied with the changes transforming society in his own lifetime. He believed that what holds society together is shared values and customs. His analysis of social change was based on the development of the *division of labour* (the growth of complex distinctions between different occupations). Durkheim argued that the division of labour gradually replaced religion as the basis of social cohesion. As the division of labour expands, people become more and more dependent on one another, because each person needs goods and services that those in other occupations supply. According to Durkheim, processes of change in the modern world are so rapid and intense that they give rise to major social difficulties, which he linked to **anomie**, a feeling of aimlessness or despair provoked by modern social life. Traditional moral controls and standards, which used to be supplied by religion, are largely broken down by modern social development, and this leaves many individuals in modern societies feeling that their daily lives lack meaning.

One of Durkheim's most famous studies was concerned with the analysis of suicide (Durkheim 1952; originally published in 1897). Suicide seems to be a purely personal act, the outcome of extreme personal unhappiness. Durkheim showed, however, that social factors exert a fundamental influence on suicidal behaviour – anomie being one of these influences. Suicide rates show regular patterns from year to year and these patterns must be explained sociologically. Many objections can be raised to Durkheim's study, but it remains a classic work whose relevance to sociology is by no means exhausted today.

Karl Marx

The ideas of Karl Marx (1818–83) contrast sharply with those of Comte and Durkheim, but like them, he sought to explain the changes in society that took place at the time of the Industrial Revolution. As a young man, Marx's political activities brought him into conflict with the German authorities; after a brief stay in France, he settled permanently in exile in Britain. His writings covered a diversity of areas. Even his sternest critics regard his work as important for the development of sociology. Much of his writing concentrated on economic issues, but

Karl Marx,
1818–1883

since he was always concerned to connect economic problems to social institutions, his work was, and is, rich in sociological insights.

Marx's viewpoint was founded on what he called the **materialist conception of history**. According to this view, it is not (as Durkheim claimed) the ideas or values human beings hold that are the main sources of social change. Rather, social change is prompted primarily by economic influences. Conflicts between classes – the rich versus the poor – provide the motivation for historical development. In Marx's words, 'All human history thus far is the history of class struggles.'

Though he wrote about various phases of history, Marx concentrated on change in modern times. For him, the most important changes were bound up with the development of **capitalism**. Capitalism is a system of production that contrasts radically with previous economic systems in history, involving as it does the production of goods and services sold to a wide range of consumers. Those who own capital – factories, machines and large sums of money – form a ruling class. The mass of the population make up a class of wage workers, or a working class, who do not own the means of their livelihood but must find employment provided by the owners of capital. Capitalism is thus a class system, in which conflict between classes is a commonplace occurrence.

According to Marx, capitalism will in the future be supplanted by a society in which there are no classes – no large-scale divisions between rich and poor. He didn't mean by this that all inequalities between individuals will disappear. Rather, societies will no longer be split into a small class that monopolizes economic and political power and the large mass of people who benefit little from the wealth their work creates. The economic system will come under communal ownership and a more equal society than we know at present will be established.

Marx's work has had a far-reaching effect on the twentieth-century world. Until recently, before the fall of Soviet communism, more than a third of the earth's population lived in societies whose governments claimed to derive their inspiration from Marx's ideas. In addition, many sociologists have been influenced by Marx's ideas about classes and class divisions.

Max Weber

Like Marx, Max Weber (pronounced 'Vaber', 1864–1920) cannot simply be labelled a sociologist; his interests and concerns ranged across many areas. Born in Germany, where he spent most of his academic career, Weber was an individual of wide learning. His writings covered the fields of economics, law, philosophy and comparative history as well as sociology, and much of his work was also concerned with the development of modern capitalism. Like other thinkers of his time, Weber sought to understand social change. He was influenced by Marx but was also strongly critical of some of Marx's major views. He rejected the materialist conception of history and saw class conflict as less significant than did Marx. In Weber's view, economic factors are important, but ideas and values have just as much impact on social change.

Max Weber,
1864–1920

Some of Weber's most influential writings were concerned with analysing the distinctiveness of Western society as compared with other major civilizations. He studied the religions of China, India and the Near East, and in the course of these researches made major contributions to the sociology of religion. Comparing the leading religious systems in China and India with those of the West, Weber concluded that certain aspects of Christian beliefs strongly influenced the rise of capitalism. This outlook did not emerge, as Marx supposed, only from economic changes. In Weber's view, cultural ideas and values help shape society and shape our individual actions.

Weber's understanding of the nature of modern societies and the reasons for the spread of Western ways of life across the world also contrasts substantially with that of Marx. According to Weber, capitalism – a distinct way of organizing economic enterprise – is one among many major factors shaping social development. Underlying capitalism, and in some ways more fundamental, is the impact of science and bureaucracy. Science has shaped modern technology and will continue to do so in any future society. Bureaucracy is the only way of organizing large numbers of people effectively, and therefore inevitably expands with economic and political growth. The development of science, modern technology, and bureaucracy was described by Weber collectively as rationalization – the organization of social and economic life according to principles of efficiency and on the basis of technical knowledge.

LATER THINKERS

Michel Foucault and Jürgen Habermas

Among the most prominent sociological thinkers of more recent times must be listed the French author Michel Foucault (1926–84) and the German writer Jürgen Habermas (b. 1929). Like the classical founders of sociology, neither was simply a sociologist; each has written widely also in philosophy and history.

Foucault was by common agreement one of the most brilliant figures in twentieth-century social thought. His works concern a subject matter similar to that analysed by Weber in his studies of bureaucracy: the development of prisons, hospitals, schools and other large-scale organizations. Foucault's later research on sexuality and the self has also been very influential, particularly in the work of feminist authors. According to Foucault, 'sexuality' (as we noted earlier of romantic love) has not always existed but has been created by processes of social development. In modern society, sexuality becomes something we 'have' – a property of the self.

The study of power – how individuals and groups achieve their ends as against those of others – is of fundamental importance in sociology. Marx and Weber, among the classical founders, laid particular emphasis on power; Foucault continued some of the lines of thought they pioneered. For instance, sexuality, as he saw it, is always bound up with social power. And he challenged the idea that acquiring knowledge leads to increasing freedom. He saw knowledge instead as a means of 'keeping tabs' on people and controlling them.

Habermas is perhaps the leading sociological thinker in the world today. He has been influenced by Marx and Weber in particular, but has drawn on other traditions of thought besides. According to Habermas, capitalist societies, in which change is ever present, tend to destroy the moral order on which they in fact depend. We live in a social order where economic growth tends to take precedence over all else – but this situation creates a lack of meaning in everyday life. Here Habermas comes back to Durkheim's concept of anomie, although he applies it in a new and original way.

IS SOCIOLOGY A SCIENCE?

Durkheim, Marx and the other founders of sociology thought of it as a SCIENCE. But can we really study human social life in a scientific way? To answer this question, we must understand what the word means. What is science?

Science is the use of *systematic methods of empirical investigation, the analysis of data, theoretical thinking and the logical assessment of arguments* to develop a body of knowledge about a particular subject matter. According to this definition, sociology is a scientific endeavour. It involves systematic methods of empirical investigation, the analysis of data and the assessment of theories in the light of evidence and logical argument.

Studying human beings, however, is different from observing events in the physical world, and sociology shouldn't be seen as like a natural science in a direct way. Unlike objects in nature, humans are self-aware beings who confer sense and purpose on what they do. We can't even describe social life accurately unless we first grasp the concepts that people apply in their behaviour. For instance, to describe a death as a suicide means knowing what the person in question was intending at the time. Suicide can occur only when an individual has self-destruction actively in mind. Someone who accidentally steps in front of a car and is killed cannot be said to have committed suicide.

The fact that we cannot study human beings in exactly the same way as objects in nature is in some ways an advantage to sociology. Sociological researchers profit from being able to pose questions directly to those they study – other human beings. In other respects, sociology creates difficulties not encountered by natural scientists. People who are aware that their activities are being scrutinized frequently will not behave in the same way as they do normally. They may consciously or unconsciously portray themselves in a way that differs from their usual attitudes. They may even try to 'assist' the researcher by giving the responses they believe are wanted.

HOW CAN SOCIOLOGY HELP US IN OUR LIVES?

Sociology has many practical implications for our lives, as Mills emphasized when developing his idea of the sociological imagination.

Awareness of cultural differences

First, sociology allows us to see the social world from many perspectives. Quite often, if we properly understand how others live, we also acquire a better understanding of what their problems are. Practical policies that are not based on an informed awareness of the ways of life of people they affect have little chance of success. Thus, a white social worker operating in a predominantly black community won't gain the confidence of its members without developing a sensitivity to the differences in social experience that often separate white and black.

Assessing the effects of policies

Second, sociological research provides practical help in *assessing the results of policy initiatives*. A programme of practical reform may simply fail to achieve what its designers sought, or may produce unintended consequences of an unfortunate kind. For instance, in the years following World War Two, large public housing blocks were built in city centres in many countries. These were planned to provide high standards of accommodation for low-income groups from slum areas, and offered shopping amenities and other civic services close at hand. However, research showed that many people who had moved from their previous dwellings to large tower blocks felt isolated and unhappy. High-rise blocks and shopping centres in poorer areas often became dilapidated and provided breeding grounds for mugging and other violent crimes.

Self-enlightenment

Third, and in some ways most important, sociology can provide us with **self-enlightenment** – increased self-understanding. The more we know about why we act as we do, and about the overall workings of our society, the more likely we are to be able to influence our own futures. We should not see sociology as assisting only policy-makers – that is, powerful groups – to make informed decisions. Those in power cannot be assumed always to consider the interests of the less powerful or underprivileged in the policies they pursue. Self-enlightened groups can often benefit from sociological research and respond in an effective way to government policies or form policy initiatives of their own. Self-help groups such as Alcoholics Anonymous and social movements such as the environmental movement are examples of social groups that have directly sought to bring about practical reforms, with considerable success.

The sociologist's role in society

Finally, many sociologists concern themselves directly with practical matters as professionals. People trained in sociology are to be found as industrial consultants, urban planners, social workers and personnel managers, as well as in many other practical jobs.

Should sociologists themselves actively advocate, and agitate for, programmes of reform or social change? Some argue that sociology can preserve its intellectual independence only if sociologists are studiously neutral in moral and political controversies. Yet there is often a connection between studying sociology and the prompting of social conscience. No sociologically sophisticated person can be unaware of the inequalities that exist in the world today, the lack of social justice in many social situations and the deprivations suffered by millions of people. It would be strange if sociologists did not take sides on practical issues, and it would be illogical to try to ban them from drawing on their expertise in so doing.

CONCLUSION

In this chapter, we have seen that sociology is a discipline in which we set aside our personal view of the world to look more carefully at the influences that shape our lives and those of others. Sociology emerged as a distinct intellectual endeavour with the development of modern societies, and the study of such societies remains its principal concern. But sociologists are also preoccupied with a broad range of issues about the nature of social interaction and human societies in general.

Sociology isn't just an abstract intellectual field but has major practical implications for people's lives. Learning to become a sociologist shouldn't be a dull academic endeavour! The best way to make sure it doesn't become so is to approach the subject in an imaginative way and to relate sociological ideas and findings to situations in your own life.

One way to do this is to become aware of differences between ways of life we in modern societies take to be normal and those of other human groups. All human beings share a lot in common. Equally, there are many variations between different societies and cultures. We look at these similarities and differences in Chapters 2 and 3.

SUMMARY

1 Sociology can be identified as the systematic study of human societies, giving special emphasis to modern, industrialized systems.

2 Sociology came into being as an attempt to understand the far-reaching changes that have occurred in human societies over the past two or three centuries. The changes involved are not just large-scale ones. Major shifts have also occurred in the most intimate and personal characteristics of people's lives. The development of a stress on romantic love as a basis for marriage is an example of this.

3 In sociological research it is important to distinguish between intended and unintended results of human action.

4 The practice of sociology involves the ability to think imaginatively and to detach oneself from preconceived ideas about social life.

5 Among the classical founders of sociology, four figures are particularly important: Auguste Comte, Karl Marx, Émile Durkheim and Max Weber. Comte and Marx, working in the mid-nineteenth century, established some of the basic issues of sociology, later elaborated on by Durkheim and Weber. These issues concern the nature of sociology and the impact of the development of modern societies on the social world.

6 Michel Foucault and Jürgen Habermas are among the more important sociological thinkers of the present day. Their work further develops themes set out by the classical founders.

7 According to its founders, sociology is a science in the sense that it involves systematic methods of investigation and the evaluation of theories in the light of evidence and logical argument. But it cannot be modelled directly on the natural sciences, because studying human behaviour is in fundamental ways different from studying the world of nature.

8 Sociology is a subject with important practical implications. It can contribute to social criticism and practical social reform in several ways. First, the improved understanding of a given set of social circumstances often gives us all a better chance of controlling them. Second, sociology provides the means of increasing our cultural sensitivities, allowing policies to be based on an awareness of divergent cultural values. Third, we can investigate the consequences (intended and unintended) of the adoption of particular policy programmes. Finally, and perhaps most important, sociology provides self-enlightenment, offering groups and individuals an increased opportunity to alter the conditions of their own lives.

IMPORTANT TERMS

- *the sociological imagination*
- *unintended consequences*
- *social reproduction*
- *social transformation*
- *anomie*
- *materialist conception of history*
- *capitalism*
- *self-enlightenment*

2

CULTURE, SOCIETY AND THE INDIVIDUAL

The concepts of CULTURE and SOCIETY, which we will explore in this chapter, are among the most widely used notions in sociology. When we use the word 'culture' in ordinary daily conversation, we often think of it as equivalent to the 'higher things of the mind' – art, literature, music and painting. As sociologists use the term, it includes such activities, but also far more. Culture refers to the ways of life of the members of a society, or of groups within a society. It includes how they dress, their marriage customs and family life, their patterns of work, religious ceremonies and leisure pursuits.

'Culture' can be conceptually distinguished from 'society', but there are very close connections between these notions. A society is a *system of interrelationships* which connects individuals together. Britain, France and the United States are societies in this sense. They include millions of people; as we shall see in the next chapter, some societies are very much smaller.

No cultures could exist without societies. But, equally, no societies could exist without culture. Without culture, we would not be 'human' at all, in the sense in which we usually understand that term. We would have no language in which to express ourselves, no sense of self-consciousness, and our ability to think or reason would be severely limited. How far do characteristics like these distinguish human beings from the animals? Where do our distinctively 'human' characteristics come from? What is the nature of human nature? These questions are crucial to sociology, because they set the foundation for the whole field of study. To answer them, we shall analyse both what as human beings we share and how we differ.

THE HUMAN SPECIES

Charles Darwin, an ordained minister of the Church of England, published his book *On the Origin of Species* in 1859, after two journeys around the world on HMS *Beagle*. Painstakingly amassing observations of the different animal species, Darwin set out a view of the development of human beings and animals quite different from any previously held. While in earlier times it was not uncommon for people to believe in beings that are half beast, half human, with Darwin's findings such possibilities were swept away. Darwin claimed to find a continuity of development from animals to human beings. Our characteristics as humans, according to him, have emerged from a process of biological change which can be traced back to the origins of life on earth, more than three billion years ago. Darwin's view of humans and animals was for many even harder to accept than that of half-beast, half-human creatures. He set in motion one of the most debated, yet persuasive, theories in modern science – the theory of **evolution**.

Evolution

According to Darwin, the development of the human species has come about as a result of a *random* process. In many religions, including Christianity, animals and human beings are seen as created by divine intervention. Evolutionary theory, by contrast, regards the development of the animal and human species as devoid of purpose. Evolution is a result of what Darwin called **natural selection**. The idea of natural selection is simple. All organic beings need food and other resources, such as protection from climatic extremes, in order to survive; but not enough resources exist to support all the types of animal that exist at any given time, because they produce far more offspring than the environment can provide food for. Those best adapted to their environment survive, while others, less well able to cope with its demands, perish. Some animals are more intelligent, move faster or have keener eyesight than others. In the struggle for survival, they have advantages over those less well endowed. They live longer, and are able to breed, passing on their characteristics to subsequent generations. They are 'selected' to survive and reproduce.

There is a continuous process of natural selection because of the biological mechanism of **mutation**. A mutation is a random genetic change which alters the biological characteristics of some individuals in a species. Most mutations are either harmful or useless in terms of survival value, but some give an animal a competitive advantage over others: individuals possessing the mutant genes will then tend to survive at the expense of those without them. This process explains both minor changes within species and major changes leading to the disappearance of entire species. For example, many millions of years ago giant reptiles flourished in various regions of the world. Their size became a handicap as mutations occurring in other, smaller species gave them superior adaptive capabilities. The early ancestors of humans were among these more adaptable species.

Although the theory of evolution has been refined since Darwin's day, the essentials of Darwin's account are still widely accepted. Evolutionary theory allows us to piece together a clear understanding of the emergence of different species and their relation to one another.

Human beings and the apes

The evolution of life, it is now generally agreed, began in the oceans. About four hundred million years ago, the first land-based creatures emerged. Some of these gradually evolved into the large reptiles, who were later displaced by mammals. Mammals are warm-blooded creatures who reproduce through sexual intercourse. Although the mammals were much smaller in bodily size than the giant reptiles, they were more intelligent and manoeuvrable. Mammals have a greater capacity to learn from experience than other animals, and this capacity has reached its highest development in the human species. Human beings are part of a group of higher mammals, the *primates*, which originated some seventy million years ago.

Our closest relatives among animal species are the chimpanzee, gorilla and orang-utan. On learning about Darwin's account of evolution, the wife of the Bishop of Worcester is said to have remarked: 'Descended from monkeys? My dear, let us hope that it is not true. But if it is true, let us hope that it does not become widely known.' Like many others since, she misunderstood what evolution involves. Human beings are not descended from the apes; humans and apes all trace their evolution from much more primitive groups of ancestor species living many millions of years ago.

Sociobiology

Although they recognized the evolutionary continuity between the animals and human beings, until recently most biologists tended to emphasize the distinctive qualities of the human species. This position has been challenged by the work of *sociobiologists*, who see close parallels between human behaviour and that of animals. The term **sociobiology** derives from the writings of the American Edward Wilson (Wilson 1975, 1978). It refers to the application of biological principles in explaining the social activities of all social animals, including human beings. According to Wilson, many aspects of human social life are grounded in our genetic make-up. For instance, some species of animals have elaborate courtship rituals, whereby sexual union and reproduction are achieved. Human courtship and sexual behaviour, according to sociobiologists, generally involve similar rituals, based also on inborn characteristics. In most animal species, to take a second example, males are larger and more aggressive than females, and tend

'Evolution's been good to you, Sid.'
Drawing by Lorenz; © 1980 *The New Yorker Magazine, Inc.*

to dominate the 'weaker sex'. Perhaps genetic factors explain why, in all human societies we know of, men tend to hold positions of greater authority than women.

One way in which sociobiologists have tried to illuminate the relations between the sexes is by means of the idea of 'reproductive strategy'. A reproductive strategy is a pattern of behaviour, arrived at through evolutionary selection, which favours the chances of survival of offspring. The female body has a very large investment in its reproductive cells compared to the male. Thus women will not squander that investment, and are not driven to have sexual relations with many partners; their overriding aim is the care and protection of offspring. Men, on the other hand, tend towards promiscuity. Their wish to have sex with many partners is sound strategy from the point of view of the species; they fulfil their role, which is to maximize the possibility of impregnation, and move on. In this way, it has been suggested, we can explain differences in the sexual behaviour and attitudes of men and women and account for phenomena such as rape.

The major issues raised by such explanations have been extensively debated over recent years. They remain highly controversial. Scholars tend to fall into two camps, depending to some degree on their intellectual background. Authors sympathetic to the sociobiological viewpoint are mostly trained in biology rather than the social sciences, while the large majority of sociologists and anthropologists tend to be sceptical of sociobiology's claims. Probably they know rather little about the genetic foundations of human life, and biologists have similarly limited knowledge of sociological or anthropological research. Each side finds it difficult to understand fully the force of the arguments advanced by the other.

Some of the passions generated early on by Wilson's work have now abated, and it seems possible to produce a reasonably clear assessment of the issues involved. Sociobiology is important – but more for what it has shown about the life of the animals than for what it has demonstrated about human behaviour. Drawing on the studies of ethologists (biologists who carry out 'fieldwork' among animal groups rather than studying animals in artificial circumstances in zoos or laboratories), sociobiologists have shown that many animal species are more 'social' than was previously thought. Animal groups have a considerable influence over the behaviour of individual members of the species. On the other hand, little evidence has been found to demonstrate that genetic inheritance controls complex forms of human activity. The ideas of sociobiologists about human social life are thus at best no more than speculative. Many critics entirely reject the interpretation of human sexual behaviour given above. There is no way, they say, in which it could be proved. Moreover, not all men are promiscuous, and if we look at sexual behaviour in modern societies, where women are much freer to choose their sexual involvements than they used to be, on average they have as many affairs as men do. Even if the generalization were correct, there are many psychological, social and cultural factors which could account for it. For example, men hold most power in society; in seeking many partners they could be driven by the desire to exert that power and keep women under their overall control.

Instincts and biological needs

Most biologists and sociologists agree that human beings do not have any 'instincts'. Such a statement runs contrary not only to the hypotheses of sociobiology, but also to what most people believe. Aren't there many things we do 'instinctively'? If someone throws a punch, don't we instinctively blink or shy away? In fact, this is not an example of an instinct when the term **instinct** is used precisely. As understood in biology and sociology, an instinct is a *complex* pattern of behaviour that is genetically determined. The courtship rituals of many of the lower animals are instinctive in this sense. The stickleback (a small freshwater fish), for example, has an extremely complicated set of rituals which have to be followed by both male and female if mating is to occur (Tinbergen 1974). Each fish produces an elaborate array of movements, to which the other responds, creating an elaborate 'mating dance'. This is genetically patterned for the whole species. A spontaneous blinking of the eye, or movement away of the head, in the face of an anticipated blow is a *reflex act* rather than an instinct. It is a single, simple response, not an elaborate behaviour pattern. This is not regarded as 'instinctive' in the technical sense.

Human beings are born with a number of basic reflexes similar to the eye-blink reaction, and most of them seem to have some evolutionary survival value. Very young human infants, for example, will suck when presented with a nipple or a nipple-like object. A young child will throw up its arms, to catch at support, when suddenly losing its balance, and pull its hand back sharply if it touches a very hot surface. Each of these reactions is obviously useful in coping with the environment.

Human beings also have a number of biologically given *needs*. There is an organic basis to our needs for food, drink, sex and the maintenance of certain levels of body temperature. But the ways in which these needs are satisfied or coped with vary widely between – and within – different cultures.

For example, all cultures tend to have some kind of standardized courtship behaviour. While this is related to the universal nature of sexual needs, their expression in different cultures – even including the sexual act itself – varies enormously. A common position for the sexual act in Western culture involves the woman lying on her back, and the man on top of her. This position is seen as absurd by people in some other societies, who are more likely to have intercourse lying side by side, or with the woman on top of the man, or with the man facing the woman's back, or in other positions. The ways in which people seek to satisfy their sexual needs thus seem to be culturally learned, not genetically implanted.

Moreover, humans can override their biological needs in ways which appear to have no parallel among the animals. Religious mystics may fast for very long periods. Individuals may choose to remain celibate for some part or all of their adult lives. All animals, including human beings, have a drive towards self-preservation, but humans are unlike other animals in being able deliberately to go against that drive, risking their lives in mountaineering or other hazardous pursuits, and even committing suicide.

CULTURAL DIVERSITY

The diversity of human culture is remarkable. Acceptable forms of behaviour vary widely from culture to culture, often contrasting in a radical way with what people from Western societies consider 'normal'. For example, in the modern West we regard the deliberate killing of infants or young children as one of the worst of all crimes. Yet in traditional Chinese culture, female children were frequently strangled at birth, because they were regarded as a liability rather than an asset to the family.

In the West, we eat oysters, but we do not eat kittens or puppy dogs, both of which are regarded as delicacies in some parts of the world. Jews do not eat pork, while Hindus eat pork but avoid beef. Westerners regard kissing as a normal part of sexual behaviour, but in many other cultures the practice is either unknown or regarded as disgusting. All these different traits of behaviour are aspects of broad cultural differences which distinguish societies from one another.

Small societies (like the 'hunting and gathering' societies discussed in chapter 2) tend to be culturally uniform, but industrialized societies are themselves culturally diverse, involving numerous different **subcultures**. In modern cities, for example, many subcultural communities live side by side – West Indians, Pakistanis, Indians, Bangladeshis, Italians, Greeks and Chinese in some areas of central London today. All these may have their own territories and ways of life.

CULTURAL IDENTITY AND ETHNOCENTRISM

Every culture has its own unique patterns of behaviour, which seem alien to people from other cultural backgrounds. As an example, we can take the Nacirema, a group described in a celebrated research investigation by Horace Miner (1956). Miner concentrated his attention on the elaborate body rituals in which the Nacirema engage, rituals which have strange and exotic characteristics. His discussion is worth quoting at length:

> The fundamental belief underlying the whole system appears to be that the human body is ugly and that its natural tendency is to debility and disease. Incarcerated in such a body, man's only hope is to avert these characteristics through the use of the powerful influences of ritual and ceremony. Every household has one or more shrines devoted to this purpose. . . . The focal point of the shrine is a box or chest which is built into the wall. In this chest are kept the many charms and magical potions without which no native believes he could live. These preparations are secured from a variety of specialized practitioners. The most powerful of these are the medicine men, whose assistance must be rewarded with substantial gifts. However, the medicine men do not provide the curative potions for their clients, but

decide what the ingredients should be and then write them down in an ancient and secret language. This writing is understood only by the medicine men and by the herbalists who, for another gift, provide the required charm . . .

The Nacirema have an almost pathological horror of and fascination with the mouth, the condition of which is believed to have a supernatural influence on all social relationships. Were it not for the rituals of the mouth, they believe that their teeth would fall out, their gums bleed, their jaws shrink, their friends desert them, and their lovers reject them. They also believe that a strong relationship exists between oral and moral characteristics. For example, there is a ritual ablution of the mouth for children which is supposed to improve their moral fibre.

The daily body ritual performed by everyone includes a mouth-rite. Despite the fact that these people are so punctilious about care of the mouth, this rite involves a practice which strikes the uninitiated stranger as revolting. It was reported to me that the ritual consists of inserting a small bundle of hog hairs into the mouth, along with certain magical powders, and then moving the bundle in a highly formalized series of gestures. (Miner 1956, pp. 503–4)

Who are the Nacirema, and in which part of the world do they live? You can answer these questions for yourself, as well as identify the nature of the body rituals described, simply by spelling 'Nacirema' backwards. Almost any familiar activity will seem strange if described out of context rather than being seen as part of the whole way of life of a people. Western cleanliness rituals are no more, or less, bizarre than the customs of some Pacific groups who knock out their front teeth to beautify themselves, or of certain South American tribal groups who place discs inside their lips to make them protrude, believing that this enhances their attractiveness.

We cannot understand these practices and beliefs separately from the wider cultures of which they are part. A culture has to be studied in terms of its own meanings and VALUES – a key presupposition of sociology. Sociologists endeavour as far as possible to avoid **ethnocentrism**, which is judging other cultures by comparison with one's own. Since human cultures vary so widely, it is not surprising that people coming from one culture frequently find it difficult to sympathize with the ideas or behaviour of those from a different one.

SOCIALIZATION

Animals low down on the evolutionary scale, such as most species of insects, are capable of fending for themselves very soon after they are born, with little or no help from adults. There are no generations among the lower animals, because the behaviour of the 'young' is more or less identical to that of 'adults'. As we go up the evolutionary scale, however, these observations apply less and less; the higher animals have to *learn* appropriate ways of behaviour. Among mammals, the young are quite often completely helpless at birth, and have to be cared for by their elders, and the human infant is the most helpless of all. A human child cannot survive unaided for at least the first four or five years of life.

SOCIALIZATION is the process whereby the helpless infant gradually becomes a self-aware, knowledgeable person, skilled in the ways of the culture into which she or he is born. Socialization is not a kind of 'cultural programming', in which the child absorbs passively the influences with which he or she comes into contact. Even the most recent new-born infant has needs or demands that affect the behaviour of those responsible for its care: the child is from the beginning an active being.

Socialization connects the different generations to one another. The birth of a child alters the lives of those who are responsible for its upbringing – and they themselves therefore undergo new learning experiences. Parenting usually ties the activities of adults to children for the remainder of the lives of both. Older people remain parents when they become grandparents, of course, thus forging another set of relationships connecting different generations with each other. Although the process of cultural learning is much more intense in infancy and early childhood than later, learning and adjustment go on throughout the whole life-cycle.

In the sections to follow, we shall continue the theme of 'nature' versus 'nurture'. We first analyse the development of the human individual from infancy to early childhood, identifying the main stages of change involved.

Unsocialized children

What would children be like if, somehow, they were raised without the influence of human adults? Obviously no humane person could bring up a child away from human influence as an experiment. There have been, however, a number of much-discussed cases of children who spent their early years away from normal human contact.

The 'wild boy of Aveyron'

On 9 January 1800 a strange creature emerged from the woods near the village of Saint-Serin in southern France. In spite of walking erect, he looked more animal than human, although he was soon identified as a boy of about eleven or twelve. He spoke only in shrill, strange-sounding cries. The boy apparently had no sense of personal hygiene, and relieved himself where and when he chose. He was brought to the attention of the local police and taken to a nearby orphanage. At first he constantly tried to escape, being recaptured only with some difficulty. He refused to wear clothes, tearing them off as soon as they were put on him. No parents ever came forward to claim him.

The child was subjected to a thorough medical examination, which turned up no abnormalities of a major kind. On being shown a mirror, he seems to have seen the image but not to have recognized himself. On one occasion he tried to reach through the mirror to seize a potato he saw in it. (The potato was in fact being held behind his head.) After several attempts, without turning his head, he took the potato by reaching back over his shoulder. A priest who observed the boy from day to day described the potato incident thus:

All these little details, and many others we could add, prove that this child is not totally without intelligence, reflection, and reasoning power. However, we are obliged to say that, in every case not concerned with his natural needs or satisfying his appetite, one can perceive in him only animal behaviour. If he has sensations, they give birth to no idea. He cannot even compare them with one another. One would think that there is no connection between his soul or mind and his body . . . (Shattuck 1980, p. 69; see also Lane 1976)

Later the boy was moved to Paris and a systematic attempt was made to change him 'from beast to human'. The endeavour was only partly successful. He was toilet-trained, accepted wearing clothes and learned to dress himself. Yet he was uninterested in toys or games, and was never able to master more than a few words. So far as we can tell, on the basis of detailed descriptions of his behaviour and reactions, this was not because he was mentally retarded. He seemed either unwilling or unable fully to master human speech. He made little further progress, and died in 1828, aged about forty.

Of course, we have to be cautious about interpreting cases of this sort. It is possible that a mental abnormality had remained undiagnosed. Alternatively, the experiences to which the child was subjected may have inflicted psychological damage that prevented him from mastering the skills most children acquire at a much earlier age. Yet there is sufficient similarity between this case history and others that have been recorded to suggest how limited our faculties would be in the absence of an extended period of early socialization.

Let us now look directly at the early phases of child development. In so doing, we will be able to understand in a more comprehensive way the processes by which the infant becomes recognizably 'human'.

THE EARLY DEVELOPMENT OF THE INFANT

Perceptual development

All human infants are born with the capacity to make certain perceptual distinctions and respond to them (Richards and Light 1986). It used to be thought that the new-born infant was swamped by a mass of sensations without any means of differentiating among them. In a famous observation, the psychologist and philosopher William James wrote: 'The baby, assailed by eyes, ears, nose, skin and entrails all at once, feels it all as one great blooming, buzzing confusion' (James 1890). This is no longer seen as an accurate portrayal by most students of infant behaviour – even new-born infants react selectively to their environment.

From the age of one week, a patterned surface (stripes, concentric circles or a face-like picture) is looked at more often than even a brightly coloured plain surface. Under the age of one month, these perceptual capacities are still weak, and images more than about a foot away are blurred. Thereafter, visual and auditory abilities increase rapidly. By the age of about four months a baby will keep in sight a person moving about the room. Sensitivity to touch and pleasure in warmth are present from birth.

Crying and smiling

Just as infants respond selectively to the environment, adults discriminate among the patterns of behaviour of the baby, assuming that these give clues to what she or he wants or needs. Crying is seen to indicate hunger or discomfort, smiling or certain other facial expressions to mean contentment. This very recognition treats these responses as social actions on the part of the infant. Cultural assumptions are deeply involved in this process, however. Crying is a good example. In many cultures, the baby is physically separate from the mother for most of the day, in a cot, pram or play area. Crying here tends to be a signal that the infant needs attention. In many other cultures, the new-born infant spends much of the day, for a period of many months, in direct contact with the mother's body, carried in a sling. Where this is the practice, a mother may pay attention only to extreme bouts of crying, which are treated as emergencies. Squirming movements of the infant are taken as the main signal that it needs food or some special treatment.

Cultural differences have also been demonstrated in the interpretation of smiling. All normal babies smile, in certain circumstances, after about a month or six weeks. An infant will smile if presented with a face-like shape simply containing two dots in place of eyes. It will also smile at a human face if the mouth is hidden just as readily as when it is not. Smiling seems to be an inborn response, not learned, or even triggered, by seeing another smiling face. One reason why we can be sure of this is that children born blind begin smiling at the same age as sighted children, although they have had no chance to copy others doing so. The situations in which smiling is regarded as appropriate, however, vary between cultures, and this is related to the early reactions adults give to the smiling response of infants. Infants do not have to learn to smile, but they have to learn when and where it is thought proper to do so. Thus the Chinese, for example, smile less often in 'public' settings than Westerners do – say, when greeting a stranger.

Infants and caretakers

An infant is able to distinguish its mother – or other prime caretaker – from other people by as early as three weeks of age. The baby still does not recognize the other individual as a *person*; rather, it responds to certain characteristics, probably the eyes, voice, and manner in which it is held. A mother knows she is recognized when the infant stops crying only when she (rather than anyone else) picks it up, smiles more at her than at other people, lifts the arms or claps to mark her appearance in the room, or, once the child is mobile, crawls to be close to her. Cultural differences influence which reactions tend to appear regularly. In a study of a Ugandan culture, Ainsworth found that embracing, hugging and kissing between mothers and infants was rare, while clapping hands to express pleasure, on the part of both mother and child, was much more common than is usual in European families (Ainsworth 1977).

The infant's attachment to its caretaker becomes firm only after about the first seven months of life. Before this time, separation from the mother will not produce any specific protest, and other people caring for the baby will be accepted without any change in the usual levels of responsiveness. At about the same age, children will start to smile only at some individuals rather than indiscriminately. It is also at this stage that an infant begins to get an understanding of the mother as a distinct person. The child recognizes that the mother exists even when she is absent from his or her immediate presence, and can hold some sort of image of her in mind. This also implies the beginning of the experience of time, because the child both has a memory of the mother and anticipates her return. Infants of eight or nine months are able to look for hidden objects, beginning to understand that objects have an independent existence regardless of whether or not they are in view at any particular moment.

Selma Fraiberg has illustrated this phase of the infant's behaviour in the course of a work designed to inform parents about children's growth.

> Have you a six- or seven-month-old baby who snatches the glasses off your nose? If you do, you hardly need this piece of advice. Remove the glasses when the baby reaches for them, slip them in a pocket or behind a sofa pillow (and don't forget where *you* hid them!). Don't trouble to be sneaky about it, let the baby see you hide them. He will not go in search of them. He will stare at the place he last saw them – on your nose – then lose interest in the problem. He does not search for the glasses because he cannot imagine that they have an existence when he does not see them.
>
> When the baby is around nine months old, don't rely on the old tricks. If he sees you remove your glasses and slip them behind a sofa pillow he will move the pillow and pounce on your glasses. He has learned that an object can be hidden from sight, yet can still exist! He can follow its movements in your hand to the place of hiding and actively search for it there. This is a tremendous step in learning and one that is unlikely to be overlooked by the parents whose glasses, earrings, pipes, fountain pens and key-cases are now not only lifted from their persons, but defy safekeeping. Parents who have babies in this stage of development are little interested in the theoretical aspects of the problem as posed here, but a theory can always bring some practical benefits. We still have some tricks up our sleeve. Let's try this: let the baby see you slip your glasses behind the pillow. Let him find them, persuade him to give them to you, then hide the glasses under a second pillow. Now he is confused. He will search for the glasses under the *first* pillow, in the first hiding place, but he will not search for them in the second hiding place. This means that the baby can conceive of the glasses having an existence when hidden, but only in one place, the first hiding place where his search had earlier been successful. When the baby does not find the glasses under the first pillow, he continues to search for them there, but it does not occur to him to search for them in the second hiding place or anywhere else. An object can still vanish. In a few weeks he will extend his search from the first hiding place to the second one and he is on his way to the discovery that an object can be moved from place to place and still have a permanent existence. (Fraiberg 1959, pp. 49–50)

The early months of a child's life are also a period of learning for the mother. Mothers, and other people who care for the child, like fathers or older children, learn to grasp the communications conveyed by the infant's behaviour and to respond to them appropriately. Some mothers are much more sensitive to these cues than others, and different cues tend to be emphasized, and reacted to, in varying cultural settings. The 'readings' mothers make of their children's behaviour strongly influence the pattern of interaction that develops between them. For instance, one mother might see a child's restlessness as indicating fatigue and put the infant to bed. Another might interpret the same behaviour as meaning that the child wants to be entertained. Mothers often project their own characteristics onto their babies, so one who finds it hard to maintain a stable caring relationship with her child might perceive the infant as aggressive and rejecting towards herself.

The forming of attachments to specific individuals marks a fundamental threshold in socialization. The primary relationship, usually between infant and mother, becomes one in which strong feelings are invested, and on its basis complex social learning processes start to occur.

The development of social responses

The relationship between child, mother and other people caring for the child alters around the end of the baby's first year of life. Not only does the child then begin to speak, but he or she is able to stand – most children are able to walk alone at about fourteen months. In their second and third years, children develop an increasing capacity to understand the interactions and emotions of other family members. The child learns how to comfort, as well as how to annoy, others. Children of two years old show distress if one parent gets angry with the other, and may hug one or the other if that person is visibly upset. A child of the same age is also able to tease a brother or sister, or a parent.

From about the age of one onwards, play starts to occupy much of the child's life. At first, a child will mainly play alone, but increasingly demands someone else to play with. Through play, children further improve their bodily coordination and start to expand their knowledge of the adult world. They try out new skills, and they imitate the behaviour of grown-ups.

In an early study, Mildred Parten set out some categories of the development of play which are still generally accepted today (Parten 1932). Young children first of all engage in *solitary independent play*. Even when in the company of other children, they play alone, making no reference to what the others are doing. This is followed by *parallel activity*, in which a child copies what the others are doing, but does not try to intervene in their activities. Subsequently (at age three or thereabouts), children engage more and more in *associative play*, in which they relate their own behaviour to that of others. Each child still acts as he or she wishes, but takes notice of and responds to what the others do. Later, at around age four, children take up *cooperative play* – activities which demand that each child collaborates with the other (as in playing at 'mummies and daddies').

Over the period from age one to four or five, the child is also learning discipline and self-regulation. One thing this means is learning to control bodily needs and deal with them appropriately. Children become toilet-trained (a difficult and extended process), and learn how to eat their food in a polite way. They also learn to 'behave themselves' in the various contexts of their activity, particularly when interacting with adults.

By about five, the child has become a fairly autonomous being, no longer just a baby, but almost independent in the elementary routines of life at home. He or she is ready to venture further into the outside world, able to spend long hours away from the parents without too much worry. The child is becoming more than ever an individual. One of the most distinctive features of human beings, compared to other animals, is that humans are *self-aware*. How should we understand the emergence of a sense of self – the awareness that the individual has a distinct identity, separate from others? During the first months of its life, the infant possesses little or no understanding of differences between human beings and material objects in its environment, and has no awareness of self. Children do not begin to use concepts like 'I', 'me' and 'you' until the age of two or after. Only gradually do they then come to understand that others have distinct identities, consciousness and needs separate from their own.

THEORIES OF CHILD DEVELOPMENT

The problem of the emergence of self is a much-debated one, and is viewed rather differently in contrasting theoretical perspectives. To some extent, this is because the most prominent theories about child development emphasize different aspects of socialization. The work of the great psychologist and founder of psychoanalysis Sigmund Freud concentrates above all on how the infant controls anxieties and on the emotional aspects of child development. The American philosopher and sociologist George Herbert Mead gives attention mainly to how children learn to use the concepts of 'I' and 'me'. The Swiss student of child behaviour Jean Piaget worked on many aspects of child development, but his most well-known writings concern **cognition** – the ways in which children learn to *think* about themselves and their environment.

Freud and psychoanalysis

Sigmund Freud, a Viennese physician who lived from 1856 to 1939, not only strongly influenced the formation of modern psychology, he was one of the major intellectual figures of the twentieth century. The impact of his ideas has been felt in art, literature and philosophy, as well as in the human social sciences. Freud was not simply an academic student of human behaviour, but concerned himself with the treatment of neurotic patients. **Psychoanalysis**, the technique of therapy he invented, involves getting patients to talk freely about their lives, particularly about what they can remember of their very early experiences. Freud came to the view that much of what governs our behaviour is in THE UNCONSCIOUS, and involves the persistence into adulthood of modes of coping with anxieties developed very early on in life. Most of these early childhood experiences are lost to our conscious memory, although they are the basis on which our SELF-CONSCIOUSNESS is established.

Personality development

According to Freud, the infant is a demanding being, with energy it cannot control because of its essential helplessness. A baby has to learn that its needs or desires cannot always be satisfied immediately – a painful process. In Freud's view, infants have needs not just for food and drink, but for erotic satisfaction. Freud did not mean that infants have sexual desires in the same way as older children or adults do. The 'erotic' refers to a general need for close and pleasurable bodily contact with others.

As Freud describes it, human psychological development is a process involving major tensions. The infant learns progressively to control his or her drives, but these remain as powerful motives in the unconscious. Freud distinguishes several typical stages in the development of the abilities of the infant and young child. He gives particular attention to the phase – at around age four to five – at which most children are able to relinquish the constant company of their parents and enter a wider social world. Freud calls this phase the _Oedipal_ stage. The early attachments which infants and young children form to their parents have a defined erotic element, in the sense noted above. If such attachments were allowed to continue and develop further, as a child matured physically she or he would become sexually involved with the parent of the opposite sex. This does not happen because children learn to repress erotic desires towards their parents.

Little boys learn that they cannot continue to be 'tied to their mother's apron strings'. According to Freud, the young boy experiences intense antagonism towards his father, because the father has sexual possession of the mother. This is the basis of the **Oedipus complex**. The Oedipus complex is overcome when the child represses both his erotic attachments to his mother and his antagonism towards his father (most of this happens on the unconscious level). This marks a major stage in the development of an autonomous self, because the child has detached himself from his early dependence on his parents, particularly his mother.

Freud's portrayal of female development is much less well worked out. He believes that something of a reverse process occurs to that found in boys. The little girl represses her erotic desires for the father and overcomes her unconscious rejection of her mother by striving to become like her – to become 'feminine'. In Freud's view, how children cope with the Oedipus complex strongly influences later relationships, especially sexual relationships, entered into by the individual.

Criticisms

Freud's theories have been widely criticized and have often met with very hostile responses. Some have rejected the idea that infants have erotic wishes, as well as the thesis that what happens in infancy and early childhood establishes unconscious modes of coping with anxiety that endure throughout life. Feminist critics have seen Freud's theory as directed too much towards male experience, giving too little attention to female psychology. Yet Freud's ideas continue to exert a powerful influence. Even if we do not accept them in their entirety, some of them are probably valid. There almost certainly are unconscious aspects to human behaviour, resting on modes of coping with anxiety established first of all in infancy.

The theory of G. H. Mead

The background and intellectual career of G. H. Mead (1863–1931) were in most respects quite different from those of Freud. Mead was primarily a philosopher, who spent most of his life teaching at the University of Chicago. He wrote rather little, and the publication for which he is best known, *Mind, Self and Society* (1934), was put together by his students on the basis of their lecture notes and other sources. Since they form the main basis of a general tradition of theoretical thinking, *symbolic interactionism*, Mead's ideas have had a very broad impact in sociology. (For further discussion of symbolic interactionism see chapter 21, 'Sociological theory'.) But Mead's work provides in addition an interpretation of the main phases of child development, giving particular attention to the emergence of a sense of self.

There are some interesting similarities between Mead's views and those of Freud, although Mead sees the human personality as less racked by tension. According to Mead, infants and young children develop as social beings first of all by imitating the actions of those around them. Play is one way this takes place. In their play, as has been noted above, small children often imitate what adults do. A small child will make mud pies, having seen an adult cooking, or dig with a spoon, having observed someone gardening. Children's play evolves from simple imitation to more complicated games in which a child of four or five will act out an adult role. Mead calls this *taking the role of the other* – learning what it is like to be in the shoes of another person. It is only at this stage that children acquire a developed sense of self. Children achieve an understanding of themselves as separate agents – as a 'me' – by seeing themselves through the eyes of others.

We achieve self-awareness, according to Mead, when we learn to distinguish the 'me' from the 'I'. The 'I' is the unsocialized infant, a bundle of spontaneous wants and desires. The 'me', as Mead uses the term, is the **social self**. Individuals develop *self-consciousness*, Mead argues, by coming to see themselves as others see them. Both Freud and Mead see the child becoming an autonomous agent, capable of self-understanding and able to operate outside the context of the immediate family, at about age five. For Freud, this is the outcome of the Oedipal phase, while for Mead it is the result of a developed capacity of self-awareness.

A further stage of child development, according to Mead, occurs when the child is about eight or nine. This is the age at which children tend to take part in organized games, rather than unsystematic 'play'. It is not until this period that children begin to understand the overall *values and morality* according to which social life is conducted. To learn organized games, one must understand the rules of play and notions of fairness and equal participation. The child at this stage learns to grasp what Mead terms the **generalized other** – the general values and moral rules involved in the culture in which he or she is developing. This is placed at a somewhat later age by Mead than by Freud, but once more there are clear similarities between their ideas on this point.

Mead's views are less controversial than those of Freud. They do not contain so many startling ideas, and they do not depend on the theory of an unconscious basis to personality. Mead's theory of the development of self-consciousness has deservedly been very influential. On the other hand, Mead's views were never published in a comprehensive form, and are useful as suggestive insights rather than as providing a general interpretation of child development.

Piaget: cognitive development

The influence of Jean Piaget's work has been not far short of that of Freud. Born in Switzerland in 1896, Piaget spent most of his life directing an institute of child development in Geneva. He published an extraordinary number of books and scientific papers, not just on child development, but on education, the history of thought, philosophy and logic. He continued his prodigious output right up to his death in 1980.

Although Freud gave so much importance to infancy, he never studied children directly. His theory was developed on the basis of observations made in the course of treating his adult patients in psychotherapy. Mead did not study children's behaviour either, working out his ideas in the context of philosophical discussion. Piaget, by contrast, spent most of his life observing the behaviour of infants, young children and adolescents. He based much of his work on the detailed observation of limited numbers of individuals, rather than studying large samples. None the less, he claimed his major findings to be valid for child development in all cultures.

The stages of cognitive development

Piaget placed great emphasis on the child's ability actively to make sense of the world. Children do not passively soak up information, but select and interpret what they see, hear and feel in the world around them. From his observations of children and the numerous experiments he conducted on their ways of thinking, he concluded that human beings go through several distinct stages of cognitive development – that is, learning to *think* about themselves and their environment. Each stage involves the acquisition of new skills and depends on the successful completion of the preceding one.

The first stage is the **sensorimotor**, which lasts from birth up to about age two. Until aged about four months, an infant cannot differentiate itself from the environment. For example, the child does not realize that its own movements cause the sides of its cot to rattle. Objects are not differentiated from persons, and the infant is unaware that anything exists outside the range of its vision. As research we have already looked at shows, infants gradually learn to distinguish people from objects, coming to see that both have an existence independent of their immediate perceptions. Piaget calls this early stage *sensorimotor* because infants learn from their senses, mainly by touching objects, manipulating them and physically exploring their environment. The main accomplishment of this stage is that by its close the child understands its environment to have distinctive and stable properties.

The next phase, called the **pre-operational stage**, is the one to which Piaget devoted the bulk of his research. This stage lasts from age two to age seven, when children acquire a mastery of language and become able to use words to represent objects and images in a symbolic fashion. A four-year-old might use a sweeping hand, for example, to represent the concept 'aeroplane'. Piaget terms the stage pre-operational because children are not yet able to use their developing mental capabilities systematically. The characteristic outlook of children in this stage is one of **egocentrism**. As Piaget uses it, this concept does not refer to selfishness, but to the tendency of the child to interpret the world exclusively in terms of its own position. She or he does not understand, for instance, that others see objects from a different perspective from her or his own. Holding a book upright, the child may ask about a picture in it, not realizing that the person sitting opposite can only see the back of the book.

Children at the pre-operational stage are not able to hold connected conversations with someone else. In egocentric speech, what each child says is more or less unrelated to what the previous speakers said. Children talk together, but not *to* one another in the same sense as adults. During this phase of development, children have no general understanding of categories of thought that adults tend to take for granted: concepts such as causality, speed, weight or number. Even if the child sees water poured from a tall, thin container into a shorter, wider one, he or she will not understand that the volume of water remains the same – concluding that there is less water in the new container, because the water level is lower.

A third phase, the **concrete operational stage**, lasts from ages seven to eleven. During this phase, children master abstract, logical notions. They are able to handle ideas such as causality without much difficulty. A child at this stage of development will recognize the false reasoning involved in the idea that the wide container holds less water than the thin, narrow one, even though the water levels are different. She or he becomes capable of carrying out the mathematical operations of multiplying, dividing and subtracting. Children by this stage are much less egocentric. In the pre-operational stage, if a girl is asked 'How many sisters have you?', she may correctly answer 'one'. But if asked, 'How many sisters does your sister have?' she will probably answer 'none', because she cannot see herself from the point of view of her sister. In the concrete operational stage the child is able to answer such a question correctly with ease.

The years from eleven to fifteen cover what Piaget calls the **formal operational period**. During adolescence, the developing child becomes able to grasp highly abstract and hypothetical ideas. When faced with a problem, children at this stage are able to review all the possible ways of solving it and go through them theoretically in order to reach a solution. The young person at the formal operational stage is able to understand why some sorts of questions are trick ones. To the question 'What creatures are both poodles and dogs?' the child might or might not be able to give the correct reply (the answer is 'poodles'), but he or she will understand why this answer is right and appreciate the humour in it.

According to Piaget, the first three stages of development are universal; but not all adults reach the formal operational stage. The development of formal operational thought depends in part on processes of schooling. Adults of limited educational attainment tend to continue to think in more concrete terms and retain large traces of egocentrism.

Criticisms

Margaret Donaldson has questioned Piaget's view that children are highly egocentric compared to adults (Donaldson 1979). The tasks which Piaget set the children he studied, as she sees it, were presented from an adult standpoint rather than in terms that were understandable to them. Egocentrism is equally characteristic of adult behaviour – in some situations. To make the point, she quotes a passage from the autobiography of the British poet Laurie Lee, describing his first day at school as a small boy.

> I spent that first day picking holes in paper, then went home in a smouldering temper.
> 'What's the matter, Love? Didn't he like it at school then?'
> 'They never gave me a present.'
> 'Present? What present?'
> 'They said they'd give me a present.'
> 'Well now, I'm sure they didn't.'
> 'They did! They said, "You're Laurie Lee, aren't you? Well; just you sit there for the present." I sat there all day but I never got it. I ain't going back there again.' (Lee 1965, p. 50)

As adults we tend to think that the child has misunderstood, in a comic way, the instructions of the teacher. Yet on a deeper level, Donaldson points out, the adult has failed to understand the child, not recognizing the ambiguity in the phrase 'sit there for the present'. The adult, not the boy, is guilty of egocentrism.

Piaget's work has also been much criticized on grounds of his methods. How can we generalize from findings based on observations of small numbers of children all living in one city? Yet for the most part Piaget's ideas have stood up well in the light of the enormous amount of subsequent research they have helped to generate. The stages of development he identifies are probably less clear-cut than he claimed, but many of his ideas are now generally accepted.

Connections between the theories

There are major differences between the perspectives of Freud, Mead and Piaget; yet it is possible to suggest a picture of child development which draws on them all.

All three authors accept that, in the early months of infancy, a baby has no distinct understanding of the nature of objects or persons in its environment or of its own separate identity. Throughout the first two or so years of life, before the mastery of developed linguistic skills, most of the child's learning is unconscious because she or he has as yet no awareness of self. Freud was probably right to claim that ways of coping with anxiety established during this early period – related, in particular, to interaction with mother and father – remain important in later personality development.

It is likely that children learn to become self-aware beings through the process suggested by Mead – the differentiating of an 'I' and a 'me'. Children who have acquired a sense of self retain egocentric modes of thinking, however, as Piaget indicated. The development of the child's autonomy probably involves greater emotional difficulties than either Mead or Piaget seemed to recognize – which is where Freud's ideas are particularly relevant. Being able to cope with early anxieties may well influence how far a child is later able to move successfully through the stages of cognition distinguished by Piaget.

So far, especially in discussing Freud and Mead, we have concentrated mainly on infancy and early childhood – with good reason, because the first few years of life are so vital. What about later phases of the life course? Everyone's life goes through a number of such phases, from childhood, adolescence, young adulthood to middle age and old age. In contrast to the earlier sections of the chapter, we will look at these not so much from the standpoint of the individual, but more in terms of how the phases of development are socially organized. For we need to understand individual development in its wider social context.

THE LIFE COURSE

The various transitions through which individuals pass during their lives seem at first sight to be biologically fixed – from childhood to adulthood and eventually to death. Things are much more complicated than this, however. The stages of the human **life course** are social as well as biological in nature. They are influenced by cultural differences and also by the material circumstances of people's lives in given types of society. For example, in the modern West, death is usually thought of in relation to old age, because most people enjoy a life-span of seventy years or more. In traditional societies, however, more people died in younger age groups than survived to old age.

Childhood

Most of us tend to think of *childhood* as a clear and distinct stage of life. 'Children', we suppose, are distinct from 'babies' or 'toddlers'. Childhood intervenes between infancy and the onset of adolescence. Yet the concept of childhood, like so many other aspects of our social life today, has only come into being over the past two or three centuries. In traditional cultures, the young moved directly from a lengthy infancy into working roles within the community. The French historian Philippe Ariès has argued that 'childhood', as a separate phase of development, did not exist in medieval times (Ariès 1973). In the paintings of medieval Europe, children were portrayed as 'little adults', having mature faces and the same style of dress as their elders. Children

FREUD, MEAD AND PIAGET COMPARED

Freud

Freud's account of child development is distinctive because it heavily emphasizes *unconscious* and *emotional* sources of child development. According to Freud, basic aspects of each individual's personality are established very early on in life, particularly as a result of interaction with the mother. Since these early patterns of behaviour are learned before the child has mastered the use of language, they tend to remain at an unconscious level.

The infant has to learn that its needs cannot always be immediately satisfied. All mothers impose some sort of feeding discipline on their children. The infant gradually comes to *repress* – unconsciously block – its demands for immediate need satisfaction. According to Freud, repression is at the origin of some of the most important features of child development. The child has both a positive and a negative relation to his or her mother, in which love and antagonism mingle.

The *Oedipal transition*, which normally occurs at about age four or five, has a central role in Freud's theory. The idea comes from the ancient Greek myth of Oedipus, who unknowingly killed his father and married his mother. In the Oedipal stage, the child is required by the wider society to break away from the emotional shelter offered in infancy by the mother. The father is the main agent within the family of this demand for greater autonomy and independence. The child must repress its hatred of the father, and at the same time repress much of its former dependence on the mother.

Mead

Mead's approach differs in some fundamental respects from that of Freud. Freud was a medical doctor and a therapist. Mead was a philosopher and sociologist. He was less concerned with the inner emotional workings of the individual personality and more with processes of social interaction. Mead placed much less emphasis than Freud did on the unconscious. The idea of repression hardly appears in Mead's writings at all. Moreover, Mead did not accept the Freudian idea that what happens in infancy and very early childhood substantially governs much of our later experience. For Mead, adolescence is as important as childhood in terms of social learning.

Mead placed much stress on the significance of play in child development. Through the imaginative aspects of play, the child learns to *take the role of the other* – to see the world as others see it, and break away from an egoistic viewpoint. Children separate the 'I' from the 'me' as a result of this process. The 'me' is the *social self*, the self as reacted to by others. In later childhood and early adolescence the boy or girl learns to take the role of the *generalized other* – the more abstract norms and values on which the wider society is based. This also tends to be learned first of all through cooperative play.

Piaget

The third great theorist of child development, Piaget, differed from each of the other two. Piaget was a psychologist who based most of his ideas on direct observations of children. Neither Freud nor Mead studied children directly. Like Mead, Piaget placed less emphasis on the unconscious than Freud; he did, however, write much more extensively than did Mead about the emotional development of the child.

For Piaget, the infant is originally *egocentric* – it sees the world exclusively from the perspective of its own position in it. Children have to learn that others exist who have thoughts and feelings comparable to their own, and they take many months to grasp concepts which adults take for granted, such as those of speed, weight or number. Learning to handle language is an essential part of mastering such notions. The path from infantile egocentrism to full adulthood goes through a number of distinct stages. In each of these, Piaget argues, the child is gradually extending his or her capability to grasp abstract concepts and to understand the feelings of others. Not until age fifteen or so are children able to master more complex notions of logic and reasoning, and some children in fact never get to this stage at all.

took part in the same work and play activities as adults, and did not have the distinct toys or games that we now take for granted.

Right up to the start of the twentieth century, in Britain and most other Western countries, children as young as seven or eight years old were put to work at what now seems a very early age. There are many countries in the world today, in fact, in which young children are engaged in full-time work, often in physically demanding circumstances (coalmines, for example) (UNICEF 1987). The idea that children have distinctive rights, and the notion that the use of child labour is morally repugnant, are quite recent developments.

Some historians, developing the view suggested by Ariès, have suggested that in medieval Europe most people were indifferent, or even hostile, to their children. This view has been rejected by others, however, and is not borne out by what we know of traditional cultures still existing today. Many parents, particularly mothers, almost certainly formed the same kinds of attachments to their children as are usual now. However, because of the long period of 'childhood' which we recognize today, modern societies are in some respects more 'child-centred' than traditional ones. Both parenting and childhood have become more clearly distinct from other stages than was true of traditional communities.

A child-centred society, it must be emphasized, is not one where all children experience love and care from parents or other adults. The physical and sexual abuse of children is a commonplace feature of family life in present-day society – although the full extent of such abuse has only recently come to light. Child abuse has clear connections with what, by public standards today, appears as the frequent mistreatment of children in premodern Europe.

It seems possible that, as a result of changes currently occurring in modern societies, 'childhood' is again becoming eroded as a distinct status. Some observers have suggested that children now 'grow up so fast' that the separate character of childhood is diminishing once more (Suransky 1982; Winn 1983). For example, even quite small children may watch the same television programmes as adults, becoming much more familiar early on with the 'adult world' than did preceding generations.

Adolescence

The concept of 'teenager' is relatively recent. The biological changes involved in puberty (the point at which a person becomes capable of adult sexual activity and reproduction) are universal. Yet in many cultures these do not produce the degree of turmoil and uncertainty often found among young people in modern societies. When there is an age-grade system, for example, coupled with distinct rites that signal the person's transition to adulthood, the process of psychosexual development generally seems easier to negotiate. Adolescents in traditional societies have less to 'unlearn' than their counterparts in modern ones, since the pace of change is slower. There is a time at which our children are required to be children no longer: to put away their toys and break with childish pursuits. In traditional cultures, where children are already working alongside adults, this process of 'unlearning' is normally much less severe.

The distinctiveness of being a 'teenager' in current times is related both to the general extension of child rights and to the process of formal education. Teenagers often try to follow adult ways, but are treated in law as children. They may wish to go to work, but are constrained to stay in school. Teenagers are 'in between' childhood and adulthood, growing up in a society subject to continuous change.

The young adult

Young adulthood seems increasingly to be becoming a specific stage in personal and sexual development in the modern world. Particularly among more affluent groups, but not limited to them, people in their early twenties are taking 'time out' to travel and explore sexual, political and religious affiliations. The importance of this 'moratorium' is likely to grow, given the extended period of education which many now undergo.

Mature adulthood

Most young adults in the West today can look forward to a life stretching right through to old age. In premodern times, few could anticipate such a future with much confidence. Death through sickness, plague or injury was much more frequent among all age groups than it is today, and women in particular were at great risk because of the high rate of mortality in childbirth.

On the other hand, some of the strains we experience now were less pronounced in previous eras. People usually maintained a closer connection with their parents and other kin than in today's more mobile populations, and the routines of work they followed were the same as those of their forebears. In our society, major uncertainties have to be resolved in marriage, family life and other social contexts. We have to 'make' our own lives more than people did in the past. The creation of sexual and marital ties, for instance, now depends on individual initiative and selection, rather than being fixed by parents. This represents greater freedom for the individual, but the responsibility can also impose strains and difficulties.

Keeping a 'forward-looking outlook' in middle age has a particular importance for us now. Most people do not expect to be 'doing the same thing all their lives' – as was usually the case for the majority of the population in traditional cultures. Men or women who have spent their lives in one career may find the level they have reached in middle age unsatisfying and further opportunities blocked. Women who have spent their early adulthood raising a family, and whose children have left home, may feel themselves to be without any social value. The phenomenon of a 'mid-life crisis' is very real for many middle-aged people. A person may feel he or she has thrown away the opportunities that life had to offer, or will never attain goals cherished since childhood. Yet the transitions involved need not lead to resignation or bleak despair; a release from childhood dreams can be liberating.

Old age

In earlier forms of society, older people were normally accorded a great deal of respect. The 'elders' – the older age groups – usually had a major, often the final, say over matters of importance to the community as a whole. Within families, the authority of both men and women often increased with age. In industrialized societies, by contrast, older people tend to lack authority both within the family and in the wider social community. Having retired from the labour force, they may be poorer than ever before in their lives. At the same time, there has been a great increase in the proportion of the population aged over sixty-five. Only one in thirty people in Britain in 1900 was over sixty-five; the proportion today is one in five.

Transition to the age-grade of elder in a traditional culture often marked the pinnacle of the status an individual could achieve. In our own society, retirement tends to bring the very opposite consequences. No longer living with their children and ejected from the economic arena, it is not easy for older people to make the final period of their life rewarding. It used to be thought that those who successfully cope with old age do so by turning to their inner resources, becoming less interested in the external rewards that social life has to offer. While no doubt this may often be true, it seems likely that, in a society in which many are physically healthy in old age, an 'outward-looking' view will come more and more to the fore. Those in retirement might find renewal in what has been called the 'third age' (following childhood and adulthood), in which a new phase of education begins.

THE SUCCESSION OF THE GENERATIONS

In medieval Europe, death was much more visible than it is today. In the modern world most people die in the enclosed environments of hospitals, removed from contact with their relatives and friends. Death is seen by many people in the West today as the end of an individual life, not as part of the process of the renewal of the generations. The weakening of religious beliefs has also altered our attitudes towards death. For us death tends to be a subject that goes undiscussed. It is taken for granted that people are frightened of dying, and thus doctors or relatives quite commonly hide from a mortally ill person the news that she or he will shortly die.

According to Elisabeth Kübler-Ross, the process of adjusting to the imminence of death is a compressed process of socialization that involves several stages. The first is *denial* – the individual refuses to accept what is happening. The second stage is *anger*, particularly among those dying relatively young, who feel resentful at being robbed of the full span of life. This is followed by a stage of *bargaining*. The individual concludes a deal with fate, or with the deity, to die peace-fully if allowed to live to see some particular event of significance, such as a family marriage or birthday. Subsequently, the individual fre-quently lapses into *depression*. Finally, if this state can be overcome, she or he might move towards a phase of *acceptance*, in which an attitude of peace is achieved in the face of approaching death.

Kübler-Ross notes that when she asks her lecture audiences what they fear most about dying, the majority of people say they are afraid of the unknown, pain, separation from loved ones or leaving cherished pro-jects unfinished. According to her, these things are really only the tip of the iceberg. Most of what we associate with death is unconscious, and this has to be brought to light if we are to be able to die in an accepting way. Unconsciously, people cannot conceive of their own death except as a malicious entity come to punish them. If they can see that this asso-ciation is an irrational one – that being terminally ill is not a punish-ment for wrongdoing – the process is eased (Kübler-Ross 1987).

In traditional cultures, in which children, parents and grandparents often live in the same household, there is usually a clear awareness of the connection of death with the succession of the generations. Individuals feel themselves to be part of a family and a community which endure indefinitely, regardless of the transience of personal exis-tence. In such circumstances, death may perhaps be looked on with less anxiety than in the more rapidly changing, individualistic social cir-cumstances of the modern world.

SOCIALIZATION AND INDIVIDUAL FREEDOM

Since the cultural settings in which we are born and come to maturity so influence our behaviour, it might appear that we are robbed of any individuality or free will. We might seem to be merely stamped into pre-set moulds which society has prepared for us. Some sociologists do tend to write about socialization – and even about sociology more generally! – as though this were the case; but such a view is fundamen-tally mistaken. The fact that from birth to death we are involved in interaction with others certainly conditions our personalities, the values we hold and the behaviour we engage in. Yet socialization is also at the origin of our very individuality and freedom. In the course of socializa-tion each of us develops a sense of IDENTITY and the capacity for inde-pendent thought and action.

This point is easily illustrated by the example of learning language. None of us invents the language we learn as a child, and we are all con-strained by fixed rules of linguistic usage. At the same time, however, understanding a language is one of the basic factors making possible our self-awareness and creativity. Without language, we would not be self-conscious beings, and we would live more or less wholly in the here-and-now. Mastery of language is necessary for the symbolic rich-ness of human life, for awareness of our distinctive individual charac-teristics and for our practical mastery of the environment.

SUMMARY

1 The concept of culture is one of the most important notions in sociology. Culture refers to the ways of life of the members of a society, or of groups within a society. It includes art, literature and painting, but also ranges much more widely. Other cultural items, for example, are how people dress, their customs, their patterns of work and religious ceremonies.

2 Culture is a large part of what makes us human. As human beings, however, we also share a common biological inheritance. The human species emerged as a result of a long process of biological evolution. Human beings are part of groups of higher mammals, the primates, with whom they have a good deal physiologically in common.

3 Sociobiology is important primarily for its insights concerning animal behaviour; the ideas of the sociobiologists about human social life are highly speculative. Our behaviour is genetically influenced, but our genetic endowment probably conditions only the potentialities of our behaviour, not the actual content of our activities.

4 Human beings have no instincts in the sense of complex patterns of unlearned behaviour. A set of simple reflexes, plus a range of organic needs, are innate characteristics of the human individual.

5 Forms of behaviour found in all, or virtually all, cultures are called cultural universals. Language, the prohibition against incest, institutions of marriage, the family, religion and property are the main types of cultural universals – but within these general categories there are many variations in values and modes of behaviour between different societies.

6 We learn the characteristics of our culture through the process of socialization. Socialization is the process whereby, through contact with other human beings, the helpless infant gradually becomes a self-aware, knowledgeable human being, skilled in the ways of the given culture.

7 The work of Sigmund Freud suggests that the young child learns to become an autonomous being only as she or he learns to balance the demands of the environment with pressing desires coming from the unconscious. Our ability to be self-aware is built, painfully, on the repression of unconscious drives.

8 According to G. H. Mead, the child achieves an understanding of being a separate agent by seeing others behave towards him or her in regular ways. At a later stage, entering into organized games, learning the rules of play, the child comes to understand 'the generalized other' – general values and cultural rules.

9 Jean Piaget distinguishes several main stages in the development of the child's ability to make sense of the world. Each stage involves the acquisition of new cognitive skills and depends on the successful completion of the preceding one. According to Piaget these stages of cognitive development are universal features of socialization.

10 Socialization continues throughout the life course. At each distinct phase of life there are transitions to be made or crises to be overcome. This includes facing up to death, as the termination of personal existence.

FURTHER READING

Philippe Ariès, _Centuries of Childhood_ (Harmondsworth: Penguin, 1973). A classical – although controversial – discussion of the historical emergence of 'childhood' as a distinct phase of human development.

Ruth Benedict, _Patterns of Culture_ (New York: Mentor Books, 1946). A classic study of cultural differences, still worth reading.

Ralph Fasold, _The Sociolinguistics of Language_ (Oxford: Blackwell, 1991). A useful textbook covering many aspects of the nature of language and culture.

Elisabeth Kübler-Ross, _Living with Death and Dying_ (London: Souvenir Press, 1987). A sensitive account of attitudes to death.

Elly Singer, _Childcare and the Psychology of Development_ (London: Routledge, 1992). A discussion of child development and the problem of releasing women from the obligation of full-time mothering.

Frances C. Waksler, _Studying the Social Worlds of Children: Sociological Readings_ (London: Falmer, 1991). A collection of texts on child development.

Raymond Williams, _Culture_ (Glasgow: Fontana, 1981). A useful general discussion of the concept of culture.

IMPORTANT TERMS

- _evolution_
- _natural selection_
- _mutation_
- _sociobiology_
- _instinct_
- _subculture_
- _ethnocentrism_
- _cognition_
- _psychoanalysis_
- _Oedipus complex_
- _social self_
- _generalized other_
- _sensorimotor stage_
- _pre-operational stage_
- _egocentrism_
- _concrete operational stage_
- _formal operational period_
- _life course_

3

TYPES OF SOCIETY

To understand human cultural diversity, we must have some sense of the different types of society that have existed in history. In this chapter, we look at the main types of premodern society, but concentrate on the changes that have transformed the social world over the recent past. We also consider an important recent global event whose consequences affect all of us today: the disappearance of a whole type of social system, Second World societies, or Soviet communism.

First of all, we consider some of the earliest forms of society, whose origins date back many thousands of years.

THE EARLIEST SOCIETIES: HUNTERS AND GATHERERS

For all but a tiny part of our existence on this planet, human beings have lived in **hunting and gathering societies**, small groups or tribes often numbering no more than thirty or forty people. Hunters and gatherers gain their livelihood from hunting, fishing and gathering edible plants growing in the wild. These cultures continue to exist in some parts of the world, such as in a few arid parts of Africa and the jungles of Brazil and New Guinea. Most hunting and gathering cultures, however, have been destroyed or absorbed by the spread of Western culture, and those that remain are unlikely to stay intact for much longer. Currently, less than a quarter of a million people in the world support themselves through hunting and gathering – only 0.001 per cent of the world's population (see figure 3.1).

Compared with larger societies – particularly modern societies, such as Britain or the United States – little inequality is found in most hunting and gathering groups. The material goods they need are limited to weapons for hunting, tools for digging and building, traps and cooking utensils. Thus there is little difference among members of the society in the number or kinds of material possessions – there are no divisions of rich and poor. Differences of position or rank tend to be limited to age and sex; men are almost always the hunters, while women gather wild crops, cook, and bring up the children. This division of labour between men and women, however, is very important: men tend to dominate public and ceremonial positions.

The 'elders' – the oldest and most experienced men in the community – usually have an important say in major decisions affecting the group. But just as there is little variation in wealth among members of a community, differences of power are much less than in larger types of society. Hunting and gathering societies are usually 'participatory' – all adult male members tend to assemble together when important decisions are taken or crises faced.

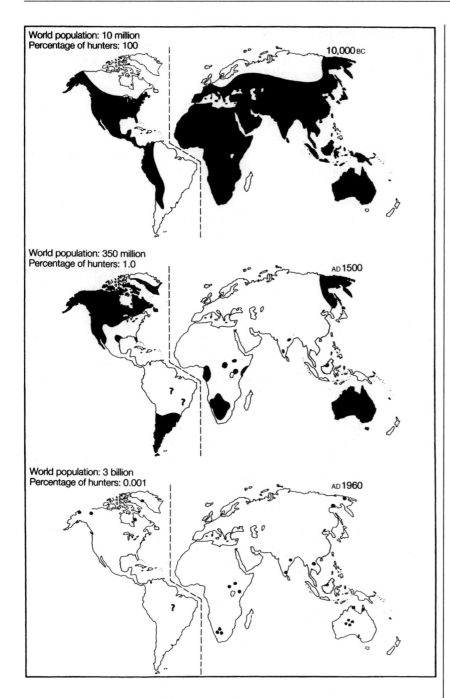

World population: 10 million
Percentage of hunters: 100

10,000 BC

World population: 350 million
Percentage of hunters: 1.0

AD 1500

World population: 3 billion
Percentage of hunters: 0.001

AD 1960

Fig. 3.1 How hunting and gathering societies declined as world population grew

Source: Richard B. Lee and Irven de Vore (eds), *Man the Hunter* (Aldine de Gruyter 1968), frontispiece. (3 billion = 3,000 million)

Hunters and gatherers do not just move about in a completely erratic way. Most have fixed territories and migrate regularly round them from year to year. Many hunting and gathering communities do not have a stable membership; people often move between different camps, or groups split up and join others within the same overall territory.

The Mbuti pygmies

Of the hundreds of descriptions of hunting and gathering societies that have been written, we shall look at just one, to illustrate their way of life: the society of the Mbuti (pronounced 'Mubooti') pygmies, who live in an area of Zaire, in Central Africa (Turnbull 1983). The Mbuti inhabit a heavily forested area, difficult for outsiders to penetrate. They themselves know the forest intimately and move about in it as they please. There is plenty of water and there are edible wild plants and animals to be hunted. The houses of the Mbuti are not permanent dwellings, but are made of leaves on a framework of branches. They can be set up in a matter of hours, and abandoned when the Mbuti move on – as they do continuously, never staying more than a month at any one site.

The Mbuti live in small bands made up of four or five families. The bands have a fairly permanent membership, but there is nothing to stop either an individual or a family leaving one group and joining another. Nobody 'runs' any band – there are no chiefs. Older men have a duty, however, to quiet 'noise' – bickering or quarrelling – which the pygmies believe displeases the spirits of the forest. If a conflict gets too severe, the members of a band split up and go to join others.

The Mbuti were first studied in the 1960s, when their traditional way of life remained intact. Since then, it has come under increasing strain. The outside world has encroached more and more on the forest, and the Mbuti are becoming drawn into the money economy of the villages around the forest's perimeters. I have presented the account of their way of life in the present tense, but it is now on the verge of extinction. Much the same is true of the examples of other types of small traditional society which are given later in the chapter.

The original 'affluent societies'?

Unlike the Mbuti, most hunting and gathering societies remaining in existence today are confined to inhospitable areas. Such groups may live close to starvation level, because the environment is too harsh to provide more than a minimal living. Hunters and gatherers have long since been driven out of most of the more fertile areas of the world, and the fact that they now live in circumstances where survival is a perennial struggle has led many scholars to assume that all such peoples lived in conditions of material deprivation. This was probably not the case in the past. A prominent anthropologist, Marshall Sahlins, has called hunter-gatherers the 'original affluent societies' – because they had more than enough to provide for their wants (Sahlins 1972). Past hunters and gatherers living in the more hospitable regions of the world did not have to spend most of the day working, 'engaged in production'. Many may have worked for a shorter average number of hours per day than the modern factory or office employee.

Hunters and gatherers have little interest in developing material wealth beyond what is needed to cater for their basic wants. Their main preoccupations are normally with religious values and with ceremonial and ritual activities. Many hunters and gatherers participate regularly in elaborate ceremonials, and may spend a large amount of their time preparing the dress, masks, paintings or other sacred objects used in such rituals.

Some authors, especially those influenced by sociobiology, have seen the prominence of hunting in these societies as related to universal human impulses towards war, but in fact hunting and gathering societies mostly seem to be unwarlike. The implements used for hunting are rarely employed as weapons against other human beings. Occasionally, clashes may occur between different groups, but these are usually very limited: few or no casualties are involved. Warfare in the modern sense is completely unknown among hunters and gatherers, who have no specialist warriors. Hunting is itself in an important sense a cooperative activity. Individuals may go off hunting alone, but they almost always share the results of the hunt – say, the meat from a wild pig or boar – with the rest of the group.

Hunters and gatherers are not merely 'primitive' peoples whose ways of life no longer hold any interest for us. Studying their cultures allows us to see more clearly that some of our institutions are far from being 'natural' features of human life. Of course, we should not idealize the circumstances in which hunters and gatherers have lived, but none the less, the absence of war, the lack of major inequalities of wealth and power, and the emphasis on cooperation rather than competition are all instructive reminders that the world created by modern industrial civilization is not necessarily to be equated with 'progress'.

PASTORAL AND AGRARIAN SOCIETIES

About twenty thousand years ago, some hunting and gathering groups turned to the raising of domesticated animals and the cultivation of fixed plots of land as their means of livelihood. **Pastoral societies** are those relying mainly on domesticated livestock, while **agrarian societies** are those that grow crops (practise agriculture). Many societies have had mixed pastoral and agrarian economies.

Pastoral societies

Depending on the environment in which they live, pastoralists rear and herd animals such as cattle, sheep, goats, camels or horses. Many pastoral societies still exist in the modern world, concentrated especially in areas of Africa, the Middle East and Central Asia. These societies are usually found in regions where there are dense grasslands, or in deserts or mountains. Such regions are not amenable to fruitful agriculture, but may support various kinds of livestock.

Pastoral societies usually migrate between different areas according to seasonal changes. Because they have animal transport, they move across much larger distances than the hunting and gathering peoples. Given their nomadic habits, people in pastoral societies do not normally accumulate many material possessions, although their way of life is more complex in material terms than that of hunters and gatherers. Since the domestication of animals permits a regular supply of food, these societies are usually much larger than hunting and gathering communities. Some pastoral societies number a quarter of a million people or more.

Ranging as they often do over large tracts of territory, pastoralists regularly come into contact with other groups. They frequently engage in trade – and also in warfare. Many pastoral cultures have been peaceful, wishing only to tend to their livestock and engage in community ritual and ceremonial. Others have been highly warlike, deriving their livelihood from conquest and pillage as well as from the herding of animals. Pastoral societies display greater inequalities of wealth and power than hunting and gathering communities. In particular, chiefs, tribal leaders or warlords often wield considerable personal power.

A classic description of a pastoral society was given by E. E. Evans-Pritchard, who studied the Nuer, a society in the Southern Sudan in Africa (Evans-Pritchard 1940). The livelihood of the Nuer depends mainly on the raising of cattle, although they also grow some crops as well. The people live in villages situated from five to twenty miles apart from one another. In the 1930s, when Evans-Pritchard carried out his study, the Nuer numbered about 200,000 people. They all speak the same language and follow similar customs, but there is no central political authority or form of government. The Nuer are divided into tribes, which sometimes collaborate with one another, but mostly live separately.

Each tribe has its own area of land, the divisions mostly being marked by water-courses. The Nuer attach no particular significance to land, however, except in so far as it provides a place to graze their cattle. Part of the year, during the dry season, they move to live in camps near water-holes. Much of the life of the Nuer is bound up with their cattle, which are in many ways central to their culture. They have a profound contempt for neighbouring peoples having few or no cattle. Every major phase of life – birth, entering adulthood, marriage and death – is marked by rituals to do with cattle. Men are often addressed by the names of their favourite oxen and women by the names of their favourites among the cows they milk.

The Nuer tribes quite often wage war on one another, and also sometimes form an alliance to fight outsiders. Just as they live for their cattle, so they fight wars for them – for instance, raiding the nearby Dinka, another pastoral society, to steal their herds. A Nuer saying goes: 'more people have died for the sake of a cow than for any other cause.'

Agrarian societies

Agrarian societies seem to have originated at about the same date as pastoral ones. At some point, hunting and gathering groups began to sow their own crops rather than simply collect those growing in the wild. This practice first developed as what is usually called 'horticulture', in which small gardens are cultivated by the use of simple hoes or digging instruments. Many peoples in the world still rely primarily on horticulture for their livelihood. (Figure 3.2 shows how the agricultural way of life has persisted into the modern world.)

Percentage of the workforce in agriculture

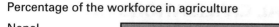

Nepal	91.7
Rwanda	91.3
Uganda	80.9
Ethiopia	74.5
Bangladesh	68.5

Industrialized societies:

Australia	7.4
Japan	6.4
Germany	4.6
Canada	3.3
United States	2.3
United Kingdom	2.0

Fig. 3.2 The persistence of the agricultural way of life compared with industrialized societies today: percentage of the workforce in agriculture, 1990

Source: Nikos Alexandratos (ed.), *World Agriculture: Towards 2010: An FAO Study*, 1995.

Like pastoralism, horticulture provides for a more assured supply of food than is possible by hunting and gathering, and therefore can support much larger communities. Since they are not on the move, peoples gaining a livelihood from horticulture can develop larger stocks of material possessions than can either pastoral or hunting and gathering communities. Once groups are settled in particular places, regular trading and political ties can be developed between separate villages. Warlike behaviour is common in horticultural societies, although the level of violence tends to be less pronounced than among some pastoral groups. Those who grow crops are not ordinarily practised in arts of combat; nomadic pastoral tribesmen, on the other hand, can mass together as marauding armies.

As an example, we will consider the Gururumba, a New Guinea tribe of just over a thousand people living in six villages (Newman 1965). In each village there are several gardens, fenced off from one another. Plots are owned by different families within these fenced areas. All, adults and children, are involved in tending the plots, although men and women are responsible for different types of fruit and vegetables. Each family has more than one plot and cultivates different plants at certain times of the year, thus providing a constant food supply. Gururumba culture involves a complicated system of ceremonial gift exchanges between families, through which prestige in the community can be achieved. The people thus have gardens in which they grow crops to cater for their day-to-day needs, and other plots in which they cultivate 'prestige' crops. 'Prestige' crops are given far more care than those relating to ordinary needs.

The Gururumba also raise pigs, which are not kept mainly for food but as items of gift exchange designed to achieve status in the community. Every few years a massive pig feast is held in which hundreds of pigs are killed, cooked and given as gifts. As in pastoral groups, among the Gururumba there is more inequality than in hunting and gathering cultures. Chiefs and tribal leaders play a prominent role, and there are substantial differences in the material wealth people possess.

NON-INDUSTRIAL CIVILIZATIONS OR TRADITIONAL STATES

From about 6000 BC onwards we find evidence of larger societies than ever existed before, which contrast in distinct ways with earlier types (Burns and Ralph 1974). These societies were based on the development of cities, showed very pronounced inequalities of wealth and power, and were associated with the rule of kings or emperors. Because they involved the use of writing, and science and art flourished, they are often called *civilizations*. However, since they developed more coordinated government than other forms of society, the term **traditional states** is also often used to refer to them.

Most traditional states were also *empires*; they achieved the size they did through the conquest and incorporation of other peoples (Eisenstadt 1963; Claessen and Skalnik 1978; Kautsky 1982). This was true, for instance, of traditional China and Rome. At its height, in the first century AD, the Roman empire stretched from Britain in north-west Europe to beyond the Middle East. The Chinese empire, which lasted for more than two thousand years, up to the threshold of the present century, covered most of the massive region of eastern Asia now occupied by modern China. No traditional states still exist in the world today. Although some, like China and Japan, remained more or less intact up to the start of the twentieth century, all have now been destroyed or dissolved into more modern systems.

The earliest traditional states developed in the Middle East, usually in fertile river areas (see figure 3.3). The Chinese empire originated in about 2000 BC, at which time powerful states were also found in what is now India and Pakistan. A number of large traditional states existed in Mexico and Latin America, such as the Aztecs of the Mexican peninsula and the Inca of Peru. The Inca state had been established for about a century before the arrival of the Spanish adventurer Pizarro, who landed in South America in 1535 with only a small force of soldiers. Yet by building alliances with other native tribes hostile to the Inca, Pizarro was able to bring about the rapid downfall of the Inca state and claim the area for Spain. His was one of the first of a series of encounters between Western influences and traditional states that was eventually to lead to the latter's complete disappearance.

The Maya

As an example of a traditional state we shall look at a third American civilization, that of the Maya, based in the Yucatan peninsula, by the Mexican Gulf. Maya civilization flourished from AD 300 to 800. The Maya built elaborate religious centres, surrounding them with their dwellings, all built in stone. The religious shrines took the form of large pyramids, and at the top of each was a temple. At Tikal, the biggest of the pyramids, the surrounding city held some 40,000 inhabitants. It was the main administrative centre – effectively the capital city – of the Maya state.

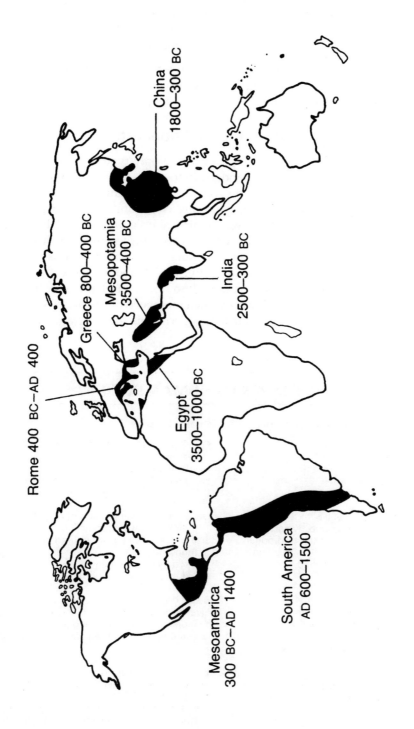

Fig. 3.3 Some of the major traditional civilizations of the past with approximate dates and locations (though all went through periods of expansion and decline)

Maya society was ruled by an aristocratic class of warrior-priests. They were the highest religious dignitaries in the society, but were also military leaders and fought continuous wars with surrounding groups. The majority of the population were peasant farmers, all of whom were required to give up a proportion of their production to their aristocratic rulers, who lived in conditions of some luxury.

It is not known for certain why Maya civilization collapsed, but it was probably conquered by neighbouring tribes. By the time the Spanish arrived, the Maya state had long since disappeared.

Features of the traditional state

The traditional state was the only type of society in history, before the emergence of modern industrialism, in which a significant proportion of the population was not directly engaged in the production of food. In hunting and gathering communities and in pastoral and agrarian societies, there was a fairly simple division of labour. The most important separation of tasks was between men and women. In traditional states, by contrast, a more complicated occupational system existed. There was still strict division of labour by sex, the activities of women being mainly confined to the household and the fields. However, among men we see the emergence of specialized trades, such as those of merchant, courtier, government administrator and soldier.

EARLY TYPES OF HUMAN SOCIETY

Type	Period of existence	Characteristics
Hunting and gathering societies	50,000 BC to the present (now on the verge of complete disappearance).	Consist of small numbers of people gaining their livelihood from hunting, fishing, and the gathering of edible plants. Few inequalities. Differences of rank limited by age and sex.
Pastoral societies	12,000 BC to the present. Today mostly part of larger states; their traditional ways of life are being undermined.	Dependent on the tending of domesticated animals for their material subsistence. Size ranges from a few hundred people to many thousands. Marked by distinct inequalities. Ruled by chiefs or warrior kings.
Agrarian societies	12,000 BC to the present. Most are now part of larger political entities, and are losing their distinct identity.	Based on small rural communities, without towns or cities. Livelihood gained through agriculture, often supplemented by hunting and gathering. Greater inequalities than among hunters and gatherers. Ruled by chiefs.
Traditional states or civilizations	6000 BC to the nineteenth century. All traditional states have disappeared.	Based largely on agriculture. Some cities exist where trade and manufacture are concentrated. Very large in size, some numbering millions of people (though small compared with larger industrialized societies). Distinct apparatus of government headed by a king or emperor. Major inequalities exist among different classes.

There was also a basic division of classes between aristocratic groups and the remainder of the population. The ruler was at the head of a 'ruling class' that maintained the exclusive right to hold the higher social positions. The members of this class usually lived in considerable material comfort or luxury. The lot of the mass of the population, on the other hand, was frequently very hard. Slave-owning was a common feature of these societies.

A few traditional states were mainly built up through trade, and were ruled by merchants, but most either were established through military conquest or involved a substantial build-up of armed forces (McNeill 1983; Mann 1986). Traditional states saw the development of professional armies, anticipating modern types of military organization. The Roman army, for example, was a highly disciplined and intensively trained body of men, and was the foundation on which the expansion of the Roman empire was built. We also find in traditional states the beginning of the mechanization of war. The swords, spears, shields and siege equipment carried by the Roman army were manufactured by specialized craftsmen. In the wars conducted between traditional states, and between these states and 'barbarian' tribes, casualties were far higher than they had ever been before.

THE MODERN WORLD: INDUSTRIAL SOCIETIES

Traditional states have now completely disappeared from the face of the earth. Although hunting and gathering, pastoral and agrarian societies continue to exist in some regions, they are only to be found in relatively isolated territories – and, in most cases, even these last surviving examples are disintegrating. What has happened to destroy the forms of society which dominated the whole of history up to two centuries ago? The answer, in a word, is INDUSTRIALIZATION – the emergence of machine production, based on the use of inanimate power resources (like steam or electricity). The INDUSTRIAL SOCIETIES (sometimes also simply called 'modern societies') are utterly different from any previous type of social order, and their development has had consequences stretching far beyond their European origins.

Industrialization originated in eighteenth-century England as a result of the Industrial Revolution, a shorthand name for a complex set of technological changes affecting the means by which people gained their livelihood. These changes included the invention of new machines (like the spinning jenny for spinning yarn), the harnessing of power resources (especially water and steam) to production, and the use of science to improve production methods. Since discoveries and inventions in one field provoke more in others, the pace of technological innovation in industrial societies is extremely rapid compared with traditional social systems.

In even the most advanced of traditional civilizations, most people were engaged in working on the land. The relatively low level of technological development did not permit more than a small minority to be freed from the chores of agricultural production. By contrast, a prime feature of industrial societies today is that the large majority of the employed population work in factories, offices or shops rather than in agriculture. And over 90 per cent of people live in towns and cities, where most jobs are to be found and new job opportunities are created. The largest cities are vastly greater in size than the urban settlements found in traditional civilizations. In the cities, social life becomes more impersonal and anonymous than before, and many of our day-to-day encounters are with strangers rather than with individuals known to us. Large-scale organizations, such as business corporations or government agencies, come to influence the lives of virtually everyone.

A further feature of modern societies concerns their political systems, which are more developed and intensive than forms of government in traditional states. In traditional civilizations, the political authorities (monarchs and emperors) had little direct influence on the customs and habits of most of their subjects, who lived in fairly self-contained local villages. With industrialization, transportation and communications became much more rapid, making for a more integrated 'national' community.

The industrial societies were the first nation-states to come into existence. **Nation-states** are political communities, divided from each other by clearly delimited borders rather than the vague frontier areas that used to separate traditional states. Nation-state governments have extensive powers over many aspects of citizens' lives, framing laws that apply to all those living within their borders. Britain is a nation-state, as are virtually all other societies in the world today.

The application of industrial technology has by no means been limited to peaceful processes of economic development. From the earliest phases of industrialization, modern production processes have been put to military use, and this has radically altered ways of waging war, creating weaponry and modes of military organization much more advanced than those of non-industrial cultures. Together, superior economic strength, political cohesion and military superiority account for the seemingly irresistible spread of Western ways of life across the world over the past two centuries.

Britain as an example of an industrial society

Britain is one country among over two hundred nation-states which exist in the world today. It is small compared to some other states of the present day, in terms of both land area and population. Britain has 58 million people. Germany, another industrialized country, by contrast has 81 million, Japan 125 million and the United States 258 million. Although relatively small in terms of population, Britain still has more people than were included in the Roman empire at its height – an indication of how much more densely populated the world is than two thousand years ago.

The industrialized character of Britain is well demonstrated by the tiny numbers of people working in agriculture – less than 2 per cent of the workforce. Like other industrial states, Britain imports a variety of foodstuffs from all over the world – tea from South Asia, apples from New Zealand, wine from France and thousands of other foodstuffs from other countries. Yet the 2 per cent working in agriculture produces more than enough to feed the British population as a whole.

As measured by the average income per head of its population, Britain is not a rich society – as compared to a number of other industrial nations. It ranks only twenty-first in the league of industrial countries. Switzerland is top, Luxemburg second and Japan third. However, Britons are very rich compared to the mass of the population in premodern societies – and compared to most of the Third World countries in current times. Britain is what is sometimes called a *First World* society, different from Second and Third World countries. It is to these nations that we now turn.

FIRST, SECOND AND THIRD WORLD SOCIETIES

Origins of the division

From the seventeenth to the early twentieth century, the Western countries established colonies in numerous areas previously occupied by traditional societies, using their superior military strength where necessary. Although virtually all these colonies have now attained their independence, the process of **colonialism** was central to shaping the social map of the globe as we know it today. In some regions, such as North America, Australia and New Zealand, which were only thinly populated by hunting and gathering communities, Europeans became the majority population. In other areas, including much of Asia, Africa and South America, the local populations remained in the majority.

Societies of the first of these types, including the United States, have become industrialized. Those in the second category are mostly at a much lower level of industrial development and are often referred to as **Third World** societies. Such societies include China, India, most of the African countries (such as Nigeria, Ghana and Algeria) and countries in South America (for example, Brazil, Peru and Venezuela). Since many of these societies are situated south of the United States and Europe, they are sometimes referred to collectively as the *South*, and contrasted to the wealthier, industrialized *North*.

The term 'Third World' was originally part of a contrast drawn between three main types of society found in the early twentieth century. **First World** countries were (and are) the industrialized states of Europe, the United States, Australasia (Australia, New Zealand, Tasmania and Melanesia) and Japan. Nearly all First World societies have multiparty, parliamentary systems of government. **Second World** societies meant the communist societies of what was then the Soviet Union (USSR) and of Eastern Europe, including Czechoslovakia, Poland, East Germany and Hungary. Second World societies had centrally planned economies, which allowed little role for private property or competitive economic enterprise.

The Soviet Union as a Second World society

The Soviet Union had a very distinct form of social, political and economic organization. It was essentially a commonwealth, made up of a diversity of different national and cultural groups. Russia was the largest of these, and Russian was the official language of the country. Many other languages were spoken, however, such as Latvian, German, Arabic and Georgian.

The Soviet Union was dominated by the rule of the Communist Party. Based on a version of Marxism (see chapter 1, pp. 9–10), Soviet communism was a system of *one-party rule*. The Communist Party dominated both the political and the economic system. The First World countries are *capitalist* and have *market economies*: business firms are privately owned, and compete with each other to sell their goods to consumers. In the Soviet Union and Eastern Europe, by contrast, most industry and agriculture was *owned by the state*: few businesses were in private hands.

Following Marx's teachings, the communist leaders believed that a collectively owned system of production would become more prosperous than the Western free market system. This proved not to be the case. The Soviet Union and East European societies were politically authoritarian and economically inefficient. These limitations led to their downfall (for more information, see chapter 13).

With the collapse of communism in 1989, the Soviet Union fell apart. Russia became a separate state again, as it had been before the revolution of 1917 and a large number of other regions broke away to form independent nation-states – such as the Ukraine, Georgia or Lithuania.

For some seventy-five years, world history was affected by a global rivalry between the Soviet Union and Eastern European countries on the one hand and the capitalistic societies of the West and Japan on the other. Today that rivalry is over. With the ending of the Cold War and the disintegration of communism in the former USSR and Eastern Europe, the Second World has effectively disappeared.

The end of the Second World

Russia and the other former Second World societies are today in the process of moving towards a competitive market system like that of the Western countries. They are also trying to build democratic political institutions based on Western models.

What's going on in Russia and the other ex-communist countries might seem to have little to do with the lives of people in Britain. But this isn't so at all. In common with all the other industrial societies, the United Kingdom is increasingly locked into a global economy such that events in other parts of the world have immediate effects on our own activities. What happens in the former Soviet Union, for instance, might actually determine whether you are able to get a good job, or even a job at all, when you leave college. For continuing economic prosperity depends on stable economic conditions worldwide. If Russia is able to achieve economic and political development, fruitful trade with Britain could be of benefit to both countries. Should there be an economic collapse in the societies of the former Soviet Union, however, damaging consequences might ensue for social and economic stability in other societies too.

Third World societies

The term *Third World* (originally coined by the French demographer Alfred Sauvy) has become a conventional way of referring to the less developed societies, but in some respects it is not very satisfactory. The label makes it sound as though these societies are quite separate from the industrialized countries – a world apart from ours. But this is not true at all; the Third World societies have long been bound up with the industrialized countries, and the other way round. They were shaped by the impact of colonialism (see figure 3.4) and by the trading links forged with the Western states. In turn, the connections which the West established with other parts of the world have strongly affected their own development. For example, the fact that there is a large black population in the United States, and in Brazil, is a result of the 'trade in people' – the slave trade – which the colonizers developed.

The large majority of Third World societies are in areas that underwent colonial rule in Asia, Africa and South America. One or two are still colonies (Hong Kong remained a British colony right up to 1997, with arrangements for control to pass to China in that year). A few colonized areas gained independence early, like Haiti, which became the first autonomous black republic in January 1804. The Spanish colonies in South America acquired their freedom in 1810, while Brazil broke away from Portuguese rule in 1822.

Some countries that were never ruled from Europe were none the less strongly influenced by colonial relationships, the most notable example being China. By force of arms, China was compelled from the seventeenth century on to enter into trading agreements with European powers, with Europeans being allocated the government of certain areas, including major seaports. Hong Kong was the last remnant of these. Most Third World nations have become independent states only since World War Two, often following bloody anti-colonial struggles. Examples include India, a range of other Asian countries (like Burma, Malaysia and Singapore), and countries in Africa (including, for example, Kenya, Nigeria, Zaire, Tanzania and Algeria).

While they may include peoples living in traditional fashion, Third World countries are very different from earlier forms of traditional societies. Their political systems are modelled on systems first established in the societies of the West – that is to say, they are nation-states. While most of the population still live in rural areas, many of these societies are experiencing a rapid process of city development. Although agriculture remains the main economic activity, crops are now often produced for sale in world markets rather than for local consumption.

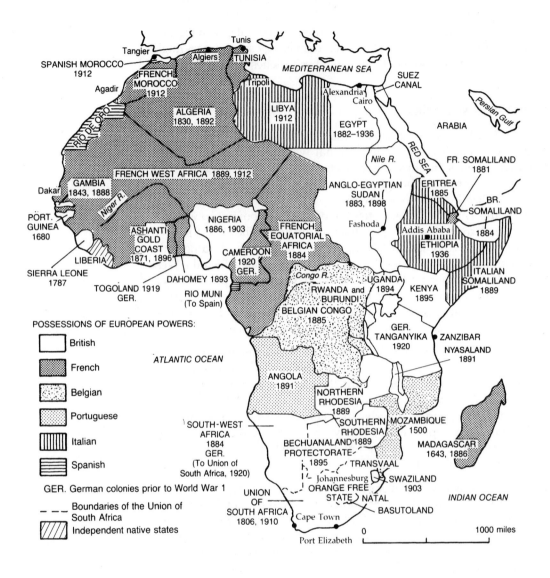

Fig. 3.4 European colonization of Africa: a map from earlier in the twentieth century showing the 'possessions' of the European powers from the eighteenth century on.

Source: Philip Lee Ralph et al., *World Civilizations*, 8th edn, vol. 2, 1991.

Conditions in the more impoverished of these societies have deteriorated rather than improved over the past few years. It has been estimated that in 1993 there were 1.2 billion people living in poverty in Third World countries, nearly a quarter of the population of the world. Some half of the world's poor live in South Asia, in countries such as India, Burma and Cambodia. About a third are concentrated in Africa. Others are in Central and South America. Over the decade from 1984 to 1994, living standards in Africa fell by 2 per cent annually. Unemployment has risen by 400 per cent, with more than 100 million people unemployed. Sub-Saharan Africa has a debt crisis as well. Its total debt has more than tripled. Repayments on that debt each year amount to four times what African governments spend on health and welfare.

India as an example of a Third World country

India and China are easily the two largest countries in the world in terms of population. India has 900 million people. China has 1,200 million – twenty-two times as many as the UK. India was colonized by the British, beginning some two centuries ago, and became part of the British empire. The country gained independence from the British after World War Two, but split into two: Pakistan, which is predominantly Islamic, split away from the main body of India, which is dominated by Hinduism.

India remains a heavily agricultural country: 33 per cent of the workforce is in agriculture. Average life expectancy is above that of many other developing countries, but well below that typical for the industrialized nations. Life expectancy for both men and women in India in 1996 was 63 years; in Britain it is currently 74 for men and 79 for women; in Japan, where people tend to live longer than anywhere else, it is 77 for men and 83 for women.

Unlike most First World countries, India is a society whose population is still growing rapidly. Population growth puts enormous strain on economic and educational resources. Only 50 per cent of the Indian population are literate (compared to 99 per cent in the UK). Many people have moved from rural areas to cities over the past thirty years. Indian cities such as Delhi, Calcutta and Bombay are overflowing with people, many of whom sleep on the streets and have no work.

Yet it would be a mistake to see India as simply 'lagging behind' the Western countries. It has a very rich and diverse culture, the inheritance of its long history as a traditional civilization. The country is also at present undergoing a rapid process of economic development. India contains large numbers of very poor people, who have to live a hand-to-mouth existence. But it has many millions of affluent people too, and prosperous industries, including high-tech industries. Its cities may be overcrowded, but they include neighbourhoods as elegant and chic as anything found in First World countries.

Third World poverty

In most Third World societies, poverty tends to be at its worst in rural areas. Malnutrition, lack of education, low life expectancy and substandard housing are generally most severe in the countryside. Many of the poor are to be found in areas where arable land is scarce, agricultural productivity low, and drought or floods common. Women are usually more disadvantaged than men. They encounter cultural, social and economic problems that even the most underprivileged men do not. For instance, they often work longer hours and, where they are paid at all, earn lower wages.

The poor in Third World countries live in conditions almost unimaginable to people in Britain or the other industrial societies. Many have no permanent dwellings apart from shelters made of cartons or loose pieces of wood. Most have no running water, sewerage or electricity. None the less, there are millions of poor people in Britain, Europe and the United States, and there are connections between poverty in these societies and global poverty. Almost half of the people living in poverty in the United States, for example, originate from the global South. This is true of the descendants of the black slaves brought over by force centuries ago; and it is true of more recent, and willing, immigrants who have arrived from Latin America, Asia and elsewhere.

THE NEWLY INDUSTRIALIZING COUNTRIES

The Third World is not a unity. While the majority of Third World countries economically lag well behind societies of the West, some have now successfully embarked on a process of industrialization. These are sometimes referred to as **newly industrializing countries** (NICs), and they include Brazil and Mexico in South America, together with Hong Kong, South Korea, Singapore and Taiwan in East Asia. The rates of economic growth of the most successful NICs, such as Taiwan, are several times those of the Western industrial economies. No Third World country figured among the top thirty exporters in the world in 1968, but twenty-five years later Hong Kong and South Korea were in the top fifteen.

The Asian NICs, as of the 1990s, have shown the most sustained levels of economic prosperity. They are investing abroad as well as promoting growth at home. South Korea's production of steel has doubled in the last decade, and its shipbuilding and electronics industries are among the world's leaders. Singapore is becoming the major financial and commercial centre of South East Asia. Taiwan is an important presence in the manufacturing and electronics industries. All these developments have directly affected Britain, whose share of global steel production, for example, has dropped significantly over the past thirty years.

Ways of life are changing rapidly in these societies. The more affluent within the Asian countries are plunging with enthusiasm into a new world of consumption.

> A global Asian affluent looks something like this: He wears Ferragamo-designed shirts and ties, sports a Rolex or Cartier watch, has a Louis Vuitton attaché case, signs his signature with a Montblanc pen, goes to work in his flashy BMW, endlessly talks on a mobile Motorola cellular phone, puts all his charges on the American Express card, travels Singapore Airlines, maintains a city apartment, and keeps a country home. (Naisbitt 1995, p. 31)

Affluence and consumer glitz exist alongside traditional forms of marriage and the family, and sometimes alongside subsistence farming and rural poverty too.

SOCIAL CHANGE TODAY: GLOBALIZATION

Take a close look at the array of products on offer the next time you walk into the local shop or supermarket. The diversity of goods which we in the West have come to take for granted as available, for anyone

SOCIETIES IN THE MODERN WORLD

Type	Period of existence	Characteristics
First World societies	Eighteenth century to the present.	Based on industrial production and generally free enterprise. Majority of people live in towns and cities, a few work in rural agricultural pursuits. Major class inequalities, though less pronounced than in traditional states. Distinct political communities or nation-states, including the nations of the West, Japan, Australia and New Zealand.
Second World societies	Early twentieth century (following the Russian Revolution of 1917) to the early 1990s.	Based on industry, but the economic system is centrally planned. Small proportion of the population work in agriculture; most live in towns and cities. Major class inequalities persist. Distinct political communities or nation-states. Until 1989, composed of the Soviet Union and Eastern Europe, but social and political changes began to transform them into free enterprise economic systems, making them First World societies.
Third World societies	Eighteenth century (mostly as colonized areas) to the present.	Majority of the population work in agriculture, using traditional methods of production. Some agricultural produce sold on world markets. Some have free enterprise systems, others are centrally planned. Distinct political communities or nation-states, including China, India and most African and South American nations.
Newly industrializing countries	1970s to the present.	Former Third World societies now based on industrial production and generally free enterprise. Majority of people live in towns and cities, a few work in agricultural pursuits. Major class inequalities, more pronounced than First World societies. Average per capita income considerably less than First World societies. Include Hong Kong, South Korea, Singapore, Taiwan, Brazil and Mexico.

with the money to buy them, depends on amazingly complex economic connections stretching across the world. The products on display have been made in, or use ingredients or parts from, a hundred different countries. All these have to be regularly transported across the globe, and constant flows of information are necessary to coordinate the millions of daily transactions involved.

'Until our day', the anthropologist Peter Worsley has written, 'human society has never existed' (Worsley 1984, p. 1), meaning that it is only in quite recent times that we can speak of forms of social association which span the earth. The world has become in important respects a single social system as a result of growing ties of interdependence which now affect virtually everyone. The global system is not just an environment within which particular societies – like Britain – develop and change. The social, political and economic connections which

➡ cross-cut borders between countries decisively condition the fate of those living within each of them. The general term for the increasing interdependence of world society is GLOBALIZATION.

No society on earth any longer lives in complete separation from others, and even in the wealthiest countries everyone is dependent on goods transported from abroad. In Britain for example, nearly all TV sets sold are made and assembled abroad, mainly in the Far East. Another case in point is the motor-car industry. Forty or so years ago, US car production was greater than that of the whole of the rest of the world put together. Today the United States stands only third; more cars are made in both Europe and Japan. Moreover, the parts used to construct the cars are made in many different countries. A Ford Mondeo car, for example, involves parts made in 112 different locations spanning sixteen countries and three continents. The very name of the car, 'Mondeo', carries a sense of the global nature of the car industry. Globalizing processes have brought numerous benefits to many in the industrialized societies: a much greater variety of goods and foodstuffs is available than ever before. At the same time, the fact that we are all now caught up in a much wider world has helped to create some of the most serious problems we now face.

Processes of globalization are among the most important social changes occurring today. Sociological analysis that confines itself to the study of single societies is becoming increasingly archaic. As human beings, we more and more share a common fate. Fundamental problems that beset human life, such as coping with ecological decay or avoiding large-scale military confrontations, are necessarily global in scope.

CONCLUSION

In spite of growing economic and cultural interdependence, the global order is riven with inequalities, and divided up into a patchwork of states with divergent as well as common concerns. There is no real indication of a political convergence that will overcome the conflicting interests of states in the near future. One of the most worrying features of world society is that, in spite of the existence of the United Nations, increasing globalization is not matched either by political integration or by a reduction of international inequalities of wealth and power.

SUMMARY

1 Several types of premodern society – forms of society which precede the development of industrial societies – can be distinguished. In hunting and gathering societies, people do not grow crops or keep livestock, but live by gathering plants and hunting animals. Pastoral societies are those in which the raising of domesticated animals provides a major source of livelihood. Agrarian societies depend on the cultivation of fixed plots of land. Larger, more developed agrarian societies form traditional states or civilizations.

2 The development and expansion of the West led to the conquest of many parts of the world, radically changing long-established social systems and cultures. This process was associated with colonialism – the imposition of Western government and Western control.

3 In industrial societies, industrial production becomes the main basis of the economy. First World industrialized countries include the nations of the 'West', plus Japan, Australia and New Zealand.

4 Second World countries were industrialized societies ruled by communist governments. Since the revolutions of 1989 in Eastern Europe, which led to the overthrow of communism there and in the former Soviet Union, Second World societies no longer exist.

5 Third World or developing countries, in which most of the world's population live, were almost all formerly colonized areas. The majority of the population work in agricultural production. Although most Third World societies are impoverished compared with the industrial nations, a minority (the NICs, or newly industrial countries) have recently experienced rapid economic development.

6 The countries of the world have become increasingly interdependent – a process known as globalization. The development of world social relations involves large-scale inequalities between the industrial and poor Third World societies.

7 Globalization is today affecting people's lives in all countries, rich and poor, altering not just global systems but everyday life. Globalization has not produced a unified world. Rather to the contrary, it has created some of the main social divisions and conflicts analysed in the various chapters of this book.

FURTHER READING

Brian M. Fagan, *People of the Earth* (London: HarperCollins, 1992). The latest edition of an authoritative survey of the origins and development of the different forms of human culture.

Stephan Haggard, *Pathways from the Periphery: The Politics of Growth in the Newly Industrialized Countries* (Ithaca, N.Y.: Cornell University Press, 1990). An analysis of political and economic aspects of industrialization in developing countries.

Leslie Holmes, *Post-Communism: An Introduction* (Cambridge: Polity Press, 1996). A first comprehensive single-authored analysis of societies after the collapse of communist power in Eastern Europe and the USSR.

Sheilagh C. Ogilvie and **Markus German (eds)**, *European Proto-Industrialisation* (Cambridge: Cambridge University Press, 1996). An extended analysis of the processes of industrialization in Europe.

Robert Skidelsky, *The World after Communism: A Polemic for Our Times* (London: Macmillan, 1995). A discussion of the likely future for the Eastern European societies following the fall of communism.

IMPORTANT TERMS

- *hunting and gathering societies*
- *pastoral societies*
- *agrarian societies*
- *traditional states*
- *nation-state*

- *colonialism*
- *Third World*
- *First World*
- *Second World*
- *newly industrializing countries*

SOCIAL INTERACTION AND EVERYDAY LIFE

Two people pass each other on a city street. At a distance, they briefly exchange glances, each rapidly scanning the other's face and style of dress. As they come close and pass by, each looks away, avoiding the other's eyes. This goes on millions of times a day in the towns and cities of the world.

When passers-by quickly glance at one another and then look away again, they demonstrate what Erving Goffman (1967, 1971) calls the **civil inattention** we require of one another in many situations. Civil inattention is not the same as merely ignoring another person. Each individual indicates recognition of the other person's presence, but avoids any gesture that might be taken as too intrusive. Civil inattention is something we engage in more or less unconsciously, but it is of fundamental importance in our everyday lives.

The best way to see why is by thinking of examples where it doesn't apply. When a person stares fixedly at another, allowing his or her face openly to express a particular emotion, it is normally with a lover, family member or close friend. Strangers or chance acquaintances, whether met with on the street, at work or at a party, virtually never hold the gaze of another in this way. To do so may be taken as an indication of hostile intent. It is only where two groups are strongly antagonistic to one another that strangers might indulge in such a practice. Thus whites in the United States have been known in the past to give a 'hate stare' to blacks walking past.

Even friends in close conversation need to be careful about how they look at one another. Each individual demonstrates attention and involvement in the conversation by regularly looking at the eyes of the other, but not staring into them. To look too intently might be taken as a sign of mistrust about, or at least failure to understand, what the other is saying. Yet someone who does not engage the eyes of the other at all is likely to be thought evasive, shifty or otherwise odd.

THE STUDY OF EVERYDAY LIFE

Why should we concern ourselves with such seemingly trivial aspects of social behaviour? Passing someone on the street and exchanging a few words with a friend seem minor and uninteresting activities, things we do countless times a day without giving them any thought. In fact, the study of such apparently insignificant forms of SOCIAL INTER-ACTION is of major importance in sociology – and, far from being uninteresting, is one of the most absorbing of all areas of sociological investigation. There are two reasons for this.

First, our day-to-day routines, with their almost constant interactions with others, give structure and form to what we do. We can learn a great deal about ourselves as social beings, and about social life itself, from studying them. Our lives are organized around the repetition of similar patterns of behaviour from day to day, week to week, month to month and year to year. Think of what you did yesterday, for example, and the day before that. If they were both weekdays, in all probability you got up at about the same time each day (an important routine in itself). You may have gone off to lessons or lectures fairly early in the morning, making a journey from home to school or college that you make virtually every weekday. You perhaps met some friends for lunch, returning to classes or private study in the afternoon. Later, you retraced your steps back home, possibly going out later in the evening with other friends.

Of course, the routines we follow from day to day are not identical, and our patterns of activity at weekends usually contrast with those on weekdays. And if we make a major change in our life, like leaving college to take up a job, alterations in our daily routines are usually necessary; but then we establish a new and fairly regular set of habits again.

Second, studying social interaction in everyday life sheds light on larger social systems and institutions. All large-scale social systems, in fact, depend on the patterns of social interaction we engage in daily. This is easy to demonstrate. Consider again the case of two strangers

The Far Side by Gary Larson

'Ordinary life would be impossible if we had to think consciously about every daily routine.'
The Far Side © 1992, Farworks Inc. Dist. by Universal Press Syndicate.

passing in the street. Such an event may seem to have little direct relevance to large-scale, more permanent forms of social organization. But when we take into account many such interactions, this is no longer so. In modern societies, most people live in towns and cities and constantly interact with others whom they do not know personally. Civil inattention is one among other mechanisms that give city life, with its bustling crowds and fleeting, impersonal contacts, the character it has.

In this chapter, we shall first learn about the non-verbal cues (facial expressions and bodily gestures) all of us use when interacting with each other. We will then move on to analyse everyday speech – how we use language to communicate to others the meanings we wish to get across. Finally, we focus on the ways in which our lives are structured by daily routines, paying particular attention to how we coordinate our actions across space and time.

NON-VERBAL COMMUNICATION

Social interaction requires numerous forms of **non-verbal communication** – the exchange of information and meaning through facial expresions, gestures and movements of the body. Non-verbal communication is sometimes referred to as 'body language', but this is misleading, because we characteristically use such non-verbal cues to eliminate or expand on what is said in words.

The face, gestures and emotion

One major aspect of non-verbal communication is the facial expression of emotion. Paul Ekman and his colleagues have developed what they call the Facial Action Coding System (FACS) for describing movements of the facial muscles that give rise to particular expressions (Ekman and Friesen 1978). By this means, they have tried to inject some precision into an area notoriously open to inconsistent or contradictory interpretations – for there is little agreement about how emotions are to be identified and classified. Charles Darwin, the originator of evolutionary theory, claimed that basic modes of emotional expression are the same in all human beings. Although some have disputed the claim, Ekman's researches among people from widely different cultural backgrounds seem to confirm this. Ekman and Friesen carried out a study of an isolated community in New Guinea, whose members had previously had virtually no contact with outsiders. When they were shown pictures of facial expressions expressing six emotions (happiness, sadness, anger, disgust, fear, surprise), the New Guineans were able to identify these emotions.

According to Ekman, the results of his own and similar studies of different peoples support the view that the facial expression of emotion and its interpretation are innate in human beings. He acknowledges that his evidence does not conclusively demonstrate this, and it may be that widely shared cultural learning experiences are involved; however, his conclusions are supported by other types of research. I. Eibl-

Eibesfeldt studied six children born deaf and blind to see how far their facial expressions were the same as those of sighted, hearing individuals in particular emotional situations (1973). He found that the children smiled when engaged in obviously pleasurable activities, raised their eyebrows in surprise when sniffing at an object with an unaccustomed smell, and frowned when repeatedly offered a disliked object. Since they could not have seen other people behaving in these ways, it seems that these responses must have been innately determined.

Using the FACS, Ekman and Friesen identified a number of the discrete facial muscle actions in new-born infants that are also found in adult expressions of emotion. Infants seem, for example, to produce facial expressions similar to the adult expression of disgust (pursing the lips and frowning) in response to sour tastes. But although the facial expression of emotion seems to be partly innate, individual and cultural factors influence what exact form facial movements take and the contexts in which they are deemed appropriate. How people smile, for example, the precise movement of the lips and other facial muscles, and how fleeting the smile is all vary between cultures.

There are no gestures or bodily postures that have been shown to characterize all, or even most, cultures. In some societies, for instance, people nod when they mean no, the opposite of Anglo-American practice. Gestures Europeans and Americans tend to use a great deal, such as pointing, seem not to exist among certain peoples (Bull 1983). Similarly, a straightened forefinger placed in the centre of the cheek and rotated is used in parts of Italy as a gesture of praise, but appears to be unknown elsewhere.

Like facial expressions, gestures and bodily posture are continually used to fill out utterances, as well as conveying meanings when nothing is actually said. All three can be used to joke, show irony or show scepticism. The non-verbal impressions that we convey inadvertently often indicate that what we say is not quite what we really mean. Blushing is perhaps the most obvious example, but there are innumerable more subtle indicators that can be picked up by other people. Genuine facial expressions tend to evaporate after four or five seconds. A smile that lasts longer could indicate deceit. An expression of surprise that lasts too long may deliberately be used as a parody – to show that the individual is not in fact surprised at all, even though she or he might have reason to be.

'Face' and culture

The word 'face' can also refer to the *esteem* in which an individual is held by others. In daily social life, we normally pay a good deal of attention to 'saving face'. Much of what we call politeness or etiquette in social gatherings consists of disregarding aspects of behaviour that might otherwise lead to a loss of face. We don't refer to episodes in an individual's past or personal characteristics that might produce embarrassment if mentioned. We refrain from making jokes about baldness if we realize that someone is wearing a hairpiece – unless we are among close friends. Tact is a sort of protective device that each person employs in the expectation that, in return, her or his own weaknesses will not be deliberately exposed to general view. Our day-to-day lives, therefore, do not just happen. Without realizing it most of the time, we skilfully maintain a close and continuous control over facial expression, body posture and gesture in our interactions with others.

Some people are specialists in the control of facial expressions and in tactful commerce with other people. A good diplomat, for example, must be able – giving every appearance of ease and comfort – to interact with others whose views he might disagree with or even find repellent. The degree to which this is managed successfully can affect the fate of whole nations. Skilful diplomacy, for instance, might defuse tensions between countries and prevent a war.

SOCIAL RULES AND TALK

Although we routinely use non-verbal cues in our own behaviour and in making sense of the behaviour of others, much of our interaction occurs through **talk** – casual verbal exchange – carried on in informal **conversations** with others. It has always been accepted by sociologists that language is fundamental to social life. Recently, however, an approach has been developed that is specifically concerned with how people use language in the ordinary contexts of everyday life. The study of conversations has been strongly influenced by the work of Erving Goffman. But the most important influence in this type of research is Harold Garfinkel, the founder of ethnomethodology (Garfinkel 1984).

Ethnomethodology is the study of the 'ethnomethods' – the folk, or lay, methods – people use to *make sense* of what others do, and particularly what they say. We all apply these methods, normally without having to give any conscious attention to them. Often we can only make sense of what is said in conversation if we know the social context, which does not appear in the words themselves. Take the following conversation (Heritage 1984):

    A: I have a fourteen-year-old son.
    B: Well, that's all right.
    A: I also have a dog.
    B: Oh, I'm sorry.

What do you think is happening here? What is the relation between the speakers? Knowing that this is a conversation between a prospective tenant and landlord makes the conversation understandable. Some landlords accept children but don't permit their tenants to keep pets. Yet if we don't know the social context, the responses of individual B seem to bear no relation to the statements of A. *Part* of the sense is in the words, and *part* is in the way in which the social context structures what is said.

Shared understandings

The most inconsequential forms of daily talk presume complicated, **shared understandings** and knowledge brought into play by those concerned. In fact, our small talk is so complex that it has so far proved impossible to program even the most sophisticated computers to converse with human beings. The words used in ordinary talk do not always have precise meanings, and we 'fix' what we want to say through the unstated assumptions that back it up. If Maria asks Tom, 'What did you do yesterday?' there is no obvious answer suggested by the words themselves. A day is a long time, and it would be logical for Tom to answer: 'Well, at seven-sixteen, I woke up. At seven-eighteen, I got out of bed, went to the bathroom and started to brush my teeth. At seven-nineteen, I turned on the shower . . .' We understand the type of response the question calls for by knowing Maria, what sort of activities she and Tom normally carry on together, and what Tom usually does on a particular day of the week, among other things.

Garfinkel's experiments

The 'background expectancies' with which we organize ordinary conversations were highlighted by some experiments Garfinkel undertook with student volunteers. The students were asked to engage a friend or relative in conversation, and to insist that casual remarks or general comments be actively pursued to make their meaning precise. If someone said, 'Have a nice day', the student was to respond, 'Nice in what sense, exactly?', 'Which part of the day do you mean?' and so forth. One of the exchanges that resulted ran as follows (Garfinkel 1963):

> S: How are you?
> E: How am I in regard to what? My health, my finance, my school work, my peace of mind, my . . .
> S: (*red in the face and suddenly out of control*) Look! I was just trying to be polite. Frankly, I don't give a damn how you are.

Why do people get so upset when apparently minor conventions of talk are not followed? The answer is that the stability and meaningfulness of our daily social life depend on the sharing of unstated cultural assumptions about what is said and why. If we weren't able to take these for granted, meaningful communication would be impossible. Any question or contribution to a conversation would have to be followed by a massive 'search procedure' of the sort Garfinkel's subjects were told to initiate, and interaction would simply break down. What seem at first sight to be unimportant conventions of talk, therefore, turn out to be fundamental to the very fabric of social life, which is why their breach is so serious.

Note that in everyday life, people on occasion deliberately feign ignorance of unstated knowledge. This may be done to rebuff the others, poke fun at them, cause embarrassment, or call attention to a double meaning in what was said. Consider, for example, this classic exchange between parent and teenager:

> P: Where are you going?
> T: Out.
> P: What are you going to do?
> T: Nothing.

The responses of the teenager are effectively the opposite of those of the volunteers in Garfinkel's experiments. Rather than pursuing inquiries where this is not normally done, the teenager declines to provide appropriate answers at all – essentially saying, 'Mind your own business!'

The first question might elicit a different response from another person in another context:

A: Where are you going?
B: I'm going quietly round the bend.

B deliberately misreads A's question in order ironically to convey worry or frustration. Comedy and joking thrive on such deliberate misunderstandings of the unstated assumptions involved in talk. There is nothing threatening about this so long as the parties concerned recognize the intent to provoke laughter.

Forms of talk

It is a sobering experience to hear a tape recording or read a transcript of a conversation to which one has contributed. Conversations are much more fractured, hesitant and ungrammatical than most people realize. When we take part in everyday talk, we tend to think that what we say is fairly polished, because we unconsciously fill in the background to the actual words; but real conversations are quite different from conversations in novels, where characters speak in well-formed and grammatical sentences.

As with Goffman's work on civil inattention, it might be presumed that the analysis of ordinary conversations is rather marginal to the main concerns of sociology; indeed, many sociologists have been critical of ethnomethodological research for just this reason. Yet some of the arguments used to show why Goffman's work is so important to sociology also apply to ethnomethodology. Studying everyday talk has shown how complicated is the mastery of language that ordinary people command. The immense difficulties involved in programming computers to do what human speakers are able to carry out without effort is evidence of this complexity. In addition, talk is an essential element of every realm of social life. The Watergate tapes of President Nixon and his advisers were nothing more than a transcript of conversation, but they provided a glimpse of the exercise of political power at the highest levels (Molotch and Boden 1985).

Response cries

Some kinds of utterances are not talk but consist of muttered exclamations, or what Goffman has called **response cries** (Goffman 1981). Consider someone saying 'Oops!' after knocking over or dropping something. 'Oops!' seems to be merely an uninteresting reflex response to a mishap, rather like blinking the eye when a person moves a hand sharply towards your face. It is not, however, an involuntary response, as is shown by the fact that people do not usually make the exclamation when alone. 'Oops!' is normally directed towards others present. The exclamation demonstrates to witnesses that the lapse is only minor and momentary, not something that should cast doubt on a person's command of his actions.

'Oops!' is used only in situations of minor failure, rather than in major accidents or calamities – which also demonstrates that the exclamation is part of our controlled management of the details of social life. Moreover, the word may be used by someone observing another individual; or it may be used to sound a warning to another. 'Oops!' is normally a curt sound, but the 'oo' may be prolonged in some situations. Thus someone might extend the sound to cover a critical moment in performing a task. For instance, a parent may utter an extended 'Oops!' or 'Oops-a-daisy!' when playfully tossing a child in the air. The sound covers the brief phase when the child may feel a loss of control, reassuring the infant and probably at the same time developing understanding of response to the child's cries.

The term 'Oops' is itself culturally defined. When Russians drop something, for example, they don't say 'Oops', but instead make an exclamation which sounds in English like 'Ayee'.

This may all sound very contrived and exaggerated. Why bother to analyse such an inconsequential utterance in this detail? Surely we don't pay as much attention to what we say as this example suggests? Of course we don't – on a conscious level. The crucial point, however, is that we take for granted an immensely complicated, continuous control of our appearance and actions. In situations of interaction, we are never expected just to be present on the scene. Others expect, as we expect of them, that we display what Goffman calls 'controlled alertness'. A fundamental part of being human is continually demonstrating to others our competence in the routines of daily life.

Slips of the tongue

'Oops!' is a response to a minor mishap. We also make mistakes in speech and pronunciation in the course of conversations, lectures and other situations of talk. In his investigations into the 'psychopathology of everyday life', Sigmund Freud, the founder of psychoanalysis, analysed numerous examples of such **slips of the tongue** (Freud 1975). According to Freud, mistakes in speaking, including mispronounced or misplaced words and stammering, are never in fact accidental. They are unconsciously motivated by feelings that are repressed from our conscious minds, or that we try consciously but unsuccessfully to suppress. These feelings often, but not always, involve sexual associations. Thus one may mean to say 'organism' but instead say 'orgasm'. In an example Freud gave, when a woman was asked, 'What regiment is your son with?' she answered, 'With the Forty-Second Murderers' (*Mörder* in German, rather than the word she intended to say, *Mörser*, or 'Mortars').

Slips of the tongue are often humorous and could pass as jokes. The difference lies simply in whether or not the speaker consciously intended the words to come out as they did. Slips of the tongue shade over into other types of 'inappropriate' speech, which Freud also believed are often unconsciously motivated – as when a person fails to see that something she says has a clear double meaning. These again can be taken as jokes if deliberately intended, but are otherwise lapses in the controlled production of talk that we expect people to sustain.

One of the best ways of illustrating these points is to look at lapses in the speech of radio and television announcers. Announcers' speech is not like ordinary talk, because it is not spontaneous but scripted. It is also expected to be more nearly perfect than ordinary talk, delivered with fewer hesitations and more clearly articulated. Hence fluffs or blunders made by newsreaders, are much more obvious than those made in casual conversations. Yet announcers do, of course, make slips of the tongue, and many are funny or have the 'only too true' nature to which Freud called attention. Here are two examples (Goffman 1981):

> This is the Dominion Network of the Canadian Broadcorping Castration.

> Beat the egg yolk and then add the milk, then slowly blend in the sifted flour. As you do, you can see how the mixture is sickening.

Other examples come into the category of inappropriate speech, where a double meaning that should have been spotted comes through:

> Ladies who care to drive by and drop off their clothes will receive prompt attention.

> Folks, try our comfortable beds. I personally stand behind every bed we sell.

> The loot and the car were listed as stolen by the Los Angeles Police Department.

> And here in Hollywood, it is rumored that the former movie starlet is expecting her fifth child in a month.

We tend to laugh more at verbal mistakes when announcers (or teachers in lectures) make them than when they occur in ordinary conversation. The humour resides not only in what is missaid, but also in the discomfiture the broadcaster or teacher might show at delivering a less than perfect performance. We temporarily see behind the mask of cool professionalism to the ordinary individual behind.

FACE, BODY AND SPEECH IN INTERACTION

Let us summarize at this point what we have learned so far. Everyday interaction depends on subtle relationships between what we convey with our faces and bodies and what we express in words. We use the facial expressions and bodily gestures of other people to fill in what they communicate verbally, and to check how far they are sincere in what they say. Mostly without realizing it, each of us keeps a tight and continuous control over facial expression, bodily posture and movement in the course of our daily interaction with others.

Sometimes, however, we make verbal slips that, as Freud's example of the 'murderers' indicates, briefly reveal what we wish to keep concealed, consciously or unconsciously. Many verbal slips inadvertently display our true feelings – like the one in the example of the cake mix, which the announcer probably thinks is really 'sickening'.

Face, bodily management and speech, then, are used to convey certain meanings and to hide others. We also organize our activities in the *contexts* of social life to achieve the same ends, as we shall now see.

Encounters

In many social situations, we engage in what Goffman calls **unfocused interaction** with others. Unfocused interaction takes place whenever individuals exhibit mutual awareness of one another's presence. This is usually the case wherever large numbers of people are assembled together, as on a busy street, in a theatre crowd or at a party. When people are in the presence of others, even if they do not directly talk to them, they continually engage in non-verbal communication through their posture and facial and physical gestures.

Focused interaction occurs when individuals directly attend to what others say or do. Except when someone is standing alone, say at a party, all interaction involves both focused and unfocused exchanges. Goffman calls an instance of focused interaction an ENCOUNTER, and much of our day-to-day life consists of encounters with other people – family, friends, workmates – frequently occurring against the background of unfocused interaction with others present on the scene. Small talk, seminar discussions, games and routine face-to-face contacts (with ticket clerks, waiters, shop assistants and so forth) are all examples of encounters.

Encounters always need 'openings', which indicate that civil inattention is being discarded. When strangers meet and begin to talk – as at a party – the moment of ceasing civil inattention is always risky, since misunderstandings can easily occur about the nature of the encounter being established (Goffman 1971). Hence the making of eye contact may first be ambiguous and tentative. A person can then act as though he had made no direct move if the overture is not accepted. In focused interaction, each person communicates as much by facial expression and gesture as by the words actually exchanged. Goffman distinguishes between the expressions individuals 'give' and those they 'give off'. The first are the words and facial expressions people use to produce certain impressions on others. The second are the clues that others may spot to check their sincerity or truthfulness. For instance, a restaurant owner listens with a polite smile to the statements of customers about how much they enjoyed their meals – at the same time noting how pleased they seemed to be while eating the food, whether a lot was left over, and the tone of voice they use to express their satisfaction.

Markers

Most of us meet and talk to a variety of people in the course of an average day. Catherine, for example, gets up, breakfasts with her family, and perhaps accompanies her children to school, stopping briefly to exchange pleasantries with a friend at the school gates. She drives to work, probably listening to the radio. During the course of the day, she enters into interchanges with colleagues and visitors, ranging from

STREETWISE

In American cities, where crime rates are often high and urban dwellers live with caution and fear, diverse populations must be wise to the ways of one another and the streets. Both African Americans and whites hold similar views about public safety, including a wariness to venture out after dark.

Elijah Anderson, an urban sociologist at the University of Pennsylvania, studied the types of social interaction on the streets of two adjacent urban neighbourhoods. His book, *Streetwise* (1990), looks at the way that blacks and whites interact on the street 'with minimum risk and maximum mutual respect in a world full of uncertainty and danger'. As other sociologists who observed social interaction have concluded, Anderson found that studying everyday life sheds light on how social order is created by individual interactions. He was particularly interested in understanding interaction when at least one party is viewed as threaten-ing. How do strangers quickly become less strange to one another?

Before looking to the streets to answer this question, Anderson recalled Erving Goffman's description of how social definitions come into existence in particular contexts or locations: 'When an individual enters the presence of others, they commonly seek to acquire information about him or bring into play information already possessed.... Information about the individual helps to define the situation, enabling others to know in advance what he will expect of them and they may expect of him.'

Following Goffman's lead, Anderson asked what types of behavioural cues and signs make up the vocabulary of public interaction. He concluded that

skin color, gender, age, companions, clothing, jewelry, and the objects people carry help identify them, so that assumptions are formed and communication can occur. Movements (quick or slow, false or sincere, comprehensible or incomprehensible) further refine this public communication. Factors like time of day or an activity that 'explains' a person's presence can also affect in what way and how quickly the image of 'stranger' is neutralized. If a stranger cannot pass inspection and be assessed as 'safe', the image of predator may arise, and fellow pedestrians may try to maintain a distance consistent with that image.

What kind of people pass inspection on the streets? According to Anderson, 'children readily pass inspection, white women and white men do so more slowly, black women, black men, and black male teenagers most slowly of all.' Only with experience do urban dwellers learn to distinguish between real danger and false alarms.

transitory conversations to formal meetings. Each of these encounters is likely to be separated by markers, or what Goffman calls brackets, which distinguish each episode of focused interaction from the one before and from unfocused interaction taking place in the background (Goffman 1974).

At a party, for example, people talking together will tend to position themselves and control their voice levels so as to create a 'huddle', separate from others. They may stand facing one another, effectively making it difficult for others to intrude until they decide to break up, or until they soften the edges of their focused interaction by moving to different positions in the room. On more formal occasions, recognized devices are often used to signal the opening and ending of a particular encounter. To signal the opening of a play, for instance, the lights go down and the curtain is raised. At the end of the performance, the auditorium lights are turned on again and the curtain falls.

Markers are particularly important either when an encounter is especially out of the ordinary or when there might be ambiguity about what is going on. For example, when a model poses naked in front of an art class, he does not usually undress or dress in the presence of the group. Undressing and dressing in private allows the body to be suddenly exposed and hidden. This both marks the boundaries of the episode and conveys that it is devoid of the sexual meanings that otherwise might be conveyed.

In very confined spaces, such as lifts, it is difficult to mark off an area of focused interaction. It is not easy, either, for other people present to indicate, as they will do in other situations, that they are not listening to whatever conversation is carried on. It is also difficult for strangers not to be seen looking at one another more directly than the norms of civil inattention allow. Thus, in lifts, people often adopt an exaggerated 'not listening' and 'not looking' pose, staring into space or at the panel of buttons – anywhere but at their fellow passengers. Conversation is usually suspended or confined to brief exchanges. Similarly, in an office or at home, if several people are talking to one another and one is interrupted to take a phone call, the others cannot readily show complete inattention and they may carry on a sort of hesitant, limp conversation.

Impression management

Goffman and other writers on social interaction often use notions from the theatre in analysing social interaction. The concept of SOCIAL ROLE, for example, originated in a theatrical setting. Roles are socially defined expectations that a person in a given SOCIAL POSITION follows. To be a teacher is to hold a specific position; the teacher's role consists of acting in specified ways towards her pupils. Goffman sees social life as though played out by actors on a stage – or on many stages, because how we act depends on the roles we are playing at a particular time. This approach is sometimes referred to as the **dramaturgical model** – social life as like a theatre drama. People are sensitive to how they are seen by others, and use many forms of **impression management** to compel others to react to them in the ways they wish. Although we may sometimes do this in a calculated way, usually it is among the things we do without conscious attention. When Philip attends a business meeting, he wears a suit and tie and is on his best behaviour; that evening, when relaxing with friends at a football match, he wears jeans and sweatshirt and tells a lot of jokes. This is impression management.

Front and back regions

Much of social life, Goffman suggested, can be divided into front regions and back regions. **Front regions** are social occasions or encounters in which individuals act out formal roles; they are 'onstage performances'. Teamwork is often involved in creating front region performances. Two prominent politicians in the same party may put on an elaborate show of unity and friendship before the television cameras, even though each cordially detests the other. A wife and husband may take care to conceal their quarrels from their children, preserving a front of harmony, only to fight bitterly once the children are safely tucked up in bed.

The **back regions** are where people assemble the props and prepare themselves for interaction in the more formal settings. Back regions resemble the backstage of a theatre or the off-camera activities of filming. When they are safely behind the scenes, people can relax and give vent to feelings and styles of behaviour they keep in check when on front stage. Back regions permit 'profanity, open sexual remarks, elaborate griping . . . rough informal dress, "sloppy" sitting and standing posture, use of dialect or substandard speech, mumbling and shouting, playful aggressiveness and "kidding", inconsiderateness for the other in minor but potentially symbolic acts, minor self-involvement such as humming, whistling, chewing, nibbling, belching and flatulence' (Goffman 1969). Thus a waitress may be the soul of quiet courtesy when serving a customer but become loud and aggressive once behind the swing doors of the kitchen. There are probably few restaurants customers would patronize if they could see all that goes on in the kitchens.

Adopting roles: intimate examinations

For an example of collaboration in impression management that also borrows from the theatre, let's look at one particular study in some detail. James Henslin and Mae Briggs studied a specific, highly delicate type of encounter: a woman's visit to a gynaecologist (Henslin and Briggs 1971). At the time of the study, most pelvic examinations were carried out by male doctors, and hence the experience was (and sometimes is) fraught with potential ambiguities and embarrassment for both parties. Men and women in the West are socialized to think of the genitals as the most private part of the body, and seeing, and particularly feeling, the genitals of another person is ordinarily associated with intimate sexual encounters. Some women feel so worried by the prospect of a pelvic examination that they refuse to visit the doctor, male or female, even when they suspect there is a strong medical reason to do so.

Henslin and Briggs analysed material collected by Briggs, a trained nurse, from a large number of gynaecological examinations. They interpreted what they found as having several typical stages. Adopting a dramaturgical metaphor, they suggested that each phase can be treated as a distinct scene, in which the parts the actors play alter as the episode unfolds. In the prologue, the woman enters the waiting room preparing to assume the role of patient, temporarily discarding her outside identity. Called into the consulting room, she adopts the 'patient' role, and the first scene opens. The doctor assumes a businesslike, professional manner and treats the patient as a proper and competent person, maintaining eye contact and listening politely to what she has to say. If he decides an examination is called for, he tells her so and leaves the room; scene one is over.

As he leaves, the nurse comes in. She is an important stagehand in the main scene shortly to begin. She soothes any worries that the patient might have, acting as both a confidante – knowing some of the 'things women have to put up with' – and a collaborator in what is to follow. Crucially, the nurse helps alter the patient from a person to a 'non-person' for the vital scene – which features a body, part of which is to be scrutinized, rather than a complete human being. In Henslin and Briggs's study, the nurse not only supervises the patient's undressing, but takes over aspects that normally the patient would control. Thus she takes the patient's clothes and folds them. Most women wish their underwear to be out of sight when the doctor returns, and the nurse makes sure that this is so. She guides the patient to the examining table and covers most of her body with a sheet before the physician returns.

The central scene now opens, with nurse as well as doctor taking part. The presence of the nurse helps ensure that the interaction between doctor and patient is free of sexual overtones, and also provides a legal witness should the physician be charged with unprofessional conduct. The examination proceeds as though the personality of the patient were absent; the sheet across her separates the genital area from the rest of her body, and her position does not allow her to watch the examination itself. Save for any specific medical queries, the doctor ignores her, sitting on a low stool, out of her line of vision. The patient collaborates in becoming a temporary non-person, not initiating conversation and keeping any movements to a minimum.

In the interval between this and the final scene, the nurse again plays the role of stagehand, helping the patient to become a full person once more. At this juncture, the two may again engage in conversation, the patient expressing relief that the examination is over. Having dressed and regroomed herself, the patient is ready to face the concluding scene. The doctor re-enters and, in discussing the results of the examination, again treats the patient as a complete and responsible person. Resuming his polite, professional manner, he conveys that his reactions to her are in no way altered by the intimate contact with her body. The epilogue is played out when she leaves the physician's office, taking up again her identity in the outside world. Patient and doctor have thus collaborated in such a way as to manage the interaction and the impression each participant forms of the other.

Personal space

There are cultural differences in the definition of **personal space**. In Western culture, people usually maintain a distance of at least three feet when engaged in focused interaction with others; when standing side by side, they may stand more closely together. In the Middle East, people often stand closer to one another than is thought acceptable in the West. Westerners visiting that part of the world are likely to find themselves disconcerted by this unexpected physical proximity.

Edward T. Hall, who has worked extensively on non-verbal communication, distinguishes four zones of personal space. *Intimate distance*, of up to one and a half feet, is reserved for very few social contacts. Only those involved in relationships in which regular bodily touching is permitted, such as lovers or parents and children, operate within this zone of private space. *Personal distance* (from one and a half to four feet) is the normal spacing for encounters with friends and close acquaintances. Some intimacy of contact is permitted, but this tends to be strictly limited. **Social distance**, from four to twelve feet, is the zone usually maintained in formal settings such as interviews. The fourth zone is that of **public distance**, beyond twelve feet, preserved by those who are performing to an audience.

In ordinary interaction, the most fraught zones are those of intimate and personal distance. If these zones are invaded, people try to recapture their space. We may stare at the intruder as if to say, 'Move away!' or elbow him aside. When people are forced into proximity closer than they deem desirable, they might create a kind of physical boundary: a reader at a crowded library desk might physically demarcate a private space by stacking books around its edges (Hall 1959, 1966).

INTERACTION IN TIME AND SPACE

Understanding how activities are distributed in time and space is fundamental to analysing encounters, and also to understanding social life in general. All interaction is *situated* – it occurs in a particular place and has a specific duration in time. Our actions over the course of a day tend to be 'zoned' in time as well as in space. Thus, for example, most people spend a zone – say, from 9 a.m. to 5 p.m. – of their daily time working. Their weekly time is also zoned: they are likely to work on weekdays and spend weekends at home, altering the pattern of their activities on the weekend days. As we move through the temporal zones of the day, we are also often moving across space as well: to get to work, we may take a bus from one area of a city to another, or perhaps commute in from the suburbs. When we analyse the contexts of social interaction, therefore, it is often useful to look at people's movements, and to recognize this **time–space convergence**.

The concept of **regionalization** will help us understand how social life is zoned in time-space. Take the example of a private house. A modern house is regionalized into rooms and hallways, and floors if there is more than one storey. These spaces are not just physically separate areas, but are zoned in time as well. The living rooms and kitchen are used most in the daylight hours, the bedrooms at night. The interaction that occurs in these regions is bound by both spatial and temporal divisions. Some areas of the house form back regions, with 'performances' taking place in the others. At times, the whole house can become a back region. Once again, this idea is beautifully captured by Goffman:

> Of a Sunday morning, a whole household can use the wall around its domestic establishment to conceal a relaxing slovenliness in dress and civil endeavour, extending to all rooms the informality that is usually restricted to kitchen and bedrooms. So, too, in American middle-class neighbourhoods, on afternoons the line between children's playground and home may be defined as backstage by mothers, who pass along it wearing jeans, loafers, and a minimum of make-up. . . . And, of course, a region that is thoroughly established as a front region for the regular performance of a particular routine often functions as a back region before and after each performance, for at these times the permanent fixtures may undergo repairs, restoration, and rearrangement, or the performers may hold dress rehearsals. To see this we need only glance into a restaurant, or store, or home, a few minutes before these establishments are opened to us for the day. (Goffman 1969)

Clock time

In modern societies, the zoning of our activities is strongly influenced by **clock time**. Without clocks and the precise timing of activities, and thereby their coordination across space, industrialized societies could not exist (Mumford 1973). The measuring of time by clocks is today standardized across the globe, making possible the complex international transport systems and communications we now depend on. World standard time was first introduced in 1884 at a conference of nations held in Washington. The globe was then partitioned into twenty-four time zones, each one hour apart, and an exact beginning of the universal day was fixed.

Fourteenth-century monasteries were the first organizations to try to schedule the activities of their inmates precisely across the day and week. Today, there is virtually no group or organization that does not do so – the greater the number of people and resources involved, the more precise the scheduling must be. Eviatar Zerubavel demonstrated this in his study of the temporal structure of a large modern hospital (1979, 1982). A hospital must operate on a twenty-four-hour basis, and coordinating the staff and resources is a highly complex matter. For instance, the nurses work for one time period in ward A, another time period in ward B, and so on, and are also called on to alternate between day- and night-shift work. Nurses, doctors and other staff, plus the resources they need, must be integrated together both in time and in space.

EVERYDAY LIFE IN CULTURAL AND HISTORICAL PERSPECTIVE

Some of the mechanisms of social interaction analysed by Goffman, Garfinkel and others seem to be universal. The use of markers to signal the opening and closing of encounters, for example, is characteristic of human interaction everywhere. Ways of organizing encounters, such as keeping the body turned away from others to form a conversational knot, are also found in all human gatherings. But much of Goffman's discussion of civil inattention and other kinds of interaction primarily concerns societies in which contact with strangers is commonplace. What about very small traditional societies, where there are no strangers and few settings in which more than a handful of people are together at any one time?

To see some of the contrasts between social interaction in modern and traditional societies, let's take as an example one of the least developed cultures in terms of technology remaining in the world: the !Kung (sometimes known as the Bushmen), who live in the Kalahari Desert area of Botswana and Namibia, in southern Africa (Lee 1968, 1969; the exclamation mark refers to a click sound made when pronouncing the name). Although their way of life is changing because of outside influences, their traditional patterns of social life are still evident.

The !Kung live in groups of some thirty or forty people, in temporary settlements near water holes. Food is scarce in their environment, and they must walk far and wide to find it. Such roaming takes up most of the average day. Women and children often stay back in the camp, but equally often the whole group spends the day walking. Members of the community will sometimes fan out over an area of up to a hundred square miles in the course of a day, returning to the camp at night to eat and sleep. The men may be alone or in groups of two or three for much of the day. There is one period of the year, however, when the routines of their daily activities change: the winter rainy season, when water is abundant and food much easier to come by. The everyday life of the !Kung during this period is centred around ritual and ceremonial activities, and preparing for them and enacting them are very time consuming.

The members of most !Kung groups never see anyone they don't know reasonably well. Until contacts with the outside became more common in recent years, they had no word for 'stranger'. While the !Kung, particularly the males, may spend long periods of the day out of contact with others, in the community itself there is little opportunity for privacy. Families sleep in flimsy, open dwellings, with virtually all activities open to public view. No one has studied the !Kung with Goffman's observations on everyday life in mind, but it is easy to see that some aspects of his work have limited application to !Kung social life. There are few opportunities, for example, to create front and back regions. The closing off of different gatherings and encounters by the walls of rooms, separate buildings and the various neighbourhoods of cities common in modern societies are remote from the activities of the !Kung.

The compulsion of proximity

In modern societies, in complete contrast to the !Kung – as will be explored in the chapters that follow – we are constantly interacting with others whom we may never see or meet. Almost all of our everyday transactions, such as buying groceries or making a bank deposit, bring us into contact – but *indirect* contact – with people who may live thousands of miles away. The banking system, for example, is international. Any money you deposit is a small part of the financial investments the bank makes worldwide.

Now that it's relatively easy, why aren't more of our interactions with others indirect? Why don't we always use the phone, fax or other means of remote communication when contacting friends or colleagues? People in business, for instance, continue to attend meetings, sometimes flying halfway around the world to do so, when it would seem much simpler and more effective to transact business through a computer or a multiparty phone line.

Deirdre Boden and Harvey Molotch have studied what they call the compulsion of proximity: the need of individuals to meet with one another in situations of co-presence, or face-to-face interaction. People put themselves out to attend meetings, Boden and Molotch suggest, because situations of co-presence, for reasons documented by Goffman in his studies of interaction, supply much richer information about how other people think and feel, and about their sincerity, than any form of electronic communication. Only by actually being in the presence of people who make decisions affecting us in important ways do we feel able to learn what is going on, and confident that we can impress them of our own views and our own sincerity. 'Copresence', Boden and Molotch say, 'effects access to the body part that "never lies", the eyes – the "windows on the soul". Eye contact itself signals a degree of intimacy and trust; copresent interactants continuously monitor the subtle movements of this most subtle body part' (1994).

MICROSOCIOLOGY AND MACROSOCIOLOGY

The study of everyday behaviour in situations of face-to-face interaction is usually called **microsociology**. **Macrosociology** is the analysis of large-scale social systems, like the political system or the economic order. It also includes the analysis of long-term processes of change, such as the development of industrialism. At first sight, it might seem as though micro and macro analysis are distinct from one another. In fact, the two are closely connected (Knorr-Cetina and Cicourel 1981; Giddens 1984), as we have seen throughout this chapter.

Macro analysis is essential if we are to understand the institutional background of daily life. The ways in which people live their everyday lives are greatly affected by the broader institutional framework, as is obvious when the daily cycle of activities of a culture like that of the !Kung is compared with life in an industrialized urban environment. In modern societies, as has been pointed out, we are constantly in contact with strangers. This contact may be indirect and impersonal. However, no matter how many indirect or electronic relations we enter into today, even in the most complex societies, the presence of other people remains crucial. While we may choose to send an acquaintance an e-mail message on the Internet, we can also choose to fly thousands of miles to spend the weekend with a friend.

Micro studies are in their turn necessary for illuminating broad institutional patterns. Face-to-face interaction is clearly the main basis of all forms of social organization, no matter how large-scale. Suppose we are studying a business corporation. We could understand much about its activities simply by looking at face-to-face behaviour. We could analyse, for example, the interaction of directors in the boardroom, people working in the various offices, or the workers on the shop floor. We would not build up a picture of the whole corporation in this way, since some of its business is transacted through printed materials, letters, the telephone and computers. Yet we could certainly contribute significantly to understanding how the organization works.

In later chapters, we will see further examples of how interaction in micro contexts affects larger social processes, and how macro systems in turn influence more confined settings of social life.

SUMMARY

1 Social interaction is the process by which we act and react to those around us. Many apparently trivial aspects of our day-to-day behaviour turn out on close examination to be both complex and important aspects of social interaction. An example is the gaze – looking at other people. In most interaction, eye contact is fairly fleeting. To stare at another person could be taken as a sign of hostility – or, on some occasions, of love. The study of social interaction is a fundamental area in sociology, illuminating many aspects of social life.

2 Various different expressions are conveyed by the human face. It is widely held that basic aspects of the facial expression of emotion are innate. Cross-cultural studies demonstrate quite close similarities between the members of different cultures both in facial expression and the interpretation of emotions registered on the human face. 'Face' can also be understood in a broader sense to refer to the esteem in which an individual is held by others. Generally, in our interaction with other people, we are concerned to 'save face' – protect our self-esteem.

3 The study of ordinary talk and conversation has come to be called ethnomethodology, a term first coined by Harold Garfinkel. Ethnomethodology is the analysis of the ways in which we actively – although usually in a taken-for-granted way – make sense of what others mean by what they say and do.

4 We can learn a great deal about the nature of talk by 'response cries' (exclamations) and studying slips of the tongue (what happens when people mispronounce or misapply words and phrases). Slips of the tongue are often humorous, and are in fact closely connected psychologically to wit and joking.

5 Unfocused interaction is the mutual awareness individuals have of one another in large gatherings, when not directly in conversation with one another. Focused interaction, which can be divided up into distinct encounters – or episodes of interaction – occurs when two or more individuals are directly attending to what the other or others are saying and doing.

6 Social interaction can often be studied in an illuminating way by applying the dramaturgical model – studying social interaction as if those involved were actors on a stage, having a set and props. As in the theatre, in the various contexts of social life there tend to be clear distinctions between front regions (the stage itself) and back regions, where the actors prepare themselves for the performance and relax afterwards.

7 Social roles are socially defined expectations of an individual in a given status or social position.

8 All social interaction is situated in time and space. We can analyse how our daily lives are 'zoned' in time and space combined by looking at how activities occur during definite periods and at the same time involve spatial movement.

9 The study of face-to-face interaction is usually called microsociology – which is contrasted to macrosociology, which studies larger groups, institutions and social systems. Micro and macro analysis are in fact very closely related, and each complements the other.

FURTHER READING

Michael Argyle, _Experiments in Social Interaction_ (Aldershot: Dartmouth, 1993). An overview of social and psychological aspects of interpersonal relations.

Erving Goffman, _Behaviour in Public Places_ (New York: Free Press, 1963). An analysis of the rituals enacted by individuals in public settings of interaction.

Erving Goffman, _The Presentation of Self in Everyday Life_ (Harmondsworth: Penguin, 1969). One of Goffman's main works, in which he discusses how individuals organize their interaction with others to foster particular views of themselves.

Henri Lefebvre, _Everyday Life in the Modern World_ (London: Allen Lane, 1971). A discussion of how social change in modern times has affected the nature of daily life.

Eric Livingstone, _Making Sense of Ethnomethodology_ (London: Routledge and Kegan Paul, 1987). A useful general account of ethnomethodology, setting out clearly the basic ideas involved.

Phil Manning, _Erving Goffman and Modern Sociology_ (Cambridge: Polity Press, 1992). An excellent overview of Goffman's writings as a whole.

IMPORTANT TERMS

- _civil inattention_
- _non-verbal communication_
- _talk_
- _conversation_
- _ethnomethodology_
- _shared understandings_
- _response cries_
- _slips of the tongue_
- _unfocused interaction_
- _focused interaction_
- _dramaturgical model_
- _impression management_
- _front region_
- _back region_
- _personal space_
- _social distance_
- _public distance_
- _time–space convergence_
- _regionalization_
- _clock time_
- _microsociology_
- _macrosociology_

5

GENDER AND SEXUALITY

➡

BASIC CONCEPTS

● *sex* ● *gender*

What is it to be a man? What is it to be a woman? Jan Morris, the celebrated travel writer, used to be a man. As James Morris, she was a member of the British expedition, led by Sir Edmund Hillary, that successfully climbed Mount Everest. She was, in fact, a very 'manly' man – a racing driver and active in many sports. Yet she had always felt herself to be a woman in a male body. So she underwent a sex-change operation and since then has lived as a woman.

The book Morris wrote describing the experience of changing sex provides some perceptive insights into the different worlds men and women inhabit:

> We are told that the social gap between the sexes is narrowing, but I can only report that having, in the second half of the twentieth century, experienced life in both roles [male and female], there seems to me no aspect of existence, no moment of the day, no contact, no arrangement, no response, which is not different for men and for women. The very tone of voice in which I was now addressed, the very posture of the person next in [line], the very feel in the air when I entered a room or sat at a restaurant table, constantly emphasized my change of status.
>
> And if others' responses shifted, so did my own. The more I was treated as a woman, the more woman I became. I adapted willy-nilly. If I was assumed to be incompetent at reversing cars, or opening bottles, oddly incompetent I found myself becoming. If a case was thought too heavy for me, inexplicably I found it so myself . . . .
>
> It amuses me to consider, for instance, when I am taken out to lunch by one of my more urbane men friends, that not so many years ago that fulsome waiter would have treated me as he is now treating him. Then he would have greeted me with respectful seriousness. Now he unfolds my napkin with a playful flourish, as if to humour me. Then he would have taken my order with grave concern, now he expects me to say something frivolous (and I do). (Morris 1974)

It brings most of us up short to think that a person who was a 'he' can become a 'she', because sexual differences are so influential in our lives. Usually we don't even notice them – precisely because they are so pervasive. They are ingrained in us from the very beginning.

In this chapter, we shall study the nature of human sexual behaviour, as well as analysing the complex character of **sexuality** – human sexual patterns – and sexual differences. Sexual life in modern societies, like so much else, is undergoing important changes that affect the emotional lives of most of us. We shall learn what these changes are and seek to interpret their wider significance towards the end of the chapter.

We begin by inquiring into the origins of the differences between boys and girls, men and women. Scholars are divided about the degree to which inborn biological characteristics have an enduring impact on our gender identities and our sexual activities. The debate is really one about how much learning there is. No one any longer supposes that our sexuality is instinctive in the sense in which the sexual activity of many lower animals – like the celebrated birds and bees – is instinctive. Some scholars, however, allow more prominence than others to social influences in analysing gender and sexuality.

SEX, GENDER AND BIOLOGY

The word 'sex', as used in ordinary language, is ambiguous, referring both to a category of person and to acts in which people engage, as in 'having sex'. For the sake of clarity, we must distinguish sex, meaning biological or anatomical differences between women and men, from sexual activity. We need also to make a further important distinction, between SEX and GENDER. While sex refers to physical differences of the body, gender concerns the psychological, social and cultural differences between males and females. The distinction between sex and gender is fundamental, since many differences between males and females are not biological in origin.

Gender differences: nature versus nurture

How far are differences in the behaviour of women and men the result of sex rather than gender? In other words, how much are they the result of biological differences? Some authors hold that there are innate differences of behaviour between women and men that appear in some form in all cultures, and that the findings of sociobiology point strongly in this direction. Such researchers are likely to draw attention to the fact, for example, that in almost all cultures, men rather than women take part in hunting and warfare. Surely, they argue, this indicates that men possess biologically based tendencies towards aggression that women lack?

Other researchers are unconvinced by this argument. The level of aggressiveness of males, they say, varies widely between different cultures, and women are expected to be more passive or gentle in some cultures than in others (Elshtain 1987). Moreover, they add, because a trait is more or less universal, it does not follow that it is biological in origin; there may be cultural factors of a general kind that produce such characteristics. For instance, in the majority of cultures, most women spend a significant part of their lives caring for children and could not readily take part in hunting or war. According to this view, differences in the behaviour of men and women develop mainly through the social learning of female and male identities, of **femininity** and **masculinity**.

The evidence from animals

What does the evidence show? One possible source of information is the differences in hormonal make-up between the sexes. Some have claimed that the male sex hormone, testosterone, is associated with the male propensity to violence. Research has indicated, for instance, that if male monkeys are castrated at birth, they become less aggressive; conversely, female monkeys given testosterone will become more aggressive than normal females. However, it has also been found that providing monkeys with opportunities to dominate others actually increases the testosterone level. Aggressive behaviour may thus affect the production of the hormone, rather than the hormone causing increased aggression.

Another possible source of evidence is direct observations of animal behaviour. Writers who connect male aggression with biological influences often stress male aggressiveness among the higher animals. If we look at the behaviour of chimpanzees, they say, male animals are invariably more aggressive than females. Yet there are in fact large differences between types of animals. Among gibbons, for instance, there are few noticeable differences in aggression between the sexes. Moreover, many female apes or monkeys are highly aggressive in some situations, such as when their young are threatened.

The evidence from humans

So far as humans are concerned one basic source of information comes from the experience of identical twins. Identical twins derive from a single egg and have exactly the same genetic make-up. In one particular case, one of a pair of identical male twins was seriously injured while being circumcised and the decision was made to reconstruct his genitals as a female. He was thereafter raised as a girl. The twins at six years old demonstrated typical male and female traits as found in Western culture. The little girl enjoyed playing with other girls, helped with the housework and wanted to get married when she grew up. The boy preferred the company of other boys, his favourite toys were cars and trucks, and he wanted to become a fireman or policeman.

For some time, this case was treated as a conclusive demonstration of the overriding influence of social learning on gender differences. However, when the girl was a teenager, she was interviewed during a television programme. The interview showed that she felt some unease about her gender identity, even perhaps that she was 'really' a boy after all. She had by then learned of her unusual background, and this knowledge may very well have been responsible for this altered perception of herself (Ryan 1985).

This case does not refute the possibility that there are biological influences on observed behaviour differences between men and women. If these do exist, though, their physiological origins have not yet been identified. The issue remains controversial; but the conclusion of geneticist Richard Lewontin is one with which many would agree:

> the primary self-identification of a person as a man or a woman, with the multitude of attitudes, ideas, and desires that accompany that identification, depends on what label was attached to him or her as a child. In the normal course of events, these labels correspond to a consistent biological difference in chromosomes, hormones, and morphology. Thus biological differences become a signal for, rather than a cause of, differentiation in social roles. (Lewontin 1982)

GENDER SOCIALIZATION

While biological evidence contributes to our understanding of the origins of gender differences, another route to take is the study of **gender socialization**, the learning of gender roles through social factors such as the family and the media.

Reactions of parents and adults

Many studies have been carried out on the degree to which gender differences are the result of social influences. Studies of mother–infant interaction show differences in the treatment of boys and girls even when parents believe their reactions to both are the same. Adults asked to assess the personality of a baby give different answers according to whether or not they believe the child to be a girl or a boy. In one classic experiment, five young mothers were observed in interaction with a six-month-old called Beth. They tended to smile at her often and offer her dolls to play with. She was seen as 'sweet', having a 'soft cry'. The reaction of a second group of mothers to a child the same age, named Adam, was noticeably different. The baby was likely to be offered a train or other 'male toys' to play with. Beth and Adam were actually the same child, dressed in different clothes (Will et al. 1976).

Gender learning

Gender learning by infants is almost certainly unconscious. Before children can accurately label themselves as either a boy or a girl, they receive a range of preverbal cues. For instance, male and female adults usually handle infants differently. The cosmetics women use contain different scents from those the baby might learn to associate with males. Systematic differences in dress, hairstyle and so on provide visual cues for the infant in the learning process. By the age of two, children have a partial understanding of what gender is. They know whether they are boys or girls and they can usually categorize others accurately. Not until five or six, however, does a child know that a person's gender does not change, that everyone has gender and that sex differences between girls and boys are anatomically based.

The toys, picture books and television programmes experienced by young children all tend to emphasize differences between male and female attributes. Toy shops and mail-order catalogues usually categorize their products by gender. Even some toys that seem neutral in terms of gender are not so in practice. For example, toy kittens and rabbits are recommended for girls, while lions and tigers are seen as more appropriate for boys.

Vanda Lucia Zammuner studied the toy preferences of children aged between seven and ten in Italy and Holland (Zammuner 1987). Children's attitudes towards a variety of toys were analysed; stereotypically masculine and feminine toys as well as toys presumed not to be sex-typed were included. Both the children and their parents were asked to assess which toys were suitable for boys and which for girls.

There was close agreement between the adults and children. On average, the Italian children chose sex-differentiated toys to play with more often than the Dutch children – a finding that conformed to expectations, since Italian culture tends to hold a more traditional view of gender divisions than Dutch society. As in other studies, girls from both societies chose gender-neutral or boys' toys to play with far more than boys wanted to play with girls' toys.

Storybooks and television

Twenty-five years ago, Lenore Weitzman and her colleagues carried out an analysis of gender roles in some of the most widely used books for preschool children and found several clear differences in gender roles (Weitzman et al. 1972). Males played a much larger part in the stories and pictures than females, outnumbering females by a ratio of 11 to 1. Including animals with gender identities, the ratio was 95 to 1. The activities of males and females also differed. The males engaged in adventurous pursuits and outdoor activities demanding independence and strength. Where girls did appear, they were portrayed as passive and confined mostly to indoor activities. Girls cooked and cleaned for the males, or awaited their return. Much the same was true of the adult men and women represented in the storybooks. Women who were not wives and mothers were imaginary creatures like witches or fairy godmothers. There was not a single woman in all the books analysed who held an occupation outside the home. By contrast, the men were depicted as fighters, policemen, judges, kings and so forth.

More recent research suggests that things have changed somewhat, but that the large bulk of children's literature remains much the same (Davies 1991). Fairy tales, for example, embody traditional attitudes towards gender and towards the sorts of aims and ambitions girls and boys are expected to have. 'Some day my prince will come' – in versions of fairy tales from several centuries ago, this usually implied that a girl from a poor family might dream of wealth and fortune. Today its meaning has become more closely tied to the ideals of romantic love. Some feminists have tried to rewrite some of the most celebrated fairy tales, reversing their usual emphases:

> I really didn't notice that he had a funny nose.
> And he certainly looked better all dressed up in fancy clothes.
> He's not nearly as attractive as he seemed the other night.
> So I think I'll just pretend that this glass slipper feels too tight.
> (Viorst 1987)

Like this version of Cinderella, however, these rewrites are found mainly in books directed at adult audiences and have hardly affected the tales told in innumerable children's books.

Although there are some notable exceptions, analyses of television programmes designed for children conform to the findings about children's books. Studies of the most frequently watched cartoons show that most of the leading figures are male, and that males dominate the active pursuits. Similar images are found in the commercials that appear throughout the programmes.

The difficulty of non-sexist child-rearing

June Statham studied the experiences of a group of parents committed to non-sexist child-rearing. Thirty adults in eighteen families were involved in the research, which included children aged six months to twelve years. The parents were of middle-class background, mostly involved in academic work as teachers or lecturers. Statham found that most of the parents did not simply try to modify traditional sex roles by seeking to make girls more like boys, but wanted to foster new combinations of the feminine and masculine. They wished boys to be more sensitive to others' feelings and capable of expressing warmth, while girls were encouraged to seek opportunities for learning and self-advancement. All the parents found existing patterns of gender learning difficult to combat. They were reasonably successful at persuading the children to play with toys that were not gender-typed, but even this proved more difficult than many of them had expected. One mother commented to the researcher:

> If you walk into a toy shop, it's full of war toys for boys and domestic toys for girls, and it sums up society the way it is. This is the way children are being socialized: it's all right for boys to be taught to kill and hurt, and I think it's terrible, it makes me feel sick. I try not to go into toy shops, I feel so angry.

Practically all the children in fact possessed, and played with, gender-typed toys, given to them by relatives.

There are now some storybooks available with strong, independent girls as the main characters, but few depict boys in non-traditional roles. A mother of a five-year-old boy told of her son's reaction when she reversed the sexes of the characters in a story she read to him:

> In fact he was a bit upset when I went through a book which has a boy and a girl in very traditional roles, and changed all the he's to she's and the she's to he's. When I first started doing that, he was inclined to say 'you don't like boys, you only like girls.' I had to explain that that wasn't true at all, it's just that there's not enough written about girls. (Statham 1986)

Clearly, gender socialization is very powerful, and challenges to it can be upsetting. Once a gender is 'assigned', society expects individuals to act like 'females' and 'males'. It is in the practices of everyday life that these expectations are fulfilled and reproduced (Lorber 1994; Bourdieu 1990).

Doing gender

Our conceptions of gender identity, as well as the sexual attitudes and inclinations linked to them, are formed so early in life that as adults we mostly take them for granted. Yet gender is more than learning to act like a girl or boy. Gender differences are something we live with every day.

In other words, gender does not just exist; we all, as some sociologists put it, 'do gender' in our daily social interactions with others (West and Zimmerman 1987). For instance, Jan Morris had to learn how to do gender when she discovered how differently she was expected to behave in the restaurant as a woman rather than as a man. As she says, there is

Transsexuals, like Jan Morris, are people who wish to live as a member of the other sex and who have surgery in order to do so. They also have hormone treatment to alter their body shape and hair distribution, and to develop secondary sexual characteristics, such as beards or breasts. Such 'gender reassignment' is not a complete change of sex: their chromosomes and their internal organs, such as wombs, remain unchanged. One transsexual, now called Mark Rees, observes: 'The total conviction of living in the wrong body simply doesn't yield to psychiatric treatment. The only alternative to constant and agonising conflict between body and mind lies in the tedious, emotionally exhausting, often embarrassing and always painful business of gender reassignment. But the reward is freedom to be one's real self.'

Unfortunately, this freedom is circumscribed under a system which, to say the least, appears illogical — and on which Britain is out of step with countries including Canada, Italy, Germany, Holland, Norway, Sweden, Poland, Switzerland, Turkey and Indonesia, as well as 48 states in the US.

Rees points out: 'The Government allows other documents to be altered, from passports and university degrees to driving licences and library tickets. It recognises transsexualism as a medical condition and even pays for psy-

Brenda Rees then ...

... and Mark Rees now

chological assessment, hormone treatment and surgery; yet after all that, it refuses amendment of the one document vital to confer legal recognition and full human rights' – that is, the birth certificate.

Source: Guardian, 1996 (text only)

'no aspect of existence' that is not gendered. Yet she didn't notice that such was the case until she changed her sex. The subtle ways in which we do gender are so much a part of our lives that we don't notice them until they are missing or radically altered.

The fact that gender is continuously learned and relearned illustrates the importance of the concept of social reproduction (see chapter 1). We socially reproduce – make and remake – gender in a thousand minor actions in the course of a day. This same process helps us to understand gender as a social institution, created and recreated in our interactions with others. As we shall see in later chapters, gender differences are also an important part of other social institutions such as the family, religion, work and class.

GENDER IDENTITY AND SEXUALITY: TWO THEORIES

Freud's theory of gender development

Perhaps the most influential – and controversial – theory of the emergence of gender identity is that of Sigmund Freud. According to Freud, the learning of gender differences in infants and young children is centred on the presence or absence of the penis. 'I have a penis' is equivalent to 'I am a boy', while 'I am a girl' is equivalent to 'I lack a penis'. Freud is careful to say that it is not just the anatomical distinctions that matter here; the presence or absence of the penis is symbolic of masculinity and femininity.

At around the age of four or five, the theory goes, a boy feels threatened by the discipline and autonomy his father demands of him, fantasizing that the father wishes to remove his penis. Partly consciously, but mostly on an unconscious level, the boy recognizes the father as a rival for the affections of his mother. In repressing erotic feelings towards the mother and accepting the father as a superior being, the boy identifies with the father and becomes aware of his male identity. The boy gives up his love for his mother out of an unconscious fear of castration by his father. Girls, on the other hand, supposedly suffer from 'penis envy' because they do not possess the visible organ that distinguishes boys. The mother becomes devalued in the little girl's eyes, because she is also seen to lack a penis and to be unable to provide one. When the girl identifies with the mother, she takes over the submissive attitude involved in the recognition of being 'second best'.

Once this phase is over, the child has learned to repress erotic feelings. The period from about five years old to puberty, according to Freud, is one of latency – sexual activities tend to be suspended until the biological changes involved in puberty reactivate erotic desires in a direct way. The latency period, covering the early and middle years of school, is the time when same-sex peer groups are most important in the child's life.

Major objections have been raised against Freud's views, particularly by feminists, but also by many other authors (Mitchell 1973; Coward 1984). First, Freud seems to identify gender identity too closely with genital awareness; other, more subtle factors are surely involved. Second, the theory seems to depend on the notion that the penis is superior to the vagina, which is thought of as just a lack of the male organ. Yet why shouldn't the female genitals be considered superior to those of the male? Third, Freud treats the father as the primary disciplining agent, whereas in many cultures the mother plays the more significant part in the imposition of discipline. Fourth, Freud believes that gender learning is concentrated at the age of four or five. Most later authors have emphasized the importance of earlier learning, beginning in infancy.

Chodorow's theory of gender development

While many writers have made use of Freud's approach in studying gender development, they have usually modified it in major respects. An example is the sociologist Nancy Chodorow (1978, 1988). Chodorow argues that learning to feel male or female derives from the infant's attachment to its parents from an early age. She places much more emphasis than Freud does on the importance of the mother rather than the father. A child tends to become emotionally involved with the mother, since she is easily the most dominant influence in its early life. This attachment has at some point to be broken in order to achieve a separate sense of self – the child is required to become less closely dependent.

Chodorow argues that the breaking process occurs in a different way for boys and girls. Girls remain closer to the mother – able, for example, to go on hugging and kissing her and imitating what she does. Because there is no sharp break from the mother, the girl, and later the adult woman, develops a sense of self that is more continuous with other people. Her identity is more likely to be merged with or dependent on another's: first her mother, later a man. In Chodorow's view, this tends to produce characteristics of sensitivity and emotional compassion in women.

Boys gain a sense of self via a more radical rejection of their original closeness to the mother, forging their understanding of masculinity from what is not feminine. They learn not to be 'sissies' or 'mummy's boys'. As a result, boys are relatively unskilled in relating closely to others; they develop more analytical ways of looking at the world. They take a more active view of their lives, emphasizing achievement, but they have repressed their ability to understand their own feelings and those of others.

To some extent, Chodorow reverses Freud's emphasis. Masculinity, rather than femininity, is defined by a loss, the forfeiting of continuing close attachment to the mother. Male identity is formed through separation; thus men later in life unconsciously feel that their identity is endangered if they become involved in close emotional relationships with others. Women, on the other hand, feel that the absence of a close relation to another person threatens their self-esteem. These patterns are passed on from generation to generation, because of the primary role women play in the early socialization of children. Women express and define themselves mainly in terms of relationships. Men have repressed these needs, and adopt a more manipulative stance towards the world.

Chodorow's work has met with various criticisms. Janet Sayers, for example, has suggested that Chodorow does not explain the struggle of women, particularly in current times, to become autonomous, independent beings (Sayers 1986). Women (and men), she points out, are more contradictory in their psychological make-up than Chodorow's theory suggests. Femininity may conceal feelings of aggressiveness or assertiveness, which are revealed only obliquely or in certain contexts (Brennan 1988). Chodorow has also been criticized for her narrow conception of the family, one based on a white, middle-class model. What happens, for example, in one-parent households or families where children are cared for by more than one adult?

These criticisms don't undermine Chodorow's ideas, which remain important. They teach us a good deal about the nature of femininity, and they help us to understand the origins of what has been called **male inexpressiveness** – the difficulty men have in revealing their feelings to others.

HUMAN SEXUALITY

As with the study of gender differences, scholars have also differed over the importance of biological versus social and cultural influences on human sexual behaviour. An important similarity in the research on gender differences and on sexuality is that both fields have looked to the animal world for understanding humans. We will first look at some of the biological arguments and the criticisms these arguments have provoked. We will then examine the social influences on sexual behaviour, which will lead us into a discussion of the tremendous variations in human sexuality.

Biology and sexual behaviour

There is clearly a biological basis to sexuality, because female anatomy differs from that of the male, and the experience of orgasm is also different. There also exists a biological imperative to reproduce, otherwise the human species would become extinct. Some biologists argue that there is an evolutionary explanation of why men tend to be more sexually promiscuous than women (see chapter 2). The argument is that men are biologically disposed to impregnate as many women as possible in order to ensure that their seed has the greatest chance of survival. Women, who at a given time have only one egg that can be fertilized, have no such biological interests. Instead, they want stable partners to protect the biological inheritance invested in the protection of their children. This argument is supported by studies of the sexual behaviour of animals claiming to show that males are normally more promiscuous than females of the same species.

More recent studies, however, have shown that female infidelity is actually quite common in the animal kingdom, and the sexual activities of many animals are more complex than was thought. It was once believed that females mated with males that had the highest potential for a superior genetic inheritance for their offspring. But a recent study of female birds has disputed this argument, claiming that female birds take an extra mating partner not for its genes, but because it may be a better parent and offer a better home territory for raising offspring. As this study concluded, 'There's more to copulation than a transfer of sperm. These females may be thinking of their futures' (quoted in Angier 1994).

The conclusions of such research are tentative, especially as regards any implications for human sexual behaviour. As we shall see, sexuality is far too complicated to be wholly attributable to biological traits.

Social influences on sexual behaviour

Most people, in all societies, are heterosexual – they look to the other sex for emotional involvement and sexual pleasure. **Heterosexuality** is in every society the basis of marriage and the family.

Yet there are many minority sexual tastes and inclinations too. Judith Lorber distinguishes as many as ten different sexual identities among human beings: heterosexual woman, heterosexual man, lesbian woman, gay man, bisexual woman, bisexual man, transvestite woman (a woman who regularly dresses as a man), transvestite man (a man who regularly dresses as a woman), transsexual woman (a man who becomes a woman, like Jan Morris) and transsexual man (a woman who becomes a man). Sexual practices themselves are even more diverse. Freud called human beings 'polymorphously perverse'. By this he meant that humans have a wide range of sexual tastes and may follow these even when, in a given society, some are regarded as immoral or illegal. Freud first began his researches during the late nineteenth century, when many people were sexually prudish; yet his patients still revealed an amazing diversity of sexual pursuits. Among possible sexual practices are the following. A man or woman can have sexual relations with women, men, or both. This can happen one at a time or with three or more participating. One can have sex with oneself (masturbation) or with no one (celibacy). Someone can have sexual relations with transsexuals or people who erotically cross-dress; use pornography or sexual devices; practise sado-masochism (the erotic use of bondage and the inflicting of pain); have sex with animals; and so on (Lorber 1994). In all societies there are sexual norms that approve of some practices while discouraging or condemning others. Such norms, however, vary widely between different cultures. Homosexuality is a case in point. As will be discussed later, some cultures have either tolerated or actively encouraged homosexuality in certain contexts. Among the ancient Greeks, for instance, the love of men for boys was idealized as the highest form of sexual love.

Accepted types of sexual behaviour also vary between different cultures, which is one way we know that most sexual responses are learned rather than innate. The most extensive study was carried out forty decades ago by Clellan Ford and Frank Beach (1951), who surveyed anthropological evidence from more than two hundred societies. Striking variations were found in what is regarded as 'natural' sexual behaviour and in norms of sexual attractiveness. For example, in some cultures, extended foreplay, perhaps lasting hours, is thought desirable and even necessary prior to intercourse; in others, foreplay is virtually non-existent. In some societies, it is believed that overly frequent intercourse leads to physical debilitation or illness. Among the Seniang of the South Pacific, advice on the desirability of spacing out love-making is given by the elders of the village – who also believe that a person with white hair may legitimately copulate every night!

In most cultures, norms of sexual attractiveness (held by both females and males) focus more on physical looks for women than for men, a situation that seems to be gradually changing in the West as women increasingly become active in spheres outside the home. The traits seen as most important in female beauty, however, differ greatly. In the modern West, a slim, small body build is admired, while in other cultures a much more generous shape is regarded as most attractive (see chapter 6). Sometimes the breasts are not seen as a source of sexual stimulus, whereas in some societies great erotic significance is attached to them. Some societies place great store on the shape of the face, while others emphasize the shape and colour of the eyes or the size and form of the nose and lips.

Sexuality in Western culture

Western attitudes towards sexual behaviour were for nearly two thousand years moulded primarily by Christianity. Although different Christian sects and denominations have held divergent views about the proper place of sexuality in life, the dominant view of the Christian church was that all sexual behaviour is suspect except that needed for reproduction. At some periods, this view produced an extreme prudishness in society at large. But at other times, many people ignored or reacted against the church's teachings, commonly engaging in practices (such as adultery) forbidden by religious authorities. As was mentioned in chapter 1, the idea that sexual fulfilment can and should be sought through marriage was rare.

In the nineteenth century, religious presumptions about sexuality became partly replaced by medical ones. Most of the early writings by doctors about sexual behaviour, however, were as stern as the views of the church. Some argued that any type of sexual activity unconnected with reproduction causes serious physical harm. Masturbation was said to bring on blindness, insanity, heart disease and other ailments, while oral sex was claimed to cause cancer. In Victorian times, sexual hypocrisy abounded. Virtuous women were believed to be indifferent to sexuality, accepting the attentions of their husbands only as a duty. Yet in the expanding towns and cities, prostitution was rife and often openly tolerated, 'loose' women being seen as in an entirely different category from their respectable sisters.

Many Victorian men who were on the face of things sober, well-behaved citizens, devoted to their wives, regularly visited prostitutes or kept mistresses. Such behaviour was treated leniently, whereas 'respectable' women who took lovers were regarded as scandalous and shunned in polite society if their behaviour came to light. The differing attitudes towards the sexual activities of men and women formed a double standard, which has long existed and whose residues still linger on today.

In current times, traditional attitudes exist alongside much more liberal attitudes towards sexuality, which developed particularly strongly in the 1960s. Some people, particularly those influenced by Christian teachings, believe that premarital sex is wrong and generally frown on all forms of sexual behaviour except heterosexual activity within the confines of marriage – although it is now much more commonly accepted that sexual pleasure is a desirable and important feature. Others, by contrast, condone or actively approve of premarital sex and hold tolerant attitudes towards different sexual practices. Sexual attitudes have undoubtedly become more permissive over the past thirty years in most Western countries. In films and plays, scenes are shown that previously would have been completely unacceptable, while pornographic material is readily available to most adults who want it.

Sexual behaviour: Kinsey's study

We can speak much more confidently about public values concerning sexuality than we can about private practices, for by their nature such practices mostly go undocumented. When Alfred Kinsey began his research in the United States in the 1940s and 1950s, it was the first time a major investigation of actual sexual behaviour had been undertaken. Kinsey and his co-researchers faced condemnation from religious organizations, and his work was denounced as immoral in the newspapers and in Congress. But he persisted, and eventually obtained sexual life histories of eighteen thousand people, a reasonably representative sample of the white American population (Kinsey et al. 1948, 1953).

Kinsey's results were surprising to most and shocking to many, because they revealed a great difference between the public expectations of sexual behaviour prevailing at that time and actual sexual conduct. He found that almost 70 per cent of men had visited a prostitute, and 84 per cent had had premarital sexual experience. Yet, following the double standard, 40 per cent of men expected their wives to be virgins at the time of marriage. More than 90 per cent of males had engaged in masturbation and nearly 60 per cent in some form of oral sexual activity. Among women, about 50 per cent had had premarital sexual experience, although mostly with their prospective husbands. Some 60 per cent had masturbated, and the same percentage had engaged in oral-genital contacts.

The gap between publicly accepted attitudes and actual behaviour that Kinsey's findings demonstrated was probably especially great at that particular period, just after World War Two. A phase of sexual liberalization had begun rather earlier, in the 1920s, when many younger people felt freed from the strict moral codes that had governed earlier generations. Sexual behaviour probably changed a good deal, but issues concerning sexuality were not openly discussed in the way that has become familiar now. People participating in sexual activities that were still strongly disapproved of on a public level concealed them, not realizing the full extent to which others were engaging in similar practices. The more permissive era of the 1960s brought openly declared attitudes more into line with the realities of behaviour.

Sexual behaviour after Kinsey

In the 1960s, the social movements that challenged the existing order of things, like those associated with countercultural, or 'hippy', lifestyles, also broke with existing sexual norms. These movements preached sexual freedom, and the invention of the contraceptive pill for women allowed sexual pleasure to be clearly separated from reproduction. Women's groups also started pressing for greater independence from male sexual values, the rejection of the double standard and recognition of the need for women to achieve greater sexual satisfaction in their relationships.

Until recently it was difficult to know with accuracy how much sexual behaviour had changed since the time of Kinsey's research. In the late 1980s, Lillian Rubin interviewed a thousand Americans between the ages of thirteen and forty-eight to try to discover what changes had occurred in sexual behaviour and attitudes over the preceding thirty years or so. According to her findings, there were indeed significant developments. Sexual activity was typically beginning at a younger age than was true for the previous generation; moreover, the sexual practices of teenagers tended to be as varied and comprehensive as those of adults. There was still a double standard, but it was not as powerful as it had been. One of the most important changes was that women had come to expect, and actively pursue, sexual pleasure in relationships. They were expecting to receive, not only to provide, sexual satisfaction – a phenomenon that Rubin argues has major consequences for both sexes.

Women are more sexually liberated than once was the case; but along with this development, which most men applaud, has come a new assertiveness many men find difficult to accept. The men Rubin talked to often said they 'felt inadequate', were afraid they could 'never do anything right', and found it 'impossible to satisfy women these days' (Rubin 1990).

Men feel inadequate? Doesn't this contradict all that we have come to expect? For in modern society, men continue to dominate in most spheres, and they are in general much more violent towards women than the other way round. Such violence is substantially aimed at the control and continuing subordination of women. Yet a number of authors have begun to argue that masculinity is a burden as much as a source of reward. Much male sexuality, they add, is compulsive rather than satisfying. If men were to stop using sexuality as a means of control, not only women but they themselves would gain.

A new fidelity?

In 1994 a team of researchers published *The Social Organization of Sexuality: Sexual Practices in the United States*, the most comprehensive study of sexual behaviour in any country since Kinsey. To the surprise of many, their findings suggested an essential sexual conservatism among Americans. For instance, 83 per cent of their subjects had had only one partner (or no partner at all) in the preceding year and among married people the figure rises to 96 per cent. Fidelity to one's spouse is also quite common: only 10 per cent of women and less than 25 per cent of men reported having an extramarital affair during their lifetime. According to the study, Americans average only three partners during their entire lifetime. Despite the apparently settled nature of sexual behaviour, some distinct changes emerge from this study, the most significant being a progressive increase in the level of premarital sexual experience, particularly among women. In fact, over 95 per cent of Americans getting married today are sexually experienced (Laumann et al. 1994).

Surveys of sexual behaviour are fraught with difficulties. We simply don't know how far people tell the truth about their sexual lives when asked by a researcher. *The Social Organization of Sexuality* seems to show that Americans are much less adventurous in their sexual lives than they used to be at the time of the Kinsey reports. It may be that the Kinsey reports were themselves inaccurate. Perhaps the fear of AIDS has led many people to restrict the range of their sexual activities. Or perhaps in the quite conservative political climate of today, people are more prone to hide aspects of their sexual activities. We cannot be sure.

The validity of surveys of sexual behaviour has recently been the focus of intense debate (Lewontin 1995). Critics of the research just discussed have asserted that such surveys do not generate reliable information about sexual practices. Part of the controversy centred on replies from older people questioned. The researchers reported that 45 per cent of men aged between eighty and eighty-five years old say they have sex with their partner. The critics feel this is so obviously untrue that it calls into doubt the findings of the whole survey. The researchers defended themselves against the charge, and received some support from specialists in the study of older people, who accused the critics of having negative stereotypes of ageing. They pointed out that in one study of older men living outside institutions 74 per cent were sexually active. One study in fact found that most men even in their nineties sustained an interest in sex.

Homosexuality

Homosexuality exists in all cultures. Yet the idea of a homosexual person – someone clearly marked off in terms of his or her sexual tastes from the majority of the population – is only a relatively recent one. In his studies of sexuality, Michel Foucault has shown that before the eighteenth century, the notion seems barely to have existed (Foucault 1878). The act of sodomy was denounced by church authorities and by the law; in England and several other European countries, it was punishable by death. However, sodomy was not defined specifically as a homosexual offence. It applied to relations between men and women, men and animals, as well as men among themselves. The term 'homosexuality' was coined in the 1860s, and from then on, homosexuals were increasingly regarded as being a separate type of people with a particular sexual aberration (Weeks 1986). Use of the term 'lesbian' to refer to female homosexuality dates from a slightly later time.

The death penalty for 'unnatural acts' was abolished in the United States following independence, and in Europe in the late eighteenth and early nineteenth centuries. Until just a few decades ago, however, homosexuality remained a criminal activity in virtually all Western countries. This fact helps explain why antagonism towards homosexuals, though no longer enshrined in law, persists in many people's emotional attitudes.

Homosexuality in non-Western cultures

In some non-Western cultures, homosexual relations are accepted or even encouraged among certain groups. The Batak people of northern Sumatra, for example, permit male homosexual relationships before marriage. At puberty, a boy leaves his parents' house and sleeps in a dwelling with a dozen to fifteen males of his age or older. Sexual partnerships are formed between couples in the group, and the younger boys are initiated into homosexual practices. This situation continues until young men marry. Once married, most, but not all, men abandon homosexual activities (Money and Ehrhardt 1972).

Among the people of East Bay, a village in Melanesia in the Pacific, homosexuality is similarly tolerated, although again only in males. Prior to marriage, while living in the men's house, young men engage in mutual masturbation and anal intercourse. Homosexual relationships also exist, however, between older men and younger boys, often involving boys too young to be living in the men's house. Each type of relationship is completely acceptable and discussed openly. Many married men are bisexual, having relations with younger boys while maintaining an active sexual life with their spouses. But homosexuality without an interest in heterosexual relationships seems to be unknown in such cultures (Davenport 1965; see also Shepherd 1987).

Homosexuality in Western culture

Kenneth Plummer, in a classic study, distinguished four types of homosexuality within modern Western culture. *Casual homosexuality* is a passing homosexual encounter that does not substantially structure a person's overall sexual life. Schoolboy crushes and mutual masturbation are examples. *Situated activities* refer to circumstances in which homosexual acts are regularly carried out but do not become an individual's overriding preference. In settings such as prisons or military camps, where men live without women, homosexual behaviour of this kind is common, regarded as a substitute for heterosexual behaviour rather than as preferable.

Personalized homosexuality refers to individuals who have a preference for homosexual activities but who are isolated from groups in which this is easily accepted. Homosexuality here is a furtive activity, hidden away from friends and colleagues. Homosexuality as a *way of life* refers to individuals who have 'come out' and have made associations with others of similar sexual tastes a key parts of their lives. Such people usually belong to gay subcultures, in which homosexual activities are integrated into a distinct lifestyle (Plummer 1975).

The proportion of the population (both male and female) who have had homosexual experiences or experienced strong inclinations towards homosexuality is much larger than those who follow an openly gay lifestyle. The probable extent of homosexuality in Western cultures first became known with the publication of Alfred Kinsey's research.

According to his findings, no more than half of all American men are completely heterosexual, judged by their sexual activities and inclinations after puberty. Of Kinsey's sample, 8 per cent had been involved in exclusively homosexual relationships for periods of three years or more. A further 10 per cent had engaged in homosexual and heterosexual activities more or less equally. Kinsey's most striking finding was that 37 per cent of men had had at least one homosexual experience to the level of orgasm. An additional 13 per cent had felt homosexual desires but had not acted on them.

Rates of homosexuality among women indicated by the Kinsey researches were lower. About 2 per cent of females were exclusively homosexual. Homosexual experiences were reported by 13 per cent, while a further 15 per cent admitted they had felt homosexual desires without acting on them. Kinsey and his colleagues were startled by the level of homosexuality their studies revealed, so the results were rechecked using different methods, but the conclusions remained the same (Kinsey et al. 1948, 1953).

The results from *The Social Organization of Sexuality* call into question the findings of Kinsey's study on the prevalence of homosexuality. In contrast to Kinsey's 37 per cent, only 9 per cent of men in the later study reported having a homosexual encounter to the level of orgasm, only about 8 per cent of men reported having homosexual desires (compared to 13 per cent), and just under 3 per cent reported a sexual encounter with another man in the preceding year.

As the authors of this study acknowledged, the stigma that remains attached to homosexuality probably contributed to a general under-reporting of homosexual behaviour. And, as one critic noted, the authors' random sample failed to address the geographical concentration of homosexuals in large cities, where homosexuals probably constitute close to 10 per cent of the overall population (Robinson 1994).

Lesbian groups tend to be less highly organized than male gay subcultures and include a lower proportion of casual relationships. Male homosexuality tends to receive more attention than **lesbianism**, and lesbian activist groups are often treated as if their interests were identical with those of male organizations. But while there is sometimes close cooperation between male gays and lesbians, there are also differences, particularly where lesbians are actively involved in feminism. The specific character of lesbian women's lives is now being studied by sociologists in more detail.

Lesbian couples often have children, some through a relationship with a man, others through artificial insemination, but it has been difficult for lesbians to gain custody.

Coming out remains a difficult process for many. Parents, other relatives and friends, and children, if there are any, must be told. However, the experience can be a rewarding one. In *There's Something I've Been Meaning to Tell You*, Loralee MacPike collected descriptions from women who had chosen to disclose their homosexuality. Of her own experience she wrote:

Like many 'born-again Lesbians', I was overjoyed at my new-found self and my newly-defined life. Neither my partner nor I had ever been in a lesbian relationship before, so neither brought to our lives the social foundations and friendships that are part of gay communities; but we began making subtle approaches to others who in one way or another appeared to be coming out to us . . . [We] have been very fortunate . . . the results have been more positive and enriching than I could have imagined. (MacPike 1989)

Attitudes towards homosexuality

Attitudes of intolerance towards homosexuality have been so pronounced in the past that it is only during recent years that some of the myths surrounding the subject have been dispelled. Homosexuality is not a sickness and is not distinctively associated with any forms of psychiatric disturbance. Homosexual males are not limited to any particular sector of occupations, such as hairdressing, interior decorating or the arts.

Some kinds of male gay behaviour might be seen as attempts to alter the usual connections of masculinity and power – one reason, perhaps, why homosexuals are so often thought to be threatening by the heterosexual community. Gay men tend to reject the image of the effeminate popularly associated with them, and they deviate from this in two ways. One is through cultivating outrageous effeminacy – a 'camp' masculinity that parodies the stereotype. The other is by developing a 'macho' image. This also is not conventionally masculine; men dressed as motorcyclists or cowboys are again parodying masculinity, by exaggerating it (Bertelson 1986).

In some ways, however, homosexuality has become more normalized – more of an accepted part of everyday society.

Several countries in Europe, such as Denmark, Norway and Sweden, now permit homosexual partners to register with the state and to claim most of the prerogatives of marriage. Cities and local governments in Holland, France and Belgium have also started to give recognition to homosexual relationships. In Hawaii, homosexual marriage can be legally obtained by means of a court case.

More and more gay activists are seeking for homosexual marriage to be fully legalized. Why do they care, when among heterosexual couples marriage appears to be losing its importance? They care because they want the same status, rights and obligations as anyone else. Marriage today is above all an emotional commitment, but as recognized by the state it also has definite legal implications. It gives to partners rights to make life-or-death medical decisions, rights of inheritance and rights to a share in pensions and other economic benefits. 'Ceremonies of commitment' – non-legal marriages – which have become popular among both homosexuals and heterosexuals in America, don't confer these rights and obligations. Conversely, of course, this is one reason why many heterosexual couples now decide either to defer marriage or not to get married at all.

Opponents of homosexual marriage condemn it as either frivolous or unnatural. They see it as legitimating a sexual orientation which the

Two homosexual men outside a register office in Russia

state should be doing its best to curb. There are pressure groups in America dedicated to getting homosexuals to change their ways and marry people of the opposite sex. Some still see homosexuality as a perversion and are violently opposed to any provisions that might normalize it.

Yet the majority of gay people simply want to be seen as ordinary. They point out that homosexuals need economic and emotional security as much as others do. In his book *Virtually Normal* (1995) Andrew Sullivan argues forcefully for the virtues of homosexual marriage. Himself a Catholic and a homosexual, he has agonized over how his religious beliefs can be reconciled with his sexuality. He argues that homosexuality is at least in part given in nature – it is not something which most simply 'choose'. To ask that someone renounce homosexuality is to ask that he or she give up the chance of loving, and being loved, by another. That love should be capable of expression inside marriage. If homosexuals are not to become an alienated minority, he concludes, gay marriage must be legalized.

In the concluding part of this chapter we turn to look at the issue of prostitution. Male prostitution is commonplace in some gay male subcultures. Female prostitution, however, is much more widespread in society at large and it is this we shall concentrate on.

Prostitution

Prostitution can be defined as the granting of sexual favours for monetary gain. The word 'prostitute' began to come into common usage in the late eighteenth century. In the ancient world, most purveyors of sexuality for economic reward were courtesans, concubines (kept mistresses) or slaves. Courtesans and concubines often had a high position in traditional societies.

A key aspect of modern prostitution is that women and their clients are generally unknown to one another. Although men may become 'regular customers', the relationship is not initially established on the basis of personal acquaintance. This was not true of most forms of the dispensing of sexual favours for material gain in earlier times. Prostitution is directly connected to the break-up of small-scale communities, the development of large impersonal urban areas and the commercializing of social relations. In small-scale traditional communities, sexual relations were controlled by their very visibility. In newly developed urban areas, more anonymous social connections were easily established.

Prostitution today

Prostitutes in the UK today mainly come from poorer social backgrounds, as they did in the past, but they have been joined by considerable numbers of middle-class women. The increasing divorce rate has tempted some newly impoverished women into prostitution. In addition, some women unable to find jobs after graduation work in massage parlours, or in call-girl networks, while looking for other employment opportunities.

Paul J. Goldstein has classified types of prostitution in terms of *occupational commitment* and *occupational context*. *Commitment* refers to the frequency with which a woman is involved in prostitution. Many women are involved only temporarily, selling sex a few times before abandoning prostitution for a long time or for ever. 'Occasional prostitutes' are those who quite often accept money for sex, but irregularly, to supplement income from other sources. Others are continually involved in prostitution, deriving their main source of income from it. *Occupational context* means the type of work environment and interaction process in which a woman is involved. A 'street-walker' solicits business on the street. A 'call-girl' solicits clients over the phone, men either coming to her home or being visited by her. A 'house prostitute' is a woman who works in a private club or brothel. A 'massage-parlour prostitute' provides sexual services in an establishment supposedly offering only legitimate massage and health facilities.

Many women also engage in barter (payment in goods or other services rather than money) for sexual services. Most of the call-girls Goldstein studied regularly engaged in sexual bartering – sex in exchange for television sets, repairs of cars and electrical goods, clothes, legal and dental services (Goldstein 1979).

A United Nations resolution passed in 1951 condemns those who organize prostitution or profit from the activities of prostitutes, but does not ban prostitution as such. A total of fifty-three member states, including the UK, have formally accepted the resolution, although their legislation about prostitution varies widely. In some countries, prostitution itself is illegal. Others, like Britain, prohibit only certain types, such as street soliciting or child prostitution. Some national or local governments license officially recognized brothels or sex parlours – such as the 'Eros centres' in Germany or the sex houses in Amsterdam. Only a few countries license male prostitutes.

Legislation against prostitution rarely punishes clients. Those who purchase sexual services are not arrested or prosecuted, and in court procedures their identities may be kept hidden. There are far fewer studies of clients than of those selling sexuality and it is rare for anyone to suggest – as is often stated or implied about prostitutes – that they are psychologically disturbed. The imbalance in research surely expresses an uncritical acceptance of orthodox stereotypes of sexuality, according to which it is 'normal' for men to actively seek a variety of sexual outlets, while those who cater to these needs are condemned.

Child prostitution

Prostitution frequently involves children. A study of child prostitutes in the United States, Britain and West Germany indicated that the majority are children who have run away from home and have no income, turning to prostitution to gain a livelihood.

The fact that many runaway children resort to prostitution is in part an unintended consequence of laws which protect children against under-age employment, but by no means all child prostitutes have run away from home. Three broad categories of child prostitute can be distinguished (Janus and Hein Bracey 1980): *runaways*, who either leave home and are not traced by their parents, or who persistently leave each time they are found and brought back; *walkaways*, who are basically living at home, but spend periods away, for example staying out periodically for several nights; *throwaways*, whose parents are indifferent to what they do or actively reject them. All categories involve males as well as females.

Child prostitution is part of the 'sex tourism' industry in several areas of the world – in, for instance, Thailand and the Philippines. Package tours, oriented towards prostitution, draw men to these areas from Europe, the United States and Japan – although these have now been made illegal in the United Kingdom. Members of Asian women's groups have organized public protests against these tours, which none the less continue. Sex tourism in the Far East has its origins in the provision of prostitutes for American troops during the Korean and Vietnam wars. 'Rest and recreation' centres were built in Thailand, the Phillippines, Vietnam, Korea and Taiwan. Some still remain, particularly in the Philippines, catering to regular shipments of tourists as well as to the military stationed in the region.

Why does prostitution exist? Certainly it is an enduring phenomenon, which resists the attempts of governments to eliminate it. It is also almost always a matter of women selling sexual favours to men, rather than the reverse – although there are some instances, as in Hamburg, in Germany, where 'houses of pleasure' exist to provide male sexual services for women. Of course, boys or men also prostitute themselves with other men.

No single factor can explain prostitution. It might seem that men simply have stronger, or more persistent, sexual needs than women, and therefore require the outlets that prostitution provides. But this explanation is implausible. Most women seem capable of developing their sexuality in a more intense fashion than men of comparable age.

If prostitution existed simply to serve sexual needs, there would surely be many male prostitutes catering to women.

The most persuasive general conclusion to be drawn is that prostitution expresses, and to some extent helps perpetuate, the tendency of men to treat women as objects who can be 'used' for sexual purposes. Prostitution expresses in a particular context the inequalities of power between men and women. Of course, many other elements are also involved. Prostitution offers a means of obtaining sexual satisfaction for people who, because of their physical shortcomings or the existence of restrictive moral codes, cannot find other sexual partners. Prostitutes cater for men who are away from home, desire sexual encounters without commitment, or have unusual sexual tastes that other women will not accept. But these factors are relevant to the extent of the occurrence of prostitution rather than to its overall nature.

CONCLUSION: GENDER, SEXUALITY AND INEQUALITY

In recent years, few areas of sociology have developed as significantly or have emerged as so central to the discipline as a whole as the study of gender relations. In large part, this reflects changes in social life itself. Established differences between male and female identities, outlooks and typical modes of behaviour are coming to be seen in a new light.

The study of gender poses difficult problems for contemporary sociology – all the more so because it has not traditionally been seen as one of the central concerns of the discipline. What concepts can we use to understand the importance of gender in society? Could we imagine a society in which gender differences disappeared, so that we were all androgynous (had the same gender characteristics)?

Sexuality also emerges as an enormously complex area of human behaviour, undergoing fundamental changes in modern societies. Our attitudes towards sex, and our sexual behaviour, reflect wider social transformations which we shall look at in the chapters to follow.

SUMMARY

1 The term 'sex' is ambiguous. As commonly used, it denotes physical and cultural differences between males and females (as in 'the male sex', 'the female sex') as well as the sexual act. It is useful to distinguish between sex, in the physiological or biological sense, and gender, which is a cultural construct (a set of learned behaviour patterns).

2 Some people argue that differences in behaviour between the sexes are genetically determined, but there is no conclusive evidence for this.

3 Gender socialization begins as soon as an infant is born. Even parents who believe they treat children equally tend to react differently to boys and girls. These differences are reinforced by many other cultural influences.

4 The two leading theories of gender identity development are those of Sigmund Freud and Nancy Chodorow. According to Freud, the presence or absence of the penis, the symbols of masculinity and femininity, are critical to the boy's identification with the father and the girl's with the mother. Chodorow stresses the importance of the mother. Both girls and boys identify early with the mother, but boys break with her to assert their masculinity, while girls stay attached to her longer. Chodorow reverses Freud's emphasis: masculinity, rather than femininity, is defined by a loss, the loss of continuing close attachment of the mother. This accounts for male inexpressiveness, or the difficulty men have in expressing their feelings.

5 Gender is not given. It is something all of us have to 'do' in our everyday actions, day in and day out. The experience of transsexuals – people who have undergone medical treatment to physically change their sexual anatomy – bears out how difficult it is to move between one gender and another.

6 In the West, Christianity has been important in shaping sexual attitudes. In societies with rigid sexual codes, double standards and hypocrisy are common. The gulf between norms and actual practice can be tremendous, as studies of sexual behaviour have shown. Sexual practices vary widely between and within cultures. In the West, repressive attitudes to sexuality gave way to a more permissive outlook in the 1960s, the effects of which are still obvious today.

7 Sexual identity is a complicated matter. Some writers have distinguished as many as ten different sexual identities, including heterosexuals, homosexuals, bisexuals and transsexuals.

8 Homosexuality seems to exist in all cultures, yet the concept of 'a homosexual' is a relatively recent idea. Only in the last hundred years has homosexual activity been considered something that a certain type of person does – a category of abnormality and deviance constructed in opposition to the category of the 'normal heterosexual'.

9 Prostitution is the granting of sexual favours for payment. Various different types of prostitution exist in modern societies, including male and child prostitution. Licensed prostitution is accepted by national or regional governments in some countries, but in most states prostitutes operate outside the law.

FURTHER READING

Henning Bech, *When Men Meet* (Cambridge: Polity Press, 1997). An interpretation of the nature of masculinity and its connections with homosexuality.

Nancy Chodorow, *The Reproduction of Mothering* (Berkeley: University of California Press, 1978). A now classic study of gender using psychoanalytic theory to explain gender socialization.

R. W. Connell, *Masculinities* (Cambridge: Polity Press, 1995). A comprehensive introduction to a new field of knowledge and politics.

Warren Farrell, *The Myth of Male Power* (London: Fourth Estate, 1994). An analysis of social conditions forming psychological aspects of masculinity.

Marilyn French, *The War Against Women* (London: Hamish Hamilton, 1992). Documents in detail the long road yet to be trodden if women are to achieve equality with men.

Lynne Segal, *Slow Motion: Changing Masculinities, Changing Men* (London: Virago, 1990). A controversial discussion of the changing nature of men's lives and experiences in modern society.

Maryon Tysoe, *Love Isn't Quite Enough: The Psychology of Male/Female Relationships* (London: Fontana, 1992). An interesting and perceptive discussion of love, romance and relationships in contemporary social life.

Jeffrey Weeks, *Sexuality and its Discontents: Meanings, Myths and Modern Sexuality* (London: Routledge, 1989). One of the best general discussions of problems of sexuality in relation to modern societies.

IMPORTANT TERMS

- *sexuality*
- *femininity*
- *masculinity*
- *gender socialization*
- *male inexpressiveness*
- *heterosexuality*
- *homosexuality*
- *lesbianism*
- *prostitution*

6

THE BODY: EATING, ILLNESS AND AGEING

➡

Look at the two photographs on page 117. The images of a sunken face and an emaciated body are almost identical. The young girl on the left is Somalian, dying from a simple lack of food. The young woman on the right is an American teenager, dying because, in a society with a superabundance of food, she chose not to eat or to eat so sparingly that her life was endangered.

The social dynamics involved in each case are utterly different. Starvation from lack of food is caused by factors outside people's control and affects only the very poor. The American teenager is suffering from **anorexia**, an illness with no known physical origin; obsessed with the ideal of achieving a slim body, she has eventually almost given up eating altogether. Anorexia and other eating disorders are illnesses of the affluent, not of those who have little or no food. They are completely unknown in the Third World countries where food is scarce, such as Somalia.

For much of human history, a few people such as saints or mystics have deliberately chosen to starve themselves for religious reasons. They were almost always men. Today, anorexia primarily affects women, and it has no specific connection to religious beliefs. It is an illness of the body, and thus we might think that we would have to look to biological or physical factors to explain it. But health and illness, like other topics we've studied, are affected by social and cultural influences.

Although it is an illness, anorexia is closely related to the idea of being on a diet, which in turn is connected with changing views of physical attractiveness, particularly of women, in modern society. In most premodern societies, such as those described in chapter 3, the ideal female shape was a fleshy one. Thinness wasn't regarded as desirable at all – partly because it was associated with lack of food and therefore with poverty. Even in Europe in the 1600s and 1700s, the ideal female shape was well rounded. Anyone who has seen paintings of the period, such as those by Rubens, will have noticed how curvaceous the women depicted in them are. The notion of slimness as the desirable feminine shape originated among some middle-class groups in the late nineteenth century, but it has become generalized as an ideal for most women only recently.

Anorexia thus has its origins in the changing body image of women in the recent history of modern societies. It was first identified as a disorder in France in 1874, but it remained obscure until the past thirty or forty years (Brown and Jasper 1993). Since then, it has become increasingly common among young women. So has **bulimia** – bingeing on food, followed by self-induced vomiting. Anorexia and bulimia are often found together in the same individual. Someone may get extremely thin and then enter a phase of eating enormous amounts and becoming grossly overweight, followed by a period of again becoming very thin.

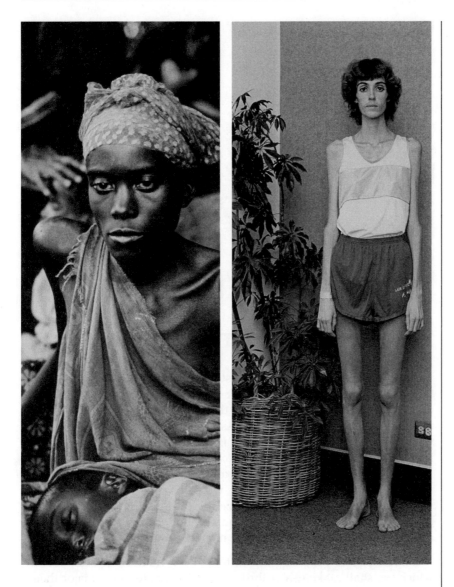

Anorexia and other eating disorders are no longer obscure forms of ill-ness in modern societies. Some 20 per cent of women in Britain suffer serious problems with eating disorders at some point in their lives. An even higher percentage experience bulimic episodes. Sixty per cent of girls age thirteen have already begun to diet; this proportion rises to over 80 per cent for young women of eighteen.

Eating disorders have become common among the rich and the famous. In 1995, in an interview on British television Princess Di publicly admit-ted having experienced severe episodes of anorexia and bulimia.

Once again, something that may seem to be a purely personal trouble – difficulties with food and despair over one's appearance – turns out to be a sociological issue. If we include not just life-threatening forms of anorexia but also obsessive concern with dieting and bodily appear-ance, eating disorders are now part of the lives of millions of people; they are found not only in Britain, but in all the industrial countries.

THE BODY AND SOCIETY

The spread of eating disorders is astonishing, and brings home clearly the influence of social factors on our lives. The field known as the SOCI-OLOGY OF THE BODY investigates the ways in which our bodies are affected by such social influences. As human beings, we are corporeal – we all possess bodies. But the body isn't something we just have, and it isn't only something physical that exists outside of society. Our bodies are deeply affected by our social experiences, as well as by the norms and values of the groups to which we belong. It is only recently that sociologists have begun to recognize the profound nature of the inter-connections between social life and the body. This field is therefore quite a new area, but it is one of the most exciting.

The sociology of the body draws together a number of basic themes which we shall make use of throughout the chapter. One major theme concerns the effects of social change on the body – as social change itself is emphasized throughout the book. A second theme is the increasing separation of the body from 'nature' – from what is taken for granted in our lives. Our bodies are being invaded by the influence of science and technology, creating new dilemmas. The invention of a range of reproductive technologies, for example, has introduced new options but has also generated intense social controversies. We shall look at two such controversies, concerning genetic engineering and abortion, later in the chapter.

The term 'technology' shouldn't be understood in too narrow a way here. In its most basic sense, it refers to material technologies such as those involved in modern medicine – for example, the scanning machine that allows a doctor to chart a baby's development prior to birth. But we must also take account of what Michel Foucault (1988) has called *social technologies* affecting the body. By this phrase, he means that the body is increasingly something we have to 'create' rather than simply accept. A social technology is any kind of regular intervention we make into the functioning of our bodies in order to alter them in specific ways. An example is dieting, so central to anorexia.

In what follows, we will first analyse why eating disorders have become so common. We shall then look at the sociological importance of reproductive technologies. From there, we will study the care of the body in modern social conditions – in other words, health and health care. Finally, we will consider the question of the ageing body. Like so many other aspects of our lives in modern societies, ageing is not what it once was! The ageing process is not simply a physical one, and the position of older people in society today is changing in basic ways.

EATING DISORDERS AND THE CULTIVATION OF THE BODY

To understand why eating disorders have become so commonplace in current times, we should think back to the social changes analysed earlier in the book. Anorexia actually reflects broad aspects of social change, including the impact of globalization.

The rise of eating disorders in Western societies coincides directly with the globalization of food production, which has accelerated from three or four decades ago. The invention of new modes of refrigeration plus the use of container transportation have allowed food to be stored for long periods and to be delivered from one side of the world to the other. Since the 1950s (and for those who can afford it – now the majority of the population in Western societies), supermarket shelves have been crammed with foods from all parts of the world. Most such foodstuffs are available all the time, not just, as was true before, when they are in season locally.

For the past few years, almost *everyone* in Britain and the other developed societies has been on a diet. This does not mean that everyone is desperately trying to get thin. Rather, when all foods are available more or less all the time, we must *decide* what to eat – construct a diet where 'diet' means the foods we habitually consume. First, we have to decide what to eat in relation to the many sorts of new medical information with which science now bombards us – for instance, that cholesterol levels are a factor in causing heart disease. Second, we now worry about the calorie content of different foods. In a society in which food is abundant, we are able for the first time to design our bodies in relation to our lifestyle habits (jogging, aerobics) and what we eat. Eating disorders have their origins in the opportunities, but also the profound strains and tensions, this situation produces.

Eighty per cent of anorexics show an addiction to exercise. An **addiction** is a compulsive pattern of behaviour which the individual finds it difficult or impossible to resist. Sally, for example, a twenty-eight-year-old single mother from the Midlands, fell prey to anorexia after having become, in her own words, 'a compulsive exerciser'. She started exercising after splitting up with the father of her son. 'I felt demoralized and worthless when the relationship broke down, and I wanted to prove I still had a life and that I was strong. Initially the exercise made me feel good about myself; I got attention from men and my self-esteem was boosted. Now I need a constant calorie burn just to feel normal.' Her obsessiveness about exercise persisted even after she recovered from her anorexia (Walker 1995).

Why do eating disorders affect women in particular and young women most acutely? To begin with, it should be pointed out that not all those suffering from eating disorders are women; about 10 per cent are men. But men don't suffer from anorexia or bulimia as often as women, partly because widely held social norms stress the importance of physical attractiveness more for women than for men, and partly because desirable body images of men differ from those of women.

When men have concerned themselves with the careful cultivation of the body, the muscular body has been the ideal. For many men who have taken it up, muscle building becomes as compulsive or addictive as eating disorders are for women. In his book *Muscle*, for example, Sam Fussell describes how he took up muscle building to help control his feelings of inadequacy and anxiety about himself as 'weedy'. From being skinny, he became very muscular indeed – but then couldn't stop. He was unable to carry on his daily activities without including hours of weight training each day. The muscle builder can never be muscular enough, just as the anorexic can't ever be thin enough (Fussell 1991).

Some women have now taken up muscle building, but most don't look in this direction when trying to achieve a body that conforms to their ideals. Their anxieties concentrate on fear of fatness. The modern ideal of the desirable woman is one who is thin and trim. Anorexia and bulimia are illnesses of the *active* woman. They don't just happen; they have to be actively accomplished. The anorectic individual sticks to a rigid, minimal diet and may do aerobics every day of the week.

Anorexia and other eating disorders reflect a situation in which women play a much larger part in the wider society than they used to, but are still judged as much by their appearance as their attainments. Eating disorders are rooted in feelings of shame about the body. The individual feels herself to be inadequate and imperfect; and her anxieties about how others perceive her become focused through her feelings about her body. Ideals of slimness at that point become obsessive – shedding weight becomes the means of making everything all right in her world. Once she starts to diet and exercise compulsively, she can become locked into a pattern of refusing food altogether, or of vomiting up what she has eaten. If the pattern is not broken (and some forms of psychotherapy and medical treatment have proved effective here), the sufferer might actually starve herself to death.

THE BODY AND REPRODUCTIVE TECHNOLOGIES

The spread of eating disorders reflects the influence of science and technology on our ways of life today: calorie counts have only been possible with the advance of technology. But the impact of technology is always conditioned by social factors. We have much more autonomy over the body than ever before, a situation that creates new possibilities of a positive kind as well as new anxieties and problems.

What is happening is part of what sociologists call the **socialization of nature**. This phrase refers to the fact that phenomena that used to be 'natural', or given in NATURE, have now become social – they depend on our own social decisions. An example is human reproduction. For hundreds of years, the lives of most women were dominated by child-birth and child-rearing. In premodern times, contraception was ineffective or, in some societies, unknown. Even in Europe as late as the eighteenth century, it was common for women to experience as many as twenty pregnancies (often involving miscarriages and infant deaths). Improved methods of contraception have helped to alter this situation in a fundamental way. Far from any longer being 'natural', it is almost unknown in the industrial countries for women to undergo so many pregnancies. Advances in contraceptive technology enable most women and men to control whether and when they have children.

Contraception is only one example of a **reproductive technology**. Some of the other areas in which natural processes have become social are described below.

Childbirth

Medical science has not always been involved with the major life transitions from birth to death. The medicalization of pregnancy and childbirth developed slowly, as local physicians and midwives were displaced by paediatric specialists. Today in the industrialized societies, most births occur in a hospital with the help of a specialized medical team.

In the past, new parents had to wait until the day of birth to learn the sex of their new-born and whether the child would be healthy. Today, prenatal tests such as the sonogram (an image of the foetus produced by using ultrasonic waves) and amniocentesis (which draws off some of the amniotic fluid from around the foetus) can be used to discover structural or chromosomal abnormalities prior to birth. Such new technology presents couples and society with new ethical and legal decisions. When a disorder is detected, the couple are faced with the decision of whether or not to have the baby, knowing it may be seriously handicapped.

Genetic engineering: designer babies

A great deal of scientific endeavour these days is being devoted to the expansion of genetic engineering; that is, intervening in the genetic make-up of the foetus so as to influence its subsequent development. The likely social impact of genetic engineering is starting to provoke debates almost as intense as those that surround the issue of abortion. According to its supporters, genetic engineering will bring us many benefits. It is possible, for example, to identify the genetic factors that make some people vulnerable to certain diseases. Genetic reprogramming will ensure that these illnesses are no longer passed on from generation to generation. It will be possible to 'design' our bodies before birth in terms of skin colour, colour of hair and eyes, weight and so forth.

There could be no better example of the mixture of opportunities and problems that the increasing socialization of nature creates for us. What choices will parents make when they can design their babies, and what limits should be placed on those choices? Genetic engineering is unlikely to be cheap. Will this mean that those who can afford to pay will be able to programme out from their children anything they see as socially undesirable physical traits? What will happen to the children of more deprived groups, who will continue to be born naturally?

Some sociologists have argued that differential access to genetic engineering might lead to the emergence of a 'biological underclass'. Those who don't have the physical advantages genetic engineering can bring might be subject to prejudice and discrimination by those who do enjoy these advantages. They might have difficulty finding employment and life or health insurance.

The abortion debate

The most controversial ethical dilemma created by modern reproductive technologies in modern societies is this: under what conditions should abortion be available to women? The abortion debate has become so intense precisely because it centres on basic ethical issues to which there are no easy solutions. Those who are 'pro life' believe that abortion is always wrong except in extreme circumstances, because it is equivalent to murder. For them, ethical issues are above all subject to the value that must be placed on human life. Those who are 'pro choice' argue that the mother's control over her own body – her own right to live a rewarding life – must be the primary consideration.

The debate has led to numerous episodes of violence. Can it ever be resolved? At least one prominent social and legal theorist, Ronald Dworkin (1993), has suggested that it can. The intense divisions between those who are pro life and those who are pro choice, he argues, hide deeper sources of agreement between the two sides, and in this there is a source of hope. At previous periods of history, life was often relatively cheap. In current times, however, we have come to place a high value on the sanctity of human life. Each side agrees with this value, but they interpret it differently, the one emphasizing the interests of the child, the other the interests of the mother. If the two sides can be persuaded to see that they share a common ethical value, Dworkin suggests, a more constructive dialogue might be possible.

THE WELL-FUNCTIONING BODY: IMAGES OF HEALTH AND ILLNESS

The sanctity of human life is also the prime value underlying the development of health care systems in modern societies. 'Health' and 'illness' are terms that are culturally and socially defined. Cultures differ in what they consider healthy and normal, as the discussion of eating disorders showed. All cultures have known concepts of physical health and illness, but most of what we now recognize as medicine is a consequence of developments in Western society over the past three centuries. In premodern cultures, the family was the main institution coping with sickness or affliction. There have always been individuals who specialized as healers, using a mixture of physical and magical remedies, and many of these traditional systems of treatment survive today in non-Western cultures throughout the world. For instance, ayurvedic medicine (traditional healing) has been practised in India for nearly two thousand years. It is founded on a theory of the equilibrium of psychological and physical aspects of the personality, imbalances of which are treated by nutritional and herbal remedies. Chinese folk medicine is similarly based on a conception of the overall harmony of the personality, involving the use of herbs and acupuncture, a technique in which needles are strategically inserted into a patient's skin.

Modern medicine introduced a view of disease that sees its origins and treatment as physical and explicable in scientific terms. The application of science to medical diagnosis and cure was the major feature of the development of modern health care systems. Other, closely related, features were the acceptance of the hospital as the setting within which serious illnesses were to be dealt with and the development of the medical profession as a body with recognized codes of ethics and significant social power. The scientific view of disease was linked to the requirement that medical training be systematic and long-term; self-taught healers were excluded. Although professional medical practice is not limited to hospitals, the hospital provided an environment in which doctors for the first time were able to treat and study large numbers of patients, in circumstances permitting the concentration of medical technology.

In medieval times, the major illnesses were infectious diseases such as tuberculosis, cholera, malaria and plague. The plague, or Black Death, of the fourteenth century (which was spread by fleas carried by rats) killed a quarter of the population of England and devastated large areas of Europe. Infectious diseases have now become a minor cause of death in the industrialized countries, and several have been substantially eradicated. In the industrialized countries, the most common causes of death are non-infectious diseases such as cancer and heart disease. Whereas in premodern societies the highest rates of death were among infants and young children, today death rates (the proportion of the population who die each year) rise with increasing age.

In spite of the prestige that modern medicine has acquired, improvements in medical care accounted for only a relatively minor part of the decline in death rates prior to the twentieth century. Effective sanitation, better nutrition and improved sewerage and hygiene were more consequential, particularly in reducing the infant mortality rates and deaths of young children. Drugs, advances in surgery, and antibiotics did not significantly decrease death rates until well into the twentieth century. Antibiotics used to treat bacterial infections first became available in the 1930s and 1940s, while immunizations (against diseases such as polio) were developed later.

Health and illness in the developed countries

Within the industrial societies, there are striking differences in the distribution of the major diseases. Around 70 per cent of deaths in Western countries are attributable to four major types of illness: cancer, heart disease, strokes and lung disease. Some progress has been made in understanding their origins and in controlling their effects, but none can be effectively cured. Since the distribution of these four diseases varies between countries, regions and classes, it seems evident that they are related to diet and lifestyle. Individuals from higher socioeconomic positions are on average healthier, taller and stronger, and live longer than those lower down the social scale. Differences are greatest in respect to infant mortality (children dying in the first year of life) and child death, but poorer people are at greater risk of dying at all ages than more affluent people.

There are several reasons for this. People in wealthier sectors of society tend to have superior diets and better access to medical care, and they are more likely to take advantage of that access. Working conditions also directly affect health. Those who work in offices or in domestic settings are at less risk of injury or exposure to hazardous materials. The extent of industry-based disease is difficult to calculate, because it is not always possible to determine whether an illness is acquired from working conditions or from other sources. However, some work-related diseases are well documented: lung disease is widespread in mining, as a result of dust inhalation; work in environments using asbestos has been shown to produce certain types of cancer.

Jake Najman has recently surveyed the evidence linking health to economic inequalities. He also considered what strategies might best be used to improve the health of the poorer groups in society. After studying data for a number of different countries, he concluded that for people in the poorest 20 per cent, as measured in terms of income, death rates were 1.5 to 2.5 times those of the highest 20 per cent of income earners. The contrast is also becoming greater rather than smaller. The same is true of **life expectancy** – the age to which individuals at birth can expect to live.

How might the influence of poverty on health be countered? Extensive programmes of health education and disease prevention are one possibility. But such programmes tend to work better among more prosperous, well-educated groups and in any case usually produce only small changes in behaviour. Increased access to health services would help, but probably to a limited degree. The only really effective policy option, Najman argues, would be to attack poverty itself, so as to reduce the income gap between rich and poor (Najman 1993).

Illness as stigma: the impact of AIDS

Not all illnesses are found more frequently among poorer than among more affluent groups. Anorexia, for instance, is more common among people from higher socioeconomic backgrounds. The same is true of AIDS (Acquired Immuno-Deficiency Syndrome), at least in Britain and other industrial countries.

AIDS is a mysterious disease, which has come from nowhere to become a major health hazard in less than twenty-five years. AIDS causes the body's immune system to collapse; it does not cause death itself, but the sufferer becomes prey to a range of fatal illnesses. Everyone who becomes infected with the virus to which most medical researchers believe it is linked, HIV (Human Immuno-Deficiency Virus), seems sooner or later to develop AIDS. AIDS is believed to be transmitted either by direct blood-to-blood contact (as occurs in blood transfusions or when drug users share needles) or through sexually emitted fluids (semen or vaginal secretion).

No one knows whether AIDS had its origins in the socialization of nature, as an unintended outcome of human intervention into the world around us. Some have suggested as much, however. It has been speculated, for example, that the disease might be the result of experiments with forms of germ warfare, which unsuspectingly created a lethal virus. Others argue that AIDS and the HIV virus have been around a long while, perhaps for centuries, in certain parts of the world. According to this theory, the symptoms now recognized as AIDS might previously have been mistaken for other diseases.

A distinctive characteristic of AIDS, compared with the majority of other illnesses, is that it can be transmitted sexually. The disease first made its appearance in North America among male homosexual groups and initially, both among medical researchers and in the eyes of the public, was seen as a homosexual disease. AIDS came into the public consciousness at a time, the early 1980s, when it seemed that many of the pre-established prejudices against homosexuality were collapsing. But the disease seemed to those repelled by homosexuality, especially some religious groups, to provide concrete justification for their hostile views. The idea that AIDS is a plague sent by God to punish perversion even found expression in some respectable medical quarters. An editorial in a medical journal asked: 'Might we be witnessing, in fact, in the form of a modern communicable disorder, a fulfillment of St Paul's pronouncement: "The due penalty of their error"?' (Altman 1986).

The rapid spread of AIDS was undoubtedly due in some degree to the increased opportunities for homosexual encounters provided by gay subcultures in North America and elsewhere. In fact, at first AIDS seemed to be limited almost exclusively to large American cities with significant gay populations. Headlines in the press set the early tone: 'Gay plague baffling medical detectives' (*Philadelphia Daily News*,

9 August 1982); 'Being gay is a health hazard' (*Saturday Evening Post*, October 1982); 'Gay plague has arrived in Canada' (*Toronto Star*). The magazine *Us* reported: 'Male homosexuals aren't so gay any more.' At the time, it was already known that probably a third of those with AIDS in the United States were not homosexual, but in the initial publicity this was virtually ignored.

When the film actor Rock Hudson died of AIDS in 1985, what shocked much of the world's press was not the nature of his illness but the fact that this symbol of male virility was homosexual. Rather than looking for the source of the disease in a particular virus, medical researchers first tried to discover its origins in specific aspects of gay practices. The discovery that AIDS can be transmitted through heterosexual contact then forced a reappraisal; most of the evidence for this came from central Africa, where AIDS was widespread but had no particular relation to male homosexuality. The 'gay plague' soon became redefined by the press as a 'heterosexual nightmare'.

The impact of AIDS is likely to influence many forms of sexual behaviour. In the homosexual community, marked changes are already noticeable; the level of casual sexual encounters has been radically reduced. Some of the most widely condemned homosexual practices, paradoxically, turn out to be the safest. For example, sado-masochistic activities involving the infliction of discomfort or pain on a partner are safe because no direct genital contact is involved. The dilemma facing male gay communities is how to foster procedures of 'safe sex' while warding off the renewed attacks to which the gay community is subject.

AIDS and the heterosexual population

In medical terms, AIDS is a moving target, new and elusive. Medical knowledge about the disease dates very quickly. And today it is becoming a global epidemic. The true number of people infected with the HIV virus is unknown, but conservative estimates put the figure at

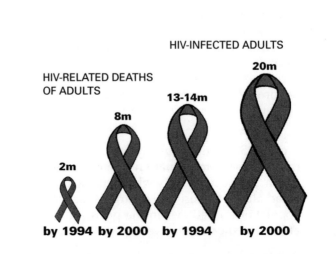

HIV-INFECTED ADULTS

HIV-RELATED DEATHS OF ADULTS

2m

8m

13–14m

20m

by 1994   by 2000   by 1994   by 2000

Fig. 6.1 AIDS: a growing threat

Source: Michael Kidron and Ronald Segal, *The State of the World Atlas*, 5th edn, 1995.

13 million worldwide (see figure 6.1). About 500,000 of these are in Europe, 1 million each in North America, Latin America and the Caribbean, and more than 8 million in Africa. The main impact of the epidemic is still to come, because of the time it takes for HIV infection to develop into full-blown AIDS. The majority of people affected in the world today are heterosexuals. Worldwide, at least four HIV infections are contracted heterosexually for every instance of homosexual spread. The World Health Organization estimates that by the year 2000, more than 30 million adults and 10 million children will have become infected.

The fact that at first AIDS was most prevalent among homosexuals has served to revive prejudices against homosexuality. However, new and terrifying as it is, AIDS raises fears and hostilities independent of this. Some of these were explored in the film *Philadelphia*, in which an AIDS sufferer, played by Tom Hanks, loses his job when his employers learn about his disease. He is fired not because he is homosexual, but because of anxieties provoked by his disease. The film traces his struggle to sue his firm for wrongful dismissal.

AIDS is an example of illness as **stigma**. A stigma is any characteristic that sets an individual or group apart from the majority of the population, with the result that the individual or group is treated with suspicion or hostility. Most forms of illness arouse feelings of sympathy or compassion among non-sufferers. When an illness is seen as uncommonly infectious, however, or is perceived as somehow a mark of dishonour or shame, sufferers may be rejected by the 'healthy' population. This was true of people afflicted with leprosy in the Middle Ages, who were popularly thought to be sinners punished by God, and were hence disowned and forced to live in separate leper colonies. In a less extreme way, AIDS often provokes such stigmatization today – in spite of the fact that, like leprosy, the danger of contracting the disease in ordinary day-to-day situations is almost nil.

There are no effective treatments for AIDS, although some drugs seem to delay its progression. While a person who is HIV positive may live for many years without developing AIDS, once the disease appears, it is effectively a death sentence. Its effects are particularly tragic, as it is most common among younger age groups. In this respect, it is unlike the other major killer illnesses in the industrial societies today, which mostly strike at older age groups.

Ageing and a propensity to illness are by no means the same, as will be discussed towards the end of the chapter. But ever since infectious illnesses like cholera and tuberculosis were conquered in the industrialized areas of the world, health care systems have concentrated mainly on combating and treating illnesses that become more common with advancing age. In the following sections, we take a closer look at systems of health care, concentrating on the health care systems of Britain and the United States. We shall then look at the issue of ageing directly.

HEALTH CARE SYSTEMS

Health care in the United Kingdom

Virtually all industrialized countries, with the exception of the United States, have comprehensive systems of publicly provided medical services. The National Health Service (NHS) in Britain, for example, was set up in 1948. The stated principle underlying its founding was that access to health care should depend on medical need rather than ability to pay.

The NHS is funded from central government revenues, collected as part of income tax. Access to a general practitioner (GP) and hospital treatment is free to all users. Drugs obtained by prescriptions given by doctors were originally supplied without charge, but legislation by recent governments has introduced a system of partial payments. When the NHS was first established to give **public health care**, pressure from the medical profession, among other influences, ensured that there would remain **private health care**, operating alongside. While the majority of general practitioners work exclusively for the NHS, a high proportion of consultants also maintain private practices. Some purely private hospitals and health care facilities exist, together with medical personnel working exclusively in the private sector, and funding and fees are often linked to private health insurance schemes. Only a small minority of the population, however, are members of such schemes.

General practitioners have a basic role in filtering the access patients have to more specialized medical treatments. The average British citi-

'The doctor doesn't visit any more. He says why don't you drop in when you're feeling better?'

zen sees a GP about four times a year. GPs deal directly with some 90 per cent of all illness, every GP having a 'list' of patients registered with him or her (up to a maximum number set by the NHS). Patients who see GPs have no intrinsic right to be referred to specialists; this is a matter for the judgement of the practitioner. Since specialists are not able to advertise, even self-referral to private consultants may not be easy if a GP disapproves.

The basic unit which administers the NHS today is the District Health Authority (DHA). DHAs are composed of local government nominees, members of the medical profession and lay people drawn from local interest groups and voluntary associations. In principle the DHAs are supposed to reflect the composition of the wider community in terms of characteristics such as class and ethnic background; in practice they tend to be a middle-class preserve. The presence of individuals from the medical profession on DHAs is justified in terms of their specialized expertise. It is worth noting, however, that this situation is not found in other areas of local government, where employees are prohibited by law from standing for election to committees within their own organizations (Kingdom 1991).

A White Paper on the NHS produced by the Conservative government in 1989 introduced basic changes in the service. A stress was put on the need to combat bureaucracy, to introduce greater 'internal competition' and to promote greater managerial efficiency. Local management, oriented to local needs, the reform suggested, is the best guarantee of effectiveness. Health authorities should be given greater freedom from supervision by higher government bodies. NHS organizations should become more like the 'flexible firms' emerging in industry (see chapter 12, 'Work and economic life').

One of the most controversial innovations was that individual hospitals could opt to become self-governing trusts. Under this scheme, hospitals are encouraged to become autonomous in their funding. They are able to depart from nationally agreed wage rates, raise capital from commercial sources and generate surpluses. As of 1996, many major hospitals have opted out in this way, and others look likely to follow suit. Critics argue, however, that such hospitals are likely to prosper only in more affluent areas, that they will duplicate unnecessarily expensive equipment which other nearby hospitals might also have, and that they may be reluctant to treat patients whose treatment could be particularly expensive (Mohan 1991).

As in most aspects of health care, evaluating the NHS reforms is not easy. The implications are complex; little research has been done on the reforms; and the long-term consequences will by definition take many years to assess. Moreover, the reforms include a wide variety of organizational changes. Surveying the available evidence, Julian Le Grand concludes that there is at least the potential for real gains in quality of patient care and in efficiency. The introduction of competitiveness within different sectors of the NHS, he thinks, has probably on the whole brought more benefits than negative results (Le Grand 1994).

Health care in the United States

An enormous sum of money is spent each year on health care in the United States – a higher proportion of total expenditure, in fact, than in any other nation (see table 6.1). American medical services are supported primarily by private insurance programmes, supplemented by government programmes – Medicare for the elderly and Medicaid for the poor. The health care system in the United States is much more fragmented and diverse than in most other countries where comprehensive government-run national health programmes exist. For example, US hospitals are owned by federal or state governments, city or county authorities, private organizations, religious orders, voluntary non-profit groups, or some combination of these.

In spite of the country's high level of wealth and the vast sums spent on health care industries, the United States does not fare well in some basic indices of health. The country ranks quite low, for example, in the two most common measures of the physical well-being of a population: average life expectancy and the rate of infant mortality. Life expectancy is higher in most European countries, and rates of infant mortality are lower. One reason is that there are an estimated 37 million people in the United States who have no private health insurance and virtually no access to public health care.

The logic of the American health care system is based on the idea that competition produces the cheapest services, since it allows consumers to pick and choose. The weaknesses in this position are well known. Consumers cannot readily shop around when they are sick, and are usually unable to judge technically the services they are offered. Those with inadequate resources have limited access to medical services. Affluent people are more often able to buy superior medical provision than those who are less well off. People who are fully covered by medical insurance have little incentive to seek less expensive care. The gen-

Table 6.1	**Life-span, health and wealth**			
Countries in order of life expectancy	Rank order in world	Life expectancy at birth, 1992, in years	Total expenditure on health, % of GDP	Expenditure on health per capita, 1991 (US dollars)
Japan	1	78.6	6.8	1,771
Sweden	4	77.7	8.8	2,372
Spain	5	77.4	6.5	877
Greece	6	77.3	4.8	274
Canada	7	77.2	9.9	1,847
Netherlands	8	77.2	8.7	1,664
Australia	11	76.7	8.6	1,466
France	12	76.6	9.1	1,912
Israel	13	76.2	4.2	509
UK	14	75.8	6.6	1,003
Germany	17	75.6	9.1	1,782
US	18	75.6	13.3	2,932
Ireland	22	75.0	8.0	886

Source: World Bank, *World Development Report 1994*; data on total expenditure on health as % of GDP were similar in 1996, see *The Economist*, *The Pocket World in Figures*, 1996.

eral result is a health care system that is expensive to run in proportion to the health levels achieved, and in which there are serious gaps in overall provision for the population.

Assessment

The assessment of health care schemes in the end brings us to certain basic questions that somehow must be answered. We have, collectively, to make some basic decisions. For example, does the age of the patient matter? Should we make more of an effort to save the lives of younger people rather than older ones? Are some aspects of health and bodily appearance to be ranked as more important than others? If so, why? There are no easy answers here. In Britain and the other industrialized countries, the future probably lies with initiatives that have to do not with cost but with shifting current practices away from the 'last ditch' treatment of illness and towards preventative medicine and the adoption of healthier ways of life.

HEALTH AND THE ENVIRONMENT

Our health is plainly connected with the environment around us, on both a local and a global level. No one knows exactly how far the threats to global ecosystems that currently exist connect to patterns of health and disease, but some forms of environmental degradation certainly produce health hazards. Protection of the environment is thus an important part of preventative medicine.

Take as an example city smog, caused mainly by car exhaust emissions. Smog is a persistent problem in London and most major European and American cities.

For a long time, it was believed that air pollution adversely affected only people with asthma or emphysema – particularly children. Now it is thought that impaired lung function and other respiratory problems can take hold in any adult when air quality falls below a certain standard. What can be done? The only feasible solution is to break the stranglehold of the car or to convert wholesale to electric vehicles.

Modern economies, however, are heavily centred on the car and associated industries. Major social changes would be needed to produce a cleaner, healthier environment. The problem of air pollution and the car is only one in a large catalogue of environmental issues. According to one estimate, 'more destruction has been wrought to the fragile framework of the biosphere during the last 40 years, since global development has really got under way, than during the preceding two or three million years' (Goldsmith 1988). Ross Hume Hall believes that health care systems should in fact be geared to environmental protection:

> On the one hand we have the environmentalists detailing the downward slide of the earth's ecology; on the other hand we have the health authorities who fail to see the slide. . . . [At the moment] we identify a health haz-

ard and a connecting curative action. . . . The opposite of this approach, the preventative mode, is less concerned with waiting to identify specific evidence of cause-and-effect links. Very simply we say we do not know exactly what effect any environmental impact has on health so we do not dump toxic wastes, for example, or destroy ecosystems – period. (Hall 1990)

HEALTH AND AGEING

Problems of health care reform cannot be disentangled from the fact that we live in an ageing society, in which the proportion of people sixty-five or over is steadily increasing. At the same time, the issue of the social importance of ageing is one that ranges much more broadly. For what old age actually *is* – the opportunities it offers and the burdens it carries – is changing dramatically.

Two rather contradictory processes are involved here. On the one hand, older people in modern societies tend to have lower status and less power than they used to have in premodern cultures. In these cultures, as in non-Western societies today (such as India or China), old age was believed to bring wisdom, and the oldest people in any given community were commonly its main decision makers. Today, increasing age normally brings with it something of the reverse. In a society undergoing constant change, as ours is, the accumulated knowledge of older people often seems to the young no longer a valuable store of wisdom, but simply behind the times.

On the other hand, however, older people today are much less prone to accept ageing as an inevitable process of the decay of the body. Here once more we can trace the impact of the socialization of nature. The ageing process was once generally accepted as an inevitable manifestation of the ravages of time. But increasingly, ageing is not something taken for granted as natural; advances in medicine and nutrition have shown that much that was once regarded as inevitable about ageing can either be countered or slowed down. On average, people live to much older ages than was true over a century ago, as a result of improvements in nutrition, hygiene and health care (see table 6.2).

In Britain in 1850, the proportion of the population over sixty-five was around 5 per cent. The figure today is over 15 per cent, and will continue to grow (see table 6.3). The average age of people in Britain has been rising for more than a century and a half. In 1800, the average age was probably as low as sixteen. At the turn of the twentieth century, it had risen to twenty-three. By 1970, it was twenty-eight, and today it has reached over thirty. The average age will continue to rise for some time to come, if no major changes in current demographic trends occur. It is likely to be thirty-five by 2000 and may climb to thirty-seven by 2030.

There has also been an expansion in the numbers of the very old. According to some estimates, the number of people in Britain over eighty-five years of age will be 50 per cent above present levels by the year 2000, comprising over 1.2 per cent of the whole population.

Table 6.2	**Expectation of life, by gender and age, in the United Kingdom**							
	1901	**1931**	**1961**	**1991**	**1993**	**1996**	**2001**	**2021**
Males								
At birth	45.5	57.7	67.8	73.2	73.6	74.4	75.4	77.6
At age								
1 year	54.6	62.4	69.5	73.8	74.1	74.8	75.7	77.9
10 years	60.4	65.2	69.9	73.9	74.2	75.0	75.9	78.0
20 years	61.7	66.3	70.3	74.2	74.5	75.3	76.1	78.2
40 years	66.1	69.3	71.4	75.1	75.4	76.3	77.2	79.3
60 years	73.3	74.3	74.9	77.7	77.8	78.6	79.5	81.4
80 years	84.9	84.7	85.2	86.4	86.4	86.8	87.2	88.2
Females								
At birth	49.0	61.6	73.6	78.7	78.9	79.7	80.6	82.6
At age								
1 year	56.8	65.3	75.1	79.2	79.3	80.1	80.9	82.8
10 years	62.7	67.9	75.4	79.4	79.5	80.3	81.1	83.0
20 years	64.1	69.0	75.6	79.5	79.6	80.4	81.2	83.1
40 years	68.3	71.9	76.3	80.0	80.1	80.9	81.7	83.5
60 years	74.6	76.1	78.8	81.9	81.9	82.6	83.3	84.9
80 years	85.3	85.4	86.3	88.3	88.3	88.8	89.1	90.0

Expectation of life in this table is the total number of years which a person might expect to live.

Source: Government Actuary's Department. From *Social Trends*, 1996, p. 130.

Table 6.3	**Percentages of elderly people (aged 65+) in selected countries in 1988 with projections for 2010**	
	1988	**2010**
UK	15.5	15.9
USA	12.1	13.9
Denmark	15.4	16.7
France	13.6	16.9
West Germany	15.4	20.5
Italy	13.7	20.2
Ireland	11.0	12.8

Source: S. Arber and J. Ginn, *Gender and Later Life*, 1991, table 1.3, p. 8.

The physical effects of ageing

Old age cannot as such be identified with ill health or disability, but advancing age of course brings increased health problems. Only during the past twenty years or so have biologists made a systematic attempt to distinguish the physical effects of ageing from traits associated with diseases. Precisely to what extent the body inevitably wears out with advancing age is a debated issue. The effects of social and economic losses are also difficult to disentangle from the effects of physical deterioration. Loss of relatives and friends, separation from children who live elsewhere and loss of employment may all take a physical toll.

In general, however, research findings demonstrate that poor health and advancing age are by no means synonymous. There are many people over sixty-five who claim to be in almost perfect health.

The ageing of the body is affected by social influences, but of course it is also governed by genetic factors. Biologists generally accept that the human being has a maximum life-span governed by its genes – this is thought to be about 120 years of age. Like all animals, the human body is genetically programmed to die.

But for how much longer? If geneticists found a way to control ageing and death, it would be one of the most profoundly important aspects of the socialization of nature mentioned earlier. Scientists have already shown that ageing cells in animals can be manipulated to make them act like young cells. Ronald Klatz, chairman of the American Academy of Anti-Ageing Medicine, has commented: 'I believe we shall see much longer lifespans, perhaps within our lifetimes. The new technologies are already here. They need to be developed. We need to start preparing for an ageless society. Ageing is a disease which can be treated' (quoted in Kelsey 1996, p. 2).

The future of ageing

In a society that places a high value on youth, vitality and physical attractiveness, older people tend to become invisible. Recent years, however, have seen some changes in attitudes towards old age. Older people are unlikely to recover the full authority and prestige that used to be accorded to elders of the community in ancient societies. Yet as they have come to comprise a larger proportion of the population, older people have acquired more political influence than they used to have. They have already become a powerful political lobby.

Activist groups have also started to fight against **ageism** – discrimination against people on the basis of their age – seeking to encourage a positive view of old age and older people. Ageism is an ideology just as sexism and racism are. There are as many false stereotypes of older people as there are in other areas. For instance, it is often believed that most people over sixty-five are in hospitals or homes for the elderly; that a high proportion are senile; and that older workers are less competent than younger ones. All these beliefs are erroneous. Ninety-five per cent of people over sixty-five live in private dwellings; only about 7 per cent of those between sixty-five and eighty show pronounced symptoms of senile decay; and the productivity and attendance records of workers over sixty are superior on average to those of younger age groups.

In their book *Life After Work: The Arrival of the Ageless Society*, Michael Young and Tom Schuller (1991) argue that age has become an oppressive device used to slot people into fixed, stereotyped roles. Many older people are rebelling against such treatment and exploring new activities and modes of self-fulfilment. They are contesting what Young and Schuller call the 'age-locked society'.

In modern societies, both young and old are categorized by age rather than in terms of their characteristics, pursuits and identities. The two groups should form an alliance, according to Young and Schuller, to break out of the categories and create an ageless society. They could be pioneers in the interests not only of their own social positions, but of the majority of the population in paid work also.

Young and Schuller argue that the young and the old could help shift the modern society order away from the treadmill of consumerism. More and more people, they say, quoting Virginia Woolf, could be freed from the constraints of labour, 'always to be doing work that one did not wish to do, and to do it like a slave, flattering and fawning'. They could develop their own unique qualities and concerns, as Woolf did in a spectacular way. Otherwise, her talent for writing, 'a small one, but dear to the possessor', she thought would 'perish and with it myself, my soul . . . like rust eating away the bloom of the spring'.

CONCLUSION

In this chapter, we have looked at some of the diverse social influences that affect us as corporeal beings – that affect the protection and care of the body. As a result of both social and technological developments, we no longer experience our bodies as just a given part of our lives. There are aspects of our bodily experiences into which science and technology now intrude – with mixed consequences. Many advances have been made in medicine and health care, and these have allowed people to live on average to older ages than once was common. At the same time, ageing has changed its meaning and older people are demanding the right to remain full members of society rather than being 'pensioned off' by the young. These developments are important politically as well as socially. Making up as they do an increasing proportion of the population as a whole, older people are potentially a group with a good deal of political power.

SUMMARY

1 The field of the sociology of the body focuses on how our bodies are affected by social influences. The rise of anorexia and other eating disorders forms an example of these influences. Anorexia and eating problems, which are found mainly among young women, are associated with basic changes going on in modern societies – particularly changes in patterns of food consumption and in women's position in society.

2 Eating disorders are also related to the wider process of the socialization of nature. This phrase means that many phenomena which used to be 'natural' – part of nature – are now determined by social factors and by technological change. An example is reproduction. Women's lives are no longer dominated by childbirth and child-rearing, as they used to be. Modern contraception and other innovations mean that 'choice' replaces 'nature'.

3 All societies have images of the 'well-functioning body' – in other words, of health and illness. The study of health and illness is one of the main areas of the sociology of the body.

4 Sociological research reveals close connections between illness and inequality. Within industrial countries, poorer groups have a shorter average life expectancy, and are more susceptible to disease, than more affluent strata. Richer countries also have higher average life expectancies than poorer ones.

5 However, not all diseases are more common among poorer groups. An example is AIDS, which in industrial countries is more common among people from higher socioeconomic backgrounds. AIDS today is becoming a global epidemic. No cure is as yet in sight for this worrying, and apparently new, disease.

6 Health care systems differ between different societies. The UK has a strongly developed system of public health care – the National Health Service. In some other countries, such as the United States, health care is more widely dependent on private health schemes, with public health care taking a lesser role. Many controversies exist about which direction health care should take in the future.

7 Environmental factors are probably coming more and more to influence patterns of health and illness. Pollution of the air, for example, may affect the health of thousands, or millions, of people. It follows that health care in the future should concentrate on creating more favourable environmental conditions for people to live and work in.

8 A further important area in the sociology of the body is the study of ageing. Ageing has been radically affected by the socialization of nature. How we age is more and more influenced by social factors: on average, people live for much longer than once was the case.

9 Ageing creates many opportunities for people to free themselves from the constraints of work. It also, however, generates social, economic and psychological problems for individuals (and often for households). For most people retirement is a major transition, usually signalling loss of status. It can be lonely and disorientating, since people must restructure much of their daily routine.

10 In recent years, older people, who now make up a large proportion of the population of the industrialized countries, have started to press for more recognition of their distinctive interests and needs. The struggle against 'ageism' (discrimination against people on grounds of their age) is an important aspect of this development.

FURTHER READING

Ellen Annandale, *The Contemporary Sociology of Health and Illness* (Cambridge: Polity Press, 1996). A discussion of both traditional and new topics in the field and an up-to-date assessment of the state of the sociology of health, illness and health care.

Kenneth R. Dutton, *The Perfectible Body: The Western Ideal of Physical Development* (London: Cassell, 1995). An introduction to the art of bodybuilding.

Ross Hume Hall, *Health and the Global Environment* (Cambridge: Polity Press, 1990). Argues the case for a comprehensive reassessment of health care, putting the emphasis on prevention and environmental protection.

Sarah Nettleton, *The Sociology of Health and Illness* (Cambridge: Polity Press, 1995). An introduction to key contemporary debates within the sociology of health and illness.

Michael Young and **Tom Schuller**, *Life After Work: The Arrival of the Ageless Society* (London: HarperCollins, 1991). A provocative discussion of the role of older people in modern societies.

IMPORTANT TERMS

- *anorexia*
- *bulimia*
- *addiction*
- *socialization of nature*
- *reproductive technologies*
- *life expectancy*
- *AIDS*
- *stigma*
- *public health care*
- *private health care*
- *ageism*

FAMILY, MARRIAGE AND PERSONAL LIFE

7

BASIC CONCEPTS

● *family* ● *kinship* ● *marriage*

The theme of much of this book is change. We live in a turbulent, difficult and unfamiliar world. Whether we like it or not, we all must come to terms with the mixture of opportunity and risk such a world presents. Nowhere is this observation more apt than in our personal and emotional lives.

In our personal lives, we now have to deal with 'relationships'. When someone asks you, 'How is your relationship going?' he or she is usually asking about a sexual involvement. But we are increasingly involved in relationships with parents, friends and others. The term 'relationship', as applied to personal life, came into general use only twenty or thirty years ago, as did the idea that there is a need for 'intimacy' or 'commitment' in personal life.

The fact that most of us, whether we resist these changes or not, now think about them a great deal is indicative of the basic transformations that have affected our personal and emotional lives over the past few decades. A relationship is something *active* – you have to work at it. It depends on winning the trust of the other person if it is going to survive over time. Most kinds of sexual relations have become like this now, and so has marriage.

It's only possible to understand what is going on in our intimate lives today if we know something about how people lived in the past. So in this chapter we will first look at the development of the family and marriage in earlier times, before analysing the consequences of present-day changes.

KEY CONCEPTS

We need first of all to define some basic concepts, particularly those of family, kinship and marriage. A FAMILY is a group of persons directly linked by kin connections, the adult members of which assume responsibility for caring for children. KINSHIP ties are connections between individuals, established either through marriage or through the lines of descent that connect blood relatives (mothers, fathers, offspring, grandparents, etc.). MARRIAGE can be defined as a socially acknowledged and approved sexual union between two adult individuals. When two people marry, they become kin to one another; the marriage bond also, however, connects together a wider range of kinspeople. Parents, brothers, sisters and other blood relatives become relatives of the partner through marriage.

Family relationships are always recognized within wider kinship groups. In virtually all societies we can identify what sociologists and anthropologists call the **nuclear family**, two adults living together in a household with their own or adopted children. In most traditional societies, the nuclear family was part of a larger kinship network of some type. When close relatives other than a married couple and children live either in the same household or in a close and continuous relationship with one another, we speak of an **extended family**. An extended family may include grandparents, brothers and their wives, sisters and their husbands, aunts and nephews.

In Western societies, marriage, and therefore the family, are associated with **monogamy**. It is illegal for a man or woman to be married to more than one individual at any one time. Monogamy is not the most common type of marriage in the world as a whole. In a famous comparison of several hundred present-day societies, George Murdock found that **polygamy**, which allows a husband or wife to have more than one spouse, was permitted in over 80 per cent (Murdock 1949). There are two types of polygamy: **polygyny**, in which a man may be married to more than one woman at the same time, and **polyandry**, much less common, in which a woman may have two or more husbands simultaneously.

THE FAMILY IN HISTORY

Sociologists once thought that prior to the modern period the predominant form of family in western Europe was of the extended type. Research has shown this view to be mistaken. The nuclear family seems long to have been pre-eminent. Premodern household size was larger than in the present day, but the difference is not especially great. In England, for example, throughout the seventeenth, eighteenth and nineteenth centuries, the average household size was 4.75 persons. The current average in the UK is 3.04. Since the earlier figure includes domestic servants, the difference in family size is small. Extended family groups were more important in eastern Europe and Asia.

Children in premodern Europe were often working – helping their parents on the farm – from seven or eight years old. Those who did not remain in the family enterprise frequently left the parental household at an early age to do domestic work in the houses of others or to follow apprenticeships. Children who went away to work in other households would rarely see their parents again.

Other factors made family groups then even more impermanent than they are now, in spite of the high rates of divorce in current times. Rates of mortality (numbers of deaths per thousand of the population in any one year) for people of all ages were much higher. A quarter or more of all infants in early modern Europe did not survive beyond the first year of life (in contrast to well under 1 per cent today), and women frequently died in childbirth. The death of children or of one or both spouses often dislocated or shattered family relations.

The development of family life

The historical sociologist Lawrence Stone has charted some of the changes leading from premodern to modern forms of family life in Europe. Stone distinguished three phases in the development of the family from the 1500s to the 1800s. In the early part of this period, the main family form was a type of nuclear family that lived in fairly small households but maintained deeply embedded relationships within the community, including with other kin. This family structure was not clearly separated from the community. According to Stone (although some historians have challenged this), the family at that time was not a major focus of emotional attachment or dependence for its members. People didn't experience, or look for, the emotional intimacies we associate with family life today. Sex within marriage was not regarded as a source of pleasure but as a necessity to propagate children.

Individual freedom of choice in marriage and other aspects of family life was subordinated to the interests of parents, other kin or the community. Outside aristocratic circles, where it was sometimes actively encouraged, erotic or romantic love was regarded by moralists and theologians as a sickness. As Stone puts it, the family during this period 'was an open-ended, low-keyed, unemotional, authoritarian institution. . . . It was also very short-lived, being frequently dissolved by the death of the husband or wife or the death or very early departure from the home of the children' (Stone 1977).

This type of family was succeeded by a transitional form that lasted from the early seventeenth century to the beginning of the eighteenth. This type was largely confined to the upper reaches of society but was nevertheless very important, because from it spread attitudes that have since become almost universal. The nuclear family became a more separate entity, distinct from ties to other kin and to the local community. There was a growing stress on the importance of marital and parental love, although there was also an increase in the authoritarian power of fathers.

In the third phase, the type of family system we are most familiar with in the West now gradually evolved. This family is a group tied by close emotional bonds, enjoying a high degree of domestic privacy and preoccupied with the rearing of children. It is marked by the rise of **affective individualism**, the formation of marriage ties on the basis of personal selection, guided by sexual attraction or romantic love. Sexual aspects of love began to be glorified within marriage instead of in extramarital relationships. The family became geared to consumption rather than production, as a result of the increasing spread of workplaces separate from the home.

As John Boswell, whom we referred to in chapter 1, has noted:

> In premodern Europe marriage usually began as a property arrangement, was in its middle mostly about raising children, and ended about love. Few couples in fact married 'for love', but many grew to love each other in time as they jointly managed their household, reared their offspring, and shared life's experiences. Nearly all surviving epitaphs to spouses evince profound affection. By contrast, in most of the modern West, marriage

begins about love, in its middle is still mostly about raising children (if there are children), and ends – often – about property, by which point love is absent or a distant memory. (Boswell 1995, p. xxi)

CHANGES IN FAMILY PATTERNS WORLDWIDE

A diversity of family forms continues to exist in different societies across the world. In some areas, such as more remote regions in Asia, Africa and the Pacific, traditional family systems are little altered. In most countries, however, widespread changes are occurring. The origins of these changes are complex, but several factors can be picked out as especially important. One is the spread of Western culture. Western ideals of romantic love, for example, have spread to societies in which it was previously unknown. Another factor is the development of centralized government in areas previously composed of autonomous smaller societies. People's lives become influenced by their involvement in a national political system; moreover, governments make active attempts to alter traditional ways of behaviour. For example, in China or Mongolia, because of the problem of rapidly expanding population growth, states frequently introduce programmes advocating smaller families, the use of contraception, and so forth.

These changes are creating a worldwide movement towards the predominance of the nuclear family, breaking down extended family systems and other types of kinship groups. This was first documented thirty years ago by William J. Goode in his book *World Revolution in Family Patterns* (1963) and has been borne out by subsequent research.

Directions of change

The most important changes occurring worldwide are the following:

1 Extended families and other kin groups are declining in their influence;
2 There is a general trend towards the free choice of a spouse;
3 The rights of women are becoming more widely recognized, in respect to both the initiation of marriage and decision-making within the family;
4 Kin marriages are becoming less common;
5 Higher levels of sexual freedom are developing in societies that were very restrictive;
6 There is a general trend towards the extension of children's rights.

It would be a mistake to exaggerate these trends, or to suppose that the nuclear family has everywhere become the dominant form. In most societies today, extended families are still the norm, and traditional family practices continue. Moreover, there are differences in the speed at which change is occurring, and there are reversals and countertrends. A study in the Philippines, for example, found a higher proportion of extended families in urban areas than in surrounding rural regions. These had not just developed from traditional extended family households, but represented something new. Leaving the rural areas, cousins, nephews and nieces went to live with their relatives in the cities to take advantage of the employment opportunities available there.

FAMILY AND MARRIAGE IN THE UNITED KINGDOM

Given the culturally diverse character of the United Kingdom today, there are considerable variations in family and marriage within the country. Some of the most striking include differences between white and non-white family patterns, and we need to consider why this is so. We will then move on to examine divorce, remarriage, and step-parenting in relation to contemporary patterns of family life.

Let us first, however, describe some basic characteristics which nearly all families in Britain share.

Overall characteristics

Features of the family as a whole in the UK are the following:

1 Like other Western families, the British family is monogamous, monogamy being established in law. Given the high rate of divorce that now exists in the United Kingdom, however, some observers have suggested that the British marriage pattern should be called **serial monogamy**. That is to say, individuals are permitted to have a number of spouses in sequence, although no one may have more than one wife or husband at any one time. It is misleading, though, to muddle legal monogamy with sexual practice. It is obvious that a high proportion of Britons engage in sexual relations with individuals other than their spouses.

2 British marriage is based on the idea of romantic love. Affective individualism has become the major influence. Couples are expected to develop mutual affection, based on personal attraction and compatibility, as a basis for contracting marriage relationships. Romantic love as part of marriage has become 'naturalized' in contemporary Britain; it seems to be a normal part of human existence, rather than a distinctive feature of modern culture. Of course, the reality is divergent from the ideology. The emphasis on personal satisfaction in marriage has raised expectations which sometimes cannot be met, and this is one factor involved in increasing rates of divorce.

3 The British family is patrilineal and neo-local. **Patrilineal inheritance** involves children taking the surname of the father, and property usually passes down the male line. (Many societies in the world are **matrilineal** – surnames, and often property, pass down the female line.) A *neo-local residence* pattern involves a married couple moving into a dwelling away from both of their families. Neo-localism, however, is not an absolutely fixed trait of the British family. Many families, particularly in lower-class neigh-

bourhoods, are matrilocal – the newly-weds settle in an area close to where the bride's parents live.

4 The British family is nuclear, consisting of one or two parents living in a household with their children. However, nuclear family units are by no means completely isolated from other kin ties.

Trends of development

Variations in family patterns

According to Rapoport, 'families in Britain today are in a transition from coping in a society in which there was a single overriding norm of what family life should be like to a society in which a plurality of norms are recognized as legitimate and, indeed, desirable' (Rapoport and Rapoport 1982, p. 476). Substantiating this argument, Rapoport identifies five types of diversity: *organizational, cultural, class, life course* and *cohort*.

Families *organize* their respective individual domestic duties and their links with the wider social environment in a variety of ways. The contrasts between 'orthodox' families – the woman as 'housewife', the husband as 'breadwinner' – and dual-career or one-parent families illustrate this diversity. *Culturally*, there is greater diversity of family beliefs and values than used to be the case. The presence of ethnic minorities (such as West Indian, Asian, Greek and Italian communities) and the influence of movements such as feminism have produced considerable cultural variety in family forms. Persistent *class* divisions, between the poor, the skilled working class, and the various groupings within the middle and upper classes, sustain major variations in family structure. Variations in family experience during the *life course* are fairly obvious. For instance, one individual might come from a family in which both parents had stayed together, and herself or himself go on to marry and then divorce. Another person might be brought up in a single-parent family, be multiply married and have children by each marriage.

The term *cohort* refers to generations within families. Connections between parents and grandparents, for example, have probably become weaker than they were. On the other hand, more people now live into old age, and three 'ongoing' families might exist in close relation to one another: married grandchildren, their parents, and the grandparents.

South Asian families

Among the variety of British family types, there is one pattern distinctively different from most others – that associated with South Asian groups. The South Asian population of the UK numbers more than one million people. Migration began in the 1950s from three main areas of the Indian subcontinent: Punjab, Gujarat and Bengal. In Britain, these migrants formed communities based on religion, area of origin, caste and, most importantly, kinship. Many migrants found their ideas of honour and family loyalty almost entirely absent among the indigenous British population. They tried to maintain family unity, but

'If anyone here knows of any reason why these two people cannot move their stuff into a flat…'

Daily Telegraph: The Best of Matt, Orion, 1995

housing proved a problem. Large old houses were available in run-down areas; moving up-market usually meant moving into smaller houses and breaking up the extended family.

South Asian children born in the UK today are exposed to two very different cultures. At home their parents expect or demand conformity to the norms of cooperation, respect and family loyalty. At school they are expected to pursue academic success in a competitive and individualistic social environment. Most choose to organize their domestic and personal lives in terms of the ethnic subculture, as they value the close relationships associated with traditional family life. Yet involvement with British culture has brought changes. Young people of both sexes are demanding greater consultation in the arrangement of their marriages.

The strength of the Asian family, both among Asian groups in the UK and in the Asian countries themselves, has been the subject of considerable recent discussion. Francis Fukuyama (1994) has spoken of the 'social capital' created by the Asian family – forms of trust and mutual reliance provided by the family in Asian countries. In his view, such social capital is one of the main factors promoting rapid economic development in Asian societies such as Taiwan, Hong Kong and Singapore.

Yet, just as traditional forms of Asian family are coming under strain in Britain, so they are in the Asian countries themselves. Divorce rates are rising in the countries just mentioned, and fertility rates are dropping (see figure 7.1). Economic development plus increasing democratization are starting to generate a higher degree of individualism and pressures for increased equality between the sexes.

Black families

Families of West Indian origin in Britain have a different structure again. There are far fewer black women aged twenty to forty-four living with a husband than among white women in the same age group. Much the same is true of African-American women in the US, where this fact has given rise to heated debates. Thirty years ago, Senator Daniel Patrick Moynihan described black families as 'disorganized' and caught up in a 'tangle of pathology' (Moynihan 1965).

Fig. 7.1 Convergence: divorce and fertility rates East and West (the scales for the different countries are not comparable; fertility rates are average number of babies per woman)

Sources: National statistics; World Bank. From *The Economist*, 28 May 1994, p. 77.

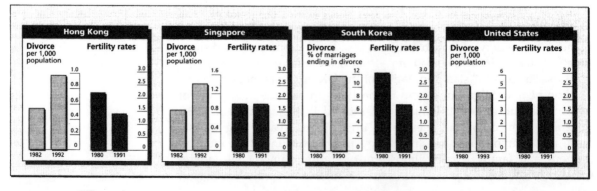

The divergence between black and white family patterns in the US has become much greater since the early 1960s, when Moynihan's study was undertaken. In 1960, 21 per cent of African-American families were headed by females; among white families, the proportion was 8 per cent. By 1993 the proportion for black families had risen to more than 58 per cent, while that for white families was 26 per cent. Female-headed families are more prominently represented among poorer blacks. African Americans in inner city neighbourhoods have experienced little rise in living conditions over the past two decades: the majority are confined to low-wage jobs or are more or less permanently unemployed. In these circumstances, there is little to foster continuity in marital relationships. The same factors seem to be at work among black families in poorer neighbourhoods of London and in other cities in the UK.

We should not see the situation of black families purely in a negative light. Extended kinship networks are important in West Indian groups – much more significant, relative to marital ties, than in most white communities. A mother heading a lone-parent family is likely to have a close and supportive network of relatives to depend on. This contradicts the idea that black single parents and their children necessarily form unstable families. A far higher proportion of female-headed families among African Americans have other relatives living with them than white families headed by females.

In her book *Lifelines* (1983), Joyce Aschenbrenner provided a comprehensive portrayal of extended kin relationships in African-American families. Aschenbrenner gained a new perspective on both white and black family types in the United States as a result of fieldwork she had earlier carried out in Pakistan. From the point of view of the Pakistanis, the *white* family in the United States seemed weak and 'disorganized'. They could not understand how a mere couple, let alone a single parent, could bring up children. They viewed with abhorrence the practice of hiring a stranger to baby-sit while the parents went out. Where were the uncles and grandparents? Why weren't a woman's brothers on hand to lend assistance if she was left on her own to bring up her children? The way they thought of the family was closer to the situation of African-American families than to the usual family structure among whites.

Discussions of the black family, Aschenbrenner suggests, have focused too strongly on the marriage relationship. This emphasis is in line with the overriding importance of marriage in modern society, but this relationship does not necessarily form the structure of the black family. In most societies that include extended families, relationships such as mother–daughter, father–son or brother–sister may be more socially significant than that between husband and wife.

DIVORCE AND SEPARATION IN THE WEST

The growth in divorce

For many centuries in the West marriage was regarded as virtually indissoluble. Divorces were granted only in very limited cases, such as non-consummation of marriage. One or two industrial countries still do not recognize divorce. Yet these are now isolated examples. Most countries have moved rapidly towards making divorce more easily available. The so-called *adversarial system* used to be characteristic of virtually all industrialized countries. For a divorce to be granted, one spouse had to bring charges (for example, cruelty, desertion or adultery) against the other. The first 'no fault' divorce laws were introduced in some countries in the mid-1960s. Since then, many Western states have followed suit, although the details vary. In the UK, the Divorce Reform Act, which made it easier for couples to obtain a divorce and contained 'no fault' provisions, was passed in 1969, and came into effect in 1971. The 'no fault' principle was further consolidated in a new bill passed in 1996.

Between 1960 and 1970, the divorce rate in Britain grew by a steady 9 per cent each year, doubling within that decade. By 1972, it had doubled again, partly as a result of the 1969 Act, which made it easier for many in marriages that had long been 'dead' to become divorced. Since 1980, the divorce rate has stabilized to some degree, but remains at a very high level compared to any previous period (Clark and Haldane 1990; and see table 7.1).

Divorce makes an increasing impact on the lives of children. It has been estimated that nearly 40 per cent of children born in the UK in 1980 will at some stage before adulthood have been members of a one-parent

Table 7.1	Divorces per 1,000 population in the European Community, 1981 and 1993	
	1981	**1993**
United Kingdom	2.8	3.1
Denmark	2.8	2.5
Finland	2.0	2.5
Sweden	2.4	2.5
Belgium	1.6	2.1
Austria	1.8	2.0
Netherlands	2.0	2.0
France	1.6	1.9
Germany	2.0	1.9
Luxembourg	1.4	1.9
Portugal	0.7	1.2
Greece	0.7	0.7
Spain	0.3	0.7
Italy	0.2	0.4
EC average	1.5	1.8

Source: Eurostat. From *Social Trends*, 1996, p. 57.

family. Although 75 per cent of women and 83 per cent of men who are divorced remarry within three years, they will none the less have grown up in a family environment.

Divorce rates are obviously not a direct index of marital unhappiness. For one thing, rates of divorce do not include people who are separated but not legally divorced. Moreover, people who are unhappily married may choose to stay together – because they believe in the sanctity of marriage, or worry about the financial or emotional consequences of a break-up, or wish to remain with one another to give their children a 'family' home.

Why is divorce becoming more common? Several factors are involved, to do with wider social changes. Except for a very small proportion of wealthy people, marriage today no longer has much connection with the desire to perpetuate property and status from generation to generation. As women become more economically independent, marriage is less of a necessary economic partnership than it used to be. Greater overall prosperity means that it is easier to establish a separate household, in case of marital disaffection, than used to be the case. The fact that little stigma now attaches to divorce is in some part the result of these developments, but also adds momentum to them. A further important factor is the growing tendency to evaluate marriage in terms of the levels of personal satisfaction it offers. Rising rates of divorce do not seem to indicate a deep dissatisfaction with marriage as such, but an increased determination to make it a rewarding and satisfying relationship.

The experience of divorce

It is extremely difficult to draw up a balance sheet of the social advantages and costs of high levels of divorce. More tolerant attitudes mean that couples can terminate an unrewarding relationship without incurring social ostracism. On the other hand, marriage break-up is almost always emotionally stressful, and may create financial hardship for one or both parties.

Uncoupling

Diane Vaughan has analysed relationships between partners during the course of separation or divorce (Vaughan 1986). She carried out a series of interviews with over one hundred recently separated or divorced people (mainly from middle-class backgrounds) to chart the transition from living together to living apart. The notion of *uncoupling* refers to the break-up of a long-term intimate relationship. She found that in many cases before the physical parting there had been a *social separation* – at least one of the partners developed a new pattern of life, becoming interested in new pursuits and making new friends in contexts in which the other was not present. This usually meant keeping secrets from the other – especially, of course, when a relationship with a lover was involved.

According to Vaughan's research, uncoupling is often unintentional at first. One individual – whom she called the *initiator* – becomes less

'Is this where my marriage was made?'

satisfied with the relationship than the other, and creates a 'territory' independent of the activities in which the couple engages together. For some time before this, the initiator may have been trying unsuccessfully to change the partner, to get him or her to behave in more acceptable ways, foster shared interests and so forth. At some point, the initiator feels that the attempt has failed and that the relationship is fundamentally flawed. From then onwards, he or she becomes preoccupied with the ways in which the relationship or the partner is defective. Vaughan suggested that this is the opposite of the process of 'falling in love' at the beginning of a relationship, when an individual focuses on the attractive features of the other, ignoring those which might be less acceptable.

Initiators seriously considering a break normally discuss their relationship extensively with others, 'comparing notes'. In so doing, they weigh the costs and benefits of separation. Can I survive on my own? How will friends and parents react? Will the children suffer? Will I be financially solvent? Having thought about these and other problems, some decide to try again to make the relationship work. For those who proceed with a separation, these discussions and enquiries help make the break less intimidating, building confidence that they are doing the right thing. Most initiators become convinced that a responsibility for their own self-development takes priority over commitment to the other.

Of course, uncoupling is not always wholly led by one individual. The other partner may also have decided that the relationship cannot be saved. In some situations, an abrupt reversal of roles occurs. The person who previously wanted to save the relationship becomes determined to end it, while the erstwhile initiator wishes to carry on.

Changing attitudes

There seem to be substantial class differences affecting reactions to the changing character of family life and the existence of high levels of divorce. In her book *Families on the Fault Line* (1994), Lillian Rubin interviewed the members of thirty-two working-class families in depth. As compared to middle-class families, she concluded, working-class parents tend to be more traditional. The norms that many middle-class parents have accepted, such as the open expression of premarital sex, are more widely disapproved of by working-class people, even where they are not particularly religious. In working-class households there tends therefore to be more of a conflict between the generations.

The young people in Rubin's study agree that their attitudes towards sexual behaviour, marriage and gender divisions are distinct from those of their parents. But they insist that they are not just concerned with pleasure seeking. They simply hold to different values from those of the older generation.

Rubin found that the young women she interviewed are much more ambivalent about marriage than were their parents' generation. They were keenly aware of the imperfections of men and spoke of exploring the options available and of living life more fully and openly than was possible for their mothers. The generational shift in men's attitudes was not as great.

Rubin's research was done in the United States, but her findings accord closely with those of researchers in Britain and other European countries. Helen Wilkinson and Geoff Mulgan carried out two large-scale studies of men and women aged between eighteen and thirty-four in the UK (Wilkinson 1994; Wilkinson and Mulgan 1995). They found major changes happening in the outlook of young women in particular; and that the values of the 18–34 generation contrasted in a general way with those of the older generations in Britain.

Among young women there is 'a desire for autonomy and self-fulfilment, through work as much as family' and 'the valuing of risk, excitement and change'. In these terms there is a growing convergence between the traditional values of men and the newer values of women. The values of the younger generation, Wilkinson and Mulgan suggest, have been shaped by their inheritance of freedoms largely unavailable to earlier generations – freedom for women to work and control their own reproduction, freedom of mobility for both sexes and freedom to define one's own style of life. Such freedoms lead to greater openness, generosity and tolerance; but they can also produce a narrow, selfish individualism and a lack of trust in others. Of those in the sample, 29 per cent of women and 51 per cent of men wanted to 'delay having children as long as possible'. Of women in the 16–24 age group, 75 per cent believed that single parents can bring up children as well as a couple can do. The study found that marriage was losing its appeal for both women and men in this age group.

Divorce and children

The effects of parental divorce on children are difficult to gauge. How much conflict there is between the parents before separation, the age of the children at the time, whether or not they have brothers or sisters, the availability of grandparents and other relatives, the children's relationships with their individual parents, how far they continue to see both parents frequently – all these and other influences can affect the process of adjustment. Since children whose parents are unhappily married but stay together may be affected by the resulting tension, assessing the consequences of divorce for children is doubly difficult.

Research indicates that children do often suffer marked emotional anxiety after the separation of their parents. Judith Wallerstein and Joan Kelly studied the children of sixty separated couples in Marin County, California (Wallerstein and Kelly 1980). They contacted the children at the time of the divorce in court, a year and a half afterwards, and five years later. According to the authors, almost all the 131 children involved experienced intense emotional disturbance at the time of the divorce. The children of pre-school age were confused and frightened, and tended to blame themselves for the separation. Older children were better able to understand their parents' motives for divorce, but frequently worried deeply about its effects on their future and often expressed sharp feelings of anger. At the end of the five-year period, however, the researchers found that two-thirds of the children were coping at least reasonably well with their home lives and their commitments outside. A third remained actively dissatisfied with their lives, subject to depression and feelings of loneliness.

Wallerstein continued her study of this same group of children, following 116 of the original 131 into young adulthood with interviews at the end of ten-year and fifteen-year periods. The interviews revealed that these children brought memories and feelings of their parents' divorce into their own romantic relationships. Almost all felt that they had suffered in some way from their parents' mistakes. Not surprisingly, most of them shared a hope for something their parents had failed to achieve – a good, committed marriage based on love and faithfulness. Nearly half the group entered adulthood as 'worried, underachieving, self-deprecating, and sometimes angry young men and women'. Although many of them got married themselves, the legacy of their parents' divorce lived with them. Those who appeared to manage the best were often helped by supportive relationships with one or both parents (Wallerstein and Blakeslee 1989).

Martin Richards (1995) has analysed a large range of research materials, coming from Britain, the US, Australia, New Zealand and other countries, concerning the impact of parental separation and divorce on children. Such research, he argues, has come up with a reliable body of conclusions. Children from similar social backgrounds whose parents are separated or divorced show small but consistent differences in their later lives from children of parents who stay together. On average, they have lower levels of self-esteem and school achievement; they change jobs more as adults and have a greater propensity to become divorced themselves.

Consistent though they may be, such findings are far from easy to interpret. Some children whose parents are divorced are successful at school and show no particular signs of low self-esteem. Conversely, many children whose parents remain together have unhappy childhoods, do poorly at school and are unsuccessful in their working lives.

A key difficulty in interpreting research results is that long-term follow-up studies by definition refer to the past. Attitudes to divorce are changing rapidly. Even a few years ago there was more of a stigma attaching to divorce than is generally the case today. As well as attitudes to divorce, such things as welfare and housing provision, availability of child care and other factors may have important effects. There is some evidence – far from conclusive, however – to suggest that separation and divorce have fewer damaging effects in Scandinavia, which has a highly developed welfare system, than elsewhere.

Rather than simply ask whether or not separation and divorce harm children, we should probably assess the changing nature of the family in terms of a challenging balance of costs and benefits. It is probably not just the presence or absence of two parents in a child's life which is important, but the style and content of the parenting. Children seem to prosper most when they are loved, when parents are authoritative – not authoritarian – and when parents have a sensitivity to their needs (Amato 1993). Divorce, of course, may make it difficult to sustain such a parenting style; but then discord between partners who stay together can also have harmful consequences for children.

Lone-parent households

Lone-parent households have become increasingly common. The vast majority are headed by women, since the wife usually obtains custody of the children following a divorce (in a small proportion of lone-parent households, the individual, again almost always a woman, has never been married). There are well over a million lone-parent households in Britain today, and the number is increasing (see figure 7.2). Such households comprise one in five of all families with dependent children. On average, they are among the poorest groups in contemporary society. Many lone parents, whether they have ever been married or not, still face social disapproval as well as economic insecurity. Earlier and more judgemental terms such as 'deserted wives', 'fatherless families' and 'broken homes' are tending to disappear, however.

The category of lone-parent household is an internally diverse one. For instance, more than half of widowed mothers are owner-occupiers, but the vast majority of never-married lone mothers live in rented accommodation. Lone parenthood tends to be a changing state, and its boundaries are rather blurred. In the case of a person who is widowed, the break is obviously clear-cut – although even here a person might have effectively been living on his or her own for some while if the partner was in hospital prior to death. About 60 per cent of lone-parent households today, however, are brought about by separation or

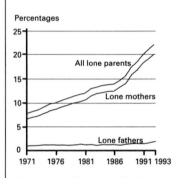

Fig. 7.2 Families headed by lone parents as a percentage of all families with dependent children, Great Britain

Sources: General Household Survey, Office of Population Censuses and Surveys. From *Social Trends*, 1996, p. 54.

divorce. In such cases, individuals may live together sporadically over a quite lengthy period. As one lone mother remarks:

> I think it takes a time to come to terms with being a single mother. In my case I've only accepted what I am in the past year. I suppose before I always thought that we might get back together but when he got married I had to give up. I felt very bad at the time, but now I think it was the best thing that could have happened because it made me come to terms with my life. (Quoted in Crow and Hardey 1992, p. 149)

Most people do not wish to be lone parents, but there is a growing minority who choose to become so – who set out to have a child or children without the support of a spouse or partner. 'Single mothers by choice' is an apt description of some lone parents, normally those who possess sufficient resources to manage satisfactorily as a single-parent household. For the majority of unmarried or never-married mothers, however, the reality is different: there is a high correlation between the rate of births outside marriage and indicators of poverty and social deprivation. As we saw earlier, these influences are very important in explaining the high proportion of lone-parent households among families of West Indian background in the UK.

The 'absent father'

The time from the late 1930s up to the 1970s has sometimes been called the period of the '**absent father**'. During World War Two, many fathers rarely saw their children because of their war service. In the period following the war, in a high proportion of families, most women were not in the paid labour force and stayed at home to look after the children. The father was the main breadwinner and consequently was out at work all day; he would see his children only in the evenings and at weekends.

With rising divorce rates in more recent years, and the increasing number of lone-parent households, the theme of the 'absent father' has come to mean something different. It has come to refer to fathers who, as a result of separation or divorce, either have only infrequent contact with their children or lose touch with them altogether. In both Britain and the United States, which have among the highest divorce rates in the world, this situation has provoked intense debate.

The increasing proportion of fatherless families has been said to be at the origin of a whole diversity of social problems, from rising crime to mushrooming welfare costs for child support. American authors who have figured prominently in the debate have had a great deal of influence over discussion of the issue in the UK. In his book *Fatherless America* (1995) David Blankenhorn argues that societies with high divorce rates are facing not just the loss of fathers but the very erosion of the idea of fatherhood – with lethal social consequences, because many children are growing up now without an authority figure to turn to in times of need. Marriage and fatherhood in all societies up to the present provided a means of channelling men's sexual and aggressive energies. Without them, these energies are likely to be expressed in criminality and violence. As one reviewer of Blankenhorn's book put it, 'better to have a dad who comes home from a nasty job to drink beer in

Table 7.2 International comparisons of non-marital births and single parenthood

Country	Percentage of all births to unmarried women		Percentage of families headed by single parents	
	1960	1990	1960	1988
United Kingdom	5	28	6	13
United States	5	28	9	23
Canada	4	24	9	15
Denmark	8	46	17	20
France	6	30	9	12
Germany	6	11	8	14
Italy	2	6	n.a.	n.a.
The Netherlands	1	11	9	15
Sweden	11	47	9	13

Sources: US Bureau of the Census, *Statistical Abstract of the United States*, 1993; Constance Sorrentino, 'The changing family in international perspective', *Monthly Labor Review* (March 1990), pp. 41–58. From Sara McLanahan and Gary Sandefur, *Growing Up with a Single Parent: What Hurts, What Helps* (Harvard University Press 1994).

front of the television than no dad at all' (*The Economist*, 8 April 1995, p. 121).

Yet, is it? The issue of absent fathers overlaps with that of the more general question of the effects of divorce on children – and there, as we saw, the implications of the available evidence are far from clear. As the same reviewer put it: 'Does not a yobbish father spawn yobbish sons? Are not some fathers bad for the family?'

Evidence relevant to this controversy comes from Sweden (actually the only country in Western Europe where the birth rate has increased since 1970). About half the babies in Sweden are born to unmarried mothers (see table 7.2). Nineteen out of twenty of these are born in homes with a father, but many will grow up without their own fathers at home, as half of all Swedish marriages end in divorce and unmarried parents split up three times more often than married ones. Twenty per cent of children in Sweden were in lone-parent families in 1994.

Research in Sweden turns up little sign of the social problems fatherlessness is supposed to bring in its wake. This might be because, in societies such as the UK or the US, it is poverty rather than the family which is the true origin of, for example, criminality and violence. In Sweden, generous welfare benefits mean that lone-parent families do not slip into poverty. In 1994 only 6.8 per cent of Swedish children lived in families with less than half the average income – a much lower proportion than in either Britain or the US (*The Economist*, 9 September 1995).

REMARRIAGE AND STEP-PARENTING

Remarriage

Remarriage can involve various circumstances. Some remarried couples are in their early twenties, neither bringing a child to the new relationship. A couple who remarry in their late twenties, their thirties or early forties each might take one or more children from the first marriage to live in the same dwelling as his or her new partner. Those who remarry at later ages might have adult children who never live in the new homes the parents establish. There may also be children within the new marriage itself. Either partner of the new couple may previously have been single, divorced or widowed, adding up to eight possible combinations. Generalizations about remarriage therefore have to be made with considerable caution, although some general points are worth making.

In 1900, about nine-tenths of all marriages in the United Kingdom were first marriages. Most remarriages involved at least one widowed person. With the rise in the divorce rate, the level of remarriage also began to climb, and an increasing proportion of remarriages began to involve divorced people. In the 1960s, the remarriage rate increased rapidly, tailing off during the 1980s and early 1990s.

Today, twenty-eight out of every hundred marriages involve at least one previously married person. Up to the age of thirty-five, the majority of remarriages involve divorced people. After that age, the proportion of remarriages involving widows or widowers rises, and by fifty-five the proportion of such remarriages is larger than the proportion of remarriages following divorce.

Odd though it might seem, the best way to maximize the chances of getting married, for both sexes, is to have been married before! People who have been married and divorced are more likely to marry again than single people in comparable age groups are to marry for the first time. At all age levels, divorced men are more likely to remarry than divorced women: three in every four divorced women, but five in every six divorced men, remarry. In statistical terms, at least, remarriages are less successful than first marriages. Rates of divorce from second marriages are higher than those from first marriages.

This does not show that second marriages are doomed to fail. People who have been divorced may have higher expectations of marriage than those who have not. Hence they may be more ready to dissolve new marriages than those only married once. It is possible that the second marriages which endure might be more satisfying, on average, than first marriages.

Step-families

A **step-family** may be defined as a family in which at least one of the adults is a step-parent. Using such a definition, the number of step-families is much greater than shown in available official statistics, since these usually refer only to families with whom step-children live. Many who remarry become step-parents of children who visit regularly, but don't live permanently in the same household.

An added feature is adoption. Brenda Maddox has estimated that more than one-third of all adoptions in the United States are of step-children. The proportion in Britain is lower, but the rate is climbing. Adoption is a method by which the non-biological parent makes up in some way for the lack of genetic connection, by making a public declaration of affiliation to the child. Adoptive parents have legal rights and obligations towards their children. Other step-parents lack these, and in most cases their relationship with their step-children endures only as long as the marriage lasts. According to the law in most countries, if the biological parent in a step-family dies or is divorced from the step-parent, the step-parent has no legal rights of custody over the children. Even if a child has lived with a step-parent for many years, if the natural parent dies the step-parent has little recourse in law if the other natural parent wishes to have custody.

Certain difficulties tend to arise in step-families. In the first place, there is usually a biological parent living elsewhere whose influence over the child or children is likely to remain powerful. Second, cooperative relations between divorced individuals are often strained when one or both remarries. Take the case of a woman with two children who marries a man who also has two, and all live together. If the 'outside' parents insist that children visit them at the same times as before, the major tensions involved in welding such a newly established family together will be exacerbated. For example, it may prove impossible ever to have the new family together at weekends.

Third, step-families merge children from different backgrounds, who may have varying expectations of appropriate behaviour within the family. Since most step-children 'belong' to two households, the likelihood of clashes in habits and outlook is considerable. Here is a step-mother describing her experience, after the problems she faced led to separation:

> There's a lot of guilt. You cannot do what you would normally do with your own child, so you feel guilty, but if you do have a normal reaction and get angry, you feel guilty about that, too. You are always so afraid you will be unfair. Her [stepdaughter's] father and I did not agree and he would say I nagged if I disciplined her. The more he did nothing to structure her, the more I seemed to nag . . . I wanted to provide something for her, to be an element of her life which was missing, but perhaps I am not flexible enough. (Smith 1990, p. 42)

There are few established norms which define the relationship between step-parent and step-child. Should a child call a new step-parent by name, or is 'Dad' or 'Mum' more appropriate? Should the step-parent discipline the children as a natural parent would? How should a step-parent treat the new spouse of his or her previous partner when collecting the children?

This letter and response appeared in Dear Abbie, a 'problem column' syndicated in many American newspapers.

> *Dear Abbie*
> A year ago I married Ted. His wife (Maxine) died and left him with two children, ages six and eight. This is my first marriage. I say that after Maxine died, Ted is no longer related to Maxine's relatives. Ted says Maxine's parents will always be his in-laws. Well, I have parents, too, so where does that leave them? A person can only have one set of in-laws at a time, and *my* parents should be regarded as grandparents, too, and they aren't. The titles of 'grandma' and 'grandpa' go to Maxine's parents. My

parents are called 'papa Pete' and 'mama Mary'. Do you think this is fair? . . . and what can I do about it? [*signed In-law trouble*]

Dear In-law trouble

Even though technically Ted is no longer the son-in-law of Maxine's parents, I advise you not to be so technical. There is a strong bond between Ted's former in-laws and their grandchildren, so if you're wise you won't tamper with these bonds because they were established before you came into the picture. Grandparents are grandparents for ever. (Quoted in Vischer and Vischer 1979, p. 132)

Step-families are developing types of kinship connection which are new to modern Western societies, although the problem experienced by 'In-law trouble' would have been common in medieval Europe and other traditional societies. The difficulties created by remarriage *after divorce* are really new. Members of these families are developing their own ways of adjusting to the relatively uncharted circumstances in which they find themselves. Some authors today speak of *binuclear families*, meaning that the two households which form after a divorce still comprise one family system where there are children involved.

The possible range of family connections and variations organized in this way, as mentioned above, is very large. Suppose, for example, a husband and wife with two children divorce and each remarries. In the new household of the wife there may be her two children, plus perhaps one or more children of her new husband. Her previous spouse also marries a woman with children, who come to live with them. All the spouses involved may continue to see their own children regularly as well as their new step-children, regardless of who lives with whom. Such connections might also bring with them other kin ties, with the parents of the previous spouses, for example. Moreover, each of the new marriages might produce further children. Perhaps the most appropriate conclusion to be drawn is that while marriages are broken up by divorce, families on the whole are not. Especially where children are involved, many ties persist despite the reconstructed family connections brought into being through remarriage.

Say 'good-bye' to the kids?

A survey carried out by the British Family Formation Survey in 1976 found that only 1 per cent of married women at that time did not want to have children. A recent report of the Office of Population Censuses and Surveys, by contrast, predicted that 20 per cent of women born between 1960 and 1990 will remain childless – by choice. Women in Britain today approach the decision to have a child in the context of other motivations they have in life, including the goals of success at work and autonomy in private life. Fertility rates are declining in virtually all other West European countries too (figure 7.3).

The childless woman is no longer the sad spinster. Whether married or not, she may have taken the decision to remain childless as an assertion of her freedom to choose. There are negative reasons as well, however. New career opportunities in Britain have not gone along with welfare provisions for parental leave and child care. Some may be wary of having children because they are worried about the likelihood of divorce and about relapsing into poverty.

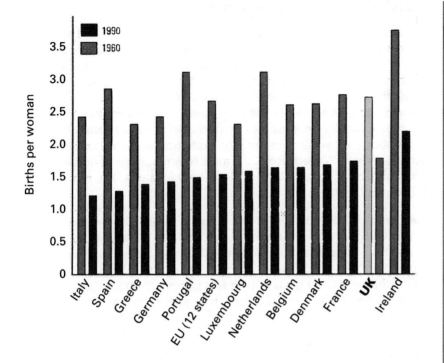

Fig. 7.3 Fertility rates in countries of the European Union, 1960 and 1990

Source: Eurostat 1993. From *Sociology Review*, November 1995 (Philip Allan Publishers), p. 34.

Whether you are male or female, you should think about these trends in relation to your own future. Will you be one of those who claim they never want children? Will you still feel the same in ten to fifteen years' time?

THE DARK SIDE OF THE FAMILY

Since family or kin relations form part of everyone's existence, family life encompasses virtually the whole range of emotional experience. Family relationships – between wife and husband, parents and children, brothers and sisters, or between distant relatives – can be warm and fulfilling. But they can equally well be full of the most pronounced tensions, driving people to despair or filling them with a deep sense of anxiety and guilt. The 'dark side' of family life is extensive, and belies the rosy images of harmony that are quite often emphasized in TV commercials and elsewhere in the popular media. There are many aspects of the oppressive side of the family, including the conflicts and hostilities that lead to separation and divorce, just discussed, and the association of family relationships with the onset of mental illness. Among the most devastating in their consequences, however, are the incestuous abuse of children and domestic violence.

Sexual abuse of children and incest

The **sexual abuse of children** is a widespread phenomenon and much of it happens in the context of the family. Sexual abuse of children can most easily be defined as the carrying out of sexual acts by adults with children below the age of consent (sixteen years old in Britain). **Incest** refers to sexual relations between close kin. Not all incest is child sexual abuse. For example, sexual intercourse between brother and sister close in age is incestuous, but does not necessarily fit the definition of abuse. In child sexual abuse, an adult is essentially exploiting an infant or child for sexual purposes. Nevertheless, the most common form of incest is one that is also child sexual abuse – incestuous relations between fathers and young daughters.

Incest, and child sexual abuse more generally, are phenomena which have been 'discovered' only over the past ten to twenty years. Of course it has long been known that such sexual acts occur, but it was assumed by most social observers that the strong taboos which exist against this behaviour meant that it was extremely uncommon. Such is not the case. Child sexual abuse has proved to be disturbingly commonplace and exists at all levels of the social hierarchy.

It is almost certain that this increase results from more direct attention being paid to the problem by welfare agencies and the police. It is equally certain that such statistics represent no more than the tip of the iceberg. In some surveys carried out in Britain and the US in the 1980s, more than a third of women were found to have been victims of sexual abuse in childhood, meaning that they had experienced unwanted sexual touching. The figure for males is about 10 per cent (Russell 1984).

Although in its more obvious versions its nature is plain, the full extent of child sexual abuse is difficult, if not impossible, to calculate because of the many forms it can assume. A general definition can be offered, but it is bound to be subject to varying interpretations. Thus one widely used formulation is that child sexual abuse exists when 'another person, who is sexually mature, involves the child in any activity which the other person expects to lead to their own sexual arousal. This might involve intercourse, touching, exposure of sexual organs, showing pornographic material or talking about things in an erotic way' (quoted in Taylor 1992, pp. 26–7).

No fully agreed definitions, however, of either child abuse in general, or child sexual abuse in particular, have been reached either by researchers or in the courts. A section of the Children Act of 1989 speaks of 'significant harm' being caused by lack of reasonable care – but what is 'significant' is left quite vague. The National Society for the Protection of Children defines four categories of abuse: 'neglect', 'physical abuse', 'emotional abuse' and 'sexual abuse'. Sexual abuse is defined as 'sexual contact between a child and adult for the purpose of the adult's sexual gratification' (Lyon and de Cruz 1993).

There were some forty child abuse enquiries held in Britain between the early 1980s and mid-1990s. The most discussed was the Cleveland enquiry of 1987. The Cleveland case involved two doctors, Marietta

Higgs and Geoffrey Wyat. They had identified a number of children in the area as having been sexually abused within their families. Parents whose children had been as a consequence removed from them by social workers made angry protests, asserting their innocence.

Police doctors disagreed with the diagnoses and nationwide debate ensued, with many articles appearing in the press about the affair. The director of social services in Cleveland subsequently acknowledged that twelve of the families, involving twenty-six children, were wrongly accused. Few issues create such strong emotions and the perpetrators of sexual abuse against children are likely to strongly deny any such offence. On the other hand, where parents or family members are mistakenly accused the emotional pain caused is great.

Why have incest and child sexual abuse come into public view so suddenly? Part of the answer seems to be that the taboos against such activity led welfare workers and social researchers in the past to be wary of asking questions about it of parents or children. The women's movement played an important role in initially drawing public attention to child sexual abuse as one element in wider campaigns against sexual harassment and exploitation. Once researchers began to probe into suspected cases of child sexual abuse, many more came to light. The 'discovery' of child sexual abuse, beginning in the United States, has been an international phenomenon (La Fontaine 1990).

We do not know exactly what proportion of child sexual abuse is incestuous, but it is likely that most cases occur in a family context. Both the nature of the incestuous relation and the sexual acts committed vary quite widely. Most studies indicate that 70–80 per cent of incest cases are father–daughter or stepfather–daughter relationships. However, uncle–niece, brother–sister, father–son, mother and child and even grandparent–grandchild relationships also occur. Some incestuous contacts are transitory and involve a fondling of the child's sexual organs by the adult, or the child being encouraged to touch the adult's genitals. Others are much more extensive and may be repeated over several years. The children involved are usually over two years old, but there are many reported instances of sexual acts with infants.

Sometimes multiple incestuous relationships exist within the same family group. One study, for instance, reported a case in which the father had had sexual intercourse with his daughter, aged fourteen, and had also committed buggery with his thirteen-year-old son, who in turn had had sexual intercourse with his sister, as had another brother. The mother knew of these activities, but was too frightened of her husband to report any of them to the authorities. The full extent of the abuse only came to light when the father was arrested for physically beating his daughter (CIBA Foundation 1984, p. 128).

Force or the threat of violence is involved in many cases of incest. Children are in some instances more or less willing participants, but this seems quite rare. Children are sexual beings, of course, and quite often engage in mild sexual play or exploration with one another. But the large majority of children subjected to sexual contact with adult family members find the experience repugnant, shameful or disturbing.

There is now considerable material to indicate that child sexual abuse may have long-term consequences for its sufferers. Studies of prostitutes, juvenile offenders, adolescent runaways and drug users show that a high proportion have a history of child sexual abuse. Of course, correlation is not causation. Demonstrating that people in these categories have been sexually abused as children does not show that such abuse was a causal influence over their later behaviour. Probably a range of factors is involved, such as family conflicts, parental neglect and physical violence.

Explanations

To explain why incest and, more broadly, child sexual abuse occur, we need to account for two things. First, why adults should be attracted to sexual activities involving children and, second, why men should make up the vast majority of abusers. Each of these raises complex issues, given the variable nature of the acts and the relationships concerned. We can say with some certainty that only a minority of the perpetrators of child sexual abuse are mentally ill. In other words, we cannot explain adult attraction to sexual involvement with children in terms of mental disorder.

Most child abusers do not seem to have a *preference* for sexual relationships with children as opposed to other adults. Rather, it is a matter of availability coupled with power. Children within the family are dependent beings and highly vulnerable to parental demands or pressures. Adults involved in incest with their children often seem to be timid, awkward and inadequate in their dealings with other adults. Many appear not just to be satisfying sexual impulses, but searching for affection they cannot obtain elsewhere. We can make a connection here with the fact that the large majority of abusers are men. In chapter 51, 'Gender and sexuality', we discussed 'male inexpressiveness' – the difficulty many men have in expressing feelings, a phenomenon which probably has deep psychological origins. Men come to associate the expression of feeling directly with sexuality, whereas women focus more on whole relationships. Males also associate sexuality with the assertion of power and with submissiveness in their partners. Therefore there is less of a difference for men between adult sexuality and sexual attraction to children than for women.

As one of the leading students of child abuse, David Finkelhor, has argued, such an interpretation provides clear implications about some of the social and psychological changes which would help to reduce the sexual exploitation of children:

> First, men might benefit from the opportunity to practise affection and dependency in relationships that did not involve sex, such as male-to-male friendships and nurturant interaction with children. Second, the accomplishment of heterosexual sex might be de-emphasized as the ultimate criterion of male adequacy. Third, men might learn to enjoy sexual relationships based on equality. Men who are comfortable relating to women at the same level of maturity and competence will be less likely to exploit children sexually. As men's relations with women change, so will their relations with children. (Finkelhor 1984, p. 13)

Violence within the family

Violence within family settings is also primarily a male domain. We may define domestic violence as physical abuse directed by one member of the family against another or others. Studies show that the prime targets of physical abuse are again children, especially small children under the age of six. Violence by husbands against wives is the second most common type. Women, however, can also be the perpetrators of physical violence in the household, violence directed against young children and husbands.

The home is in fact the most dangerous place in modern society. In statistical terms, a person of any age or of either sex is far more likely to be subject to physical attack in the home than on the street at night. One in four murders in the UK is committed by one family member against another.

It is occasionally claimed that women are almost as violent as men in the home towards both spouses and children. Some surveys indicate that wives hit husbands nearly as often as the reverse. However, violence by females is more restrained and episodic than that of men, and much less likely to cause enduring physical harm. 'Wife battering' – the regular physical brutalizing of wives by husbands – has no real equivalent the other way round. Men who physically abuse children are also much more likely to do so in a consistent way, causing long-standing injuries, than women.

Why is domestic violence so commonplace? Several sets of factors are involved. One is the combination of emotional intensity and personal intimacy characteristic of family life. Family ties are normally charged with strong emotions, often mixing love and hate. Quarrels which break out in the domestic setting can unleash antagonisms that would not be felt in the same way in other social contexts. What seems only a minor incident can precipitate full-scale hostilities between spouses or between parents and children. A man tolerant towards eccentricities in the behaviour of other women may become furious if his wife talks too much at a dinner party or reveals intimacies he wishes to keep secret.

A second influence is the fact that a good deal of violence within the family is actually tolerated, and even approved of. Although socially sanctioned family violence is relatively confined in nature, it can easily spill over into more severe forms of assault. There are few children in Britain who have not at some time been slapped or hit, if only in a minor way, by one of their parents. Such actions quite often meet with general approval on the part of others, and they are probably not even thought of as 'violence'. If a stranger slapped a child in a shop because he disapproved of something she said or did, it would be a different matter. Yet there is no difference in the assault involved.

Although it is less clear-cut, there is, or has been in the past, also social approval of violence between spouses. The cultural acceptability of this form of domestic violence is expressed in the old ditty:

> A woman, a horse and a hickory tree
> The more you beat 'em the better they be.

In the workplace and other public settings, it is a general rule that no one can hit anyone else, no matter how objectionable or irritating they may be. This is not the case within the family. Many research studies have shown that a substantial proportion of couples believe that in some circumstances it is legitimate for a spouse to strike the other. About one in four Americans of both sexes takes the view that there can be a good reason for a husband to strike a wife. A somewhat lower proportion believe that the reverse also holds (Greenblat 1983).

However, violence within the family does also reflect broader patterns of violent behaviour. Many husbands who physically abuse their wives and children have records of violence in other contexts. A study by Jeffrey Fagan and his co-researchers of a national sample of battered wives showed that more than half their husbands were violent with others as well as with their partners. More than 80 per cent of these men had in fact been arrested at least once for episodes of violence of a non-domestic kind (Fagan et al. 1983).

ALTERNATIVES TO MARRIAGE AND THE FAMILY

Communes

The family has long had its critics. In the nineteenth century, numerous thinkers proposed that family life should be replaced by more communal forms of living. Some of these ideas were acted on, one of the best-known examples being the Oneida Community, of New England in the USA, set up in the middle of the nineteenth century. It was based on the religious beliefs of John Humphrey Noyes. Every man in the community was married to every woman, and all were supposed to be parents to the community's children. After various initial difficulties, the group expanded to include about three hundred people, and endured for about thirty years before breaking up. Many other communes have been founded since then, in Britain as well as many other Western countries. A large variety of communal groups were established in the 1960s, often involving free sexual relations within the group and collective responsibility for the raising of children. A small number of these are still in existence.

The most important current example of communal domestic life is that of the **kibbutzim** in Israel. A kibbutz is a community of families and individuals which cooperates in the raising of children. Most of the kibbutzim were originally collective farming enterprises, but today many have also moved into industrial production. There are more than 240 kibbutzim in Israel, having nearly 100,000 members in all. Some are small, with no more than fifty members, while others include as many as 2,000 people. Each kibbutz operates as though it were a single household, child care being treated as the responsibility of the whole community rather than the family. In some, children live in special 'children's houses' rather than with their parents, although they usually spend weekends with their families.

The kibbutzim were originally established with a radical intent. Communal ownership of property, together with the group rearing of children, were to allow kibbutzim members to escape the individualistic, competitive nature of life in modern societies. These ideals have by no means been abandoned; yet over the years the majority of kibbutzim have opted for more conventional living arrangements than those favoured in the early stages. It is more common for children to sleep in their parents' quarters, for instance, than used to be the case. The children's houses in the kibbutz are today perhaps better described as providing extensive child-care facilities rather than expressing communal responsibility for the raising of children.

Cohabitation

Cohabitation – where a couple live together in a sexual relationship without being married – has become increasingly widespread in most Western societies. In Britain until very recently cohabitation was generally regarded as somewhat scandalous. During the 1980s, however, the number of unmarried men and women sharing a household went up sharply. Cohabitation has become widespread among college and university students. Surveys in the United States indicate that about one in four students there live with partners with whom they are involved in a sexual relationship at some point during the course of their college careers.

Cohabitation in Britain today seems to be for the most part an experimental stage before marriage. Young people come to live together usually by drifting into it, rather than through calculated planning. A couple who are already having a sexual relationship spend more and more time together, eventually giving up one or other of their individual homes. Young people living together almost always anticipate getting married at some date, but not necessarily to their current partners. Only a minority of such couples pool their finances.

Over the past forty years, there has been a 400 per cent increase in the number of people in the UK cohabiting before marriage. Only 4 per cent of women born in the 1920s cohabited and 19 per cent of those born in the 1940s – but nearly half the women born in the 1960s. It has been forecast that four out of five married couples will have lived together before marriage by the year 2000 (Wilkinson and Mulgan 1995).

The close connection between cohabitation and marriage is indicated in figure 7.4, which comes from research carried out at the University of Essex. The majority of couples will probably be together after ten years and almost two-thirds will marry each other. This is not surprising, since surveys indicate that most young people see cohabitation as 'trial marriage'.

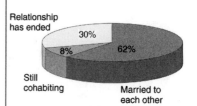

Relationship has ended 30%

Still cohabiting 8%

Married to each other 62%

Fig. 7.4 What happens to cohabiting relationships over time: likely outcomes for cohabiting couples in the UK after a period of ten years

Source: 'Living in Britain', report to survey respondents, University of Essex, 1995.

In some other European countries, particularly in rural areas, cohabitation has a long history as a legitimate practice. This is the case with the Nordic countries, which in fact have the highest rates of cohabitation today. There is not, however, a direct continuity with the past. In Sweden in 1960, for example, only 1 per cent of couples cohabited; today that figure has risen to an estimated 40 per cent. As in other countries in Europe, the majority of cohabiting couples marry after a certain time, or when they have children. Cohabitation has quite often been given a legal status, such that, should a relationship break up, individuals can sue for property settlement and maintenance.

Gay-parent families

Many homosexual men and women now live in stable relationships as couples, and some gay couples have been formally 'married' even if these ceremonies have no standing in law. Relaxation of previously intolerant attitudes towards homosexuality has been accompanied by a growing tendency for courts to allocate custody of children to mothers living in gay relationships. Techniques of artificial insemination mean that gay women may have children and become **gay-parent families** without any heterosexual contacts. While virtually every gay family with children in Britain involves two women, for a period in the late 1960s and early 1970s social welfare agencies in several cities in the US placed homeless gay teenage boys in the custody of gay male couples. The practice was discontinued, largely because of adverse public reaction (see also chapter 5, 'Gender and sexuality').

Staying single

Several factors have combined to increase the numbers of people living alone in modern Western societies. One is a trend towards later marriages – people now marry on average about three years later than was the case in 1960; another is the rising rate of divorce. Yet another is the growing number of old people in the population whose partners have died. Being single means different things at different periods of the life-cycle. A larger proportion of people in their twenties are unmarried than used to be the case. By their mid-thirties, however, only a small minority of men and women have never been married. The majority of single people aged thirty to fifty are divorced and 'in between' marriages. Most single people over fifty are widowed.

Peter Stein interviewed sixty single individuals in the age range twenty-five to forty-five (Stein 1980). Most felt ambivalent about being single. They recognized that being single often helped their career opportunities, because they could concentrate whole-heartedly on work; it made available a wider variety of sexual experiences, and promoted overall freedom and autonomy. On the other hand, they acknowledged the difficulty of being single in a world where most people their age were married, and suffered from isolation or loneliness. On the whole, most found the pressures to marry greater than the incentives to stay single.

THE DEBATE ABOUT 'FAMILY VALUES'

'The family is collapsing!' cry the advocates of family values, surveying the changes of the past few decades – a more liberal and open attitude towards sexuality, steeply climbing divorce rates and a general seeking for personal happiness at the expense of older conceptions of family duty. We must recover a moral sense of family life, they argue. We must reinstate the traditional family, which was much more stable and ordered than the tangled web of relationships in which most of us find ourselves now.

'No!' reply their critics. 'You think the family is collapsing. In fact, it is merely diversifying. We should actively encourage a variety of family forms and sexual life, rather than supposing that everyone has to be compressed into the same mould.'

Which side is right? We should probably be critical of both views. A return to the traditional family isn't a possibility. This is not only because, as explained earlier, the traditional family as it is usually thought of never existed, or because there were too many oppressive facets to families in the past to make them a model for today. It is also because the social changes that have transformed earlier forms of marriage and the family are mostly irreversible. Women won't return in large numbers to a domestic situation from which they have painfully managed to extricate themselves. Sexual partnerships and marriage today, for better or worse, can't be like they used to be. Emotional communication – more precisely, the active creation and sustaining of relationships – has become central to our lives in the personal and family domain.

What will be the result? The divorce rate may have levelled off from its previous steep increase, but it is not dropping. All measures of divorce are to some extent estimates, but on the basis of past trends, we can guess that some 60 per cent of all marriages contracted now might end in divorce within ten years.

Divorce, as we've seen, is not always a reflection of unhappiness. People who may in former times have felt constrained to remain in miserable marriages can make a fresh start. But there can be no doubt that the trends affecting sexuality, marriage and the family create deep anxieties for some people at the same time as they generate new possibilities for satisfaction and self-fulfilment for others.

Those who argue that the great diversity in family forms that exists today is to be welcomed, as freeing us from the limitations and sufferings of the past, surely have a certain amount of right on their side. Men and women can remain single if they wish, without having to face the social disapproval that once came from being a bachelor or, even more, a spinster. Couples in live-in relationships no longer face social rejection by their more 'respectable' married friends. Gay couples can set up house together and bring up children without facing the same level of hostilities they would have in the past.

These things having been said, it is difficult to resist the conclusion that we stand at a crossroads. Will the future bring about the further decay of long-term marriages or partnerships? Will we more and more inhabit an emotional and sexual landscape scarred by bitterness and violence? None can say for certain. But such a sociological analysis of marriage and the family as we have just concluded strongly suggests that we won't resolve our problems by looking to the past. We must try to reconcile the individual freedoms most of us have come to value in our personal lives with the need to form stable and lasting relations with other people.

SUMMARY

1 Kinship, family and marriage are closely related terms of key significance for sociology and anthropology. Kinship comprises either genetic ties or ties initiated by marriage. A family is a group of kin having responsibility for the upbringing of children. Marriage is a bond between two people living together in a socially approved sexual relationship.

2 A nuclear family is a household in which a married couple (or single parent) live together with their own or adopted children. Where kin other than a married couple and children live in the same household, or are involved in close and continuous relationships, we speak of the existence of an extended family.

3 In Western societies, marriage, and therefore the family, are associated with monogamy (a culturally approved sexual relationship between one woman and one man). Many other cultures tolerate or encourage polygamy, in which an individual may be married to two or more spouses at the same time. Polygyny, in which a man may marry more than one wife, is far more common than polyandry, in which a woman may have more than one husband.

4 In Western Europe and the USA, nuclear family patterns were strongly implanted well before the development of industrialization, although they were profoundly influenced by it. Changes in family patterns were produced by such factors as the development of centralized government, the expansion of towns and cities, and employment within organizations outside family influence. These changes are tending to produce a worldwide movement towards nuclear family systems, eroding extended family forms and other types of kinship group.

5 Most industrial countries include a diversity of family forms. In Britain, for example, families of South Asian and West Indian origin differ from the dominant family types.

6 There have been major changes in patterns of family life in the West during the postwar period. A high percentage of women are in the paid labour force, divorce rates are rising and substantial proportions of the population are either in single-parent households or living within step-families. Cohabitation (where a couple lives together in a sexual relationship outside of marriage) has become increasingly common in many industrial countries.

7 Many people today live in step-families. A step-family is created whenever a parent with a child or children remarries or cohabits with a new partner.

8 Family life is by no means always a picture of harmony and happiness. The 'dark side' of the family is found in the patterns of sexual abuse and domestic violence which often occur within it. Most sexual abuse of children is carried out by males, and seems to connect with other types of violent behaviour in which some men are involved.

9 Marriage has ceased to be (if it ever was) the condition for regular sexual experience, for either sex; it is no longer the basis of economic activity. It seems certain that varying forms of social and sexual relationships will flourish still further. Marriage and the family remain firmly established institutions, yet are undergoing major stresses and strains.

FURTHER READING

Stewart Asquith and **Anne Stafford**, *Families and the Future* (Edinburgh: HMSO, 1995). An analysis of issues to do with children and the future of family.

Diana Gittins, *The Family in Question* (London: Macmillan, 1992). An updated version of an established text dealing with the major aspects of family life in modern societies.

Helen O'Connell, *Women and the Family* (London: Zed Books, 1994).

A revision of the role of women in family relationships.

Roderick Phillips, *Untying the Knot: A Short History of Divorce* (Cambridge: Cambridge University Press, 1991). A readable study of the history of divorce in Europe and the United States.

Ann Phoenix, *Young Mothers?* (Cambridge: Polity Press, 1991). A discussion of the problems of teenage mothers in modern society.

IMPORTANT TERMS

- *nuclear family*
- *extended family*
- *monogamy*
- *polygamy*
- *polygyny*
- *polyandry*
- *affective individualism*
- *serial monogamy*
- *patrilineal inheritance*

- *matrilineal inheritance*
- *lone-parent household*
- *absent father*
- *step-families*
- *sexual abuse of children*
- *incest*
- *kibbutzim*
- *cohabitation*
- *gay-parent families*

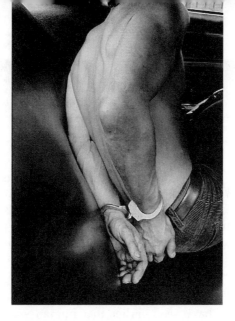

8

DEVIANCE AND CRIME

BASIC CONCEPTS

● *deviance* ● *norms* ● *conformity* ● *crime*

We all know who deviants are, or so we tend to think. Deviants are those individuals who refuse to live by the rules that the majority of us follow. They're violent criminals, drug addicts or 'down-and-outs', who don't fit in with what most people would define as normal standards of acceptability. Yet things are not quite as they appear – a lesson sociology often teaches us, for it encourages us to look beyond the obvious. The notion of the deviant, as we shall see, is actually not an easy one to define.

We have seen earlier that human social life is governed by rules or norms. Our activities would collapse into chaos if we didn't stick to rules that define some kinds of behaviour as proper in particular contexts and others as inappropriate. Orderly behaviour on the roads, for example, would be impossible if drivers didn't observe the rule of driving on the left. No deviants here, you might think, except perhaps for the drunken or reckless driver. If you did think this, though, you would be wrong. Most drivers are not just deviants but criminals. For most drivers regularly drive at well above the legal speed limits – assuming there isn't a police car in sight.

We are all rule breakers as well as conformists. We are all also rule creators. Drivers may break the law on the motorways, but in fact they have evolved informal rules that are superimposed on the legal rules. When the legal speed limit on the motorway is 70 mph, most drivers don't go above 80 or so, and tend to go more slowly when driving through urban areas.

Conventional rules about what is and isn't reckless driving also vary. Northern Europeans who drive in the south of Italy, for example, where drivers break other traffic rules as well, are apt to find the experience a hair-raising one. In Brazil, traffic lights and other traffic controls are not treated as binding rules, but as mere suggestions. Motorists in Rio de Janeiro drive through red lights without stopping, unless another car enters the intersection. Where there is a main street crossing a lesser one, the driver on the main road presumes right of way, no matter what the traffic signals might indicate. Someone entering from the smaller street must hoot or flash the headlights to warn other drivers (Lull 1995).

When we begin the study of deviant behaviour, we must consider which rules people are observing and which they are breaking. Nobody breaks *all* rules, just as no one conforms to all rules. Even individuals who might seem wholly outside the pale of respectable society, such as bank robbers, are likely to be following rules of the groups of which they are members. Some distinctly disreputable groups, such as motorcycle gangs, have strict codes of conduct for their members; those who deviate from them are either punished or expelled.

THE STUDY OF DEVIANT BEHAVIOUR

The study of deviant behaviour is one of the most intriguing yet complex areas of sociology. It teaches us that none of us is quite as normal as we might like to think. It also helps us see that people whose behaviour might appear incomprehensible or alien can be seen as rational beings when we understand why they act as they do.

The study of deviance, like other fields of sociology, directs our attention to social *power*, as well as the influence of social class – the divisions between rich and poor. When we look at deviance from or conformity to social rules or norms, we always have to bear in mind the question, *whose* rules? As we shall see, social norms are strongly influenced by divisions of power and class.

What is deviance?

DEVIANCE may be defined as non-conformity to a given set of norms that are accepted by a significant number of people in a community or society. No society, as has already been stressed, can be divided up in a simple way between those who deviate from norms and those who conform to them. Most of us on some occasions transgress generally accepted rules of behaviour. We may, for example, have at some point committed minor acts of theft, like shoplifting or taking small items from work – such as office note-paper and pens – for personal use.

The scope of the concept of deviance is very wide, as some examples will illustrate. The billionaire Howard Hughes built up his massive fortune through a mixture of hard work, inventive ideas and shrewd decisions. In terms of his drive to succeed, his activities conformed to some of the key values in Western societies, values emphasizing the desirability of material rewards and individual achievement. On the other hand, in some areas, his behaviour deviated sharply from orthodox norms. He lived the last few years of his life almost completely isolated from the outside world, hardly ever venturing out of the hotel suite he had made his home. He let his hair grow very long and cultivated a long, straggly beard, making him look more like a biblical prophet than a successful businessman.

Hughes was both highly successful and highly deviant in his behaviour. As a contrasting example, we might take the career of Ted Bundy. Bundy's way of life, on the face of things, conformed to the norms of behaviour of a good citizen. He led what seemed not only a normal life, but a most worthy one. For example, he played an active role in the Samaritans, an association that organizes a twenty-four-hour phone-in service for people who are distressed or suicidal. Yet Bundy also carried out a series of horrific murders. Before sentencing him to death, the judge at his trial praised Bundy for his abilities (he had prepared his own defence) but finished by noting what a waste he had made of his life. Bundy's career shows that a person can seem entirely normal while secretly engaging in acts of extreme deviance.

Deviance does not refer only to individual behaviour; it concerns the activities of groups as well. An illustration is the Hare Krishna cult, a religious group whose beliefs and mode of life are different from those of the majority of people in Britain. The cult was established in the 1960s when Sril Prabhupada came to the West from India to spread the word of Krishna consciousness. He aimed his message particularly at young people who were drug users, proclaiming that one could 'stay high all the time, discover eternal bliss' by following his teachings. The Hare Krishnas became a familiar sight, dancing and chanting in the streets, airports and other venues. They were regarded in a tolerant light by most of the population, even if their beliefs seemed eccentric.

The Hare Krishnas represent an example of a **deviant subculture**. Although their membership today has declined, they have been able to survive fairly easily within the wider society. The organization is wealthy, financed by donations from members and sympathizers. Their position diverges from that of another deviant subculture, who might be mentioned here by way of contrast: the permanently homeless. People who are down-and-out live on the streets by day, spending their time in parks or in public buildings (like libraries). They may sleep outside or find refuge in shelters. Most of the permanently homeless eke out a miserable existence on the fringes of the wider society.

Norms and sanctions

All social NORMS are accompanied by sanctions that promote CONFORMITY and protect against non-conformity. A **sanction** is any reaction from others to the behaviour of an individual or group that is meant to ensure that the person or group complies with a given norm. Sanctions may be positive (the offering of rewards for conformity) or negative (punishment for behaviour that does not conform). They can also be formal or informal. Formal sanctions are applied by a specific body of people or an agency to ensure that a particular set of norms is followed. Informal sanctions are less organized and more spontaneous reactions to non-conformity, such as when a student is teasingly accused by friends of working too hard or being a 'nerd' if he decides to spend an evening studying rather than going to a party.

The main types of formal sanctions in modern societies are those represented by the courts and prisons. The police, of course, are the agency charged with bringing offenders to trial and possible imprisonment. **Laws** are formal sanctions defined by governments as principles that their citizens must follow; they are used against people who do not conform. Where there are laws, there are also crimes, since CRIME can most simply be defined as any type of behaviour that breaks a law.

At this point, we can move on to look at the main theories that have been developed to interpret and analyse deviance. Most accounts of deviance have been based particularly on studies of criminal activity, which will be our main focus as well.

THEORIES OF CRIME AND DEVIANCE

The biological view

Some of the first attempts to explain crime were essentially biological in character. The Italian criminologist Cesare Lombroso, working in the 1870s, believed that criminal types could be identified by the shape of the skull. He accepted that social learning could influence the development of criminal behaviour, but he regarded most criminals as biologically degenerate or defective. Lombroso's ideas became thoroughly discredited, but similar views have repeatedly been suggested. Another popular method of trying to demonstrate the influence of heredity on criminal tendencies was to study family trees. But this demonstrates virtually nothing about the influence of heredity, because it is impossible to disentangle inherited and environmental influences.

A later theory distinguished three main types of human physique and claimed that one type was directly associated with delinquency. Muscular, active types (mesomorphs), the theory went, are more likely to become delinquent than those of thin physique (ectomorphs) or more fleshy people (endomorphs) (Sheldon 1949; Glueck and Glueck 1956). Such views have also been widely criticized. Even if there were an overall relationship between bodily type and delinquency, this would show nothing about the influence of heredity. People of the muscular type may be drawn towards criminal activities because these offer opportunities for the physical display of athleticism. Moreover, nearly all studies in this field have been restricted to delinquents in reform schools, and it may be that the tougher, athletic-looking delinquents are more liable to be sent to such schools than fragile-looking, skinny ones.

Some individuals might be inclined towards irritability and aggressiveness, and this could be reflected in crimes of physical assault on others. Yet there is no decisive evidence that any traits of personality are inherited in this way, and even if they were, their connection to criminality would at most be only a distant one.

The psychological view

Like biological interpretations, psychological theories of crime associate criminality with particular types of personality. Some have suggested that in a minority of individuals, an amoral, or psychopathic, personality develops. **Psychopaths** are withdrawn, emotionless characters who delight in violence for its own sake.

Individuals with psychopathic traits do sometimes commit violent crimes, but there are major problems with the concept of the psychopath. It isn't at all clear that psychopathic traits are inevitably criminal. Nearly all studies of people said to possess these characteristics have been of convicted prisoners, and their personalities inevitably tend to be presented negatively. If we describe the same traits positively, the personality type sounds quite different, and there seems no reason why people of this sort should be inherently criminal. Were we to be looking for psychopathic individuals for a research study, we might place the following ad (Widom and Newman 1985):

ARE YOU ADVENTUROUS?
Researcher wishes to contact adventurous, carefree people who've led exciting, impulsive lives. If you're the kind of person who'd do almost anything for a dare, call 337-XXXX any time.

Such people might be explorers, spies, gamblers, or just bored with the routines of day-to-day life. They *might* be prepared to contemplate criminal adventures, but would seem just as likely to look for challenges in socially respectable ways.

Psychological theories of criminality can at best explain only some aspects of crime. While some criminals may possess personality characteristics distinct from the remainder of the population, it is highly improbable that the majority of criminals do so. There are all kinds of crimes, and it is implausible to suppose that those who commit them share some specific psychological characteristics. Even if we confine ourselves to one category of crime, such as crimes of violence, different circumstances are involved. Some such crimes are carried out by lone individuals, while others are the work of organized groups. It is not likely that the psychological make-up of people who are loners will have much in common with the members of a close-knit gang. Even if consistent differences could be linked to forms of criminality, we still couldn't be sure which way the line of causality would run. It might be that becoming involved with criminal groups influences people's outlooks, rather than that the outlooks actually produce criminal behaviour in the first place.

Society and crime: sociological theories

Any satisfactory account of the nature of crime must be sociological, for what crime is depends on the social institutions of a society. One of the most important emphases of sociological thinking about crime is on the interconnections between conformity and deviance in different social contexts. Modern societies contain many different subcultures, and behaviour that conforms to the norms of one particular subculture may be regarded as deviant outside it. For instance, there may be strong pressure on a member of a boys' gang to prove himself by stealing a car. Moreover, there are wide divergences of wealth and power in society, which greatly influence opportunities open to different groups. Theft and burglary, not surprisingly, are carried out mainly by people from the poorer segments of the population; embezzling and tax evasion are by definition limited to persons in positions of some affluence.

Learned deviance: differential association

Edwin H. Sutherland linked crime to what he called **differential association** (Sutherland 1949). This idea is very simple. In a society that contains a variety of subcultures, some social environments tend to encourage illegal activities, whereas others do not. Individuals become delinquent through associating with people who are the carriers of criminal norms. For the most part, according to Sutherland, criminal behaviour is learned within primary groups, particularly peer groups.

This theory is in contrast to the view that psychological differences separate criminals from other people; it sees criminal activities as learned in much the same way as law-abiding ones, and as directed towards the same needs and values. Thieves try to make money just like people in orthodox jobs, but they choose illegal means of doing so.

Structural strain: anomie as a cause of crime

Robert K. Merton's interpretation of crime, which links criminality to other types of deviant behaviour, similarly emphasizes the normality of the criminal (Merton 1957). Merton drew on the concept of *anomie* to construct a highly influential theory of deviance. As we saw in chapter 1, the notion of anomie was first introduced by Émile Durkheim, one of the founders of sociology, who suggested that in modern societies traditional norms and standards become undermined without being replaced by new ones. Anomie exists when there are no clear standards to guide behaviour in a given area of social life. In these circumstances, Durkheim believed, people feel disoriented and anxious; anomie is therefore one of the social factors influencing dispositions to suicide.

Merton modified the concept of anomie to refer to the strain put on individuals' behaviour when accepted norms conflict with social reality. In American society – and to some degree in other industrial societies – generally held values emphasize material success, and the means of achieving success are supposed to be self-discipline and hard work. Accordingly, people who really work hard can succeed, no matter what their starting point in life. This idea is not in fact valid, because most of the disadvantaged are given only limited conventional opportunities for advancement, or none at all. Yet those who do not 'succeed' find themselves condemned for their apparent inability to make material progress. In this situation, there is great pressure to try to get ahead by any means, legitimate or illegitimate. According to Merton, then, deviance is a by-product of economic inequalities.

Merton identifies five possible reactions to the tensions between socially endorsed values and the limited means of achieving them. *Conformists* accept both generally held values and the conventional means of realizing them, whether or not they meet with success. The majority of the population fall into this category. *Innovators* continue to accept socially approved values but use illegitimate or illegal means to follow them. Criminals who acquire wealth through illegal activities exemplify this type.

Ritualists conform to socially accepted standards although they have lost sight of the values behind these standards. The rules are followed for their own sake without a wider end in view, in a compulsive way. Ritualists would be people who dedicate themselves to boring jobs, even though the jobs have no career prospects and provide few rewards. *Retreatists* have abandoned the competitive outlook altogether, thus rejecting both the dominant values and the approved means of achieving them. An example would be the members of a self-supporting commune. Finally, *rebels* reject both the existing values and the means, but wish actively to substitute new ones and reconstruct the social system. The members of radical political groups fall into this category.

Later researchers linked Sutherland's notion of differential association (the idea that the group of people with whom individuals associate influences them for or against crime) to Merton's typology. In their study of delinquent boys' **gangs**, Richard A. Cloward and Lloyd E. Ohlin (1960) argued that such gangs arise in subcultural communities where the chances of achieving success legitimately are small, such as deprived ethnic minorities. Their work rightly emphasized connections between conformity and deviance. Lack of opportunity for success in the terms of the wider society is the main differentiating factor between those who engage in criminal behaviour and those who do not.

We should be cautious about the idea that people in poorer communities aspire to the same level of success as more affluent people. Most tend to adjust their aspirations to what they see as the reality of their situation. Yet it would also be wrong to suppose that a mismatch of aspirations and opportunities is confined to the less privileged. There are pressures towards criminal activity among other groups too, as is indicated by the so-called white-collar crimes of embezzlement, fraud and tax evasion, which we will study later.

Labelling theory

One of the most important approaches to the understanding of criminality is called **labelling theory** – although this term itself is a label for a cluster of related ideas rather than a unified view. Labelling theorists interpret deviance not as a set of characteristics of individuals or groups, but as a *process* of interaction between deviants and non-deviants. In their view, we must discover why some people become tagged with a 'deviant' label in order to understand the nature of deviance itself.

People who represent the forces of law and order, or are able to impose definitions of conventional morality on others, do most of the labelling. The labels that create categories of deviance thus express the power structure of society. By and large, the rules in terms of which deviance is defined are framed by the wealthy for the poor, by men for women, by older people for younger people, and by ethnic majorities for minority groups. For example, many children wander into other people's gardens, steal fruit, or play truant. In an affluent neighbourhood, these might be regarded by parents, teachers and police alike as innocent pastimes of childhood. In poor areas, they might be seen as evidence of tendencies towards juvenile delinquency.

Once a child is labelled a delinquent, he or she is stigmatized as a criminal and is likely to be considered untrustworthy by teachers and prospective employers. The individual then relapses into further criminal behaviour, widening the estrangement from orthodox social conventions. Edwin Lemert (1972) called the initial act of transgression primary deviance. **Secondary deviance** occurs when the individual comes to accept the label and sees himself as deviant.

Take, for example, Luke, who smashes a shop window while spending a Saturday night out on the town with his friends. The act may perhaps

Prescribed drugs **LEGAL**

Legal if prescribed. These include barbiturates and tranquillizers, commonly prescribed to calm people down or help them sleep. Many lead to dependence. Withdrawal effects can include anxiety, sleeplessness and mental confusion.

Alcohol **LEGAL**

Legal to buy, sell and drink by adults. Produced when fruit, vegetables or grain ferments. Users feel less shy and more relaxed. Heavy drinking leads to stomach and liver disorders and malnutrition and judgement is impaired. There is a strong risk of dependence.

LSD **ILLEGAL**

Lysergic Acid (LSD) is usually taken in capsule form; makes people see or hear things in a different way. There are no known physical side-effects but a bad experience can cause anxiety and depression. The drug ecstasy combines the stimulant effects of amphetamines with versions of the effects of LSD.

Cannabis **ILLEGAL**

A bushy plant found wild in most parts of the world. Usually smoked. It can make people more relaxed, more talkative and more aware of sound, taste etc. It can cause confusion, anxiety and depression. Cannabis is not thought to lead to dependence.

Solvents **RESTRICTED**

It is illegal for shops to sell to children under 16 if they think they will inhale them. Vapours inhaled from glue, paints, nail-varnish removers etc. Most common among 12- to 16-year-olds. Effects include feelings of well-being or drowsiness. Use can cause brain damage. Risk of dependence. Risk of death due to poisoning or accidental suffocation.

Heroin **ILLEGAL**

The most commonly misused form of opiate. Opiates depress the nervous system often producing a feeling of well-being. Dependence can follow repeated use. Withdrawal symptoms include aches, tremors and spasms. Risk of infection if using shared or unsterilized needles.

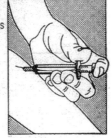

Legality and illegality: drugs and the law in modern Britain. Drug-taking provides a good illustration of labelling theory, because people generally have more tolerant attitudes towards alcohol, for example, than towards drugs like cannabis or heroin. Yet alcohol is a drug like the others, and is the cause of many health problems.

Source: © *Guardian*, first published in *Education Guardian,* 12 November 1991, p. 2; graphics Paddy Allen.

be called the accidental result of over-boisterous behaviour, an excusable characteristic of young men. Luke might escape with a reprimand and a small fine. If he is from a 'respectable' background, this is a likely result. And the smashing of the window stays at the level of primary deviance if the youth is seen as someone of good character who on this occasion became too rowdy. If, on the other hand, the police and courts hand out a suspended sentence and make Luke report to a social worker, the incident could become the first step on the road to secondary deviance. The process of 'learning to be deviant' tends to be accentuated by the very organizations supposedly set up to correct deviant behaviour – prisons and asylums.

Labelling theory is important because it begins from the assumption that no act is intrinsically criminal. Definitions of criminality are established by the powerful, through the formulation of laws and their interpretation by police, courts and correctional institutions. Critics of labelling theory have sometimes argued that there are certain acts that are consistently prohibited across virtually all cultures, such as murder, rape and robbery. This view is surely incorrect; even within our own culture, killing is not always regarded as murder. In times of war, killing of the enemy is positively approved, and until recently the laws in Britain did not recognize sexual intercourse forced on a woman by her husband as rape.

We can more convincingly criticize labelling theory on other grounds. First, in emphasizing the active process of labelling, labelling theorists neglect the processes that *lead* to acts defined as deviant. For labelling certain activities as deviant is not completely arbitrary; differences in socialization, attitudes and opportunities influence how far people engage in behaviour likely to be labelled deviant. For instance, children from deprived backgrounds are more likely than richer children to steal from shops. It is not the labelling that leads them to steal in the first place so much as the background from which they come.

Second, it is not clear whether labelling actually does have the effect of increasing deviant conduct. Delinquent behaviour tends to increase following a conviction, but is this the result of the labelling itself? Other factors, such as increased interaction with other delinquents or learning about new criminal opportunities, may be involved.

Theoretical conclusions

What should we conclude from this survey of theories of crime? We must first recall a point made earlier: even though crime is only one subcategory of deviant behaviour as a whole, it covers such a variety of forms of activity – from shoplifting a bar of chocolate to mass murder – that it is unlikely that we could produce a single theory that would account for all forms of criminal conduct.

Each of the above theories contributes to our understanding of some aspects or types of crime. Biological and psychological approaches may identify personality characteristics that, in particular contexts of social learning and experience, predispose certain individuals to contemplate criminal acts. For example, people with traits usually termed psycho-pathic may be more heavily represented among some categories of vio-lent criminals than among the general population. On the other hand, they are probably also overrepresented among those who carry out acts of extreme heroism or risk.

The contributions of the sociological theories of crime are twofold. First, these theories correctly emphasize the continuities between crimi-nal and 'respectable' behaviour. The contexts in which particular types of activity are seen as criminal and punishable by law vary widely. Second, all agree that context is important in criminal activities. Whether someone engages in a criminal act or comes to be regarded as a criminal is influenced fundamentally by social learning and social surroundings.

In spite of its deficiencies, labelling theory is perhaps the most widely used approach to understanding crime and deviant behaviour. This theory sensitizes us to the ways in which some activities come to be defined as punishable in law, and the power relations that form such definitions, as well as to the circumstances in which particular individ-uals fall foul of the law.

Now let's look directly at the nature of the criminal activities occurring in modern societies, paying particular attention to crime in the United Kingdom.

CRIME AND CRIME STATISTICS

How much crime actually exists, and what are the most common forms of criminal offence? To answer these questions, we can begin by look-ing at the official crime statistics. Since such statistics are published reg-ularly, there would seem to be no difficulty in assessing crime rates – but this assumption is quite erroneous. Statistics about crime and delin-quency are probably the least reliable of all officially published figures on social issues.

The most basic limitation of official crime statistics is that they only include crimes actually recorded by the police. There is a long chain of problematic decisions between a possible crime and its registration by the police (see figure 8.1). The majority of crimes, especially petty thefts, are never reported to the police at all. People vary in their ability to recognize crimes and their willingness to report them. Of the crimes that do come to the notice of the police, a proportion are not recorded in the statistics; for instance, the police may be sceptical of the validity of some information about purported crimes that comes their way. Surveys estimate that at least half of all serious crimes, including forcible rape, robbery and aggravated assault (assault with the purpose of inflicting severe injury) are not reported to the police.

The Bureau of the Census in the United States has been interviewing people in a random sample of 60,000 households since 1973, to see how many were victims of particular crimes during the preceding six

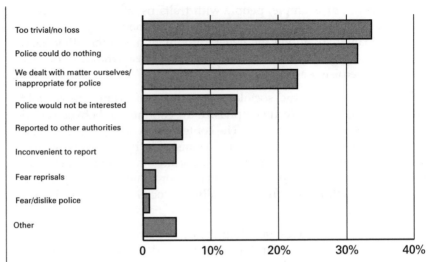

Fig. 8.1 Reasons for not reporting crime (as a percentage of those who experienced a crime and did not report it to the police; more than one reason could be given), England and Wales, 1993

Source: British Crime Survey, Home Office. From *Social Trends*, 1996, p. 165.

months. This research, which is called the National Crime Survey, has confirmed that much serious crime goes unreported. Reporting is highest for commercial robbery (86 per cent) and lowest for household thefts of under 50 dollars (15 per cent). Until the 1982 and 1984 British Crime Surveys (BCS) there was no official estimate of unrecorded crime in the United Kingdom. The patterns of unreported crime in Britain, as disclosed by the BCS, closely mirror the American findings.

To find the true rates of crime, we cannot simply add unreported crimes to the official police rate, because practices of local police forces in reporting crime vary. Some report fewer crimes than others, either because of inefficiency or because their arrest record thereby looks better. In Britain, the government conducts a regular General Household Survey, sampling households nationally. The survey included a question about burglary in 1972, 1973, 1979 and 1980. Households were asked to mention any burglaries occurring in the twelve months preceding the interview. The 1981 survey concluded that there had been almost no change in the incidence of burglaries between 1972 and 1980, yet over this period the official British crime statistics, based on crimes reported to the police, showed an increase of 50 per cent (Bottomley and Pease 1986, pp. 22–3). The apparent rise probably stemmed from increasing public awareness of crime which led to more reporting, plus more effective modes of data collection by the police.

As measured by statistics of crimes reported to the police, rates of crime in the UK have been increasing more or less continuously for well over half a century. Prior to the 1920s, there were fewer than 100,000 offences recorded each year in England and Wales. This number had reached 500,000 by 1950, and over 5 million by 1991. The police today thus record over nine offences annually for every one hundred people. Northern Ireland may be associated with a high level of terrorist violence, but the overall level of crime there, in the police statistics, is well below that of England and Wales, at only four offences for every hundred persons (see figure 8.2). In terms of official statistics, crimes of violence have risen steeply over the past two decades. The British Crime Survey data also suggest that from 1981 to 1991 property crime rose by

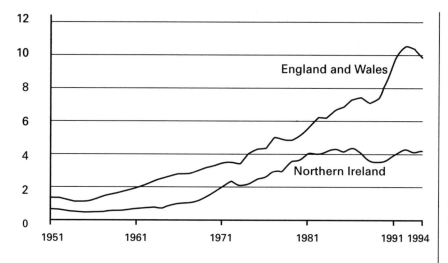

Fig. 8.2 Notifiable offences recorded by the police per 100 population, 1951–1994

Sources: Home Office; Royal Ulster Constabulary. From _Social Trends_, 1996, p. 159.

95 per cent, while crimes against the person rose by 21 per cent. There seems to be a fairly close correlation between such rises in crime and increases in the male unemployment rate. Unemployed young men aged 16–29 are heavily overrepresented in relation to both categories of crime. Regional analysis adds further support for this link. The main employment black spots of the country, such as Merseyside, Greater Manchester, the West Midlands, South Wales and Greater London are also crime black spots (Wells 1995).

New Left Realism

For a long while many criminologists, particularly those of a more liberal or leftist persuasion, tended to minimize the importance of rises in official crime rates. They sought to show that the media created unnecessary public disquiet about the issue, or argued that most crime was a disguised form of protest against inequality – much as Merton's scheme of anomie might suggest. New Left Realism (NLR), associated particularly with the work of Jock Young, moved away from that position (Young 1988).

NLR contends that the increases in crime have actually occurred, and that the public is right to be worried by them. In line with this emphasis, the approach seeks to draw attention to the victims of crime, rather than being concerned only with those who undertake criminal acts. Victim surveys, it is claimed, provide a more valid picture of extent of crime than either the official statistics or the British Crime Survey (Evans 1992). Victim studies, Young says, show that the police are losing the struggle against crime, especially in the impoverished inner city areas (for more material on the inner city and its problems, see chapter 17, 'Cities and the development of modern urbanism'). Street crime, including crimes of violence of various sorts, drug-dealing and vandalism, has increased sharply.

The approach draws on Merton, Cloward and Ohlin and others to suggest that, in the inner cities, criminal subcultures develop. Such subcultures do not derive from poverty as such, but from lack of inclusion within the wider community. Criminalized youth groups, for example, operate at the margins of 'respectable society' and pit themselves against it. The fact that rates of crime carried out by blacks have risen over recent years is attributed to the fact that policies of racial integration have failed.

Critics of the approach accept the importance of the stress on victimization. They point out, however, that public perceptions of crime are often based on stereotypes – false images. NLR might unintentionally lend support to the stereotype: black = criminal. The approach has also been criticized for moving attention too much towards the victim. What is needed is an exploration of the experiences of both victim and offender (Hughes 1991).

Homicide and other violent crime

Homicide

Rates of homicide (murder) are probably the most accurate of crime statistics. Yet even here there are problems. For a death to be classified as a murder it has to be known to have occurred. This usually means a body has to be found; few deaths where a body remains undiscovered are categorized as homicide. Given that a body is located, murder will only be suspected if there are circumstances which indicate that the death was 'non-natural' – such as severe bruising or lacerations of the skull. Once a case is brought against someone, it may be decided that the accused was guilty of manslaughter (killed another person unintentionally but unlawfully), rather than murder (figure 8.3).

Public health statistics, based on coroners' reports, provide a way of measuring the homicide rate that is more or less independent of police reports. These reports are not entirely accurate, since coroners may mistakenly call a homicide an accident, or misinterpret a homicide as a sui-

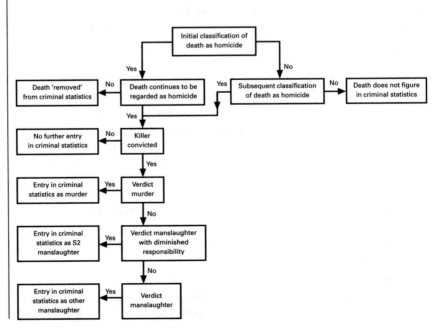

Fig. 8.3 The various ways in which a homicide may be recorded (or not recorded) in criminal statistics

Source: A. K. Bottomley and K. Pease, *Crime and Punishment: Interpreting the Data* (Open University Press 1986), p. 9.

cide. However, such statistics are generally quite close to rates of homicide in police reports, suggesting that these might in fact be fairly accurate.

Violent crime in the USA

Nobody disputes one phenomenon disclosed by the crime statistics – the exceptionally high level of violent crime that occurs in the United States as compared with other industrialized countries, including Britain (though not compared with some Third World countries – see table 8.1). There are more reported murders each year in Detroit, with a population of just over one-and-a-half million, than in the whole of the United Kingdom, which has a population of fifty-eight million people. Viewed in this context, the United States is a culture in which crimes of violence flourish. Why should this be?

The answer is sometimes given as the widespread availability of handguns and other firearms. This is surely relevant, but cannot on its own be the full answer. Switzerland has very low rates of violent crime, yet firearms are easily accessible: all males there are members of the citizen army and keep weapons in their homes, including rifles, revolvers and sometimes other automatic weapons, plus ammunition. Nor are gun licences difficult to obtain (Clinard 1978). The most likely explanation for the high level of violent crime in the United States is a combination of the availability of firearms, the general influence of the 'frontier tradition' and the existence of subcultures of violence in the large cities. Violence on the part of frontiersmen and vigilantes is an honoured part of American history. Some of the first immigrant areas established in the cities developed their own informal modes of neighbourhood social control, backed by violence or threat of violence. Young people in black

Table 8.1	Countries with high murder rates (number per 100,000 population, based on police records), 1990	
1	Bahamas	52.61
2	Philippines	30.12
3	Guatemala	27.40
4	Jamaica	20.85
5	Botswana	19.50
6	Zimbabwe	17.88
7	Peru	12.01
8	Barbados	11.67
9	Sri Lanka	11.60
10	Malta	10.44
11	Paraguay	10.00
12	Thailand	9.50
13	United States	9.40
14	Ex-Soviet Union	8.67
15	Trinidad & Tobago	8.42
16	Papua New Guinea	7.78
17	Sweden	7.02
18	Taiwan	6.40
19	United Kingdom	6.00

Source: The Economist, The Pocket World in Figures (Profile Books Ltd 1996), p. 81.

and Hispanic communities have similarly developed subcultures of manliness and honour associated with rituals of violence.

It is important to note the relatively mundane character of many crimes of violence. Most assaults and homicides bear little resemblance to the murderous, rampaging acts of gunmen given most prominence in the media. Murders generally happen in the context of family and other interpersonal relationships. They are far more often carried out by people under the influence of alcohol than by those under the influence of narcotics – which is hardly surprising, given the prevalence of alcohol consumption.

A substantial proportion of homicides are 'victim precipitated' – the victim initiates the fatal outburst by making the first menacing gesture or striking the first blow. Many examples appear in Wolfgang's research in the United States, which initially drew attention to the phenomenon. For example: 'A victim became incensed when his eventual slayer asked for money which the victim owed him. The victim grabbed a hatchet and started in the direction of his creditor, who pulled out a knife and stabbed him' (Wolfgang 1958, p. 253; see also Campbell and Gibbs 1986).

Let us now look at what happens to those actually convicted of crimes. The wages of crime are limited to *punishment*. The most widespread form of punishment for crime today is imprisonment (although fining is common for minor crimes).

PRISONS AND PUNISHMENT

Changes in modes of punishment

Before the early nineteenth century, imprisonment was rarely used to punish crime. Most towns of any size had a local jail, but these were normally very small and were not capable of holding more than three or four prisoners at any time. They were used to 'cool off' drunks for the night, or occasionally as places where accused persons awaited trial. In the bigger European cities, there were prisons of some size; most of the people interned in these were convicted criminals awaiting execution. These institutions were very different from the prisons that were built in great numbers from the turn of the nineteenth century onwards. Prison discipline was lax or non-existent. Sometimes those who were to be executed were plunged into dungeons, and saw only the jailer before being taken to execution, but more often the prison atmosphere was amazingly free and easy by modern standards.

Jonathon Atholl, a historian of crime, has described life in Newgate, one of the early London prisons. It was a bustling, lively place, full of visitors at most times of the day. In 1790 one of the condemned men held a ball at the prison, apparently not an uncommon event: 'Tea was served at 4 p.m. to the music of violins and flutes, after which the company danced until 8 p.m. when a cold supper was produced. The party broke up at 9 o'clock, the usual hour for closing the prison' (Atholl

1954, p. 66). The main forms of punishment for crime until the nineteenth century were putting people in the stocks, whipping, branding with hot irons or hanging. These were usually carried out publicly, and were well attended. Some executions attracted thousands of people. Prisoners about to be hanged might make speeches, justifying their actions or proclaiming themselves innocent. The crowd would cheer, boo or hiss, according to their assessment of the accused's claims.

Modern prisons have their origins, not in the jails and dungeons of former times, but in workhouses. Workhouses date from the seventeenth century in most European countries, and were established during the period when feudalism was breaking down; many peasant workers could not get work on the land, and so became vagrants. In the workhouses they were provided with food, but forced to spend most of their time in the institution and made to work extremely hard. The workhouses also, however, became places where other groups were interned if no one was prepared to care for them outside: the sick, aged, feebleminded and mentally ill.

During the eighteenth century, prisons, asylums and hospitals gradually became distinct from one another. Reformers came to object to traditional punishments, seeing deprivation of liberty as a more effective way of coping with criminal activities. Murder became recognized as the most serious crime, as rights of individual freedom developed within the wider political system: for to kill another person is the ultimate attack on that individual's rights. Since prisons were supposed to have the effect of training criminals in sober habits of discipline and conformity, the idea of punishing people in public progressively dropped away.

Prisons and moral improvement

Imprisonment is a mode of punishing wrong-doers and of protecting citizens from them. But the underlying principle of the prison system is that of 'improving' the individual to play a fit and proper part in society. Do prisons have this effect on those interned in them for specific periods of time? The evidence strongly suggests that they do not.

Prisoners are no longer generally physically maltreated, as was once common practice – although physical beatings are by no means unknown, even in women's prisons (as will be shown below). However, prisoners suffer many other types of deprivation. They are deprived not only of their freedom, but of a proper income, the company of their families and previous friends, heterosexual relationships, their own clothing and other personal items. They frequently live in overcrowded conditions, and have to accept strict disciplinary procedures and the regimentation of their daily lives.

Living in these conditions tends to drive a wedge between prison inmates and the outside society, rather than adjust their behaviour to the norms of that society. Prisoners have to come to terms with an environment quite distinct from 'the outside', and the habits and attitudes they learn in prison are quite often exactly the opposite of those they are supposed to acquire. For instance, they may develop a grudge against the ordinary citizenry, learn to accept violence as normal, gain contacts with seasoned criminals which they maintain when freed, and acquire criminal skills about which they previously knew little. It is therefore not surprising that rates of **recidivism** – repeat offending by those who have been in prison before – are disturbingly high. Over 60 per cent of all men set free after serving prison sentences in the UK are rearrested within four years of their original crimes. The actual rate of reoffending is presumably higher than this, as no doubt some of those returning to criminal activities are not caught.

Although prisons do not seem to succeed in rehabilitating prisoners, however, it is possible that they deter people from committing crimes. While those who are actually imprisoned are not deterred, the unpleasantness of prison life might well deter others. There is an almost intractable problem here for prison reformers. Making prisons thoroughly unpleasant places to be in probably helps deter potential offenders, but it makes the rehabilitating goals of prisons extremely difficult to achieve. But the less harsh prison conditions are, the more imprisonment loses its deterrent effect.

Prison protest and alternatives to imprisonment

Prisons in Britain today, in common with those of most other industrialized societies, are massively overcrowded (for prison populations, see figure 8.4). Since imprisonment mostly does not rehabilitate, and perhaps does not even deter, why not consider alternatives to prison as a way of coping with crime? Several alternatives are either in use or being considered in various countries.

One is supervision within the community, including *probation, parole* and *bail supervision*. It is already the case in the UK that, at any one time, many more people who have been convicted of crimes are on probation or parole than in prison. Probation is widely used as a means of dealing with relatively minor crimes; it means that a person has to be 'on good behaviour' for a certain period, and report regularly to the authorities. At the end of that period the case is closed. Parole is a reduction in the length of a sentence, given to reward good behaviour while an individual is in prison. Bail supervision, often used in the US,

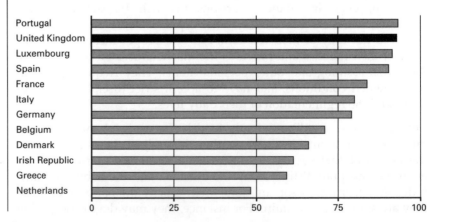

Fig. 8.4 Prison population in the European Community (per 100,000 population), 1992

Sources: Council of Europe; Home Office. From *Social Trends*, 1995, chart 9.27.

keeps people out of jail with responsible supervision while they are awaiting trial, before guilt or innocence has been determined.

Another alternative is *diversion*, which refers to programmes that divert the individual away from the courts altogether. Most existing programmes, again widely used in various countries, concern first or minor offenders. With the help of a diversion worker, the offender begins by accepting his or her own responsibility for the action in question, and then plans what can be done in response. The idea is to reduce guilt and stigma, and to plan rehabilitation positively.

Many other possibilities exist, including *community service work orders*; replacing sentences with *fines* that have to be worked off; *repayment by the offender to the victim*, in terms of money or services; *victim–offender reconciliation programmes; therapeutic communities*; and *temporary absence passes*, to allow prisoners to spend time out of jail. Some have argued that prisons should be abolished altogether. In historical terms, as noted previously, they are a relatively recent invention, and they have never worked well in terms of their main objectives. For the time being, however, it is more likely that most countries will retain imprisonment but mix it with a variety of other options (Vass 1990).

The death penalty

Ever since prison sentencing became the main form of criminal punishment, the death penalty has been increasingly controversial. Executing people for crimes has seemed barbaric to most reformers. Moreover, where the death penalty is in use, it is impossible to correct cases of injustice afterwards, should evidence come to light which shows that an individual was wrongly convicted.

The United States is almost the only Western country in which the death penalty is still applied. The death penalty was in fact abolished by the Supreme Court in 1972, but reinstated in 1976. Executions have been resumed in a substantial number of states. The number of people sentenced to death each year is growing, but so far appeals and other factors have limited the proportion of those actually executed.

In various other countries there is public pressure to bring back the death penalty, at least for certain types of crime (such as terrorism or murdering a policeman). In Britain, opinion polls consistently show that a majority of the population would like the death penalty reinstated. Many members of the public apparently believe that the threat of execution deters potential murderers, but although the arguments continue, there is little or no evidence to support the idea. Countries which have abolished the death penalty do not have notably higher homicide rates than before. Although the United States retains the death penalty, American rates of homicide are easily the highest in the industrialized world.

Of course, the strength of public feeling on this issue may reflect attitudes towards punishment, rather than the idea that the death penalty is a deterrent. People may consider that someone who takes another person's life should be punished in kind. The alternative view is that it

METHODS USED FOR EXECUTING PEOPLE

METHOD: Electrocution
Used in: Twelve US states
What happens: The prisoner is strapped into the chair. Electrodes are attached to the head and legs and the switch is thrown, sending a blast of 1,500 to 2,000 volts through the body.

METHOD: Gas chamber
Used in: Five US states
What happens: A cyanide pellet is dropped into a container of sulphuric acid and placed under the victim's chair. A deadly gas then fills the sealed chamber, sending the body into convulsions.

METHOD: Lethal injection
Used in: Thiry-two US states
What happens: Deadly chemicals are injected; many states use an anaesthetic that puts the prisoner to sleep, then a muscle relaxant that stops the lungs functioning, and a final agent that stops the heart.

METHOD: Hanging
Used in: Iran, Iraq, Afghanistan, Jamaica, Japan, Malaysia, four US states
What happens: A noose is tied around the neck. A trap-door is flung open beneath the feet and the weight of the body dislocates the upper vertebrae of the neck. The spinal cord separates from the brain and the heart stops. If the drop is too short, the prisoner is gradually strangled; if it's too long, the head may be ripped off.

METHOD: Stoning
Used in: Iran
What happens: The public is invited to throw stones, but must not select ammunition that's too small (it might not work) or too big (it might kill on the first try).

METHOD: Firing squad
Used in: Indonesia, Iran, Iraq, Nigeria, Taiwan, two US states
What happens: The convict is strapped into a chair and hooded, with a target pinned to the chest. Five marksmen, one of whom is shooting blanks, fire.

METHOD: Decapitation
Used in: Saudi Arabia
What happens: The head is severed from the body with a sword. The blade should cut through the spinal cord, causing unconsciousness from spinal shock, but more than one swipe of the blade may be necessary.

Source: Amnesty International. Map from Arbie Jones, 'Sentenced to death', *Cosmopolitan*, March 1996, p.17.

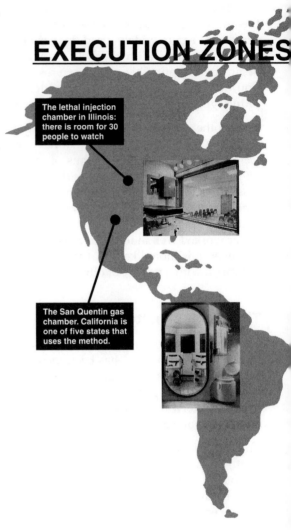

EXECUTION ZONES

The lethal injection chamber in Illinois: there is room for 30 people to watch

The San Quentin gas chamber. California is one of five states that uses the method.

is morally wrong for a society to put its citizens to death, whatever their crime. This second view, together with the lack of a deterrent effect, is what has swayed most Western legislators.

GENDER AND CRIME

Like other areas of sociology, criminological studies have traditionally ignored half the population. Many textbooks in criminology still include virtually nothing about women, save for sections on rape and

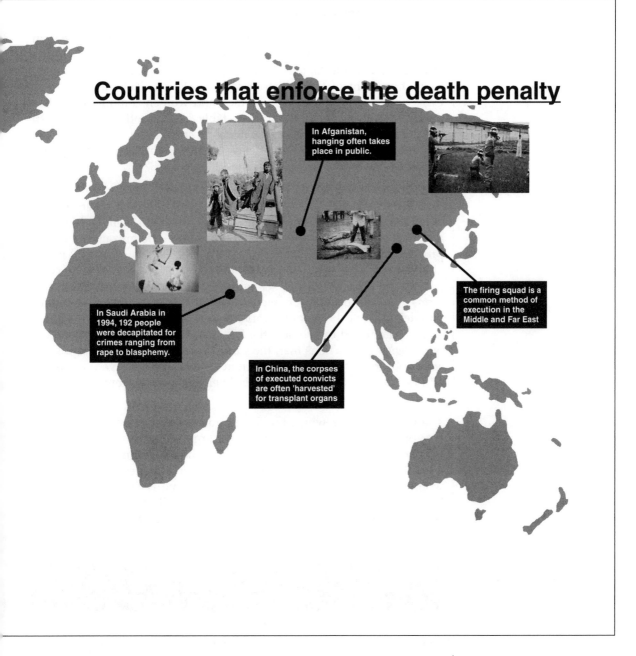

Countries that enforce the death penalty

In Afganistan, hanging often takes place in public.

In Saudi Arabia in 1994, 192 people were decapitated for crimes ranging from rape to blasphemy.

In China, the corpses of executed convicts are often 'harvested' for transplant organs

The firing squad is a common method of execution in the Middle and Far East

prostitution, and most theories of deviance similarly disregard women almost completely. An example is Merton's account of social structure and anomie. The 'pressure to succeed' is supposed to reach virtually everyone in modern societies. Logically, therefore, one could argue that women should figure more prominently than men in the various categories of deviance identified by Merton, including crime, as there are fewer opportunities open for women 'to get on' than for men. Yet rates of criminality among women are – or seem to be – exceptionally low. Even if women are for some reason less prone to participate in deviant activities than men, this is hardly a reason to omit them from consideration.

Male and female crime rates

The statistics on gender and crime are startling. For example, there is an enormous imbalance in the ratio of men to women in prison, not only in Britain but in all the industrialized countries. Women make up only some 3 per cent of the British prison population. There are also contrasts between the types of crime men and women commit, at least as indicated in the official statistics (see table 8.2). The offences of women rarely involve violence, and are almost all small-scale. Petty thefts like shoplifting, and public order offences such as public drunkenness and prostitution, are typical female crimes (Flowers 1987).

Of course, it may be that the real gender difference in crime rates is less than the official statistics show. For example, police and other officials may regard female offenders as less dangerous than men, and let pass activities for which males would be arrested. Victimization surveys provide a means of checking on such a possibility. In one study in the United States, the National Crime Survey materials of 1976 were compared with FBI statistics to see whether there was any divergence in terms of proportions of women involved in criminal activities (Hindelang et al. 1978). Little variation was found in respect of serious crimes committed by women, the FBI statistics actually showing somewhat *higher* proportions than the survey reports. It has been argued by some observers that the proportion of women involved in 'male' crimes, such as armed robbery, is likely to increase, but there is no clear-cut evidence of such a trend.

The only crime for which the female rate of conviction approximates that of men is shoplifting. Some have argued that this indicates that women will engage in criminal activities where they find themselves in a 'public' context – out shopping – rather than a domestic one. In other words, where the opportunity to commit crime is more or less equal between men and women, they are equally likely to commit offences. However, there have been few investigations comparing female and

Table 8.2 **Female and male offenders found guilty in all courts by type of offence, England and Wales 1993**				
	Females		**Males**	
Indictable offences	**Nos (000)**	**%**	**Nos (000)**	**%**
Violence against the person	3.4	8.7	35.5	91.3
Sexual offences	0.1	2.0	4.3	98.0
Burglary	1.0	2.5	39.2	97.5
Robbery	0.3	5.9	4.8	94.1
Theft and handling stolen goods	22.1	18.2	99.5	81.8
Fraud and forgery	3.9	22.3	13.6	77.7
Criminal damage	0.8	8.5	8.6	91.5
Drug offences	2.0	9.1	19.9	90.9
Other (excluding motoring)	3.6	9.5	34.2	90.5
Motoring	0.5	4.6	10.3	95.4
Total	**37.7**	**12.3**	**269.9**	**87.7**

Source: Home Office, 1993. From *Sociology Review,* September 1995 (Philip Allan Publishers), p. 4.

male rates of shoplifting, and this conclusion at the moment has to remain somewhat speculative (Buckle and Farrington 1984).

The girls in the gang

There has been little work on female members of youth gangs, or on female gangs where these exist. Numerous accounts of male street-corner groups and male gangs have been written, but in these studies women appear only fleetingly. Anne Campbell, however, has studied girls in New York street gangs (Campbell 1986a). She selected three gangs for intensive study: one was ethnically mixed, one Puerto Rican, the other black. The members' ages ranged from fifteen to thirty. Campbell spent six months living with each gang, focusing especially on the gang leaders.

Connie was the leader of the Sandman Ladies, a female group associated with the Sandman Bikers, a gang headed by her husband. She was thirty at the time of the research, and led a mixed Hispanic and black gang in Harlem, New York. The major source of income of the Sandman Bikers was drug-dealing. The group was involved in a long-standing feud with the Chosen Ones, a female gang from uptown Manhattan. Those who joined the Sandman Ladies had to prove their fighting capabilities; entry was decided by Connie, who made an initial judgement about whether a girl could 'hang around' for a trial period, and whether she later got her 'patches' (insignia). Connie always carried a flick-knife, and also possessed a gun. She said that when she fought, it was to kill. Fighting involving physical brawls was just as constant a preoccupation of the female as of the male group.

Weeza and the Sex Girls were a Hispanic gang, with a male and a female section. Weeza could not read or write, and was unsure of her true age – which was probably twenty-six. At the gang's height, there were more than fifty female members. The women cultivated a reputation for physical toughness; fighting and beatings were commonplace. The male members of the gang admired the women for this, while still encouraging traditional roles in other respects, such as caring for children, cooking and sewing.

The third group studied were the Five Percent Nation, which was a black religious organization. Members believed that 10 per cent of the population exploits 85 per cent of the population, the other 5 per cent being enlightened believers in Islam, who have the duty of educating blacks. The police regarded the Five Percent Nation as a street gang. The individual on whom Campbell concentrated her attention, Sun-Africa, had rejected what she called her 'government name'. As with the other groups, she and other female members frequently engaged in fighting. Group members had been arrested for robbery, possession of dangerous weapons, burglary and car theft.

In another study Campbell interviewed working-class schoolgirls about fighting. She found this to be an activity in which they engaged more often than is commonly believed (Campbell 1986b). Almost all those she contacted admitted to having been involved in a fight; a quarter had been in more than six fights. The majority rejected the statement 'I think fighting is only for boys.'

In the 1990s, girls have started joining America's inner-city gangs in substantial numbers. They find a sense of status through their gang activities and they achieve this through violence. One member of the Brooklyn scar-face gang commented, 'I'd just see something I wanted so bad, I'd just take it, I'd pull a knife, I'd just want things.' A group of girls killed a fifteen-year-old on the New York subway to take her earrings. Names of new all-women gangs include the 6th Street Whores, the Crochet Girls and the Wise Intelligent Sisters. Some gangs of this kind now exist in parts of London, such as Stockwell and Brixton, although as yet they seem both less formalized and less violent (Nicoll 1995).

Prison violence among women

The autobiographical accounts collected by Pat Carlen of women prisoners in British prisons contain numerous episodes of violence, which is portrayed as a constant feature of female prison life (Carlen et al. 1985). Josie O'Dwyer, an inmate of Holloway Prison in London, describes how the 'heavy mob' of female guards specialized in violent retribution towards prisoners they saw as ill behaved. Beatings by the 'heavy mob' and by other prisoners were common:

> One particular officer always steamed in and started poking you in the chest because she wanted you to hit her – that's what she got off on, the struggling and the fighting. They carry you by the 'necklace', the key chains, and you can have three chains round your neck at any one time. You get purple bruises round your neck, a necklace of purple . . . you begin to black out and you think, 'This is it, I'm going to die now' . . . I could have died. But I didn't and I was lucky. I was a survivor. (Carlen et al. 1985, p. 149)

Evaluation

The studies by Campbell and Carlen show that violence is not exclusively a characteristic of male criminality. Women are much less likely than men to participate in violent crime, but are not always inhibited from taking part in violent episodes. Why, then, are female rates of criminality so much lower than those of men?

There is some evidence that female law-breakers are quite often able to escape coming before the courts because they are able to persuade the police or other authorities to see their actions in a particular light. They invoke what has been called the 'gender contract' – the implicit contract between men and women whereby to be a woman is to be erratic and impulsive, on the one hand, and in need of protection on the other. Worrall, for example, describes the case of a woman who killed her sister with a kitchen knife. Instead of being sent to prison, she was put on probation for three years, on condition that she receive therapeutic treatment. The details of what happened in court suggest that the judge considered that being a 'very typical young woman' and being murderously violent were incompatible with one another. Thus she was not considered the responsible author of her crime (Worrall 1990).

Yet differential treatment could hardly account for the vast difference between male and female rates of crime. The reasons are almost certainly the same as those which explain gender differences in other spheres. There are, of course, certain specifically 'female crimes' – most notably, prostitution – for which women are convicted while their male clients are not. 'Male crimes' remain 'male' because of differences in socialization and because men's activities and involvements are still more non-domestic than those of most women. The gender difference in crime used often to be explained by supposedly innate biological or psychological differences – in terms of differential strength, passivity or preoccupation with reproduction. Nowadays 'womanly' qualities are seen as largely socially generated, in common with the traits of 'masculinity'. Many women are socialized to value different qualities in social life (caring for others and the fostering of personal relationships) from those valued by males. Equally important, through the influence of ideology and other factors – such as the idea of the 'nice girl' – women's behaviour is often kept confined and controlled in ways that male activities are not.

Ever since the late nineteenth century criminologists have predicted that gender equalization would reduce or eliminate the differences in criminality between men and women, but as yet these differences remain pronounced. Whether the variations between female and male crime rates will one day disappear we still cannot say with any certainty.

CRIME AND THE 'CRISIS OF MASCULINITY'

Crime, therefore, is gendered. While there are a few girls' gangs, the high levels of crime found in poorer areas of cities are associated particularly with the activities of young men. Why should so many young men in these areas turn to crime? Some answers we have already touched on. Boys are often part of gangs from an early age, a subculture in which some forms of crime are a way of life. And once gang members are labelled as criminals by the authorities, they embark on regular criminal activities. In spite of the existence today of girl gangs, such subcultures are fundamentally masculine and infused with male values of adventure, excitement, and comradeship.

On the basis of an empirical study of the violent behaviour of young men in a number of cities, Beatrix Campbell has suggested that their behaviour is in part a response to a 'crisis of masculinity' in modern societies (Campbell 1993). In the past, young men, even in neighbourhoods where the level of criminality was high, had a clear set of goals to aim for in life: getting a legitimate job and becoming the breadwinner for a wife and family. But such a male role, Campbell argues, is now under strain, particularly for young men in more deprived areas. Where long-term unemployment is the only prospect, aiming to support a family isn't an option. Moreover, women have become more independent than they used to be, and don't need a man to achieve status in the wider society. The result is a spiral of social deterioration of

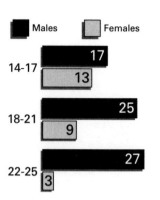

Males ■   Females □

14-17 | Males: 17 | Females: 13

18-21 | Males: 25 | Females: 9

22-25 | Males: 27 | Females: 3

Fig. 8.5 Getting older: percentage of age group involved in property theft in Britain, 1992

Source: Home Office. From the *Guardian*, 19 January 1996, p. 1.

the sort found in deprived inner-city areas today. Campbell's study fits closely with other recent sociological work on poverty, crime, and the city.

The level of crime of young men is closely related to unemployment. Some have suggested that high levels of male unemployment are beginning to create a new category of career criminal. A report published by the Home Office in 1996, *Young People and Crime*, provides research materials relevant to this thesis. The research described in the report involved interviews with 2,500 young people, of both sexes, aged between fourteen and twenty-five.

The researchers didn't depend on police statistics, but asked the interviewees to state in confidence whether they had committed crimes. The results showed that by age twenty-five, fully 30 per cent of young men had engaged in some form of criminal activity – excluding illegal drug use and motoring offences. Criminal activities of young men used to drop off sharply by their early twenties, but the research indicates that this is no longer so. For instance, the proportion of young men aged 22–25 engaging in property theft is higher than for the age group 18–21 (see figure 8.5). The report concludes that the lack of the prospect of a stable job is making it difficult for a large segment of the younger generation to become responsible adults.

The research showed that teenage girls were almost as likely to be involved in property theft as boys; however, the girls' rates fall steeply for those aged twenty-two and above.

VICTIMS OF CRIME

Crimes against women

We now turn to consider some basic problems which very many women face, directly or indirectly. They are all to do with ways in which males use their superior social or physical power against women: domestic violence, sexual harassment and rape. While each of these has been practised by women against men, in the vast majority of cases men are the aggressors and women the victims.

Domestic violence

The home is often idealized as a haven of security and happiness, but **domestic violence** – violence in the context of the home – is part of the experience of many women. This is not a new social ill. Violence towards women was a common aspect of marriage in medieval times and in the early days of industrialization. Until the late nineteenth century, there were no laws in the UK prohibiting a man from physically abusing his wife, short of serious injury or murder. Women now have more legal protection, yet such violence remains widespread.

In spite of an improving legal position, recourse to the law for women subjected to domestic violence is difficult. The attitude of the police, who normally have a policy of non-intervention in 'domestic disputes', is very often unhelpful. When called out in such circumstances, they tend to restrict their intervention to calming down the dispute, rather than pressing charges. Women in relationships involving violence often find it difficult to leave the household for a variety of economic and social reasons, including their responsibility for children. Local government housing departments are sometimes wary of women who come to them with complaints of physical abuse, suspecting these to be exaggerated for the purposes of securing alternative housing rapidly.

Sexual harassment

In the work setting, the rights of women are more easily enforceable, and levels of actual violence against women are low. **Sexual harassment**, nevertheless, is extremely common. Sexual harassment in the workplace may be defined as the use of occupational authority or power to try to enforce sexual demands. This may take blatant forms, as when it is suggested to a female employee that she consent to a sexual encounter or be dismissed. Most kinds of sexual harassment are somewhat more subtle. They involve hints, for example, that the granting of sexual favours would bring other rewards; or that if such favours are not offered, some kind of punishment, such as a blocked promotion, will ensue.

It is obviously not easy to draw a line between harassment and what might be regarded as a legitimate approach from a man to a woman. On the basis of self-reporting, however, it has been estimated that seven out of ten women in the UK are affected by sexual harassment in a prolonged way during the course of their working lives. Sexual harassment may be a single occurrence or a consistent pattern of behaviour (Kelly 1988). Where the second of these is involved, women frequently experience difficulty in maintaining their usual work rate, may take sick leave or quit their jobs altogether.

Rape

The extent of **rape** is very difficult to assess with any accuracy. Only a small proportion of rapes actually come to the attention of the police and are recorded in the statistics. The real figure might be as much as five times as high as the official statistics show – although estimates vary widely. A study of 1,236 women in London revealed that one in six had been raped; one in five of the remainder had fought off an attempted rape. Half the assaults had taken place either in the woman's own house or in that of her assailant (Hall 1985). The majority of women who are raped either wish to put the incident out of their minds, or are unwilling to participate in what can be a humiliating process of medical examination, police interrogation and courtroom cross-examination. The legal process often takes a long time; it may be as much as eighteen months after the incident before a court verdict is reached.

The trial itself can be intimidating. Courtroom procedure is public and the victim must come face to face with the accused. Proof of penetration, the identity of the rapist and the fact that the act occurred without the woman's consent all have to be forthcoming. Corroborative evidence of the identity of an assailant is likely to be hard to obtain if the crime occurred in a dark street or alleyway. A woman who walks alone at night is liable to be seen as encouraging the attentions of men. A woman's capacity to give a definite 'no' in the face of male sexual initiatives is affected by popular stereotypes and images, which may also influence courtroom judgements. If a woman consents to go with a man to his home, or engage in sexual contact with him, this is often seen as agreement to full intercourse or other sexual practices that he may desire. Her right to say 'no' at a later stage is not recognized; in effect, she has to carry the responsibility for the man's failure to control his behaviour. Wherever the rape occurs, the woman may be interrogated about the history of her previous sexual relationships, although a man's sexual history is not deemed relevant in the same way. In fact, prior convictions for rape or assault on the part of an accused cannot be mentioned in rape cases.

According to Sir Matthew Hale, a judge delivering a ruling in 1736, a husband 'cannot be guilty of rape committed by himself upon his lawful wife, for by their mutual matrimonial consent and contract the wife hath given up herself in this kind unto her husband which she cannot retract' (quoted in Hall et al. 1984, p. 20). This formulation remained the law in England and Wales until 1991. In October of that year, the House of Lords dismissed a lorry driver's appeal against conviction for attempting to rape his wife. In giving judgement, Lord Keith said: 'Hale's proposition reflected the state of affairs in these respects at the time it was enunciated . . . In modern times, any reasonable person must regard that conception as quite unacceptable.' Rape within marriage is, however, illegal only in a minority of Western countries, including Denmark, Sweden, Norway and Canada. In the United States, the first case of prosecution for rape in marriage was won against James K. Chretien in 1979. Before the Chretien case, rape within marriage was illegal in five states. Since then, many others have brought in legislation or introduced test cases establishing the crime.

Conventional attitudes as to what is and what is not rape can be very strong. Researchers studying forcible sex within established relationships reported the following case. A man who was drunk started to attempt anal intercourse with his girlfriend. She refused and screamed, at which point he became violent, held her down so that she could not move and forced her to submit. Yet when asked by the researchers whether she had ever been forced to have sex against her will, she said 'No' (Finkelhor and Yllo 1982).

Research has shown many common beliefs about rape to be false. It is not true, for example, that rape cannot happen if the victim resists; that only young, 'attractive' women are likely to be raped; that some women enjoy the experience of being raped; or that most rapists are in some way psychologically disturbed (Hall 1985). Most rapes are not spontaneous but are, at least partly, planned in advance. Rape is clearly related to the association of masculinity with power, dominance and toughness. It is not for the most part the result of overwhelming sexual desire, but of the ties between sexuality and feelings of power and superiority. There seems to be little connection between lust and rape. A substantial proportion of rapists in fact are only able to become sexually aroused once they have terrorized and degraded the victim. The sexual act itself is less significant than the debasement of the woman (Estrich 1987).

Over the last few years, women's groups have pressed for change in both legal and public thinking about rape. They have stressed that rape should not be seen as a sexual offence, but as a type of violent crime. It is not just a physical attack but an assault on an individual's integrity and dignity. As one writer put it, rape is 'an act of aggression in which the victim is denied her self-determination. It is an act of violence which, if not actually followed by beatings or murder, nevertheless carries with it the threat of death' (Griffin 1978, p. 342). The campaign has had some real results in changing legislation, and rape is today generally recognized in law to be a specific type of criminal violence.

There is a sense in which all women are victims of rape. Women who have never been raped often experience anxieties similar to those who have. They may be afraid to go out alone at night, even on crowded streets, and may be almost equally fearful of being on their own in a house or flat. Emphasizing the close connection between rape and orthodox male sexuality, Susan Brownmiller has argued that rape is part of a system of male intimidation that keeps all women in fear. Those who are not raped are affected by the anxieties thus provoked, and by the need to be much more cautious in everyday aspects of life than men have to be (Brownmiller 1975).

Brownmiller's view may sound extreme, but a moment's thought shows how careful a woman has to be if she wishes to minimize the chance of assault. The following is a list of 'dos' and 'don'ts' for women trying to reduce the risk of rape, published by a women's organization in the United States. This list supplies compelling support for the view that rape is a crime that affects the behaviour of all women (Katz and Mazur 1979, p. 307).

1 Make your home as safe as possible; locks, windows, and doors should be in good working condition. If you move to a new apartment or home, change the locks. The Crime Prevention Unit of the local police can give advice on making the residence burglar-proof – and thus rape-proof.
2 If you live alone:
   a) leave lights on to give the impression of more than one occupant;
   b) pretend that there is a male in the house when you answer the door (call out loudly, 'I'll get the door, Bob!');
   c) do not list your first name on the doorbell or in the telephone book; instead, use initials.
3 In general, be aloof to strangers and never open the door to a stranger. Always ask for identification from a delivery or service man (their I.D. card can be slipped beneath the door). If children live in the house, be sure that they do not open the door to a stranger.
4 If you live in an apartment house, do not enter or remain alone in a deserted basement, garage, or laundry room.
5 If you receive an obscene telephone call, say nothing but hang up immediately and report the call to the police.
6 Avoid being alone on the streets or on a university campus late at night. However, if necessary, carry in your hand a 'practical' weapon,

such as a lighted cigarette, a hat pin, a plastic lemon, an umbrella, a pen, a kitchen fork, a key chain, a hair brush or comb (to slash his face), or a police whistle (not tied around the neck, but on a key chain).

7 Do not hitchhike. (Everyone agrees that this is primary!) If absolutely necessary, go in groups and only in heavy traffic.

8 If you drive a car:
   a) be sure your gas tank is never below one-quarter full;
   b) always lock your car when you leave it;
   c) check back seat and floor before getting into a car;
   d) if you have car trouble, do not accept help from a man or group of men; instead, lift the hood, and wait inside the locked car for the police to come.

9 Be wary of picking up strange men in bars, particularly if you have been drinking heavily or using drugs.

10 Do not ride the elevators alone with a man. Either get off immediately or stand by the control panel.

11 On a date, communicate your limits of sexual activity early so that no misunderstandings occur later.

12 Babysitters should check on the family's reputation before taking the job. Parents should be very careful in the selection of a babysitter.

13 If you are attacked, do *not* cry 'rape', cry 'fire!'

Male rape

Male rape (still perpetuated exclusively by men) is more common than was once thought – particularly in closed institutions like prisons. Surveys conducted in male prisons estimate that some 15 per cent of inmates are raped. Rape in prison may continue over a period of years and is often part of a pattern of intimidation and continuous control. 'Few female rape victims must repay their rapist for the violence he inflicted upon them by devoting their existence to serving his every need. But rape victims in the world of the prison must' (Rideau and Wikberg, quoted in M. Walker 1994, p. 13).

Officially, rape doesn't exist in British prisons. A prisoner in Bristol brought a case against the Home Office in 1994, alleging that he was raped by his cell-mate in 1991. According to him, when he told prison officials they displayed no interest and took no action. Survivors, a group concerned with helping male victims of sex abuse, counsel sixty to seventy men a year and say that each year two or three of these have been raped while in prison. A spokesman for the organization claimed that male rape is the most underreported crime in the country.

CRIMES OF THE AFFLUENT AND POWERFUL

Although poorer members of society make up the bulk of the prison population, engaging in criminal activities is by no means confined to them. Many wealthy and powerful people carry out crimes, whose consequences can be much more far-reaching than the often petty crimes of the poor. We shall go on to consider some of these forms of crime.

White-collar crime

The term 'white-collar crime' was first introduced by Edwin Sutherland (1949), and refers to crime carried out by those in the more affluent sectors of society. The term covers many types of criminal activity, including tax frauds, illegal sales practices, securities and land frauds, embezzlement, the manufacture or sale of dangerous products and illegal environmental pollution, as well as straightforward theft. The distribution of white-collar crimes is even harder to measure than that of other types of crime; most such forms of crime do not appear in the official statistics at all. We can distinguish between **white-collar crime** and **crimes of the powerful**. White-collar crime mainly involves the use of a middle-class or professional position to engage in illegal activities. Crimes of the powerful are those in which the authority conferred by a position is used in criminal ways – as when an official accepts a bribe to favour a particular policy.

Although it is regarded by the authorities in a much more tolerant light than crimes of the less privileged, the cost of white-collar crime is enormous. Far more research has been carried out on white-collar crime in the United States than in Britain. In America, it has been calculated that the amount of money involved in white-collar crime (defined as tax fraud, securities frauds involving drugs and medical services, home improvement frauds and car repair frauds) is forty times as great as that in ordinary crimes against property (robberies, burglaries, larceny, forgeries and car thefts) (President's Commission on Organized Crime 1985). Some forms of white-collar crime, moreover, affect much larger

'Kickbacks, embezzlement, price fixing, bribery . . .
this is an extremely high-crime area.'

numbers of people than lower-class criminality. An embezzler might rob thousands – or today, via computer fraud, millions – of people, and tainted foods or drugs sold illegally can affect the health of many, and might lead to fatalities.

Violent aspects of white-collar crime are less visible than in cases of homicide or assault, but are just as real – and may on occasion be much more serious in their consequences. For example, flouting regulations concerning the preparation of new drugs, safety in the workplace, or pollution may cause physical harm or death to large numbers of people. Deaths from hazards at work far outnumber murders, although precise statistics about job accidents are difficult to obtain. Of course, we cannot assume that all, or even the majority, of these deaths and injuries are the result of employer negligence about safety factors for which they are legally liable. Nevertheless, there is some basis for supposing that many are due to the neglect of legally binding safety regulations by employers or managers.

It has been estimated that about 40 per cent of job injuries in the USA each year are the direct result of illegal working conditions, while a further 24 per cent derive from legal but unsafe conditions. No more than a third are due to unsafe acts by workers themselves (Hagen 1988). There are many documented examples of employers knowingly introducing or maintaining hazardous practices even where these are contrary to the law. Some argue that deaths resulting from these circumstances should be called *corporate homicides*, because they effectively involve the illegal (and avoidable) taking of life on the part of business corporations.

Governmental crime

Can government authorities ever be said to engage in crime? If 'crime' is defined more broadly than it was above, to refer to moral wrongdoing which has harmful consequences, the answer is resoundingly clear. States have perpetrated many of the most dreadful crimes in history, including the wiping out of whole peoples, indiscriminate mass bombings, the Nazi holocaust and Stalin's concentration camps. However, even if we limit our definition of crime to the breaking of codified laws, governments not infrequently act in criminal ways. That is to say, they ignore or transgress the very laws their authority is supposed to defend. In British colonial history, this was the case, for example, when legal guarantees offered to African peoples promising protection of their land and way of life were repeatedly flouted.

The police, the government agency established to control crime, are sometimes themselves involved in criminal activities. This involvement does not consist just of isolated acts, but is a widespread feature of police work. Criminal activities of police officers include intimidating, beating up or killing suspects, accepting bribes, helping to organize criminal networks, fabricating or withholding evidence, and keeping some or all of the proceeds when money, drugs or other stolen goods are recovered.

ORGANIZED CRIME

Organized crime refers to forms of activity that have many of the characteristics of orthodox business, but in which the activities engaged in are illegal. Organized crime in America is a massive business, rivalling any of the major orthodox sectors of economic enterprise, such as the car industry. National and local criminal organizations provide illegal goods and services to mass consumers, and some criminal networks also extend internationally. Organized crime embraces illegal gambling, prostitution, large-scale theft and protection rackets, among other activities.

Precise information about the nature of organized crime is obviously difficult to obtain. In romantic portrayals of gangsters, organized crime in the United States is controlled by a secret society of national dimensions, 'the Mafia'. The Mafia as such – like the cowboy – is in some degree a creation of American folklore. There is almost certainly no group of mysterious mobsters of Sicilian origin who sit at the top of a coherent nationwide organization. Yet it does seem that established criminal organizations exist in nearly all major American cities, some of which have connections with one another.

Organized crime in the United States is much more firmly established, pervasive and tenacious than in other industrialized societies. In France, for example, such crime is quite prominent, but is largely limited in its influence to two major cities, Paris and Marseilles. In southern Italy, the region of the stereotypical gangster, criminal networks are very powerful, but they are linked to traditional patterns of family organization and community control within largely poor, rural areas. Organized crime has probably become so significant in American society because of an early association with – and in part a modelling on – the activities of the industrial 'robber barons' of the late nineteenth century. Many of the early industrialists made fortunes by exploiting immigrant labour, largely ignoring legal regulations on working conditions and often using a mixture of corruption and violence to build their industrial empires. Organized crime flourished in the deprived ethnic ghettos (where people were ignorant of their legal and political rights), using similar methods to curtail competition and build networks of corruption.

Illicit gambling, on horse races, lotteries and sporting events, represents the greatest source of income generated by organized crime in the United States. Many Western countries, unlike the United States, have legal off-course betting; in the United Kingdom there are licensed public betting shops. While these do not escape all criminal influence, gambling is not controlled by illegal organizations to anything like the same extent as in the United States.

Although we have little systematic information on organized crime in the United Kingdom, it is known that extensive criminal networks exist in areas of London and other large cities. Some of these have international connections. London in particular is a centre for criminal operations based in the United States and elsewhere.

CRIMINAL NETWORKS: THE MAJOR OPERATORS

TRIADS
Who they are: Chinese gangsters, originally from Hong Kong and South-East Asia. Four main societies: 14K, Wo Shing Wo, Wo On Lock, San Yee On.
Where they are based: London, also in Manchester, Hull, Glasgow.
How they make money: drug trafficking, prostitution, credit card fraud, protection, extortion, illegal gambling and immigration. Also counterfeiting, video piracy, money laundering.
Power rating: expanding their interests in the UK. They use violence and intimidation within Chinese communities to maintain power. There is great difficulty in persuading witnesses to come forward because of brutal reprisals and intimidation.

YARDIES
Who they are: often inaccurate term used to describe drug dealers with links to the Caribbean, in particular Jamaica. No evidence that they are run by bosses; usually a Yardie with a reputation for violence and murder obtains the services of British Afro-Caribbeans to help to run drug rackets. Many simply appropriate the Yardie title to gain respect.
Where they are based: mainly in south London, particularly Brixton, also Manchester, Bristol, Birmingham, Leicester, Nottingham, and Leeds.
How they make money: almost exclusively through drug dealing. Jamaican gangs now control most of the supply of crack cocaine in the UK. Also gun trafficking and protection rackets.
Power rating: Yardies are distinguished by their readiness to use extreme violence and firearms. There are also concerns about their increasing use of witness intimidation. Police believe that with the increase in the crack cocaine market, the Yardies are the group most likely to push the police into arming themselves more widely.

TRADITIONAL FAMILY GANGS
Who they are: often working-class groups of criminals who operate in a specific patch, frequently controlling the distribution of drugs. Families make up the core of gangs, which have a strong regional identity.
Where they are based: every major city has its gangs, but there is evidence of growing links between the different outfits, particularly in the distribution of drugs. Major centres: London, Glasgow, Manchester, Liverpool, Newcastle.
How they make money: mainly enterprise crime with little penetration of the financial world, and in drug trafficking, often through control of pubs and clubs. They have moved from traditional crimes such as armed robbery to counterfeiting and fraud, and are also involved in extortion, protection rackets, and theft of heavy goods vehicles.
Power rating: recent outbreaks of killings between rival drug gangs in Glasgow, Manchester and Liverpool illustrate their willingness to revert to violence. However, they do not have the ambition or power to expand much beyond a single city, though there is some evidence of a loose network.

OTHER ORGANIZED CRIME GROUPS:

Eastern Europeans
Particularly from the former Soviet Union. They use the British banking system to launder money, but are also involved in gun running.

Terrorists
Despite the ceasefire, both Republican and Loyalist terrorist groups are still fund raising in Northern Ireland through armed robberies, extortion, protection rackets, smuggling, illegal gaming, video piracy, and gun running. The groups also control many pubs and clubs. Sections of some Loyalist groups are involved in drug dealing, but the IRA refuses to handle drugs.

Mafia
The National Criminal Intelligence Service has reported an increase in Mafia-related activities in the UK in the past five years, particularly in London. In the UK they have focused on fraud and drug trafficking, but are also involved in gaming.

Bikers
These include the Hell's Angels, who have 12 chapters in the UK – an estimated 250 members, involved in firearms, drug trafficking, car theft and extortion. Several gangs are believed to have set up legitimate businesses with an underground banking system.

West Africans
Particularly Nigerians, who have been involved in housing and benefit frauds, forgery and fraud. Only a small number of 'cells' in operation, comprising about 50 people, mainly in London.

Colombian cartels
Almost exclusively involved in drug trafficking and money laundering.

Turks and Kurds
There is evidence of a small number of clans involved in drug trafficking, extortion and car theft. Political groups, Dev Sol and PKK, have become involved in criminal activities to bankroll terrorism. About 1,000 members here.

Vietnamese
There is some evidence that the Triad gangs are hiring the Vietnamese to carry out violent hits and high-risk jobs.

Asians
A growing number in the Pakistani and Bangladeshi communities, often set up in response to racist attacks. The Home Office has warned that a demographic time bomb is about to explode, with young Asian criminals about to come of age. Favoured crimes: extortion and protection, credit-card fraud, drugs, immigration, smuggling and car theft, mainly in Bradford, London, and Bolton.

Japanese Yakuza
Members of the Japanese organised crime Boryokudan ('group of violence'). Little direct involvement here, but some evidence of laundering money by buying up UK property.

Source: Jason Bennetto, 'Caution: you are about to enter gangland Britain', *Independent*, 21 August 1995, pp. 2–3, (part entry).

Organized crime in Britain is more complex than it was some years ago (see the box). There is no single national organization linking different criminal groups, but such crime has become more sophisticated than ever before. For example, some of the larger criminal organizations launder money through the big clearing banks; using their 'clean' money they then invest in legitimate businesses. Police believe that between £2.5 and £4.0 billion of criminally generated money passes through UK banks each year. Concern about the increasing sophistication of organized crime has prompted the police to compile a national gangland register. Six police forces from different parts of the country, together with customs officers, collaborate to provide details of suspected criminal activities. The register contains the names of some 400 'criminals of major significance'.

British organized crime has its 'families', modelled along the lines of Mafia families in the United States. One of the most powerful recent criminal families has been the Arifs, from Stockwell, in South London. The Arifs were involved in armed robberies and drug smuggling in the 1980s. They also owned a string of pubs, restaurants and clubs, almost certainly bought from the proceeds of their criminal enterprises. Bekir Arif was jailed for five years at the end of the 1980s after being convicted of robbery with violence.

The reign of the Arifs ended in the early 1990s, following a series of successful police operations. In the course of an attempted armed robbery in 1990 one of the gang was shot dead by the police. The head of the family, Dogan Arif, is currently serving a fourteen-year prison sentence for his part in an £8.5 million drug smuggling deal (Bennetto 1995).

Japanese Yakuza gangs and Italian and American Mafia operators have established themselves in Britain. Among the newest arrivals are criminals from the former Soviet Union. Two recent commentators have spoken of the new Russian mafia as 'the world's deadliest crime syndicate' (Elliot and Lin 1995). The Russian criminal networks are deeply involved in money laundering, linking up their activities with Russia's largely unregulated banks. Some think the Russian groups may come to be the world's largest criminal networks. They have their basis in a mafia-riddled Russian state, where underworld 'protection' is now routine for many businesses. The most worrying possibility is that Russia's new mobsters are smuggling nuclear materials on an international scale, materials taken from the Soviet nuclear arsenal.

Despite numerous campaigns by the government and the police, the narcotics trade is one of the most rapidly expanding international criminal industries, having an annual growth rate of more than 10 per cent in the 1980s and early 1990s and an extremely high level of profit. Heroin networks stretch across the Far East, particularly South Asia, and are located also in North Africa, the Middle East and Latin America. Supply lines also pass through Paris and Amsterdam, from where drugs are commonly supplied to Britain.

CRIME, DEVIANCE AND SOCIAL ORDER

It would be a mistake to regard crime and deviance wholly in a negative light. Any society which recognizes that human beings have diverse values and concerns must find space for individuals or groups whose activities do not conform to the norms followed by the majority. People who develop new ideas, in politics, science, art or other fields, are often regarded with suspicion or hostility by those who follow orthodox ways. The political ideals developed in the American revolution, for example – freedom of the individual and equality of opportunity – were fiercely resisted by many people at the time, yet they have now become accepted across the world. To deviate from the dominant norms of a society takes courage and resolution, but is often crucial in securing processes of change which later are seen to be in the general interest.

Is 'harmful deviance' the price a society must pay when it allows considerable leeway for people to engage in non-conformist pursuits? For example, are high rates of criminal violence a cost which is exacted in a society in exchange for the individual liberties its citizens enjoy? Some have certainly suggested as much, arguing that crimes of violence are inevitable in a society where rigid definitions of conformity do not apply. But this view does not hold much water when examined closely. In some societies which recognize a wide range of individual freedoms and tolerate deviant activities (such as Holland), rates of violent crime are low. Conversely, countries where the scope of individual freedom is restricted (like some Latin American societies) may show high levels of violence.

A society that is tolerant towards deviant behaviour need not suffer social disruption. This outcome can probably only be achieved, however, where individual liberties are joined to social justice – in a social order where inequalities are not glaringly large and in which the population as a whole has a chance to lead a full and satisfying life. If freedom is not balanced with equality, and if many people find their lives largely devoid of self-fulfilment, deviant behaviour is likely to be channelled towards socially destructive ends.

SUMMARY

1 Deviant behaviour refers to actions which transgress commonly held norms. What is regarded as deviant can shift from time to time and place to place; 'normal' behaviour in one cultural setting may be labelled 'deviant' in another.

2 Sanctions, formal or informal, are applied by society to reinforce social norms. Laws are norms defined and enforced by governments; crimes are acts which are not permitted by those laws.

3 Biological and psychological theories have been developed claiming to show that crime and other forms of deviance are genetically determined; but these have been largely discredited. Sociologists argue that conformity and deviance are differently defined in dif-

ferent social contexts. Divergences of wealth and power in society strongly influence what opportunities are open to different groups of individuals and what kinds of activities are regarded as criminal. Criminal activities are learned in much the same way as law-abiding ones, and in general are directed towards the same needs and values.

4 Labelling theory (which assumes that labelling someone as deviant will reinforce their deviant behaviour) is important because it starts from the assumption that no act is intrinsically criminal (or normal). However, this theory needs to be supplemented with the enquiry: what caused the behaviour (which has come to be labelled deviant) in the first place?

5 The extent of crime in any society is difficult to assess, as not all crimes are reported. But some societies seem to experience much higher levels of crime than others – as is indicated by the high rates of homicide in the US compared to other Western countries.

6 As 'crime' has varied between different periods and cultures, so have forms of punishment. Prisons have developed partly to protect society and partly with the intention of 'reforming' the criminal. In this they seem to be mostly ineffective. The death penalty has been abolished in most countries.

7 Prisons do not seem to deter crime, and the degree to which they rehabilitate prisoners to face the outside world without relapsing into criminality is dubious. Many alternatives to prison have been suggested, including probation, community service work, fines, repayment to the victim and other measures. Some of these are already in widespread use in certain countries.

8 Rates of criminality are much lower for women than for men, probably because of general socialization differences between men and women, plus the greater involvement of men in non-domestic spheres.

9 Rape is almost certainly much more common than the official statistics reveal. There is a sense in which all women are victims of rape, since they have to take special precautions for their protection and live with the fear of rape.

10 White-collar crime and crimes of the powerful refer to crimes carried out by those in the more affluent sectors of society. Organized crime refers to institutionalized forms of criminal activity, in which many of the characteristics of orthodox organizations appear, but the activities engaged in are systematically illegal.

FURTHER READING

Patricia Adler and **Peter Adler** (eds), *Constructions of Deviance: Social Power, Context, and Interaction* (Belmont, Calif.: Wadsworth, 1994). An analysis of deviant behaviour from the interactionist perspective.

Stanley Cohen and **Laurie Taylor**, *Escape Attempts* (London: Routledge, 1992). A revised edition of a study which examines the different ways in which individuals seek to escape from the habits and routines of ordinary life.

Janet Foster, *Villains: Crime and Community in the Inner City* (London: Routledge, 1990). An intriguing account of the development of criminal subcultures in an area of central London.

Stephen Hester and **Peter Eglin**, *A Sociology of Crime* (London: Macmillan, 1992). A useful general textbook on criminology.

M. Maguire et al. (eds), *The Oxford Handbook of Criminology* (Oxford: Clarendon Press, 1994).

Stephen Pilling, *Rehabilitation and Community Care* (London: Routledge, 1991). Analyses the implications of hospital closure and argues for a programme of careful planning for community services.

Robert Reiner, *The Politics of the Police* (London: Harvester, 1992). A new edition of an established text dealing with the history and sociology of the police force in Britain.

John Wells, *Crime and Unemployment* (London: Employment Policy Institute, 1995). A useful discussion of the effects of unemployment on patterns of criminal behaviour.

Ann Worrall, *Offending Women* (London: Routledge, 1990). An interesting and important analysis of gender and the law.

IMPORTANT TERMS

- *deviant subculture*
- *sanction*
- *law*
- *psychopath*
- *differential association*
- *gang*
- *labelling theory*
- *secondary deviance*
- *recidivism*
- *domestic violence*
- *sexual harassment*
- *rape*
- *white-collar crime*
- *crimes of the powerful*
- *organized crime*

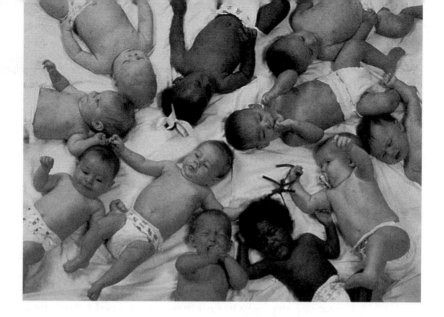

9

ETHNICITY AND RACE

➡

BASIC CONCEPTS

• *ethnicity* • *racism* • *prejudice* • *discrimination*

In many parts of the world today, struggles between different cultural and racial groups are being played out, some leading to intense bitterness and appalling bloodshed. Bloody wars having such origins have been fought out in, among other areas, Bosnia Herzegovina (in what used to be Yugoslavia), Ethiopia (in Africa) and Georgia (part of the former Soviet Union).

At the same time, floods of refugees and immigrants move restlessly across different regions of the globe, either trying to escape from such conflicts or fleeing poverty in search of a better life. Often they reach a new country only to find they are resented by people who some generations ago were immigrants themselves.

Such is the case, for example, for many people coming to the United States. The US is culturally the most diverse society in the world. It is a society of immigrants: the original population, the American Indians, make up less than 1 per cent of the US population as a whole. Yet Britain and Europe are rapidly becoming almost as culturally mixed as the US. It was the Europeans, of course, who were the first immigrants to North America, and who until fairly recently dominated immigration into what became the United States and Canada. Today, there are new waves of immigration, legal and illegal, into Western Europe itself. Immigrants are coming from Eastern Europe, Africa, from the Near East and from Asia. Many of the dilemmas, conflicts and clashes – as well as the benefits and opportunities – which the US has faced as a result of immigration are now being experienced in Europe.

Europe is becoming more *ethnically heterogeneous* than ever before.

ETHNICITY

ETHNICITY refers to the cultural practices and outlooks of a given community of people that set them apart from others. Members of ethnic groups see themselves as culturally distinct from other groups in a society, and are seen by those other groups to be so in return. Different characteristics may serve to distinguish ethnic groups from one another, but the most usual are language, history or ancestry (real or imagined), religion and styles of dress or adornment. Ethnic differences are *wholly learned*, a point that seems self-evident until we remember how often some groups have been regarded as 'born to rule' or 'shiftless', 'unintelligent', and so forth. (For the diversity of ethnic groups in Great Britain, see table 9.1.)

In this chapter, we will investigate why ethnic divisions so frequently produce social conflicts. The idea of 'race' has had an enormous influence on such conflicts, and we shall consider its nature and origins. We

Table 9.1 **Ethnic group composition of the population in Great Britain in 1992 (per cent)**

Ethnic group	Great Britain	England and Wales	England	Wales	Scotland
White	94.5	94.1	93.8	98.5	98.7
Ethnic minorities	5.5	5.9	6.2	1.5	1.3
Black	1.6	1.8	1.9	0.3	0.1
Black-Caribbean	0.9	1.0	1.1	0.1	0.0
Black-African	0.4	0.4	0.4	0.1	0.1
Black-Other	0.3	0.4	0.4	0.1	0.1
South Asian	2.7	2.9	3.0	0.6	0.6
Indian	1.5	1.7	1.8	0.2	0.2
Pakistani	0.9	0.9	1.0	0.2	0.4
Bangladeshi	0.3	0.3	0.3	0.1	0.0
Chinese and others	1.2	1.2	1.3	0.6	0.5
Chinese	0.3	0.3	0.3	0.2	0.2
Other-Asian	0.4	0.4	0.4	0.1	0.1
Other-Other	0.5	0.6	0.6	0.3	0.2
Total population (000s)	54,888.9	49,890.3	47,055.2	2,835.1	4,998.6

Source: D. Owen, *Ethnic Minorities in Britain: Settlement Patterns*, 1992, p. 2. Census data is Crown Copyright.

then analyse why some groups come to despise or hate others so much, concentrating on forms of racial or ethnic prejudice. In subsequent sections of the chapter, we study ethnic relations in different national contexts, giving particular attention to the US, Britain and Continental Europe.

Minority groups

The notion of **minority groups** (or **ethnic minorities**) is widely used in sociology and is more than a merely numerical distinction. There are many minorities in a statistical sense, such as people over six feet tall or weighing more than 250 pounds, but these are not minorities according to the sociological concept. In sociology, members of a minority group are *disadvantaged* as compared with the majority population and have some sense of *group solidarity*, of belonging together. The experience of being the subject of prejudice and discrimination usually heightens feelings of common loyalty and interests.

Members of minority groups often tend to see themselves as a people apart from the majority. Minority groups are usually physically and socially isolated from the larger community. They tend to be concentrated in certain neighbourhoods, cities or regions of a country. There is little intermarriage between those in the majority and members of the minority group, or between minority groups. People within the minority sometimes actively promote endogamy (marriage within the group) in order to keep alive their cultural distinctiveness.

Many minorities are both ethnically and physically distinct from the rest of the population. This is the case with West Indians and Asians in Britain, for example, and with African Americans, Chinese and other groups in the United States. Physical differences such as skin colour are commonly called racial. Ethnic distinctions are rarely neutral, but are commonly associated with inequalities of wealth and power, as well as with antagonisms between groups. Among ethnic-group tensions, those based on race are particularly prevalent.

Race and biology

Many people today believe, mistakenly, that humans can be readily separated into biologically different races. This is not surprising considering the numerous attempts by scholars to establish racial categorizations of the peoples of the world. Some authors have distinguished four or five major races, while others have recognized as many as three dozen. But too many exceptions to these classifications have been found to make any of them workable.

A commonly used type, for example, Negroid, is supposed to be composed of people with dark skin, tightly curled black hair, and certain other physical characteristics. Yet the original inhabitants of Australia, the Aboriginals, possess dark skin but wavy, and sometimes blond, hair. A host of other examples can be found that defy any simple classification. There are no clear-cut 'races', only a range of physical variations in human beings. Differences in physical type between groups of human beings arise from population inbreeding, which varies according to the degree of contact between different social or cultural groups. Human population groups are a continuum. The genetic diversity *within* populations that share visible physical traits is as great as the diversity between them. In virtue of these facts, many biologists, anthropologists and sociologists believe the concept of race should be dropped altogether.

There are clear physical differences between human beings, and some of these differences are inherited. But the question of why some differences and not others become matters for social discrimination and prejudice has nothing to do with biology. Racial differences, therefore, should be understood as *physical variations singled out by the members of a community or society as socially significant*. Differences in skin colour, for example, are treated as significant, whereas differences in colour of hair are not. RACISM is prejudice based on socially significant physical distinctions. A racist is someone who believes that some individuals are superior or inferior to others as a result of these racial differences.

PREJUDICE AND DISCRIMINATION

The concept of race is modern, but prejudice and discrimination have been widespread in human history, and we must first clearly distinguish between them. PREJUDICE refers to *opinions or attitudes* held by members of one group towards another. A prejudiced person's preconceived views are often based on hearsay rather than on direct evidence, and are resistant to change even in the face of new information. People may harbour favourable prejudices about groups with which they identify and negative prejudices against others. Someone who is prejudiced against a particular group will refuse to give it a fair hearing.

DISCRIMINATION refers to _actual behaviour_ towards the other group. It can be seen in activities that disqualify members of one group from opportunities open to others, as when a black Briton is refused a job made available to a white person. Although prejudice is often the basis of discrimination, the two may exist separately. People may have prejudiced attitudes that they do not act on. Equally important, discrimination does not necessarily derive directly from prejudice. For example, white house-buyers might steer away from purchasing properties in predominantly black neighbourhoods not because of attitudes of hostility they might feel towards those who live there, but because of worries about declining property values. Prejudiced attitudes in this case influence discrimination, but in an indirect fashion.

Psychological interpretations

Psychological theories can help us understand the nature of prejudiced attitudes and also why ethnic differences matter so much to people. Two types of psychological approach are important. One employs the concept of stereotypical thinking to analyse prejudice. The other says that there is a particular type of person who is most prone to hold prejudiced attitudes against minority groups.

Stereotypes and scapegoats

Prejudice operates mainly through the use of **stereotypical thinking**, which means thinking in terms of fixed and inflexible categories. Stereotyping is often closely linked to the psychological mechanism of **displacement**, in which feelings of hostility or anger are directed against objects that are not the real origin of those feelings. People vent their antagonism against 'scapegoats', people blamed for things that are not their fault. The term 'scapegoat' originated with the ancient Hebrews, who each year ritually loaded all their sins onto a goat, which was then chased into the wilderness. **Scapegoating** is common when two deprived ethnic groups come into competition with one another for economic rewards. People who direct racial attacks against blacks, for example, are often in an economic position similar to theirs. They blame blacks for grievances whose real causes lie elsewhere.

Scapegoating is normally directed against groups that are distinctive and relatively powerless, because they make an easy target. Protestants, Catholics, Jews, Italians, black Africans and others have played the unwilling role of scapegoat at various times throughout Western history.

Scapegoating frequently involves **projection**, the unconscious attribution to others of one's own desires or characteristics. Sexuality may be involved. Research has consistently demonstrated that when the members of a dominant group practise violence against a minority and exploit it sexually, they are likely to believe that the minority group itself displays these traits of sexual violence. For instance, the bizarre ideas held by white men in the old American South about the lustful nature of African-American men probably originated in their own frustrations, since sexual access to white women was limited by the formal nature of courtship. Similarly, in South Africa the belief that black males are exceptionally potent sexually and that black women are voluptuous used to be widespread among whites. Black males are thought to be highly dangerous sexually to white women – while in fact, virtually all sexual contact was initiated by white men towards black women.

The authoritarian personality

It is possible that some types of people, as result of early socialization, are particularly prone to stereotypical thinking and projection. A famous piece of research carried out by Theodor Adorno and his associates in the 1940s diagnosed a character type they termed the **authoritarian personality** (Adorno et al. 1950). The researchers developed several measurement scales for assessing levels of prejudice. On one scale, for instance, people were asked to agree or disagree with a series of statements expressing strongly anti-Semitic views. Those who were diagnosed as prejudiced against Jews also tended to express negative attitudes towards other minorities. People with an authoritarian personality, the investigators concluded, tend to be rigidly conformist, submissive to their superiors and dismissive towards inferiors. Such people are also highly intolerant in their religious and sexual attitudes.

The characteristics of an authoritarian personality, it was suggested by the researchers, result from a pattern of upbringing in which parents are unable to express direct love for their children and are aloof and disciplinarian. As adults, these individuals suffer from anxieties that can be controlled only by the adoption of a rigid outlook. They are unable to cope with ambiguous situations, and they ignore inconsistencies, tending to think in a stereotypical way.

Adorno's research was subjected to a barrage of criticism. Some have doubted the value of the measurement scales used. Others have argued that authoritarianism is not a characteristic of personality, but reflects the values and norms of particular subcultures within the wider society. The investigation may be more valuable as a contribution to understanding authoritarian patterns of thought in general, rather than distinguishing a particular personality type. Yet there are clear similarities between these findings and other research on prejudice. For example, a classic study by Eugene Hartley investigated attitudes towards thirty-five ethnic minorities and also found that those prejudiced against one ethnic group were likely to express negative feelings against others. Jews and African Americans were disliked just as much as Wallonians, Pireneans and Danireans (Hartley 1946). The three latter groups in fact are non-existent; the names were coined by Hartley in order to see whether people would be prejudiced against groups they could not have even heard of.

Sociological interpretations

The psychological mechanisms of stereotypical thinking, displacement and projection are found among members of all societies, and help to explain why ethnic antagonism is such a common element in different cultures. However, they tell us little about the social processes involved in discrimination. To study such processes, we must call on three sociological ideas.

Ethnocentrism, group closure and allocation of resources

Sociological concepts relevant to ethnic conflicts on a general level are those of *ethnocentrism, ethnic group closure* and *resource allocation*. Ethnocentrism – a suspicion of outsiders combined with a tendency to evaluate the culture of others in terms of one's own culture – is a concept we have encountered previously (chapter 2). Virtually all cultures have been ethnocentric to some degree, and it is easy to see how ethnocentrism combines with stereotypical thought. Outsiders are thought of as aliens, barbarians or morally and mentally inferior. This was how most civilizations viewed the members of smaller cultures, for example, and the attitude has fuelled innumerable ethnic clashes in history.

Ethnocentrism and **group closure** frequently go together. 'Closure' refers to the process whereby groups maintain boundaries separating themselves from others. These boundaries are formed by means of exclusion devices, which sharpen the divisions between one ethnic group and another. Such devices include limiting or prohibiting intermarriage between the groups, restrictions on social contact or economic relationships like trading, and the physical separation of groups (as in the case of ethnic ghettos). African Americans in the US have experienced all three exclusion devices: racial intermarriage has been illegal in some states, economic and social segregation was enforced by law in the South, and segregated black ghettos still exist in most major cities.

Sometimes groups of equal power mutually enforce lines of closure: their members keep separate from each other, but neither group dominates the other. More commonly, however, one ethnic group occupies a position of power over another. In these circumstances, group closure coincides with **resource allocation**, instituting inequalities in the distribution of wealth and material goods.

Some of the fiercest conflicts between ethnic groups centre on the lines of closure between them precisely because these lines signal inequalities in wealth, power or social standing. The concept of ethnic group closure helps us understand both the dramatic and the more insidious differences that separate communities of people from one another – not just why the members of some groups get shot, lynched, beaten up or harassed, but also why they don't get good jobs, a good education or a desirable place to live. Wealth, power and social status are scarce resources – some groups have more of them than others. To hold on to their distinctive positions, privileged groups sometimes undertake extreme acts of violence against others. Similarly, members of underprivileged groups may also turn to violence as a means of trying to improve their own situation.

ETHNIC ANTAGONISM: A HISTORICAL PERSPECTIVE

To fully analyse ethnic relations and **ethnic antagonism** in current times, we must take a historical perspective. It is impossible to understand the divisions today without giving prime place to the impact of the expansion of Western colonialism on the rest of the world.

From the fifteenth century onward, Europeans began to venture into previously uncharted seas and unexplored land masses, pursuing the aims of exploration and trade but also conquering and subduing native peoples. They poured out by the millions from Europe to settle in these new areas. In the shape of the slave trade, they also occasioned a large-scale movement of people from Africa to the Americas (see figure 9.1). The following are the extraordinary shifts in population that have occurred over the past 350 years or so:

● *Europe to North America* From the seventeenth century to the present, some 45 million people have emigrated from Europe to what is now the United States and Canada. About 150 million in North America today can trace their ancestry to this migration.

● *Europe to Central and South America* About 20 million people from Europe, mostly from Spain, Portugal and Italy, migrated to Central and South America. Some 50 million in these areas today are of European ancestry.

● *Europe to Africa and Australasia* Approximately 17 million people in these continents are of European ancestry. In Africa, the majority emigrated to the state of South Africa, which was colonized mainly by the British and Dutch.

● *Africa to the Americas* Starting in the sixteenth century, about 15 million blacks were unwillingly transported to the North and South American continents. Almost 1 million arrived in the sixteenth century; some 1.3 million in the seventeenth century; 6 million in the eighteenth century; and 2 million in the nineteenth century. Black Africans were brought to the Americas in chains to serve as slaves; families and whole communities were brutally destroyed in the process.

These population flows formed the basis of the current ethnic composition of the United States, Canada, the countries of Central and South America, South Africa, Australia and New Zealand. In all of these societies, the indigenous populations were subjected to European rule and, in North America and Australasia, became tiny ethnic minorities. Since the Europeans were from diverse backgrounds, they implanted numerous ethnic divisions in their new homelands. At the height of the colonial era, in the nineteenth and early twentieth centuries, Europeans also ruled over native populations in many other regions: India, Burma, Malaya and parts of the Middle East.

For most of the period of European expansion, ethnocentric attitudes were rife among the colonists, who believed that they were on a civilizing mission to the rest of the world. Even the more liberal Europeans

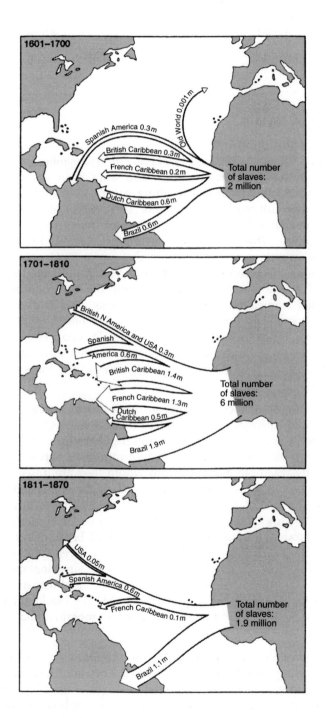

Fig. 9.1 The Atlantic slave trade, 1601–1870. By far the largest single destination was Brazil, with 3.6 million people being taken there over less than 300 years

Source: Ben Crow and Mary Thorpe, *Survival and Change in the Third World* (The Open University 1988), p. 15.

thought themselves superior to the indigenous peoples they encountered. The fact that many of those peoples thought precisely the same about the colonists is not so relevant, since the Europeans possessed the power to make their outlook count. The early period of colonialism coincided with the rise of racism, and ever since then racial divisions and conflicts have tended to occupy a prime place in ethnic conflicts as a whole. In particular, racist views separating whites from blacks became central to European attitudes.

The rise of racism

Why has racism flourished? There are several reasons. One is that an opposition between white and black, as cultural symbols, was deeply rooted in European culture. White had long been associated with purity, black with evil (there is nothing natural about this symbolism; in some other cultures, it is reversed). The symbol of blackness held negative meanings *before* the West came into extensive contact with black peoples. These symbolic meanings tended to infuse the Europeans' reactions to blacks when they were first encountered on African shores. The sense that there was a radical difference between black and white peoples combined with the 'heathenism' of the Africans led many Europeans to regard blacks with disdain and fear. As a seventeenth-century observer expressed it, blacks 'in colour as in condition are little other than Devils incarnate' (Jordan 1968). Although the more extreme expressions of such attitudes have disappeared today, it is difficult not to believe that elements of this black–white cultural symbolism remain widespread.

A second important factor leading to modern racism was simply the invention and diffusion of the concept of **race** itself. Quasi-racist attitudes have been known to exist for hundreds of years. In China in AD 300, for example, we find recorded descriptions of barbarian peoples 'who greatly resemble monkeys from whom they are descended'. But the notion of race as a cluster of inherited characteristics comes from European thought of the eighteenth and nineteenth centuries. Count Joseph Arthur de Gobineau (1816–1882), who is sometimes called the father of modern racism, proposed ideas that became influential in many circles. According to de Gobineau, three races exist: the white, black and yellow. The white race possesses superior intelligence, morality and will-power, and these inherited qualities underlie the spread of Western influence across the world. The blacks are the least capable, marked by an animal nature, a lack of morality, and emotional instability.

The ideas of de Gobineau and others who proposed similar views were presented as supposedly scientific theories. They later influenced Adolf Hitler, who transformed them into the ideology of the Nazi party. The notion of the superiority of the white race, although completely without value factually, remains a key element of white racism. It is an explicit element, for example, in the ideology of the Ku Klux Klan, and it was the basis of *apartheid* (separate racial development) in South Africa – which we shall consider below.

A third reason for the rise of modern racism lies in the exploitative relations that Europeans established with non-white peoples. The slave trade could not have been carried on had it not been widely believed by Europeans that blacks belonged to an inferior, even subhuman, race. Racism helped justify colonial rule over non-white peoples and denied them the rights of political participation that were being won by whites in their European homelands.

The relations between whites and non-whites varied according to different patterns of colonial settlement, and were also influenced by cultural differences between the Europeans themselves. To demonstrate these points, we now turn to look at race relations in Brazil, South Africa and the US, before analysing racial and ethnic divisions in the UK at greater length.

ETHNIC RELATIONS IN HISTORICAL PERSPECTIVE: SOME EXAMPLES

Comparing ethnic relations in other societies with those in Britain illustrates the ways in which prejudice and discrimination vary with different patterns of historical development. Brazil is sometimes quoted as an example of a society free from ethnic prejudice between black and white, although, as we shall see, this is not wholly accurate. South Africa, by contrast, is a country where prejudice and discrimination developed in an extreme form, and segregation of black and white became institutionalized, prior to the recent changes which have introduced majority rule. For the US we begin with the campaign for black civil rights.

Ethnic relations in Brazil

A little under four million Africans were transported to Brazil before the end of the slave trade in the middle of the nineteenth century. In the United States blacks coming from different African cultures were usually dispersed, but in Brazil people shipped from the same areas were normally kept together. Hence they were able to retain more of their original culture than was possible for those in the United States. Slaves in Brazil were allowed to marry even if their masters disapproved, as long as they continued serving them as before, and once married, a couple could not be sold as individual slaves. Sexual contact between white men and slave women was frequent, and the children of such unions were often freed, sometimes being fully accepted as part of the white family. Slavery was finally abolished in 1888, but well before then whites had become used to the existence of free blacks (Swartz, 1985).

After the ending of slavery, many black Brazilians moved into the towns and cities. There most of them lived (and live today) in considerable poverty, yet they were not debarred from membership of labour unions, and a proportion have risen to positions of wealth and power. There is a much-quoted Brazilian saying that 'A rich black man is a white and a poor white man is a black.' The phrase neatly catches the relatively relaxed views of racial differences, as well as the fact that 'whiteness' is still clearly identified with superiority. Whites continue to dominate the higher positions in all sectors of the society.

For a long while Brazilians had interpreted their system of race relations in a charitable light, comparing it positively to the more segregated patterns of the USA, but in the 1960s and 1970s, as moves to secure greater civil rights for American blacks gathered strength, such comparisons became less favourable to Brazil. In the early 1960s, the Brazilian Congress passed a law forbidding discrimination in public places after a touring American black, Katherine Dunham, complained of being refused accommodation in a São Paulo hotel. The law was largely a symbolic gesture, however, with no effort being made by the government to investigate the extent of possible discrimination.

Most observers agree that such discrimination has been fairly rare in Brazil, but there have been few government programmes designed to improve the social and economic opportunities of non-whites. The Brazilian belief in 'whitening' stands in some contrast to the continued concentration of blacks in the poorest sections of the society. Brazil has none the less avoided the recurrent lynchings and riots which have punctuated the history of the United States, and has escaped most of the more extreme forms of anti-black prejudice.

The social development of South Africa

In South Africa, the first European settlers were Dutch. Finding the local population resistant to working in European enterprises, they began importing large numbers of slaves from elsewhere in Africa and from the Dutch East Indies. The British later established a dominant position in South Africa, putting an end to slavery in the 1830s. Divisions between whites and indigenous Africans were not at first as absolute as they later became. When slavery was abolished, new taxes were introduced for blacks, which effectively forced many of them to contract themselves to European employers, and young African men had to look for employment away from home in order to pay the tax. A system of 'migrant labour' developed which set the pattern for the subsequent evolution of the South African economy. Many Africans went to work in gold or diamond mines, living in special camps well away from the neighbourhoods where Europeans lived. Gradually a segregated system grew up which was later formalized in law.

Under the **apartheid** system, introduced after World War Two, the population of South Africa was classified into four 'registration groups' – the 4.5 million white descendants of European immigrants; the 2.5 million so-called 'coloured people', whose descent is traced from members of more than one 'race'; the 1 million people of Asian descent; and the 23 million black Africans. Pierre van den Berghe distinguished three main levels of segregation in South African society during the years of apartheid (van den Berghe 1970).

1 **Microsegregation** – the segregation of public places (such as used also to be the case in the American South). Washrooms, waiting

rooms, railway carriages and other public areas have separate facilities for whites and non-whites.
2 Mezzosegregation – the segregation of whites and non-whites in
terms of the neighbourhoods where they live in urban areas. Blacks
are compelled to live in specially designated zones.
3 Macrosegregation – the segregation of whole peoples in distinct
territories set up as *native reserves*.

The South African economy was unable to function without the labour
power of millions of non-whites, living in or near the cities. Originally
there used to be some ethnically mixed neighbourhoods in the major
urban areas, but more and more of the blacks were placed in 'model
townships', situated a number of miles away from the white areas. In
addition, millions of people were herded into so-called *homelands* well
away from the cities. These regions were organized into partially
autonomous states subject to the overall control of the white central
government. Under apartheid, non-whites had no vote, and so no representation, in the central government.

The homelands were supposed to be separate territories where the
black majority could exercise the political rights denied them in white
South Africa. Under the provisions of the 1970 Homelands Citizenship
Act, those in a homeland were automatically deprived of their South
African citizenship on the day it became 'independent'. So-called *frontier commuters* lived with their families in the homelands and travelled
daily across the 'national borders' into white South Africa.

Apartheid was universally condemned by the international community, and opposed by many from within the society. For a lengthy period
South Africa was subject to economic sanctions designed to put pressure on the country to discontinue the system; in addition, South Africa
was excluded from a range of international sporting events. The sanctions almost certainly had some influence, as did internal protest, but
one of the major reasons why apartheid began to disintegrate in the
1980s was that many black people deliberately acted counter to it – in
spite of punishments meted out by the authorities. For instance, large
numbers of people migrated to urban areas in search of work in spite of
laws that debarred them from doing so.

In 1990, President de Klerk lifted the ban on the African National
Congress (ANC), the Communist Party and a range of other opposi-
tional groups which had previously been prohibited, driven underground or forced into exile. Nelson Mandela, the ANC leader, who had
been in prison since 1962, was freed. A new constitution was drawn up
which, for the first time, gave every person the vote. A referendum was
held in March 1992 among white voters, and a large majority was in
favour of pressing ahead with such reform.

South Africa has today become a functioning democracy, with Nelson
Mandela as its elected president. Apartheid has quickly become a thing
of the past. The country for the moment seems reasonably harmonious.
Yet there is a great deal of violent crime in the townships, as well as in
some of the prosperous white neighbourhoods, and it will be some

while before anyone can be sure that the country will not again experience violent ethnic conflicts.

Since the ending of apartheid there has been a surge of investment in South Africa. Many large South African companies have also begun to invest in other parts of Africa. For example, in 1994–5 South African Breweries bought large holdings in the state-run brewing companies of Tanzania and Zambia. It already has outlets in Botswana, Lesotho and Swaziland. A subsidiary of Pepkor, the biggest retailer in South Africa, opened three stores in Zambia in 1995 and plans four more for the future.

Such an expansion of South African capitalism is not without its problems. The head of a retail chain in Zimbabwe was cheered at a conference in that country when she accused South Africans of trying to 'gobble up Africa'. Farmers in Mozambique have staged demonstrations aimed at preventing the government from selling arable land to South African investors. Such tensions are hardly surprising, given the fact that South African governments during the period of apartheid backed military intervention in Mozambique and other surrounding countries. Racial and ethnic hostilities still simmer in these encounters, given that virtually all South African business leaders are white.

In his book about the transition from minority government in South Africa, *The Bondage of Fear* (1995), Fergal Keane notes that

> it remains a country with deep and dangerous fault lines. The years of minority rule might have created a solid infrastructure and the most developed economy in Africa, but they have also been enormously wasteful in terms of misdirected spending . . . Six million people unemployed; ten million with no access to running water and twenty-three million without electricity; fewer than 50 per cent of black children under the age of fourteen attending school and nine million destitute. (p. 238)

Black civil rights in the United States

The abolition of slavery and early developments

Slavery was ended in North America as a result of the Civil War between the northern and southern states. The emancipation proclamation was in fact signed in 1863, a year before the war ended. The end of slavery, however, did not signal a dramatic advance in the fortunes of blacks, most of whom remained in circumstances of dire poverty. A series of 'Jim Crow' laws passed in the South between 1890 and 1912 banned blacks from 'white' railway carriages, public toilets and cafés. Such segregation was officially recognized by a Supreme Court decision in 1896, which declared 'separate but equal' facilities constitutional. The activities of the Ku Klux Klan, a violent secret society, were directed to ensuring that segregation was maintained.

Struggles by minority groups to achieve equal rights and opportunities, from the revolution onwards, have been important in American history. Most minorities have been successful in achieving access to political influence and economic rewards, and in pressing claims to equal status with the majority, but blacks were largely excluded from such processes of self-advancement until the early 1940s. The National Association for the Advancement of Colored People (NAACP) and the National Urban League were founded in 1909 and 1910 respectively. Both fought for black civil rights, but their struggle began to have some real effect only during and after World War Two.

Before the United States entered the war, the leaders of the NAACP and the Urban League met with President Franklin D. Roosevelt, petitioning for the desegregation of the armed forces. Not only was this refused, but Roosevelt made a public statement to the effect that the civil rights leaders had agreed at the meeting to the continuation of segregation. Angry at this apparent deception, a black union leader who had attended the meeting, A. Philip Randolph, called for a march of a hundred thousand blacks as a protest in Washington. A few days before the march was due to take place, Roosevelt signed an order forbidding discrimination in employment on the grounds of ethnic differences and pledging action on the issue of segregation in the armed forces.

Two years later, the newly established Congress of Racial Equality (CORE) began challenging segregation in restaurants, swimming pools and other public areas in Chicago. Although not a great deal was gained, and whites reacted fiercely, this marked the beginning of militant action on behalf of black civil rights – which fifteen years later became a mass movement.

Shortly after World War Two, the NAACP instituted a campaign against segregated public education, which came to a head when the organization sued five school boards, challenging the concept of separate and equal schooling which then held sway. In 1954 the Supreme Court unanimously decided that 'separate educational facilities are inherently unequal'. This decision became the platform for struggles for civil rights for the next two decades. When the Supreme Court decision was first reached, several state and local governments made efforts to limit its effects. School integration proceeding under federal orders was violently resisted by the Ku Klux Klan, 'White Citizens' Councils' and local vigilante groups. Even as late as 1960, well under 1 per cent of Southern black students attended desegregated schools.

The very strength of the resistance from recalcitrant whites served to persuade black leaders that mass militancy was necessary to give civil rights any real substance. In 1956 a black woman called Rosa Parks was arrested in Montgomery, Alabama, for declining to give up her seat on a bus to a white man. As a result almost everyone among the black population of the town, led by a Baptist minister, Dr Martin Luther King Jr, boycotted the transportation system for 381 days. Eventually the city was forced to abolish segregation in that transport system.

Further boycotts and sit-ins followed, with the object of desegregating other public facilities. The marches and demonstrations began to achieve a mass following from blacks and white sympathizers. King planned campaigns of active but non-violent resistance to discrimination, but responses to the movement were far from non-violent.

Governor Faubus of Arkansas called out state troopers to stop black students entering the Central High School in Little Rock. In Birmingham, Alabama, Sheriff 'Bull' Connor ordered the police to disperse protesters with fire hoses, clubs and police dogs.

After the episode in Birmingham several hundred demonstrations took place in many American cities over a period of some ten weeks, more than 15,000 protesters being arrested. In 1963 a quarter of a million civil rights supporters staged a march in Washington, where King declared: 'We will not be satisfied until justice rolls down like the waters and righteousness like a mighty stream.' In 1964 a Civil Rights Act was passed by Congress, comprehensively banning discrimination in public facilities, education, employment and any agency receiving government funds. Further bills in following years were aimed at ensuring that blacks became fully registered voters, and outlawed discrimination in housing.

The civil rights movement

The civil rights movement provided a sense of cultural freedom and affirmation for black activists, going well beyond the formal objects for which they were fighting. The Student Nonviolent Coordinating Committee (SNCC) had its 'Freedom Singers', who translated their aspirations into music and song. Vincent Harding has described the energy and sense of a fresh beginning felt by many blacks at the time:

> There was an indescribable hope, idealism, courage and determination in those early months of organizing, marching, singing and going to jail . . . They were believers. When they sang in jail, in mass-meetings, in front of policemen and state troopers, 'We shall overcome', they meant it . . . overcoming meant 'freedom' and 'rights' and 'dignity' and 'justice' and black and white together and many other things that people in a movement feel more than they define. (Harding 1980)

Attempts to implement the new civil rights legislation again met with ferocious resistance from opponents. Civil rights marchers were insulted and beaten up, and some lost their lives. One response was the development of more aggressive black militant groups under the title of 'Black Power'. Moderates dissociated themselves from this development, and continued to press for reforms in line with established laws. Major riots broke out in black ghetto areas in cities across America between 1965 and 1968.

In spite of the barriers which hampered the full realization of its provisions, the Civil Rights Act proved to be fundamentally important. Its principles applied not just to blacks, but to anyone subject to discrimination, including other ethnic groups and women. It served as the starting point for a range of movements concerned with developing the rights of oppressed groups.

During the struggles of the 1960s, the goals of the black civil rights movement were somewhat altered. The ambition of most civil rights leaders had always been the full integration of blacks into wider American culture. The rise of militant black power groups helped shift these ideals towards a stress on the dignity of being black and the intrinsic value of black culture. Blacks now began to demand an independent position in the community, looking towards the development of a genuinely plural society rather than assimilation within the white social order. This change in outlook was also prompted by the feeling that equality before the law is of little use if discrimination persists in practice.

Integration and antagonism

Over the period of some thirty years since the passing of the Civil Rights Act, major changes have taken place. By the mid-1990s, the number of black elected officials had increased from barely a hundred in the early 1960s to seven thousand. Four times as many blacks were enrolled in colleges and universities at the end of that period as at the beginning. An expanding black middle class of business people and professionals had come into being. Blacks became mayors of some of the largest cities in the country, including New York, Chicago, Atlanta and Baltimore. Blacks also became much more prominent in literature, the theatre and the performing arts (Marable 1991).

Yet one cannot speak of the emergence of a new period of racial harmony and integration. On the contrary: in the late 1980s and early 1990s hundreds of acts of racially motivated violence occurred in different parts of the US. Racial tensions in cities such as New York, Boston and Chicago rose to a high pitch; in 1991 massive public demonstrations were organized by both black and white groups, each accusing the other of racism. In 1992 there were major outbreaks of violence in Los Angeles and several other US cities. Further riots took place in the mid-1990s in Los Angeles. In spite of the gains made over the longer period mentioned above, the overall social and economic status of blacks again suffered a decline. The average income of black families, for example, fell quite sharply in the early 1990s, and college enrolments tailed off.

In inner-city areas there was an explosion of illegal drug use and spiralling violence. Murder was the leading cause of death for black American men throughout the 1980s. A 1990 report of the _New England Journal of Medicine_ reported that the life expectancy of a young black male living in Harlem in New York was shorter than that of a man of the same age in Bangladesh. In his speech in Washington in 1963, Martin Luther King dreamed of a 'colour-blind society', in which his children would be 'judged not by the colour of their skin but by the content of their character'; but such a goal still seems a long way off.

Latinos and Asians in the United States

The wars of conquest that created the modern United States were not only directed against the Indian population. Much of the south-west – along with a quarter of a million Mexicans – was taken by the United States in 1848 as a result of the American war with Mexico. The term 'Chicano' includes the descendants of these people, together with subsequent immigrants from Mexico. The term 'Latino' refers to anyone from Spanish-speaking areas living in the United States.

The three main groups of Latinos in the United States are Mexican Americans (around 13.5 million), Puerto Ricans (2.7 million) and Cubans (1 million). A further 5 million Spanish-speaking residents are from areas in Central and South America. The Latino population has been increasing at an extraordinary rate – 53 per cent between 1980 and 1990 – mainly as a result of the large-scale flow of new immigrants from across the Mexican border. If current trends continue, the Latino residents will outnumber African Americans within the next decade.

The Asian connection

About 3 per cent of the population of the United States is of Asian origin – 8 million people. Chinese, Japanese and Filipinos (immigrants from the Philippines) form the largest groups. But now there are also significant numbers of Asian Indians, Pakistanis, Koreans and Vietnamese living in America. And as a result of the war in Vietnam, some 350,000 refugees from that country entered the United States in the 1970s.

Most of the early Chinese immigrants settled in California, where they were employed mainly in heavy industries such as mining and railroad construction. The retreat of the Chinese into distinct Chinatowns was not primarily their choice, but was made necessary by the hostility they faced. Since Chinese immigration was ended by law in 1882, the Chinese remained largely isolated from the wider society, at least until recently.

The early Japanese immigrants also settled in California and the other Pacific states. During World War Two, following the attack on Pearl Harbor by Japan, all Japanese Americans in the United States were made to report to 'relocation centers', which were effectively concentration camps, surrounded by barbed wire and gun turrets. In spite of the fact that most of these people were American citizens, they were compelled to live in the hastily established camps for the duration of the war. Paradoxically, this situation eventually led to their greater integration within the wider society, since, following the war, Japanese Americans did not return to the separate neighbourhoods in which they had previously lived. They have become extremely successful in reaching high levels of education and income, marginally outstripping whites. The rate of intermarriage of Japanese Americans with whites is now nearly 50 per cent.

Asian Americans, particularly Japanese Americans, have today become very successful. On average, they achieve better results in school and have a higher rate of entrance to university than whites. They also have a higher average income.

Let us now consider ethnic divisions in Britain. We will look not only at blacks versus whites, but more broadly at the diversity of ethnic groups.

ETHNIC DIVERSITY IN THE UNITED KINGDOM

Early immigration

The considerable number of Irish, Welsh and Scottish names scattered among the English people today is a reminder of the traditional flow of people from the 'Celtic fringes' to the urban centres of England. In the early nineteenth century, long before the advent of major immigration from distant colonies, developing English cities attracted migrants from the less prosperous areas of the British Isles. In 1867 *The Times* lamented the fact that 'There is hardly such a thing as a pure Englishman in this island.' The monarchy, which is today depicted as the most distinctively 'English' of English institutions, has included many 'foreign' elements. England has had French, Scots, Dutch and German monarchs; the present royal family has so many non-English forebears that it could best be described as 'European'!

There has been a thriving Irish community in London since the seventeenth century. Although at first they worked mainly in unskilled manual jobs, Irish immigrants were able in time to move into more skilled and better-paid positions. Alone among countries in Western Europe, the population of Ireland actually fell in the nineteenth century. London, Manchester, Liverpool and Glasgow received tens of thousands of Irish immigrants, while many more left for the US. Between 1830 and 1847, 300,000 Irish landed in Liverpool alone. By 1851, half a million Irish people had settled in England and Wales. Why did so many come? Persistent famines in Ireland forced people to seek a new life elsewhere, and the proximity of Ireland to England made it relatively easy for the Irish to travel to cities in Great Britain and keep up some communication with their native country.

The Irish in mid nineteenth-century England were the largest immigrant group in a society which, outside London, had largely been sheltered from foreign 'incursions'. The capital itself, however, contained many 'exotic' groups. A Jewish community had existed for centuries but increased substantially over the following hundred years, as harsh repression drove Jews in other countries to the relative safety of England. By 1800 it was calculated that there were some 6,000 Jews in provincial towns and between 15,000 and 20,000 in London. Criticized when poor, the Jews were also condemned when rich. When Charles Dickens created Fagin in *Oliver Twist*, he employed an immediately recognizable and common caricature.

During the Industrial Revolution, Dutch immigrants in Britain helped to establish a network of banking and financial agencies known as 'Dutch finance' – which was to prove vital in the economic transformation of the country. Enterprising, well-educated Dutch entrants brought to England social and economic qualities which were of abiding and revolutionary importance. Non-British people thus made a significant contribution to the creation of a new socioeconomic climate in England.

The influx of Chinese immigrants during the period of English industrial expansion was for employers a welcome source of cheap labour for English factories. Yet on several occasions in the late

HISTORY OF BLACK PEOPLE IN BRITAIN: SOME IMPORTANT DATES

1596	Elizabeth I issues proclamation to send 'Blackmoores' out of England.
1772	Judge Mansfield rules black people cannot be forcibly removed from England.
1807	The Slave Trade is abolished in the British Empire.
1823	The 1823 Navigation Act denies Lascars the right to work on British ships, except in times of war.
1834–38	Slavery is abolished in the British Empire, with a five-year 'apprenticeship' system for the former slaves.
1892	Dadabhai Naoroji is the first Asian elected to House of Commons.
1919	Anti-black riots in Liverpool in which Charles Wootton is murdered.
1925	The Special Restrictions (Coloured Alien Seamen) Order prohibits black British sailors from working on British ships, and forces some black sailors born in Britain out of the country.

Source: *Sociology Review*, 3.4 (April 1994).

nineteenth century union leaders spoke out against Chinese immigration because of the threat posed to the wage levels of local workers.

Black settlement in Britain was given an impetus in the late nineteenth century by the expansion of shipping to West Africa and the Caribbean. A few African and West Indian students were admitted to British universities at this period, but the largest black immigrant group consisted of black sailors who had settled in British cities. These were the founders of the first modern black communities in Britain (notably in Cardiff). The need for more fighting men to bolster the British forces during World War One led to the recruitment of over 15,000 men from the British Caribbean islands to form a black West Indian regiment, and a number of West Indian troops settled in Britain when hostilities ended, preferring to sample whatever Britain had to offer rather than return to the economically depressed West Indies (Fryer 1984).

Later developments

The Nazi persecutions of the early 1930s sent a generation of European Jews fleeing westwards to safety. One survey estimated that 60,000 Jews settled in the UK between 1933 and 1939, but the real figure may well have been higher. Between 1933 and 1939 some 80,000 refugees arrived from Central Europe, and a further 70,000 came during the war itself. By May 1945, Europe faced an unprecedented refugee problem: millions of people had become refugees. Several hundred thousand of these settled in Britain.

In the period after World War Two Britain experienced immigration on an unprecedented scale – most of the new residents came from the Commonwealth countries in response to job opportunities here. There was something of a class division in the way the British reacted to this new influx of immigrants. Those in governing circles were influenced by the notion of Britain's great imperial heritage, and therefore felt that West Indians, Indians, Pakistanis and Africans were all British subjects and entitled to settle in Britain. There was also a marked shortage of labour in postwar Britain; employers were for a while keen to attract immigrant labour. Many working people, however, living in the poorer areas (to which the new immigrants gravitated), were more aware of disruptions to their own everyday lives. Their attitudes to the newcomers were often hostile. Nearly a third of all Commonwealth immigrants came to live in certain parts of London; there were further concentrations of immigrants in the West Midlands, in Bradford, and in other impoverished urban areas.

Successive governments saw the full integration of the new immigrants into British society as a goal that was both desirable and possible. Roy Jenkins, Labour Home Secretary during the 1960s, offered a definition of integration 'not as a flattening process of assimilation but as equal opportunity, accompanied by cultural diversity, in an atmosphere of mutual tolerance'. In 1966, under the Race Relations Act introduced by the Labour government, a Race Relations Board was established. It provided for intervention in cases of proven discrimination on racial grounds. In 1968, a more substantial Bill against discrimination was introduced, but this was coupled with new legislation to control entry, which thenceforth sharply reduced the number of new immigrants. In the same year, while parliament was discussing race relations, Enoch Powell (then Conservative front-bench spokesman for defence) delivered a speech in Birmingham in which he envisaged an extraordinary growth of the non-white population: 'Like the Romans, I seem to see "the River Tiber flowing with much blood".' A Gallup poll showed that 75 per cent of the population were broadly sympathetic to Powell's views.

The Race Relations Act of 1976 set out to curb racial discrimination. The Act prohibited discrimination in respect of job applications, housing and the membership of organizations or clubs. The new body set up to apply the Act, the Commission for Racial Equality, was given an extensive range of powers, and its judgements were treated as legally binding. The period of the 1970s, however, also saw the emergence of an explicitly racist party of the extreme right, the National Front. Other organizations subjected it to direct challenge: the Anti-Nazi League, for example, was set up in 1977 to counter National Front propaganda.

Before it was abolished by the Conservative government, the Greater London Council created an ethnic minorities committee which had wide powers to correct underrepresentation of ethnic minorities in local government posts. Greater London was declared an 'anti-apartheid zone', and an 'anti-racist' year of festivals and concerts was organized for 1984. Brockwell Park in South London was renamed Zephania Mothopeng Park, after an anti-apartheid campaigner. In reaction to such ethnically defined politics, the Tory Party widely displayed a new advertising slogan, a picture of a black man bearing the statement 'Labour calls him Black, we call him British'. Yet the ethnocentric definitions of 'Britishness' which flourished in conservative circles were hardly easy for ethnic minorities in the country to identify with.

A leading Tory minister, John Patten, however, in a letter to Muslim groups presented what it means to be British in a way which stressed pluralism. Patten sketched a picture of a 'Britain where Christians, Muslims, Jews, Hindus, Sikhs and others can all work and live together, each retaining proudly their own faith and identity, by each sharing in common the bond of being, by birth or choice, British'. The very statement enshrines the difficulties of creating a multicultural society. The 'proud retaining of faith and identity' is likely to go against the goal of being definitively 'British'. The British Muslim community, for example, clashed with the government over the Islamic blasphemy law which the British courts refused to accept.

By 1990 people in the UK from West Indian or South Asian backgrounds were more likely to have been born in the UK than not (the proportion had increased to more than 55 per cent). The proportion is still growing, emphasizing that such groups now constitute a non-white British population, with full citizenship rights, rather than an immigrant one. These groups now make up approximately 5 per cent of the population.

A British Nationality Act, passed in 1981, tightened up on the conditions under which people from former or existing dependent territories could enter the UK. British citizenship was separated from citizenship of British dependent territories. A category of 'British Overseas Citizens' was created, referring mainly to people living in Hong Kong, Malaysia and Singapore; they were not entitled to settle in the UK, and their children could not inherit their citizenship. Commonwealth citizens, who could previously register as British citizens after living in the country for five years, now had to apply for naturalization under the same conditions as people from anywhere else in the world. Other restrictions on entry and right of residence were also added. Legislation introduced in 1988 increased these restrictions even further.

Britain has also reduced the possibilities for refugees from political or religious persecution to enter the country. Further legislation on asylum was passed in 1991 introducing stringent checks on people claiming refugee status, including fingerprinting, a reduction in access to free legal advice and the doubling of fines levied on airlines which bring in passengers not holding valid visas. The new regulations were heavily criticized by church leaders and by the United Nations Commissioner for Refugees; but they have remained in place.

British immigration policy has not been particularly coherent over the past several decades. It has been said to be marked by two main traits. One is the absence of a concern with labour market needs – no attempts have been made (as they have in the US, for example) to create easier conditions of entry for people having high qualifications or bringing in substantial wealth. The other has been called an obsession 'to detect or keep out that one extra black' (Plummer 1979, p. 8). Any implication of racism is of course officially denied, but it is difficult to resist the conclusion that in a covert way its influence is strong. A German observer has noted that 'the antics of preventing illegal entry, often in breach of international human rights conventions, from denying visas to visiting family members, fingerprinting and "virginity tests" to rabid acts of detention, which mostly happen to be directed against coloured per-

	Unemployed rates				
Ethnic group	Unemployed (000s)	On scheme (000s)	Persons (%)	Males (%)	Females (%)
White	2,246.1	318.6	8.8	10.7	6.3
Ethnic minorities	238.4	33.1	18.3	20.3	15.6
Black	94.0	13.3	21.1	25.2	16.6
Black-Caribbean	53.8	6.7	18.9	23.8	13.5
Black-African	26.1	4.1	27.0	28.9	24.7
Black-Other	14.1	2.5	22.2	25.5	18.3
South Asian	105.0	12.9	18.2	19.2	16.5
Indian	51.7	7.2	13.1	13.4	12.7
Pakistani	40.1	4.4	28.8	28.5	29.6
Bangladeshi	13.2	1.3	31.7	30.9	34.5
Chinese and others	39.4	6.9	14.1	15.5	12.1
Chinese	7.0	1.2	9.5	10.5	8.3
Other-Asian	12.8	2.7	13.4	14.2	12.3
Other-Other	19.5	3.0	17.7	19.7	14.8
Entire population	2,484.5	351.7	9.3	11.2	6.8

Table 9.2 Unemployment rates by ethnic group, Great Britain, 1991

Source: D. Owen, *Ethnic Minorities in Britain: Economic Characteristics*, 1993. Census data is Crown Copyright.

sons of New Commonwealth origins, carry a clear message: that blacks are unwanted' (Jopke 1995, p. 38).

Race, racism and inequality

There is considerable variation in the occupational distribution of non-whites in Britain. Among blacks, much higher proportions are found in manual occupations; higher proportions are unemployed than among whites (see table 9.2). Some 80 per cent of black males and 70 per cent of South Asians, as compared with around 50 per cent of white males, are in manual jobs. Among those of West Indian origin there are very few non-manual workers, but a high proportion of people in skilled occupations. The large majority of Bangladeshis are in semi-skilled and unskilled work. Asians who came to Britain from East Africa actually have higher proportions on average in non-manual jobs than is the case for whites. Non-white women fare considerably worse than non-white men: they have much lower proportions in non-manual or skilled manual work than do comparable males (Hamnett et al. 1990).

Many non-white people, including a majority of South Asians, live away from the central areas of cities. But there is a strong association between ethnic background and place of dwelling; thus West Indians are seven times more likely to live in inner London, Birmingham or Manchester than are whites. Male unemployment rates in these areas are very high. Most black people do not live in the inner city by choice; they moved there because such areas were least favoured by the white population and empty properties became available as whites moved out.

Blacks and Asians still at a social disadvantage

BLACK and Asian people remain disadvantaged on most main social and economic indicators . . . Some groups, particularly Indians, are doing relatively well in certain areas such as education and home ownership, but ethnic minorities generally fare markedly worse than the white population on grounds of unemployment, pay, housing, or as victims of crime.

A report published in 1996 by the Office for National Statistics, *Social Focus on Ethnic Minorities,* is a compilation of data mostly already in the public domain.

Until recently there was official reluctance to collect statistics broken down by race. The report, the first of its kind, does not pretend to paint a complete picture of ethnic minority lifestyles.

More than 3 million people, just under 6 per cent of the population, are non-white.

Only 34 per cent of children of black Caribbean descent are living with a married man and woman, 54 per cent are with a lone mother. By contrast, 90 per cent of children from Asian communities are with a married couple.

Similarly, 83 per cent of Indian households own or are buying their own homes, compared with 36 per cent of Bangladeshi and 40 per cent of black households.

In education, Asian children do better at GCSEs than all other groups, including whites. At age 18, 65 per cent of Indians, 61 per cent of Pakistanis and Bangladeshis, 72 per cent of other Asians and 50 per cent of blacks are still in full-time education, compared with 38 per cent of whites. However, unemployment is far higher among all minority groups than among whites.

Black and Pakistani/Bangladeshi people in particular have jobless rates three times as high as whites.

On pay, average hourly full-time rates are as low as £4.78 for Pakistani/Bangladeshi women, compared with £6.59 for white women, and only £6.87 for Pakistani/Bangladeshi men, compared with £8.34 for whites.

On crime, all minority groups are statistically more likely than whites to

be victims of both personal and property offences. However, the report points out that crime rates are higher in inner city areas, where most black and Asian people live.

A quarter of all Bangladeshis in Britain are concentrated in the east London borough of Tower Hamlets.

The report includes some unpublished data from a forthcoming analysis by the Policy Studies Institute. This shows that almost half black and Asian people visit their family's country of origin every five years, the proportion rising to 60 per cent among Chinese.

The PSI data also shows that eight out of 10 Pakistani/Bangladeshi women living in Britain always wear traditional clothing, compared with fewer than one out of 10 men from the same communities.

Wearing of traditional clothing is most common among older Asian people. Among blacks, however, it is younger people who make up most of the 25 per cent who say they sometimes wear clothes or style their hair in ways meant to show a connection with Africa or the Caribbean.

Source: Guardian, 8 August 1996.

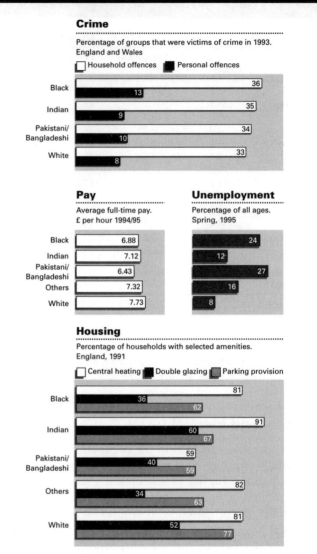

Crime

Percentage of groups that were victims of crime in 1993. England and Wales

☐ Household offences ■ Personal offences

	Household	Personal
Black	13	36
Indian	9	35
Pakistani/Bangladeshi	10	34
White	8	33

Pay

Average full-time pay. £ per hour 1994/95

Black	6.88
Indian	7.12
Pakistani/Bangladeshi	6.43
Others	7.32
White	7.73

Unemployment

Percentage of all ages. Spring, 1995

Black	24
Indian	12
Pakistani/Bangladeshi	27
Others	16
White	8

Housing

Percentage of households with selected amenities. England, 1991

☐ Central heating ■ Double glazing ▨ Parking provision

	Central heating	Double glazing	Parking provision
Black	81	36	62
Indian	91	60	67
Pakistani/Bangladeshi	59	40	59
Others	82	34	63
White	81	52	77

The most successful non-whites, as measured in terms of level of income, are those South Asians who are self-employed or small employers. The proportion of people in this category has risen steadily over the past twenty years: 23 per cent of East African Asian men are in this group, compared with 14 per cent for the white male population. Asian corner shops and other forms of Asian-run business have become such a prominent aspect of British society that some have suggested that they could lead an economic revival of inner-city areas. The case is almost certainly overstated, because many self-employed Asians work extremely long hours for relatively low levels of overall income. They are registered as self-employed, but are in effect employed by other members of the family who run the business; and they do not have the usual advantages that employees enjoy of sick pay, paid holidays and employer contributions to National Insurance.

However affluent they may be, non-white groups are all vulnerable to racism of one kind or another – including racially motivated attacks. Most escape such treatment, but for a minority the experience can be disturbing and brutal. A research report describes the following instances:

> As a boy sleeps, a pig's head, its eyes, ears, nostrils and mouth stuffed with lighted cigarettes, is hurled through the window of his bedroom. A family does not leave its home after seven in the evening; they stay in one large room, having barricaded their ground floor. A family is held prisoner in its own flat by a security cage bolted to the front door by white neighbours. A youth is slashed with a knife by an older white boy as he walks along a school corridor between classes. (Gordon 1986)

Ethnicity and policing

The deprivations to which people exposed to racism are subject, as mentioned previously, both help to produce, and are produced by, the decaying environment of the inner cities (see also chapter 17, 'Cities and the development of modern urbanism'). Here there are clear correlations between race, unemployment and crime, which tend to centre particularly on the position of young black males. In 1982 the police decided to start issuing a racial breakdown of street robberies, a statistic not previously reported. The core issue picked up by the television and newspapers was the 'disproportionate involvement' of young blacks in such crimes as mugging and robbery from stores. The result was the public creation of a link between race and crime. The *Daily Telegraph* commented: 'Many young West Indians in Britain, and, by a connected process, growing numbers of young whites, have no sense that the nation in which they live is part of them. So its citizens become to them mere objects of violent exploitation' (quoted in Solomos and Rackett 1991, p. 44). Yet the experience of many young blacks is that it is precisely *they* who are the 'objects of violent exploitation' in their encounters with whites and to some extent also, unfortunately, the police.

A study of the police by Roger Graef found racist attitudes to be widespread among police officers. He concluded that the outlook of the police was 'actively hostile to all minority groups'. Blacks in particular were spoken of in terms of crude stereotypes, jokes and mocking comments. Noting the interviewer's disapproval, one officer remarked, by way of humorous reassurance: 'Policemen are insulting about every-one. It's not specifically the coons. You hear remarks about poofs, Pakis, lesbos, women, students, the Irish – you name it. We hate every-body' (Graef 1989, p. 124).

It is hardly surprising, therefore, that research should show hostility to the police to be a common phenomenon among black groups. To some extent, such attitudes are simply the result of direct experience; the attitudes of young blacks in particular are shaped by the policing strategies they encounter. A study published in 1983 concluded that 'the lack of confidence in the police among young West Indians can be described as disastrous' (Smith and Small 1983, p. 326), and this situation does not seem to have altered appreciably over the intervening years.

Black women are equally a focus of prejudice and discrimination. A substantial proportion of black women are lone heads of households, a situation which seems to expose them to critical attitudes in the media as well as among the white public. Thus an article in the *London Evening Standard* declared: 'Young black men commit a disproportionately high number of violent crimes in London because most black mothers, when they are young girls, have children out of wedlock and are not sup-ported by the fathers' (quoted in Chigwada 1991, p. 138).

Studies of views of black women on the part of police show that blacks are often seen as hostile, aggressive and 'hard to deal with'. Women who are 'in trouble' with the police frequently face situations of double jeopardy; they risk being ostracized by the black community as well. The Black Women's Prison Scheme was set up by community associa-tions to encourage black groups to be more supportive towards women offenders. Research indicates that young black women are just as criti-cal of the police as their male counterparts. Thus one investigation among black women concluded: 'Without exception, all the black women in the study held staunchly anti-police feelings and accused the police of racial prejudice and corruption' (Player 1991, p. 122).

ETHNIC RELATIONS ON THE CONTINENT

Large-scale migrations took place in Europe during the first two decades after World War Two. The Mediterranean countries provided the nations in the north and west with cheap labour. Migrants moving from areas like Turkey, North Africa, Greece and southern Spain and Italy were for a period actively encouraged by host countries facing acute shortages of labour. Switzerland, Germany, Belgium and Sweden all have considerable populations of migrant workers. At the same time, countries that used to be colonial powers experienced an influx of immigrants from their former colonies: this applied primarily to France (Algerians) and the Netherlands (Indonesians) as well as the UK.

Labour migration into and within Western Europe slowed down appreciably two decades ago, as the boom turned into a recession. Although the transition from migration to settlement is everywhere well advanced, most members of the developing ethnic minorities still suffer serious legal disabilities. In some countries, legal frameworks originally designed to manage temporary labour migration have simply been maintained, despite the fact that they are ill suited to the current situation. In other nations (such as France and Germany), new restrictive policies have been introduced to control minority populations – for example, limiting the rights of established immigrants to bring in close relatives.

Many West European countries have witnessed campaigns for returning migrants to their countries of origin, threats of deportation in the event of unemployment or committing an offence, and other related policies. Such proposals must seem a particularly disturbing threat to minority youth, often born in their host country, who face the prospect of being forced to 'return' to countries with which they have no real links.

Immigration, and the racism associated with it, have become explosive issues in Europe in the 1990s. Illegal immigrants from North Africa have entered European countries, particularly France and Italy, in large numbers. The dissolution of the Soviet Union and the other changes in Eastern Europe have led governments in the western part of the Continent to fear a massive influx of immigration from the East. Hundreds of attacks on foreigners – and on Turkish workers, some of whom had been in the country for more than twenty years – took place in newly unified Germany in 1991 and 1992.

In Austria, the rightist group, the Freedom Party, is campaigning to stop foreigners gaining access to the country. A comparable organization in Italy, the Lombard League, has strong voting support in the north of the country. Even in the Scandinavian countries, long the bastions of liberalism in race relations, rightist groups with substantial support have arisen.

Over the period from the end of World War Two to the opening of the Berlin Wall, over 18 million people immigrated into Germany – or what was then West Germany. Yet successive German governments clung to the idea that theirs was not a country of immigration. The Germanic notion of citizenship was one associated with blood, not place of birth. The children of 'guest workers', who did not have full citizenship rights, have none the less quite often prospered economically. With the reunification of Germany, some erstwhile East Germans have become resentful that they are poorer than those who do not enjoy the same citizenship rights they do (Baldwin-Evans and Schain 1995).

Legislation pursued by the German federal parliament in 1990 included some liberalizing measures in favour of the rights of immigrants. For instance, immigrants are entitled to file for a permanent residence permit after eight years of stay. The law still talked, however, of 'foreigners', rather than using the term 'immigrant'. The Green Party denounced the legislation as a product of 'institutional racism' and called for a 'minute of silence' in the parliament to 'commemorate the future victims of this law'.

More generally in Europe, many human rights and immigration organizations have reacted with dismay at what they see as a rising tide of racism, coupled to an attempt to construct a 'fortress Europe'. Yet the trends do not all go in the direction of decreasing tolerance. Anti-racist organizations have developed strongly in all the countries referred to above, and most governments have promoted measures designed to reduce discrimination.

LIKELY FUTURE DEVELOPMENTS IN ETHNIC RELATIONS

Ethnic conflicts and divisions are by no means limited to the countries we have mentioned. Since the dissolution of Soviet communism, a host of ethnic struggles have broken out in republics which were once part of the Soviet Union, including Russia itself. Ethnic battles have raged in parts of India and in Sri Lanka. In Rwanda, in Africa, such divisions produced a civil war as savage and bloodthirsty as that which happened in Bosnia in Europe. The issue of accommodating ethnic diversity has thus become a problem of fundamental importance for global society.

The US is the most ethnically diverse nation in the West, having been constructed as an 'immigrant society'. The models of possible future ethnic development worked out there have distinct relevance to potential paths of change in Europe and elsewhere. Three models have been suggested as characterizing the development of ethnic relations in the United States. One is **assimilation**, meaning that immigrants abandon their original customs and practices, moulding their behaviour to the values and norms of the majority. Generations of immigrants were subjected to pressure to become 'assimilated' in this way, and many of their children became more or less completely 'American' as a result.

A second model is that of the **melting pot**. Rather than the traditions of the immigrants being dissolved in favour of those dominant among the pre-existing population, all become blended to form new, evolving cultural patterns. Many have believed this to be the most desirable outcome of ethnic diversity. To a limited degree, this model is an accurate expression of aspects of American cultural development. Although the 'Anglo' culture has remained the pre-eminent one, its character in some part reflects the impact of the many different groups that now compose the American population.

The third model is that of **cultural pluralism**. In this view, the most appropriate course is to foster the development of a genuinely plural society, in which the equal validity of numerous different subcultures is recognized. The United States has long been pluralistic, but ethnic differences have for the most part been associated with inequalities rather than equal but independent membership of the national community.

In Europe we can see similar tensions and similar options. Most official governmental policies, in Britain and elsewhere, are directed towards the first path, that of assimilation. As in the United States, this is likely to prove most problematic where ethnic minorities are physically quite distinct from the majority of the population – as is the case with West Indians and Asians in Britain. The persistence of racism (often institutionalized) in Europe makes the notion of the melting pot of fairly limited relevance.

The leaders of most ethnic minorities have increasingly emphasized the path of pluralism. To achieve 'distinct but equal' status will demand major struggles, and as yet this is a very distant option. Ethnic minorities are still perceived by many people as a threat: a threat to their job, their safety and the 'national culture'. The scapegoating of ethnic minorities is a persistent tendency. With the young in Western Europe quite often still holding similar prejudices to those of older generations, ethnic minorities in most countries face a future of continued discrimination, in a social climate characterized by tension and anxiety.

For the foreseeable future, as in the past, the most likely path is a mixture of the three types, with a stronger emphasis on pluralism than used to be the case. It would be a mistake, however, to see ethnic pluralism as resulting only from differing cultural values and norms 'brought in' to a society from the outside. Cultural diversity has also been *created* by the experience of ethnic groups as they adapt to the wider social environments in which they find themselves.

SUMMARY

1 Sections of a population form ethnic groups by virtue of sharing common cultural characteristics which separate them from others within that population. Ethnicity refers to cultural differences that set one group apart from another. The main distinguishing characteristics of an ethnic group are language, history or ancestry, religion and styles of dress or adornment. Ethnic differences are wholly learned, although they are sometimes thought of as 'natural'.

2 A minority group is one whose members are discriminated against by the majority population in a society. Members of minority groups often have a strong sense of group solidarity, deriving in part from the collective experience of exclusion.

3 Race refers to physical characteristics, such as skin colour, treated by members of a community or society as ethnically significant – as signalling distinct cultural characteristics. Many popular beliefs about race are mythical. There are no clear-cut characteristics by means of which human beings can be allocated to different races.

4 Racism means falsely ascribing inherited characteristics of personality or behaviour to individuals of a particular physical appearance. A racist is someone who believes that a biological explanation can be given for characteristics of inferiority supposedly possessed by people of one physical stock or another.

5 Displacement and scapegoating are psychological mechanisms associated with prejudice and discrimination. In displacement, feelings of hostility become directed against objects that are not the real origin of these anxieties. People project their anxieties and insecurities on to scapegoats. Prejudice involves holding preconceived views about an individual or group; discrimination refers to actual behaviour which deprives members of a group from opportunities open to others.

6 Ethnic attitudes are assimilated by children at a very young age. They learn, for example, to think of whites as superior and blacks as inferior.

7 Group closure and privileged access to resources are an important part of many situations of ethnic antagonism. However, some of the fundamental aspects of modern ethnic conflicts, especially racist attitudes held by whites against blacks, have to be understood in terms of the history of the expansion of the West and of colonialism.

8 Historical examples illustrate various ways in which societies have dealt with ethnic minorities, ranging from slavery and apartheid to relative acceptance, and the ways those minorities have reacted.

9 Immigration has led to the existence of numerous different ethnic groups within Britain, the US and other industrial countries. Major ethnic divisions exist in the United States, particularly between whites and blacks. Divisions in the UK and other European countries are not so severe, but major conflicts have become common.

10 Three models of possible future developments in ethnic relations can be distinguished – the first stressing assimilation, the second the melting pot, and the third cultural pluralism. Assimilation: new immigrant groups adopt the attitudes and language of the dominant community. Melting pot: the different cultures and outlooks of the ethnic groups in a society are merged together. Pluralism: ethnic groups exist separately and participate in economic and political life. In recent years there has been an emphasis on the third of these avenues, whereby different ethnic identities are accepted as equally valid within the context of the overall national culture.

FURTHER READING

Frances Abound, *Children and Prejudice* (Oxford: Blackwell, 1989). A discussion of how prejudiced attitudes are formed in childhood.

Steven Fraser, *The Bell Curve Wars: Race, Intelligence and the Future of America* (New York: Basic Books, 1995). A collection of critical articles centred on the claims of the book by Murray and Herrnstein, *The Bell Curve*.

Geoffrey Harris, *The Dark Side of Europe: The Extreme Right Today* (Edinburgh: Edinburgh University Press, 1990). A comparative discussion of the rise of extreme right-wing groups in contemporary Europe.

Trevor Jones, *Britain's Ethnic Minorities* (London: Policy Studies Institute, 1993). A survey of minority groups in Britain.

David Mason, *Race and Ethnicity in Modern Britain* (Oxford: Oxford University Press, 1995). An analysis of the role and importance of race and ethnicity in contemporary British society; the historical background to migration and ethnic diversity; and ethnic issues of public policy.

IMPORTANT TERMS

- *minority group (or ethnic minority)*
- *stereotypical thinking*
- *displacement*
- *scapegoating*
- *projection*
- *authoritarian personality*
- *group closure*
- *resource allocation*

- *ethnic antagonism*
- *race*
- *apartheid*
- *microsegregation*
- *mezzosegregation*
- *macrosegregation*
- *assimilation*
- *melting pot*
- *cultural pluralism*

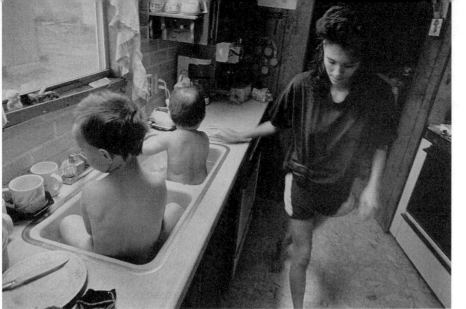

STRATIFICATION AND CLASS STRUCTURE

➡

BASIC CONCEPTS
• *social stratification* • *class* • *status* • *class structure* • *social mobility*

Why are some groups in a society more wealthy or powerful than others? How unequal are modern societies? How much chance has someone from a lowly background of reaching the top of the economic ladder? Why does poverty persist in affluent countries today? These are some of the questions we shall pose and try to answer in this chapter. The study of social inequalities is one of the most important areas of sociology, because the material resources to which people have access determine a great deal about their lives.

SYSTEMS OF SOCIAL STRATIFICATION

➡

Inequalities exist in all types of human society. Even in the simplest cultures, where variations in wealth or property are virtually non-existent, there are inequalities between individuals, men and women, the young and old. A person may have a higher status than others, because of particular prowess at hunting, for instance, or because he or she is believed to have special access to the ancestral spirits. To describe inequalities, sociologists speak of SOCIAL STRATIFICATION. Stratification can be defined as *structured inequalities between different groupings of people*. It is useful to think of stratification as rather like the geological layering of rock in the earth's surface. Societies can be seen as consisting of 'strata' in a hierarchy, with the more favoured at the top and the less privileged nearer the bottom.

Four basic systems of stratification can be distinguished: *slavery, caste, estates* and *class*. These are sometimes found in conjunction with one another: slavery, for instance, existed alongside classes in ancient Greece and Rome, and in the southern United States before the Civil War.

Slavery

Slavery is an extreme form of inequality in which some individuals are literally owned by others as their property. The legal conditions of slave ownership have varied between different societies. Sometimes slaves were deprived of almost all rights in law – as was the case in the southern United States – while in other instances their position was more akin to that of servant.

In the United States, South America and the West Indies in the eighteenth and nineteenth centuries, slaves were used almost exclusively as plantation workers and as domestic menials. In classical Athens, by contrast, they were found in many settings, sometimes in positions of great responsibility. Slaves were excluded from political positions and the military, but were found in most other types of occupation. Some were literate and worked as government administrators; many were trained in craft skills. In Rome, where the ruling groups held a low opinion of trade and commerce, slaves sometimes became very wealthy through their business activities, and some rich slaves even owned slaves themselves. At the bottom of the scale, however, those working on plantations or in mines in the ancient world were often treated harshly (Finley 1968, 1980).

Slavery has frequently provoked resistance and struggle from those subjected to it. History is punctuated with slave rebellions, and sometimes slaves managed collectively to free themselves from their masters. Systems of forced slave labour – such as on plantations – have tended to be unstable; high productivity can only be achieved through constant supervision and the use of brutal methods of punishment. Slave-labour systems break down partly because of the struggles they provoke and partly because economic or other incentives motivate people more effectively than direct compulsion. Slavery is simply not very efficient. The slave trade carried on by the Western powers up to the nineteenth century was the last – but also the most extensive – system of trading in slaves to be carried on. Since freedom was granted to slaves in North and South America, well over a century ago, slavery as a formal institution has been gradually eradicated, and today has almost completely disappeared from the world.

Caste

Caste is associated above all with the cultures of the Indian subcontinent. The term 'caste' itself is not an Indian one, coming from the Portuguese *casta*, meaning 'race' or 'pure stock'. Indians themselves have no single term for describing the caste system as a whole, but a variety of words referring to different aspects of it, the two main ones being *varna* and *jati*. The *varna* consist of four categories, each ranked differently in terms of social honour. Below these four groupings are the 'untouchables', those in the lowest position of all. The *jati* are locally defined groups within which the caste ranks are organized.

The caste system is extremely elaborate, and varies in its structure from area to area – so much so that it does not really constitute one 'system' at all, but a loosely connected diversity of varying beliefs and practices. But certain principles are widely shared. Those in the highest *varna*, the Brahmins, represent the most elevated condition of purity, the untouchables the lowest. The Brahmins must avoid certain types of contact with the untouchables, and only the untouchables are allowed physical contact with animals or substances regarded as unclean. The caste system is closely bound up with the Hindu belief in rebirth; individuals who fail to abide by the rituals and duties of their caste, it is believed, will be reborn in an inferior position in their next incarnation. The Indian caste system has never been completely static. Although individuals are debarred from moving between castes, whole groups can change, and frequently have changed, their position within the caste hierarchy.

The concept of caste is sometimes used outside the Indian context where two or more ethnic groups are largely segregated from one another, and where notions of racial purity prevail. In such circumstances, there are strong taboos (or sometimes legal prohibitions) preventing intermarriage between the groups concerned. When slavery was abolished in the southern states of the US, the degree of separation between blacks and whites remained so strong that some have used the term caste to refer to the stratification system. The concept of caste has also been applied to South Africa, where strict segregation was until recently maintained between black and white, and intermarriage or sexual contact between them was forbidden by law (see chapter 9, 'Ethnicity and race').

Estates

Estates were part of European feudalism, but also existed in many other traditional civilizations. The feudal estates consisted of strata with differing obligations and rights towards each other, some of these differences being established by law. In Europe, the highest estate was composed of the aristocracy and gentry. The clergy formed another estate, having lower status but possessing various distinctive privileges. Those in what came to be called the 'third estate' were the commoners – serfs, free peasants, merchants and artisans. In contrast to castes, a certain degree of intermarriage and individual mobility was tolerated between estates. Commoners might be knighted, for example, to repay special services given to the monarch; merchants could sometimes purchase titles. A remnant of the system persists in Britain, where hereditary titles are still recognized, and business leaders, civil servants and others may be knighted or receive peerages in recognition of their services.

Estates have tended to develop in the past wherever there was a traditional aristocracy based on noble birth. In feudal systems, such as in medieval Europe, estates were closely bound to the local manorial community: they formed a local, rather than a national, system of stratification. In more centralized traditional empires, such as China or Japan, they were organized on a more national basis. Sometimes the differences between the estates were justified by religious beliefs, although rarely in as strict a way as in the Hindu caste system.

Class

CLASS systems differ in many respects from slavery, castes or estates. Four differences should be mentioned in particular:

1 Unlike the other types of strata, classes are not established by legal or religious provisions; membership is not based on inherited position as specified either legally or by custom. Class systems are typically more fluid than the other types of stratification and the boundaries between classes are never clear-cut. There are no formal restrictions on intermarriage between people from different classes.
2 An individual's class is at least in some part *achieved*, not simply 'given' at birth as is common in other types of stratification system.

Social mobility – movement upwards and downwards in the class structure – is much more common than in the other types. (In the caste system, individual mobility from one caste to another is impossible.)

3 Classes depend on *economic* differences between groupings of individuals – inequalities in possession and control of material resources. In the other types of stratification system, non-economic factors (such as the influence of religion in the Indian caste system) are generally most important.

4 In the other types of stratification system, inequalities are expressed primarily in personal relationships of duty or obligation – between serf and lord, slave and master, or lower- and higher-caste individuals. Class systems, by contrast, operate mainly through large-scale connections of an impersonal kind. For instance, one major basis of class differences is to be found in inequalities of pay and working conditions; these affect all the people in specific occupational categories, as a result of economic circumstances pertaining in the economy as a whole.

We can define a class as a large-scale grouping of people who share common economic resources, which strongly influence the type of lifestyle they are able to lead. Ownership of wealth, together with occupation, are the chief bases of class differences. The major classes that exist in Western societies are an **upper class** (the wealthy, employers and industrialists, plus top executives – those who own or directly control productive resources); a **middle class** (which includes most white-collar workers and professionals); and a **working class** (those in blue-collar or manual jobs). In some of the industrialized countries, such as France or Japan, a fourth class – **peasants** (people engaged in traditional types of agricultural production) – has also until recently been important. In Third World countries, peasants are usually still by far the largest class.

'I said, we must have lunch sometime.'

We will now turn to a discussion of the major theories of stratification that have been developed in sociology, concentrating especially on their relevance to modern societies.

THEORIES OF STRATIFICATION IN MODERN SOCIETIES

The most influential theoretical approaches are those developed by Karl Marx and Max Weber; most subsequent theories of stratification have been heavily indebted to their ideas. We shall also analyse two later theories, those put forward by Erik Olin Wright and Frank Parkin. The ideas of Marx and Weber have made a deep impact on the development of sociology, and have influenced many other areas of the discipline too. Aspects of their writings are discussed in various other chapters.

Karl Marx's theory

Most of Marx's works were concerned with stratification and, above all, with social class, yet surprisingly he failed to provide a systematic analysis of the concept of class. The manuscript Marx was working on at the time of his death (subsequently published as part of his major work, *Capital*) breaks off just at the point where he posed the question 'What constitutes a class?' Marx's concept of class thus has to be reconstructed from the body of his writings as a whole. Since the various passages where he discusses class are not always fully consistent, there have been many disputes between scholars about 'what Marx really meant'. The main outlines of his views, however, are fairly clear.

The nature of class

For Marx a class is a group of people who stand in a common relationship to the **means of production** – the means by which they gain a livelihood. Before the rise of modern industry, the means of production consisted primarily of land and the instruments used to tend crops or pastoral animals. In preindustrial societies, therefore, the two main classes were those who owned the land (aristocrats, gentry or slaveholders) and those actively engaged in producing from it (serfs, slaves and free peasantry). In modern industrial societies, factories, offices, machinery and the wealth or capital needed to buy them become more important. The two main classes are those who own these new means of production – industrialists or **capitalists** – and those who earn their living by selling their labour to them – the working class or, in the now somewhat archaic term Marx sometimes favours, the 'proletariat'.

The relationship between classes, according to Marx, is an exploitative one. In feudal societies, exploitation often took the form of the direct transfer of produce from the peasantry to the aristocracy. Serfs were compelled to give a certain proportion of their production to their aristocratic masters, or had to work for a number of days each month in the lord's fields to produce crops consumed by the lord and his retinue. In modern capitalist societies, the source of exploitation is less obvious, and Marx devotes much attention to trying to clarify its nature. In the course of the working day, Marx reasons, workers produce more than is actually needed by employers to repay the cost of hiring them. This **surplus value** is the source of profit, which capitalists are able to put to their own use. A group of workers in a clothing factory, say, might be able to produce a hundred suits a day. Selling half the suits provides enough income for the manufacturer to pay the workers' wages. Income from the sale of the remainder of the garments is taken as profit.

Marx was struck by the inequalities the capitalist system creates. Although in earlier times aristocrats lived a life of luxury, completely different from that of the peasantry, agrarian societies were relatively poor. Even if there had been no aristocracy, standards of living would inevitably have been meagre. With the development of modern industry, however, wealth is produced on a scale far beyond anything seen before, but workers have little access to the wealth their labour creates. They remain relatively poor, while the wealth accumulated by the propertied class grows. Moreover, with the development of modern factories and the mechanization of production, work frequently becomes dull and oppressive in the extreme. The labour which is the source of our wealth is often both physically wearing and mentally tedious – as in the case of a factory hand whose job consists of routine tasks carried on day in, day out, in an unchanging environment.

The complexity of class systems

Although in Marx's theory there are two main classes in society, those who own the means of production and those who do not, he recognizes that actual class systems are much more complex than this model suggests. In addition to the two basic classes, there exist what Marx sometimes calls **transitional classes**. These are class groups left over from an earlier type of production system, such as the peasantry in modern societies.

Marx also draws attention to splits which occur within classes. Some examples can be given as follows:

1 Within the upper class there are often conflicts between financial capitalists (like bankers) and industrial manufacturers.
2 There are divisions of interest between people with small businesses and those who own or manage large corporations. Both belong to the capitalist class, but policies which favour large businesses are not always in the interests of small ones.
3 At the bottom of the working class, the long-term unemployed have worse conditions of life than the majority of workers. These groups often consist largely of ethnic minorities.

Marx's concept of class directs us towards objectively structured economic inequalities in society. Class does not refer to the beliefs people hold about their position, but to objective conditions which allow some to have greater access to material rewards than others.

Max Weber's theory

Weber's approach to stratification is built on the analysis developed by Marx, but he modifies and elaborates it. There are two main differences between the two theories.

First, although Weber accepts Marx's view that class is founded on objectively given economic conditions, he sees a greater variety of economic factors as important in class formation than are recognized by Marx. According to Weber, class divisions derive not only from control or lack of control of the means of production, but from economic differences which have nothing directly to do with property. Such resources include especially the skills and credentials or qualifications which affect the types of job people are able to obtain. Those in managerial or professional occupations earn more, and have more favourable conditions of work, for example, than people in blue-collar jobs. The qualifications they possess, such as degrees, diplomas and the skills they have acquired, make them more 'marketable' than others without such qualifications. At a lower level, among blue-collar workers, skilled craftsmen are able to secure higher wages than the semi- or unskilled.

Secondly, Weber distinguishes two other basic aspects of stratification besides class. One he calls *status* and the other *party*. He in fact adapted the notion of status groups from the example of medieval estates, the word he used in German (*Stand*) meaning both.

Status

STATUS in Weber's theory refers to differences between social groups in the social honour or prestige they are accorded by others. Status distinctions often vary independently of class divisions, and social honour may be either positive or negative. Positively privileged status groups include any groupings of people who have high **prestige** in a given social order. For instance, doctors and lawyers have high prestige in British society. **Pariah groups** are negatively privileged status groups, subject to discrimination that prevents them from taking advantage of opportunities open to most others. The Jews were a pariah group in medieval Europe, banned from participating in certain occupations and from holding official positions.

Possession of wealth normally tends to confer high status, but there are many exceptions. The term 'genteel poverty' refers to one example. In Britain, individuals from aristocratic families continue to enjoy considerable social esteem even when their fortunes have been lost. Conversely, 'new money' is often looked on with some scorn by the well-established wealthy.

Whereas class is objectively given, status depends on people's subjective evaluations of social differences. Classes derive from the economic factors associated with property and earnings; status is governed by the varying *styles of life* groups follow.

Party

In modern societies, Weber points out, party formation is an important aspect of power, and can influence stratification independently of class and status. 'Party' defines a group of individuals who work together because they have common backgrounds, aims or interests. Marx tended to explain both status differences and party organization in terms of class. Neither, in fact, Weber argues, can be reduced to class divisions, even though each is influenced by them; both can in turn influence the economic circumstances of individuals and groups, thereby affecting class. Parties may appeal to concerns cutting across class differences; for example, parties may be based on religious affiliation or nationalist ideals. A Marxist might attempt to explain the conflicts between Catholics and Protestants in Northern Ireland in class terms, since more Catholics than Protestants are in working-class jobs. A follower of Weber would argue that such an explanation is ineffective, because many Protestants are also working class in background. The parties to which people are affiliated express religious as well as class differences.

Weber's writings on stratification are important, because they show that other dimensions of stratification besides class strongly influence people's lives. Most sociologists hold that Weber's scheme offers a more flexible and sophisticated basis for analysing stratification than that provided by Marx.

The ideas developed by Marx and Weber are still used extensively in sociology today, although rarely without modification. Those working in the Marxian tradition have further developed the ideas Marx himself set out; others have tried to elaborate Weber's concepts. Since the two standpoints are similar in many ways, though complementary in others, some common ways of thinking have emerged. We can give some indication of these by looking briefly at two more recent theoretical perspectives.

Erik Olin Wright's theory of class

The American sociologist Erik Olin Wright has developed a theoretical position which owes much to Marx, but also incorporates ideas from Weber (Wright 1978, 1985). According to Wright, there are three dimensions of control over economic resources in modern capitalist production, and these allow us to identify the major classes which exist.

1 Control over investments or money capital.
2 Control over the physical means of production (land or factories and offices).
3 Control over labour power.

Those who belong to the capitalist class have control over each of these dimensions within the production system. Members of the working class have control over none of them. In between these two main classes, however, there are groups whose position is more ambiguous.

These people are in what Wright calls **contradictory class locations**, because they are able to influence some aspects of production, but are denied control over others. White-collar and professional employees, for example, have to contract their labour power to employers in order to obtain a living, in the same way as manual workers do. Yet at the same time they have a greater degree of control over the work setting than most people in blue-collar jobs. Wright terms the class position of such workers 'contradictory', because they are neither capitalists nor manual workers, yet share certain common features with each.

Frank Parkin: a Weberian approach

Frank Parkin, a British author, has proposed an approach drawing more heavily on Weber than on Marx (Parkin 1971, 1979). Parkin agrees with Marx, as Weber did, that ownership of property – the means of production – is the basic foundation of class structure. Property, however, according to Parkin, is only one form of **social closure** which can be monopolized by a minority and used as a basis of power over others. We can define social closure as any process whereby groups try to maintain exclusive control over resources, limiting access to them. Besides property or wealth, most of the characteristics Weber associated with status differences, such as ethnic origin, language or religion, may be used to create social closure.

Two types of process are involved in social closure. *Exclusion* refers to strategies that groups adopt to separate outsiders from themselves, preventing them from having access to valued resources. Thus white unions in the US have in the past excluded blacks from membership, as a means of maintaining their own privileges. *Usurpation* refers to the attempts of the less privileged to acquire resources previously monopolized by others – as where blacks struggle to achieve rights of union membership.

Both strategies may be used simultaneously in some circumstances. Trade unions, for instance, may engage in usurpatory activities against employers (going on strike to obtain a greater share of the resources of a firm), but at the same time may exclude ethnic minorities from membership. Parkin calls this *dual closure*. Here there is clearly a point of similarity between Parkin and Wright. Dual closure concerns much the same processes as those discussed by Wright under the heading of contradictory class locations. Both notions indicate that those in the middle of the stratification system to some extent cast their eyes towards the top, yet are also concerned to distinguish themselves from others lower down.

CLASSES IN WESTERN SOCIETIES TODAY

Some authors argue that class today has become relatively unimportant in modern Western societies. It is generally agreed that a century and a half ago, in the early period of the development of industrial capitalism, there were major class differences. Even those who are most critical of Marx's thought acknowledge that there were yawning gaps between the labouring poor and the wealthy industrialists who employed them. Since then, it has been claimed, material inequalities have been greatly lessened in the industrialized countries. Taxes directed against the rich, combined with welfare benefits for those who cannot easily earn a living for themselves, have flattened out the top and bottom of the scale of inequality. Moreover, with the spread of public education, those who have the necessary talent can find their way to the top levels of the social and economic system.

Yet this picture is far from accurate. The influence of class may be less than Marx supposed, but there are few spheres of social life left untouched by class differences. Even physical differences are correlated with class membership. Working-class people have on average lower birth-weight and higher rates of infant mortality, are smaller at maturity, less healthy, and die at a younger age, than those in higher-class categories. Major types of mental disorder and physical illness, including heart disease, cancer, diabetes, pneumonia and bronchitis, are all more common at lower levels of the class structure than towards the top (Waitzkin 1986).

Differences in wealth and income

Marx believed that the maturing of industrial capitalism would bring about an increasing gap between the wealth of the minority and the poverty of the mass of the population. According to him, the wages of the working class could never rise far above subsistence level, while wealth would pile up in the hands of those owning capital. At the lowest levels of society, particularly among those frequently or permanently unemployed, there would be an 'accumulation of misery, agony of labour, slavery, ignorance, brutality, moral degradation . . .' (Marx 1970, p. 645). Marx was right, as we shall see, about the persistence of poverty within the industrialized countries and in anticipating that large-scale inequalities of wealth and income would continue. He was wrong, however, to suppose that the income of most of the population would remain extremely low, as well as to claim that a minority would become more and more wealthy relative to the majority. Most people in Western countries today are much better off materially than were comparable groups in Marx's day. To examine how far, and why, this is the case, we have to look at changes in the distribution of wealth and income over the past century or so.

Wealth refers to all the assets individuals own (stocks and shares, savings and property such as homes or land; items which can be sold). **Income** refers to wages and salaries coming from paid occupations, plus 'unearned' money deriving from investments (usually interest or dividends). While most people get what money they have from their work, the wealthy derive the bulk of their income from investments.

Wealth

Reliable information about the distribution of wealth is difficult to obtain. Some countries keep more accurate statistics than others, but

Table 10.1	Distribution of wealth in the United Kingdom				
	1976	**1981**	**1986**	**1991**	**1993**
Marketable wealth					
Percentage of wealth owned by:					
Most wealthy 1%	21	18	18	17	17
Most wealthy 5%	38	36	36	35	36
Most wealthy 10%	50	50	50	47	48
Most wealthy 25%	71	73	73	71	72
Most wealthy 50%	92	92	90	92	92
Total marketable wealth (£ billion)	280	565	955	1,711	1,809
Marketable wealth plus occupational and state pension rights					
Percentage of wealth owned by:					
Most wealthy 1%	13	11	10	10	10
Most wealthy 5%	26	24	24	23	23
Most wealthy 10%	36	34	35	33	33
Most wealthy 25%	57	56	58	57	56
Most wealthy 50%	80	79	82	83	82
Total marketable wealth (£ billion)	472	1,036	1,784	3,014	3,383

Estimates are based on the estates of persons dying in those years or, for 1993, on estates notified for probate.

Source: Inland Revenue. From *Social Trends*, 1996, p. 111.

there is always a considerable amount of guesswork involved. The affluent do not usually publicize the full range of their assets; it has often been remarked that we know far more about the poor than we do about the wealthy. What is certain is that wealth is concentrated in the hands of relatively few. In Britain the top 1 per cent own some 17 per cent of all personal wealth (wealth owned by individuals rather than organizations). The most wealthy 10 per cent of the population own about half the total wealth (see table 10.1).

Ownership of stocks and bonds is more unequal than holdings of wealth as a whole. The top 1 per cent in the UK own some 75 per cent of privately held corporate shares; the top 5 per cent own over 90 per cent of the total. But there has also been more change in this respect. Some 25 per cent of the population own shares, which compares with 14 per cent in 1986. Many people bought shares for the first time during the Conservative government's privatization programme. The increase is even more dramatic when looked at over a longer period, for in 1979 only 5 per cent of the population held shares. Most of these holdings are small (worth less than £1,000 at 1991 prices), and institutional share ownership – shares held by companies in other firms – is growing faster than individual share ownership. The proportion of total share value held by individuals halved between 1963 and 1990 (HMSO 1992).

In the US, the distribution of total wealth is about the same as in the UK, while ownership of corporate shares is even more concentrated. More specifically, the wealthiest 10 per cent of families own 90 per cent of corporate stocks and business assets and 95 per cent of bonds. The richest 0.5 per cent (400,000 households) own 40 per cent of corporate stocks and bonds.

Income

One of the most significant changes in Western countries over the past century has been the rise in real income of the majority of the working population (real income is actual income excluding the effects of inflation, so as to provide a fixed standard of comparison from year to year). Blue-collar workers in Western societies now earn between three and four times as much as their counterparts at the turn of the century. Relative gains for white-collar, managerial and professional workers have been slightly higher. In terms of earnings per head of the population and the range of goods and services which can be purchased, the majority of the population in the West today are vastly more affluent than most people have been before in human history. One of the most important reasons for the growth in earnings is the increasing *productivity* – output per worker – that has been secured through technological development in industry. The value of the goods and services produced per worker has risen more or less continually, in many industries at least, since the 1900s.

Nevertheless, just as in the case of wealth, income distribution remains unequal. The top 20 per cent of households in 1994 received half of the total income for the population. The top 5 per cent of earners in the United States receive 17.6 per cent of total income; the highest 20 per cent obtain 44.6 per cent; and the bottom 20 per cent receive only 4.4 per cent. The average pretax earnings of the poorest fifth of people in the United States declined by about 5 per cent in the period from 1977 to 1992. During the same period, the richest fifth saw their incomes grow by 9 per cent before taxes – and the tax burden on these people was lower in 1992 than it had been in 1977.

Let us look now at CLASS STRUCTURE, the pattern of class divisions in the United Kingdom, making a few comments about other countries along the way.

Social class divisions

The upper class

The upper class in British society consists of relatively small numbers of individuals and families who own considerable amounts of property – thinking of them as the top 1 per cent of wealth-holders provides an approximate statistical guide. There tend to be fairly clear status divisions within the upper class between 'old' and 'new' money. Families whose property has been inherited through several generations often look down on those whose wealth is self-made. While they may mix in some contexts, those who have risen from humbler origins often find themselves excluded from most of the circles in which the longer-established wealthy move.

Property, as both Marx and Weber emphasize, confers power, and members of the upper class are disproportionately represented at the higher levels of power. Their influence stems in part from direct control of industrial and financial capital, and in part from their access to leading positions in the political, educational and cultural spheres.

John Scott has described the three sectors of the upper class in the nineteenth century: large landowners, financial entrepreneurs and industrialists (Scott 1991). The first of these saw itself as an aristocracy, but came gradually during the course of the century to extend such recognition to the more successful of the financial groups. The industrialists, many of whose enterprises were located in the north, were kept, and to some extent kept themselves, at arm's length. As the century progressed and their wealth grew, they were accepted more and more by the other two sectors. By the end of the century, the industrialists had acquired interests in land and in banks and insurance companies, while landowners were supplementing their income with earnings from directorships in the industrial companies.

*'So when we got back both the Ferrari and the Rolls had been clamped. I mean
Sarah isn't that just typical of my luck.'*

The merger of the different groupings within the upper class, Scott argues, has continued throughout the twentieth century – although some conflicts continue and divisions persist. For example, financial leaders in the City of London sometimes find themselves at odds with the heads of business corporations; policies which benefit one group do not always favour the other. Landowners have today largely disappeared as a separate sector of the upper class. Many of the old landed estates have come into public ownership; the only people who can afford to run the others in the traditional manner are those who have made money by other means.

The middle class

The phrase *the middle class* covers people working in many different occupations. According to some observers, the majority of the population of Britain today falls into this class, because the proportion of white-collar jobs has risen markedly relative to blue-collar ones (see chapter 12, 'Work and economic life').

There are three fairly distinct sectors within the middle class. The *old middle class* consists of self-employed owners of small businesses, proprietors of local shops, and small farmers.

The proportion of people who are self-employed has been declining for most of the century. Over the past fifteen years, however, this trend has gone into reverse. In 1981, 6.7 per cent of the workforce was self-employed. By 1991 this figure had risen to 10 per cent. One study looked at what a group of people who were self-employed in 1981 were doing in 1991. Not all were still in the labour market, and of those only two-thirds were still in self-employment (Fielding 1995).

Even then, during that time, they might have been involved with several businesses.

Small businesses are much more unstable than larger ones, and most fail within two years of being set up. Only some 20 per cent of those established in any one year in the UK are still in business five years later. Small firms and shops are often unable to compete effectively with the large companies, supermarkets and restaurant chains. If the old middle class has not shrunk as much as some (including Marx) once thought would be the case, it is because there is a large reservoir of people wanting to try their hand at starting a business of their own. Most of those who go out of business are thus replaced by others. Small-business men and women tend to have a fairly distinct social and political outlook. In some countries, such as France, many have been persistent supporters of political parties of the extreme right.

The *upper middle class* is made up mainly of those holding managerial or professional positions. This category includes large numbers of individuals and families, and generalizing about their attitudes and outlook is risky. Most have experienced some form of higher education, and the proportion holding liberal views on social and political issues, especially among professional groups, is fairly high.

Rather than speak of the 'upper middle class', the Oxford sociologist John Goldthorpe prefers the term 'service class'. The service class refers to professional, managerial and technical workers, a category which, as we shall see later, is expanding in modern societies. The term is potentially confusing. Goldthorpe does not mean workers who are in the service sector. Rather, the term signifies workers who 'service' the needs of employers – who provide an administrative apparatus for the conduct of their businesses or organizations. They provide specialized knowledge and managerial know-how; in return they enjoy privileges including high salaries, job security and fringe benefits such as private pension rights. Over the past two decades or so, however, as firms shed workers as part of an attempt to thin down and become more competitive, the economic conditions of the service class have become more unstable, some groups turning to self-employment.

The *lower middle class* is a heterogeneous category, including people working as office staff, sales representatives, teachers, nurses and others. For the most part, in spite of the merging of some of their conditions of work, the majority of members of the lower middle class have different social and political attitudes from most blue-collar workers.

The diverse character of the middle class as a whole is captured to some degree by concepts such as those offered by Wright and Parkin. Middle-class people find themselves in 'contradictory' situations of 'dual closure' in the sense that they are caught between conflicting pressures and influences. Many lower-middle-class people, for example, identify with the same values as those in more remunerative positions, but may find themselves living on incomes below those of the better-paid manual workers.

The working class

The working class consists of those working in blue-collar, manual occupations. As with the middle class, there tend to be marked divisions within the working class as a whole. One important source of such divisions is skill level. The *upper working class*, consisting of skilled workers, has frequently been seen as an 'aristocracy of labour', its members having incomes, conditions of work and job security superior to those in other blue-collar occupations. Although some skills have been undermined by technological developments and the position of the workers in the occupations concerned weakened – as among printers – on the whole the economic circumstances of skilled workers have become even more favourable in recent years. In many trades, their earnings have remained relatively high, and their jobs stable; they have been much less affected by increasing levels of unemployment than those in less skilled blue-collar jobs.

The *lower working class* is made up of those in unskilled or semi-skilled jobs, for which little training is needed. Most of these jobs carry lower incomes than, and inferior job security to, skilled occupations.

Working-class occupations differ in terms of whether they are full-time or part-time, and how much job security workers have. A distinction between *central* and *peripheral* areas of the economy helps to illuminate this. Central sectors are those where workers are in full-time jobs, obtaining relatively high earnings and enjoying long-term job security. Peripheral sectors are those where jobs are insecure, with low earnings and a high proportion of part-time workers. Skilled workers and a proportion of semi- and unskilled employees (mostly white males) predominate in the central sectors – which are also more often unionized. Others find themselves in the peripheral sector, where the level of unionization is low.

The underclass

A major line of demarcation within the working class is between the ethnic majority and underprivileged minorities – who compose an **underclass**. Members of the underclass have markedly worse work conditions and living standards than the majority of the population. Many are among the long-term unemployed, or drift in and out of jobs. In Britain, blacks and Asians are disproportionately represented in the underclass. In some European countries, migrant workers who found jobs in times of greater prosperity twenty years ago now make up a large part of this sector of the working class. This is true, for instance, of Algerians in France and Turkish migrants in West Germany.

The nature of underclasses has been hotly debated in sociology. Much of this debate has concentrated on the US, particularly as regards the position of poor blacks living in inner-city areas. William Julius Wilson has argued that the black population of the US has become divided in two.

In *The Declining Significance of Race*, drawing on research done in Chicago, Wilson argued that a substantial black middle class – white-collar workers and professionals – has emerged over the past three or four decades in the United States. Not all African Americans still live in city ghettos, and those who remain are kept there, Wilson maintained, not so much by active discrimination as by economic factors – in other words, by class rather than by race. The old racist barriers are disappearing; blacks are stuck in the ghetto as a result of economic disadvantages (Wilson 1978).

Wilson's work ignited a controversy that still burns fiercely. The conservative political writer Charles Murray agreed about the existence of a black underclass in most big cities. According to Murray, however, African Americans find themselves at the bottom of society as a result of the very welfare policies designed to help improve their position. People become dependent on welfare handouts and build a 'culture of poverty' around such welfare dependency. They then have little incentive to find jobs, build solid communities, or make stable marriages (Murray 1984).

In reply to Murray's claims, Wilson reiterated and extended his previous arguments, again using research carried out in Chicago. The movement of many whites from the cities to the suburbs, the decline of urban industries, and other urban economic problems, he suggested, led to high rates of joblessness among African-American men. The forms of social disintegration to which Murray pointed, including the high proportion of unmarried black mothers, Wilson explained in terms of the shrinking of the available pool of 'marriageable' (employed) men.

Murray subsequently applied his arguments to the UK (1990). According to him, there isn't as yet a clearly defined underclass in existence in the UK, but one is rapidly developing. It will include not only members of ethnic minorities, but whites from impoverished areas where social disintegration is advancing. Murray's work has been sharply criticized, however, by other sociologists working in this country.

We shall consider the validity of Murray's claims later. First, however, we look at changes affecting those at the higher levels of the class structure.

Changes in class structure

Decomposition of the upper class?

As noted earlier, the upper class (like all other class groups) has always been internally divided. Some authors have argued, however, that the upper class has today become so disaggregated that effectively it has disappeared as a coherent class category. In the nineteenth century and the earlier part of the current century, so the argument runs, membership of the upper class was based on ownership of property – businesses, financial organizations, or land. Today land, as mentioned, is no longer a significant source of power, and the economy is dominated by large business corporations, which are not owned by individuals. They have thousands of different shareholders, who have little influence over the running of the companies. Control of the large corporations has fallen into the hands of their top executives, who do not own the firms they run: they are simply high-grade white-collar workers or professionals.

Thus in John Goldthorpe's scheme of classes in modern societies there is no longer an upper class, only the 'service class', made up, at its highest levels, of business managers, higher-grade professionals and administrators. Other authors have pointed to the phenomenon of institutional shareholding (see chapter 12, 'Work and economic life') as accentuating a move away from the importance of private ownership of capital. A high percentage of shares today are owned by insurance companies, pension funds and unit trusts, and these cater for very large sections of the population. About half the population of the UK, for example, has today invested in private pension schemes.

Yet the view that there is no longer a distinguishable upper class is questionable. John Scott, whose analysis of the changing nature of the upper class was referred to earlier, has argued that the upper class today has changed shape, but retains its distinctive position. It consists of people linked by what he terms a 'constellation of interests' to the power of big business. Senior executives in large corporations may not own their companies, but they are often able to accumulate shareholdings, and these connect them both to old-style entrepreneurs and to 'finance capitalists'. 'Finance capitalists', a category including the people who run the insurance companies and other organizations that are large institutional shareholders, are at the core of the upper class today.

Professionals, managers, administrators

The growing number of people working in professional, managerial and administrative occupations is related to the importance of large-scale organizations in modern societies (see chapter 11, 'Modern organizations'). It is also connected with the expanding numbers of people working in sectors of the economy where the state plays a major role – for example, in government, education, health and social welfare. In spite of widespread privatization, in 1994 some 28 per cent of the labour force was working in state-owned industries. The majority of people working in professional occupations – doctors, accountants, lawyers and so forth – are in fact employed by the state.

Professionals, managers and higher-level administrators gain their position largely from their possession of 'credentials' – degrees, diplomas and other qualifications. As a whole they enjoy relatively secure and remunerative careers, and their separation from people in more routine non-manual jobs has probably grown more pronounced in recent years. Some have seen professionals and the other higher white-collar groups, indeed, as coming to form a specific class, the 'professional managerial class'. The degree of division between them and white-collar workers, however, does not seem either deep or clear-cut enough to make such a position defensible.

White collar, blue collar: feminization and proletarianization

Far more people today work in non-manual jobs than formerly was the case; but whether or not they have thereby become 'middle class' is a fiercely debated question in sociology. Two issues are involved here. First, many of the more routine non-manual jobs that have been created are filled by women. There has taken place a process of what has come to be called, somewhat clumsily, the *feminization* of routine white-collar labour. As we will see, the issue of class and gender is a complex one.

Second, the conditions of work for many people in such jobs have become downgraded or *deskilled* – the skills which the jobs used to require from human workers have become obsolete as machinery has been introduced to take over some of their functions. This applies, for example, to clerical and secretarial work in offices; calculating, writing and organizational skills have been partly superseded by the introduction of typewriters, adding machines, photocopying machines and, more recently, computers and word-processors.

Feminization and deskilling, in fact, are directly connected. For example, the more the proportion of people working in clerical and related occupations has grown, the higher the percentage of women in those occupations – and the more routinized those occupations become. Women also greatly outnumber men in the jobs at lower levels in the expanding sector of the marketing, retail and leisure industries. Jobs such as sales assistant, or check-out assistant, are largely feminized.

In his influential study *Labour and Monopoly Capital*, written some twenty years ago, Harry Braverman argued that most routine, white-collar jobs have become deskilled to such a degree that they now differ little from manual work. Far from more and more people becoming middle class, what we see here, it is said, is a process of 'proletarianization'. These groups are being thrust down into an expanding working class, which has to be seen as including many 'non-manual' jobs (Braverman 1974).

Most sociologists believe that Braverman overstated his case. Some occupations become *reskilled*, rather than deskilled, with the progress of technological change – more skill, rather than less, is required. This is true, for example, of some jobs affected by the introduction of computers (although others are actually downgraded by the same process). Moreover, the social class of a married individual depends also on the spouse's position. Women in routine non-manual jobs are often married to men in higher white-collar occupations: the household as a whole is middle class.

Studies of routine white-collar jobs, and of the workers in them, have produced somewhat conflicting results as regards the idea of proletarianization. Rosemary Crompton and Gareth Jones (1984) studied white-collar workers in a bank, local authority and insurance company. They found that women clerical workers were much less likely to be promoted to higher-level white-collar work than were men. Most of the jobs they studied they saw as proletarianized: workers simply follow a set of routines, without much place for initiative. Men are quite often able to escape from such positions, while women mostly cannot; hence it is mainly female white-collar jobs that have become downgraded.

Gordon Marshall et al. (1988) are critical of these conclusions, as well as of the views of Braverman. They interviewed men and women in a range of occupations and asked them if their jobs today required more skill than when they started work. They found that only 4 per cent claimed that their work needed less skill, and that the proportion was little different for feminized than for other white-collar jobs. White-collar workers, they concluded, still have greater autonomy in their jobs than most manual workers do; in terms of class consciousness, they are much more likely to think of themselves as 'middle class' than are manual workers.

Changes affecting the working class

As will be discussed later in the chapter, British society, in common with most other industrialized countries, has considerable numbers of poor people. However, the majority of individuals working in blue-collar occupations no longer live in poverty. As was mentioned earlier, the income of manual workers has increased considerably since the turn of the century. This rising standard of living is expressed in the increased availability of consumer goods across all classes. About 50 per cent of blue-collar workers now own their own homes. Cars, washing machines, televisions and telephones are owned by a very large proportion of households.

The phenomenon of working-class affluence suggests yet another possible route towards a more 'middle-class society'. Perhaps, as blue-collar workers grow more prosperous, they become more middle class? This idea, with the sociologist's characteristic fondness for cumbersome names, came to be known as the *embourgeoisement* thesis. Embourgeoisement means 'becoming more bourgeois', a Marxian-style term for 'becoming more middle class'.

In the 1960s, John Goldthorpe and his colleagues carried out what came to be a very well-known study of the embourgeoisement hypothesis. Based on interviews with workers in the car and chemical industries in Luton, the research was published in three volumes. It is often referred to as the *Affluent Worker* study (Goldthorpe et al. 1968–9). A total of 229 manual workers were studied, together with 54 white-collar workers for purposes of comparison. Many of the blue-collar workers had migrated to the area in search of well-paid jobs; compared to most other manual workers, they were in fact highly paid and earned more than most lower-level white-collar workers.

The results of the study, in the eyes of its authors, were clear-cut: the embourgeoisement thesis was false. These workers were not in the process of becoming more middle class. They held what Goldthorpe and his colleagues termed an 'instrumental' attitude towards their work: they saw it as a means to an end, the end of gaining good wages. Their work was mostly repetitive and uninteresting, and they had little direct commitment to it. Yet they did not associate with white-collar workers in their leisure-time, and did not aspire to rise up the class ladder; the money they earned they earmarked for various kinds of goods and possessions.

No strictly comparable research has been carried out in the intervening years, and it is not clear how far, if the conclusions reached by Goldthorpe et al. were valid at the time, they remain true now. It is generally agreed that the old, traditional working-class communities have tended to become fragmented, or have broken down altogether, with the decline of manufacturing industry and the impact of consumerism. Just how far such fragmentation has proceeded, however, remains open to dispute.

Divisions within the working class reflect contrasts between households, not just individuals. Ray Pahl's work, *Divisions of Labour* (1984), reports a study of working-class families in the Isle of Sheppey, in Kent. He found a schism between 'work-rich' and 'work-poor' households. The former refers to a situation where two or more members of a household are in stable jobs; such people tend to own their own dwellings and have a comfortable lifestyle. Those in 'work-poor' households, on the other hand, find making ends meet much more of a struggle.

In general it would be difficult to dispute that stratification within the working class, as well as between classes, has come to depend not only on occupational differences but on differences in consumption and lifestyle. Modern societies have become in important respects consumer societies, geared to the acquisition of material goods. In some respects a consumer society is a 'mass society', where class differences are to a degree overridden; thus people from different class backgrounds may all watch similar television programmes. Yet class differences can also become *intensified* through variations in lifestyle and 'taste' (Bourdieu 1986).

The question of the underclass

Whether tendencies towards the formation of an underclass have gone as far in the UK and Europe as Murray claims is open to dispute. Lydia Morris reports on research she carried out in Hartlepool, in the northeast of England. It is in areas in Britain where there has been a decline in manufacturing industry and a large-scale rise in unemployment that an underclass is likely to emerge. Hartlepool is one such area.

Morris studied three groups of unemployed workers: the first consisted of couples in which the man had been unemployed for at least twelve months; the second of couples in which the man had held the same job for the last twelve months; and the third of couples in which the man had started a new job within the last twelve months. The people studied were nearly all white. Morris points out that unemployment in the UK is not so distinctively a 'black' issue as in the US.

In terms of social inclusion – whether individuals and families have networks of support on which they can rely – Morris found little difference between the three groups. Those who had been unemployed for more than a year were still concerned with the search for work; they had not created an anti-work culture. The situation of these men resulted from the long-term economic decline of the area, lack of skills and a relative absence of work-based informal contacts which might have helped them to find local employment. Morris did find, however, that most of the long-term unemployed had partners who were also unemployed, and that they had the highest proportion of unemployed friends. Nevertheless, she concluded that 'There is no direct evidence in my study of a distinctive culture of the "underclass"' (Morris 1993, p. 410).

Morris's research is by no means conclusive. It was conducted in only one part of the country, and that was one where ethnic minorities were not heavily represented. West Indian and Asian men are more concentrated in semi-skilled work, and have higher average rates of employment, than white males (Pilkington 1992).

The tendencies towards economic division and social exclusion now characteristic of America do seem to be hardening both in Britain and Western Europe. The racial and ethnic element here is prominent. In cities such as London, Manchester, Rotterdam, Frankfurt, Paris and Naples the position of the urban poor is worsening. Hamburg is Europe's richest city, as measured by average personal income, and has the highest proportion of millionaires in Germany. It also has the highest proportion on welfare and unemployment – 40 per cent above the national average. A third of industrial jobs in and around the city have disappeared in the fifteen years up to 1994.

The majority of poor and unemployed people in West European countries are native to their countries, but there are also many first and second generation immigrants in poverty and trapped in deteriorating city neighbourhoods, and the proportion of lone-parent families is increasing. Moss Side in Manchester, Gallusviertel in Frankfurt and Nieuwe Western in Rotterdam are examples.

A group of Dutch sociologists interviewed several hundred people living in the poorer city areas of Holland. They found (contrary to Morris's conclusions) that 55 per cent of the long-term unemployed among the interviewees had stopped looking for work. The researchers concluded that most had taken a decision to give up work and live on welfare (Engbersen et al. 1993).

GENDER AND STRATIFICATION

Studies of stratification were for many years 'gender blind' – they were written as though women did not exist, or as though, for purposes of analysing divisions of power, wealth and prestige, women were unimportant and uninteresting. Yet gender itself is one of the most profound examples of stratification. There are no societies in which men do not, in some aspects of social life, have more wealth, status and influence than women.

Class divisions and gender

One of the main problems posed by the study of gender and stratification in modern societies sounds simple, but turns out to be difficult to resolve. This is the question of how far we can understand gender inequalities in modern times mainly in terms of class divisions. Inequalities of gender are more deep-rooted historically than class systems; men have superior standing to women even in hunting and gathering societies, where there are no classes. Yet class divisions are so marked in modern societies that there is no doubt that they 'overlap' substantially with gender inequalities. The material position of most women tends to reflect that of their fathers or husbands; hence it can be argued that we have to explain gender inequalities mainly in class terms.

In a classic work on stratification, Frank Parkin expressed this point of view very well:

> Female status certainly carries with it many disadvantages compared with that of males in various areas of social life including employment opportunities, property ownership, income, and so on. However, these inequalities associated with sex differences are not usefully thought of as components of stratification. This is because for the great majority of women the allocation of social and economic rewards is determined primarily by the position of their families and, in particular, that of the male head. Although women today share certain status attributes in common, simply by virtue of their sex, their claims over resources are not primarily determined by their own occupation but, more commonly, by that of their fathers or husbands. And if the wives and daughters of unskilled labourers have something in common with the wives and daughters of wealthy landowners, there can be no doubt that the *differences* in their overall situation are far more striking and significant. Only if the disabilities attaching to female status were felt to be so great as to override differences of a class kind would it be realistic to regard sex as an important dimension of stratification. (Parkin 1971, pp. 14–15)

Women, it can be argued, tend even today to be confined to a 'private' domain – the domestic world of the family, children and the household. Men, on the other hand, live more of a 'public' life, and they determine how wealth and power are distributed. Their world is that of paid work, industry and politics.

The view that class inequalities largely govern gender stratification was often an unstated assumption until recently, but the issue has now become the subject of some debate. John Goldthorpe has defended what he calls the 'conventional position' in class analysis – that the paid work of women is relatively insignificant compared to that of men, and that therefore women can be regarded as being in the same class as their husbands (Goldthorpe 1983). This is not, Goldthorpe emphasizes, a view based on an ideology of sexism. On the contrary, it recognizes the subordinate position in which most women find themselves in the labour force. Women have part-time jobs more often than men, and tend to have more intermittent experience of paid employment because of withdrawing for lengthy periods to bear and care for children. Since the majority of women are in a position of economic dependence on their husbands, it follows that their class position is most often governed by the husbands' class situation.

Goldthorpe's argument can be criticized in several ways. First, in a substantial proportion of households the income of women is essential to maintaining the family's economic position and mode of life. In these circumstances women's paid employment in some part determines the class position of households. Second, a wife's employment may strongly influence that of her husband, not simply the other way round. Even where a woman earns less than her husband, her working situation may still be the 'lead' factor in influencing the class of her husband. This could be the case, for instance, if the husband is an unskilled or semi-skilled blue-collar worker and the wife, say, the manageress of a shop. The wife's occupation may set the standard of the position of the family as a whole.

Third, many 'cross-class' households exist, in which the work of the husband is in a higher class category than that of the wife, or (less commonly) the other way round. Since few studies of such households have been carried out, we cannot be confident that it is always appropriate to take the occupation of the male as the determining influence. There may be some purposes for which it is more realistic to treat men and women, even within the same households, as being in different class positions. Fourth, the proportion of families in which women are the sole breadwinners is increasing. Unless the woman has an income derived from alimony which puts her on the same economic level as her ex-husband, she is by definition the determining influence on her own class position (Stanworth 1984; Walby 1986).

Research supports the conclusion that the economic position of a woman cannot simply be 'read off' from that of her husband. A study carried out in Sweden showed cross-class families to be common (Leiuffsrud and Woodward 1987). In most such cases, the husband had the superior occupation, although in a minority of instances the reverse was the case. The research showed that individuals in such families tended to 'import' aspects of their differing class position into the family. Decisions, for instance, about who stays home to care for a sick child were related to the interaction of class and gender in the family. Where the wife's job was superior to that of the husband, he would usually have this responsibility.

The debate continues

Goldthorpe and others have defended the view he proposed and added some further observations. For research purposes, they say, it is reasonable to use the partner of the higher class to classify a household, whether that person be a man or a woman. Moreover, they argue, where material on wives has been included in research, the result is only to modify, rather than radically alter, the findings of the 'conventional position' (Goldthorpe et al. 1988).

Developing the debate further, some authors have suggested that the class position of an individual should be determined without reference to the household. Social class, in other words, would be assessed from occupation independently for each individual, without specific reference to that person's domestic circumstances. This approach was taken, for example, in the work of Gordon Marshall and his colleagues in a study of the class system of the UK (Marshall et al. 1988).

Such a perspective, however, also has its difficulties. It leaves on one side those who are not in paid employment, including not only full-time housewives, but also retired people and the unemployed. The latter two groups can be categorized in terms of the last occupations they held, but this can be problematic if they have not worked for some while. Moreover, it seems potentially very misleading to ignore the household altogether. Whether individuals are single or in a domestic partnership can make a large difference in the opportunities open to them.

Research carried out by Norman Bonney (1992) shows that high-earning women tend to have high-earning partners, and that the wives of men in professional and managerial occupations have higher earnings than other employed female partners. This finding suggests that the growing involvement of women in paid employment may lead to an accentuation of class divisions between households, which would not be picked up if individuals were considered only separately. Marriage tends to produce partnerships where both individuals are relatively privileged or disadvantaged in terms of occupational attainment.

We now turn to look at the issue of social mobility. Here, as in other areas of class analysis, for a long while the question of gender was largely ignored.

SOCIAL MOBILITY

In studying stratification, we have to consider not only the differences between economic positions or occupations, but what happens to the individuals who occupy them. The term SOCIAL MOBILITY refers to the movement of individuals and groups between different socioeconomic positions. **Vertical mobility** means movement up or down the socioeconomic scale. Those who gain in property, income or status are said to be *upwardly mobile*, while those who move in the opposite direction are *downwardly mobile*. In modern societies there is also a great deal of **lateral mobility**, which refers to geographical movement between neighbourhoods, towns or regions. Vertical and lateral mobility are often combined. For instance, an individual working in a company in one city might be promoted to a higher position in a branch of the firm located in another town, or even in a different country.

There are two ways of studying social mobility. First, we can look at individuals' own careers – how far they move up or down the social scale in the course of their working lives. This is usually called **intra-generational mobility**. Alternatively, we can analyse how far children enter the same type of occupation as their parents or grandparents. Mobility across the generations is called **intergenerational mobility**.

Comparative mobility studies

The amount of vertical mobility in a society is a major index of the degree of its 'openness', indicating how far talented individuals born into lower strata can move up the socioeconomic ladder. How 'open' are the industrialized countries in terms of social mobility? Is there more equality of opportunity in Britain than elsewhere? Studies of social mobility have been carried on for a period of more than fifty years, frequently involving international comparisons. One of the earliest works in the field was that of Pitirim Sorokin (1927). Sorokin covered a vast array of different societies, including traditional Rome and China, and also carried out one of the first detailed studies of mobility in the United States. He concluded that opportunities for rapid ascent in the US were much more limited than American folklore suggested. The techniques Sorokin used to gather his data, however, were relatively primitive.

Research carried out by Peter Blau and Otis Dudley Duncan forty years later was far more sophisticated and comprehensive (Blau and Duncan 1967). Their investigation remains the most detailed study of social mobility yet carried out in any single country. (Wide-ranging though it may have been, like most other studies of mobility, it bears out the points made previously – all those studied were men.) Blau and Duncan collected information on a national sample of 20,000 males. They concluded that there is much vertical mobility in the United States, but nearly all of this is between occupational positions quite close to one another. 'Long-range' mobility is rare. Although downward movement does occur, both within the careers of individuals and intergenerationally, it is much less common than upward mobility. The reason for this is that white-collar and professional jobs have grown much more rapidly than blue-collar ones, a shift that has created openings for sons of blue-collar workers to move into white-collar positions.

Perhaps the most celebrated international study of social mobility was that carried out by Seymour Martin Lipset and Reinhard Bendix (1959). They analysed data from nine industrialized societies – Britain, France, West Germany, Sweden, Switzerland, Japan, Denmark, Italy and the United States, concentrating on mobility of men from blue-collar to white-collar work. Contrary to their expectations, they discovered no evidence that the United States was more open than the European societies. Total vertical mobility across the blue-collar/white-collar line was 30 per cent in the United States, with the other societies varying between 27 and 31 per cent. Lipset and Bendix concluded that all the industrialized countries were experiencing similar changes in respect of the expansion of white-collar jobs. This led to an 'upward surge of mobility' of comparable dimensions in all of them. Others have questioned their findings, arguing that significant differences between countries are found if more attention is given to downward mobility, and if long-range mobility is also brought into consideration (Heath 1981; Grusky and Hauser 1984).

In their work *The Constant Flux* (1993), Robert Erikson and John Goldthorpe report on their most recent research into social mobility.

They studied mobility in Western and Eastern Europe, the US, Australia and Japan. Data from twelve national studies of mobility, covering roughly the first seventy years of this century, were analysed. They found that there was no long-term tendency for mobility rates to increase. Total mobility rates 'move in what would appear to be an essentially directionless fashion' (p. 367). The United States did not have significantly higher rates of mobility than the other countries which were looked at.

Downward mobility

Although **downward mobility** is less common than upward mobility, it is still a widespread phenomenon. Downward intragenerational mobility is also common. Mobility of this type is quite often associated with psychological problems and anxieties, where individuals become unable to sustain the lifestyles to which they have become accustomed. Redundancy is another of the main sources of downward mobility. Middle-aged people who lose their jobs, for example, either find it hard to gain new employment at all, or can only obtain work at a lower level of income than before.

Thus far there have been very few studies of downward mobility in the UK. It is probable, however, that downward mobility, in inter- and intragenerational terms, is on the increase in Britain as it is in the United States. In the US there have been several recent studies of the phenomenon. Over the 1980s and early 1990s, for the first time since World War Two, there was a general downturn in the average real earnings (earnings after inflation) of people in middle-level white-collar jobs in the US. Thus even if such jobs continue to expand relative to others, they may not support the lifestyle aspirations they once did.

Corporate restructuring and 'downsizing' are the main reasons why these changes are happening. In the face of increasing global competition, many companies have trimmed their workforces. White-collar as well as full-time blue-collar jobs have been lost – to be replaced by poorly paid, part-time occupations.

Downward mobility in the US is particularly common today among divorced or separated women with children. As an illustration, we might take the life of Sandra Bolton, described by John Schwarz in his book *The Forgotten Americans*. Sandra's fate belies the idea that people who work hard and follow the rules will be able to prosper. Sandra's husband had regularly assaulted her during the six years of their marriage, and child welfare officials considered him a threat to their two children. She divorced her husband after the Child Protective Services told her that the state would take her children if she didn't leave him.

Sandra receives no maintenance from her ex-husband, who, two weeks before the divorce was finalized, piled their furniture and valuables into a truck and drove away, not to be seen again. Whereas while married she sustained a moderately comfortable, middle-class way of life, Sandra now lives a hand-to-mouth existence. She tried to remain in college, supporting herself and her children by doing various menial jobs, but was unable to earn enough money to keep up.

A neighbour looked after her children while she took a full-time job as a secretary at a medical centre. Taking courses at night and during the summers, she eventually completed a college degree. Although she has applied at many places, she hasn't been able to find a position paying more than her secretarial job. The money she earns isn't enough to pay for the ordinary expenses she and her children incur, so she has taken on a second job, as check-out person in a supermarket, in the evenings – and even then can only just make ends meet.

'You try to do the responsible thing,' she says, 'and you're penalized, because the system we have right now doesn't provide you with a way to make it. I mean, I work so hard. There's only so much a person can do' (Schwarz 1991).

As a result of her divorce, Sandra has sunk from a life of some comfort to living in poverty. She is not alone – in the US, or in Britain.

Social mobility and success

Many people in modern societies believe that it is possible for anyone to reach the top if they work hard and persistently enough, yet the figures indicate that very few succeed. Why should it be so difficult? In one respect, the answer is very simple. Even in a 'perfectly fluid' society, in which everyone had an exactly equal chance of reaching the highest positions, only a small minority would do so. The socioeconomic order at the top is shaped like a pyramid, with only relatively few positions of power, status or wealth. No more than two or three thousand people, out of a total population of fifty-eight million in Britain, could become directors of one of the two hundred largest corporations.

In addition, however, those who hold positions of wealth and power have many openings available to them to perpetuate their advantages and to pass them on to their offspring. They can make sure their children have the best available education, and this will often lead them into good jobs. In spite of wealth taxes and death duties, the rich have normally found means of passing on much of their property to their descendants. Most of those who make it to the top have a head start – they come from professional or affluent backgrounds. Studies of people who have become wealthy show that hardly anyone begins with nothing. The large majority of people who have 'made money' did so on the basis of inheriting or being given at least a modest amount initially – which they then used to make more.

William Rubinstein carried out a study of the backgrounds of British millionaires in the 1980s (Rubinstein 1986). He based his work on people who died in 1984 and 1985 leaving at least one million pounds. (It is almost impossible to discover reliable facts about living millionaires.) Rubinstein found that those whose fathers were wealthy businessmen or landowners still make up 42 per cent of the ranks of millionaires. People likely to have received material encouragement from their families (those with parents who were higher professionals) account for an additional 29 per cent. Forty-three per cent of millionaires inherited over £100,000 each, and a further 32 per cent inherited between £10,000 and £100,000. In Britain the surest way to become rich is still to be born rich.

Levels of mobility

Overall levels of mobility have been extensively studied in Britain over the postwar period – although again virtually all the research has concentrated on men. An early study was directed by David Glass (1954). Glass's work analysed intergenerational mobility for a longish period up to the 1950s. His findings correspond to those noted above in respect of international data (around 30 per cent mobility from blue-collar to white-collar jobs). Glass's research was in fact widely drawn on by those making international comparisons. While a good deal of mobility occurred, most of this was short range. Upward mobility was much more common than downward mobility, and was mostly concentrated at the middle levels of the class structure. People right at the bottom tended to stay there; almost 50 per cent of sons of workers in professional and managerial jobs were themselves in similar occupations.

A further study was carried out by John Goldthorpe and his colleagues at Oxford, based on a survey carried out in 1972 (Goldthorpe et al. 1980). They sought to investigate how far patterns of social mobility had altered since the time of Glass's work, and concluded that the overall level of mobility of men was in fact higher than in the previous period, with rather more long-range movement being noted. The main reason for this, however, was not that the occupational system had become more egalitarian. Rather, the origin of the changes was the accelerating growth in the number of higher white-collar jobs relative to blue-collar ones. The researchers found that two-thirds of the sons of unskilled or semi-skilled manual workers were themselves in manual occupations. About 30 per cent of professionals and managers were of working-class origins, while some 4 per cent of men in blue-collar work were from professional or managerial backgrounds.

Although the data are incomplete, research by Anthony Heath indicates that the mobility chances of women are severely limited by the lack of opportunities for female employees in professional and managerial occupations (Heath 1981). Over half the daughters of professionals or managers are in routine office jobs, no more than 8 per cent obtaining positions at a level comparable to those of their fathers. Only 1.5 per cent of women from blue-collar homes are to be found in such occupations (although 48 per cent are in routine office work).

The original Oxford mobility study was updated on the basis of new material collected about ten years later (Goldthorpe and Payne 1986). The major findings of the earlier work were corroborated, but some further developments were found. The chances of boys from blue-collar backgrounds getting professional or managerial jobs, for example, had increased. Once again, this was traced to changes in the occupational structure, producing a reduction of blue-collar occupations relative to higher white-collar jobs. Downward mobility was even less frequent than in the preceding research. However, a much higher proportion than before of men from working-class backgrounds were unemployed, reflecting the spread of mass unemployment from the early 1970s onwards.

Marshall et al. produced results in the 1980s which largely corroborated the findings of Goldthorpe and others. They found about a third of people in higher white-collar or professional jobs were from blue-collar backgrounds. Findings such as these demonstrate a substantial amount of fluidity in British society. For many people it is indeed possible to move up the social hierarchy, in terms of both intragenerational and intergenerational mobility; but the scales are still biased against women, and the fluid character of modern society derives mostly from its propensity to upgrade occupations. Marshall and his co-workers conclude: 'More "room at the top" has not been accompanied by great equality in the opportunities to get there' (Marshall et al. 1988, p. 138). However, one should bear in mind a point made earlier: mobility is a long-term process, and if the society is becoming more 'open', the full effects will not be seen for a generation.

Problems in studying social mobility

The study of social mobility presents various problems. For example, it is not clear whether mobility from blue-collar to white-collar work is always correctly defined as 'upward'. Skilled blue-collar workers may be in a superior economic position to many people in more routine white-collar jobs. The nature of jobs alters over time, and it is not always obvious that what are regarded as the 'same' occupations are in fact still such. Clerical occupations, for instance, as we have seen, have changed greatly over the past several decades, through the mechanization and computerization of office work. Another difficulty is that, in studies of intergenerational mobility, it is difficult to decide at what point of the respective careers to make comparisons. A parent may still be at mid-career when a child begins his or her work life; parents and their offspring may simultaneously be mobile, perhaps in the same direction or (less often) in different directions. Should we compare them at the beginning or the end of their careers?

All these difficulties can be dealt with to some extent. Care can be taken to alter occupational categories when it is clear that the nature of jobs has shifted radically over the period covered by a particular study. For example, we might decide to group higher blue-collar and routine white-collar jobs together, examining mobility into and out of these jobs as a whole. The problem about where in individuals' careers to make comparisons in studying intergenerational mobility can be resolved – where the data permit – by comparing parents and children both at the beginning and at the end of their careers. But these strategies are not entirely satisfactory. What may appear to be precise figures in mobility studies have to be approached with caution. We can only draw general conclusions from mobility research, particularly where international comparisons are involved.

Your own mobility chances

What implications might be drawn from mobility studies about the career opportunities which face you, as someone searching for a good job in the 1990s? Like previous generations, you are likely to enjoy upward mobility if you do not already come from a privileged background. It seems probable that the proportion of managerial and professional jobs will continue to expand relative to lower-level positions. Those who have done well in the educational system are most likely to fill these 'empty places'.

Yet there are not nearly enough higher-status positions open for all who wish to enter them, and some of you are bound to find that your careers do not match up to what you had hoped for. Although a higher proportion of jobs is being created at managerial and professional levels than existed before, the overall number available in the economy is declining, as compared to people actively seeking work. One reason for this is the growing number of women competing with men for a finite number of jobs. Another (whose consequences are difficult to sort out fully as yet) is the increasing use of information technology in production processes. Because computerized machinery can now handle tasks – even of a highly complicated kind – which once only human beings could do, it is possible, and perhaps even likely, that many jobs will be eliminated in future years.

If you are a woman, although your chances of entering a good career are improving, you face two major obstacles to your progress. Male managers and employers still discriminate against women applicants. They do so at least partly because of their belief that 'women are not really interested in careers', and that they are likely to leave the workforce when they begin a family. The second of these factors does indeed still very substantially affect the chances of women. This is less because they are uninterested in a career than because they are often effectively forced to choose between a career and having children. Men are rarely willing to share full responsibility for domestic work and child care. Although many more women than before are organizing their domestic lives in order to pursue a career, there are still major barriers in their way.

POVERTY AND INEQUALITY

Right at the bottom of the class system, large numbers of people in the United Kingdom exist in conditions of poverty. Many do not have a proper diet, and live in insanitary conditions, having a lower life expectancy than the majority of the population. Yet more affluent people often have little accurate knowledge about the extent of poverty.

This is not a new phenomenon. In 1889, Charles Booth published a work which showed that a third of Londoners were living in dire poverty (Booth 1889). The result was a public outcry. How could it happen that, in a country which at the time was probably the wealthiest on earth, at the centre of a massive empire, poverty should be so widespread? Booth's work was taken up by his namesake, General William Booth of the Salvation Army. His *In Darkest England and the Way Out* (1970, originally published in 1890) opened with figures derived from Charles Booth's calculations, showing there to be 387,000 'very poor' people in London, 220,000 'near starving' and 300,000 'starving'. Almost a quarter of a million copies of William Booth's book were sold within a year, so effectively did he capture the public imagination. Poverty, he proposed, could be drastically reduced by the means of practical programmes of reform and welfare.

What is poverty?

How should *poverty* be defined? A distinction is usually made between *subsistence* or **absolute poverty** and **relative poverty**. Charles Booth was one of the first to try to establish a consistent standard of subsistence poverty, which refers to lack of basic requirements to sustain a physically healthy existence – sufficient food and shelter to make possible the physically efficient functioning of the body. Booth assumed that these requirements would be more or less the same for people of equivalent age and physique living in any country. This is essentially the concept still used most frequently in the analysis of poverty worldwide.

Subsistence definitions of poverty have various inadequacies, especially when formulated as a specific income level. Unless it is set quite high, even allowing for adjustments, a single criterion of poverty tends to mean that some individuals are assessed as above the poverty line when in fact their income does not meet even their basic subsistence needs. Some parts of the country, for example, are much more expensive to live in than others. Moreover, the subsistence calculation of poverty does not take into account the impact of generally rising living standards. It is more realistic to adjust ideas about levels of poverty to the changing norms and expectations in a society as economic growth occurs. The majority of the world's population live in dwellings that do not contain a bath or shower; but it would be hard not to see piped water as a necessity in an industrialized society. Problems with formulations of relative poverty are also complex, however. Income criteria are again generally used, but these conceal variabilities in the actual needs people have.

Poverty today

In contrast to the United States and many other countries, where there is an officially set 'poverty line', in Britain interpretations of poverty as such are not provided by the government.

Studies in the UK used to define anyone having an income on or below the level of supplementary benefit as living 'in poverty'. 'Supplementary benefit' referred to cash benefits paid to people whose income did not reach a level deemed necessary for subsistence. People with incomes of between 100 and 140 per cent of supplementary benefit were defined as living 'on the margins of poverty'. Supplementary benefit no longer exists, but the latest available figures still relate to the period when it was in use.

The numbers of people living in, or on the margins of, poverty increased dramatically throughout the 1980s. In 1979, 6 million people, 12 per cent of the population, were in the first category, and 22 per cent in the two categories combined. The figures for 1987 were 19 per cent and 28 per cent respectively; 10 million people were living in poverty and a further 5 million were living near the margins (Blackburn 1991). About two-thirds of the overall increase in the two categories was a result of the rise in unemployment over the period.

Who are the poor? People in the following categories are particularly likely to be living in poverty: the unemployed, those in part-time or insecure jobs, older people, the sick and disabled, and members of large families and/or single-parent families. About half of all old age pensioners are living in poverty. Many people who may have been reasonably paid during their working lives experience a sharp reduction in income on retirement. Single-parent families, nearly all headed by women, make up an increasing proportion of the poor. The high unemployment of the 1980s and early 1990s seems unlikely to decline in the near future, and prolonged unemployment for principal breadwinners and their offspring is pushing more and more families into poverty.

The proportion of children (those under fifteen years of age) living in households with income 50 per cent below the national average – one way of defining poverty – has risen over recent years. In 1979, 10 per cent of children were living in such households. By 1991, this proportion had grown to 31 per cent. Surveying this and other research, Vinod Kumar concludes that a 'review of the evidence, based on a variety of measures of poverty, indicates the continuation of an unmistakable trend towards sharply rising child poverty' (Kumar 1993, p. 187).

The most important influences on the spread of child poverty are high rates of unemployment, an increase in the proportion of low-paid jobs in the economy and the growth in the number of single-parent households.

Why are the poor still poor?

Some general influences on the level of poverty have been well established. Well-developed and systematically administered welfare programmes, in conjunction with government policies which actively assist in keeping down unemployment, reduce poverty levels. Some societies do exist – such as Sweden – in which subsistence poverty has been almost completely eliminated. A social price probably has to be paid for this, not just in terms of high levels of taxation, but in the development of bureaucratic government agencies which may appropriate a great deal of power. Yet the more the distribution of wealth and income in a country is left open to mechanisms of the market – as was the case in the UK in the 1980s – the greater the material inequalities found. The theory underlying the policies of Mrs Thatcher's governments was that cutting tax rates for individuals and corporations would generate high levels of economic growth, the fruits of which would 'trickle down' to the poor. The evidence does not support this thesis. Such an economic policy may or may not generate acceleration of economic development, but the result tends to expand the differentials between the poor and the wealthy, actually swelling the numbers of those living in subsistence poverty. (For international comparisons of the size and impact of social programmes, see table 10.2.)

Surveys have shown that the majority of Britons regard the poor as responsible for their own poverty and are suspicious of those who live 'for free' on 'government handouts'. Many believe that people on welfare could find work if they were determined to do so. These views are out of line with the realities of poverty. About a quarter of those officially living in poverty are in work anyway, but earn too little to bring them over the poverty threshold. Of the remainder, the majority are children under fourteen, those aged sixty-five and over, and the ill

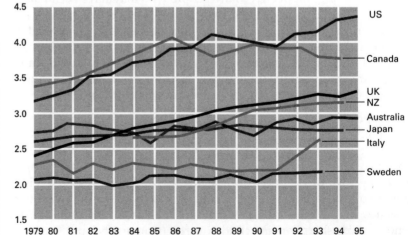

Income of richest 10% divided by income of poorest 10%

Fig. 10.1 The graph shows the ratio of male earnings in the top 10 per cent of the population to male earnings in the bottom 10 per cent. The higher the figure (see vertical axis), the greater the inequality

Source: Independent on Sunday, 21 July 1996.

Table 10.2	Relative size and impact of social programmes in seven Western nations		
	Percentage of all low-income persons whom governmental benefits lift to half the median income	**Percentage of all low-income two-parent families that governmental benefits lift to half the median income**	**Percentage of all elderly low-income families that governmental benefits lift to half the median income**
United Kingdom	68.5	63.1	77.0
United States	38.1	19.4	71.5
Israel	50.0	42.9	58.1
Canada	52.7	40.5	84.4
Norway	80.1	56.4	94.0
(West) Germany	78.8	69.8	88.4
Sweden	87.8	76.5	99.9

Source: Adapted from Timothy M. Smeeding et al. (eds), *Poverty, Inequality, and Income Distribution in Comparative Perspective*, 1990, pp. 30–1, table 2.1, and p. 67, table 3.5.

or disabled. In spite of popular views about the high level of welfare cheating, fewer than 1 per cent of welfare applications involve fraudulent claims – much lower than in the case of income tax returns, where it is estimated that more than 10 per cent of tax is lost through misreporting or evasion.

Poverty and welfare dependency

Being poor does not necessarily mean being mired in poverty. A substantial proportion of people in poverty at any one time have either enjoyed superior conditions of life previously or can be expected to climb out of poverty at some time in the future. For many, however, it is a lifetime sentence, particularly for those who are among the long-term unemployed.

Critics of existing welfare institutions have argued that these produce 'welfare dependency', meaning that people become dependent on the very programmes that are supposed to allow them to forge an independent and meaningful life for themselves. They become not just materially dependent, but psychologically dependent on the arrival of the welfare payment. Instead of taking an active attitude towards their lives, they tend to adopt a resigned and passive one, looking to the welfare system to support them.

The idea of **welfare dependency** is a controversial one and some deny that such dependency is widespread. 'Being on welfare' is commonly regarded as a source of shame, they say, and most people who are in such a position probably strive actively to escape from it as far as possible.

Carol Walker has analysed research into how people living on income support manage to organize their lives. She found a picture very different from that painted by those who argue that living on welfare is an easy option. Of unemployed respondents in one study, 80 per cent had experienced a deterioration in their living standards since living on welfare. For nearly all, life became much more of a struggle. For a minority, on the other hand, social assistance can bring improvements in living standards. For instance, someone who is unemployed and reaches age sixty is relabelled a 'pensioner claimant' and can claim benefits 30 per cent higher than those previously obtained.

The category of those whose circumstances may improve does in fact include single parents. Research indicates that as many as a third of single parents – almost all of them women – were better off after the break-up of their marriage than they were before. The large majority, however, became worse off.

Only 12 per cent of people living on social assistance in the 1990s say they are 'managing quite well'. Most say they are 'just getting by' or 'getting into difficulties'. Planning ahead is difficult. Money cannot be put aside for the future, and bills are a matter of constant concern. In spite of its importance, food is often treated as an item which can be cut back on when money is short. Walker concludes: 'Despite sensational newspaper headlines, living on social assistance is not an option most people would choose if they were offered a genuine alternative. Most find themselves in that position because of some traumatic event in their lives: loss of a job, loss of a partner or the onset of ill health' (Walker 1994, p. 9).

However widespread it may or may not be, tackling welfare dependency has become a main target of attempts at reform of welfare institutions. Among the most significant of such reforms have been welfare-to-work programmes, whose driving force is to move recipients from public assistance into paid jobs. These are being introduced in the UK and some other European countries, but have already existed for some while in the United States. There has therefore been some opportunity there to study their implications.

Daniel Friedlander and Gary Burtless studied four different government-initiated programmes designed to encourage welfare recipients to find paid work. The programmes were roughly similar. They provided financial benefits for welfare recipients who actively searched for jobs, as well as guidance in job-hunting techniques and opportunities for education and training. The target populations were mainly single-parent family heads of households who were recipients of Aid to Families with Dependent Children, the largest cash welfare programme in the country. Friedlander and Burtless found that the programmes did achieve results. People involved in them were able either to enter employment or to start working sooner than others who didn't participate. In all four programmes, the earnings produced were several times greater than the net cost of the programme. They were least effective, however, in helping those who needed them the most – those who had been out of work for a lengthy period, the long-term unemployed.

Welfare-to-work programmes are designed to provide positive encouragement for welfare recipients to find paid jobs. But some welfare analysts have suggested that a more ruthless attitude should be adopted. They propose that welfare payments, under certain circumstances, should be either substantially reduced or abolished altogether. For example, benefits might be cut off if a single mother with one child had another child while still on welfare. The idea of such schemes is to dissolve the conditions that create welfare dependency and force people to look for paid work. Critics argue that such schemes are likely to lead those whose welfare benefits are reduced or taken away to turn to crime or prostitution in order to sustain a livelihood. There have been only a few experiments of this kind so far, and it is not yet possible adequately to judge what their consequences have been (Friedlander and Burtless 1994).

The homeless

Most poor people live in some sort of home or permanent shelter. Those who do not, the homeless, have become very visible in the streets of cities over the past twenty years.

'Over the edge' is how Martha Burt describes the problem of homelessness in America (Burt 1993). Burt began research on the problem in the 1980s in an attempt to evaluate the Emergency Fund and Shelter Program, set up to respond to the great increase in the numbers of people who became homeless or hungry in that decade. A few, she found, deliberately choose to roam the streets, sleeping rough, free from the constraints of property and possessions. But the large majority have no such wish at all; they have been pushed over the edge into homelessness by factors beyond their control. Once they find themselves without a permanent dwelling, their lives sometimes deteriorate into a spiral of hardship and deprivation. In Britain, too, homelessness can be associated with a 'vicious street cycle' (see the box).

Like poverty, homelessness isn't as easy to define as we might imagine. Two generations ago, most people still thought of 'home' as the family home. Homeless people were seen as individuals who lived in hostels on skid row. They were called homeless because they lived alone and rarely saw their families or kin.

Over the past two or three decades, far more people have come to live alone by choice. The homeless hence have become defined as people who have nowhere to sleep, and who either stay in free street shelters on a temporary basis or sleep in places not meant for habitation, such as in doorways, on park benches, in railway stations or in derelict buildings.

Who are the homeless in Britain? The category is in fact a mixed one. About a quarter are people who have spent time in a mental hospital. At least some of these individuals would have been long-term inmates before the 1960s, when people with chronic mental illnesses began to be released from institutions as a result of changes in health care policy. This process of deinstitutionalization was prompted by several factors. One was the desire of the government to save money – the cost of keeping people in mental hospitals, as in other types of hospitals, is high. Another, more praiseworthy motive was the belief on the part of leaders of the psychiatric profession that long-term hospitalization often did more harm than good. Anyone who could be cared for on an outpatient basis, therefore, should be. The results haven't borne out the hopes of those who saw deinstitutionalization as a positive step. Some

The vicious street cycle

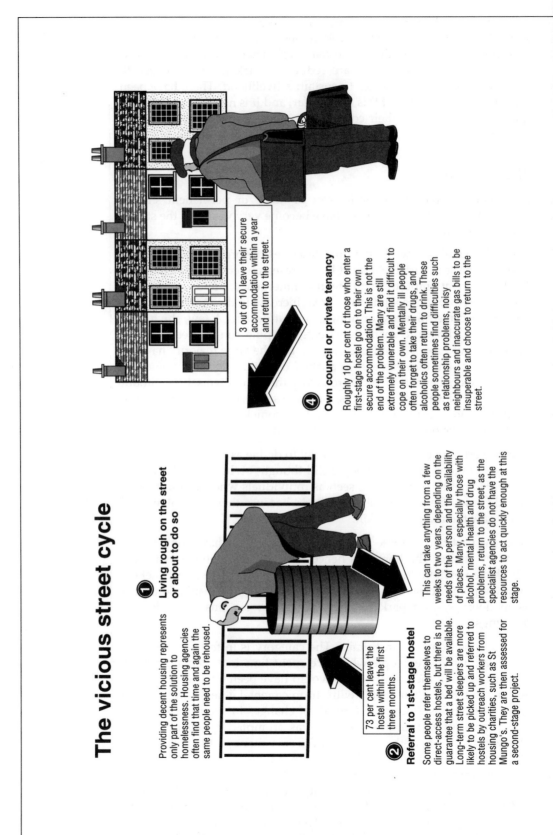

① Living rough on the street or about to do so

Providing decent housing represents only part of the solution to homelessness. Housing agencies often find that time and again the same people need to be rehoused.

② Referral to 1st-stage hostel

Some people refer themselves to direct-access hostels, but there is no guarantee that a bed will be available. Long-term street sleepers are more likely to be picked up and referred to hostels by outreach workers from housing charities, such as St Mungo's. They are then assessed for a second-stage project.

73 per cent leave the hostel within the first three months.

This can take anything from a few weeks to two years, depending on the needs of the person and the availability of places. Many, especially those with alcohol, mental health and drug problems, return to the street, as the specialist agencies do not have the resources to act quickly enough at this stage.

3 out of 10 leave their secure accommodation within a year and return to the street.

④ Own council or private tenancy

Roughly 10 per cent of those who enter a first-stage hostel go on to their own secure accommodation. This is not the end of the problem. Many are still extremely vunerable and find it difficult to cope on their own. Mentally ill people often forget to take their drugs, and alcoholics often return to drink. These people sometimes find difficulties such as relationship problems, noisy neighbours and inaccurate gas bills to be insuperable and choose to return to the street.

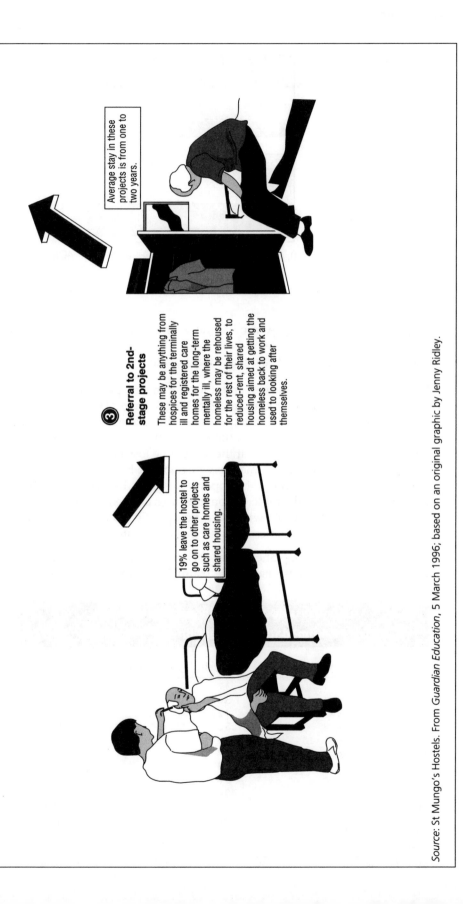

Average stay in these projects is from one to two years.

③ **Referral to 2nd-stage projects**

These may be anything from hospices for the terminally ill and registered care homes for the long-term mentally ill, where the homeless may be rehoused for the rest of their lives, to reduced-rent, shared housing aimed at getting the homeless back to work and used to looking after themselves.

19% leave the hostel to go on to other projects such as care homes and shared housing.

Source: St Mungo's Hostels. From *Guardian Education*, 5 March 1996; based on an original graphic by Jenny Ridley.

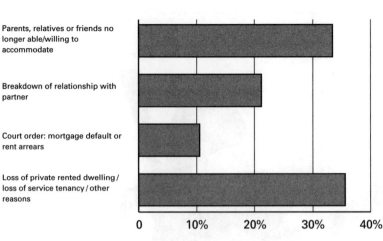

Fig. 10.2 Reasons for homelessness among homeless households found accommodation by local authorities, England, Wales and Northern Ireland, 1994

Sources: Department of the Environment; Welsh Office; Department of the Environment, Northern Ireland. From *Social Trends*, 1996, p. 187.

hospitals discharged people who had nowhere to go, and who perhaps hadn't lived in the outside world for years. Often, little concrete provision for proper out-patient care was in fact made.

Most of the homeless, however, aren't former mental patients, and they aren't alcoholics or regular consumers of illegal drugs. They are people who find themselves on the streets because they have experienced personal disasters, often several at a time (see Figure 10.2). A woman, for instance, may get divorced and at the same time lose not only her home but her job. A young person may have trouble at home and make for the big city without means of support. Research has indicated that those who are most vulnerable to homelessness are people from lower-working-class backgrounds who have no specific job skills and very low incomes. Long-term joblessness is a major indicator.

The housing action group Shelter has carried out some local researches and on the basis of these has made estimates of the numbers of the

Table 10.3	Homeless households living in temporary accommodation in Great Britain, 1982–1994 (000s)			
	Bed and breakfast	**Hostels**	**Short-life leasing**	**All**
1982	2.0	3.7	4.8	10.5
1983	3.0	3.6	4.5	11.1
1984	4.2	4.2	5.3	13.7
1985	5.7	5.0	6.7	17.4
1986	9.4	5.0	8.3	22.7
1987	10.6	5.7	10.5	26.8
1988	11.2	6.8	14.2	32.2
1989	12.0	8.6	19.9	40.5
1990	11.7	10.4	27.0	49.1
1991	12.9	11.7	39.7	64.3
1992	8.4	12.6	46.6	67.6
1993	5.4	11.9	40.7	58.0
1994	4.7	11.9	35.7	52.3

Source: Department of the Environment; Welsh Office; Scottish Office. From *Social Trends*, 1996, p. 187.

homeless. According to Shelter, homelessness grew by 300 per cent over the years from 1978 to 1992. During 1995, local authorities in England and Wales registered 450,000 people as living without a semi-permanent residence. Shelter, however, puts the true number considerably higher than that. Government statistics on 'homeless households' living in temporary accommodation are shown in table 10.3.

Even though it isn't the whole answer, most sociologists who have studied the problem agree that the provision of more adequate forms of housing is of key importance in tackling homelessness, whether the housing is directly sponsored by the government or not. As Christopher Jencks concludes in his book, *The Homeless* (1994): 'Regardless of why people are on the streets, giving them a place to live that offers a modicum of privacy and stability is usually the most important thing we can do to improve their lives. Without stable housing, nothing else is likely to work.'

CLASS, INEQUALITY AND ECONOMIC COMPETITIVENESS

Inequalities between the poor and the more affluent have expanded in Britain over the past twenty years. Is growing class inequality a price which has to be paid to secure economic development? This assumption was particularly prominent during the period of the Thatcher governments. The pursuit of wealth, the reasoning was, creates economic development because it is a motivating force encouraging innovation and drive. But a good deal of evidence has accumulated that runs counter to this assumption. In his book *Capitalism vs Capitalism* (1993), Michel Albert systematically compares two models of enterprise and economic organization. One, which he terms the 'American model' (but which applies to the UK too), is based on largely deregulated markets and low levels of state welfare systems, and is marked by a high degree of economic inequality between rich and poor. The other he calls the 'Rhine model', because it is based on the sort of economic system found in countries that lie close to the Rhine river in Europe – Germany, Switzerland and Holland – although it has important qualities in common with Japan and the other successful Asian economies.

In the Rhine model, collective interests tend to take precedence over individual ones. These are not aggressively individualistic societies. The communities of which the individual forms a part, whether these are business enterprises, towns or labour unions, are regarded as crucial in providing stability. Particularly important, the Rhine model countries are egalitarian societies; the differences between rich and poor are less than in Britain or the US.

The Rhine model has been more successful than the American one in global economic competition, Albert argues, largely because of its egalitarian character. Support for Albert's view can be drawn from the study of the successful Asian countries, such as Japan, Singapore, South Korea and Taiwan, over the past thirty years. Countries where inequality is relatively low on the whole have prospered more than those where the divisions between rich and poor are greater. Including poorer people in the wider society rather than cutting them off from it probably gives them the means as well as the will to improve their earning power. The relation between inequality and economic growth, however, remains controversial.

CONCLUSION

Economic inequality is a persistent feature of all social systems except for hunting and gathering societies – in which little wealth is produced in any case. Class divisions form the core economic inequalities in modern societies. Class exerts a great influence in our lives. But our activities are never completely determined by class divisions: many people experience some social mobility. Others, however, find themselves in situations of poverty from which it is very difficult to escape. Relative poverty is in fact a measure of inequality; British society tends to be more unequal than most other Western societies. Some have argued that such high levels of inequality, far from encouraging economic development, tend to act against it. Combating poverty and hopelessness, which is surely desirable for its own sake, might also help the UK to be more competitive in the global economy.

SUMMARY

1 Social stratification refers to the division of society into layers or strata. When we talk of social stratification, we draw attention to the unequal positions occupied by individuals in society. Stratification by gender and age is found in all societies. In the larger traditional societies and in industrialized countries today, there is stratification in terms of wealth, property and access to material goods and cultural products.

2 Four major types of stratification system can be distinguished: slavery, caste, estates and class. Whereas the first three depend on legal or religiously sanctioned inequalities, class divisions are not 'officially' recognized, but stem from economic factors affecting the material circumstances of people's lives.

3 The most prominent and influential theories of stratification are those developed by Marx and Weber. Marx places the primary emphasis on class, which he sees as an objectively given characteristic of the economic structure of society. He sees a fundamental split between the owners of capital and the workers who do not own capital. Weber accepts a similar view, but distinguishes two other aspects of stratification, status and party. Status refers to the esteem or 'social honour' given to individuals or groups; party refers to the active mobilizing of groups to secure definite ends.

4 Most people in modern societies are more affluent today than was the case several generations ago, yet the distribution of wealth and income remains highly unequal. The wealthy use various means to transmit their property from one generation to the next. Wealth refers to all assets individuals own: cash, savings and current accounts, investments in stocks, bonds and property, and other investments. Income refers to wages and salaries from paid occupations, plus money derived from investments.

5 Possession of substantial amounts of wealth, especially when the wealth is passed on from generation to generation, is the main characteristic distinguishing the upper class from other class groups in society. The middle class is composed broadly of those working in white-collar occupations, but it can be divided into the old middle class (such as small business owners), the upper middle class (professionals and managers) and the lower middle class (office staff, teachers, nurses, etc.). The working class is composed of people working in blue-collar or manual occupations. The underclass is composed of those who are chronically poor and without permanent occupation. Most people in the underclass are from ethnic minority groups.

6 Change is affecting each of these class groups. As a result of changes in the occupational structure, the working class is contracting relative to other classes. A particularly important controversy concentrates on how far a rootless, disaffected underclass is developing.

7 Analyses of stratification have traditionally been written from a male point of view. This is partly because of the assumption that gender inequalities simply reflect class differences; this assumption is highly questionable. Gender influences stratification in modern societies to some degree independently of class.

8 An individual's class position is at least in some part achieved; it is not simply 'given' from birth. Social mobility, both upwards and downwards in the class structure, is a fairly common feature.

9 In the study of social mobility, a distinction is made between intragenerational and intergenerational mobility. The first of these refers to movement up or down the social scale within an individual's working life. The second concerns movement across the generations, as when a daughter or son from a blue-collar background becomes a professional. Social mobility is mostly of limited range. Most people remain close to the level of the families from which they came, though the expansion of white-collar jobs in the last few decades has provided the opportunity for considerable short-range upward mobility.

10 Poverty remains widespread within the affluent nations. There are two methods of assessing poverty: one involves the notion of 'subsistence poverty', which is a lack of the basic resources needed to maintain health and effective bodily functioning; the other, 'relative poverty', involves assessing the gaps between the living conditions of some groups and those enjoyed by the majority of a population.

11 Economic inequality is probably relevant to a country's competitiveness in the global economy. Some claim that the most successful industrial countries in the world economy tend to be those where inequalities are relatively low.

FURTHER READING

Richard Breen and **David Rottman**, *Class Stratification* (London: Harvester Wheatsheaf, 1995). An updated review of social classes.

T. Butler and **M. Savage**, *Social Change and the Middle Classes* (London: UCL Press, 1995). An analysis of recent trends in the development of the middle classes.

Rosemary Crompton, *Class and Stratification* (Cambridge: Polity Press, 1993). A comprehensive review of the theoretical and methodological approaches to the study of class and stratification which have been developed since World War Two.

Robert Erikson and **John Goldthorpe**, *The Constant Flux: A Study of Class Mobility in Industrial Societies* (Oxford: Clarendon Press, 1993). A historical analysis of social mobility in twentieth-century Europe.

Frank Field, *Losing Out: The Emergence of Britain's Underclass* (Oxford: Blackwell, 1989). A discussion of the underclass issue in Britain, written by a prominent Labour MP.

David Lockwood, *The Black Coated Worker: A Study in Class Consciousness* (Oxford: Oxford University Press, 1989). A reissue of a classic study of class, together with a lengthy postscript.

Peter Saunders, *Social Class and Stratification* (London: Routledge, 1990). A short and accessible text covering the main issues in the study of class and stratification.

John Westergaard, *Who Gets What?* (Cambridge: Polity Press, 1995). A defence of the continuing importance of class analysis for the study of contemporary societies.

IMPORTANT TERMS

- *slavery*
- *caste*
- *estate*
- *upper class*
- *middle class*
- *working class*
- *peasants*
- *means of production*
- *capitalists*
- *surplus value*
- *transitional classes*
- *prestige*
- *pariah groups*
- *contradictory class locations*
- *social closure*
- *wealth*
- *income*
- *underclass*
- *vertical mobility*
- *lateral mobility*
- *intragenerational mobility*
- *intergenerational mobility*
- *downward mobility*
- *absolute poverty*
- *relative poverty*
- *welfare dependency*

11

MODERN ORGANIZATIONS

Once upon a time, we were all born in our own dwellings. Women virtually always gave birth in the place where they lived, and people attached a great deal of significance to the exact spot where they were born – in the local community or village, in this house or that house, in this room or that. Usually, birth took place in the main, or communal, room of the mother's home. As soon as the first contractions started, local women would gather to assist her. Women usually gave birth in front of the hearth, especially if the weather outside was cold. Straw was brought in and scattered on the floor, in more or less the same way as it was done in the cowshed when a calf was born.

Women in childbirth had no other resources save for those the community could offer. For centuries, the idea of calling on help outside the community was alien to the ways of thinking of women of the villages. 'Women helping one another' and 'giving mutual assistance' are phrases that crop up constantly in the writings of priests and administrators who reported on childbirth in the eighteenth and early nineteenth centuries. The key figure was the midwife, a woman experienced in assisting at births. A midwife was originally known as the 'good mother': she was someone who could cope with the pains and problems of younger women at key times in their pregnancy and at the birth itself. A document written in France in the 1820s indicates the qualities the midwife was expected to have. She needed to be 'strong, sturdy, nimble, graceful, with no bodily defects, with long supple hands'. The spiritual side was no less important: she should be 'virtuous, discreet, prudent, of good conduct and regular habits' (Gelis 1991).

Until about the 1950s, most people in Britain were born in their own homes, and the midwife continued to play an important role. Today, however, the practice of giving birth in a hospital is most common, and this change has brought other important transformations in its wake. Few of us any longer feel an emotional connection with our place of birth. Why should we? That place is now a large, impersonal hospital. After having existed for many centuries, midwives have now either disappeared completely or simply play a role in helping out in earlier phases of pregnancy. The birth process itself is controlled and monitored by the professionals within the hospital – doctors, nurses and other medical staff.

ORGANIZATIONS AND MODERN LIFE

A modern hospital is a good example of an organization. An ORGAN-IZATION is a large grouping of people, structured on impersonal lines and set up to achieve specific objectives; in the case of the hospital, these objectives are curing illness and providing other forms of medical attention.

In current times, organizations play a much more important part in our everyday lives than was ever true previously. Besides delivering us into this world, they also mark our progress through it and see us out of it when we die. Even before we are born, our mothers, and probably our fathers too, are involved in classes, pregnancy check-ups and so forth, carried out within hospitals and other medical organizations. Every child born today is registered by government organizations, which collect information on us from birth to death. Most people today die in a hospital – not at home, as was once the case – and each death must be formally registered with the government too.

Every time you use the phone, turn on the tap or TV, or get into a car, you are in contact with, and to some extent dependent on, organizations. And usually this will mean many organizations, all interacting in a regular way with each other as well as with you. The water company, for example, makes it possible to take for granted that water will pour out when you turn on the tap. But the water company is also dependent on other organizations, such as those that construct and service reservoirs, which are themselves dependent on others . . . and so on almost indefinitely. You turn on the tap in your own home, but the water probably comes from miles away. The water company – or, more normally, a whole group of water companies – must supply not only you but thousands or millions of others simultaneously. You can multiply what the water company does dozens of times; for counting on a regular supply of water is only one way in which we are dependent on organizations.

It should be remembered that for most of human history, before the level of organizational development became as great as it is now, people couldn't count on aspects of life to which we now give barely a second thought. For example, a century ago in Britain few houses were equipped with a regular supply of piped water, and much of the water people used was polluted and responsible for numerous illnesses and epidemics. Even today, in large areas of the less developed societies (for example, Asia or Africa), there is no piped water; people gather water each day from a spring or well, and much of it contains bacteria that spread disease. In modern societies, drinking water is carefully checked for contamination; this involves yet more organizations, the health standards authorities.

But the tremendous influence organizations have come to exert over our lives cannot be seen as wholly beneficial. Organizations often have the effect of taking things out of our own hands and putting them under the control of officials or experts over whom we have little influence. For instance, we are all *required* to do certain things the government tells us – pay taxes, abide by laws, go off to fight wars – or face punishment. As sources of social power, organizations can thus subject the individual to dictates he or she may be powerless to resist.

In this chapter, we look at the rise of modern organizations and the consequences this development has for our lives today. We shall first analyse the ideas of two writers who have had an especially strong impact on how sociologists think of organizations: Max Weber and Michel Foucault. We shall then look at some of the ways in which organizations work – whether they are business corporations or hospitals, schools or government offices, colleges or prisons – and we will study what differences exist between these various types. We shall give particular attention to large business organizations, which are coming to operate more and more on a world level. In the concluding sections, we shall consider how far business corporations and other organizations in modern societies are becoming subject to major processes of change.

THEORIES OF ORGANIZATION

Max Weber developed the first systematic interpretation of the rise of modern organizations. Organizations, he argued, are ways of coordinating the activities of human beings, or the goods they produce, in a stable way across space and time. Weber emphasized that the development of organizations depends on the control of information, and he stressed the central importance of writing in this process: an organization needs written rules for its functioning, and files in which its 'memory' is stored. Weber saw organizations as strongly hierarchical, with power tending to be concentrated at the top. In this chapter, we shall examine whether Weber was right. If he was, it matters a great deal to us all. For Weber detected a clash as well as a connection between modern organizations and democracy that he believed had far-reaching consequences for social life.

Weber's view of bureaucracy

All large-scale organizations, according to Weber, tend to be bureaucratic in nature. The word 'bureaucracy' was coined by a Monsieur de Gournay in 1745, who added to the word 'bureau', meaning both an office and a writing table, a term derived from the Greek verb 'to rule'. BUREAUCRACY is thus the rule of **officials**. Bureaucracy as a term was first applied only to government officials, but it gradually became extended to refer to large organizations in general.

The concept was from the beginning used in a disparaging way. De Gournay spoke of the developing power of officials as 'an illness called bureaumania'. The French novelist Honoré de Balzac saw bureaucracy as 'the giant power wielded by pygmies'. This sort of view has persisted into current times: bureaucracy is frequently associated with red tape, inefficiency and wastefulness. Other writers, however, have seen bureaucracy in a different light – as a model of carefulness, precision and effective administration. Bureaucracy, they argue, is in fact the most efficient form of organization human beings have devised, because all tasks are regulated by strict rules of procedure. Weber's account of bureaucracy steers a way between these two extremes.

A limited number of bureaucratic organizations, Weber pointed out, existed in the traditional civilizations. For example, a bureaucratic officialdom in imperial China was responsible for the overall affairs of government. But it is only in modern times that bureaucracies have developed fully.

According to Weber, the expansion of bureaucracy is inevitable in modern societies; bureaucratic authority is the only way of coping with the administrative requirements of large-scale social systems. However, Weber also believed bureaucracy to exhibit a number of major failings, as we will see, which have important implications for the nature of modern social life.

In order to study the origins and nature of the expansion of bureaucratic organizations, Weber constructed an **ideal type** of bureaucracy. ('Ideal' here refers not to what is most desirable, but to a pure form of bureaucratic organization. An ideal type is an abstract description constructed by accentuating certain features of real cases so as to pinpoint their most essential characteristics.) Weber listed several characteristics of the ideal type of bureaucracy (1978):

- *There is a clear-cut hierarchy of authority* Thus tasks in the organization are distributed as 'official duties'. A bureaucracy looks like a pyramid, with the positions of highest authority at the top. There is a chain of command stretching from top to bottom, making coordinated decision-making possible. Each higher office controls and supervises the one below it in the hierarchy.

- *Written rules govern the conduct of officials at all levels of the organization* This does not mean that bureaucratic duties are just a matter of routine. The higher the office, the more the rules tend to encompass a wide variety of cases and demand flexibility in their interpretation.

- *Officials are full-time and salaried* Each job in the hierarchy has a definite and fixed salary attached to it. Individuals are expected to make a career within the organization. Promotion is possible on the basis of capability, seniority, or a mixture of the two.

- *There is a separation between the tasks of an official within the organization and the official's life outside* The home life of the official is distinct from activities in the workplace, and is also physically separated from it.

- *No members of the organization own the material resources with which they operate* The development of bureaucracy, according to Weber, separates workers from the control of their means of production. In traditional communities, farmers and craft workers usually had control over their processes of production and owned the tools they used. In bureaucracies, officials do not own the offices they work in, the desks they sit at or the office machinery they use.

Weber believed that the more an organization approaches the ideal type of bureaucracy, the more effective it will be in pursuing the objectives for which it was established. He often likened bureaucracies to sophisticated machines.

Formal and informal relations within bureaucracies

Weber's analysis of bureaucracy gave prime place to FORMAL RELATIONS within organizations, the relations between people as stated in the rules of the organization (see examples in figure 11.1). Weber had little to say about the informal connections and small-group relations that may exist in all organizations. But in bureaucracies, informal ways of doing things often allow for a flexibility that couldn't otherwise be achieved.

In a classical study, Peter Blau studied INFORMAL RELATIONS in a government agency which had the task of investigating possible income-tax violations (Blau 1963). Agents who came across problems they were unsure how to deal with were supposed to discuss them with their immediate supervisor; the rules of procedure stated that they should not consult colleagues working at the same level as themselves. Most officials were wary of approaching their supervisors, however, because they felt this might suggest a lack of competence on their part and reduce their promotion chances. Hence, they usually consulted each other, violating the official rules. This not only helped to provide concrete advice; it also reduced the anxieties involved in working alone. A cohesive set of loyalties at a primary level of SOCIAL GROUP developed among those working at the same level. The problems these workers faced, Blau concludes, were probably coped with much more effectively as a result. The group was able to evolve informal procedures allowing for more initiative and responsibility than was provided for by the formal rules of the organization.

Informal networks tend to develop at all levels of organizations. At the very top, personal ties and connections may be more important than the formal situations in which decisions are supposed to be made. For example, meetings of boards of directors and shareholders supposedly determine the policies of business corporations. In practice, a few

Fig. 11.1 Formal relations within organizations

Source: Shaun Gregson and Frank Livesey, *Organizations and Management Behaviour*, 1993.

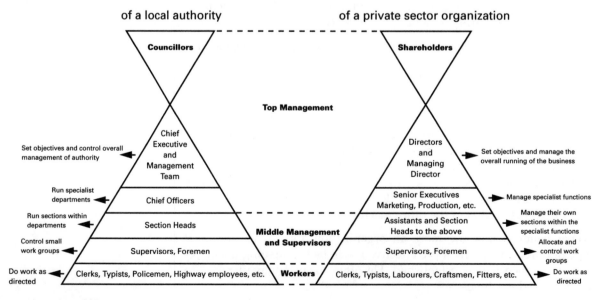

Organization hierarchy/pyramids

members of the board often really run the corporation, making their decisions informally and expecting the board to approve them. Informal networks of this sort can also stretch across different corporations. Business leaders from different firms frequently consult one another in an informal way, and may belong to the same clubs and leisure-time associations.

Deciding how far informal procedures generally help or hinder the effectiveness of organizations is not a simple matter. Systems that resemble Weber's ideal type tend to give rise to a forest of unofficial ways of doing things. This is partly because the flexibility that is lacking can be achieved by unofficial tinkering with formal rules. For those in dull jobs, informal procedures often also help to create a more satisfying work environment. Informal connections between officials in higher positions may be effective in ways that aid the organization as a whole. On the other hand, these officials may be more concerned to advance or protect their own interests than to further those of the overall organization.

The physical setting of organizations

Most modern organizations function in specially designed physical settings. A building that houses a particular organization possesses specific features relevant to the organization's activities, but it also shares important architectural characteristics with buildings of other organizations. The architecture of a hospital, for instance, differs in some respects from that of a business firm or a school. The hospital's separate wards, consulting rooms, operating rooms and offices give the overall building a definite layout, while a school may consist of classrooms, laboratories and a sports hall. Yet there is a general resemblance: both are likely to contain hallways with doors leading off, and to use standard decoration and furnishings throughout. Apart from the differing dress of the people moving through the corridors, the buildings in which modern organizations are usually housed have a definite sameness to them. And they often look similar from the outside as well as within their interiors. It would not be unusual to ask, on driving past a building, 'Is that a school?' and receive the response 'No, it's a hospital'. Although major internal modifications will be required, it can happen that a school takes over buildings that once housed a hospital.

Michel Foucault's theory of organizations: the control of time and space

Michel Foucault showed that the architecture of an organization is directly involved with its social make-up and system of authority (Foucault 1970, 1979). By studying the physical characteristics of organizations, we can shed new light on the problems Weber analysed. The offices Weber discussed abstractly are also architectural settings – rooms, separated by corridors – within organizations. The buildings of large firms are sometimes actually constructed physically as a hierarchy, in which the more elevated one's position in the hierarchy of authority, the nearer the top one's office is; the phrase 'the top floor' is sometimes used to mean those who hold ultimate power in the organization.

In many other ways, the geography of an organization will affect its functioning, especially in cases where systems rely heavily on informal relationships. Physical proximity makes forming primary groups easier, while physical distance can polarize groups, resulting in a 'them' and 'us' attitude between departments.

Surveillance in organizations

The arrangement of rooms, hallways and open spaces in an organization's buildings can provide basic clues to how its system of authority operates. In some organizations, groups of people work collectively in open settings. Because of the dull, repetitive nature of certain kinds of industrial work, like assembly-line production, regular supervision is needed to ensure that workers sustain the pace of labour. The same is often true of routine work carried out by typists, who sit together in the typing pool, where their activities are visible to their superiors. Foucault laid great emphasis on how visibility, or lack of it, in the architectural settings of modern organizations influences and expresses patterns of authority. Their visibility determines how easily subordinates can be subject to what Foucault calls **surveillance**, the supervision of activities in organizations. In modern organizations, everyone, even in relatively high positions of authority, is subject to surveillance; but the more lowly a person is, the more her or his behaviour tends to be closely scrutinized.

Surveillance takes two forms. One is the direct supervision of the work of subordinates by superiors. Consider the example of a school classroom. Pupils sit at tables or desks, usually arranged in rows, all in view

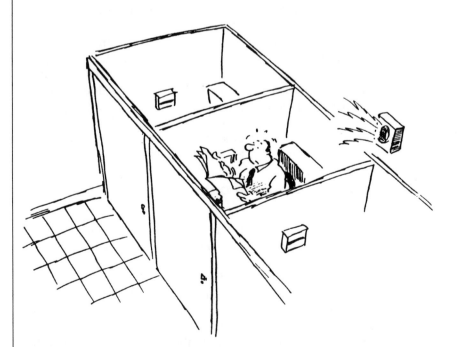

'Sensors indicate that No. 2 cubicle has been occupied for eighteen minutes. Do you require assistance?'

of the teacher. Children are supposed to look alert or otherwise be absorbed in their work. Of course, how far this actually happens in practice depends on the abilities of the teacher and the inclinations of the children to conform to what is expected of them.

The second type of surveillance is more subtle but equally important. It consists in keeping files, records and case histories about people's lives. Weber saw the importance of written records (nowadays often computerized) in modern organizations, but did not fully explore how they can be used to regulate behaviour. Employee records usually provide complete work histories, registering personal details and often giving character evaluations. Such records are used to monitor employees' behaviour and assess recommendations for promotion. In many business firms, individuals at each level in the organization prepare annual reports on the performance of those in the levels just below them. School and college records are also used to monitor the performance of individuals as they move through the organization.

Organizations cannot operate effectively if employees' work is haphazard. In business firms, as Weber pointed out, people are expected to work regular hours. Activities must be consistently coordinated in time and space, something promoted both by the physical settings and by the precise scheduling of detailed timetables. Timetables regularize activities across time and space – in Foucault's words, they 'efficiently distribute bodies' around the organization. Timetables are the condition of organizational discipline, because they slot the activities of large numbers of people together. If a university did not strictly observe a lecture timetable, for example, it would soon collapse into complete chaos. A timetable makes possible the intensive use of time and space: each can be packed with many people and many activities.

Under surveillance! The prison

Foucault paid a great deal of attention to organizations, like prisons, in which individuals are physically separated for long periods from the outside world. In such organizations, people are **incarcerated** – kept hidden away – from the external social environment. A prison illustrates in clear detail the nature of surveillance because it seeks to maximize control over inmates' behaviour. Foucault asks, 'Is it surprising that prisons resemble factories, schools, barracks, hospitals which all resemble prisons?' (1979).

According to Foucault, the modern prison has its origins in the Panopticon, an organization planned by the philosopher and social thinker Jeremy Bentham in the nineteenth century. 'Panopticon' was the name Bentham gave to an ideal prison he designed, which he tried on various occasions to sell to the British government. The design was never fully implemented, but some of its main principles were incorporated in prisons built in the nineteenth century in Britain, Europe and the US. The Panopticon was circular in shape, with the cells built around the outside edge. In the centre was an inspection tower. Two windows were placed in every cell, one facing the inspection tower and the other facing outside. The aim of the design was to make prisoners visible to guards at all times. The windows in the tower itself were equipped with venetian blinds, so that while the prison staff could keep the prisoners under constant observation, they themselves could be invisible.

Bureaucracy and democracy

Foucault was right about prisons. Even today, most prisons look remarkably like the Panopticon. He was also right about the central role of surveillance in modern societies, an issue that has become even more important now because of the growing impact of information and communications technologies. We live in what some have called the **surveillance society** (Lyon 1994) – a society in which information about our lives is gathered by all types of organizations.

As mentioned earlier, government organizations hold enormous amounts of information about us, from records of our dates of birth, schools and jobs to data on income used for tax collecting and information used to issue driving licences and allocate national insurance numbers. With the development of computers and other forms of electronic data processing equipment, surveillance threatens to move into every corner of our lives. Imagine you heard of a country, with a population of 26 million, where the government operated 2,220 databases, containing an average of 20 files on each citizen. Ten per cent of the population have their names in the central police computer. You might think this is a country labouring under a dictatorship. In fact, it is Canada (Lyon 1994).

The diminishing of democracy with the advance of modern forms of organization and information control was something that worried Weber a great deal. What especially disturbed him was the prospect of rule by faceless bureaucrats. How can democracy survive in the face of the increasing power bureaucratic organizations are wielding over us? After all, Weber reasoned, bureaucracies are necessarily specialized and hierarchical. Those near the bottom of the organization inevitably find themselves reduced to carrying out mundane tasks and have no power over what they do; power passes to those at the top. Weber's student Roberto Michels (1967) invented a phrase that has since become famous to refer to this loss of power: in large-scale organizations, and more generally a society dominated by organizations, he argued, there is an iron *law of oligarchy*. **Oligarchy** means rule by the few. According to Michels, the flow of power towards the top is simply an inevitable part of an increasingly bureaucratized world – hence the term 'iron law'.

The limits of surveillance

Weber and Foucault argued that the most effective way to run an organization is to maximize surveillance – to have clear and consistent divisions of authority. But this view is a mistake, at least if we apply it to business firms, which don't (as prisons do) exert total control over people's lives in closed settings. Prisons are not actually a good model for organizations as a whole. Direct supervision may work tolerably well when the people involved, as in prisons, are basically hostile to those in authority over them and do not want to be where they are. But in organizations where managers desire others to cooperate with them in reaching common goals, the situation is different. Too much direct supervision alienates employees, who feel they are denied any opportunities for involvement in the work they do (Grint 1991; Sabel 1982).

This is one main reason why organizations founded on the sorts of principles formulated by Weber and Foucault, such as large factories involving assembly-line production and rigid authority hierarchies, eventually ran into great difficulties. Workers weren't inclined to devote themselves to their work in such settings; continuous supervision was in fact _required_ to get them to work reasonably hard at all, but it promoted resentment and antagonism.

People are also prone to resist high levels of surveillance in the second sense mentioned by Foucault, the collection of written information about them. That was in effect one of the main reasons why the Soviet-style communist societies broke down. In these societies, people were spied on in a regular way either by the secret police or by others in the pay of the secret police – even relatives and neighbours. The government also kept detailed information on its citizenry in order to clamp down on possible opposition to their rule. The result was a form of society that was politically authoritarian and, towards the end, economically inefficient. The whole society did indeed come almost to resemble a gigantic prison, with all the discontents, conflicts and modes of opposition prisons generate – a system from which, in the end, the population broke free.

BEYOND BUREAUCRACY?

For quite a long while in the development of Western societies, Weber's model, closely mirrored by that of Foucault, held good. In government, hospital administration, universities and business organizations, bureaucracy seemed to be dominant. Even though, as Peter Blau showed, informal social selections always develop in bureaucratic settings and are in fact effective, it seemed as though the future might be just what Weber had anticipated: constantly increasing bureaucratization.

Bureaucracies still exist aplenty in the West, but Weber's idea that a clear hierarchy of authority, with power and knowledge concentrated at the top, is the only way to run a large organization is starting to look archaic. Numerous organizations are overhauling themselves to become less, rather than more, hierarchical. In so doing, many business corporations in the West are following the so-called 'Japanese model'.

The Japanese model

The economic success of Japan is frequently said to be due mainly to the distinctive characteristics of the large Japanese corporations – which differ substantially from most business firms in the West. Japanese companies diverge from the characteristics that Weber associated with bureaucracy in several ways:

- *Bottom-up decision-making* The big Japanese corporations do not form a pyramid of authority as Weber portrayed it, with each level being responsible only to the one above. Rather, workers low down in the organization are consulted about policies being considered by management, and even the top executives regularly meet with them.

- *Less specialization* In Japanese organizations, employees specialize much less than their counterparts in the West. Take the case of Sugao, as described by William Ouchi (1982). Sugao is a university graduate who has just joined the Mitsubeni Bank in Tokyo. He will enter the firm in a management training position, spending his first year learning generally how the various departments of the bank operate. He will then work in a local branch for a while as a teller, and will subsequently be brought back to the bank's headquarters to learn commercial banking. Then he will move out to yet another branch dealing with loans. From there he is likely to return to headquarters to work in the personnel department. Ten years will have elapsed by this time, and Sugao will have reached the position of section chief. But the process of job rotation does not stop there. He will move on to a further branch of the bank, perhaps dealing this time with the financing of small businesses, and then return to yet a different job at headquarters.

  By the time Sugao reaches the peak of his career, some thirty years after having begun as a trainee, he will have mastered all the important tasks. In contrast, a typical American bank management trainee of the same age will almost certainly specialize in one area of banking early on, and stay in that speciality for the remainder of her or his working life.

- *Job security* The large corporations in Japan are committed to the lifetime employment of those they hire; the employee is guaranteed a job. Pay and responsibility are geared to seniority – how many years a worker has been with the firm – rather than to a competitive struggle for promotion.

- *Group oriented production* At all levels of the corporation, people are involved in small cooperative 'teams', or work groups. The groups, rather than individual members, are evaluated in terms of their performance. Unlike their Western counterparts, the 'organization charts' of Japanese companies – maps of the authority system – show only groups, not individual positions. This is important because it contradicts the supposed iron law of oligarchy.

- *Merging of work and private lives* In Weber's depiction of bureaucracy, there is a clear division between the work of people within the organization and their activities outside. This is in fact true of most Western corporations, in which the relation between firm and employee is an economic one. Japanese corporations, by contrast, provide for many of their employees' needs, expecting in return a high level of loyalty to the firm. Japanese employees, from workers on the shop floor to top executives, often wear company uniforms. They may assemble to sing the 'company song' each morning, and they regularly take part in leisure activities organized by the corporation at weekends. (A few Western corporations, like IBM and Apple, now also have company songs.) Workers receive material benefits from the company over and above their salaries. The electrical firm Hitachi, for example, studied by Ronald Dore (1980), provided housing for all unmarried workers and nearly half of its married male employees. Company loans were available for the education of children and to help with the cost of weddings and funerals.

Studies of Japanese-run plants in Britain and the United States indicate that 'bottom-up' decision-making does work outside Japan. Workers seem to respond positively to the greater level of involvement these plants provide (White and Trevor 1983). It seems reasonable to conclude, therefore, that the Japanese model does carry some lessons relevant to the Weberian conception of bureaucracy. Organizations that closely resemble Weber's ideal type are probably much less effective than they appear on paper, because they do not permit lower-level employees to develop a sense of autonomy over, and involvement in, their work tasks.

Drawing on the example of Japanese corporations, Ouchi (1979, 1982) has argued that there are clear limits to the effectiveness of bureaucratic hierarchy, as emphasized by Weber. Overtly bureaucratized organizations lead to 'internal failures' of functioning because of their rigid, inflexible and uninvolving nature. Forms of authority Ouchi calls *clans* – groups having close personal connections with one another – are more efficient than bureaucratic types of organization. The work groups in Japanese firms are one example, but clan-type systems also often develop informally within Western organizations.

THE INFLUENCE OF THE LARGE CORPORATION

Some Japanese corporations have been highly successful in global markets, including many firms, such as Toyota, Sony or Mitsubishi, which have become household names in the West. Let us now go on to look at the **global corporations** and large-scale business companies in more detail. They are usually referred to as **transnational** (or *multinational*) **companies**. The term 'transnational' is preferable, indicating that these companies operate *across* different national boundaries rather than simply *within* several or many nations. A transnational corporation is a company that has plants or offices in two or more countries.

The biggest transnationals are gigantic companies, the value of their sales outstripping the gross national product of many countries (see figure 11.2). Half of the hundred largest economic units in the world today are nations; the other half are transnational corporations! The scope of the operations of these companies is staggering. The 600

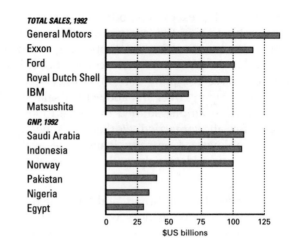

Fig. 11.2 Total sales of some of the largest multinational companies compared with the gross national product of selected countries, 1992

Source: Commission on Global Governance, *Our Global Neighbourhood* (Oxford University Press 1995).

largest transnationals account for more than one-fifth of the total industrial and agricultural production in the global economy. About seventy of these giant companies are responsible for half of total global sales (Dicken 1992). The revenues of the largest 200 companies rose tenfold between the mid-1970s and the 1990s. Over the past twenty years, the transnationals' activities have become increasingly global: only three of the world's 315 largest companies in 1950 had manufacturing subsidiaries in more than twenty countries; some fifty do so today. These are still, of course, a small minority; most of the transnationals have subsidiaries in between two and five countries.

Eighty of the top 200 transnational corporations in the world are based in the United States, contributing just over half the total sales. The share of American companies has, however, fallen significantly since 1960, a period in which Japanese companies have grown dramatically: only five Japanese corporations were in the top 200 in 1960, as compared to twenty-eight in 1991. (For a fuller international picture see figure 11.3.)

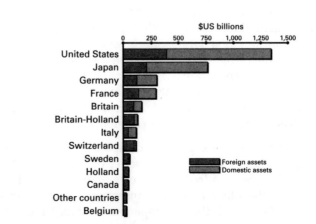

Fig. 11.3 Assets of the top hundred multinationals by their home country, 1992

Source: UNCTAD. From *The Economist*, 24 June 1995.

Contrary to common belief, most of the investment by transnational companies is within the industrialized world: three-quarters of *all* foreign direct investment is between the industrialized countries. Nevertheless, the involvements of transnationals in Third World countries are very extensive, with Brazil, Mexico and India showing the highest levels of foreign investment. Since 1970 the most rapid rate of increase in corporate investment by far has been in the Asian newly industrializing countries of Singapore, Hong Kong, South Korea and Malaysia.

The reach of the transnationals

The reach of the transnationals over the past thirty years would not have been possible without advances in transport and communications. Jet travel now allows people to move around the world at a speed that would have seemed inconceivable even half a century ago. The development of extremely large ocean-going vessels (superfreighters), together with containers that can be shifted directly from one type of transport to another, makes possible the easy transport of bulk materials.

Telecommunications technologies now permit more or less instantaneous communication from one part of the world to another. Satellites have been used for commercial telecommunications since 1965, when the first satellite could carry 240 telephone conversations at once. Current satellites can carry 12,000 simultaneous conversations! The larger transnationals now have their own satellite-based communications systems. The Mitsubishi corporation, for instance, has a massive network, across which five million words are transmitted to and from its headquarters in Tokyo each day.

Types of transnational corporation

The transnationals have assumed an increasingly important place in the world economy over the course of this century. They are of key importance in the **international division of labour** – the worldwide distribution of jobs. Just as national economies have become increasingly *concentrated* – dominated by a limited number of very large companies – so has the world economy. In the case of the United States and several of the other leading industrialized countries, the firms that dominate nationally also have a very wide-ranging international presence. Many sectors of world production (such as agribusiness) are *oligopolies* – production is controlled by three or four corporations, which dominate the market. Over the past two or three decades, international oligopolies have developed in motor-car production, microprocessors, the electronics industry and some other goods marketed worldwide.

H. V. Perlmutter divides transnational corporations into three types (see figure 11.4). One consists of **ethnocentric transnationals**, in which company policy is set, and as far as possible put into practice, from a headquarters in the country of origin. Companies and plants which the

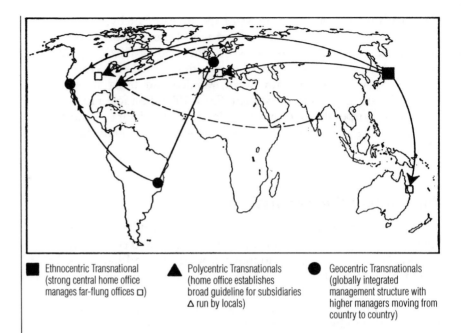

Ethnocentric Transnational
(strong central home office
manages far-flung offices □)

Polycentric Transnationals
(home office establishes
broad guideline for subsidiaries
△ run by locals)

Geocentric Transnationals
(globally integrated
management structure with
higher managers moving from
country to country)

Fig. 11.4 Three types of transnational corporations

parent corporation owns around the world are cultural extensions of the originating company – its practices are standardized across the globe. A second category is that of **polycentric transnationals**, where overseas subsidiaries are managed by local firms in each country. The headquarters in the country or countries of origin of the main company establish broad guidelines within which local companies manage their own affairs. Finally, there are **geocentric transnationals**, which are international in their management structure. Managerial systems are integrated on a global basis, and higher managers are very mobile, moving from country to country as needs dictate (Perlmutter 1972).

Of all transnationals, the Japanese companies tend to be most strongly ethnocentric in Perlmutter's terms. Their worldwide operations are usually controlled tightly from the parent corporation, sometimes with the close involvement of the Japanese government. The Japanese Ministry of International Trade and Industry (MITI) plays a much more direct part in the overseeing of Japanese-based foreign enterprise than Western governments do. MITI has produced a series of development plans coordinating the overseas spread of Japanese firms over the past two decades. One distinctive Japanese type of transnational consists of the giant trading companies or *sogo shosha*. These are colossal conglomerates whose main concern is with the financing and support of trade. They provide financial, organizational and information services to other companies. About half of Japanese exports and imports are routed through the ten largest sogo shosha. Some, like Mitsubishi, also have large manufacturing interests of their own.

New trends: downsizing and decentring

In spite of their success, organizational change is accelerating among companies operating at the global level. There are big differences between the large corporation in the later 1990s and its counterpart earlier in the century. As Robert Reich has written, speaking of US corporations:

> America's core corporation no longer plans and implements the production of a large volume of goods and services; it no longer invests in a vast array of factories, machinery, laboratories, inventories, and other tangible assets; it no longer employs armies of production workers and middle-level managers. . . . In fact, the core corporation is no longer even American. It is, increasingly, a facade, behind which teems an array of decentralized groups and subgroups continuously contracting with similarly diffuse working units all over the world. (Reich 1992)

The global company which has been most radically decentred in a short period of time is Asea Brown Boveri, one of the largest engineering firms in the world. Its annual revenues amount to more than 30 billion US dollars. It has been broken down into 1,200 different organizations, all quite loosely linked to one another. Its chairman, Percy Barvenik, says, 'We grow all the time, but we also shrink all the time.' The company has laid off many of its staff in the process. The number of staff at its headquarters in Zurich was reduced from 4,000 to less than 200 (Naisbitt 1995).

One observer has commented: 'In the year ahead all big companies will find it increasingly difficult to compete with – and in general will perform more poorly than – smaller, speedier, more innovative companies. The mindset that in a huge global economy the multinationals dominate world business could not have been more wrong. The bigger and more open the world economy becomes, the more small and middle-sized companies will dominate (ibid., p. 47).

Organizations as networks

Stanley Davis argues that business firms, and other organizations too, are increasingly coming to be networks, which involve bottom-up decision-making, rather than hierarchies. They are doing so in response to the pressures coming from globalization, with the intense new patterns of change which it stimulates. Where change becomes both more profound and ever more rapid, Weberian-style bureaucracies are too cumbersome and too entrenched in their established ways to be able readily to cope with it. As Davis puts it:

> Whether organizations shrink through down-sizing, grow through alliances, or remain the same size, they will nevertheless be reorganizing their inner space. When you divide a whole into parts, it is the space between the parts that unites them together. Space is intangible and intangibility is increasingly prominent both in the new economy and in its new organizations. The industrial image of structure, for example, is the grinder-like architecture of buildings. The image of structure in the new economy, however, will be more like the architecture of atoms, built on energy and information, not steel. (Davis 1988)

Cutting down on time is the key to reorganizing activities across space. In a global marketplace, firms are under pressure from customers to deliver as quickly as possible, and the customer is as likely as not to be on the other side of the world. The system of production called 'just in time', pioneered by Taiichi Ohno of Toyota, has been adopted by many business organizations outside Japan. It is called 'just in time' because supplies arrive at the factory only just before they need to be used. They therefore don't need to be stored in a production plant over a long period of time. Essentially, 'just in time' production means integrating all the elements of a production process – including the involvement of top management – to cut out superfluous operations where time is lost (J. Blackburn 1990).

European and American corporations have recently tried to adopt some of these practices. Michael Hammer and James Champy (1993) give an example from the IBM Credit Corporation, a subsidiary of IBM. Until recently, requests for credit were handled in a series of steps, each carried out as a separate specialist task. In other words, the company was a bureaucracy in Weber's sense. The process of deciding about credit applications took an average of seven days, although it sometimes needed up to two weeks. Some people who were seeking credit would go elsewhere during this time.

To see whether this situation could be simplified and speeded up, a group of management consultants took a financing request themselves through all the stages of the process of authorization. The people in each office were asked to process the request as they usually would, only to do it immediately rather than adding it to the pile of work on their desks. The consultants found that the actual work took altogether only ninety minutes. The rest – most of the seven days – was taken up by passing the request from one department to the next.

It was the whole process that needed to be changed to improve efficiency, not the individual steps. The specialists in each office were replaced by generalists who could deal with the credit process from beginning to end. The result was extraordinary. The seven-*day* turn-around was slashed to four *hours* – and fewer people were required than for the older, more cumbersome way.

THE REORDERING OF TECHNOLOGY AND MODERN ORGANIZATIONS

Organizations in modern society are about the reordering of space and time. Today, information technology and electronic communication are making possible the transcending of space and the control of time in ways that were unknown in even the relatively recent past. The fact that complex information, stored in computers, can be flashed around the world is altering many aspects of our lives. The globalizing processes that are both produced by and the driving force behind these technologies are also serving to change the very shape of many organizations. This is particularly true of business corporations, which have to compete with one another in a global marketplace.

Organizations have to *be* somewhere, don't they? That's certainly what Foucault thought. In an important sense, his view is valid. The business area of any large city, with its imposing array of buildings climbing up towards the sky, bears ample witness to this truth. These buildings, which house the executives and work staffs of large corporations, banks and finance houses, tend to be packed into a small area.

Yet at the same time, big organizations today are 'nowhere'. They consist of as many scattered individuals and groups as they do clusters of people working in the same physical space in office buildings. This is partly because of the ease with which people now can communicate with one another in an immediate way across the world, something the information highway will further develop. It is also because of the ever-increasing importance of information, rather than physical goods, in shaping our social existence.

Physical places and goods can't occupy the same space, but physical places and information, a series of electronic blips, can. Hence organizations themselves aren't so constrained to 'be' somewhere as used to be the case. Where, for instance, is the stock market? Is it located in the City of London, where the traders rush around the floor exchanging slips of paper? Not today. The stock market is not, as markets once were, a physical place for the buying of stocks and shares. One might say that it is everywhere and nowhere. The stock market consists of a large number of dealers, most of whom work from computer screens in different offices and settings, and who are in continuous contact across the whole world with their counterparts in New York, Paris, Tokyo and Frankfurt. The large corporation is less and less a big business than an 'enterprise web' – a central organization that links smaller firms together. IBM, for example, which used to be one of the most jealously self-sufficient of all large corporations, in the 1980s and early 1990s joined with dozens of US-based companies and more than eighty foreign-based firms to share strategic planning and cope with production problems.

Some corporations remain strongly bureaucratic and centred in a particular country. Most are no longer so clearly located anywhere. The old transnational corporation used to work mainly from its headquarters, and its overseas production plants and subsidiaries were controlled from there. Now, with the transformation of space and time noted above, groups situated in any region of the world are able, via telecommunications and computer, to work with others. Nations still try to influence flows of information, resources and money across their borders. But modern communications technologies make this more and more difficult, if not impossible. Knowledge and finances can be transferred across the world as electronic blips moving at the speed of light.

CONCLUSION

Are networks, involving a large amount of bottom-up decision-making, the path to the future, taking us completely away from Weber's more pessimistic vision? Some have suggested so, but we should be cautious about such a view. Bureaucratic systems are more internally fluid than Weber believed and are increasingly being challenged by other, less hierarchical forms of organization. But they probably won't disappear altogether, as the dinosaurs did. In the near future, there is likely to be a continuing push and pull between tendencies towards large size, impersonality and hierarchy in organizations on the one hand and opposing influences on the other.

SUMMARY

1 Organizations play a central role in our lives in the present day. An organization can be defined as a large association of people, set up to achieve specific objectives. Examples of organizations include business corporations, government agencies, schools, universities, hospitals and prisons.

2 All modern organizations are in some degree bureaucratic in nature. Bureaucracy involves a clear-cut hierarchy of authority; written rules governing the conduct of officials (who work full-time for a salary); and a separation between the tasks of the official within the organization and life outside it. Members of the organization do not own the material resources with which they work. Max Weber argued that modern bureaucracy is a highly effective means of organizing large numbers of people, ensuring that decisions are taken according to common criteria.

3 Informal networks tend to develop at all levels both within and between organizations. The study of these informal ties is as important as the more formal characteristics concentrated on by Weber.

4 The work of Weber and Michels identifies a tension between bureaucracy and democracy. On the one hand, long-term processes of centralization of decision-making are associated with the development of modern societies. On the other hand, one of the main features of the past two centuries has been growing pressure towards democracy. The trends conflict, with neither one in a position of dominance.

5 The physical settings of organizations strongly influence their social features. The architecture of modern organizations is closely connected to surveillance as a means of securing obedience to those in authority. Surveillance refers to the supervision of people's activities, as well as to the keeping of files and records about them.

6 Japanese corporations differ significantly from most Western companies in terms of their characteristics as organizations. There is more consultation of lower-level workers by managerial executives; pay and responsibility are linked to seniority; and groups, rather than individuals, are evaluated for their performance. Although it is by no means proved that these help explain why Japan's economic performance has outstripped that of most Western countries, some Western firms have adopted aspects of Japanese management systems in recent years.

7 Large business corporations dominate in modern capitalist economies. When one corporation has a commanding position in an industry, it is a monopoly. More common is the oligopoly, in which a small group of large corporations predominate in an industry.

With the globalizing of the economy, most large corporations have become transnational, or multinational, companies. They operate across different national boundaries in two or more countries.

8 The large business corporations have started to restructure themselves over recent years. As a result of 'downsizing' – the shedding of staff through internal reorganization – they are becoming leaner and less bureaucratized. Many have become loose networks of groups rather than bureaucratic hierarchies in Weber's sense.

9 Bureaucratic organizations almost certainly won't disappear, but will coexist with other types of organizations and groups.

10 All modern organizations depend on the specialization of knowledge and the transmitting of information. Professionalization, together with the increasing use of information technology, may be leading to a general increase in the flexibility of organizations. The impact of these changes – thus far, at any rate – has often been exaggerated.

FURTHER READING

John Allen et al., *Political and Economic Forms of Modernity* (Cambridge: Polity Press and Open University, 1992). Contains several useful articles on the changing nature of political and economic organizations today.

Richard Brown, *Understanding Industrial Organisations* (London: Routledge, 1992). A survey of the different theoretical approaches to the understanding of industrial organizations.

Jeff Hearn et al. (eds), *The Sexuality of Organisation* (London: Sage, 1989). Argues that the orthodox sociology of organizations has largely ignored issues concerned with gender and sexuality.

Christel Lane, *Management and Labour in Europe* (London: Elgar, 1989). A discussion of business organization in France, Germany and the UK.

David Lyon, *The Electronic Eye: The Rise of Surveillance Society* (Cambridge: Polity Press, 1994). An intriguing analysis of the role of information technology as a means of social control.

John McDermott, *Corporate Society* (Boulder, Colo.: Westview, 1991). A discussion of the role of the corporation in modern society.

Michael Reed, *The Sociology of Organisations: Themes, Perspectives and Prospects* (London: Harvester Wheatsheaf, 1992). A useful general text on the sociology of modern organizations.

IMPORTANT TERMS

- officials
- ideal type
- surveillance
- incarceration
- surveillance society
- oligarchy
- global corporations
- transnational companies
- international division of labour
- ethnocentric transnationals
- polycentric transnationals
- geocentric transnationals

WORK AND ECONOMIC LIFE

➡

BASIC CONCEPTS

- *work* • *the economy* • *division of labour*
- *unemployment*

For most of us, work occupies a larger part of our lives than any other single type of activity. We often associate the notion of work with drudgery – with a set of tasks that we want to minimize and, if possible, escape from altogether. You may have this very thought in mind as you set out to read this chapter! Is this most people's attitude towards their work, and if so, why? We shall try to find out in the following pages.

Work has more going for it than drudgery, or people would not feel so lost and disoriented when they become unemployed. How would you feel if you thought you would never get a job? In modern societies, having a job is important for maintaining self-esteem. Even where work conditions are relatively unpleasant, and the tasks involved dull, work tends to be a structuring element in people's psychological make-up and the cycle of their daily activities. Several characteristics of work are relevant here.

- *Money* A wage or salary is the main resource many people depend on to meet their needs. Without such an income, anxieties about coping with day-to-day life tend to multiply.

- *Activity level* Work often provides a basis for the acquisition and exercise of skills and capacities. Even where work is routine, it offers a structured environment in which a person's energies may be absorbed. Without it, the opportunity to exercise such skills and capacities may be reduced.

- *Variety* Work provides access to contexts that contrast with domestic surroundings. In the working environment, even when the tasks are relatively dull, individuals may enjoy doing something different from home chores.

- *Temporal structure* For people in regular employment, the day is usually organized around the rhythm of work. While this may sometimes be oppressive, it provides a sense of direction in daily activities. Those who are out of work frequently find boredom a major problem and develop a sense of apathy about time. As one unemployed man remarked, 'Time doesn't matter now as much as it used to. . . . There's so much of it' (Fryer and McKenna 1987).

- *Social contacts* The work environment often provides friendships and opportunities to participate in shared activities with others. Separated from the work setting, a person's circle of possible friends and acquaintances is likely to dwindle.

- *Personal identity* Work is usually valued for the sense of stable social identity it offers. For men in particular, self-esteem is often bound up with the economic contribution they make to the maintenance of the household.

Against the backdrop of this formidable list, it is not difficult to see why being without work may undermine individuals' confidence in their social value.

PAID AND UNPAID WORK

We often tend to think of work, as the notion of being 'out of work' implies, as equivalent to having a paid job, but in fact this is an over-simplified view. Non-paid labour (such as repairing one's own car or housework) looms large in many people's lives. Many types of work do not conform to orthodox categories of paid employment. Much of the work done in **the informal economy**, for example, is not recorded in any direct way in the official employment statistics. The term *informal economy* refers to transactions outside the sphere of regular employment, sometimes involving the exchange of cash for services provided, but also often involving the direct exchange of goods or services.

Someone who comes round to fix the television may be paid in cash, without any receipt being given or details of the job recorded. People exchange 'cheap' – that is to say pilfered or stolen – goods with friends or associates in return for other favours. The informal economy includes not only 'hidden' cash transactions, but many forms of *self-provisioning* which people carry on inside and outside the home. Do-it-yourself activities, domestic machinery and household tools, for instance, provide goods and services which would otherwise have to be purchased (Gershuny and Miles 1983).

Housework, which has traditionally mostly been carried out by women, is usually unpaid. But it is work, often very hard and exhausting work, nevertheless. **Voluntary work**, for charities or other organizations, has an important social role. Having a paid job is important for all the reasons listed above – but the category of 'work' stretches more widely.

We can define WORK, whether paid or unpaid, as being the carrying out of tasks requiring the expenditure of mental and physical effort, which has as its objective the production of goods and services that cater to human needs. An **occupation**, or job, is work that is done in exchange for a regular wage or salary. In all cultures, work is the basis of THE ECONOMY. The **economic system** consists of institutions that provide for the production and distribution of goods and services.

In this chapter, we shall analyse the nature of work in modern societies and look at the major changes affecting economic life today. Work is always embedded in the wider economic system. In modern societies, that system depends on *industrial production*. Modern industry, as has been stressed in other parts of the book, differs in a fundamental way from premodern systems of production, which were based above all on agriculture. Most people worked in the fields or cared for livestock. In modern societies, by contrast, only a tiny proportion of the population works in agriculture, and farming itself has become industrialized – it is carried on largely by means of machines rather than by human hand.

Modern industry is itself always changing – technological change is one of its main features. **Technology** refers to the harnessing of science to machinery to achieve greater productive efficiency. The nature of industrial production also changes in relation to wider social and economic influences. In this chapter, we focus on both technological and economic change, showing how these are transforming industry today.

To begin with, we concentrate on paid work – work in industrial settings. We look at changes in production processes in industry and how these have affected jobs. Industrial production is by no means always a harmonious affair. In subsequent sections, we look at the origins of industrial conflict, concentrating on the impact of strikes. From there we analyse women's role in industry. Many more women are in paid work than used to be the case, and we shall trace out the causes and consequences of this development. In the concluding part of the chapter, we study unemployment and pose the question: what is the future of work?

We start by analysing the changing patterns of modern industrial production.

THE DIVISION OF LABOUR AND ECONOMIC DEPENDENCE

One of the most distinctive characteristics of the economic system of modern societies is the existence of a highly complex DIVISION OF LABOUR: work has become divided into an enormous number of different occupations in which people specialize. In traditional societies, non-agricultural work entailed the mastery of a craft. Craft skills were learned through a lengthy period of apprenticeship, and the worker normally carried out all aspects of the production process from beginning to end. For example, a metalworker making a plough would forge the iron, shape it, and assemble the implement itself. With the rise of modern industrial production, most traditional crafts have disappeared altogether, replaced by skills that form part of more large-scale production processes. An electrician working in an industrial setting today, for instance, may inspect and repair only a few parts of one type of machine; different people will deal with the other parts and other machines.

The contrast in the division of labour between traditional and modern societies is truly extraordinary. Even in the largest traditional societies, there usually existed no more than twenty or thirty major craft trades, together with such specialized pursuits as merchant, soldier and priest. In a modern industrial system, there are literally thousands of distinct occupations. The UK census lists some 20,000 distinct jobs in the British economy. In traditional communities, most of the population worked on farms and were economically self-sufficient. They produced their own food, clothes and other necessities of life. One of the main features of modern societies, by contrast, is an enormous expansion of **economic interdependence**. We are all dependent on an immense number of other workers – today stretching right across the world – for the products and services that sustain our lives. With few exceptions, the vast majority of people in modern societies do not produce the food they eat, the houses in which they live or the material goods they consume.

Taylorism and Fordism

Writing some two centuries ago, Adam Smith, one of the founders of modern economics, identified advantages that the division of labour provides in terms of increasing productivity. His most famous work, *The Wealth of Nations*, opens with a description of the division of labour in a pin factory. A person working alone could perhaps make twenty pins per day. By breaking down that worker's task into a number of simple operations, however, ten workers carrying out specialized jobs in collaboration with one another could collectively produce 48,000 pins per day. The rate of production per worker, in other words, is increased from 20 to 4,800 pins, each specialist operator producing 240 times more than when working alone.

More than a century later, these ideas reached their most developed expression in the writings of Frederick Winslow Taylor, an American management consultant. Taylor's approach to what he called scientific management involved the detailed study of industrial processes in order to break them down into simple operations that could be precisely timed and organized. **Taylorism**, as scientific management came to be called, was not merely an academic study. It was a system of production designed to maximize industrial output, and it had a widespread impact on the organization of industrial production and technology.

Taylor was concerned with improving industrial efficiency, but he gave little consideration to the results of that efficiency. Mass production demands mass markets, and the industrialist Henry Ford was among the first to see this link. **Fordism**, an extension of Taylor's principles of scientific management, is the name used to designate the system of mass production tied to the cultivation of mass markets. Ford designed his first auto plant at Highland Park, Michigan, in 1908 to manufacture only one product – the Model T Ford – thereby allowing the introduction of specialized tools and machinery designed for speed, precision and simplicity of operation. One of Ford's most significant innovations was the construction of a moving assembly line, said to have been inspired by Chicago slaughterhouses, in which animals were disassembled section by section on a moving line. Each worker on Ford's assembly line was assigned a specialized task, such as fitting the left-side door handles as the car bodies moved along the line. By 1929, when production of the Model T ceased, over 15 million cars had been produced.

The limitations of Fordism and Taylorism

At one time, it looked as though Fordism represented the likely future of industrial production as a whole. This has not proved to be the case. The system can only be applied in industries, such as car manufacture, that produce standardized products for large markets. To set up mechanized production lines is enormously expensive, and once a Fordist system is established, it is quite rigid; to alter a product, for example, substantial reinvestment is needed. Fordist production is easy to copy if sufficient funding is available to set up the plant. But firms in countries in which labour power is expensive find it difficult to compete with those where wages are cheaper. This was one of the factors originally leading to the rise of the Japanese car industry (although Japanese wage levels today are no longer low) and, more recently, that of South Korea.

Low-trust systems and high-trust systems

Fordism and Taylorism are what some industrial sociologists call **low-trust systems**. Jobs are set by management and are geared to machines. Those who carry out the work tasks are closely supervised and are allowed little autonomy of action. Where there are many low-trust positions, the level of worker dissatisfaction and absenteeism is high, and industrial conflict is common. A **high-trust system** is one in which workers are permitted to control the pace, and even the content, of their work, within overall guidelines. Such systems are usually concentrated at the higher levels of industrial organizations.

From the early 1970s onwards, firms in Western Europe, the United States and Japan experimented with alternatives to low-trust systems. These include automated assembly lines and group production, in which a work group carries out a recognized role in influencing the nature of the work task. We shall now look at these strategies in turn.

Automation

The concept of **automation**, or programmable machinery, was introduced in the mid-1800s, when Christopher Spencer, an American, invented the Automat, a programmable lathe that made screws, nuts and gears. Automation has thus far affected relatively few industries, but with advances in the design of industrial robots, its impact is certain to become greater. A robot is an automatic device that can perform functions ordinarily done by human workers. The term was coined about fifty years ago by the playwright Karel Čapek, from the Czech word *robota*, compulsory labour.

Robots were first introduced into industry in some numbers in 1946, when a device was invented to automatically regulate machinery in the engineering industry. Robots of greater complexity, however, date only from the development of microprocessors – basically since the 1970s. The first robot controlled by a minicomputer was developed in 1974 by Cincinnati Milason. Robots today can execute numerous tasks like welding, spray-painting, lifting and carrying parts. Some robots can distinguish parts by feel or touch, while others can make out a certain range of objects visually. As Robert Ayres and Steven Miller have pointed out,

> There can be no more dedicated and untiring factory worker than a robot. Robots can repeat tasks such as spot-welding and spray-painting flaw-lessly on a variety of workpieces, and they can quickly be reprogrammed to perform entirely new tasks. . . . In the next few years, we can expect to see many industrial robots installed in medium-batch manufacturing plants. Robots will feed workpieces to clusters of automatic machines in workcells, which may be serialized to form a closed loop manufacturing system controlled by microprocessors. (Ayres and Miller 1985)

The majority of the robots used in industry worldwide are to be found in automobile manufacture. The usefulness of robots in production thus far is relatively limited, because their capacity to recognize differ-ent objects and manipulate awkward shapes is still at a rudimentary level. Yet it is certain that automated production will spread rapidly in forthcoming years; robots are becoming more sophisticated, while their costs are decreasing.

Group production

Group production, collaborative work groups in place of assembly lines, has sometimes been used in conjunction with automation as a way of reorganizing work. The underlying idea is to increase worker motivation by letting groups of workers collaborate in production processes rather than requiring each worker to spend the whole day doing a single repetitive task like inserting the screws in the door han-dle of a car.

An example of group production is quality circles (QCs), groups of between five and twenty workers who meet regularly to study and resolve production problems. Workers who belong to QCs receive extra training, enabling them to contribute technical knowledge to the dis-cussion of production issues. QCs were initiated in the United States, taken up by a number of Japanese companies, then repopularized in the West in the 1980s. They represent a break from the assumptions of Taylorism, since they recognize that workers possess the expertise to contribute towards the definition and method of the tasks they carry out.

Flexible production

One of the most important changes in worldwide production processes over the past few years has been the introduction of computer-aided design. While Taylorism and Fordism were successful at producing mass products (that were all the same) for mass markets, they were completely unable to produce small orders of goods, let alone goods specifically made for an individual customer. Computer-aided designs, coupled to other types of computer-based technology, have altered this situation in a radical way. Stanley Davis speaks of the emergence of 'mass customizing': the new technologies allow the large-scale produc-tion of items designed for particular customers. Five thousand shirts might be produced on a traditional assembly line each day. It is now possible to customize every one of the shirts just as quickly as five thousand identical shirts, and at no greater expense (Davis 1988).

Before computer-aided design came along, the Japanese pioneered what they called **flexible production**. By introducing production systems that differ in almost every respect from the mass production system Henry Ford pioneered at Detroit, Japanese car makers were able to notch up a remarkable increase in global sales from the mid-1970s to the early 1990s (Dertouzos 1989). The Japanese have placed the emphasis upon the creation of a skilled work force and on ways of increasing the speed with which new product designs are introduced and new products brought to market.

Changes taking up to twenty-four hours in European or American car plants in the early 1980s could be made in five minutes in the Japanese factories. The goal was perfect first-time quality, with no need for subsequent improvements. Group production was brought to a high level; integrated work teams consisted of assemblers, workers and suppliers. By means of these techniques, planners could work to a cycle (the time taken from the first conception of a new model until the last vehicle rolls off the production line) of seven and a half years. European and American planners, by contrast, until recently were working with thirteen-to-fifteen-year cycles. They have now caught up a good deal, basically by trying to copy Japanese practices. However, as Lester Thurow has put it with reference to the US, 'The best American plants are not quite as good as the best Japanese plants, and the worst American plants are far worse than the worst Japanese plants' (Thurow 1993).

TRENDS IN THE OCCUPATIONAL SYSTEM

The **occupational system** in all industrialized countries has changed very substantially since the opening of the present century. In 1900, over three-quarters of the employed population was in manual (blue-collar) work. Some 28 per cent of these were skilled workers, 35 per cent semi-skilled and 10 per cent unskilled. White-collar and professional jobs were relatively few in number. By the middle of the century, manual workers made up less than two-thirds of the population in paid labour, and non-manual work had expanded correspondingly.

A census of the population of the UK was taken in 1971 and another in 1981. Over that period, the proportion of people in blue-collar occupations declined from 62 per cent to 56 per cent for men and from 43 to 36 per cent in the case of women. Professional and managerial jobs filled by men increased by about one million. By 1981 there were 170,000 fewer men in routine white-collar work, but 250,000 more women in such jobs. The decline in manual jobs corresponded closely with a decrease in proportions of people involved in manufacturing industry. In 1981 there were 700,000 fewer men and 420,000 fewer women in manufacturing work than there had been ten years before.

These trends continue today, but have levelled off somewhat. A Labour Force Survey carried out by the government in 1990 showed that just over 50 per cent of men and 33 per cent of women were in manual occupations. The most extreme contrast between the sexes was between people in routine white-collar as compared to skilled blue-collar occupations. In 1990, 31 per cent of women were in the former type of job, compared with only 6 per cent of men, while 25 per cent of men were in skilled manual work, compared with only 4 per cent of women. In a number of other industrialized countries, such changes have proceeded further than in Britain. For example, according to some estimates, under 40 per cent of the US labour force is in manual occupations today (Rossides 1990).

There is considerable debate over why such changes have occurred. The reasons seem to be several. One is the continuous introduction of labour-saving machinery, culminating in the spread of information technology and computerization in industry in recent years. Another is the rise of manufacturing industry outside the West, particularly in the Far East. The older industries in Western societies have experienced major cutbacks because of their inability to compete with the more efficient Far Eastern producers, whose labour costs are lower.

Among other things, these developments have influenced patterns of industrial conflict. We now turn to look at this topic.

UNIONS AND INDUSTRIAL CONFLICT

There have long been conflicts between workers and those in economic and political authority over them. Riots against military conscription and high taxes, and food riots at periods of harvest failure, were common in urban areas of Europe in the eighteenth century. These 'pre-modern' forms of labour conflict continued up to not much more than a century ago in some countries. For example, there were food riots in several large Italian towns in 1868 (Geary 1982). Such traditional forms of confrontation were not just sporadic, irrational outbursts: the use or threat of violence had the effect of limiting the price of grain and other essential foodstuffs.

The development of unions

Industrial conflict between workers and employers in the first half of the nineteenth century was frequently only semi-organized. Where there was confrontation, workers would quite often leave their places of employment and form crowds in the streets; they would make their grievances known through their unruly behaviour or by engaging in acts of violence against the authorities. Workers in some parts of France in the late nineteenth century retained the practice of threatening disliked employers with hanging! Use of the strike, which is now associated with organized bargaining between workers and management, developed slowly and sporadically. The Combination Acts passed in

Britain in 1799 and 1800 made the meeting of organized workers' groups illegal, and banned popular demonstrations. The Acts were repealed some twenty years later, when it became apparent that they stimulated more public disturbances than they quelled. Membership of **trade unions** grew and trade unionism soon became a mass movement. Union activity was legalized in the last quarter of the nineteenth century, after which membership increased to cover 60 per cent of male manual workers in Britain by 1920. The British trade union movement is coordinated by a central body founded in 1868, the Trades Union Congress (TUC), which developed strong links with the Labour Party.

At the turn of the century, there was little direct connection between the existence of unions and the tendency to strike. Most early strikes were spontaneous, in the sense that they were not called by any specific organizations of workers. A report of the US Commissioner of Labor in 1907 showed that about half of all the strikes at the time were not initiated by unions (Ross 1954). Much the same was probably true in Britain. This situation had changed by the end of World War One, since when the proportion of strikes occurring among non-unionized workers has become small.

The development of the union movement has varied considerably between countries, as has the influence of the unions over the workforce, employers and government. In Britain and the United States unions have been established for longer than in most European societies. The German unions, for example, were largely destroyed by the Nazis in the 1930s, and set up afresh after World War Two, whereas the main development of the French union movement did not in fact occur until the 1930s, when the freedom to organize unions and negotiate collective labour contracts was formally recognized.

Why do unions exist?

Although their levels of membership and the extent of their power vary widely, union organizations exist in all Western countries. All such countries legally recognize the right of workers to strike in pursuit of economic objectives. Why have unions become a basic feature of modern societies? Why does union–management conflict seem to be a more or less ever-present feature of industrial settings?

Some have proposed that unions are effectively a version of medieval guilds – associations of people working in the same trade – reassembled in the context of modern industry. This interpretation might help us understand why unions often emerged first among craft workers, but does not explain why they have been so consistently associated with wage bargaining and industrial conflict. A more satisfactory explanation must look to the fact that unions developed to protect the material interests of workers in industrial settings which bring them together, creating solidarity, but in which they hold very little formal power.

In the early development of modern industry, workers in most countries were without political rights and had little influence over the conditions of work in which they found themselves. Unions developed in the first instance as means of redressing the imbalance of power between workers and employers. Whereas workers had little power as individuals, through collective organization their influence was considerably increased. An employer can do without the labour of any particular worker, but not without that of all or most of the workers in a factory or plant. Unions were originally mainly 'defensive' organizations, providing the means whereby workers could counter the overwhelming power over their lives which employers enjoyed.

Recent developments

Unions themselves, of course, have altered over the years. Some have grown very large and, as permanent organizations, have become bureaucratized. Unions are staffed by full-time officials, who may themselves have little direct experience of the conditions under which their members work. The activities and views of union leaders can thus become quite distant from those of the members they represent. Shop-floor groups sometimes find themselves in conflict with the strategies of their own unions. Most unions have not been successful in recruiting a high level of women workers. Although some have initiated campaigns to increase their female membership, many have in the past actively discouraged women from joining.

In current times, unions in Western countries are facing a threat from three connected sets of changes: high levels of unemployment, which weaken the unions' bargaining position; the decline of the older manufacturing industries, in which the union presence has traditionally been strong; and the increasing intensity of international competition, particularly from Asian countries, where wages are often lower than in the West. In the United States and several European countries, including Britain, France, Germany and Denmark, rightist governments came to power in the 1970s and 1980s, mostly determined to limit what they saw as excessive union influence in industry.

Employment Acts passed in Britain in 1980 and 1982 introduced new limitations on the legal rights of unions. The official definition of a 'trade union dispute' was tightened up to exclude such activities as picketing the suppliers of an employer. The Trade Union Act of 1984 required that unions hold a ballot of members before undertaking industrial action, as well as introducing other restrictions on union prerogatives. The civil servants employed at the government communications centre (GCHQ) were deprived of their right to belong to a union, a move which was justified by arguing that industrial action at GCHQ could represent a threat to national security. These measures have certainly had considerable effects on the union movement, nationally and at local level. Combined with the other, more general, factors mentioned earlier, they have quite drastically reduced union influence.

In the United States, the unions face a crisis of even greater dimensions than their counterparts in most European countries. Union-protected working conditions and wages have been eroded in several major industries over the past fifteen years. Workers in the road transport, steel and car industries have all accepted lower wages than those previously negotiated. The unions came out second-best in several major strikes, perhaps the most notable example being the crushing of the air traffic controllers' union in the early 1980s.

Decline in union membership and influence is something of a general phenomenon in the industrialized countries, and is not to be explained wholly in terms of political pressure applied by rightist governments against the unions. Unions usually become weakened during periods when unemployment is high, as has been the case for a considerable while in many Western countries (see further below). Trends towards more flexible production tend to diminish the force of unionism, which flourishes more extensively where there are many people working together in large factories.

Strikes

What is a **strike**? The answer is by no means obvious or easy to formulate. For example, can we distinguish between a strike and a short stoppage of work? In the strike statistics of many countries an attempt is made to do so, by only counting as strikes stoppages lasting more than a specific time (like half a day), or where more than a certain number of workers are involved. Are overtime bans or 'working to rule' examples of strike activity?

On the whole it seems preferable to define 'strike' in a reasonably narrow sense, or else the term loses all precision. We can define a strike as a temporary stoppage of work by a group of employees in order to express a grievance or enforce a demand (Hyman 1984). All the components of this definition are important in separating strikes from other forms of opposition and conflict. A strike is *temporary*, since workers intend to return to the same job with the same employer; where workers quit altogether, the term is not appropriate. As a *stoppage of work*, a strike is distinguishable from an overtime ban or 'going slow'. A *group* of workers has to be involved, because a strike refers to a collective action, not the response of one individual worker. That those acted against are *employers* serves to separate strikes from protests such as may be conducted by tenants or students. Finally, a strike involves *seeking to make known a grievance or press a demand*; workers who are absent solely to attend a sports event cannot be said to be on strike.

Strikes represent only one aspect or type of conflict in which workers and management may become involved. Other closely related expressions of organized conflict are *lock-outs* (where employers rather than workers bring about a stoppage of work), output restrictions, and clashes in contract negotiation. Less organized expressions of conflict may include high labour turnover, absenteeism and interference with production machinery.

Strike statistics

Since there is a fairly large arbitrary element in specifying exactly what a strike is, it is not surprising that different countries have varying practices in the registering of strike statistics. International comparisons of strike levels can be made, but have to be interpreted with caution. What is regarded as a strike in one country, and thus included in the statistics, may not count as such in another. For example, in Britain a stoppage has to involve only ten workers or more before it is reported as a strike, whereas in the United States (since 1982) only stoppages involving a thousand or more workers are registered in the strike statistics.

Three measures of strike activity are usually published – the number of strikes per year, the proportion of the labour force involved in strikes for that year, and the number of working days lost through strike activity. The three taken together provide a rough idea of differences in strike levels between countries. In terms of all three criteria, Italy and Canada are among the most strike-prone countries, the least being Germany and the Scandinavian countries. The United States and United Kingdom are in the middle range. There seems to be no particular connection between strike levels, as measured by the official statistics, and levels of economic performance. Countries with low strike rates, in other words, do not necessarily show higher levels of economic growth than those having more strikes. This is hardly surprising; the value of comparative strike statistics is in any case suspect, and industrial conflict or tensions can be expressed in many ways other than strikes. In addition, it does not follow that because industrial relations are harmonious, productivity will inevitably be high.

Recent trends in industrial conflict

In a well-known work published at the beginning of the 1960s, it was argued that strikes were 'withering away'. According to the authors, prolonged and intense disputes are mainly characteristic of the early phases of industrialization. Once agreed-on frameworks of industrial bargaining are firmly in place, they argued, strike activity declines (Ross and Hartman 1960). No sooner was this thesis proclaimed than there was an upsurge of industrial conflict in many Western countries, including Britain. A notable feature of strike activity in the British context during the 1960s and early 1970s was a sharp rise in the number of unofficial strikes. It seems that many workers at this period were as disaffected with their official union organizations as with their employers.

In the 1980s and early 1990s the focus of strike activity shifted back to the official unions. At the same time, the strike rate in Britain has declined substantially, owing in large part to the constrained political and economic climate in which the unions now find themselves. This seems to be part of an international trend. With two or three exceptions, all Western countries have experienced a lessening of strike activity over this period.

WOMEN AND WORK

Until recently, in Western countries paid work was predominantly the sphere of men. Over the past few decades this situation has changed radically: more and more women are moving into the labour force. In the following sections of the chapter we look at the origins and implications of this phenomenon – one of the most important changes happening in modern society at the present time.

Women and the workplace: the historical view

For the vast majority of the population in preindustrial societies (and many people in Third World societies today), productive activities and the activities of the household were not separate. Production was carried on either in the home or nearby. All members of the family in medieval Europe participated in work on the land or in handicrafts. In the towns, workshops were normally in the home, and family members contributed to various aspects of the production process. In the weaving trade, for instance, children did carding and combing, older daughters and mothers spun, and fathers wove. Wives and children similarly worked directly with men in tailoring, shoemaking and baking. Women often had considerable influence within the household as a result of their importance in economic processes, even if they were excluded from the male realms of politics and warfare. Wives of craftsmen often kept business accounts, as did those of farmers, and widows quite commonly owned and managed businesses.

Much of this changed with the separation of the workplace from the home brought about by the development of modern industry. The movement of production into mechanized factories was probably the largest single factor. Work was done at the machine's pace by individuals hired specifically for the tasks in question, so employers began to contract workers as individuals rather than families. The old way of treating families as one unit took a long time to fade out, however; in the early part of the nineteenth century, in Britain and many other European countries, employers still often hired family units. If the father was hired to work in the factory, for example, the wife and children would be taken on as domestic servants or farm-hands.

As the practice declined, however, an increasing division became established between home and workplace. Women came to be associated with 'domestic' values, although the idea that 'a woman's place is in the home' had different implications for women at varying levels in society. Affluent women enjoyed the services of maids, nurses and domestic servants. The burdens were harshest for poorer women, who had to cope with the household chores as well as engaging in industrial work to supplement their husbands' income.

Rates of employment of women outside the home, for all classes, were quite low until well into the twentieth century. Even as late as 1910, in Britain, more than a third of gainfully employed women were maids or house servants. The female labour force consisted mainly of young single women, whose wages, when they worked in factories or offices, were often sent by their employers direct to their parents. When they married, they withdrew from the labour force.

Since then, women's participation in the paid labour force has risen more or less continuously. One major influence was the labour shortage experienced during World War One. During the war years, women carried out many jobs previously regarded as the exclusive province of men. On returning from the war, men again took over most of those jobs, but the pre-established pattern had been broken. Today between 35 and 60 per cent of women aged between sixteen and sixty in most European countries hold paid jobs outside the home. The most significant rise has been among married women. The overall rate for the UK is 53 per cent. More than 40 per cent of married women with children aged under three are now in gainful employment. The proportion of women in the paid labour force, nevertheless, is still well below that of men: 74 per cent of the male population between twenty-five and sixty is in paid employment, and the proportion of men in paid employment has not altered much over the past century.

Inequalities at work

Women workers today are concentrated in poorly paid, routine occupations. Changes in the organization of employment as well as sex-role stereotyping have contributed to this. Alterations in the prestige and the work tasks of 'clerks' provide a good example. In 1850, in the UK, 99 per cent of clerks were men. To be a clerk was often to have a responsible position, involving knowledge of accountancy skills and sometimes carrying managerial responsibilities. Even the lowliest clerk had a certain status in the outside world. The twentieth century has seen a general mechanization of office work (starting with the introduction of the typewriter in the late nineteenth century), accompanied by a marked downgrading of the skills and status of 'clerk' – together with another related occupation, that of 'secretary' – into a low-status, low-paid occupation. Women came to fill these occupations as the pay and prestige associated with them declined. In 1991, nearly 90 per cent of clerical workers and 98 per cent of all secretaries in the UK were women.

Whether or not women have dependent children has a major impact on their participation in the paid labour force. In all socioeconomic groups women are more likely to be in full-time work if they have no children at home. However, mothers are today much more likely to return to full-time work, to the same job, and for the same employer, than they were at the beginning of the 1980s. At that time, a high proportion of mothers returning to work mostly took part-time jobs or found themselves in lower-paid positions than those they had left. In the early 1990s, women tend to resume their careers, especially in the higher-paid occupations (HMSO 1992).

Far more women are in part-time occupations, nevertheless, than are men (see figure 12.1). Most of these actively prefer to be in part-time rather than full-time paid employment. However, there is an important sense in which they have little choice. Men, by and large, do not assume prime responsibility for the rearing of children. Women who hold that responsibility (as well as other domestic obligations – see below) but still want, or need, to work in paid jobs inevitably find part-time work a more feasible option.

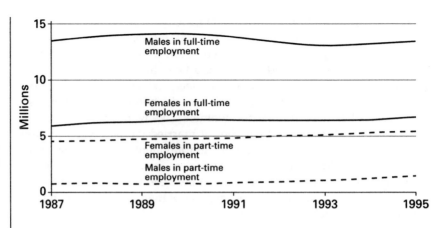

Fig. 12.1 Men and women in full-time and part-time employment in the United Kingdom, 1987–1995

Source: Labour Force Survey, Central Statistical Office. From *Social Trends*, 1996, table 4.1.

Women have recently made some inroads into occupations defined as 'men's jobs', but so far only to a limited degree. Less than 5 per cent of directorships in British companies are held by women; four out of five firms have no women directors at all. A similar story can be told in many domains of the economy. For instance, about one million women currently work for the major banks in the UK. Yet only 2 per cent of managers at the National Westminster Bank are women, 3 per cent at the Midland and 4 per cent at Barclays.

Things are not very different in the professions. The proportion of women solicitors and barristers has risen over the past twenty years, but still stands at only 14 per cent. Only 3 per cent of High Court judges are women, all of whom are in the Family Division. There are no female Lords of Appeal at all (Grint 1991).

We cannot say as yet how far these extreme inequalities of gender are likely to become less acute in the near future. It is possible that there are quite profound transitions taking place today; but it takes a long while for those embarking on careers to reach their peak attainments, and the results may only be witnessed some years hence. Take the legal profession as an example. In the early 1990s almost half of current law students in Britain were women, a very substantial rise over the prior decade. Most will presumably enter law careers; the test will be how many eventually get to the top.

The problems of success

At the moment, women who *are* successful economically have to fit in with a world where they feel they do not fully belong. The experiences of women executives have been compared to those of someone going to a foreign country for an extended stay. It is essential to take good guides and maps, and to observe the rules of the local inhabitants. A good deal of 'culture shock' is involved, and even the foreigner who stays on permanently is never totally accepted. In the longer run, however, women may exert a modifying effect on the masculine value system, bringing family responsibilities and work imperatives into line with one another.

One of the major factors affecting women's careers is the male perception that, for female employees, work comes second to having children. A British study investigated the views of managers interviewing female applicants for positions as technical staff in the health services. The researchers found that the interviewers always asked the women about whether or not they had, or intended to have, children. They virtually never followed this practice with male applicants. When asked why not, two themes ran through their answers: (a) women with children may require extra time off for school holidays or if a child falls sick, and (b) responsibility for child care is seen as a mother's problem rather than a parental one.

Some managers saw their questions on this issue as indicating an attitude of 'caring' towards women employees, but most saw such questioning as part of their task to assess how far a female applicant would prove a reliable colleague. Thus one manager remarked: 'It's a bit of a personal question, I appreciate that, but I think it's something that has to be considered. It's something that can't happen to a man really, but I suppose in a sense it's unfair – it's not equal opportunity because the man could never find himself having a family as such' (Homans 1987, p. 92). Yet, while men cannot biologically 'have a family' in the sense of bearing children, they can, of course, be involved in and responsible for

child care. Such a possibility was not taken into account by any of the managers studied. The same attitudes were held about the promotion of women: they were seen as likely to interrupt their careers to care for young children, no matter how senior a position they might have reached. A top male manager commented:

> 'Males tend to dominate the higher levels because simply the women drop out to have babies and that sort of thing . . . I don't think that is necessarily selective promotion but just the facts of life that women tend to go off and get married and have their families and therefore they have a fragmented career. They come back and have a gap in experience or training and when you come down to it and you are selecting candidates, it is not the sex of the candidate but what they can contribute to their job. You've got the candidate who is perhaps a woman who has seen three years out of a job for family reasons and a man who has been on the job. It is fairly evident, given that the rest is equal between the candidates, that he is likely to get the job.' (Homans 1987, p. 95)

The few women who were in senior management posts were all without children, and several of those who planned to have children in the future said they intended leaving their posts, perhaps retraining for other positions subsequently.

A survey of women managers carried out in East Anglia in 1992 showed similar findings (Verney 1992). Virtually all the two hundred women interviewed named problems of child care as the most difficult issue facing women who sought to make a success of a business career. Workplace nurseries were regarded by many as the biggest short-term improvement that could be made; but only 2 per cent of the companies covered in the survey provided them.

How should we interpret these findings? Are women's job opportunities hampered mainly by male prejudices? Some managers expressed the view that women with children should not seek paid work, but occupy themselves with child care and the home. Most, however, accepted the principle that women should have the same career opportunities as men. The bias in their attitudes was less to do with the workplace itself than with the domestic responsibilities of parenting. So long as most of the population take it for granted that parenting cannot be shared on an equal basis, the problems facing women employees will persist. It will remain a 'fact of life', as one of the managers put it, that women are severely disadvantaged, compared to men, in their career opportunities (Cockburn 1991).

Equal opportunities legislation

An Equal Opportunities Act was passed in the UK in 1970. According to its clauses, it is illegal for men and women to receive different rates of pay for the same job. However, the terms in which this principle was set out were sufficiently ambiguous for many employers simply to change some job titles so as to create 'different' jobs for men and women – so the Act then did not apply. The European Community introduced a more forceful Equal Pay Act in 1975, which enshrined what was called the 'principle of equal pay'. Not just the 'same work', but 'work to which equal value is attributed' should be paid equally.

NEW JOB: HOUSEHUSBAND

Jonathan Rourke, 29, has been a house-husband for two and a half years following the birth of his son Sam. He trained as a nursery teacher and lives in Hounslow, London.
What made you choose this job? My wife Lindy had a job to go back to and I didn't. Also, my background and experience is more in working with younger children than her — she teaches in a junior school.
How much do you earn? Nothing directly, but the child benefit is £41.20 a month.
What is the work like? I get Sam up around 7am and dress him. He's at playgroup three mornings a week, I pick him up after that and give him lunch. We might meet some of his friends in the park after his afternoon nap. Sam tends to go to bed a bit later than other kids of his age so that Lindy can spend more time with him. When I drop him off at the playgroup there'll be a large group of mums chatting away and I feel very much on the edge of things. And it's the same at what they still sometimes call the mothers and toddlers group.
What is Sam like? Around strangers he's very shy initially, he fiddles with a spot on one finger, but once he settles down he's fairly lively. Sometimes I take him to Heathrow, he's fascinated by the planes. The best part of it is watching him grow up — he's so talkative now and he had very little language a year ago.
What would your ideal job be? I really want to teach, but it's wonderful being at home with Sam.
What about the future? I just keep an eye on the job vacancies at the moment, but we're moving from rented property to buying soon so when he goes to school full time I may seriously have to look for work.

OLD JOB: HOUSEWIFE

Snezana Taylor, 36, has been a housewife for five years. Previously she had a variety of temporary and permanent secretarial positions and she has completed a bilingual secretarial course. Her parents are from the former Yugoslavia.
What made you choose this job? I wanted to be at home with the children.
How much do you earn? For the two children I think you get child benefit of around £70 a month.
What is the work like? I have to feed the children, wash them, organise their clothes, take them to school, take them to their activities, help them with their reading or homework, play with them and keep them stimulated (she laughs). Looking after them is enjoyable, it's trying to deal with all of the housework and other things as well that becomes a bit stressful sometimes. I also have to look after my husband Timothy; he's a quantity surveyor and works very long hours. With everyone screaming and ranting and raving and wanting their dinner and everything else it's sometimes hard to cope with it all.
What are the children like? Tanya is five and attends school, she's quite outgoing and likes bouncing around. Natasha is three and a half, she likes drawing and colouring and is a bit more shy. They go swimming and to ballet.
What would your ideal job be? This is definitely the best option for me at the moment.
What about the future? Next September Natasha will be at school full-time and I might be able to return to temping or some sort of work that I can fit in around the children.

Interviews Peter Carty; illustrations Anne Morrow
Source: Guardian, 6 March 1996, p. 3.

The contrast between the two is important. For the European legislation means that women in jobs equivalent to, but separated from, those of men can claim that what they are doing is of equivalent value and should be paid the same. The British government was in fact taken to the European Court because of the relative weakness of its equal opportunities legislation.

However, it is dubious how much difference any of this has made in practice to the occupational system. The Equal Opportunities Commission in Britain has fought some much-publicized cases of illegal discrimination against women. A case was won at an industrial tribunal in 1989, for example, by a group of female typists and secretaries at Lloyd's Bank; they successfully claimed that their work was of equal value to that of a male bank messenger, who had been receiving higher wages.

Such gains, however, have been few and far between. The extent to which some will go to get round the law is illustrated by the case of a firm which advertised for a 'rugby-playing marketing executive, male or female'. This was not discriminatory, the company argued, because there are twelve women's rugby clubs in the country. They lost the case (Neuberger 1991).

Low pay and the female poverty trap

As might be expected, the average pay of employed women is well below that of men, although the difference has narrowed somewhat over the past twenty years. Women are over-represented in the more poorly paid job sectors, but even within the same occupational categories as men, women on average have lower salaries. For instance, female clerical workers in Britain are paid 60 per cent of the earnings of their male counterparts; women sales employees earn 57 per cent of male earnings in the same occupation.

A substantial proportion of women in the UK live in poverty. This is particularly true of women who are heads of households. The percentage of women among the poor has risen steadily over the past two decades, despite the fact that the percentage of people living in poverty went down in the 1960s and was stable in the 1970s (rising again in the 1980s and early 1990s). Poverty tends to be especially acute for women with very small children who need constant care. There is a vicious circle here: a woman who can obtain a reasonably well-paid job may be financially crippled by having to pay for child care, yet if she starts working part-time, her earnings drop, whatever career prospects she may have had disappear, and she also loses other economic benefits – such as pension rights – which full-time workers receive.

How far are things different in other countries? As a basis for comparison, we shall consider Sweden, which has introduced a greater range of measures concerned with improving the economic status of women than has been the case in the UK.

The case of Sweden

Sweden leads the Western world in terms of legislation designed to promote the equality of the sexes (Scriven 1984). A high proportion of women in Sweden are in paid employment – in 1986, 80 per cent of those aged between sixteen and sixty-four did some form of paid work (Allmän/månad statistik 1987). State benefits, providing for 90 per cent of normal earnings, are available to anyone having a child to cover the period from one month before birth until six months afterwards. These six months can be divided between parents in terms of who takes time off from work to care for the child. A further 180 days' benefit are available, which may be taken by either mother or father at a subsequent period. Many child-care centres exist to provide after-school and holiday-time facilities for children up to the age of twelve.

These measures seem to have been partially successful in terms of providing opportunities for women to achieve positions of influence. For example, women hold a quarter of the seats in the Swedish parliament, one of the highest percentages internationally. Yet few women are found at the top levels of business firms, and in most occupations women are not much more significantly represented than in other Western societies. In 1985, 45 per cent of Swedish women worked in part-time occupations, which have poorer career opportunities, social benefits and pension rights than full-time jobs (only 5 per cent of men aged between sixteen and sixty-four are in part-time work in Sweden). Many women do not wish to leave their children at the day centres for the long periods necessary for them to take full-time employment, and women continue to be primarily responsible for the home and for child care. Paradoxically, because of the existence of the day centres, men may think they have less need to participate in child care than they would do otherwise.

Housework

Housework in its current form came into existence with the separation of the home and workplace (Oakley 1974). The home became a place of consumption rather than production of goods. Domestic work became 'invisible' as 'real work' was defined more and more as that which receives a direct wage. The period of the development of a separate 'home' also saw other changes. Before the inventions and facilities provided by industrialization influenced the domestic sphere, work in the household was hard and exacting. The weekly wash, for example, was a heavy and demanding task. The Maytag Washing Machine Co. carried out research reconstructing what washing involved in the nineteenth century, concluding that 'the old washday was as exhausting as swimming five miles of energetic breast stroke, arm movements and general dampness supplying an almost exact parallel' (quoted in Hardyment 1987, p. 6).

'This – iron. You-iron-shirts. I-go-out-with-the-girls. O.K.?'

The introduction of hot and cold running water into homes eliminated many time-consuming tasks; previously water itself had to be carried to the home and heated there whenever hot water was required. The piping of electricity and gas made coal and wood stoves obsolete, and chores such as the regular chopping of wood, carrying of coal and constant cleaning of the stove were thereby largely eliminated. Labour-saving equipment such as vacuum cleaners and washing machines

Table 12.1	Division of household tasks between couples, Great Britain, 1994 (per cent)					
	Always the woman	Usually the woman	About equal or both together	Usually the man	Always the man	All couples
Washing and ironing	47	32	18	1	1	100
Deciding what to have for dinner	27	32	35	3	1	100
Looking after sick family members	22	26	45	–	–	100
Shopping for groceries	20	21	52	4	1	100
Small repairs around the house	2	3	18	49	25	100

Total includes those who did not answer and where the task was done by a third person.

Source: British Social Attitudes Survey, Social & Community Planning Research. From *Social Trends*, 1996, p. 216.

reduced hard work, and declining family size meant fewer children to care for. Yet, surprisingly, the average amount of time spent on domestic work by women did not decline very markedly. The amount of time British women not in paid employment spend on housework has remained quite constant over the past half-century. Household appliances eliminated some of the heavier chores, but new tasks were created in their place. Time spent on child care, stocking up the home with purchases and meal preparation all increased.

The trend towards an increasing number of women entering the labour force has had a discernible impact on housework activities. Married women employed outside the home do less domestic work than others, although they almost always shoulder the main responsibility for care of the home (see table 12.1). The pattern of their activities is of course rather different. They do more housework in the early evenings and for longer hours at weekends than do those who are full-time housewives.

Unpaid domestic labour is of enormous significance to the economy. It has been estimated that housework accounts for between 25 and 40 per cent of the wealth created in the industrialized countries. Domestic work props up the rest of the economy by providing free services on which many of the population in paid work depend.

Housewives (occasionally today also househusbands) are without paid work. They don't, however, count in the statistics of being 'unemployed'. What does 'unemployment' in fact mean? This is one of the issues we turn to in the next section.

UNEMPLOYMENT

Rates of UNEMPLOYMENT have fluctuated considerably over the course of this century. In Western countries, unemployment reached a peak in the early 1930s, with some 20 per cent of the labour force being out of work in Britain. The ideas of the economist John Maynard Keynes strongly influenced public policy in Europe and the United States during the postwar period. Keynes believed that unemployment results from lack of sufficient purchasing power to buy goods; governments can intervene to increase the level of demand in an economy, leading to the creation of new jobs. State management of economic life, many came to believe, meant that high rates of unemployment belonged to the past. Commitment to *full employment* became part of government policy in virtually all Western societies. Until the 1970s, these policies seemed successful, and economic growth was more or less continuous.

Over the past fifteen years or so, however, unemployment rates have shot up in many countries, and Keynesianism has been largely abandoned as a means of trying to control economic activity. For some quarter of a century after World War Two, the British unemployment rate was less than 2 per cent. It rose to 12 per cent in the early 1980s, then fell, increasing again at the end of the decade. In 1995 it stood at 11 per cent.

Analysing unemployment

Interpreting official unemployment statistics, however, is not straightforward (see figure 12.2). Unemployment is not easy to define. It means 'being out of work'. But 'work' here means 'paid work', and 'work in a recognized occupation'. People who are properly registered as unemployed may engage in many forms of productive activity, like painting

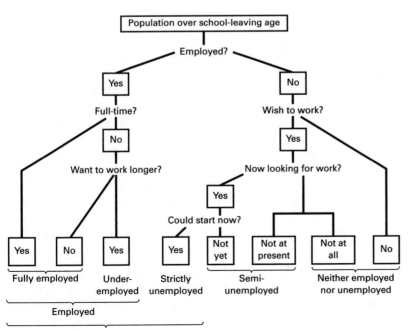

Fig. 12.2 A taxonomy of possible employment, unemployment and non-employment states

Source: Peter Sinclair, *Unemployment: Economic Theory and Evidence* (Blackwell Publishers 1987), p. 2.

the house or tending the garden. Many people are in part-time paid work, or only in paid jobs sporadically; the retired are not counted as 'unemployed'

Many economists think the standard unemployment rate should be supplemented by two other measures. 'Discouraged workers' are those who would like a job, but who despair of getting one and thus have given up looking. 'Involuntary part-time workers' are people who cannot find a full-time job even though they want one. Adding in these measures does provide a fuller demographic picture of unemployment (see figure 12.3). There were 4 million discouraged workers and 15 million involuntary part-time ones in the countries of the European Union in 1993, compared to 34 million officially unemployed (*The Economist*, 22 July 1995, p. 92). In Japan, if the extra two categories are included, total unemployment more than doubles.

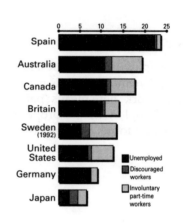

Fig. 12.3 Not working: unemployed workers, discouraged workers and involuntary part-time workers as a percentage of the labour force in various countries, 1993

Source: OECD. From *The Economist*, 22 July 1995, p. 92.

Variations in the distribution of government-defined unemployment within Britain are well documented. Unemployment is higher for men than for women, and for ethnic minorities than for whites. Ethnic minorities also have much higher rates of long-term unemployment than the rest of the population. The recent rise in unemployment has especially affected young people, again being more pronounced for ethnic minority groups than for whites. Unemployment rates for those aged between sixteen and nineteen stand at some 20 per cent. To some extent this is artificially high, because it includes numbers of students who work part-time or in casual employment. However, a substantial proportion of young people are among the long-term unemployed, especially the members of minority groups. More than half the male teenage unemployment involves those out of work for six months or more.

The experience of unemployment can be very disturbing to those accustomed to having secure jobs. Obviously the most immediate consequence is a loss of income. The effects of this vary between countries, because of contrasts in the level of unemployment benefits. In Britain, for instance, long-term welfare benefits are provided for the unemployed. Unemployment may produce acute financial difficulties, but does not affect access to health care and other welfare benefits, since these are provided by the state. In the United States, Spain and some other Western countries, on the other hand, unemployment benefits last a shorter time and the economic strain on those without work is correspondingly greater.

Why have rates of unemployment risen?

Rates of unemployment have fluctuated in Western countries in recent years, and substantial variations have existed between different societies. Outside the Western orbit, unemployment has been consistently less in Japan than elsewhere. A combination of factors probably explains the relatively high levels of unemployment found in many Western states over the past two decades or so.

- An important element is the rise of international competition in industries on which Western prosperity used to be founded. In 1947, 60 per cent of world steel production was carried out in the United States. Today the figure is only about 15 per cent, while steel production has risen threefold in Japan and the Third World countries (principally Singapore, Taiwan and Hong Kong – which are now undercutting Japanese prices).

- On several occasions, beginning with the 'oil crisis' of 1973 (the time when the main oil-producing countries got together and collectively agreed to raise the price of oil), the world economy has experienced either quite severe recession or a slowdown in production.

- The increasing use of microelectronics in industry has reduced the need for labour power.

- More women than ever before are seeking paid employment, with the result that more people are chasing the limited number of available jobs.

It is not clear whether the current high rates of unemployment will continue – or perhaps become even more pronounced – in the immediate future. Some countries seem to be better placed to combat large-scale unemployment than others. Rates of unemployment have been reduced more successfully in the United States than in Britain or some of the other major European nations. This is perhaps because the sheer economic strength of the country gives it more power in world markets than smaller, more fragile economies. Alternatively, it may be that the exceptionally large service sector in the US provides a greater source of new jobs than is available in countries where more of the population has traditionally been employed in manufacturing.

Unemployment in Europe and the US

During the 1980s and early 1990s the US economy created many more jobs than was true of the countries of Western Europe. Contrary to what many believe, these were not mainly so-called 'macjobs' –

low-paid jobs such as serving in hamburger stalls. Four out of five new jobs in the US were in managerial or professional occupations.

Why were fewer jobs created in the European countries? Some argue that the major factor was the high minimum wage which several of the leading European countries, such as France, have enshrined in their legislation. A more important reason might be the existence of barriers in product markets – markets for the sale of goods and services. For example, an average of 10 per cent of all jobs in the industrialized countries are in retailing. The retail sector has been a major source of job creation in America; in France, by contrast, employment in retailing has decreased. This is probably because of strict regulations about the zoning of shopping areas and limiting hours of opening – in the US some stores are open on a twenty-four-hour basis.

High levels of unemployment have led critics to speculate about the role of paid work in our lives in general. Perhaps many of us will experience a different relation to work from that which has dominated up to the present? In the conclusion of this chapter, we consider this problem.

THE FUTURE OF WORK

The portfolio worker

In the light of the impact of the global economy and the demand for a 'flexible' labour force, some sociologists and economists have argued that more and more people in the future will become 'portfolio workers'. They will have a 'skill portfolio' – a number of different job skills and credentials – which they will use to move between several jobs during the course of their working lives. Only a relatively small proportion of workers will have continuous 'careers' in the current sense.

Some see this move to the **portfolio worker** in a positive light: workers will not be stuck in the same job for years on end and will be able to plan their work lives in a creative way (Handy 1994). Others hold that 'flexibility' in practice means that organizations can hire and fire more or less at will, undermining any sense of security their workers might have. Employers will only have a short-term commitment to their workforces and will be able to minimize the paying of extra benefits or pension rights.

A recent study of Silicon Valley, California, claims that the economic success of the area is already founded on the portfolio skills of its workforce. The failure rate of firms in Silicon Valley is very high: about 300 new companies are established every year, but an equivalent number also go bust. The workforce, which has a very high proportion of professional and technical workers, has learned to adjust to this. The result, the authors say, is that talents and skills migrate rapidly from one firm to another, becoming more adaptable on the way. Technical specialists become consultants, consultants become managers, employees become venture capitalists – and back again (Bahrami and Evans 1995).

Such a situation is as yet very definitely the exception rather than the rule. According to the most recent employment statistics, full-time workers in Britain and the US – which have the most deregulated labour markets among industrial countries – spend as long in each job today as they did ten years ago (*The Economist*, 21 May 1995). The reasons seem to be that managers recognize that a high degree of turnover among workers is costly and bad for morale, and that they prefer to retrain their own employees rather than bring in new ones, even if this means paying above the market rate. In their book, *Built to Last* (1994) James Collins and Jerry Porras analysed eighteen American companies which have continuously outperformed the stock-market average since 1926. They found that these companies, far from hiring and firing at will, had followed highly protective policies towards their staff. Only two of these companies over the period studied brought in a chief executive from the outside, compared to thirteen of the less successful corporations included in the research.

These findings do not disprove the ideas of those who speak of the arrival of the portfolio worker. Organizational downsizing is a reality, throwing many thousands of workers who may have thought they had a lifetime job on to the labour market. To find work again, they may be forced to develop and diversify their skills. Many, particularly older people, might never be able to find jobs comparable to those they held before, or perhaps even paid work at all.

The declining importance of work?

'Everyone has the right to work' states the Universal Declaration of Human Rights, signed at the United Nations after World War Two. At the time, this meant the right to a paid job. If, however, the trend towards large-scale unemployment proves to be long term, the aim may prove to be unrealizable. Perhaps we should rethink the nature of paid work, and in particular the dominant position it often has in people's lives.

Unemployment tends to be seen by employers and workers alike as a negative phenomenon, but this outlook needs examining. After all, the identification of 'work' with 'paid employment' is peculiarly limiting. If someone expends enormous effort on a hobby, such as cultivating a beautiful garden, for interest rather than for any material reward, why should this not be regarded as work? The word 'unemployment' only came into the language in the late nineteenth century; perhaps it might disappear in the late twentieth, if not having a job ceases to be regarded as the same as being 'out of work'. Why not, some observers suggest, classify all the unemployed as self-employed, giving subsidies to those who need them to follow their chosen pursuits?

In all the industrialized countries the average length of the working week is gradually being reduced. Many workers still undertake long stretches of overtime, but some governments are introducing new limits on permissible working hours. In France, for example, overtime is restricted to a maximum of 130 hours a year. In most countries, the official retiring age is sixty-five, but there seems to be a move towards early retirement and shortening the average working career (Blyton

1985). More people would probably quit the labour force at sixty, or earlier, if they could afford to do so.

If the amount of time given to paid employment continues to shrink, and the need to have a job becomes less central, the nature of careers might be substantially reorganized. Job-sharing, or the working of flexible hours, for example, may become increasingly common. Some work analysts have suggested that sabbatical leave, such as exists in universities, should be extended to workers in other spheres, so that everyone would be entitled to take a year off to study or pursue some form of self-improvement. Perhaps more and more individuals will engage in *life planning*, by which they arrange to work in different ways (paid, unpaid, full-time or part-time, etc.) at different stages in their lives. Thus some people might choose to enter the labour force only after a period of formal education, followed by one devoted to pursuits like travel. Many people might opt to work part-time throughout their lives, rather than being forced to do so because of lack of full-time opportunities.

Some recent surveys of work indicate that, even under existing conditions, part-time workers register higher levels of job satisfaction than those in full-time employment. This may be because most part-time workers are women, who have lower expectations of their careers than men, or who are particularly relieved to escape from domestic monotony. Yet many individuals seem to find reward precisely in the fact that they are able to balance paid work with other activities and enjoy a more varied life. Some people might choose to 'peak' their lives, giving full commitment to paid work from their youth to their middle years, then perhaps changing to a second career which would open up new interests.

The French sociologist and social critic André Gorz has argued that in the future paid work will play a less and less important part in people's lives. Gorz bases his views on a critical assessment of Marx's writings. Marx believed that the working class – to which more and more people would supposedly belong – would lead a revolution that would bring about a more humane type of society, in which work would be central to the satisfactions life has to offer. Although writing as a leftist, Gorz rejects this view. Rather than the working class becoming the largest grouping in society (as Marx suggested) and leading a successful revolution, it is actually shrinking. Blue-collar workers have now become a minority – and a declining minority – of the labour force.

It no longer makes much sense, in Gorz's view, to suppose that workers can take over the enterprises of which they are a part, let alone seize state power. There is no real hope of transforming the nature of paid work, because it is organized according to technical considerations which are unavoidable if an economy is to be efficient. 'The point now', as Gorz puts it, 'is to free oneself *from* work . . .' (Gorz 1982, p. 67). This is particularly necessary where work is organized along Taylorist lines, or is otherwise oppressive or dull.

Rising unemployment, together with the spread of part-time work, Gorz argues, has already created what he calls a 'non-class of nonworkers', alongside those in stable employment. Most people, in fact, are in this 'non-class', because the proportion of the population in stable paid jobs at any one time is relatively small – if we exclude the young, the retired, the ill and housewives, together with people who are in part-time work or unemployed. The spread of microtechnology, Gorz believes, will further reduce the numbers of full-time jobs available. The result is likely to be a swing towards rejecting the 'productivist' outlook of Western society, with its emphasis on wealth, economic growth and material goods. A diversity of lifestyles, followed outside the sphere of permanent, paid work, will be pursued by the majority of the population in coming years.

According to Gorz, we are moving towards a 'dual society'. In one sector, production and political administration will be organized to maximize efficiency. The other sector will be a sphere in which individuals occupy themselves with a variety of non-work pursuits offering enjoyment or personal fulfilment.

How valid is this viewpoint? That there *are* major changes going on in the nature and organization of work in the industrialized countries is beyond dispute. It does seem possible that more and more people will become disenchanted with 'productivism' – the stress on constant economic growth and the accumulation of material possessions. It is surely valuable, as Gorz has suggested, to see unemployment not wholly in a negative light, but as offering opportunities for individuals to pursue their interests and develop their talents. Yet, thus far at least, progress in this direction has been slight; we seem to be far from the situation Gorz envisages. With women pressing for greater job opportunities, there has been a rise, not a fall, in the numbers of people actively interested in securing paid employment. Paid work remains for many the key basis of generating the material resources necessary to sustain a varied life.

SUMMARY

1 Work is the carrying out of tasks, involving the expenditure of mental and physical effort, which have as their objective the production of goods and services catering for human needs. Many important kinds of work – like housework or voluntary work – are unpaid. An occupation is work which is done in exchange for a regular wage. Work is in all cultures the basis of the economic system.

2 A distinctive characteristic of the economic system of modern societies is the development of a highly complex and diverse division of labour.

3 The division of labour means that work is divided into different occupations requiring specialization. One result is economic interdependence: we are all dependent on each other to maintain our livelihoods.

4 One manifestation of this is Taylorism, or scientific management. Taylorism divides work into simple tasks that can be timed and organized. Fordism extended the principles of scientific management to mass production tied to mass markets. Fordism and Taylorism can be seen as low-trust systems that maximize worker alienation. A high-trust system allows workers control over the pace and even content of their work.

5 Major changes have occurred in the occupational system during the course of the century. Particularly important has been the relative increase in non-manual occupations at the expense of manual ones. The interpretation of these changes, however, is disputed.

6 Union organizations, together with recognition of the right to strike, are characteristic features of economic life in all Western countries. Unions emerged as defensive organizations, concerned to provide a measure of control for workers over their conditions of labour. Today, union leaders quite often play an important role in formulating national economic policies – although this is less true of Britain at present than formerly.

7 The nature of women's work has been greatly affected by the separation of the workplace from the home. Many married women become 'housewives' and are regarded as 'not working' – even though the hours of labour they put into domestic tasks may be far more than the working hours of their husbands. Far more women are now in paid employment than was the case some decades ago; but women are disproportionately concentrated in low-paid jobs.

8 While women have been largely successful in overcoming gender typing, they also encounter the assumption that women put the concerns of their family before their career. At the same time, regardless of the percentage of women in the paid workforce, women still perform the bulk of housework, work concentrated on maintaining the home and raising children.

9 Unemployment has been a recurrent problem in the industrialized countries in the twentieth century. As work is a structuring element in a person's psychological make-up, the experience of unemployment is often disorienting. The impact of new technology seems likely further to increase unemployment rates.

10 Some speak of the arrival of the portfolio worker – the worker who has a 'portfolio' of different skills, and will be able to move readily from job to job. Such workers do exist, but for many people in the workforce 'flexibility' is more likely to be associated with poorly paid jobs with few career prospects.

11 Major changes are currently taking place in the nature and organization of work, which seem certain to become even more important in the future. None the less, paid work remains for many people the key way of generating the resources necessary to sustain a varied life.

FURTHER READING

Godfried Engbersen et al., *Cultures of Unemployment: A Comparative Look at Long-Term Unemployment and Urban Poverty* (Boulder, Colo.: Westview, 1993). A discussion of how far the long-term unemployed develop a 'culture of poverty'.

Keith Grint, *The Sociology of Work: An Introduction* (Cambridge: Polity Press, 1991). A very useful textbook dealing with most aspects of the study of work in modern societies.

Ray Pahl, *Divisions of Labour* (Oxford: Blackwell, 1984). An important discussion of work, the household and the family.

Andrew Sayer and **Richard Walker**, *The New Social Economy* (Oxford: Blackwell, 1992). A useful discussion of developments affecting the nature of industrial production today.

Neil J. Smelser and **Richard Swedberg** (eds), *The Handbook of Economic Sociology* (Princeton: Princeton University Press, 1994). A good general reader on the sociology of economic life.

IMPORTANT TERMS

- *the informal economy*
- *voluntary work*
- *occupation*
- *economic system*
- *technology*
- *economic interdependence*
- *Taylorism*
- *Fordism*
- *low-trust systems*
- *high-trust systems*
- *automation*
- *flexible production*
- *occupational system*
- *trade union*
- *strike*
- *housework (domestic labour)*
- *portfolio worker*

13

GOVERNMENT, POLITICAL POWER AND WAR

BASIC CONCEPTS

- *government* • *politics* • *power* • *authority*
- *the state* • *nation-state* • *democracy*
- *industrialization of war*

In 1989, a drama unfolded in Tiananmen Square in Beijing, the capital of China. Thousands of people gathered to demonstrate in favour of democracy. The communist government of China reacted ferociously. Red Army units attacked the demonstrators. Many were killed and hundreds of others were rounded up and imprisoned.

Democracy is still not a reality of China. Yet in many other parts of the world, pro-democracy movements have been successful in toppling authoritarian regimes. In the former Soviet Union and Eastern Europe, communism was overthrown by such movements. Democratic forms of government have also been established in recent years in much of Latin America, and some countries in Africa and Asia. Democratic governments have existed for much longer in Western Europe, North America, Australia and New Zealand.

Democratization is one of the major political forces in the world today – influencing, and influenced by, globalization. Like so many aspects of contemporary societies, the realm of government and politics is undergoing major changes. GOVERNMENT refers to the regular enactment of policies, decisions and matters of state on the part of the officials within a political apparatus. POLITICS concerns the means whereby power is used to affect the scope and content of governmental activities. The sphere of the *political* may range well beyond that of state institutions themselves.

In this chapter, we shall study the main factors affecting political life. We shall analyse the nature of democracy and consider the role of political parties. We will discuss some of the transformations in British politics in recent years, and from there move to look at politics in the international domain. Towards the end of the chapter we consider the consequences of the changes in Eastern Europe after 1989 and examine the impact of war on society.

First of all, however, let us consider some basic concepts necessary to study political life – *power, authority* and *the state*. All political life, in one sense or another, is about *power*: who holds it, how they achieve it and what they do with it.

POWER AND AUTHORITY

As mentioned in chapter 1, the study of power is of fundamental importance for sociology. POWER is the ability of individuals or groups to make their own interests or concerns count, even when others resist. It sometimes involves the direct use of force, such as when the Chinese authorities suppressed the democracy movement in Tiananmen Square. Power is an element in almost all social relationships, such as that between employer and employee. This chapter focuses on a narrower aspect of power, governmental power. In this form, it is almost always accompanied by ideologies, which are used to justify the actions of the powerful. For example, the Chinese government's use of force against the students demonstrating for democracy was a defence of the communist ideology as the ultimate form of government.

AUTHORITY is a government's legitimate use of power. **Legitimacy** means that those subject to a government's authority consent to it. Power is thus different from authority. When pro-democracy demonstrations in China broke out and the government responded by imprisoning and killing the demonstrators, it was an exercise of power but also an indication of the government's loss of authority. Contrary to what many believe, democracy is not the only type of government people consider legitimate. Dictatorships can have legitimacy as well. But as we shall see later, democracy is currently the most widespread form of government called legitimate.

THE CONCEPT OF THE STATE

A STATE exists where there is a political apparatus of government (institutions like a parliament or congress, plus civil service officials) ruling over a given territory, whose authority is backed by a legal system and by the capacity to use military force to implement its policies. All modern societies are NATION-STATES. That is, their system of government lays claim to specific territories, possesses formalized codes of law, and is backed by the control of military force. Nation-states have come into existence at various times in different parts of the world (for example, the United States in 1776 and the Czech Republic in 1993). Their main characteristics, however, contrast rather sharply with those of states in traditional civilizations, such as those described in chapter 1. They are:

- *Sovereignty* The territories ruled by traditional states were always poorly defined, the level of control wielded by the central government being quite weak. The notion of **sovereignty** – that a government possesses authority over an area with clear-cut borders, within which it is the supreme power – had little relevance. All nation-states, by contrast, are sovereign states.

- *Citizenship* In traditional states, most of the population ruled by the king or emperor showed little awareness of, or interest in, those who governed them. Neither did they have any political rights or influence. Normally only the dominant classes or more affluent groups felt a sense of belonging to an overall political community. In modern societies, by contrast, most people living within the borders of the political system are **citizens**, having common rights and duties and knowing themselves to be part of a nation. While there are some people who are political refugees or are 'stateless' almost everyone in the world today is a member of a definite national political order.

● *Nationalism* Nation-states are associated with the rise of **nationalism**, which can be defined as a set of symbols and beliefs providing the sense of being part of a single political community. Thus, individuals feel a sense of pride and belonging in being British, American, Canadian or Russian. Probably people have always felt some kind of identity with social groups of one form or another – their family, village or religious community. Nationalism, however, made its appearance only with the development of the modern state. It is the main expression of feelings of identity with a distinct sovereign community.

Nationalistic loyalties do not always fit the physical borders marking the territories of states in the world today. Virtually all nation-states were built from communities of diverse backgrounds. As a result, local nationalisms have frequently arisen in opposition to those fostered by the states. Thus, in Canada, for instance, nationalist feelings among the French-speaking population in Quebec present a challenge to the feeling of 'Canadianness'. Yet while the relation between the nation-state and nationalism is a complicated one, the two have come into being as part of the same process.

Having discussed some of the important characteristics of modern states, we now consider the nature of democracy.

DEMOCRACY

The word 'democracy' has its roots in the Greek term *demokratia*, the individual parts of which are *demos* ('people') and *kratos* ('rule'). DEMOCRACY in its basic meaning is therefore a political system in which the people, not monarchs (kings or queens) or aristocracies (people of noble birth like lords), rule. This sounds simple and straightforward, but it is not. What does it mean to be ruled by the people? As David Held has pointed out, questions can be raised about each part of that phrase (Held 1987). If we start with the 'people'.

● Who are the people?

● What kind of participation are they to be allowed?

● What conditions are assumed to be conducive to participation?

As regards 'rule':

● How broad or narrow should the scope of rule be? Should it be confined, for example, to the sphere of government, or can there be democracy in other spheres, such as industrial democracy?

● Can rule cover the day-to-day administrative decisions governments must make, or should it refer only to major policy decisions?

In the case of 'rule by':

● Must the rule of the people be obeyed? What is the place of obligation and dissent?

- Should some of the people act outside the law if they believe existing laws to be unjust?

- Under what circumstances, if any, should democratic governments use coercion against those who disagree with their policies?

Answers to these questions have taken contrasting forms at varying periods and in different societies. For example, 'the people' has been variously understood as owners of property, white men, educated men, men, and adult men and women. In some societies the officially accepted version of democracy is limited to the political sphere, whereas in others it is extended to other areas of social life.

Participatory democracy

In **participatory democracy** (or direct democracy), decisions are made communally by those affected by them. This was the original type of democracy practised in ancient Greece. Those who were citizens, a small minority of the society, regularly assembled to consider policies and make major decisions. Participatory democracy is of limited importance in modern societies, where the mass of the population have political rights, and it would be impossible for everyone actively to participate in the making of all the decisions that affect them.

Yet some aspects of participatory democracy do play a part in modern societies. The holding of referenda, for example, when the people express their views on a particular issue, is one form of participatory democracy. Direct consultation of large numbers of people is made possible by simplifying the issue down to one or two questions to be answered. Referenda are regularly used at the national level in some European countries.

Monarchies and liberal democracies

While some modern states (such as Britain and Belgium) still favour monarchs, these are few and far between. Where traditional rulers of this sort are still found, their real power is usually limited or non-existent. In a tiny number of countries, such as Saudi Arabia and Jordan, monarchs continue to hold some degree of control over government, but in most cases they are symbols of national identity rather than personages having any direct power in political life. The queen of the United Kingdom, the king of Sweden, and even the emperor of Japan are all **constitutional monarchs**: their real power is severely restricted by the constitution, which vests authority in the elected representatives of the people. The vast majority of modern states are republican – there is no king or queen; almost every one, including constitutional monarchies, professes adherence to democracy.

Countries in which voters can choose between two or more parties and in which the mass of the adult population has the right to vote are usually called **liberal democracies**. Britain and the other Western European countries, the US, Japan, Australia and New Zealand all fall into this category. Some Third World countries, such as India, also have liberal democratic systems.

The spread of liberal democracy

For a long while, the political systems of the world were divided between liberal democracy and communism, as found in the former Soviet Union (and which still exists in China and a few other countries). Communism was essentially a system of one-party rule. Voters were given a choice not between different parties but between different candidates of the same party – the Communist Party; there was often only one candidate running. There was thus no real choice at all. The Communist Party was easily the dominant power in Soviet-style societies: it controlled not just the political system but the economy as well.

Since 1989, when the hold of the Soviet Union over Eastern Europe was broken, processes of democratization have swept across the world in a sort of chain-reaction process. Countries such as Nicaragua in Central America and Zaire and South Africa in Africa have established liberal democratic governments. In China, which holds about a fifth of the world's population, the communist government is facing strong pressures towards democratization. Thousands of people remain in prison in China for the non-violent expression of their desire for democracy. But there are still groups, resisted by the communist government, working actively to secure a transition to a democratic system.

Why has democracy become so popular? The reasons have to do with the social and economic changes discussed throughout this book. First, democracy tends to be associated with competitive capitalism in the economic system, and capitalism has shown itself to be superior to communism as a wealth-generating system. Second, the more social activity becomes globalized and people find their daily lives becoming influenced by events happening far away, the more they start to push for more information about how they are ruled – and therefore for greater democracy.

Third is the influence of mass communications, particularly television. The chain reaction of the spread of democracy has probably been greatly affected by the visibility of events in the world today. With the coming of new television technologies, particularly satellite and cable, governments cannot maintain control over what their citizens see – as happened in the Tiananmen Square confrontation. As in China, the Communist Party in the Soviet Union and Eastern Europe used to maintain a strict control over television networks, which were all government-owned and government-run. But the spread of satellite transmission gave many people access to TV programmes from the West, and thus brought them into contact with different views of their conditions of life from those churned out by orthodox government propaganda.

Democracy in trouble?

As liberal democracy is becoming so widespread, we might expect it to be working in a highly successful way. Yet such is not the case. Democracy is in some difficulty almost everywhere. This is not only because it is proving difficult to set up a stable democratic order in

Russia and other erstwhile communist societies. Democracy is in trouble in its main countries of origin – in Britain, Europe and the US, surveys show that increasing proportions of people are dissatisfied with the political system, or indifferent towards it.

Why are many unhappy with the very political system that seems to be sweeping all before it across the world? The answers, curiously, are bound up with the factors that have helped spread democracy – the impact of capitalism and the globalizing of social life.

As the sociologist Daniel Bell has observed, national government is too small to respond to the big questions, such as the influence of global economic competition or the destruction of the world's environment; but it has become too big to deal with the small questions, issues that affect particular cities or regions. Governments have little power, for instance, over the activities of giant business corporations, the main actors within the global economy. A US corporation may decide to shut down its production plants in Britain and set up a new factory in Mexico instead, in order to lower costs and compete more effectively with other corporations. The result is that thousands of British workers lose their jobs. They are likely to want the government to do something, but national governments are unable to control processes bound up with the world economy. All the government can do is try to soften the blow, by providing unemployment benefits or job retraining. (See figure 13.1 for the way government spending is shared out in the UK.)

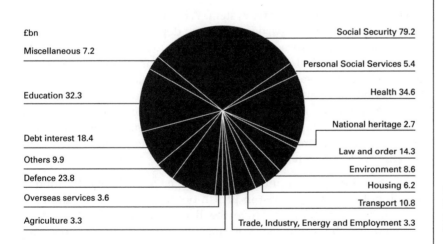

£bn
Miscellaneous 7.2
Education 32.3
Debt interest 18.4
Others 9.9
Defence 23.8
Overseas services 3.6
Agriculture 3.3

Social Security 79.2
Personal Social Services 5.4
Health 34.6
National heritage 2.7
Law and order 14.3
Environment 8.6
Housing 6.2
Transport 10.8
Trade, Industry, Energy and Employment 3.3

Fig. 13.1 UK government spending, 1992–3 (£ billions)

Source: HM Treasury. From Hutchinson Gallup, *Info 95* (Helicon 1994).

At the same time that governments have shrunk in relation to global issues, they have also become more remote from the lives of most citizens. Many resent the fact that decisions affecting their lives are made by distant 'power brokers' in London – party officials, interest groups, lobbyists and bureaucratic officials. They believe that the government is unable to deal with important local issues as well, such as crime and homelessness. The result is that faith in government has dropped substantially. This in turn affects people's willingness to participate in the political process.

We shall see how some of these influences make themselves felt in British politics a little later. Liberal democracy by definition involves the existence of several political parties. We look first of all at the different types of party system which can be grouped under the general label of liberal democracy.

POLITICAL PARTIES AND VOTING IN WESTERN COUNTRIES

A **political party** may be defined as an organization oriented towards achieving legitimate control of government through an electoral process. In some situations, there may be political organizations which seek to achieve power but are denied the opportunity to do so through orthodox means. Such organizations are best regarded as political sects or movements until they achieve recognition. In late nineteenth-century Germany, for example, the Social Democrats were outlawed by Bismarck. They were an organized political movement, operating outside orthodox channels, but later achieved recognition as a party, and have held power for several periods in this century.

Party systems

There are many types of party system. Whether a two-party system or a system involving more parties flourishes depends in large part on the nature of electoral procedures in a given country. Two parties tend to dominate the political system where elections are based on the principle of winner-takes-all. The candidate who gains the most votes wins the election, no matter what proportion of the overall vote he or she gains. Where elections are based on different principles, such as proportional representation (in which seats in a representative assembly are allocated in terms of proportions of the vote attained), two-party systems are less common.

In Western European countries various types of party organization are found, not all of which exist in British politics. Some parties are based on religious denomination (like the Belgian parties, the Parti Social Chrétien and the Katholieke Volkspartij); some are ethnic parties, representing specific nationalist or linguistic groups (such as the Scottish National Party in Britain or the Svenska Folkpartiet in Finland); others are rural parties, representing agrarian interests (for example, the Centerpartiet in Sweden or the Schweizerische Volkspartei in Switzerland); yet others are environmental parties, concerned with ecological objectives (such as the Greens in Germany).

Socialist or labour parties have formed governments at some point since World War Two in most West European societies. Until recently there were officially recognized communist parties in virtually all such countries, some of which were large (such as those in Italy, France and

Spain). Following the changes in Eastern Europe, many have now changed their titles. There are many conservative parties (like the Parti Républicain in France or the Conservative and Unionist Party in Britain) and 'centrist' parties which occupy the 'middle ground' between *left* and *right* (such as the Liberal Democrats in Britain). (The term 'left' is used to refer to radical or progressive political groups who lean towards socialism; 'right' refers to more conservative groups.)

In some countries, the leader of the majority party, or of one of the parties in a coalition, automatically becomes prime minister, the highest public official in the land. In other cases (like the United States) a president is elected separately from party elections to the main representative bodies. Hardly any of the electoral systems in Western countries are exactly the same as one another, and most are more complicated than that of the United Kingdom. Germany can serve as an example. In that country, members are elected to the Bundestag (parliament) by a system which combines winner-takes-all and proportional election rules. Half the members of the Bundestag are elected in constituencies in which the candidate getting the most votes wins. The other 50 per cent are elected according to the proportions of the vote they poll in particular regional areas. This is the system which has enabled the Green Party to win parliamentary seats. A 5 per cent limit has been set to prevent undue proliferation of small parties – at least this proportion of the vote must be achieved before a party obtains parliamentary representation. A similar system is also used in local elections.

Systems with two dominating parties, like that of Britain, tend to lead to a concentration on the 'middle ground', where most votes are to be found, and exclude more radical views. The parties in these countries usually cultivate a moderate image, and sometimes come to resemble one another so closely that the choice they offer is slight. A plurality of interests may supposedly be represented by each party, but they quite often become blended into a bland programme with few distinctive policies. Multiparty systems allow divergent interests and points of view to be expressed more directly, and provide scope for the representation of radical alternatives; on the other hand, no one party is likely to achieve an overall majority. This leads to coalitions which can suffer from an inability to make decisions because of major conflicts, or to a rapid succession of elections and new governments, none able to stay in power for long and thus very limited in their effects.

Parties and voting in Britain

In Britain until the nineteenth century parties were regarded only as temporary devices, needed to mobilize support in relation to specific events or crises. As parties developed into more stable organizations, they became associated with the idea that support for their leadership could bring specific rewards. Party membership and loyalty came to be linked to various forms of patronage, in which the faithful would be rewarded by receiving specific positions in a new administration. For most of the twentieth century, two major parties (Labour and Conservative) have dominated the national political scene, and *adversarial politics* has developed through the raising of support for two alternative governmental teams, each consisting of members of a single party.

British electoral politics has changed significantly over the past twenty years or so. One factor is structural: the proportion of the economically active population involved in traditional blue-collar occupations – in manufacture especially – has dropped considerably. There is little doubt that this has eroded some traditional sources of Labour support. A second factor is the split that occurred in the Labour Party at the beginning of the 1980s, which led to the founding of the Social Democratic Party (SDP). Although the SDP no longer exists, the more recently formed Liberal Democrats have sustained significant support. A third influence has been that of the Conservative prime minister from 1979 to 1990, Mrs Thatcher. The vigorous programme of change initiated by Mrs Thatcher and her cabinets expressed a significant move from earlier Tory philosophy. **Thatcherism** gave prime emphasis to restricting the role of the state in economic life, and made faith in market forces the basis of both individual liberties and economic growth.

Before 1970, the two major parties enjoyed stable voting support (Heath et al. 1986), and most of the electorate had strong Tory or Labour loyalties (see below). This was recognized in party campaigns, which concentrated more on rallying the faithful than on trying to convert those holding alternative views. The two elections held in 1974 showed that these traditional loyalties had become markedly weaker. The proportion of voters saying that they made up their minds during the final campaign increased markedly. It seems likely, therefore, that the campaigns have become more important to the election results than they used to be. Television has probably been a significant influence here, as a means of 'selling' the images of parties and politicians.

Voting behaviour – partisan dealignment

The pattern of **voting behaviour** found in the UK before the 1970s – committed loyalty to one or other of the two main parties – came to be known as *partisan alignment*. The idea of partisan alignment presumed that social class was the most important influence on voting behaviour and that the voters 'identified' with one party or the other. In other words, they thought of themselves as either 'Conservative' or 'Labour'. A study carried out by David Butler and Donald Stokes in the 1960s indicated that over 90 per cent of the population identified with one or other party in this way. Most said they identified 'fairly strongly' or 'very strongly' with their chosen party (Butler and Stokes 1974).

The correlation between class and voting has become distinctly more fuzzy today. In addition, a much higher proportion of voters now claim to be influenced in their voting behaviour by the policies and outlook of the parties, rather than giving one or other their unswerving loyalty. This is a process, therefore, of *partisan dealignment* – a move away from consistent party identification.

What accounts for increasing partisan dealignment? Ivor Crewe (1983) has mentioned two types of influence. One concerns the growing importance of aspects of people's lives not directly dependent on class differences – for example, whether or not people rent or own their own housing or are members of unions. Thus union members consistently vote in much higher numbers for Labour than for the Conservatives, and this applies whether they are members of blue-collar unions or white-collar unions.

The second factor is that voters have become to a decreasing degree captives of pre-existing political attitudes which determine their party preferences. They now tend to vote for whatever party they see as best supporting their **interests**. Thus in the late 1970s and the 1980s, Crewe suggests, the Labour Party offered to the electorate policies that many of its supporters disliked – hence the long period of Tory government.

The election of 1992

In the 1992 election there was a swing to Labour of just over 2 per cent; the Conservatives retained an overall majority in parliament, although the size of that majority was much reduced. The proportion of the population voting Tory remained markedly stable from 1979 (when it was 44.9 per cent) to 1992 (42.8 per cent). The Labour share of the vote was larger than its lowest ever point (under 30 per cent in the 1983 election). In 1992 Labour received 35.2 per cent of the vote. However, that proportion was still less than the party had achieved in 1979. The third party, the Liberal Democrats, took 18.3 per cent of the vote, a decline from the two previous elections.

In spite of the continuity of support for all three parties, studies carried out during the election confirmed the presence of a substantial floating vote. A study of a representative group of some 1,500 voters showed that 21 per cent decided on how they would vote only in the last week of the campaign.

The results of the election in general supported the thesis of partisan dealignment, but suggested that such dealignment had progressed further among non-Conservative than among Conservative voters. That made the problem for the Labour Party considerable; the 1992 election was the fourth in a row won by the Tories.

Thatcherism and after

As was mentioned earlier, one of the most distinctive features of British politics in the late 1970s and 1980s was the influence of the political ideas associated with Mrs Thatcher. What were the sources of Thatcherism? What was its appeal to such an apparently wide section of the British electorate? It is easy to suppose that the policies associated with Mrs Thatcher's governments were more unified and consistent than was in fact the case. Thatcherism had certain guiding threads, but was in most respects a fairly loose collection of programmes and initiatives. Some were adopted for pragmatic reasons, while others evolved, or were largely abandoned, with the progress of time (Riddell 1985; Kavanagh 1987).

During her first term of office Mrs Thatcher's policies mostly concentrated on 'monetarism'. Controlling the money supply was believed to be the key to reducing inflation and promoting the sound management of the economy. The targets set for monetary control, however, proved impossible to achieve, and monetarism was in effect largely abandoned subsequently. Following the 1983 election, the momentum of Thatcherism in economic matters was maintained by the privatizing of public companies. The sale of shares in British Telecom, British Gas, British Steel, British Airways and British Petroleum drew a wide response.

The advantages of the privatization are claimed to be several. It is held to reintroduce healthy economic competition in place of unwieldy and ineffective public bureaucracies, reduce public expenditure and end political interference in managerial decisions.

The privatization policies begun by Mrs Thatcher have had an enduring impact. At first they were hotly contested by the Labour Party. Later, however, Labour abandoned its hostile stance and came to accept that much of such privatization was irreversible.

'The lady's not for turning!' Mrs Thatcher declared in one of her more celebrated public pronouncements. Perhaps the strongest element of continuity in Thatcherism was the personality and moral style of Mrs Thatcher herself. Her crusading outlook did not win the affection of many of the electorate, but it brought respect for her qualities as a national leader. Mrs Thatcher's refusal to back down in the face of the Argentinian occupation of the Falkland Islands seemed to many to give concrete expression to these qualities, and her dominant role within the government was also reinforced by her characteristic dismissals of cabinet members who were out of sympathy with her views.

However, having won a crushing victory in the election of 1987, Mrs Thatcher's popularity among the electorate began to decline sharply. Key factors were the unpopularity of the Poll Tax (a tax not based on income or property but 'per head'), her controversial views about Britain's role in the European Community, and the movement of the economy into recession. The level of dissatisfaction with her leadership within the Conservative Party reached such a pitch that, when Michael Heseltine challenged her in November 1990, he was able to force a second ballot by denying her the 15 per cent lead needed for outright victory. At that point senior colleagues persuaded her to retire from the contest, from which John Major emerged as the new Conservative leader and the country's prime minister (Kingdom 1991).

'New Labour'

Under John Major, the Conservatives continued to privatize state enterprises, even where such plans were less than popular with the electorate. British Rail was divided and sold off to private tender, for example, although surveys showed that the majority of the population did not support such a programme. The Labour Party opposed these proposals and committed itself to putting the railways back into public ownership if it was successful in the next national election.

Partly in response to the impact of Thatcherism, and partly in reaction to wider global events, including the intensifying of global economic competition, the Labour Party has been shifting its ideological outlook.

'Excuse me, do the Thatchers live round here?'

This process was begun under Neil Kinnock, who resigned from the Labour leadership after the party lost the election of 1992. It was continued under the new leader, John Smith, whose period of leadership of the Labour Party was cut short by his premature death. Tony Blair became leader of the party in 1994 and immediately embarked on further far-reaching internal reforms. Christening his reformed party **'New Labour'**, Blair led a successful campaign within the party to abolish the notorious Clause 4 – a clause in the party's constitution which committed it to widespread public ownership of industry.

Labour has thus given formal recognition to the central importance of the market economy, which Mrs Thatcher was so determined to expand. In so doing, the party is making changes similar to those which have happened in most other socialist parties in Western Europe. A decisive influence here has been the dissolution of communism in the Soviet Union and Eastern Europe, which we shall discuss shortly in this chapter.

The outlook of the Labour Party has always been quite different from that of communism – the level of state ownership of industrial enterprise in the communist societies was much greater than anything the Labour Party ever envisaged. Yet most people accept that the disintegration of communism also signals that less extreme ideas of socialism need to be radically overhauled. The idea that a modern economy can be 'managed' through being placed under state control – an idea central both to communism and Labour-style socialism – now appears obsolete.

THE POLITICAL PARTICIPATION OF WOMEN

Voting patterns and political attitudes

Voting has a special meaning for women against the background of their struggle to obtain universal suffrage, which took a long time virtually everywhere. The members of the early women's movements saw the vote both as the symbol of political freedom and the means of achieving greater economic and social equality. In Britain and the United States, where the attempts of women to win voting rights were more active and provoked more violence than elsewhere, women's leaders underwent considerable hardship to reach this end. Even today women do not have the same voting rights as men in all countries, although Saudi Arabia is the only state where women cannot vote at the national level. Has the hard-fought struggle to acquire voting rights produced the results that were hoped for?

The short answer is 'no'. In most Western countries, when they first achieved voting rights, women voted in far smaller numbers than men. In the first national election for which all women were eligible in Britain, in 1929, only about one-third voted, as compared to two-thirds of men. The proportions were roughly the same in the US, and a similar pattern is found in other states in the early period after the instituting of universal voting rights. Women still do not vote in the same proportions as men in many nations, although in some cases the discrepancy has disappeared. Voter turnout of women in the last three US presidential elections has been only between 3 and 6 per cent less than that of men. In Britain, in parliamentary elections since 1970 (including the election of that year), the differential has not been more than 4 per cent. Gender differences in voting have completely disappeared in Sweden, West Germany and Canada, while in Italy, Finland and Japan women vote at slightly higher rates than men.

These figures indicate that the real obstacle to equality between the sexes was not denial of the vote, but the more deeply buried social divisions between men and women, which restricted women to the household and domestic tasks. Changes in these social divisions have brought about alterations in the political participation of women, rather than the other way around. As the differences in power and status between men and women begin to narrow, women's level of voting climbs.

How far do the political attitudes of women differ from those of men? Many suffragists, early supporters of women's right to vote, believed that the entry of women into politics would radically transform political activity, bringing a new sense of altruism and morality. Those who were against the extending of the vote to women similarly argued that the political participation of women would have momentous consequences – but of a disastrous kind. A prominent male opponent of

The Achievement of Women's Right to Vote on an Equal Basis with Men

1893	New Zealand	1945	France, Hungary, Italy, Japan,
1902	Australia		Vietnam, Yugoslavia, Bolivia
1906	Finland	1946	Albania, Romania, Panama
1913	Norway	1947	Argentina, Venezuela
1915	Denmark, Iceland	1948	Israel, Korea
1917	USSR	1949	China, Chile
1918	Canada	1950	El Salvador, Ghana, India
1919	Austria, Germany, The	1951	Nepal
	Netherlands, Poland, Sweden,	1952	Greece
	Luxembourg, Czechoslovakia	1953	Mexico
1920	USA	1954	Colombia
1922	Ireland	1955	Nicaragua
1928	Great Britain	1956	Egypt, Pakistan, Senegal
1929	Ecuador	1957	Lebanon
1930	South Africa	1959	Morocco
1931	Spain, Sri Lanka, Portugal	1962	Algeria
1932	Thailand	1963	Iran, Kenya, Libya
1934	Brazil, Cuba	1964	Sudan, Zambia
1936	Costa Rica	1965	Afghanistan, Guatemala
1937	Philippines	1977	Nigeria
1941	Indonesia	1979	Peru, Zimbabwe
1942	Dominican Republic, Uruguay		

Source: Lisa Tuttle, *Encyclopedia of Feminism*, 1986, pp. 370–1.

female franchise in Britain warned that 'a revolution of such boundless significance cannot be attempted without the greatest peril to England' (quoted in Currell 1974, p. 2). Women's involvement in politics, it was widely held, would trivialize political life, and at the same time undermine the stability of the family.

Neither of these extreme consequences has come to pass. The obtaining of the vote by women has not greatly altered the nature of politics. Women's voting patterns, like those of men, are shaped by party preferences, policy options and the choice of available candidates, though some differences between female and male voting are fairly consistently found. Women voters on the whole tend to be more conservative than men, as judged by level of voting for rightist parties. This is true, for example, in France, Germany and Italy. The relationship is more ambiguous in Britain and the United States. In Britain young women vote in higher numbers for the Labour Party than young men, but older women disproportionately vote Conservative. The two tendencies more or less balance one another. In the United States a conservative orientation cannot be easily associated with either of the two main parties, since the contrast between the Republicans and Democrats is not a straightforward opposition between political right and left.

A gender gap, however, has opened up in the US in voting patterns. White men support the Republicans over the Democrats by a margin of 51 per cent to 23 per cent, while white women are evenly split between the parties; at the same time, black and Hispanic voters of both sexes are strongly Democratic. Married white men in middle age have become a key source of support for the Republicans, while single women, white and black, have become a key Democratic constituency.

The influence of women on politics cannot be assessed solely in terms of voting. Feminist groups have made an impact on political life independently of the franchise, particularly in recent decades. Since the early 1960s, the National Organization of Women (NOW) and other women's groups in the US have pressed for a range of issues directly affecting women to be placed on the political agenda. Such issues include equal rights at work, the availability of abortion, changes in family and divorce law, and lesbian rights. In most European countries, comparable national women's organizations have often been lacking, but changes affecting the position of women in the wider society have brought the same issues to the centre of the political stage. Many of these matters – like the question of how far abortion should be freely available – have proved highly controversial among women as well as men.

Women's groups played a significant role in Britain in the passing of the 1967 Abortion Act and legislation against sex discrimination at work, and women's organizations have pressed for other changes which have been recognized in law, such as protection for the victims of domestic violence secured under the Domestic Violence and Matrimonial Procedures Act of 1976. A national survey carried out in 1992 highlighted further issues which count as high priority for women, but which men as a whole rank as much less important. These include, for example, the development of policies to provide nursery facilities for pre-school children and policies to do with child benefits (Kellner 1992). Whatever happens in the future, it seems clear that many problems and concerns that particularly affect women, and which have previously been neglected or regarded as being 'outside politics', are now central to political debates.

GLOBAL FORCES

In the remaining sections of the chapter, we move on from Britain to consider political forces and influences in the wider international arena. Democracy, as we have seen, has become a global force. Globalization is altering many other aspects of national politics and nation-state power too. The European Union (EU) is one response to globalization – an attempt to compensate for the declining power of the nation-state by building a supranational association of European states.

When people nowadays ask, 'Are you for or against Europe?', 'Europe' means the EU. 'Europe', of course, extends beyond the countries which are members of the EU; countries such as Norway or Switzerland, which are certainly in Europe, are not in the EU. Moreover, Europe also includes the ex-communist countries of Eastern Europe, which are also not members of the EU – although some want to be.

For centuries, Europe was a continent riven by wars. World War One and World War Two both had their origins in Europe. One of the motives of the statesmen who initiated the policies which eventually produced the EU was to prevent the further recurrence of war in Europe. Countries which are economically integrated and politically interwoven, they reasoned, wouldn't go to war with one another.

Warfare is our topic in the concluding sections of the chapter. Before this, we look at the development of the EU and the changes produced by the disintegration of communism in the Soviet Union and Eastern Europe.

The European Union and the changed map of Europe

The development of the Union

In a speech given in Zurich in 1946, Winston Churchill declared, 'We must build a kind of United States of Europe.' It was not the British who took a lead in this endeavour, however, but other European countries, most notably France and what was then West Germany. The Treaty of Paris established the European Coal and Steel Community in 1951. This was followed by the European Atomic Energy Community, and later the European Economic Community (EEC). The EEC, set up by the Treaty of Rome in 1958, established a common market for the trading of goods between the member countries. Britain, however, stood aside, immersed more fully in its links with the other Commonwealth countries and with the United States. The country did not become a member of the EEC until early in 1973.

As the EEC moved towards greater political unity, the word 'Economic' was dropped from its title and it became generally known as the European Community (EC). With further integration, it has become the **European Union**. The EU today is made up of a complicated set of representative and bureaucratic organizations. At the top is the *European Council*, made up of the heads of state or government of the member countries, who meet some three times a year. The *Council of Ministers* consists of the foreign ministers of the member states and other working groups of officials. It forms the chief policy-making body of the Union and takes legislative decisions. Such decisions used to require a unanimous vote, but most are now made on a majority basis – an important step, because it means that legislation can go through against a country's wishes.

The *European Commission* proposes policy for the Council of Ministers to adopt or amend, and is responsible for putting the Council's decisions into effect. It is headed by Commissioners nominated by the member states. The *European Parliament* has 518 elected members, who provide opinions about proposals put to the Council and provide a forum for discussion. The European Parliament lacks legislative power, a matter of concern to many who believe that the EU as it stands is essentially undemocratic. Finally, the *European Court of Justice* interprets and enforces EU law. It has no police force to back up its judgments, but its decisions are binding on the courts of the member countries.

The early Community moved from an initial membership of six to nine when Denmark and Ireland joined alongside Britain in 1973.

Subsequently this became further enlarged to twelve and, as of 1996, fifteen. Major clashes, over agricultural policy in particular, have marked its development, as well as hindering the formation of coherent agreements. In 1987 a Single Europe Act was passed which set in motion a series of innovations designed to lead to greater unity, including the abolition of all remaining trade barriers

The future development of the EU has become problematic as a result of the extraordinary changes which swept across Eastern Europe, and then the Soviet Union, from 1989 onwards. 'Europe' used to have a clear boundary when it was understood as the liberal democracies of Western Europe, set off from the communist societies of the East. The dissolution of the Soviet Union has changed all this. Now it is no longer obvious where 'Europe' ends, and many of the newly formed eastern liberal democracies propose to apply for EU membership.

What kind of entity, though, is the EU? Is it likely to become simply a sort of super nation-state, or is it something different from pre-existing political systems? Philippe Schmitter (1991) points out that there are numerous ways in which the EU differs from a nation-state at the moment. As explained above, it lacks a single form of supreme authority: the Court of Justice can override specific laws of its member states, but there is no overall means of enforcing decisions. Yet it has some of the trappings of sovereignty. For instance, it is recognized as an entity by some 130 states across the world which have entered into diplomatic relations with it.

Nation-states are firmly territorial, but the sense in which the EU has its 'own' territory is more ambiguous. The EU does not directly 'rule' over its territory, and its boundaries are not definitely fixed, for an indefinite number of further states are likely to become members in the near future. The EU has a diffuse presence; a number of 'external' states have agreements of association with it. Unlike a nation-state, the EU has no clear hierarchy of administrative offices. The various component parts outlined previously overlap in the various areas of power and competence. The Commission has a central role in decision-making processes, but it exercises its role with great respect for the views of its member states and the views of other EU bodies.

The EU, Schmitter argues, is a very specific form of political order, and may be pioneering developments which offer a model for other areas of the world to follow. It is neither nation nor state, but rather an alternative political system to both. The EU is federal in a certain sense, but not in the manner of a federal state, since it does not just consist of regions organized in a collective way, but of a whole diversity of different units and subunits. It is a unitary political actor for certain purposes, but for others is an aggregate, and depends on continual 'rolling agreements'.

> The eventual European Community will be a unique form of political domination. It may resemble some existing polities: the United States, the Federal Republic of Germany, Switzerland, Canada, Spain, etc., and it may be described in terms that could sound familiar: federal, confederal, technocratic, democratic, pluralist, and so forth, but it will be different. (Schmitter 1991, p. 29)

According to an agreement signed at Maastricht, near the end of the century Europe will become more integrated politically than at present, and will have a single currency. As of 1996, it is not clear whether the single currency will come into being by the end of the century or not. Only some nations look likely to meet the complex economic criteria needed for it to go ahead. The name for the new currency, however, has been chosen: the 'euro'.

Changes in Eastern Europe

The year 1989 was the two-hundredth anniversary of the French revolution. It was also a new 'year of revolutions' in Europe, perhaps as far-reaching in its implications as 1789 was. In 1989, one after the other, communist regimes in Eastern Europe relinquished their grip on power (for further discussion of these events, see chapter 18, 'Revolutions and social movements'). What had seemed like a solidly and pervasively established system of rule throughout Eastern Europe was thrown off almost overnight. The communists lost power in an accelerating sequence in the countries they had dominated for half a century: Hungary (February), Poland (June), Bulgaria, East Germany and Czechoslovakia (November), Romania (December). Every East European country, including the most retarded, Albania, had freely elected governments by January 1992. Even more remarkably, by this date the Communist Party had been ousted in the Soviet Union itself, and that country had broken up into myriad independent states.

With some exceptions, Eastern Europe is well advanced in the process of writing new constitutions and setting up multiparty parliamentary systems. For the most part, the spectrum of parties resembles that found in West European countries. Some ex-communist parties continue to exist, although quite often they have dropped the name 'communist' and can no longer behave as they did in single-party systems. In the mid-nineties they have in fact done surprisingly well in elections. In the 1995 elections to the Russian Duma (parliament), for example, the re-emergent Russian Communist Party secured 22 per cent of the vote, making it the largest party in the parliament.

All the East European countries face major economic as well as political difficulties in the transitions they are attempting to make. Most of the population in these societies express dissatisfaction with the development of democracy in their countries, and many express disquiet about rises in crime and violence. According to the European Bank for Reconstruction and Development (EBRD) most of the East European economies have made great advances over the past several years. Yet the promises of democratic capitalism have turned out to be empty for many in Eastern Europe. Seventy-five million 'newly poor' have been created as a result of unemployment and the erosion of the buying power of people on fixed incomes – and this figure excludes the countries of the former Soviet Union. Aid to Eastern Europe from the West has been on quite a modest scale.

The changes that have occurred seem in most countries to have affected women in a particularly adverse way (Watson 1992). The proportion of women in parliaments and other leading political bodies has in some countries fallen sharply. For instance, in the initial stages of change, in what was Czechoslovakia the percentage of female members of parliament fell from 34 per cent to 4 per cent; in Poland from 20 per cent to 8 per cent; and in Bulgaria from 21 per cent to 8 per cent. Women are heavily over-represented among the growing numbers of unemployed produced by the transition to market economies in the East.

How successful will the East European societies be in instituting stable liberal democratic systems of government? Samuel Huntington (1990) has identified six influences likely to be decisive:

1 How far a country has experienced liberal democratic government at earlier periods in its history. The former Czechoslovakia has the most favourable history judged in this way, with Albania at the other extreme. In Czechoslovakia, however, there were deep tensions between the Czechs and Slovaks, and the country has now become divided into two separate states.

2 The level of economic development attained by the country – in this respect the Czech Republic and Hungary are in the lead.

3 How effectively the country was ruled under its previous communist regime. The supposition here is that a state which governed effectively under an authoritarian system would be more likely also to do so in a democratic one.

4 The strength and variety of social and political organizations that were able to stay independent of the communist rulers.

5 How capable the new governments prove to be in constructing and putting into practice radical policies of economic reform.

6 The degree of separation and hostility between subnational or ethnic groups, regions or classes. Yugoslavia has already succumbed to disintegration as a result of such divisions, and Czechoslovakia has become divided, but how far others might follow is as yet not clear.

Much the same considerations apply to the new states formed following the break-up of the Soviet Union, including Russia itself. Most start from much further back than the East European countries. The majority have no independent history of liberal democracy whatsoever, and some have not even previously existed as separate states at all. Whatever happens in the next few years, the map of Europe has changed for good and with it the global political order – since the former Soviet Union stretched right across to the far side of Asia.

Whether liberal democracy becomes firmly established is likely to depend on how far a market economy is set up. A report from the EBRD published in late 1994 looked at economic indicators relevant to progress towards a market economy in ex-communist countries. The main indicators of change were how far the privatizing of industry had proceeded; the degree of restructuring of businesses, to escape from previous styles of management; openness to competition and foreign trade; and reform of the banking system. As measured in these terms, the level of change is greatest in the Czech Republic, Hungary and Poland; it is lowest in Azerbaijan, Georgia, Turkmenistan and the Ukraine.

Among ex-communist countries, a federal state that before 1989 seemed among the most advanced, Yugoslavia, collapsed into bloody war. The conflict in Bosnia-Herzegovina, one of the component parts of ex-Yugoslavia which claimed independence, claimed 500,000 lives. Appalling though that figure is, the Bosnian conflict remained relatively local and confined. The new relationship between East and West prevented any escalation on the scale of some of the other major wars that have occurred this century. We now turn to problems raised by the continuing importance of military power and war in human social affairs.

WAR AND THE MILITARY

The events of 1989 and after show clearly the importance of the use of military power at important social or political transitions. The sociology of **military power** is an important part of political sociology, and it is this we shall discuss in the concluding part of the chapter. We will look first at the history of warfare and then at the Cold War and its aftermath.

From limited to total war

Prior to the twentieth century, even when large battles were fought, they were limited to only small segments of the population – soldiers who did the fighting (normally a small percentage of the adult males of a society) and civilians living in the immediate regions where the wars were fought. These can be characterized as **limited wars**. But World War One (1914–18), in which enormous bodies of soldiery took part, was clearly not limited. **Total war** involves several antagonistic nations, high proportions of their male populations, the mobilization of their overall economies, and fighting throughout the world. World War One, or the 'Great War', was in many ways a watershed in military development in the twentieth century. It fully justified its name; in terms of the number of countries involved – most of the European nations, together with Russia, Japan and the United States – there were no historical parallels. The numbers of combatants and civilians killed were much higher than in any previous armed conflict.

At least two major developments promoted this transition from limited to total war: the industrialization of war and the rise of the mass military organization. The INDUSTRIALIZATION OF WAR refers to the application of modern industrial methods to the production and development of weaponry. Modern mass military systems developed into bureaucratic organizations and significantly changed the nature of organizing and fighting wars. In addition, governments introduced **universal conscription** – the drafting of all able-bodied men within a certain age range – as the scale of war increased.

Military expenditure and the Cold War

The twentieth century has been unquestionably the most war-ridden and destructive in human history. Thus far, more than 100 million human beings have been killed in war, an average of 3,500 a day. Most were killed in the two world wars. Military budgets grew progressively up to 1989; military weaponry has become increasingly sophisticated and more destructive. Large-scale nuclear weapons are capable of killing millions of people.

Until the late 1980s, global military expenditure was dominated by the **Cold War** – the antagonistic rivalry between the United States and the former Soviet Union that lasted from the late 1940s until about 1990. Each side not only spent massive sums every year on the development of armaments and on maintaining large numbers of military personnel, but constructed extensive systems of alliances with other countries, often training the armed forces of allied states. The Soviets concentrated attention on Eastern Europe but also provided weaponry and training for states in the Middle East, Asia and Africa. The United States built a system of alliances, including the North Atlantic Treaty Organization (NATO), stretching across much of the world.

The arms trade

The bulk of the world trade in armaments – the **arms trade** – is weaponry sold by the industrialized nations to Third World countries. The United States and the USSR were the world's leading arms exporters. In the years before the Gulf War of 1991, the USSR and some of the Western nations provided or sold weapons and other military-related goods to Iraq, which was in danger of losing its war with Iran. Certain of these weapons, particularly those furnished by the Soviet Union, proved to be old-fashioned or inadequate faced with the very latest Western arms technology, as the outcome of the Gulf War – in which Iraq was heavily defeated by a United Nations force, sponsored mainly by the US – showed. However, advanced technology is on offer to whoever wishes and can afford to buy.

World military expenditures followed an upward trend from the 1950s until the end of the 1980s. In 1977 world expenditure on weapons exceeded 1 billion US dollars a day, representing a rate of spending of 50 million dollars each hour. By the latter part of the 1980s, this rate had almost doubled, as measured in real terms (taking out the factor of inflation). Global military expenditure in 1993 was estimated at some 5 per cent of total world income. It is greater than the economic production of the whole African continent; it is more than that of all Asia, if Japan is left out.

In the light of the ending of the Cold War, one could hopefully anticipate a reduction in the developed world's military spending. Arms-related expenditure has dropped sharply in Russia and the other states that used to form the Soviet Union. The United States, Britain and other Western countries are also scaling back defence spending over the next few years. This will, however, increase the pressure to export arms to make up for lost domestic markets. It is not certain that the ending of the Cold War will reduce what Third World countries see as security requirements, internal as well as external. As we shall see in the next sections, to what degree we can count on a global peace dividend remains far from clear.

War and global security

Is the world becoming a safer place as a result of the recent political developments? Certainly the prospect of an all-out nuclear holocaust is much diminished. But the possibility of nuclear war has not disappeared. In 1992 there were at least 50,000 nuclear weapons still in existence (Barnaby 1992), and in 1994 nearly 20,000 were still deployed (see figure 13.2). Most of the weapons belong to the United States, Russia and other states of the former USSR. Britain, France and China possess significant stockpiles; Israel has been a nuclear weapon state for some time; India and Pakistan may also now have the capability; and others have the means to follow suit.

A major problem is how to contain **nuclear proliferation** – the spread of nuclear weapons to states that do not currently possess them (Levanthal and Tanzer 1991). It is hard to argue that global security would be enhanced if thirty, forty or more states possessed nuclear weapons. Yet the Western powers, who justify their nuclear arsenals on the grounds that they deter aggression, can hardly be surprised if other countries seek to obtain them for the same reason. And if one state acquires the capability, its rival will seek to do likewise. The likelihood of proliferation thus increases.

The immediate danger resulting from the break-up of the Soviet Union seems to have been avoided. The nuclear weapons deployed throughout what are now twelve independent republics will be concentrated on Russian territory, where adequate security and control can be provided more readily. Yet because of the expense of maintaining weapons and materials in good condition, there are doubts about their continuing safety. Moreover, former Soviet scientists may be recruited by other countries for their expertise.

At the heart of the proliferation problem is the place that the two materials required for nuclear weapons, highly enriched uranium and plutonium, occupy in the peaceful production of nuclear power. Given the technological expertise, possession of either of these materials makes possible the building of a nuclear weapon. Japan and Germany in particular possess plutonium stocks as extensive as those in the nuclear arsenals of the United States, and could construct nuclear armaments rapidly if they so chose. The reprocessing of spent fuel from nuclear power stations also creates a large-scale proliferation threat. According to existing plans, by the turn of the new century, two thousand metric tons of plutonium will have been recovered from spent fuel in reprocessing plants in Europe and Japan. Fewer than fifteen pounds is needed to make a nuclear bomb. Since plutonium lasts for thousands of years, the problem of guaranteeing its safety and peaceful use is likely to prove formidable.

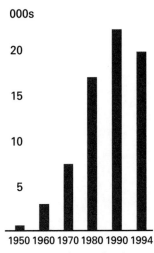

Fig. 13.2 Nuclear warheads deployed, 1950–1994

Source: Commission on Global Governance, *Our Global Neighbourhood* (Oxford University Press 1995), p. 13.

A WORLD WITHOUT WAR?

Nuclear weapons are not the only destructive armaments that people are capable of inventing. Chemical weapons, for example, are cheap to produce. Iraq used chemical weaponry in its war with Iran during the 1980s and threatened to use it in the Gulf war in 1991. Chemical weapons mostly work by bombarding enemy troops or civilians with poisonous gases, which can be instantly fatal. One of these artificially produced poison gases was used in the attack on commuters in the Tokyo subway system in 1995, in which several people were killed and many others had to be hospitalized.

This is a time of basic change in the world political order, however, and opportunities exist for producing a less dangerous world. The risks are easy to see: to possible nuclear proliferation and other weapons of mass destruction must be added the influence of new forms of nationalism, ethnic and religious antagonisms, and inequalities between rich and poorer nations – all potential sources of global conflicts. On the other hand, some of the main factors that promoted warfare in the past, particularly the drive to acquire new territories by conquest, have become less relevant today. Modern societies are much more interdependent globally, and for the most part their boundaries have been fixed and agreed on by the overall community of states. Present-day warfare, especially nuclear war, has become so destructive that it cannot be used to achieve realistic political or economic objectives.

One of the most hopeful developments in recent years has been the growing recognition that the age-old adage 'If you want peace, prepare for war' does not apply in the nuclear age. Even if nuclear confrontations are avoided, wars using conventional weapons may still be fought, and they may prove massively destructive; but there is clear cause for hope.

Michael MccGwire, a well-known defence analyst, has argued that over the next twenty or thirty years the realistic possibility exists of creating a world free of nuclear weapons (MccGwire 1995). A nuclear weapons-free world (NWW) would be one where the nuclear powers agree to scrap all their nuclear armaments over an agreed period. An NWW, he says, is the only way to halt proliferation and keep nuclear weapons out of the hands of aggressive states and terrorist groups. It is a realistic option because many military and political leaders have come to see that nuclear weapons are useless for strategic purposes. The only reason for having them is that others have them or might acquire them. The risk of war will be there whatever happens; but an NWW is the only way to avoid the possibility of calamitous nuclear confrontations which could still destroy large parts of the earth and perhaps even humanity as a whole.

SUMMARY

1 A state exists where there is a political apparatus, ruling over a given territory, whose authority is backed by a legal system and by the ability to use force to implement its policies.

2 Modern states are nation-states, usually having some form of congressional or parliamentary system. The notion of sovereignty (the authority of a government over a clearly defined territorial order) suggests both the acknowledged legitimacy of the nation-state and the recognition of the state's borders by others. Each community acquires a distinctive character through its association with nationalism.

3 Democracy is a political system in which the people rule. In participatory democracy (or direct democracy), decisions are made by those affected by them. A liberal democracy is a representative multiparty democracy (such as the United Kingdom), where citizens can vote for one of at least two parties.

While democracy has become widespread, some troubles exist. In countries such as the United Kingdom, the government is unable to address many of the needs of its citizens. Dissatisfaction with government is increasing, while political participation is decreasing.

4 A political party is an organization oriented towards achieving legitimate control of government through an electoral process. In most Western states, the largest parties are those associated with general political interests – socialism, communism, liberalism or conservatism. There is usually some connection between voting patterns and class differences. In many Western countries there has recently been a decline in allegiance to traditional parties and a growing disenchantment with the party system in general.

5 British politics over recent years has known the strong impact of Thatcherism – a set of doctrines which has survived the fall from power of Mrs Thatcher herself. Thatcherism involves a belief in the desirability of cutting back on the role of the state and in the reign of free market enterprise.

6 Thatcherism changed the outlook of the Conservative Party. The Labour Party has also undergone major changes over the past twenty years. Under the leadership of Tony Blair in particular, 'New Labour' has moved away from older socialist notions, including nationalization and planned economic enterprise.

7 The development of the European Union has had an important impact on all of its member states. While it is not completely clear what the future of the EU will be, it will probably not become a 'super nation-state', but will retain its own distinctive character.

8 The political map of Europe has been transformed by the crumbling of communism in 1989 and after. Russia and the societies of Eastern Europe are becoming parliamentary democracies and market economies, although this process of transition is a difficult and problematic one.

9 Warfare has always played a major role in politics. The nature of war has changed greatly across the ages. With the development of modern society, a process of the industrialization of war occurred – the application of industrial methods to the waging of war. In the nuclear age, there is reason to hope that major wars will decline, because the possible consequences of war are too calamitous.

FURTHER READING

Christopher Dandeker, *Surveillance, Power and Modernity* (Cambridge: Polity Press, 1990). A survey of the development of systems of power in modern societies which places strong emphasis on the role of the military.

Stephen George, *An Awkward Partner: Britain in the European Community* (Oxford: Oxford University Press, 1990). A useful survey of the often tense relation between Britain and the rest of the European Community.

David Held, *Models of Democracy, Second Edition* (Cambridge: Polity Press, 1996). A classic and highly influental account of the diverse forms of democracy.

John Kingdom, *Government and Politics in Britain* (Cambridge: Polity Press, 1991). A comprehensive and critically oriented text on British politics.

James N. Rosenau, *Turbulence in World Politics: A Theory of Change and Continuity* (London: Harvester, 1990). An attempt at a sweeping reformulation of how the global political order should be understood.

John Scott, *Who Rules Britain?* (Cambridge: Polity Press, 1991). The best book on elites and power in British society.

D. W. Urwin and **W. E. Patterson**, *Politics in Western Europe Today: Perspectives, Policies and Problems since 1980* (London: Longman, 1990). A useful overall source book offering an introduction to political life in the various countries of Western Europe.

IMPORTANT TERMS

- *legitimacy*
- *sovereignty*
- *citizen*
- *nationalism*
- *participatory democracy*
- *constitutional monarch*
- *liberal democracy*
- *political party*
- *Thatcherism*
- *voting behaviour*
- *interests*
- *New Labour*
- *European Union*
- *military power*
- *limited war*
- *total war*
- *universal conscription*
- *Cold War*
- *arms trade*
- *nuclear proliferation*

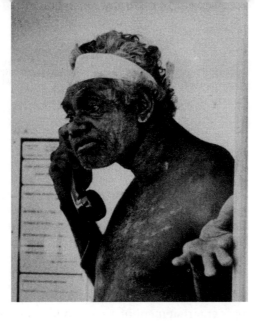

14

MASS MEDIA AND POPULAR CULTURE

'A long time ago there were no toys and everyone was bored. Then they had TV, but they were bored again. They wanted control. So they invented video games.' Thus runs the history of humanity as described by Victor, the eight-year-old son of Marsha Kinder, author of *Playing with Power* (1991), a study of the influence of television and video games on young children. Victor is the household Nintendo champion, and an avid TV watcher as well.

Victor is not alone in his tastes. Video games, especially Nintendo, are mass entertainment of a scope and appeal never seen before our global era, played by children and teenagers almost the world over. Expensive though most such games are, they sell in large numbers even in some of the poor countries of the world; millions have been sold in the more affluent countries.

A key aspect of Nintendo, and other rival systems appearing rapidly over the horizon, is the clarity of the graphics and sound. The games are becoming so 'real' that it is a serious question how far boys like Victor see the Nintendo world as just as real as the world outside. And perhaps that question needs to be asked of everyone. For most of us have become regular consumers of *popular culture*. The term POPULAR CULTURE refers to entertainments watched, read or participated in by hundreds of thousands or millions of people. The compelling stories of soap operas such as *EastEnders*, for instance, pull in millions regularly each week – some, every day.

In this chapter, we'll study the impact of such forms of popular culture, which are often referred to as mass media. The MASS MEDIA include video games and television, but also newspapers, films, magazines, advertisements, videos and CDs. As with the 'popular' in 'popular culture', these are referred to as 'mass' media because they reach mass audiences – audiences comprised of very large numbers of people. They are also sometimes referred to as *mass communications*.

The mass media are often associated only with entertainment – like Nintendo – and seen as rather marginal to most people's lives. Such a view is a partial one, however: mass communications are involved in many other aspects of our social activities too. Media like newspapers or television have a wide-ranging influence over our experience and over **public opinion**. This is not just because they affect our attitudes in specific ways, but because they are the *means of access* to the knowledge on which many social activities depend. Voting in national elections, for example, would be impossible if information about current political events, candidates and parties were not generally available. Even those who are largely uninterested in politics and have little knowledge of the personalities involved have some awareness of national and international events. Only a complete hermit could be completely detached from the 'news events' which impinge on all of us – and we might well suspect that a twentieth-century hermit would possess a radio!

We begin the study of mass media by looking at one of the earliest forms, newspapers. From there we move on to analyse the impact of television. We'll analyse some leading theories of media, and consider the rise of media entrepreneurs such as Rupert Murdoch. Finally, we shall consider the new electronic media: the Internet and the information superhighway.

EARLY MASS MEDIA: THE NEWSPAPERS

Newspapers in their modern form derive from pamphlets and information sheets printed and circulated in the 1700s. Newspapers only became 'daily', with many thousands or millions of readers, from the end of the nineteenth century onwards. The newspaper was a fundamentally important development in the history of modern media, because it packaged many different types of information within a limited and easily reproducible format. Newspapers contained in a single package information on current affairs, entertainment and advertising. News and advertising developed together, and indeed the distinctions between news, advertising and entertainment are shifting and difficult to define. For example, the announcement that a ship is leaving or arriving may in one context be news, in another an advertisement, or in another, if it concerns particular passengers and is written as part of a gossip column, it becomes entertainment.

The cheap daily press was pioneered in the United States. The one-cent daily paper was originally established in New York, then copied in other major eastern cities. By the early 1900s there were city or regional newspapers covering most of the American states. (In contrast to the smaller countries of Europe, national newspapers did not develop.) During the period of mass immigration, many foreign-language newspapers were published in the United States. For example, in 1892 ninety-seven German-language daily papers were being published in cities in the mid-west and north-east of the country. The invention of cheap newsprint (the paper used) was the key to the mass diffusion of newspapers from the late nineteenth century onwards.

The two prime examples of prestige newspapers at the turn of the century were the *New York Times* and *The Times* of London. Most of the influential papers in other countries took these as their models. Newspapers at the top end of the market became a major political force and have remained so to the present day.

For half a century or more, newspapers were the chief way of conveying information quickly and comprehensively to a mass public. Their influence has waned with the rise of radio, cinema and – much more important – television. As recently as 1960, more than one newspaper per household was sold each day in the UK – an average of 112 newspapers for every 100 households – but the ratio has steadily declined since then. Today fewer than 90 papers are sold for every 100 house-holds. Sales to young adults have fallen particularly.

Newspaper publishing

Newspapers have long been associated with the image of the powerful tycoon, the head of a publishing empire. The picture is not an inaccurate one. In many countries, newspaper ownership is concentrated in the hands of a few large corporations often owned and dominated by particular individuals or families. Many of these firms today also have extensive holdings in television and the entertainments industry. In Britain, huge companies run by *press barons*, the Lords Northcliffe, Beaverbrook and Kemsley, developed on the basis of the success of their mass circulation papers in the 1920s and 1930s. France has seen the development of the Hersant information empire; the German Springer and Grüner organizations are vast. In the United States, the number of cities in which there are competing newspaper firms has steadily declined, from more than five hundred at the turn of the century to just over thirty in 1984. Only 3 per cent of American cities have competing papers – local newspaper publishing has become a monopoly enterprise.

With the exception of the US, all Western countries boast a number of national newspapers. There is a choice between nationally available papers, often geared to different political standpoints. Although newspapers in the United States are local, they are by no means all locally owned: more than 70 per cent are controlled by publishing chains. In some of these, as with many mass circulation papers in Europe, the owners set the editorial policies which editors and journalists must follow. In the Hearst chain of newspapers, several editorials are sent every day to the editors of the eight major papers, some of which *have* to be used, while others *may* be. The editors do not write their own.

The fact that newspaper ownership is concentrated has worried most Western governments. In many countries, governments have taken action to prevent the takeover of newspapers by large chains, although such action has frequently failed. Sometimes states have tried to enforce political balance in the press: in Norway, for example, a scheme was set up in the 1970s to equalize investments between newspapers representing different sides of the political spectrum, and most local communities in that country now have two or more well-produced and comprehensive papers providing different points of view on national and international news.

It is possible that the development of computer-based technologies will lead to greater numbers of newspapers, as they have recently become much cheaper to print and produce than used to be the case. On the other hand, electronic communication might in fact bite further into newspaper circulation. For instance, teletext systems provide news information constantly updated during the course of the day and available on the TV screen.

A number of new national newspapers have in fact been introduced in the UK over recent years. Only one or two, however, have been successful.

New national papers

Among other newspapers launched in Britain in the 1980s were the *Independent, Today, News on Sunday* and *Sunday Sport*. The fate of the last two of these is instructive – and dispiriting for those who might wish to raise the standards of the British press. *News on Sunday* was launched in 1987. It was a politically independent paper, owned by a trust and not by an entrepreneur. Its aims were to be of an 'open democratic nature'. It was concerned to promote social justice and was 'opposed to all forms of sexism, racism and all discrimination which denies the capabilities and potential of the individual'.

Sunday Sport, owned by David Sullivan, was a very different kind of enterprise. Its editorial policy was stated as 'tits, bums, QPR and roll your own fags'. The paper was targeted at men aged sixteen to thirty-five. The staff of *News on Sunday* considered the paper 'junk journalism' and at one point proposed an advertising campaign with the slogan for their own paper: 'No tits but a lot of balls'. The campaign was, however, abandoned on the grounds of poor taste.

The first edition of *News on Sunday* led with a story of poverty in Latin America. On the same day, *Sunday Sport* led with 'Royal Home Sex

The Far Side by Gary Larson

'Hey, Lola. Did you see this thing in the paper?'

Orgy' – a story about a pornographic film being made in the stately home of Lord Hertford. *News on Sunday* went bankrupt after having only appeared for a few months, while *Sunday Sport* is still being published and has a circulation of 500,000 (Trowler 1994).

Newspapers as a whole play less of a role in society than once was the case. They have been challenged by the spread of other media, particularly television.

THE IMPACT OF TELEVISION

The increasing influence of television is probably the most important development in the media of the past thirty years or so. If current trends in TV watching continue, by the age of eighteen the average child born today will have spent more time watching television than in any other activity except sleep. Virtually every household now possesses a TV set. In the UK the average set is switched on for between five and six hours a day. Much the same is true in the United States and the other West European countries (Goodhardt et al. 1987). The number of hours individuals watch TV is lower than this, of course, since the set is viewed by different members of the household at different times, but the average adult in Britain watches for about three hours (see table 14.1).

Table 14.1 Use of free time by age, Great Britain, May 1995 (hours per week)

	16–24	25–34	35–44	45–59	60 and over	All aged 16 and over
Television or radio	14	15	13	17	26	19
Visiting friends (may include eating)	7	5	4	4	4	5
Reading	1	1	2	3	6	3
Talking, socializing and telephoning friends	3	3	3	4	4	3
Eating and drinking out	6	4	4	4	2	3
Hobbies, games and computing	2	2	1	3	3	2
Walks and other recreation	2	2	1	2	3	2
Doing nothing (may include illness)	1	1	1	2	2	2
Sports participation	3	1	1	1	1	1
Religious, political and other meetings	–	1	1	–	1	1
Concerts, theatre, cinema and sports spectating	1	1	–	–	–	–
Other	1	–	–	–	–	–
All free time	40	37	33	40	52	42

Source: ESRC Research Centre on Micro-social Change, from *Omnibus Survey*. From *Social Trends*, 1996, p. 217.

Over recent years video machines have come into widespread use, to record programmes for later viewing or to show films on video at home. So have home video games of all sorts. In his book *Video Kids* (1991), Eugene Provenzo analyses the impact of Nintendo. There are currently some 19 million Nintendo games in the US and many more in other countries. Nearly all are owned and operated by children. Social codes and traditions have developed based on the games and their characters. Of the thirty best-selling toys in the US in 1990, twenty-five were either video games or video equipment. The games are often directly linked to the characters or stories in films and TV programmes; in turn, television programming has been based on Nintendo games. Video games, Provenzo concludes, have become a key part of the culture and experience of childhood today.

Public broadcasting

Like mass newspapers, television today is big business, and in most countries the state has been directly involved with its administration. In Britain the British Broadcasting Corporation, which initiated the first television programmes ever produced, is a public organization. It is funded by licence fees paid by every household that owns a set. For some years the BBC was the only organization permitted to broadcast either radio or television programmes in Britain, but today, alongside the two BBC TV channels, BBC 1 and 2, there exist two terrestrial commercial TV channels (ITV and Channel 4). The frequency and duration of advertising is controlled by law, with a maximum of six minutes per hour. These regulations also apply to satellite channels, which became widely available to subscribers in the 1980s.

In the United States the three leading TV organizations are all commercial networks – the American Broadcasting Company (ABC), Columbia Broadcasting System (CBS) and the National Broadcasting Company (NBC). Networks are limited by law to owning no more than five licensed stations, which in the case of these three organizations are in the biggest cities. The 'big three', therefore, reach over a quarter of all households via their own stations. Some two hundred affiliated stations are also attached to each network, comprising 90 per cent of the seven hundred or so TV stations in the country. The networks depend for their income on selling advertising time. The National Association of Broadcasters, a private body, lays down guidelines about the proportion of viewing time per hour to be devoted to advertising: 9.5 minutes per hour during 'prime time' and 16 at other periods. TV companies use regularly collected statistics (ratings) of how many people watch specific programmes in setting advertising fees. The ratings also, of course, strongly influence whether or not a series continues.

The power of the large networks has become diminished since the advent of satellite and cable TV. The viewer in many European countries, including the UK, and in the major American cities, can select from a multiplicity of channels and programmes. In such circumstances, particularly if one adds in the influence of videos, people more and more do their own 'programming'. They construct viewing schedules of a personalized character rather than depending on the pre-supplied network scheduling.

Satellite and cable are altering the nature of television almost everywhere. Once these have started to make inroads into the domains of the orthodox television channels, it is difficult for governments to control the content of TV, as they have characteristically done in the past. Thus television and the electronic media seem to have played a basic part in the circumstances which produced the revolutions of 1989 in Eastern Europe (see chapter 18, 'Revolutions and social movements').

The future of the BBC

The position of the BBC – like that of public broadcasters in most other countries – is under strain and has been the subject of much controversy. The future of the BBC has become problematic because of the proliferation of new forms of media technology. New channels are constantly being introduced; with the development of digital technology (see later in the chapter), literally hundreds of cable and satellite channels will become available. The BBC's share of the television audience in 1995 was just over 40 per cent. It is watched by only 33 per cent of people who have cable or satellite TV.

Some have suggested that the BBC should be privatized. In other words, it should get its revenue from advertising, as other channels do, and the licence fee could disappear. So far, this idea has been resisted. A 1994 White Paper on the future of the BBC recommended the continuation of the licence fee and reaffirmed that it should stay in public ownership.

Yet the licence fee system can't endure if the BBC's audience falls a great deal further – which some think will inevitably happen. One observer recently commented: 'Perhaps with hindsight public-service broadcasting will seem a freak of technology: for a mere half-century, it was possible for one medium to communicate the same material to most of a country's population' (*Economist*, 23 Dec. 1995, p. 29).

The effect of television on behaviour

Vast amounts of research have been done to try to assess the effects of television programmes. Most such studies have concerned children – understandably enough, given the sheer volume of their viewing and the possible implications for socialization. The three most commonly researched topics are television's impact on propensities to crime and violence, the nature of TV news, and the role of television in social and cultural life.

TV and violence

The incidence of violence in television programmes is well documented. The most extensive studies have been carried out by Gerbner and his collaborators, analysing samples of prime-time and weekend daytime television for all the major American networks each year after 1967. The number and frequency of violent acts and episodes were

Violent imagery on TV: Judge Dredd

charted for a range of varying types of programme. Violence is defined in the research as the threat or use of physical force, directed against the self or others, in which physical harm or death is involved. Television drama emerged as highly violent in character: on average 80 per cent of such programmes contained violence, with a rate of 7.5 violent episodes per hour. Children's programmes showed even higher levels of violence, although killing was less commonly portrayed. Cartoons contained the highest number of violent acts and episodes of any type of television programme (Gerbner et al. 1979, 1980; Gunter 1985).

In what ways, if at all, does the depiction of violence influence the audience? F. S. Anderson collected the findings of sixty-seven studies conducted over the twenty years from 1956 to 1976 investigating the influence of TV violence on tendencies to aggression among children. About three-quarters of the studies claimed to find some such association. In 20 per cent of cases there were no clear-cut results, while in 3 per cent of the researches the investigators concluded that watching television violence actually decreases aggression (Anderson 1977; Liebert et al. 1982).

The studies Anderson surveyed, however, differ widely in the methods used, the strength of the association supposedly revealed, and the definition of 'aggressive behaviour'. In crime dramas featuring violence (and in many children's cartoons) there are underlying themes of justice and retribution. A far higher proportion of miscreants are brought to justice in crime dramas than happens with police investigations in real life, and in cartoons harmful or threatening characters usually tend to get their 'just deserts'. It does not necessarily follow that high levels of the portrayal of violence create directly imitative patterns among those watching, who are perhaps more influenced by the underlying moral themes. In general, research on the 'effects' of television on audiences has tended to treat viewers – children and adults – as passive and undiscriminating in their reactions to what they see.

It is doubtful whether violent material in video games, TV or films directly produces tendencies to violence in those who watch it. Similarly, it is dubious whether Victor's involvement with Nintendo necessarily harms his progress at school. The effects of video games are likely to be governed by other influences on school performance. In other words, where there are strong pressures deflecting students from an interest in their schoolwork, absorption with TV or video pursuits will tend to reinforce these attitudes. Video games and TV then can become a refuge from a disliked school environment.

But it is also possible that video games can act to develop skills that might be relevant both to formal education and also to wider participation in a society that depends increasingly on electronic communication. According to Marsha Kinder, her son Victor's adeptness at Nintendo transferred fruitfully to other spheres. For example, the better he became at video games, the more interested and skilful he was at drawing cartoons.

Robert Hodge and David Tripp emphasize that children's responses to TV involve interpreting or *reading* what they see, not just registering the content of programmes (Hodge and Tripp 1986). They suggest that most research has not taken account of the complexity of children's mental processes. TV watching, even of trivial programmes, is not an inherently low-level intellectual activity; children 'read' programmes by relating them to other systems of meaning in their everyday lives. For example, even very young children recognize that media violence is 'not real'. According to Hodge and Tripp, it is not the violence as such in television programmes that has effects on behaviour, but rather the general framework of attitudes within which it is both presented and 'read'.

Sociologists study TV news

Sociological studies of television have given a good deal of attention to the news. A substantial proportion of the population doesn't read newspapers; TV news is thus a key source of information about what goes on in the world. Some of the most well-known – and controversial – researches concerned with television news were those carried out by the Glasgow Media Group at Glasgow University. The group published a series of works critical of the presentation of the news: *Bad News*, *More Bad News*, *Really Bad News* and *War and Peace News*. They followed similar research strategies in each of these books, although they altered the focus of their investigations.

Bad News (1976), their first, and most influential, book was based on an analysis of news broadcasts on all channels (Channel 4 didn't yet exist at that time) between January and June 1975. The objective was to provide a systematic and dispassionate analysis of the content of the news and the ways in which it was presented. *Bad News* concentrated on the portrayal of industrial disputes. The later books concentrated more on political coverage and on the Falklands War.

The conclusion of *Bad News* was that news about industrial relations typically was presented in a selective and slanted fashion. Terms like

'trouble', 'radical' and 'pointless strike' suggested anti-union views. The effects of strikes, causing disruption for the public, were much more likely to be reported on than their causes. Film material used often made the activities of protesters appear irrational and aggressive. For example, film of strikers stopping people entering a factory would focus on any confrontations which occurred, even if they were very infrequent.

Bad News also pointed out that those who construct the news act as 'gatekeepers' for what gets on the agenda – in other words, what the public hears about at all. Strikes in which there were active confrontations between workers and management, for instance, might get widely reported. More consequential and long-lasting industrial disputes elsewhere might be largely ignored. The views of news journalists, the Media Group suggested, reflect the outlook of the dominant groups in society, who inevitably see strikers as dangerous and irresponsible.

Critical responses

The works of the Media Group were much discussed within media circles as well as within the academic community. Some news producers accused the researchers of simply exercising their own biases, which they thought lay with the strikers. They pointed out that, while *Bad News* contained a chapter on 'The trade unions and the media', there was no chapter on 'Management and the media'. This should have been discussed, the media critics argued, because news journalists are often accused by management of being biased against them, rather than against the strikers.

Academic critics made similar points. Martin Harrison (1985) gained access to transcripts of ITN news broadcasts for the period covered by the original study. On this basis he argued that the five months analysed in the study were not typical. There was an abnormal number of days lost over the period. It would have been impossible for the news to report all of these, and therefore the tendency to focus on the more colourful episodes was understandable.

In Harrison's view, the Media Group was wrong to claim that news broadcasts concentrated too much on the effects of strikes. After all, many more people are normally affected by strikes than take part in them. Sometimes millions of people find their lives disrupted by the actions of a handful of people. Finally, according to Harrison's analysis, some of the assertions made by the Media Group were simply false. For example, contrary to what the Group stated, the news did normally name the unions involved in disputes and did say whether or not the strikes were official or unofficial.

In replying to such criticism, members of the Group noted that Harrison's research had been partly sponsored by ITN, possibly compromising his academic impartiality. The transcripts scrutinized by Harrison were not complete and some passages were included that ITN did not in fact broadcast at all.

Since that date, members of the Media Group have carried out a range of further research studies. In an article called 'Seeing is believing' one of its members, Greg Philo, reported research on people's memories of past events (Philo 1991). Specifically, he asked about recollections of the miners' strike of 1984–5, a large-scale and prolonged confrontation between the miners' union, led by Arthur Scargill, and Mrs Thatcher's Conservative government.

Philo showed photographs from the strike to different groups of people and asked them to write news stories about them as if they were journalists. He also questioned them about what they remembered of the strike, asking, for example, whether it was mainly peaceful or not. He found that the stories they wrote closely resembled the original TV items which had appeared while the strike was on. Many of the phrases were the same.

Over half the people believed that the picketing that had happened during the strike was mostly violent (violence had actually been very infrequent). Philo concluded that it 'can be very difficult to criticise a dominant media account if there is little access to alternative sources of information. In these circumstances we should not underestimate the power of the media' (p. 177).

In *Getting the Message*, the Media Group collected together recent research on news broadcasting. The editor of the volume, John Eldridge, points out that the debate provoked by the original work of the group still continues (Eldridge 1993). To say what would count as objectivity in news reporting will always be difficult. As against those who say that the idea of objectivity makes no sense (see the section on Jean Baudrillard later in the chapter), Eldridge affirms the importance of continuing to look at media products with a critical eye. Accuracy in news reporting can and must be studied. After all, when the football results are reported, we expect them to be accurate. A simple example like this, Eldridge argues, reminds us that issues of truth are always involved in news reporting.

Yet the point holds that the news is never just a 'description' of what 'actually happened' on a given day or in a given week. The 'news' is a complex construction, which regularly influences what it is 'about'. For example, when a politician appears on a news programme and makes a comment about a controversial issue – say, the state of the economy and what should be done about it – that comment itself becomes 'news' in subsequent programmes.

Television and genre

Television today operates in continuous flow. Advertising may break up programmes, but there are no gaps. If the screen should go blank for a while, the television company always feels obliged to apologize. It is presumed by both producers and viewers that TV is unending – and indeed many channels now never go off the air at all.

TV is a flow, but TV programming is a jumble. A schedule for a single evening, for example, will usually have a whole array of quite different programmes, one after the other. The idea of **genre** is useful for making sense of the seemingly chaotic nature of TV programming (Abercrombie 1996). Genre refers to how programme makers and viewers understand 'what' it is that is being watched – it refers to how programmes are categorized by these groups as, for example, news, soap operas, game shows, musicals or thrillers. Each genre has its rules and conventions which mark it out and separate it from others.

These are partly rules about content. For example, soap operas happen in a domestic setting, Westerns in the historical context of nineteenth-century America. They are also about characters and contexts. Central characters in soap operas, such as families at home, are likely to be peripheral in thrillers. Genres also set up different expectations. Suspense and mystery are a necessary part of detective series, but not usually of soap operas.

TV producers by and large know what audiences expect, and operate within those boundaries. This allows them to achieve routines in what they do. Production teams of actors, directors and writers who specialize in a given genre can be built up. Props, sets and costumes can be used over and over again. Audience loyalty can be generated as people become accustomed to following regular programmes in a given genre. Of course, genres may also be stretched, or sometimes deliberately transgressed, in order to achieve a particular programme style. *Not the Nine O'Clock News*, for example, used the genre of news to create comedy. There was a certain shock value at first, but the audience rapidly became used to the fact that the programme really belonged in the genre of comedy.

The differences between genres are not always clear-cut, and the divisions between them change over time, as producing and viewing conventions change. For example, police series, such as *Hill Street Blues*, take on some of the characteristics of soap opera. The genres of drama and documentary become merged in staged re-enactments of history – as when there was a dramatized series about President Nixon and the Watergate scandal, with actors playing Nixon and his colleagues.

Soap opera

Soap opera is a genre created *by* television, and is its most popular type of programme. Of the most watched TV shows in Britain each week, almost all are soap operas – *EastEnders, Coronation Street, Brookside* and many others. No one knows where the term 'soap opera' actually came from, save that it originated in the US. Some series now thought of as belonging to the genre of soap opera were not originally conceived of in that way – they date from a time before the term 'soap opera' came into use in the UK. *Coronation Street*, for example, existed for years before it became categorized as a soap.

Soap operas fall into various different types, or subgenres, at least as represented on British TV. Soaps produced in the UK, like *Coronation Street*, tend to be gritty and down to earth, concerned often with the lives of poorer people. Second, there are American imports, many of which, like *Dallas* or *Dynasty*, portray individuals leading more glamorous lives. A third category is made up of Australian imports, such as *Neighbours*. These tend to be low-budget productions, featuring middle-class homes and lifestyles.

Soaps are like TV as a whole: continuous. Individual stories may come to an end, and different characters appear and disappear, but the soap itself has no ending until it is taken off the air completely. Tension is created between episodes by so-called 'cliff-hangers'. The episode abruptly stops just before some key event happens – the viewer has to wait until the next episode to see how things turn out.

A basic part of the genre of soap opera is that it demands regular viewing on the part of whoever watches it. A single episode makes very little sense. Soap operas presume a history, which the regular viewer knows – he or she becomes familiar with the characters, with their personalities and their life experiences. The threads which are linked to create such history are above all personal and emotional – soaps for the most part do not look at larger social or economic frameworks, which impinge only from the outside.

Such qualities are a large part of the reason why soaps are much more commonly watched on a regular basis by women rather than men. In most societies, women are regarded as specialists not only in the mechanics of domestic life, where soaps unfold – they are also thought of as having special concern with, and sensitivity to, the emotions.

Differing views have been put forward by sociologists about why soap operas are so popular – and they are popular across the world, not only in Britain or America, but in Africa, Asia and Latin America. Some think that they provide a means of escape, particularly where women find their own lives dull or oppressive. Such a view is not particularly convincing, though, given that many soaps feature people whose lives are just as problematic. More plausible is the idea that soap operas address universal properties of personal and emotional life. They explore dilemmas which everyone must face, and perhaps even help some viewers to think more creatively about their own lives.

How should we think about the wider implications of the media? This is one of the main concerns of those who have developed theoretical interpretations of the role of media in shaping social development and social organization. It is to these theories that we now turn.

THEORIES OF MEDIA

Early theories

Two influential early theorists of media were the Canadian authors, Harold Innis and Marshall McLuhan. Innis (1950, 1951) argued that different media strongly influence the organization of contrasting forms of society. Some media endure for long periods of time, but are hard to transport across space. This was true, for example, of stone hieroglyphics – writing carved on stone – found in some ancient civilizations. Stone carvings last a long time, but they cannot be easily transported. They are a poor means of keeping in touch with distant places. Hence societies which depend on such a form of communication cannot become very large. COMMUNICATION refers to the transfer of information from one individual or group to another, whether in speech or through another medium.

Messages on light material, such as papyrus (material resembling paper, but made out of the stem of a plant) can be carried much more easily to distant places, making larger forms of society possible. Papyrus, for example, allowed the Romans to maintain a large empire, with a government that could extend its control to distant regions.

McLuhan (1964) developed some of Innis's ideas, and applied them particularly to the media in modern, industrialized societies. According to McLuhan, 'the medium is the message'. That is to say, the nature of the media found in a society influences its structure much more than the content, or the messages, which the media convey. Television, for instance, is a very different medium from the printed book. It is electronic, visual and composed of fluid images. A society in which television plays a basic role is one where everyday life is experienced differently from one which only has print. Thus the TV news conveys global information instantaneously to millions of people. The electronic media, McLuhan thought, are creating what he called a **global village** – people throughout the world see major news items unfold and hence participate in the same events as one another. Millions of people in different countries, for example, know about Princess Di's life and her problems and follow the unfolding saga of the British royal family.

Jean Baudrillard, whose ideas we shall look at in a few paragraphs' time, has been strongly influenced by the ideas of Innis and McLuhan. We turn first, however, to the theories of the German sociologist and philosopher, Jürgen Habermas.

Jürgen Habermas: the public sphere

The German philosopher and sociologist Jürgen Habermas, whose work we encountered in chapter 1, is linked to the 'Frankfurt School' of social thought. The Frankfurt School was a group of authors inspired by Marx who nevertheless believed that Marx's views needed radical revision to bring them up to date. Among other things, they believed that Marx had not given enough attention to the influence of culture in modern capitalist society.

The Frankfurt School made extensive study of what they called the 'culture industry', meaning the entertainment industries of film, TV, popular music, radio, newspapers and magazines. They argued that the spread of the culture industry, with its undemanding and standardized products, undermines the capacity of individuals for critical and independent thought. Art disappears, swamped by commercialization – 'Mozart's Greatest Hits'.

Habermas has taken up some of these themes, but developed them in a different way. He analyses the development of media from the early eighteenth century up to the present moment, tracing out the emergence – and subsequent decay – of the 'public sphere' (Habermas 1989). The **public sphere** is an area of public debate in which issues of general concern can be discussed and opinions formed.

The public sphere, according to Habermas, developed first in the salons and coffee houses of London, Paris and other European cities. People used to meet in such salons to discuss issues of the moment, using as a means for such debate the news sheets and newspapers which had just begun to emerge. Political debate became a matter of particular importance. Although only small numbers of the population were involved, Habermas argues that the salons were vital to the early development of democracy. For they introduced the idea of resolving political problems through public discussion. The public sphere – at least in principle – involves individuals coming together as equals in a forum for public debate.

However, the promise offered by the early development of the public sphere, Habermas concludes, has not been fully realized. Democratic debate in modern societies is stifled by the development of the culture industry. The development of the mass media and mass entertainment causes the public sphere to become largely a sham. Politics is stage-managed in parliament and the media, while commercial interests triumph over those of the public. 'Public opinion' is not formed through open, rational discussion, but through manipulation and control – as, for example, in advertising.

Baudrillard: the world of hyperreality

One of the most influential current theorists of media is the French author Jean Baudrillard. Baudrillard regards the impact of modern mass media as being quite different from, and much more profound than, that of any other technology. The coming of the mass media, particularly electronic media such as TV, has transformed the very nature of our lives. TV does not just 'represent' the world to us, it increasingly defines what the world in which we live actually *is*.

Consider as an example the O. J. Simpson trial, a celebrated court case which unfolded in Los Angeles in 1994–5. Simpson originally became famous as an American football star, but later became known around the world as a result of appearing in several popular films, including the *Naked Gun* series. He was accused of the murder of his wife, Nicole, and after a very long trial was acquitted. The trial was televised live and was watched in many countries, including Britain. In America six television channels covered the trial on a continuous basis.

The trial did not just happen in the courtroom. It was a televisual event linking millions of viewers and commentators in the media. The trial is an illustration of what Baudrillard calls **hyperreality**. There is no longer a 'reality' (the events in the courtroom) which television allows us to see. The 'reality' is actually the string of images on the TV screens of the world which defined the trial as a global event.

Just before the outbreak of hostilities in the Gulf in 1991, Baudrillard wrote a newspaper article entitled 'The Gulf War cannot happen'. When war was declared and a bloody conflict took place it might seem obvious that Baudrillard had been wrong. Not a bit of it. After the end of the war, Baudrillard wrote a second article, 'The Gulf War did not happen'. What did he mean? He meant that the war was not like other wars that have happened in history. It was a war of the media age, a televisual spectacle, in which, along with other viewers throughout the world, George Bush and Saddam Hussein watched the coverage by CNN to see what was actually 'happening'.

Baudrillard argues that, in an age where the mass media are everywhere, in effect a new reality – hyperreality – is created, composed of the intermingling of people's behaviour and media images. The world of hyperreality is constructed of **simulacra** – images which only get their meaning from other images and hence have no grounding in an 'external reality'. The current ads for Silk Cut cigarettes, for example, don't refer to the cigarettes at all, but only to previous ads which have appeared in a long series. No political leader today can win an election who doesn't appear constantly on television: the TV image of the leader is the 'person' most viewers know.

John Thompson: the media and modern society

Drawing in some part on the writings of Habermas, John Thompson has analysed the relation between the media and the development of industrial societies (Thompson 1990, 1995). From early forms of print through to electronic communication, Thompson argues, the media have played a central role in the development of modern institutions. The main founders of sociology, including Marx, Weber and Durkheim, Thompson believes, gave too little attention to the role of media in shaping even the early development of modern society.

Sympathetic to some of the ideas of Habermas, Thompson is also critical of him, as he is of the Frankfurt School and of Baudrillard. The

Frankfurt School's attitude to the culture industry was too negative. The modern mass media, Thompson thinks, do not deny us the possibility of critical thought; in fact, they provide us with many forms of information to which we couldn't have had access before. In common with the Frankfurt School, Habermas treats us too much as the passive recipients of media messages. In Thompson's words:

> Media messages are commonly discussed by individuals in the course of reception and subsequent to it . . . [They] are transformed through an ongoing process of telling and retelling, interpretation and reinterpretation, commentary, laughter and criticism . . . By taking hold of messages and routinely incorporating them into our lives . . . we are constantly shaping and reshaping our skills and stocks of knowledge, testing our feelings and tastes, and expanding the horizons of our experience. (Thompson 1995, pp. 42–3)

Thompson's theory of the media depends on a distinction between three types of interaction (see the box). **Face-to-face interaction**, such as people talking at a party, is rich in clues which individuals use to make sense of what others say (see chapter 4 above). **Mediated interaction** involves the use of a media technology – paper, electrical connections, electronic impulses. Characteristic of mediated interaction is that it is stretched out in time and space – it goes well beyond the contexts of ordinary face-to-face interaction. Mediated interaction takes place between individuals in a direct way – for instance, two people talking on the telephone – but there isn't the same variety of clues as where people are face to face.

A third type of interaction is **mediated quasi-interaction**. This refers to the sort of social relations created by the mass media. Such interaction is stretched across time and space, but it doesn't link individuals directly: hence the term 'quasi-interaction'. The two previous types are 'dialogical': individuals communicate in a direct way. Mediated quasi-

The active audience at work. Talking back to the TV for personal and social reasons is common and clear evidence that audiences are not 'passive receivers'.

TYPES OF INTERACTION

Interactional characteristics	Face-to-face interaction	Mediated interaction	Mediated quasi-interaction
Space-time constitution	Context of co-presence; shared spatial-temporal reference system	Separation of contexts; extended availability in time and space	Separation of contexts; extended availability in time and space
Range of symbolic cues	Multiplicity of symbolic cues	Narrowing of the range of symbolic cues	Narrowing of the range of symbolic cues
Action orientation	Oriented towards specific others	Oriented towards specific others	Oriented towards an indefinite range of potential recipients
Dialogical/monological	Dialogical	Dialogical	Monological

Source: John B. Thompson, *The Media and Modernity*, Polity Press 1995.

interaction is 'monological': a TV programme, for example, is a one-way form of communication. People watching the programme may discuss it, and perhaps address some remarks to the TV set – but, of course, it doesn't answer back.

Thompson's point is not that the third type comes to dominate the other two – essentially the view taken by Baudrillard. Rather, all three types intermingle in our lives today. The mass media, Thompson suggests, change the balance between the public and the private in our lives. Contrary to what Habermas says, much more comes into the public domain than before, and this leads quite often to debate and controversy.

An example would be the *Panorama* interview which Princess Di gave in 1995. She answered many questions which curious viewers had about her life, and at the same time revealed a good deal about the institution of the monarchy. Both aspects of the interview prompted vigorous debate, not only in the newspapers and on television, but in homes, bars and cafés across the country.

Ideology and the media

The study of media is closely related to the impact of *ideology* in society. IDEOLOGY refers to the influence of ideas on people's beliefs and actions. The concept has been widely used in media studies, as well as in other areas of sociology, but it has also long been controversial. The word was first coined by a French writer, Destutt de Tracy, in the late 1700s. He used it to mean a 'science of ideas'.

In the hands of later authors, however, the term became used in a more critical way. Marx, for example, regarded ideology as 'false consciousness'. Powerful groups are able to control the dominant ideas circulating in a society so as to justify their own position. Thus, according to Marx, religion is often ideological: it teaches the poor to be content with their lot. The social analyst should uncover the distortions of ideology so as to allow the powerless to gain a true perspective on their lives – and take action to improve their conditions of life.

Thompson (1990) calls de Tracy's view the *neutral* conception of ideology and Marx's view the *critical* conception of ideology. Neutral conceptions 'characterize phenomena as ideology or ideological without implying that these phenomena are necessarily misleading, illusory or aligned with the interests of any particular group'. Critical notions of ideology 'convey a negative, critical or pejorative sense' and carry with them 'an implicit criticism or condemnation' (pp. 53–4).

Thompson argues that the critical notion is to be preferred, because it links ideology with power. Ideology is about the exercise of **symbolic power** – how ideas become used to hide, justify or legitimate the interests of dominant groups in the social order.

In their studies the Glasgow Media Group in effect were analysing ideological aspects of TV news reporting. The news tended to favour the government and management at the expense of the strikers. In general, Thompson believes, mass media – including not only the news but all varieties of programme content and genre – greatly expand the scope of ideology in modern societies. They reach mass audiences and are in his terms, based on 'quasi-interaction' – audiences cannot answer back in a direct way.

THE GLOBALIZING OF MEDIA

If today we are all aware that we live in 'one world', this is in large part a result of the international scope of the communications media. Anyone who switches on the television and watches 'the world news' usually gets just that: a presentation of some of the events which took place that day or shortly before in many different parts of the world. Television programmes and films are sold to large international markets; hundreds of millions of people watch such programmes and series.

All these developments express the emergence of a **world information order** – an international system of the production, distribution and consumption of information. Like other aspects of global society, the new information order has developed unevenly and reflects divisions between the developed societies and Third World countries.

News

Flows of news are dominated by a small number of news agencies, which supply up-to-date information to newspapers, radio and TV stations throughout the world. Reuters, a British agency, was one of the first in the field. In 1870, together with HAVAS, a French company, it divided up the globe into exclusive news territories. Reuters dealt with Britain, Holland and their imperial dependencies, which at that time stretched across large segments of Africa and Asia. HAVAS took France, Italy, Spain, Portugal and part of the Middle East. In 1876, Reuters agreed that HAVAS could have exclusive claim to South America, Reuters being given the whole of the Far East, except for what was then Indo-China but including Australasia. Both agencies exchanged news with the most prominent American agency, Associated Press (AP).

AP was thus at that time largely dependent on the two European agencies for material used by newspapers in the United States, but after World War One, the leading American agencies began to compete with their European rivals in many parts of the world. The two largest agencies, AP and UPI (United Press International) still gain much of their revenue from newspapers, radio and television in the United States, but have become very influential in providing news material used internationally.

Together with Agence France-Presse, which has replaced HAVAS, Reuters, AP and UPI are responsible for most of the international news transmitted throughout the world. UPI, today the biggest of the four, has 6,400 clients in 114 countries, and its releases are translated into 48 languages. Information assembled by these agencies, once sent by Morse code or telephone line, is now sent via computer and satellite links. Between them the four agencies send out 34 million words each day, claiming to provide nine-tenths of the total news output of the world's press, radio and television.

Cinema, television, advertising and electronic communication

American sources are dominant in the production and distribution of television programmes, films, advertisements and various forms of electronic communication.

In the 1920s, when feature films first saw the light of day, Hollywood made four-fifths of all films screened in the world, and the United States continues to be easily the largest influence in the cinema industry. The governments of many countries provide subsidies to aid their own film industries, but no other country rivals the United States as an exporter of feature films. In Britain, for instance, American films account for 40 per cent of all films shown each year in cinemas. Most of the other countries which have a film export industry, such as Italy, Japan and Germany, also import large quantities of American films. In South America the proportion is often over 50 per cent, and a similar ratio applies in many parts of Asia, Africa and the Middle East. In Thailand, as many as 90 per cent of all films shown per year are American.

In television programmes, the British are an important global presence alongside American corporations. Excluding showings on television of feature films made for the big screen, earnings for British television exports are about the same as those for the US. However, a far higher proportion of British programmes are sold to a single market – the United States itself – than in the case of American products, so the worldwide influence of American television programmes is in fact more considerable.

Nine of the ten largest advertising firms in the world are North American. Half the major agencies in Canada, Germany, France, Britain and Australia are American; in many states in Asia, Africa and South

America the largest agencies are either American or owned by US companies. The top ten advertising agencies are transnationals, some with a host of subsidiaries in other countries. The large advertising agencies are regularly employed by the giant transnational corporations to coordinate programmes of advertising put out simultaneously in many countries.

American influence is strong over the electronic channels used to communicate much of the information on which modern states and large corporations depend. Telecommunication links now essential to banking, world monetary transactions and some kinds of TV and radio broadcasting are mostly in American hands. International Business Machines (IBM), based in the United States, is one of the largest of all transnational corporations, and has enormous influence over international information flow, particularly in the supply of computer resources. It has been estimated that nine-tenths of all records held in databases throughout the world are accessible to the American government or other organizations in the United States.

The largest media company in the world, Time-Warner, formed in 1989 as a result of a merger, is also US-based. It has a workforce of some 350,000, with subsidiaries in Europe, Latin America, Asia and Australia. Its activities include film making, television, video, book publishing and music recording.

Other large media corporations – apart from the Murdoch and Berlusconi empires discussed below – include the Japanese Sony Corporation, which owns CBS Records and Hollywood studios; the German Bertelsmann group, owner of RCA Records and a large US-based set of publishing companies; and the French publishing corporation, Hachette.

Media imperialism

The paramount position of the industrialized countries, above all the United States, in the production and diffusion of media has led many observers to speak of *media imperialism*. A cultural empire, it is argued, has been established. Third World countries are held to be especially vulnerable, because they lack the resources to maintain their own cultural independence.

Via the electronic media, Western cultural products have certainly become widely diffused across the globe. Pico Iyer speaks of 'video nights in Katmandu', of frequenting discos in Bali (Iyer 1989). American videos are commonplace in the Islamic republic of Iran, as well as audiotapes of Western popular music, brought in on the black market (Sreberny-Mohammadi 1992). Not only more popular entertainment forms are at issue, however. Control of the world's news by the major Western agencies, it has been suggested, means the predominance of a 'First World outlook' in the information conveyed. Thus it has been claimed that attention is given to the Third World in news broadcasts mainly in times of disaster, crisis or military confrontation, and that the daily files of other types of news kept on the industrialized world are not maintained for Third World coverage.

THE MUSIC INDUSTRY: A GLOBAL PHENOMENON

World record sales figures 1992

Global sales of discs and tapes increased by over 9 per cent in 1992 according to statistics issued by the International Federation of the Phonographic Industry (IFPI). The retail market in the 59 countries surveyed by IFPI was worth $28.7 billion.

Almost all of the growth occurred in North America and Asia. The United States market for soundcarriers reached almost $8.9 billion due mainly to a 22 per cent increase in the numbers of Compact Discs sold there. US consumers accounted for over 400 million CD units out of the 1992 world total of 1.15 billion.

Music sales in South East Asia also expanded to reach over $2 billion in 1992. This was a 44 per cent increase over the figures reported in 1991. In this region, the main format for recorded music remains the cassette. Over 40 per cent of the world's tapes are sold here. After the US, India (240 million units) and China (150 million) are the largest national markets for music cassettes.

In contrast to Asia and the US, the record industries of Japan and Europe had a relatively poor year in 1992. Although the Japanese spent over $3 billion on records and tapes, this was only 6 per cent more than in 1991. At 181 million discs, the CD market in Japan grew by under 6 per cent. In Europe, six of the eleven European Community members which report figures to IFPI showed a net loss in the value of sales in 1992. The position was worst in Greece where the record market fell by 26 per cent. The best performance came from Portugal where sales were up by 9 per cent although France and Germany also reported slight increases.

The table below shows the year-on-year progress of the various formats in the world music market. While CD sales were up by 18 per cent this was significantly less than the 28 per cent increase shown by the format in 1990 and 1991. With the important exception of the US the Compact Disc revolution seems to have slowed considerably in the main industrialized countries and price factors have so far prevented CD from becoming a major soundcarrier in Asia, Africa and Latin America. The IFPI totals show a slight growth in cassette sales, although like the relatively low fall in vinyl LP sales this may be due to reporting variations in 1991 and 1992. The 1992 world listing includes Russia for the first time and the estimated cassette sales in that country were 100 million units. Similarly, IFPI's 1992 returns show that 30 million LPs were sold in China, although none were reported for the previous year.

While the world total of singles sales remained almost static, the two-song or three-song format is now almost extinct outside Japan, the US and Western Europe. These countries accounted for 96 out of every 100 singles sold in the world in 1992.

World sales by format 1992 (in millions of units)

Singles	331.6 (−0.4%)
LPs	126.1 (−19.5%)
Cassettes	1551.9 (+2.8%)
CDs	1152.9 (+18.0%)

Source: Dave Laing, *Popular Music*, Cambridge University Press, 1993.

Herbert Schiller has claimed that control of global communications by United States firms has to be seen in relation to various factors. He argues that American TV and radio networks have fallen increasingly under the influence of the federal government and particularly the Defense Department. He points out that RCA, which owns the NCB television and radio networks, is also a leading defence subcontractor to the Pentagon, the headquarters of the US armed forces. American television exports, coupled with advertising, propagate a commercialized culture which corrodes local forms of cultural expression. Even where governments prohibit commercial broadcasting within their borders, radio and television from surrounding countries can often be directly received.

Schiller argues that, although Americans were the first to be affected by the 'corporate-message cocoon . . . what is now happening is the creation and global extension of a new total corporate informational-cultural environment' (Schiller 1989, pp. 168, 128). Since US corporations and culture are globally dominant, they have 'overwhelmed a good part of the world', such that 'American cultural domination . . . sets the boundaries for national discourse' (Schiller 1991, p. 22).

Media entrepreneurs

Rupert Murdoch

Rupert Murdoch is an Australian-born entrepreneur who is the owner of one of the world's largest media empires – much of which is in fact based in the US. He began his career with the family-owned *Adelaide News*. Murdoch later set up Australia's first national newspaper, *The Australian*, in 1964. On the basis of its success and his developing business interests, he purchased the two British newspapers the *News of the World* and the *Sun* in 1969. In the mid-1970s he acquired the *New York Post*, which he subsequently sold, then bought back. Later American acquisitions included papers in San Antonio, Boston, Chicago and other cities.

Murdoch turned many of these newspapers towards sensationalistic journalism, built on the three themes of sex, crime and sport. The *Sun* became highly successful, with a circulation of over 4 million per day. Following the 1992 election, won by John Major, the paper carried a headline 'It was the *Sun* wot done it'. Presumably under Murdoch's guidance, the paper had waged a savage campaign against the Labour Party, and particularly against its then leader, Neil Kinnock.

In 1981 Murdoch overcame opposition to buy the up-market papers, *The Times* and the *Sunday Times*. He also started to expand into television, establishing Sky TV, a satellite and cable chain which, after initial reverses, proved commercially successful. He controls Star TV, which covers parts of the Far East.

Murdoch owns 64 per cent of the Star TV network. Star TV is based in Hong Kong and was founded by one of the old-established trading companies there, Hutchison Whampoa. Its declared strategy is to 'control the skies' in satellite transmission over an area from Japan to Turkey, taking in the gigantic markets of India and China. It transmits five channels, one of which is BBC world news. The satellite brings to these countries such programmes as Oprah Winfrey, a show which features very frank discussions of sex and relationships. It has been said that in the still quite traditional Asian countries it is as if the 1960s and 1990s were compressed together – an instantaneous, media-transmitted sexual revolution.

In 1985, Murdoch bought a half interest in Twentieth-Century Fox, the film company. Together with his partners in Fox, he then acquired seven US TV stations from Metromedia Inc., one of which he disposed of immediately. His Fox Broadcasting Company started up in 1987. Murdoch acquired the US-based publishers, Harper and Row – now renamed HarperCollins – in 1987.

Governments can cause trouble for Murdoch, because, at least within their own boundaries, they can introduce legislation limiting media cross-ownership – that is, a situation where the same firm owns several newspapers and TV stations. The European Union has also expressed concern about the dominant position of very large media companies. Yet Murdoch's power is not easily contained, given its global spread. He is weighty enough to influence governments, but it is in the nature of the telecommunications business that it is everywhere and nowhere. Murdoch's power base is very large, but also elusive.

In a speech given in October 1994, Murdoch took on those who see his media empire as a threat to democracy and freedom of debate. 'Because capitalists are always trying to stab each other in the back,' Murdoch argued, 'free markets do not lead to monopolies. Essentially, monopolies can only exist when governments support them.' He quoted George Orwell, who wrote in one of his novels, 'Whenever you see a streetmarket you know that there's hope for England yet.' In Murdoch's words,

> That's a moment of true artistic insight – albeit unsupported (as sometimes happens with artists) with any rational or scientific follow-through. The freedom, the unforced exchange of the street market, its pragmatic acceptance of human self-interest and its transformation of self-interest into something mutually, peacefully beneficial – it does mean there's hope for England. And, indeed, for all of us in the Western World.

'We at News Corporation', Murdoch went on to say, 'are enlightened.' He discovered that in India, to where Star television is beamed, thousands of private operators had invested in satellite dishes and were selling Star programming illegally. Well, what we should do, Murdoch argued, is applaud! News Corporation, he concluded, looks forward to 'a long partnership with these splendid entrepreneurs' (Murdoch 1994).

Murdoch was for a while the head of the largest media organization the world has known. In 1995, however, he was overtaken. In that year a merger was announced between the Disney Company and ABC, the American television network. The merger created a corporation larger than Murdoch's, headed by the chairman of Disney, Michael Eisner. With interests in film-making plus a host of other enterprises, Disney was already a corporation of global spread before the merger. Eisner will have unprecedented power to shape the cultural tastes of the world's population, since Disney films and other media products penetrate almost everywhere.

The new company had revenues in 1995 of 16.5 billion US dollars, compared to the 8 billion dollars of Murdoch's News Corporation. Eisner made it clear that he wants to compete with Murdoch in the rapidly expanding markets of Asia. Murdoch's response to the merger was, 'They are twice as big as me now.' Then he added: 'A bigger target.' The early years of the car age were dominated by Ford and General Motors. It looks as though Murdoch and Eisner are set to dominate the early phases of the age of 'infotainment' (Leadbetter and Helmore 1995).

Silvio Berlusconi

TV was deregulated in Italy in 1976, resulting in the setting up of over six hundred different channels. These small companies, however, were soon mostly taken over by Mondadore, a large television corporation owned by Silvio Berlusconi. Today Berlusconi's chain has about 40 per cent of the Italian television audience; RAI, the state-owned broadcasting company, has about the same, with the rest going to the remaining smaller stations. Berlusconi also set up Channel 5 in France.

In Italy, Silvio Berlusconi used his media empire to enter politics in a direct way. He led his rightist party Forza Italia to victory in the national elections in 1994 and became Italian premier. His reign, however, was short. After losing power, he faced a series of corruption charges, to do with bribing other party leaders and using his TV stations to assist his bid for power.

CNN

Ted Turner is the founder of CNN, a continuous news channel which now reaches many countries in the world. CNN was started on a relatively small budget, and initially surprised other media operators by its success. According to Turner, CNN was the first to build on intensifying globalization. Turner recognized that very large numbers of people across the world speak English, or are learning it. They are interested in seeing English-language news programmes; and so are the many English-speaking tourists and business people who populate up-market hotels across the world.

Turner says: 'We are pioneers; and our philosophy has been and continues to be that we always want to come in where we're wanted, and we never try to force our way or force anybody in any way, shape or form' (Turner 1994, p. 39).

CNN has six offices in Asia and is expanding rapidly there, operating its programmes through four satellites.

THE ISSUE OF MEDIA REGULATION

The rise and influence of the media entrepreneurs and the large media companies worries many. For these corporations are in the business not just of selling goods but of influencing opinions. The proprietors of such corporations, like Murdoch or Berlusconi, make no secret of their rightist political views, which inevitably are a cause of concern to political parties and other groups holding different political positions.

Murdoch's view that only governments create monopolies has a certain element of truth in it. Murdoch is not a monopoly supplier, and has had to take massive financial risks – and losses – to get to the position he now holds. He faces competition not only from the other media giants, such as that headed by Eisner, but from a host of other contenders. Yet the idea that market competition prevents large firms from dominating industries is questionable, to say the least.

Recognizing this, all countries have provisions that seek to control media ownership. But how tight should these be? And given the global character of media enterprises, can national governments in any case have much hope of controlling them?

The issue of **media regulation** is more complex than might appear at first sight. It seems obvious that it is in the public interest that there should be a diversity of media organizations, since this is likely to ensure that many different groups and political perspectives can be listened to. Yet placing limits on who can own what, and what forms of media technology they can use, might affect the economic prosperity of the media sector. A country which is too restrictive might find itself left behind. The media industries are one of the fastest-growing sectors of the modern economy; the audiovisual industry alone is expected to create 2 million new jobs in the next ten years.

Critics of media concentration say that the large media companies wield excessive power. Businesses, on the other hand, argue that if they are subject to regulation they cannot make effective commercial decisions and will lose out in global competition. Moreover, they ask, who is to do the regulating? Who is to regulate the regulators?

There has in fact been very little research done on how far media ownership correlates with media content (Purnell and Collins 1995). The question was already difficult to study given the diversity of forms of media which existed up to the 1970s. It is even more difficult to examine with the proliferating of new interactive media – for example, video on demand.

Attempts which have been made to clarify the issue of regulation have tended to founder. The countries of the European Union, for example, have a tangled morass of different provisions for media regulation. At a conference on mass media policy in 1991, the Council of Europe tried to reach conclusions after discussing media regulation for several years. No agreed conclusions were reached.

One guiding thread of media regulation policy might be the recognition that market dominance by two or three large media companies simultaneously threatens both proper economic competition, and democracy – since the media owners are unelected. Existing anti-monopoly legislation can be brought into play here, although it differs widely across Europe and other industrial countries. The EU, for instance, recently blocked a joint cable and pay-television venture between Deutsche Telekom, Bertelsmann and the Kirch Group.

Competitiveness means pluralism, or should do – and presumably pluralism is good for democracy. Yet is pluralism enough? Many point to the US in arguing that having a plurality of media channels does not guarantee quality and accuracy of content. In a study of US television, for example, Jay Blumler found it 'inimical to broadcasting range – of programme form, of sorts of quality favoured, of viewer effect and experience stimulated' (Blumler 1986, p. 141).

Some see the maintenance of a strong public broadcasting sector as of key importance in blocking the dominance of the large media companies. Yet public broadcasting systems, which in Britain means the BBC, create their own problems. In most countries they used themselves to be a monopoly and in many countries were effectively used as a means of government propaganda. The question of who is to regulate the regulators comes up here with particular force.

One issue which complicates the question of media regulation is the very rapid rate of technological change. The media are constantly being transformed by technical innovations. The most important among these

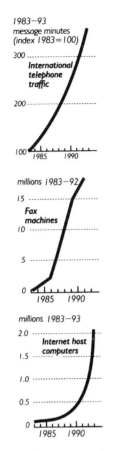

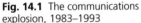

Fig. 14.1 The communications explosion, 1983–1993

Source: Commission on Global Governance, *Our Global Neighbourhood*, Oxford University Press 1995, p. 174.

at the moment concern the impact of multimedia and the Internet, which we consider in the concluding sections of the chapter.

MULTIMEDIA

Although we have concentrated so far on newspapers, television and other parts of the 'culture industry', we should not think of the media of communication only in those terms. Particularly as influenced by the computer, the media are affecting what we do in many other areas as well. New communications technologies, for example, stand behind profound changes in the world's money systems and stock markets. Money is no longer gold, or the cash in your pocket. More and more, money has become electronic, stored in computers in the world's banks. The value of whatever cash you do happen to have in your pocket is determined by the activities of traders on money markets. Such markets have been created only over the past ten to fifteen years or so: they are the product of a marriage between computers and communication satellite technology. 'Technology', it has been said, 'is rapidly turning the stock exchange into a seamless global market, open 24 hours a day' (Gibbons 1990, p. 111).

Four technological trends have contributed to these developments: the constant improvement in the capabilities of computers, together with declining costs; digitization of data, making possible the integration of computer and telecommunications technologies; satellite communications development; fibre optics, which allows many different messages to travel down a single small cable. The dramatic communications explosion of recent years (see figure 14.1) shows no signs of slowing down.

In his book *Being Digital* (1995), the founder of the media laboratory at the Massachusetts Institute of Technology, Nicholas Negroponte, analyses the profound importance of digital data in current communications technologies. Any piece of information, including pictures, moving images and sounds, can be translated into 'bits'. A bit is either a 1 or 0. For instance, the digital representation of 1, 2, 3, 4, 5, is 1, 10, 11, 100, 101 etc. Digitization – and speed – are at the origin of the development of **multimedia**: what used to be different media needing different technologies (such as visuals and sound) can now be *combined* on a single medium (CD-ROM/computer etc.). The speed of computers doubles every eighteen months and the technology has now reached the stage where a video tape can be translated into a picture on a personal computer screen, and back again.

Negroponte predicts that the personal computer (PC) will be the multimedia point of reference for the future. Current computers already have a range of multimedia capabilities. But these will become dramatically expanded. The PC will also be a TV set and an 'electronic gateway' for cable, telephone and satellite. In the future there will be no separate TV industry. Digitization also permits the development of

interactive media, allowing individuals actively to participate in, or structure, what they see or hear.

The **information superhighway** was much discussed in the mid-1990s. The term was repeatedly invoked by the Vice-President of the US, Al Gore. The superhighway is more a vision of the future than a description of the present. It envisages a situation in which most or all households will be connected via fibre optic cable. The electronic gateway of which Negroponte speaks will open into every home. At the moment four separate technologies have separate electronic paths into the home: telephone, terrestrial broadcast, cable and satellite. (Of course, not everyone has all of these.) In future, all will travel down the same cable and have as their outlet a single computer/television.

'The information superhighway' may not be the most appropriate term to refer to the implications of the digital revolution. It suggests a road map, whereas the new interactive technologies annihilate distance and make it irrelevant. The term implies order, whereas the impact of the new technologies may very well be chaotic and disruptive.

THE INTERNET

For the past few years, it has been observed, the titans of media and communications have waged a war for the digital future:

> With great fanfare, telephone and cable TV companies have launched dozens of trials to demonstrate their vision of speedy electronic networks, connecting homes to a boundless trove of information, communication, education and fun. Shambling towards their distant goal of a wired world, they have been too busy to notice the unruly bunch of computer hackers,

engineers and students scurrying about at their feet. They should have paid more attention. For while the giants have just been talking about an information superhighway, the ants have actually been building one: the Internet. ('The accidental superhighway', *The Economist*, 1st July 1995)

'I can't make my mind up – another pint or go home and surf the Internet'

'We should bid farewell to the PC, farewell to the floppy disks and file folders,' says Negroponte – and so say many others too. This seems to be the era of the PC, but in fact the reign of the PC is almost over. Larry Ellison, the chief executive of Oracle, a leading database company, has said that the PC is 'a ridiculous device' (quoted in Kelly 1995, p. 105). Most people who use one employ only a fraction of its computing power, and it is a device which separates individuals from one another. The future, they say, lies not with the individual computer but with a global system of interconnected computers – and this is exactly what

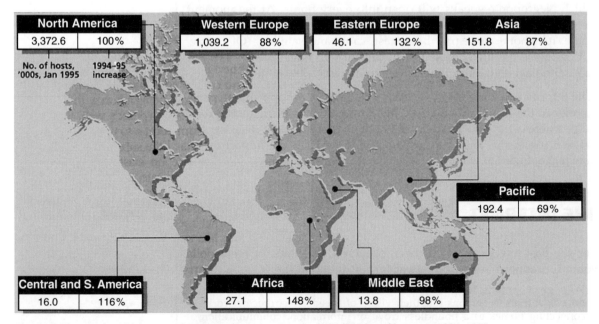

North America		Western Europe		Eastern Europe		Asia	
3,372.6	100%	1,039.2	88%	46.1	132%	151.8	87%

No. of hosts, '000s, Jan 1995 — 1994–95 increase

Pacific: 192.4 | 69%

Central and S. America: 16.0 | 116%

Africa: 27.1 | 148%

Middle East: 13.8 | 98%

Fig. 14.2 The wired world: hosts on the Internet by region, January 1995 (000s), and increases 1994–1995

Sources: Internet Society; from *The Economist*, 1 July 1995, p. 5.

the **Internet** is. The new slogan is: 'The network is the computer.' In other words, the PC becomes a terminal for events happening elsewhere – events happening on a network stretching across the planet, a network that is not owned by any individual or company (see figure 14.2).

Bill Gates, the founder of Microsoft, now one the world's biggest corporations, anticipated that this development would happen – and that realization allowed him to make his future. Even the leading visionaries in the computer world, until recently, thought that the future of the industry would be with hardware – the individual computer. Gates realized that it would be with the software which creates the computer's different functions. Yet not even Gates has any control over the Internet, which his innovations have helped to bring into being.

The Internet has come about in a spontaneous way. It is the product of an undivided world – a world after the fall of the Berlin Wall. Yet its first origins were precisely in the Cold War period which preceded 1989. The Net had its beginnings in the Pentagon, the headquarters of the American military. It was established in 1969 and was first of all named the ARPA net, after the Pentagon's Advanced Research Projects Agency. The aim was limited. The ARPA sought to allow scientists working on military contracts in different parts of America to pool their resources and to share the expensive equipment they were using. Almost as an afterthought, its originators thought up a way of sending messages too – thus electronic mail, 'e-mail', was born. E-mail is a system of correspondence where messages are sent directly from one computer to another, or to many others. Hence there is no waiting period as when a normal letter is sent: the connection is immediate.

The Pentagon Internet consisted of five hundred computers until the early 1980s, all located in military laboratories and university computer science departments. Other people in universities then started catching on, and began using the system for their own purposes. The Internet by 1987 had expanded to include 28,000 host computers, at many different universities and research labs. Those making use of it introduced a variety of innovations, creating new software which made it possible for individuals to take part in discussions and make use of research data.

For several years, the Internet remained confined to universities. With the spread of home-based PCs, however, it began to move outside – and then entered a period of explosive growth. 'On-line' services, 'bulletin boards' – electronic discussion groups – and software libraries were put on to the Net by a bewildering variety of people, situated no longer just in North America, but all over the world. Corporations also got in on the act. In 1994 companies overtook universities as dominant users of the network.

The relation between the Internet and the proclaimed information superhighway is problematic. Some say, as the quote a few paragraphs back indicates, that the Internet is in fact the information superhighway. It simply arrived in a different way from that planned by most of the cable and telephone companies (and by governments). Others hold that some basic features are missing. The real superhighway, they say, will combine not only computers but all other communications services, from telephone to TV.

A major part of the Internet is the World Wide Web. Indeed, like a cuckoo in a nest, it threatens to take over its host. The Web is in effect a global multimedia library. It was invented by a software engineer at a Swiss physics lab in 1992; the software which popularized it across the world was written by an undergraduate at the University of Illinois.

'Joanne? Oh! I was hoping to get your answering machine.'
© 1996 Boris Drucker from The Cartoon Bank, Inc.

How many people are actually connected to the Internet is unknown. It is thought there are some 35 million people on line throughout the world. In terms of global population as a whole, the number is not large – but it is as big as a medium-size country. More important is its rate of expansion. It has been estimated that the Internet has grown at a rate of 200 per cent annually since 1985.

CONCLUSION

In a world of quite stunning technological change, no one can be sure what the future holds. What is certain is that developments in media technologies are at the very heart of such change. Many see the Internet as exemplifying the new global order emerging at the close of the twentieth century. Users of the Internet live in 'cyberspace'. **Cyberspace** means the space of interaction formed by the global network of computers which compose the Internet. In cyberspace, much as Baudrillard might say, we are no longer 'people', but messages on one another's screens. Outside of e-mail, where users identify themselves, no one on the Internet knows who anyone else really is, whether they are male or female, or where they are in the world. There is a famous cartoon about the Internet, which has a dog sitting in front of a computer. The caption reads: 'The great thing about the Internet is that no one knows you are a dog.'

We know what 'dog' spells backwards. There's another story told about new communications technologies too: 'A theologian asked the most powerful supercomputer, "Is there a God?" The computer said it lacked the processing power to know. It asked to be connected to all the other supercomputers in the world. Still, it was not enough power. So the computer was hooked up to all the mainframes in the world, and then all the minicomputers, and to all the personal computers. And eventually it was connected to all the computers in cars, microwaves, VCRs, digital watches and so on. The theologian asked for the final time, "Is there a God?" And the computer replied: "There is now!"' (Naisbitt 1995, p. 80).

The story encapsulates both some of the hopes and the fears which the Internet arouses. Will we lose our identities in cyberspace? Will computerized technology dominate us rather than the reverse? Will electronic media destroy all other forms of communications media, such as the book? The answer to each of these questions, fortunately, almost certainly is 'no'. People don't use video conferencing if they can get together with others in an ordinary way. Business executives have far more forms of electronic communication available to them than ever before. At the same time, the number of face-to-face business conferences has shot up.

As individuals, we don't control technological change, and the sheer pace of such change threatens to swamp our lives. Yet the arrival of the wired-up world, thus far at any rate, hasn't led to Big Brother: rather to the contrary, it has promoted decentralization and individualism. Finally, books and other 'pre-electronic' media look unlikely to disappear. Bulky as it is, this book is handier to use than a computerized version would be. Negroponte's *Being Digital* wasn't produced for the gadgets it describes, but written as a book. Even Bill Gates has found it necessary to write a book to describe the new high-tech world he anticipates.

In the meantime, the Internet spawns its own mundane problems. A recent headline in the *Guardian* newspaper announced, 'Net addicts lead sad virtual lives'. The article describes the lives of people who spend hours every day on the network. There is even a new support group for Internet addicts, called Caught in the Net. Cyberspace contacts can't substitute for interaction with flesh-and-blood people and aren't likely to.

SUMMARY

1 The mass media have come to play a fundamental role in modern society. The mass media are media of communication – newspapers, magazines, television, radio, cinema, videos, CDs and other forms – which reach mass audiences.

2 The newspapers were among the most important of early mass media. They continue to be significant, but other, newer media, particularly radio and television, have supplemented them.

3 The influence of the mass media on our lives is profound. The media not only provide entertainment, but provide and shape much of the information which we utilize in our daily lives.

4 In spite of many studies of television and violence, it is still not clear how far, and in what ways, the portrayal of violence on TV encourages aggressive behaviour in real life. Most of the research has underestimated how far viewers selectively interpret what they see, and the complex ways in which the 'fictional' and the 'real' interrelate.

5 Sociologists have given a good deal of attention to studying television news. A series of studies of TV news was carried out by a group of researchers working at Glasgow University – the Glasgow Media Group. Their work, which claimed that news reporting was slanted in certain specific ways, gave rise to a prolonged controversy, which still continues today.

6 The idea of genre is valuable in distinguishing different types of TV programme. Genre refers to understandings which programme makers and viewers share about 'what' is being watched. News, soap opera, game shows and thrillers are examples of different genres.

7 A range of different theories of media and popular culture have been developed. Innis and McLuhan argued that media influence society more in terms of how they communicate than what they communicate. In McLuhan's words, 'the medium is the message': TV, for example, influences people's behaviour and attitudes because it is so different in nature from other media, such as newspapers or books.

8 Other important theorists include Habermas, Baudrillard and Thompson. Habermas points to the role of the media in creating a 'public sphere' – a sphere of public opinion and public debate.

Baudrillard has been strongly influenced by McLuhan. He believes that new media, particularly television, actually change the 'reality' we experience.

Thompson argues that the mass media have created a new form of social interaction – 'mediated quasi-interaction' – which is more limited, narrow and one-way than everyday social interaction.

9 The sense today of inhabiting one world is in large part a result of the international scope of media of communication. A world information order – an international system of the production, distribution and consumption of informational goods – has come into being. Given the paramount position of the industrial countries in the world information order, many believe that the Third World countries are subject to a new form of media imperialism.

10 The media industries worldwide tend to be dominated by a small number of very large companies. Several of these are headed by celebrated media entrepreneurs, the most well-known of whom is Rupert Murdoch. Many critics worry about the concentration of media power in the hands of such powerful individuals, who they say are not accountable to democratic procedures.

11 Recent years have seen the emergence of multimedia, linked to the development of the Internet and the possible construction of an 'information superhighway'. 'Multimedia' refers to the combination on a single medium of what used to be different media needing different technologies, so that a CD-ROM, for example, can carry both visuals and sound and be played on a computer. Many claims have been made about the likely social effects of these developments, but it is still too early to judge how far these will be borne out.

FURTHER READING

Nick Abercrombie, *Television and Society* (Cambridge: Polity Press, 1996). An introduction to the role of television in contemporary society and the ways in which TV programmes are produced and consumed.

James W. Carey, *Communication as Culture: Essays on Media and Society* (London: Unwin Hyman, 1989). An interesting and accessible set of essays on the importance of communication and media in traditional and modern societies.

Richard Collins and **Cristina Murroni**, *New Media, New Policies* (Cambridge: Polity Press, 1996). An overview of new communications, media technologies and their regulation.

John Eldridge (ed.), *Getting the Message: News, Truth and Power* (London: Routledge, 1993). An updated series of discussions of the work of the Glasgow Media Group.

John Eldridge (ed.), *Glasgow Media Group Reader*, vol. 1 (London: Routledge, 1995). A useful analysis of news content, language and visuals.

John Fiske, *Understanding Popular Culture* (London: Unwin Hyman, 1990). An absorbing and provocative discussion of mass culture.

James Lull, *Media, Communication, Culture* (Cambridge: Polity Press, 1995). A useful survey of the cultural impact of mass communication.

Nicholas Negroponte, *Being Digital* (London: Hodder and Stoughton, 1995). An account of the impact of new information technology.

The Polity Reader in Cultural Theory (Cambridge: Polity Press, 1994).

John Thompson, *The Media and Modernity: A Social Theory of the Media* (Cambridge: Polity Press, 1995). A major new analysis of the role of the media in the rise of modern societies.

IMPORTANT TERMS

- public opinion
- genre
- global village
- public sphere
- hyperreality
- simulacrum
- face-to-face interaction
- mediated interaction
- mediated quasi-interaction
- symbolic power
- world information order
- media regulation
- multimedia
- information superhighway
- Internet
- cyberspace

EDUCATION

15

BASIC CONCEPTS

● *education* ● *cultural reproduction*

Imagine you are in the shoes – or the wooden clogs – of Jean-Paul Didion, a peasant boy growing up in a French farming community about two centuries ago. Jean-Paul is fourteen years old in 1750. He cannot read or write, but this is not uncommon; only a few of the adults in his village have the ability to decipher more than the odd word or two of written texts. There are some schools in nearby districts, run by monks and nuns, but these are completely removed from Jean-Paul's experience. He has never known anyone who attended school, save for the local priest. For the past eight or nine years, Jean-Paul has been spending most of his days helping with domestic tasks and working in the fields. The older he gets, the longer each day he is expected to share in the hard physical work involved in intensive tilling of his father's plot of land.

Jean-Paul is likely never to leave the area where he was born, and may spend almost his whole life within the village and surrounding fields, only occasionally travelling to other local villages and towns. He may have to wait until he is in his late fifties before inheriting his father's plot, then sharing control of it with his younger brothers. Jean-Paul is aware that he is 'French', that his country is ruled by a particular monarch, and that there is a wider world beyond even France itself. But he has only a vague awareness even of 'France' as a distinct political entity. There is no such thing as 'news' or any regular means by which information about events elsewhere reaches him. What he knows of the wider world comes from stories and tales he has heard from adults, including a few visiting travellers. Like others in his community, he learns about major events – like the death of the king – only days, weeks, or sometimes months after they have occurred.

Although in modern terms Jean-Paul is uneducated, he is far from ignorant. He has a sensitive and developed understanding of the family and children, having had to care for those younger than himself since he was very young. He is already highly knowledgeable about the land, methods of crop production and modes of preserving and storing food. His mastery of local customs and traditions is profound, and he can turn his hand to many tasks other than agricultural cultivation, such as weaving or basket-making.

Jean-Paul is an invention, but the description above represents the typical experience of a boy growing up in early modern Europe. Compare our situation today. In the industrialized countries, virtually everyone can read and write. We are all aware of being members of a particular society, and have at least some knowledge of its geographical position in the world and of its past history. Our lives are influenced at all ages beyond infancy by information we pick up through books, newspapers, magazines and television. We have all undergone a process of formal schooling. The printed word and electronic communication, combined with the formal teaching provided by schools and colleges, have become fundamental to our way of life.

In this chapter, we shall study how present-day education has developed, and analyse its social influence. We begin by looking at the development of schooling in the UK, analysing the different types of schools which exist and the political debates to which education has given rise. We shall then make some comparisons between schooling in Britain and other countries before moving on to higher education. Having described some of the main theoretical approaches to education, in subsequent sections of the chapter we shall consider issues of education and inequality.

THE DEVELOPMENT OF LITERACY AND SCHOOLING

The term 'school' has its origins in a Greek word meaning leisure or recreation. In preindustrial societies, schooling was available only to the few who had the time and money available to pursue it. Religious leaders or priests were often the only fully literate groups, using their knowledge to read and interpret sacred texts. For the vast majority of people, growing up meant learning by example the same social habits and work skills as their elders. As we have seen, children normally began assisting in domestic, farm and craft work at a very young age. Reading was not necessary or even useful in their daily lives.

Another reason why so few were able to read was that all texts had to be laboriously copied by hand, and so were scarce and expensive. Printing, an invention which came to Europe from China, altered that situation. The first printing press in the West was invented by Johann Gutenberg in 1454. Printing made texts and documents widely available. These included books and pamphlets, but also many kinds of routine materials essential to the running of an ever more complex society. Codes of law, for instance, were written down and widely diffused. Records, reports and the collection of routine data increasingly became part of government, economic enterprises and organizations in general. The increasing use of written materials in many different spheres of life led to higher levels of **literacy** (the ability to read and write at a basic level) than had ever previously been the case. EDUCATION in its modern form, involving the instruction of pupils within specially constructed school premises, gradually began to emerge. Yet until a century and a half ago, and even more recently, the children of the wealthy were frequently educated by private tutors. Most of the population continued to have no schooling whatsoever until the first few decades of the nineteenth century, when in the European countries and the United States systems of primary schools began to be constructed.

The process of industrialization and the expansion of cities served to increase demands for specialized schooling. People now work in many different occupations, and work skills can no longer be passed on directly from parents to children. The acquisition of knowledge becomes increasingly based on abstract learning (of subjects like maths, science, history, literature and so forth), rather than on the practical transmission of specific skills. In a modern society people have to be furnished with basic skills, such as reading, writing and calculating and a general knowledge of their physical, social and economic environment; and it is also important that they know how to learn, so that they are able to master new, sometimes very technical, forms of information.

ORIGINS AND DEVELOPMENT OF THE BRITISH SYSTEM

The modern **educational system** first took shape in most Western societies in the early part of the nineteenth century. Britain was much more reluctant than most other countries to establish an integrated national system. Education was backward in England and Wales, although more developed in Scotland. A Select Committee on Education declared in 1818 that 'England is behind all Continental rivals in education.' By the middle of the century, Holland, Switzerland and the German states had achieved more or less universal enrolment in elementary schools, but England and Wales fell far short of such a target.

Between 1870 (when compulsory education was first established in Britain) and World War Two, successive governments increased expenditure on education. The school-leaving age rose from ten to fourteen, and more and more schools were built, but education was not really considered to be a major area for government intervention (Chapman 1986). Most schools were run by private or church authorities under the supervision of local government boards. World War Two changed this attitude. Recruits to the armed forces were given ability and learning tests; the results startled the authorities by showing a low level of educational skills. Concerned about prospects for postwar recovery, the government began to rethink the existing educational system.

Up to 1944, the vast majority of British children attended a single free school, the *elementary* school, until the age of fourteen. *Secondary* schools existed alongside the elementary system, but parents had to pay. This system divided children along clear lines of social class – children from poorer backgrounds were almost all confined to elementary schooling. Less than 2 per cent of the population attended university. The Education Act of 1944 initiated several major changes, including free secondary education for all; the raising of the school-leaving age to fifteen; and a commitment to equality of opportunity in education. Education became a major responsibility of elected local government.

As a result of the Act, the majority of local education authorities adopted academic selection as a means of providing secondary education tailored to children's needs. Academic selection at age eleven – the age of transition from primary to secondary school – was supposed to sort out the more able from duller children, regardless of social background. For most pupils, results in the 'eleven-plus' examination determined whether they went on to *grammar schools* (for the more 'academic' children) or to *secondary modern schools* (for those presumed to be more suited to vocational learning). A minority of children also went either to technical schools or to special schools. The option of staying on at school until seventeen was available for those who wanted to continue their education.

By the 1960s – partly as a result of sociological research – it had become clear that the results of the eleven-plus had not come up to expectations. The Crowther Report of 1959 showed that only 12 per cent of pupils continued in school until the age of seventeen, and early leaving was shown to be more closely related to class background than to academic performance. The Labour government which was returned to power in 1964 was committed to establishing *comprehensive schools*, abolishing the division between grammar and secondary modern, and thus mixing together children of diverse class backgrounds. However, there was confusion over what the comprehensive school should offer: 'grammar schools for all' or a completely new type of education. No one solution was found to the problem, and different schools and regions developed their own approaches. Some local authorities resisted the change, and in a few areas grammar schools still exist.

Since the early 1970s state education has been strongly affected by the jolting transition from a situation in which labour power was in short supply, and there were demands on the schools to provide the skills the economy needed, to one in which there is too much – a time of rising unemployment and reduced government revenue. Educational expansion, which had characterized the whole of the postwar period, was suddenly replaced by contraction and attempts at the reduction of government expenditure. From the mid-1970s to the early 1990s, state spending on education dropped from 6.3 per cent of public expenditure as a whole to just over 5 per cent.

An Education Act passed in 1988 introduced various significant reforms – some of which have met with great opposition. In conjunction with its policies in other spheres, the Conservative government sought to introduce an element of market competition into education. School heads were given greater financial responsibilities, and schools were permitted to 'opt out' from the control of local education authorities to become 'independent state schools'. A national curriculum was established which specifies a universal framework of teaching for the state sector (Johnson 1991).

In 1992 a new funding agency was established which was gradually to take over the provision of places in schools that opted out. In the White Paper detailing the tasks of the agency, the government said that it hoped 'that over time all schools will have become grant-maintained' – in other words, will have opted out. By 1995, however, only 1,000 schools had done so out of a total population of 23,000 state schools.

The fee-paying schools

The public schools in Britain are an oddity in more ways than one. They are not public at all but, on the contrary, private, fee-paying institutions. The degree of independence they have from the rest of the education system and the key role they play in the society at large marks them out from the systems of other countries. The public schools are nominally subject to state supervision, but in fact few major pieces of educational legislation have affected them. They were left untouched by the 1944 Act, as they were by the setting up of the comprehensive schools; and the large majority stayed single-sex schools until recently.

There are some private schools, often linked to religious dominations, in all Western societies, but in no other society are private schools either so exclusive or so important as in the UK. It has been observed that for well over a century state education has been run by people who have little interest in it and would not dream of sending their children to its schools.

There are about 2,300 fee-paying schools in England, educating some 7 per cent of the population. They include a diversity of different organizations, from prestigious establishments such as Eton, Rugby or Charterhouse, through to so-called minor public schools whose names would be unknown to most people. Some are boarding schools in isolated towns, while others, like Westminster, are set in the centre of busy cities. There are also schools linked to religious denominations, such as the Catholic school Ampleforth.

As a result of the 1988 Education Reform Act, all state schools have to follow a standard national curriculum, which involves testing pupils at seven, eleven, fourteen and sixteen. The introduction of the national curriculum was strongly resisted by some groups in the teaching profession, who were opposed to such standardized testing and who felt the curriculum to be unnecessarily confining. Teachers took strike action against the tests in the summer of 1993.

Representatives from the fee-paying schools were involved in the creation of the national curriculum. Yet these schools do not have to follow it. The fee-paying schools can teach whatever they wish and have no obligation to test children. Most have opted to follow the national curriculum, but some have simply ignored it.

The term 'public school' is limited by some educationalists to a group of the major fee-paying schools. These are schools which are members of the Headmasters' Conference (HMC), originally formed in 1871. Initially there were only fifty schools in the Conference. The number has now expanded to 233. Schools like those listed above – Eton, Rugby and the rest – are members.

Individuals who attended HMC schools dominate the higher positions in British society. A study by Ivan Reid and others, for example, published in 1991, showed that 84 per cent of judges, 70 per cent of bank directors and 49 per cent of top civil servants had attended HMC schools (Reid et al. 1991).

John Major in 1990 campaigned to become leader of the Conservative Party stating his aspiration to create a 'classless society'. On the face of things, Major himself appeared to conform to such an ideal in his own career. He left school at sixteen and obtained few educational qualifications. Yet his first cabinet showed that the classless society was a long way off (Walford 1993). Nineteen of the twenty-two members of the cabinet were from fee-paying schools (that cabinet did not include even one woman). Only one member of the cabinet, moreover, had his children educated in state secondary schools (see the box).

A CONSERVATIVE CABINET'S CHOICE OF SCHOOLS FOR THEIR CHILDREN

Minister	Children	Schools attended
John Major	2	State primary, private secondary
Kenneth Clarke	2	State primary, private secondary
Norman Lamont	2	Private
Douglas Hurd*	3*	Private
Tom King	2	Private
Kenneth Baker	2	Private
John Gummer	4	Two state primary, one private secondary, one fee-paying choir school
Tony Newton	2	State
Michael Howard	2	Private
John MacGregor	3	Private
Michael Heseltine	3	Private
Lord Mackay	1	Private
Peter Brooke	3	Private
David Hunt	4	Private
Ian Lang	2	Private
Peter Lilley	0	
David Mellor	2	Private
Chris Patten	3	State primary/one private
Malcolm Rifkind	2	Private
John Wakeham	3	Two at private
William Waldegrave	4	Private
David Waddington	5	Private

*From first marriage; two young children from second marriage not included.
Source: Guardian, 19 Feb. 1992.

Education and politics

Education has long been a political battleground and continues to be so in the 1990s. A protracted debate has centred on the impact of comprehensive schooling – on educational standards and on inequalities in the wider society. Originally comprehensive education attracted support from both ends of the political spectrum. It was the Labour government, as mentioned, which set the comprehensive system into motion, however, and therefore support for comprehensive education has tended to be associated much more with the political left than with the right. The architects of comprehensive education believed that the new schools would provide for greater equality of opportunity than was possible in selective education. They did not give much thought to the curriculum as such, being more concerned with equality of access.

When Mrs Thatcher became Prime Minister, the conservatives become more vocal in their criticisms of comprehensive schooling. They believed that grammar schools should not have been allowed more or less to disappear as happened with the introduction of the comprehensive system. They determined to create a greater variety of schools at the secondary level, with a correspondingly greater scope for parents to choose the nature of their children's education.

In the late 1980s, Mrs Thatcher started speaking of creating a 'revolution' in the running of schools. Such a revolution was due to dismantle the giant comprehensive schools and reduce the power of the local education authorities who were responsible for running them. In addition to establishing the national curriculum, the 1988 Education Act introduced a new system of school management, called the 'local management of schools'. The devolution of the administration of schools was to balance the inevitable centralization involved in the national curriculum. A new group of City Technology Colleges (CTCs) and grant-maintained schools was also to be established.

The CTC programme was not successful, and was ended in 1993 with only fifteen colleges in existence. In 1992 a new White Paper was published to speed up the process of giving independence to schools. The local education authorities are to have a markedly reduced role. Grant-maintained schools – those which opt out from local authority control – are now managed by a new governmental body, the Funding Agency for Schools.

The comprehensive system and its critics

Critics of the comprehensive system believe that it has failed in two ways. According to such critics, comprehensive schools have not promoted greater equality of opportunity, but rather the reverse. Bright children from poorer backgrounds could prosper in the days of the eleven-plus; in comprehensive schools, they are held back. Equally important, the critics say, the comprehensive schools only provide a poor standard of education, because excellence goes unrewarded and specialization is discouraged.

Before the introduction of the comprehensive school system, 20 per cent of pupils passed the eleven-plus and went on to grammar school. With the reform, the idea was to create schools with a mixture of able and less able children. Comprehensive schools would also have 20 per cent of pupils in the upper range of ability.

Things have not turned out like that. As measured by exam results, only 27 per cent of comprehensives have 20 per cent or more pupils in the upper ability range. On the other hand, 18 per cent have more than 20 per cent of children in that range. These schools in effect, if not in name, have become grammar schools. Less successful schools in the system have become more or less equivalent to the old secondary moderns. In 38 per cent of schools the proportion of pupils in the top ability range is 10 per cent or less, while in 16 per cent of schools the proportion is under 5 per cent.

The selection processes which have produced this situation operate in several ways. In the first place, the eleven-plus never disappeared completely. There are ninety-five remaining grammar schools, which still use the test; and grammar schools are still usual in Northern Ireland. Within the comprehensive system, selection processes work informally, but they are no less powerful for all that. Schools have to give priority to children within their area. Parents can thus 'buy' their children into the schools with the best results by ensuring that they have the right address.

SEVEN WAYS TO MAKE SURE YOUR CHILDREN GET INTO A 'GOOD SCHOOL'

1 Pay.

2 Move to an area which still has the 11-plus and spend a fortune on coaching.

3 Check with estate agents, pay a graphic mapper to get the right address. Mortgage yourself to the eyeballs to pay for it. Alternatively lie about your address.

4 Ensure your kids have no special needs.

5 Get to know the governors of a grant-maintained school who can admit your child under 'governors' provisions'.

6 Convert to Church of England/Catholicism/Judaism.

7 Offer to make substantial donations to school coffers.

Source: Observer, 7 Jan. 1996.

A substantial percentage of schools which have opted out of local authority control take personal and medical factors into account in deciding about entry. One such factor, for example, might be whether or not a child is considered 'difficult'. According to a recent study, over 50 per cent of such schools apply selective criteria in such a way (Hugill 1996). Proposals introduced by the conservatives in 1996 will allow all state schools to select up to 15 per cent of their pupils, either by ability or a specialist subject such as science or music. They will be able to select a higher proportion with special permission from the government.

Opting out was supposed to increase parental choice by creating diversity in the school system. But the unintended consequence might be to reduce such choice: an increasing number of children are being denied a place at their first choice of school.

The Labour Party is committed to defending the comprehensive system, but under the leadership of Tony Blair seems unlikely to go back on all of the reforms which the Tories introduced. Blair accepts that standards of British schooling, as measured by international comparisons, are not high and that further educational reform is a necessary priority. He also recognizes that diversity in education is a desirable goal. His problem is how to reconcile that diversity with Labour's commitment to reduce educational inequalities. That problem is a very large one indeed. Fee-paying schools and grant-maintained schools help provide diversity; yet they cater mainly to children from more privileged backgrounds and thus perpetuate existing inequalities.

Let us move on at this point to look briefly at schooling in another country, the US, before considering systems of higher education.

COMPARISONS OF SCHOOL SYSTEMS

Schooling in the United States has its origins in the disciplining of children. The basis of this seventeenth-century development was the Puritan belief that all children should obey their parents without question, a belief that the original American colonies had in fact made part of their legal statutes. A legal provision of 1642 promised severe sanctions against the 'great neglect of many parents and masters in training up their children in learning and labor'. Because this measure was ineffectual, however, the Puritan authorities commanded every town to provide schooling, beginning in 1647 in Massachusetts and Connecticut.

It was almost two centuries before education became a common experience for the by then much-expanded American population. All states provided free elementary schooling by the 1850s, although at first attendance was not compulsory and large numbers of the population still went without any formal schooling at all. Compulsory education was introduced in most states towards the end of the nineteenth century, a period of extremely rapid expansion in the building of schools and colleges. There were only 160 public high schools in the country in 1870, but by 1900 there were in excess of 6,000.

The diverse cultural make-up of America at the turn of the century presented a particular challenge to the school system. By that time, immigrants from Europe and elsewhere, with many different native languages and all with great hopes for the future, had settled in the United States. School then became a major transmission point in linguistically and to some extent culturally anglicizing the immigrants. In addition, the schools taught American ideals of equality of opportunity, thus encouraging the immigrants to set about making a new life. The notion that everyone is born equal led to the development of mass public education in the United States well before comparable systems were set up in other countries. Education was seen as an avenue of mobility in a society in which the aristocratic ideal – that some people are born with superior rights to others – had never held sway. And along with the idea of equality, other American values and beliefs were, and continue to be, taught more or less explicitly.

Primary and secondary education

There are wide differences between countries, both in the number of years children are expected to be in school (see table 15.1), and in ways of organizing educational systems. Some systems are highly centralized; in France, for example, all students follow nationally determined curricula and sit for exactly the same national examinations. In contrast, the American system is much more fragmentary. Individual states provide substantial funding for schools, contributing about 40 per cent of the necessary finance, with the federal government providing another 40 per cent. The rest comes from taxation revenue in local school districts. As a result, schools are administered by local school

Table 15.1	Countries with the highest mean years of schooling, 1992					
1	United States	12.4	15	Japan	10.8
2	Canada	12.2	16	New Zealand	10.7
3	Norway	12.1	17	Luxembourg	10.5
4	Australia	12.0	18	Israel	10.2
	France	12.0	19	Hungary	9.8
6	United Kingdom	11.7	20	Barbados	9.4
7	Germany	11.6	21	South Korea	9.3
	Switzerland	11.6	22	Argentina	9.2
9	Austria	11.4		Ex-Czechoslovakia	9.2
	Sweden	11.4		Iceland	9.2
	Belgium	11.2	25	Estonia	9.0
12	Netherlands	11.1		Latvia	9.0
13	Denmark	11.0		Lithuania	9.0
14	Finland	10.9		Russia	9.0

Source: The Economist, Pocket World in Figures, Profile Books Ltd, 1996.

boards, elected by community vote, which have the power to appoint teachers and other school officials and select (and occasionally ban) texts and other reading or viewing materials.

Such community control of schooling has mixed consequences. There are clear benefits in that schools are kept responsive to the needs and interests of the areas they serve. On the other hand, the system also leads to great differences in school funding, depending on how wealthy a given community is. Class size, available facilities and the capability to attract well-qualified teachers all vary enormously between different school districts.

HIGHER EDUCATION

International comparisons

There are also large differences between societies in the organization of **higher education** (education after school, usually at university or college). In some countries, all universities and colleges are public agencies, receiving their funding directly from government sources. Higher education in France, for instance, is organized nationally, with centralized control being almost as marked as in primary and secondary education. All course structures have to be validated by a national regulatory body responsible to the Minister of Higher Education. Two types of degree can be gained, one awarded by the individual university, the other by the state. National degrees are generally regarded as more prestigious and valuable than those of specific universities, since they are supposed to conform to guaranteed uniform standards. A certain range of occupations in government are only open to the holders of national degrees, which are also favoured by most industrial employers. Virtually all teachers in schools, colleges and universities in France are themselves state employees. Rates of pay and the broad framework of teaching duties are fixed centrally.

The United States is distinctive among developed countries in terms of the high proportion of colleges and universities which are in the private sector. Private organizations make up 54 per cent of organizations of higher education in the United States. These include some of the most prestigious universities, such as Harvard, Princeton and Yale. The distinction between *public* and *private* in American higher education, however, is not as clear-cut as is the case in other countries. Students at private universities are eligible for public grants and loans, and these universities receive public research funding. Public universities often possess substantial endowments, and may be given donations by private firms. They also often obtain research grants from private industrial sources.

The system in Britain

The British system of higher education is considerably more decentralized than that of France, but more unitary than that of the US. Universities and colleges are government-financed, and teachers at all levels of the educational system have their salaries determined according to national wage scales. Yet there is considerable diversity in the organization of institutions and curricula.

There were twenty-one universities in Britain in the immediate prewar period. Most of the universities at this time were very small by today's standards. In 1937, the total number of undergraduates in British universities was only slightly more than the number of full-time university academic staff in 1981 (Carswell 1985). Graduate work was only weakly developed, even in Cambridge or Oxford, the oldest universities. In 1937, 75 per cent of all the graduate students in the country were registered at the University of London.

Between 1945 and 1970, the higher education system in Britain grew to be four times as large. The older universities were expanded, and new, 'red-brick' or concrete universities built (such as Sussex, Kent, Stirling and York). A *binary* system was set up with the creation of polytechnics. This second layer of higher education became relatively large, comprising some four hundred colleges offering a wide range of courses. The polytechnics concentrated more on vocational courses than the universities. The Council for National Academic Awards was created as a validating body to ensure their degrees were of a uniform standard.

Today, British institutions of higher education have what has sometimes been called a 'standard coinage'. This means that a degree from Leicester or Leeds, at least in theory, is the same standard as one from Cambridge, Oxford or London. Yet Oxford and Cambridge are noted for a highly selective intake, about half of which comes from fee-paying schools. An Oxford or Cambridge degree confers greater chances of reaching a high economic position than a qualification from most other universities.

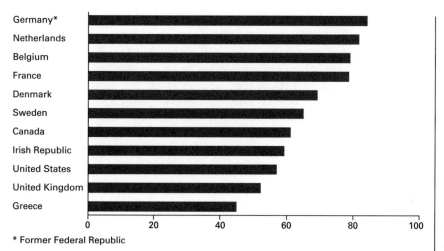

Fig. 15.1 Percentage of eighteen-year-olds in education and training (full time or part time), international comparison, 1992

Source: OECD. From *Social Trends*, 1996, p. 75.

* Former Federal Republic

In spite of postwar expansion, the proportion of the British population in universities, and in higher and further education and training more generally, is below that of other Western countries (see figure 15.1). In 1970 only 17 per cent of eighteen-year-olds entered university. The proportion of students in universities rose considerably in the late 1980s and early 1990s, to 25 per cent of the youth population. However, the rise is partly accounted for by the fact that polytechnics became relabelled universities.

While the universities have been expanding, they have had to do so while coping with steady-state, or even reduced, funding from government. The result is a crisis in funding in higher education. A special committee, led by Rod Dearing, was set up to investigate the future of universities, and of higher education more generally. As of the mid 1990's, universities and colleges are struggling to cope, and a few are on the verge of bankruptcy.

We now move on to discuss gender, ethnicity and education, going on from there to analyse theories of schooling.

GENDER AND THE EDUCATION SYSTEM

The formal curriculum in schools, apart from participation in games, no longer distinguishes in any systematic way between boys and girls. However, there are various other 'points of entry' for the development of gender differences in education. These include teacher expectations, school rituals and other aspects of a hidden curriculum. Regulations which compel girls to wear dresses or skirts in school form one of the most obvious ways in which gender typing occurs. The consequences go beyond mere appearance. As a result of the clothes she wears, a girl lacks the freedom to sit casually, to join in rough and tumble games, or sometimes to run as fast as she is able. School reading texts also help to perpetuate gender images. Although this again is changing, story books in primary schools often portray boys as showing initiative and independence, while girls, if they appear at all, are more passive and watch their brothers. Stories written especially for girls often have an element of adventure in them, but this usually takes the form of intrigues or mysteries in a domestic or school setting. Boys' adventure stories are more wide-ranging, having heroes who travel off to distant places or are sturdily independent in other ways (Statham 1986).

For many years, girls on average did better than boys in terms of school results until the middle years of secondary education. They then fell behind: boys did better at O- and A-Level, and at university. Recently, however, these trends have started to alter. Girls in British schools have started to forge ahead of boys. In 1995 all-girls schools took the top five places, and fourteen out of the top twenty places, in a league table of schools. At the end of the 1970s about the same number of boys and girls got five or more passes at O-Level. In the intervening years a gap has developed: girls are doing better than boys at O-Level and at A-Level.

Similar findings have been reported from America. Boys there are twice as likely to be in special education and twice as likely to drop out of high school altogether. This difference now carries over to higher education. Young women in the US are more likely than young men to go to university, still more likely to graduate, and even more likely to go on to do a postgraduate degree ('Career opportunities', *The Economist*, 8 July 1995).

Some suggest that the change reflects a wider transformation in the position of men and women in society. The dominance of men has been challenged in many areas and many writers now speak of a 'changed masculinity'. More men are unemployed than women, and the old male role of breadwinner has to some degree broken down. Boys might be less sure what to aim for in life than they used to be (see chapter 8, pp. 195–6).

Gender and higher education

Women's organizations in Britain and elsewhere have often attacked sex discrimination in school and higher education. Women are still heavily under-represented among the teaching staff in colleges and universities. There are currently only some 120 women professors in Britain, representing 4 per cent of the total. Women made up 31 per cent of contract researchers, but no more than 7 per cent of tenured staff in 1988 (Bogdanor 1990). The proportion of full-time lecturers in university who are women has been rising, but is still low at 17 per cent. In their book *Storming the Tower* (1990) Suzanne Lie and Virginia O'Leary analyse comparative statistics on the position of women in higher education from around the world, including the UK, the United States, Germany, Norway, India and Israel. In all the countries studied, the proportion of women students has increased steadily over the postwar period. In the US, Israel and Norway, women make up roughly half of all undergraduates. So far as academic positions go, however, the picture is much more dismal. Only a small percentage of university teachers in these countries are women, and they are everywhere disproportionately in the lower grades and in non-tenured jobs.

A comparative investigation of women academics in Britain and the United States disclosed that in both countries women on average have higher teaching loads than male colleagues, and are less often involved in postgraduate teaching. Heavy teaching loads are likely to cut into time available for research and publication; and levels of both publication and postgraduate supervision are important criteria for promotion.

EDUCATION AND ETHNICITY

Sociologists have carried out a good deal of research into the educational fortunes of ethnic minorities in Britain. Governments have also sponsored a series of investigations, including *Education for All*, the report of the Swann Committee. The Swann Report found significant differences in average levels of educational success between groups from different ethnic backgrounds. Children from West Indian families tended to fare worst in school, as measured by formal academic attainments. They had improved from ten years earlier, however. Asian children were equal to white children, in spite of the fact that on average the families from which they came were economically worse off than white families (Swann Committee 1985).

Subsequent research indicates that the picture has shifted, however. Trevor Jones (1993) carried out research which indicated that children from all minority group backgrounds were more likely to continue on in full-time education from sixteen to nineteen than were whites. Only 37 per cent of whites stayed on in education in 1988–90, compared to 43 per cent from West Indian backgrounds, 50 per cent of South Asians and 77 per cent of Chinese. Jones suggested something of a negative reason for this. Many members of ethnic minority groups might stay on in education because of the problem of finding a job.

THEORIES OF SCHOOLING

Bernstein: language codes

There are several theoretical perspectives on the nature of modern education and its implications for inequality. One approach emphasizes linguistic skills. Basil Bernstein has argued that children from varying backgrounds develop different *codes*, or forms of speech, during their early lives, which affect their subsequent school experience (Bernstein 1975). He is not concerned with differences in vocabulary or verbal skills, as these are usually thought of; his interest is in systematic differences in ways of using language, particularly contrasting poorer and wealthier children.

The speech of working-class children, Bernstein argues, represents a **restricted code** – a way of using language containing many unstated assumptions which speakers expect others to know. A restricted code is a type of speech tied to the cultural setting of a lower-class community or district. Many working-class people live in a strong familial or neighbourhood culture, in which values and norms are taken for granted, and not expressed in language. Parents tend to socialize their children directly by the use of rewards or reprimands to correct behaviour. Language in a restricted code is more suitable for communication about practical experience than for discussion of more abstract ideas, processes or relationships. Restricted code speech is thus characteristic of children growing up in lower-class families, and of the peer groups in which they spend their time. Speech is oriented to the norms of the group, without anyone easily being able to explain *why* they follow the patterns of behaviour they do.

The language development of middle-class children, by contrast, according to Bernstein, involves the acquisition of an **elaborated code** – a style of speaking in which the meanings of words can be *individualized* to suit the demands of particular situations. The ways in which children from middle-class backgrounds learn to use language are less bound to particular contexts; the child is able more easily to generalize and express abstract ideas. Thus middle-class mothers, when controlling their children, frequently explain the reasons and principles which underlie their reactions to the child's behaviour. While a working-class mother might tell a child off for wanting to eat too many sweets by simply saying, 'No more sweets for you!', a middle-class mother is more likely to explain that eating too many sweets is bad for one's health and the state of one's teeth.

Children who have acquired elaborated codes of speech, Bernstein proposes, are more able to deal with the demands of formal academic education than those confined to restricted codes. This does not imply that lower-class children have an 'inferior' type of speech, or that their codes of language are 'deprived'. Rather, the way in which they use speech clashes with the academic culture of the school. Those who have mastered elaborated codes fit much more easily within the school environment.

There is evidence to back up Bernstein's theory, although its validity is still debated. Joan Tough has studied the language of working-class and middle-class children, finding systematic differences. She backs up Bernstein's thesis that lower-class children generally have less experience of having their questions answered, or of being offered explanations about the reasoning of others (Tough 1976). The same conclusion was reached in subsequent research by Barbara Tizard and Martin Hughes (1984).

Bernstein's ideas help us understand why those from low socioeconomic backgrounds tend to be 'under-achievers' at school. The following traits have been associated with restricted code speech, all of them inhibiting the lower-class child's educational chances:

● The child probably receives limited responses to questions asked at home, and therefore is likely to be both less well informed and less curious about the wider world than those mastering elaborated codes.

- The child will find it difficult to respond to the unemotional and abstract language used in teaching, as well as to appeals to general principles of school discipline.

- Much of what the teacher says is likely to be incomprehensible, depending on different forms of linguistic usage from those to which the child is accustomed. The child may attempt to cope with this by *translating* the teacher's language into that with which she or he is familiar – but then could fail to grasp the very principles the teacher intends to convey.

- While the child will experience little difficulty with rote or 'drill' learning, she or he will have major difficulties in grasping conceptual distinctions involving generalization and abstraction.

Bowles and Gintis: schools and industrial capitalism

The work of Samuel Bowles and Herbert Gintis is concerned mainly with the institutional background to the development of the modern school system (Bowles and Gintis 1976). Bowles and Gintis base their ideas on schooling in the United States, but claim they apply also to other Western societies. Quoting studies such as that by Jencks et al. (1972), they begin from the observation that education has not been a powerful influence towards economic equality. Modern education, they suggest, should be understood as a response to the economic needs of industrial capitalism. Schools help to provide the technical and social skills required by industrial enterprise; and they instil respect for authority and discipline into the labour force. Relations of authority and control in school, which are hierarchical and include an emphasis on obedience, directly parallel those dominating the workplace. The rewards and punishments held out in school also replicate those in the world of work. Schools help to motivate some individuals towards 'achievement' and 'success', while discouraging others, who find their way into low-paid jobs.

Bowles and Gintis accept that the development of mass education has had many beneficial effects. Illiteracy has been virtually eliminated, and schooling provides access to learning experiences which are intrinsically self-fulfilling. Yet because education has expanded mainly as a response to economic needs, the school system falls far short of what enlightened reformers hoped from it.

According to Bowles and Gintis, modern schools reproduce the feelings of powerlessness which many individuals experience elsewhere. The ideals of personal development central to education can only be achieved if people can control the conditions of their own lives and develop their talents and abilities of self-expression. Under the current system, schools 'are destined to legitimate inequality, limit personal development to forms compatible with submission to arbitrary authority, and aid in the process whereby youth are resigned to their fate' (Bowles and Gintis 1976, p. 266). If there were greater democracy in the workplace and more equality in society at large, Bowles and Gintis argue, a system of education could be developed providing for greater individual fulfilment.

Illich: the hidden curriculum

One of the most controversial writers on educational theory is Ivan Illich. He is noted for his criticisms of modern economic development, which he describes as a process whereby previously self-sufficient peoples are dispossessed of their traditional skills and made to rely on doctors for their health, teachers for their schooling, television for their entertainment and employers for their subsistence. Illich argues that the very notion of compulsory schooling – now accepted throughout the world – should be questioned (Illich 1973). Like Bowles and Gintis, Illich stresses the connection between the development of education and economic requirements for discipline and hierarchy. He argues that schools have developed to cope with four basic tasks: the provision of custodial care, the distribution of people among occupational roles, the learning of dominant values and the acquisition of socially approved skills and knowledge. The school has become a *custodial* organization because attendance is obligatory, and children are 'kept off the streets' between early childhood and their entry into work.

Much is learnt in school which has nothing to do with the formal content of lessons. Schools tend to inculcate what Illich called *passive consumption* – an uncritical acceptance of the existing social order – by the nature of the discipline and regimentation they involve. These lessons are not consciously taught; they are implicit in school procedures and organization. The **hidden curriculum** teaches children that their role in life is 'to know their place and to sit still in it' (ibid.).

Illich advocates *deschooling* society. Compulsory schooling is a relatively recent invention, he points out; there is no reason why it should be accepted as somehow inevitable. Since schools do not promote equality or the development of individual creative abilities, why not do away with them in their current form? Illich does not mean by this that all forms of educational organization should be abolished. Education, he argues, should provide everyone who wants to learn with access to available resources – at any time in their lives, not just in their childhood or adolescent years. Such a system should make it possible for knowledge to be widely diffused and shared, not confined to specialists. Learners should not have to submit to a standard curriculum, and they should have personal choice over what they study.

What all this means in practical terms is not wholly clear. In place of schools, however, Illich suggests several types of *educational framework*. Material resources for formal learning would be stored in libraries, rental agencies, laboratories and information storage banks, available to any student. 'Communications networks' would be set up, providing data about the skills possessed by different individuals and whether they would be willing to train others or engage in mutual learning activities. Students would be provided with vouchers allowing them to use educational services as and when they wished.

Are these proposals wholly utopian? Many would say so. Yet if, as looks possible, paid work is substantially reduced or restructured in the future, they appear less unrealistic. Were paid employment to become less central to social life, people might instead engage in a wider variety of pursuits. Against this backdrop, some of Illich's ideas make good sense. Education would not be just a form of early training, confined to special institutions, but would become available to whoever wished to take advantage of it.

Illich's ideas have again become fashionable in the 1990s with the rise of new communications technologies. Some believe that the so-called information superhighway will revolutionize education – an issue further discussed below.

EDUCATION AND CULTURAL REPRODUCTION

Perhaps the most illuminating way of connecting some of the themes of these three theoretical perspectives is through the concept of CULTURAL REPRODUCTION (Bourdieu 1986, 1988; Bourdieu and Passeron 1977). Cultural reproduction refers to the ways in which schools, in conjunction with other social institutions, help perpetuate social and economic inequalities across the generations. The concept directs our attention to the means whereby, via the hidden curriculum, schools influence the learning of values, attitudes and habits. Schools reinforce variations in cultural values and outlooks picked up early in life; when children leave school, these have the effect of limiting the opportunities of some, while facilitating those of others.

The modes of language use identified by Bernstein no doubt connect with such broad cultural differences, which underlie variations in interests and tastes. Children from lower-class backgrounds, particularly those from minority groups, develop ways of talking and acting which clash with those dominant in the school. As Bowles and Gintis emphasize, schools impose rules of discipline on pupils, the authority of teachers being oriented towards academic learning. Working-class children experience a much greater cultural clash when they enter school than those from more privileged homes. The former find themselves in effect in a foreign cultural environment. Not only are they less likely to be motivated towards high academic performance; their habitual modes of speech and action, as Bernstein holds, do not mesh with those of the teachers, even if each is trying their best to communicate.

Children spend long hours in school. As Illich stresses, they learn much more there than is contained in the lessons they are actually taught. Children get an early taste of what the world of work will be like, learning that they are expected to be punctual and apply themselves diligently to the tasks which those in authority set for them (Webb and Westergaard 1991).

Willis: an analysis of cultural reproduction

A celebrated discussion of cultural reproduction is provided in the report of a fieldwork study carried out by Paul Willis in a school in Birmingham (Willis 1977). The question he set out to investigate was how cultural reproduction occurs – or, as he puts it, 'how working-class kids get working-class jobs'. It is often thought that, during the process of schooling, children from lower-class or minority backgrounds simply come to see that they 'are not clever enough' to expect to get highly paid or high-status jobs in their future work lives. In other words, the experience of academic failure teaches them to recognize their intellectual limitations; having accepted their 'inferiority', they move into occupations with limited career prospects.

As Willis points out, this interpretation does not conform at all to the reality of people's lives and experiences. The 'street wisdom' of those from poor neighbourhoods may be of little or no relevance to academic success, but involves as subtle, skilful and complex a set of abilities as any of the intellectual skills taught in school. Few if any children leave school thinking 'I'm so stupid that it's fair and proper for me to be stacking boxes in a factory all day.' If children from less privileged backgrounds accept menial jobs, without feeling themselves throughout life to be failures, there must be other factors involved.

Willis concentrated on a particular boys' group in the school, spending a lot of time with them. The members of the gang, who called themselves 'the lads', were white; the school also contained many children from West Indian and Asian backgrounds. Willis found that the lads had an acute and perceptive understanding of the school's authority system – but used this to fight that system rather than work with it. They saw the school as an alien environment, but one they could manipulate to their own ends. They derived positive pleasure from the constant conflict – which they kept mostly to minor skirmishes – they carried on with teachers. They were adept at seeing the weak points of the teachers' claims to authority, as well as where they were vulnerable as individuals.

In class, for instance, the children were expected to sit still, be quiet and get on with their work. But the lads were all movement, save when the teacher's stare might freeze one of them momentarily; they would gossip surreptitiously, or pass open remarks that were on the verge of direct insubordination but could be explained away if challenged.

Willis describes all this beautifully:

> 'The lads' specialise in a caged resentment which always stops just short of outright confrontation. Settled in class, as near a group as they can manage, there is a continuous scraping of chairs, a bad-tempered 'tut-tutting' at the simplest request, and a continuous fidgeting about which explores every permutation of sitting or lying on a chair. During private study, some openly show disdain by apparently trying to go to sleep with their heads sideways down on the desk, some have their backs to the desk gazing out of the window, or even vacantly at the wall. . . . A continuous hum of talk flows around injunctions not to, like the inevitable tide over barely dried sand and everywhere there are rolled-back eyeballs and exaggerated mutterings of conspiratorial secrets. . . . In the corridors there is a foot-

dragging walk, an over-friendly 'hello' or sudden silence as the deputy [senior teacher] passes. Derisive or insane laughter erupts which might or might not be about someone who has just passed. It is as demeaning to stop as it is to carry on. . . . Opposition to the school is principally manifested in the struggle to win symbolic and physical space from the institution and its rules and to defeat its main perceived purpose: to make you 'work'. (Willis 1977, pp. 12–13, 26)

The lads referred to conformist children – those who accepted the authority of the teachers and concerned themselves with academic values – as 'the ear-'oles'. The ear-'oles actually *listened* to the teachers, and did as they were told. The ear-'oles would go on to be far more 'successful', in terms of getting well-paid, comfortable jobs on leaving school, than the lads. Yet their awareness of the complexities of the school environment, according to Willis, was in many respects less profound than that of the lads. They accepted them in an unquestioning way.

Most pupils were somewhere between the lads on the one side and the ear-'oles on the other – less openly confrontational than the first group and less consistently conformist than the second. Styles and modes of opposition, however, were also strongly influenced by ethnic divisions. The teachers were mostly white, and in spite of their distaste for the school, the lads had more in common with them than black children did. Some groups of children from West Indian families were much more openly, and violently, hostile to the school than the lads. The lads themselves were openly racist, and distinguished themselves sharply from the black gangs.

The lads recognized that work would be much like school, but they actively looked forward to it. They expected to gain no direct satisfaction from the work environment, but were impatient for wages. Far from taking the jobs they did – in tyre fitting, carpet laying, plumbing, painting and decorating – from feelings of inferiority, they held an attitude of dismissive superiority towards work, as they had towards school. They enjoyed the adult status which came from working, but were uninterested in 'making a career' for themselves. As Willis points out, work in blue-collar settings often involves quite similar cultural features to those the lads created in their counterschool culture – banter, quick wit and the skill to subvert the demands of authority figures where necessary. Only later in their lives might they come to see themselves as trapped in arduous, unrewarding labour. When they have families, they might perhaps look back on education retrospectively – and hopelessly – as the only escape. Yet if they try to pass this view on to their own children, they are likely to have no more success than their own parents did.

EDUCATION AND INEQUALITY

The development of education has always been closely linked to ideals of mass democracy. Reformers value education, of course, for its own sake – for the opportunity it provides for individuals to develop their abilities and aptitudes. Yet education has also consistently been seen as a means of equalization. Universal education, it has been argued, will help reduce disparities of wealth and power by providing able young people with skills to enable them to find a valued place in society. How far has this happened? Much sociological research has been devoted to answering this question. Its results are clear: education tends to express and reaffirm existing inequalities far more than it acts to change them.

Coleman's study of inequalities in education in the US

Studies carried out in a variety of countries demonstrate that social and family background are the major influences over school performance, and are thus reflected in subsequent levels of income. One of the classic investigations was undertaken in the United States in the 1960s. The 1964 Civil Rights Act required the United States Commissioner of Education to report on educational inequalities resulting from differences of ethnic background, religion or national origin. James Coleman, a sociologist, was appointed director of the research programme. The results were published in 1966, after one of the most extensive research investigations ever carried out in sociology.

Information was collected about more than half a million pupils, who were also given a range of tests assessing verbal and non-verbal abilities, reading levels and mathematical skills. Sixty thousand teachers also completed forms providing data about four thousand schools. The results provided a general survey of schooling in the country, and gave rise to some surprising results, which had a significant practical impact on policy-making.

The report found that the large majority of children were in schools effectively segregated into black and white. In almost 80 per cent of schools attended by white students, black students accounted for only 10 per cent or less of their numbers. Whites and Asian Americans scored higher in achievement tests than blacks or other ethnic minorities. Coleman had supposed that the study would show that mainly black schools would have worse facilities, larger classes and inferior buildings compared with those that were predominantly white, but the results showed far fewer differences of this type than had been anticipated.

He concluded that the material resources provided in schools made little difference to educational performance; the decisive influence was the children's backgrounds. In Coleman's words, 'Inequalities imposed on children by their home, neighbourhood, and peer environment are carried along to become the inequalities with which they confront adult life at the end of school' (Coleman et al. 1966, p. 325). There was, however, some evidence that students from deprived backgrounds who had close friendships with others who were better off were likely to be more successful at school.

The Coleman report influenced public debates about school integration in Britain as well as the USA, since it suggested that children from minority groups would do better in school if mixed with students from more affluent backgrounds.

Later research

While subsequent research has confirmed some of Coleman's findings, aspects of his work have been challenged. Since his study was confined to a single point in time, it could not analyse changes. A study by Michael Rutter, carried out in London, looked at the educational development of groups of boys over several years. The children studied were first contacted in 1970, when they were about to finish their primary schooling, and information was collected on social background and academic performance. The survey was repeated in 1974, when the boys had been in secondary school for three years. Within the group, a number of schools were selected for intensive study: pupils and teachers were interviewed and classroom activities observed.

The findings indicated that schools do in fact have an influence on the academic development of children. The factors Rutter found to be important had been left largely unanalysed in Coleman's investigation: they included, for example, the quality of teacher–pupil interaction, an atmosphere of cooperation and caring between teachers and students, and well-organized course preparation. Schools which provided superior learning environments were not always best equipped in terms of material resources or buildings.

Rutter's results do not negate the finding that influences prior to, and outside, school are most decisive in perpetuating social inequalities. Since the factors Rutter pointed to are often maximized in schools catering to well-motivated students and which provide good support for their teachers, his results help us to understand just why schooling tends to maintain inequalities. There is a self-repeating cycle in which students from relatively privileged homes attend a particular school, and perpetuate its qualities; good teachers are attracted, and motivation is maintained. A school mainly attended by deprived children will have to work far harder to achieve a similar result. Nevertheless, Rutter's conclusions do suggest that differences in school organization and atmosphere can counteract outside influences on academic attainment. Improvements in teaching quality, the social climate of the school and patterns of school work can help deprived children improve academic performance. In later research Coleman in fact reached similar conclusions (Coleman, Hoffer and Kilgore 1981).

Christopher Jencks's *Inequality*, published in 1972, reviewed some of the empirical evidence which had accumulated by then on education and inequality, concentrating mainly on US research (Jencks et al. 1972). Jencks reaffirmed the findings that educational and occupational attainment are governed mainly by family background and non-school factors, and that educational reforms on their own can have only minor effects on existing inequalities. Jencks's work has been criticized on methodological grounds, but his overall conclusions remain persuasive (Oakes 1985).

Much information now exists on patterns of inequality in education in the United Kingdom. Research reported by A. H. Halsey and his colleagues in 1980 developed various comparisons between educational opportunities open to working-class boys and those available to boys from the 'service class' (people of professional and managerial background). A boy from the service class during the postwar period was ten times as likely as one from the working class to be in school at the age of eighteen, and was eleven times as likely to go to university.

Streaming

The practice of **streaming** – dividing schoolchildren into groups that receive different instruction on the basis of assumed similarities in ability or attainment – is a controversial feature of schooling. In some schools, students are only streamed for certain subjects; in others, for all subjects. Streaming partly explains why schooling seems to have little effect on existing social inequalities. For being placed in a particular stream labels a student as either able or otherwise. As we have seen in the case of labelling and deviance, once attached, such labels are hard to break away from. Children from more privileged backgrounds, where academic work is encouraged, are likely to find themselves in the higher streams early on – and by and large stay there.

Jeannie Oakes (1985) studied streaming in twenty-five junior and senior high schools in the US, where the practice of streaming is very common. The schools were both large and small and in both urban and rural areas. She concentrated on differences *within* schools rather than between them. She found that although several schools claimed they did not stream children, virtually all of them had mechanisms for sorting them into groups that seemed to be alike in ability and achievement, to make teaching easier. In other words, they employed streaming but did not choose to use the term itself. Even where streaming only existed in this informal fashion, she found strong labels developing – high ability, low achieving, slow, average and so on. Individual students in these groups came to be defined by teachers, other students and themselves in terms of such labels. A student in a 'high-achieving' group was considered a high-achieving *person* – clever and quick. A pupil in a 'low-achieving' group came to be seen as slow, below average – or, in more forthright terms, a dummy. What is the impact of streaming on students in the 'low' group? A subsequent study by Oakes found that these students received a poorer education in the quality of courses, teachers and textbooks made available to them (Oakes 1990).

The usual reason given for streaming is that bright children learn more quickly and effectively in a group of others who are equally able, and that clever students are held back if placed in mixed groups. Surveying the evidence, Oakes was able to show that these assumptions are questionable. The results of later research investigations are not wholly consistent, but the majority have found that the brightest students do not learn more, or more quickly, when taught in equal-ability groups. The learning of average and slow pupils, however, is reduced by streaming.

In the UK, as a consequence of the introduction of the national curriculum, with a number of subjects, such as English or maths, which all English and Welsh schoolchildren must study, 'setting' is tending to replace streaming. Children are commonly streamed only for subjects in the core curriculum, but are placed in mixed ability classes for other subjects, such as humanities. If it is true that streaming has the consequences Oakes notes for the United States, however, setting would not avoid the negative effects of labelling. In those subjects which count the most – in the core curriculum – children are still labelled either 'high' or 'low' achievers.

INTELLIGENCE AND INEQUALITY

The discussion so far neglects the possible importance of inherited differences in ability. Suppose it were the case that variations in educational attainment and in subsequent occupational position and income directly reflected differential intelligence? In such circumstances, it might be argued, there is in fact equality of opportunity in the school system, for people find a level equivalent to their innate potential.

What is intelligence?

For many years psychologists have debated whether a single human ability which can be called **intelligence** actually exists, and, if so, how far it rests on innately determined differences. Intelligence is difficult to define, because it covers many different, often unrelated, qualities. We might suppose, for example, that the 'purest' form of intelligence is the ability to solve abstract mathematical puzzles. However, people who are very good at such puzzles sometimes have low abilities in other areas, such as history or art. Since the concept has proved so resistant to accepted definition, some psychologists have proposed (and many educators have by default accepted) that intelligence can simply be regarded as 'what **IQ** (intelligence quotient) tests measure'. The unsatisfactory nature of this is obvious enough, because the definition of intelligence becomes wholly circular.

Most IQ tests consist of a mixture of conceptual and computational problems. The tests are constructed so that the average score is 100 points: anyone scoring below is thus labelled as having 'below-average intelligence', and anyone scoring above has 'above-average intelligence'. In spite of the fundamental difficulty in measuring intelligence, IQ tests are widely used in research studies, as well as in schools and businesses.

IQ and genetic factors

Scores on IQ tests do in fact correlate highly with academic performance (which is not surprising, since IQ tests were originally developed to predict success at school). They therefore also correlate closely with social, economic and ethnic differences, since these are associated with variations in levels of educational attainment. White students score better, on average, than blacks or members of other disadvantaged minorities. An article published by Arthur Jensen in 1969 caused a furore by attributing IQ differences between blacks and whites in part to genetic variations (Jensen 1967, 1979).

More recently, psychologist Richard J. Herrnstein and sociologist Charles Murray have reopened the debate about IQ and education in a controversial way. They argue in their book *The Bell Curve: Intelligence and Class Structure in American Life* (1994) that the accumulated evidence linking IQ to genetic inheritance has now become overwhelming. The significant differences in intelligence between various racial and ethnic groups, they say, must in part be explained in terms of heredity. Most of the evidence they quote comes from studies carried out in the US. According to Herrnstein and Murray, such evidence indicates that some ethnic groups on average have higher IQs than other groups. Asian Americans, particularly Japanese Americans and Chinese Americans, on average possess higher IQs than whites, though the difference is not large. The average IQs of Asians and whites, however, are substantially higher than those of blacks. Summarizing the findings of 156 studies, Herrnstein and Murray find an average difference of 16 IQ points between these two racial groups. The authors argue that such differences in inherited intelligence contribute in an important way to social divisions in American society. The more clever an individual is, the greater the chance that she or he will rise in the social scale. Those at the top are there partly because they cleverer than the rest of the population – from which it follows that those at the bottom remain there because, on average, they are not so clever.

Critics of Herrnstein and Murray deny that IQ differences between racial and ethnic groups are genetic in origin. They argue that differences in IQ result from social and cultural differences. IQ tests, they point out, pose questions – to do with abstract reasoning, for example – more likely to be part of the experience of more affluent white students rather than of blacks and ethnic minorities. Scores on IQ tests may also be influenced by factors that have nothing to do with the abilities supposedly being measured, such as whether the testing is experienced as stressful. Research has demonstrated that African Americans score six points lower on IQ tests when the tester is white than when the tester is black (Kamin 1977).

The average lower IQ score of African Americans in the United States is remarkably similar to that of deprived ethnic minorities in other countries – such as the 'untouchables' in India (who are at the very bottom of the caste system), the *maoris* in New Zealand, and the *burakumin* of Japan. Children in these groups score an average of ten to fifteen IQ points below children belonging to the ethnic majority. The *burakumin* – descendants of people who in the eighteenth century, as a result of local wars, were dispossessed from their land and became outcasts and vagrants – are a particularly interesting example. They are not in any way physically distinct from other Japanese, although they have suffered from prejudice and discrimination for centuries. In this case, the difference in average IQ results cannot derive from genetic variations since there are no genetic differences between them and the majority population; yet the IQ difference is as thoroughly fixed as that between blacks and whites. *Burakumin* children in America, where they are treated like other Japanese, do as well on IQ tests as other Japanese.

Such observations strongly suggest that the IQ variations between African Americans and whites in the United States result from social and cultural differences. This conclusion receives further support from a comparative study of fourteen nations (including the United States) showing that average IQ scores have risen substantially over the past half century for the population as a whole (Coleman 1987). IQ tests are regularly updated. When old and new versions of the tests are given to the same group of people, they score significantly higher on the old tests. Present-day children taking IQ tests from the 1930s outscored 1930s groups by an average of fifteen points – just the kind of average difference that currently separates blacks and whites. Children today are not innately superior in intelligence to their parents or grandparents; the shift presumably derives from increasing prosperity and social advantages. The average social and economic gap between whites and African Americans is at least as great as that between the different generations, and is sufficient to explain the variation in IQ scores. While there may be genetic variations between individuals that influence scores on IQ tests, that some races are on average cleverer than others remains unproven and improbable.

The Bell Curve Wars

In *The Bell Curve Wars* (Fraser 1995), a number of noted scholars got together to examine the ideas of Herrnstein and Murray. The editor of the volume describes *The Bell Curve* as 'the most incendiary piece of social science to appear in the last decade or more'. The claims and assertions in the work 'have generated flash floods of letters to the editor in every major magazine and newspaper, not to mention the over-the-air commentary on scores of radio and television shows' (p. 3).

According to Stephen Jay Gould, one of the contributors to *The Bell Curve Wars*, Herrnstein and Murray are wrong on four major counts. He disputes their claims that intelligence can be described by a single IQ number; that people can be meaningfully ranked along a single scale of intelligence; that intelligence derives substantially from genetic inheritance; and that it cannot be altered. He shows that each of these assumptions is questionable.

Howard Gardner, another contributor, argues that a century of research has dispelled the notion of 'intelligence' as a general category. There are only 'multiple intelligences' – practical, musical, spatial, mathematical and so forth. Other contributors to *The Bell Curve Wars* claim that there is no systematic relation between IQ scores and later job performance. 'Racist pseudoscience' is their common reaction.

Gould concludes: 'We must fight the doctrine of *The Bell Curve* both because it is wrong and because it will, if activated, cut off all possibility of proper nurturance for everyone's intelligence. Of course, we cannot all be rocket scientists or brain surgeons, but those who can't might be rock musicians or professional athletes (and gain far more social prestige and salary thereby) . . .' (Gould 1995, p. 22).

Emotional and interpersonal intelligence

In his book of the same name, Daniel Goleman (1996) has argued that 'emotional intelligence' might be at least as important as IQ in determining how we fare in our lives. **Emotional intelligence** refers to how people use their emotions – the ability to motivate oneself, to have self-control, enthusiasm and persistence. By and large these aren't inherited and the more children can be taught them, the more chance they have of making use of their intellectual capabilities.

According to Goleman, 'The brightest among us can founder on shoals of unbridled passion and unruly impulses; people with high IQs can be stunningly poor pilots of their private lives' (p. 34). This is one reason why measures of ordinary intelligence don't correlate very well with subsequent achievement.

Thus one research study followed ninety-five Harvard students who graduated in the 1940s. By the time they were in middle age, those who had the high IQ test scores in college were only slightly more successful than lower-scoring students in terms of their careers. Another piece of research looked at the other end of the IQ scale. Four hundred and fifty boys, two-thirds from families on welfare, and all from a slum area near Harvard, were studied. A third of the group had IQs below 90. Again IQ had only a small connection with their subsequent careers. For example, 7 per cent of men with IQs under 80 were unemployed, but so were 7 per cent with IQs over 100. Childhood abilities such as handling emotions and getting on well with others were better predictors. As Howard Gardner has put it:

> *Inter*personal intelligence is the ability to understand other people: what motivates them, how they work, how to work cooperatively with them. Successful salespeople, politicians, teachers, clinicians and religious leaders are all likely to be individuals with high degrees of interpersonal intelligence. *Intra*personal intelligence . . . is a capacity to form an accurate, veridical model of oneself and to be able to use that model to operate effectively in life. (Gardner 1993, p. 9)

We have to revise our ideas of intelligence to include the diversity of factors which make for success in life. Something similar can be said of education itself. Education, as was stressed at the opening of the chapter, is a broader notion than that of schooling. New technological developments, particularly those associated with information technology, may cause us in the future to re-examine how we see education processes.

THE FUTURE OF EDUCATION

Education and new communications technology

The spread of information technology looks set to influence education in a number of different ways, some of which may perhaps be quite fundamental. The new technologies are affecting the nature of work, replacing some types of human work by machines. The sheer pace of technological change is creating a much more rapid turnover of jobs than once was the case. Education can no longer be regarded as a stage of preparation before an individual enters work. As technology changes, necessary skills change, and even if education is seen from a purely vocational point of view – as providing skills relevant to work – most observers agree that lifelong exposure to education will be needed in the future.

One suggestion in Britain, for example, is that a 'learning bank' should be established, to which individuals could turn at more or less any time in their lives. People would invest money in the bank, or the state or their employers would do so. This could later be reclaimed, at generous rates of interest, in the form of education credits, which would allow retraining in order to acquire new technical or job skills.

No one really knows as yet what the real effects of the new information and communications technologies will be. Some suggest that they will destroy far more jobs than they are likely to create. They speak of the 'end of work' (for further discussion of the 'declining importance of work', see chapter 12). If there is no longer enough paid work to go around, the implications for modern society are profound. Many people, including an increasing number of women, define their lives largely in terms of the work they do, and their work is central to their sense of self-esteem.

Should it happen that societies become more and more 'workless', these attitudes will look more and more archaic – and the already widespread feelings of despair or worthlessness which unemployment characteristically creates will be worsened. Education should and must play a role here. But this could not be education in the narrow sense of training and retraining. It would have to be education in relation to wider human values. Education would be both a means and an end to the development of a rounded and autonomous self-education in the service of self-development and self-understanding. There is nothing utopian in this idea, which corresponds to humanistic ideals of education developed by educational philosophers. An example already in existence is the 'university of the third age'. The 'third age' is the age of retirement – older people who have given up paid work. Retirement is sometimes just as difficult to cope with as unemployment – for that is effectively what it is. The **university of the third age** provides older people with the opportunity to educate themselves as they choose, developing whatever interests they care to follow.

While the speed of information technology is very relevant to such discussions, it also bears directly on the nature of the educational process itself and it is this we shall concentrate on in the concluding section.

Technologies of education

The rise of education in its modern sense was connected with a number of other major changes happening in the nineteenth century. One was the development of the school. One might naively think that there was a demand for education and that schools and universities were set up to meet that demand. But that was not how things happened. Schools arose, as Michel Foucault has shown, as part of the administrative apparatus of the modern state. The 'hidden curriculum' was about discipline and about the control of children.

A second influence was the development of printing and the arrival of 'book culture'. The mass distribution of books, newspapers and other printed media was as distinctive a feature of the development of industrial society as were machines and factories. Education developed to provide skills of literacy and computation giving access to the world of printed media. Nothing is more characteristic of the school than the schoolbook or textbook.

© Tony Reeve and Steve Way and the *Independent*

In the eyes of many, all this is set to change with the growing use of computers and multimedia technologies in education. It has been said that 'around 70–80% of telecommunications trials conducted in the emerging multimedia technologies around the world involve education or at least have an education component' (quoted in Kenway et al. 1995). Will the computer, CD-ROM and videotape increasingly replace the schoolbook? And will schools still exist in anything like the form in which they do today if children turn on their computers in order to learn, rather than sitting in rows listening to a teacher?

The new technologies, it is said, will not just add to the existing curriculum, they will undermine and transform it. For young people now are already growing up in an information- and media-related society and are much more familiar with its technologies than most adults are – including their teachers. This is the Nintendo generation, spoken of in chapter 14 – the techno-tots, techno-toddlers and vid-kids. Some speak of a 'classroom revolution': the arrival of 'desk-top virtual reality' and the **classroom without walls**.

There seems little doubt that multimedia technologies will find their way extensively into education. Political parties have lent their support to this in the UK as elsewhere. But one of the main driving forces is business: schools as well as homes are being targeted by the large media companies. The home computer market in the US, for example, seemed to have reached saturation point before the marketing of new forms of educational software, which has served to give it new impetus. Companies also plan to use the Internet to market new educational programmes:

> Targeting the working adult population, Jones International Ltd will establish a 'cyberspace business college' that would offer a master's degree in

business communications through the Internet, cable and satellite television and videocassettes. Annual tuition for the International University
College will start at $12,280 and the format will be similar to Jones's Mind
Extension University, where students communicate with professors and
peers via e-mail, and submit their assignments electronically, 'Universities
play the major role in education, but there are millions of potential students thirsting for knowledge that they can't reach,' says Chairman Glenn
R. Jones. (Kenway et al. 1995, p. 18)

As in many other areas of contemporary social life, markets and information technology are major influences on educational change.
The reforms of the British school system introduced by Conservative
governments, for example, have been influenced by the cost-cutting
pressures of globalization. The commercializing and marketizing of
education also reflect such pressures. Schools are being 're-engineered'
in much the same way as business corporations.

Many of those likely to enter the education field will be organizations
whose relation to schooling was previously marginal or non-existent.
They include cable companies, software houses, telecommunication
groups, film-makers and equipment suppliers. These will not be limited in their influence to schools or universities. They are already forming part of what has been called 'edu-tainment' – a sort of parallel
education industry linked to the software industry in general, to muse-
ums, science parks and heritage areas.

Whether the new technologies will have the radical implications for
education which some claim is still an open question. Critics have
pointed out that, even if they do have major effects, these may act to
reinforce educational inequalities. '**Information poverty**' might become
added to the material deprivations which currently have such an effect
on schooling. The 'classroom without walls' at the moment looks some
way off. In the meantime, many schools and colleges are suffering from
underfunding and long-standing neglect.

SUMMARY

1 Education in its modern form, involving the instruction of pupils
within specially designated school premises, began to emerge with
the spread of printed materials and higher levels of literacy.
Knowledge could be retained, reproduced and consumed by more
people in more places. With industrialization, work became more
specialized, and knowledge was increasingly acquired in more abstract rather than practical ways – the skills of reading, writing and
calculating.

2 The expansion of education in the twentieth century has been
closely tied to perceived needs for a literate and disciplined workforce. Although reformers have seen the use of education for all as
a means of reducing inequalities, its impact in this respect is fairly
limited. Education tends to express and reaffirm existing inequalities more than it acts to change them.

3 Following the 1944 Education Act, everyone in the UK had the opportunity for free secondary education, and the school-leaving age was raised to fifteen. However, the fee-paying, 'public' schools continued to occupy a privileged place and play a key role in society.

State secondary education was shared among grammar schools, secondary modern schools and a small number of technical schools. The eleven-plus examination became the means of separating pupils between types of state schools according to ability.

4 In the 1960s, the comprehensive school system for secondary education was introduced. The eleven-plus exam was abolished, along with most grammar schools and all secondary moderns. In recent years, the comprehensive system has itself come under much attack. Critics feel that the comprehensives have not achieved the educational standards which their initiators hoped for.

5 The organization of and teaching within schools have tended to sustain gender inequalities. Rules specifying distinct dress for girls and boys encourage sex typing, as do texts containing established gender images. There is evidence that teachers treat girls and boys differently, and certain subjects are thought more suitable for girls than boys and vice versa. Women are still under-represented among students and teachers in higher education, and this situation is unlikely to improve until the other factors change.

6 Various sociological theories have had an impact on interpretations of education and schooling. According to Bernstein's theory, children who have acquired elaborated codes of speech are more able to deal with the demands of formal academic education than those confined to restricted codes. Intelligence tests, such as IQ tests, rely on a standardized conception of 'useful' abilities and skills; they are culture-bound and thus limited in application.

7 The formal school curriculum is only one part of a more general process of cultural reproduction influenced by many informal aspects of learning, education and school settings. The 'hidden curriculum' plays a significant role in cultural reproduction.

8 Because intelligence is difficult to define, there has been a great deal of controversy about the subject. Some argue that genes determine one's IQ; others believe that social influences determine it. The weight of the evidence appears to be on the side of those arguing for social and cultural influences. A major controversy about IQ has developed as a result of the book *The Bell Curve*. The book claims that races differ in terms of their average level of inherited intelligence. Critics reject this thesis completely.

9 David Goleman has argued for the importance of emotional intelligence, which refers to how well people manage their emotions and to their skills at getting along with others. He suggests that emotional intelligence may be at least as important as IQ in determining how successful individuals are in their working lives.

10 Education and schooling may be changed very substantially by the impact of information technology – computers and multimedia. It may be that the school itself will become less important, because pupils can learn through computer connections in the home.

FURTHER READING

Andy Green, *Education and State Formation* (London: Macmillan, 1990). An analysis of the rise of national systems of education in England, France and the United States.

Mark Holmes, *Educational Policy for the Pluralist Democracy: The Common School, Choice, and Diversity* (Washington D.C.: Falmer Press, 1992). Provides an insight into social and political aspects of education.

Sheila Riddell, *Gender and the Politics of the Curriculum* (London: Routledge, 1992). Uses case studies of two secondary schools to analyse interrelations between the curriculum and gender identity.

IMPORTANT TERMS

- *literacy*
- *educational system*
- *higher education*
- *restricted code*
- *elaborated code*
- *hidden curriculum*
- *streaming*
- *intelligence*
- *IQ*
- *emotional intelligence*
- *university of the third age*
- *classroom without walls*
- *information poverty*

RELIGION

BASIC CONCEPTS

● *religion* ● *ritual* ● *secularization*

> By the light of day, and by the fall of night, your Lord has not forsaken you, nor does He abhor you. The life to come holds a richer prize for you than this present life.
>
> You shall be gratified with what your Lord will give you. Did He not find you an orphan and give you shelter? Did He not find you in error and guide you? Did He not find you poor and enrich you? Therefore do not wrong the orphan, nor chide away the beggar.
>
> But proclaim the goodness of your Lord.

This scriptural passage gives a good insight into the hold that religion has had over the lives of human beings for thousands of years. God cares for each of us, the scripture asserts, providing us with care and comfort, food and shelter. In worshipping God and believing in his goodness, we shall reap benefits in the life to come.

Not all religions, as we shall see a little later in this chapter, share these beliefs, but in one form or another, religion is found in all known human societies. The earliest societies on record, of which we have evidence only through archaeological remains, show clear traces of religious symbols and ceremonials. Throughout subsequent history, RELIGION has continued to be a central part of human experience, influencing how we perceive and react to the environments in which we live.

The scripture just quoted presents religion as a source of personal solace and support. Yet religion has often been the origin of intense social struggles and conflicts. Consider the advice and sentiments contained in the following scriptural statement:

> Let love for our brotherhood breed warmth of mutual affection. Give pride of place to one another in esteem.
> With unflagging energy, in ardour of spirit, serve the Lord.
> Let hope keep you joyful; in trouble stand firm; persist in prayer.
> Contribute to the needs of God's people, and practise hospitality.
> Call down blessings on your persecutors – blessings, not curses . . .
> If possible, so far as it lies with you, live at peace with all men.

Like the first text, these words convey a sense of universal love and of God's goodness. It is difficult to suppose that believers who followed the teaching of the first of these scriptures would be out of sympathy with the sentiments of the second. Yet for many centuries these two groups of believers have frequently come into bloody conflict. The first quotation is in fact from the Qur'ān, the holy book of Islam. The second comes from the New Testament of the Christian Bible. Islam and Christianity have overlapping origins and recognize many of the same prophets. Each, however, rejects the God of the other, and regards those who follow the alternative religion – or any other religion at all – as outsiders.

Between the eleventh and thirteenth centuries, European armies invaded parts of the Middle East with the object of capturing the Holy

Land from the Muslims (the followers of Islam) for Christianity. These wars, which the Christians called 'Crusades', were some of the bloodiest ever fought, but were carried out in the name of both God and Allah. Thousands were slaughtered, and atrocities were committed by Christian and Islamic armies alike over the course of two hundred years. The Europeans captured large tracts of land and important cities, including Jerusalem, in the First Crusade, but by the end of the Ninth, in 1272, the Muslims had recaptured all of the Holy Land.

St Bernard, abbot of a large monastery at Clairvaux, France, was one of the most fervent advocates of the crusades. 'How blessed are the martyrs who die in the battle!' he wrote. 'Rejoice, stout champion, if you live and conquer in the Lord, but exult and glory even more if you die and join the Lord' (Koenigsburger 1987).

How can religion have such a purchase on individuals' lives that they are prepared to sacrifice themselves for its ideals? Why has religion been such a pervasive aspect of human societies? Under what conditions does religion unite communities, and under what conditions does it divide them? These are the questions that we shall try to answer in this chapter. In order to do so, we shall have to ask what religion actually is, and look at some of the different forms that religious beliefs and practices take. We shall also consider the main sociological theories of religion and analyse the various types of religious organization that can be distinguished. Finally, we will consider the fate of religion in the modern world; for it has seemed to many observers that, with the rise of science and modern industry, religion today has become a less central force in social life than it was prior to the modern age.

The study of religion is a challenging enterprise which places quite special demands on the sociological imagination. In analysing religious practices, we have to make sense of the many different beliefs and rituals found in the various human cultures. We must be sensitive to ideals that inspire profound conviction in believers, yet at the same time take a balanced view of them. We have to confront ideas that seek the eternal, while recognizing that religious groups also promote quite mundane goals – such as acquiring finance or soliciting for followers. We need to recognize the diversity of religious beliefs and modes of conduct, but also probe into the nature of religion as a general phenomenon.

DEFINING RELIGION

The variety of religious beliefs and organizations is so immense that scholars have found great difficulty in reaching a generally accepted definition of religion. In the West, most people identify religion with Christianity – a belief in a supreme being, who commands us to behave in a moral fashion on this earth, and promises an after-life to come. Yet we certainly cannot define religion as a whole in these terms. These beliefs, and many other aspects of Christianity, are absent from most of the world's religions.

What religion is not

In order to overcome the pitfalls of culturally biased thinking about religion, it is probably best to begin by saying what religion is *not*, considered in general terms. First, religion should not be identified with **monotheism** (belief in one God). Most religions involve many deities. Even in some versions of Christianity, there are several figures with sacred qualities: God, Jesus, Mary, the Holy Ghost, angels, and saints. In certain religions there are no gods at all.

Second, religion should not be identified with *moral prescriptions* controlling the behaviour of believers – like the commandments that Moses was supposed to have received from God. The idea that the gods are interested in how we behave on this earth is alien to many religions. To the ancient Greeks, for example, the gods were largely indifferent to the activities of humanity.

Third, religion is not necessarily concerned with *explaining how the world came to be as it is*. In Christianity, the myth of Adam and Eve purports to explain the origin of human existence, and many religions have *myths of origin* of this sort; but equally many do not.

Fourth, religion cannot be identified with the *supernatural*, as intrinsically involving belief in a universe 'beyond the realm of the senses'. Confucianism, for example, is concerned with accepting the natural harmony of the world, not with finding truths that 'lie behind' it.

What religion is

Characteristics that all religions *do* seem to share are as follows. Religions involve a set of *symbols*, invoking feelings of *reverence* or *awe*, and are linked to RITUALS or ceremonials (such as church services) engaged in by a community of believers. Each of these elements needs some elaboration. Whether or not the beliefs in a religion involve gods, there are virtually always beings or objects inspiring attitudes of awe or wonder. In some religions, for example, people believe in and revere a 'divine force', rather than personalized gods. In other religions, there are figures who are not gods, but are thought of with reverence – such as Buddha or Confucius.

The rituals associated with religion are very diverse. Ritual acts may include praying, chanting, singing, eating certain kinds of food – or refraining from doing so – fasting on certain days, and so on. Since ritual acts are oriented towards religious symbols, they are usually seen as quite distinct from the habits and procedures of ordinary life. Lighting a candle to honour or placate a god differs completely in its significance from doing so to provide illumination. Religious rituals are often carried on by individuals in isolation, but all religions also involve ceremonials practised collectively by believers. Regular ceremonials normally occur in special places – churches, temples or ceremonial grounds.

The existence of collective ceremonial is usually regarded by sociologists as one of the main factors distinguishing religion from magic, although the borderlines are by no means clear-cut. **Magic** is the influencing of events by the use of potions, chanting or ritual practices. It is generally practised by individuals, not by a community of believers. People often choose to resort to magic in situations of misfortune or danger. Thus Bronislaw Malinowski's classic study of the Trobriand islanders of the Pacific describes a variety of magical rites performed before any hazardous voyage by canoe (Malinowski 1982). The islanders omit such rites when they are simply going fishing on the safe and placid waters of a local lagoon.

Although magical practices have mostly disappeared from modern societies, in situations of danger magic-like superstitions are still common. Many who work in occupations that are dangerous or where chance factors can drastically affect performance – such as miners, deep-sea fishermen or sports players – indulge in small superstitious rituals or carry particular items in times of stress. An example might be a tennis player who insists on wearing a particular ring during big matches. Astrological beliefs, which have been inherited from magical ideas in pre-modern societies, still command a following, although probably most people do not take them too seriously.

VARIETIES OF RELIGION

In traditional societies, religion usually plays a central part in social life. Religious symbols and rituals are often integrated with the material and artistic culture of the society – music, painting or carving, dance, story-telling and literature. In small cultures, there is no professional priesthood, but there are always certain individuals who specialize in knowledge of religious (and often magical) practices. Although there are various sorts of such specialists, one common type is the **shaman** (a word originating among North American Indians). A shaman is an individual believed to be able to direct spirits or non-natural forces through ritual means. Shamans are sometimes essentially magicians rather than religious leaders, however, and are often consulted by individuals dissatisfied with what is offered in the religious rituals of the community.

Totemism and animism

Two forms of religion found frequently in smaller cultures are **totemism** and **animism**. The word 'totem' originated among North American Indian tribes, but has been widely used to refer to species of animals or plants believed to have supernatural powers. Usually each kinship group or clan within a society has its own particular totem, with which various ritual activities are associated. Totemic beliefs might seem alien to those living in industrialized societies, yet in certain relatively minor contexts, symbols similar to those of totemism are familiar – as when a sports team has an animal or plant for its emblem. Mascots are totems.

Animism is a belief in spirits or ghosts, thought to populate the same world as human beings. Such spirits may be seen as either benign or malevolent, and may influence human behaviour in numerous respects. In some cultures, for example, spirits are believed to cause illness or madness, and may also *possess* or take over individuals in such a way as to control their behaviour. Animistic beliefs are not confined to small cultures, but are found to some degree in many religious settings. In medieval Europe, those believed to be possessed by evil spirits were frequently persecuted as sorcerers or witches.

Small, seemingly 'simple' societies frequently have complex systems of religious belief. Totemism and animism are more common among these societies than in larger ones, but some small societies have far more complex religions. The Nuer of southern Sudan, for instance, described by E. E. Evans-Pritchard, have an elaborate set of theological ideas centred on a 'high god' or 'sky spirit' (Evans-Pritchard 1956). Religions which incline towards monotheism, however, are found relatively infrequently among smaller traditional cultures. Most are **polytheistic** – there is a belief in many gods.

Judaism, Christianity and Islam

The three most influential monotheistic religions in world history are *Judaism*, *Christianity* and *Islam*. All originated in the Middle East and each has influenced the others.

Judaism

Judaism is the oldest of the three religions, dating from about 1,000 BC. The early Hebrews were nomads, living in and around ancient Egypt. Their **prophets**, or religious leaders, partly drew their ideas from existing religious beliefs in the region, but differed in their commitment to a single, almighty God. Most of their neighbours were polytheistic. The Hebrews believed that God demands obedience to strict moral codes, and insisted on their claim to a monopoly of truth, seeing their beliefs as the only true religion (Zeitlin 1984, 1988).

Until the creation of Israel, not long after the end of World War Two, there was no state of which Judaism was the official religion. Jewish communities survived in Europe, North Africa and Asia, although they were frequently persecuted – culminating in the murder of millions of Jews by the Nazis in concentration camps during the war.

Christianity

Many Judaic views were taken over and incorporated as part of Christianity. Jesus was an orthodox Jew, and Christianity began as a sect of Judaism; it is not clear that Jesus wished to found a distinctive religion. His disciples came to think of him as the *Messiah* – a Hebrew word meaning 'the anointed', the Greek term for which was 'Christ' – awaited by the Jews. Paul, a Greek-speaking Roman citizen, was a major initiator of the spread of Christianity, preaching extensively in Asia Minor and Greece. Although the Christians were at first savagely persecuted, the Emperor Constantine eventually adopted Christianity as the official religion of the Roman empire. Christianity spread to become a dominant force in Western culture for the next two thousand years.

Christianity today commands a greater number of adherents, and is more generally spread across the world, than any other religion. Over a thousand million individuals regard themselves as Christians, but there are many divisions in terms of theology and church organization, the main branches being Roman Catholicism, Protestantism and Eastern Orthodoxy.

Islam

The origins of Islam, today the second largest religion in the world (see table 16.1), overlap with those of Christianity. Islam derives from the teachings of the prophet Muhammad in the seventh century AD. The single God of Islam, Allah, is believed to hold sway over all human and natural life. The *Pillars of Islam* are the five essential religious duties of Muslims (as believers in Islam are called). The first is the recitation of the Islamic creed, 'There is no god but Allah, and Muhammad is the apostle of Allah.' The second is the saying of formal prayers five times each day, preceded by ceremonial washing. The worshipper at these prayers must always face towards the holy city of Mecca in Saudi Arabia, no matter how far away that is.

The third pillar is the observance of Ramadan, a month of fasting during which no food or drink may be taken during daylight. The fourth is

Table 16.1 Religious populations of the world, 1993

Religion	Number	Percentage of total
Christians	1,869,282,470	33.5
Roman Catholics	1,042,501,000	18.7
Protestants	382,374,000	6.9
Orthodox	173,560,000	3.1
Anglicans	75,847,000	1.4
Other Christians	195,000,470	3.5
Muslims	1,014,372,000	18.2
Non-religious	912,874,000	16.4
Hindus	751,360,000	13.5
Buddhists	334,002,000	6.0
Atheists	242,852,000	4.3
Chinese folk religions	140,956,000	2.5
New religionists	123,765,000	2.2
Tribal religionists	99,736,000	1.8
Sikhs	19,853,000	0.4
Jews	18,153,000	0.3
Other	49,280,000	1.0

Source: Statistical Abstract of the United States, 1994, p. 855.

the giving of alms (money to the poor), set out in Islamic law, which often has been used as a source of taxation by the state. Finally, there is the expectation that every believer will attempt, at least once, to make a pilgrimage to Mecca.

Muslims believe that Allah spoke through earlier prophets – including Moses and Jesus – before Muhammad, whose teachings most directly express his will. Islam has come to be very widespread, having some 1,000 million adherents throughout the world. The majority are concentrated in North and East Africa, the Middle East and Pakistan. (For a brief discussion of Muslim beliefs, see the section on the Islamic revolution below.)

The religions of the Far East

Hinduism

There are major contrasts between Judaism, Christianity and Islam and the religions of the Far East. The oldest of all the great religions still prominent in the world today is *Hinduism*, the core beliefs of which date back some six thousand years. Hinduism is a polytheistic religion. It is so internally diverse that some scholars have suggested that it should be regarded as a cluster of related religions rather than a single religious orientation; many local cults and religious practices are linked by a few generally held beliefs.

Most Hindus accept the doctrine of the cycle of *reincarnation* – the belief that all living beings are part of an eternal process of birth, death and rebirth. A second key feature is the caste system, based on the belief that individuals are born into a particular position in a social and ritual hierarchy, according to the nature of their activities in previous incarnations. A different set of duties and rituals exists for each caste, and one's fate in the next life is governed mainly by how well these duties are performed. Hinduism accepts the possibility of numerous different religious standpoints, not drawing a clear line between believers and non-believers. There are over 750 million Hindus, virtually all living on the Indian subcontinent. Hinduism does not seek to convert others into 'true believers', unlike Christianity and Islam.

Buddhism, Confucianism, Taoism

The **ethical religions** of the East encompass *Buddhism, Confucianism* and *Taoism*. These religions have no gods. Rather, they emphasize ethical ideals that relate the believer to the natural cohesion and unity of the universe.

Buddhism derives from the teachings of Siddhartha Gautama, the Buddha (*enlightened one*), who was a Hindu prince in a small kingdom in south Nepal in the sixth century BC. According to the Buddha, human beings can escape the reincarnation cycle by the renunciation of desire. The path of salvation lies in a life of self-discipline and meditation, separated from the tasks of the mundane world. The overall objective of Buddhism is the attainment of *Nirvana*, complete spiritual fulfilment. The Buddha rejected Hindu ritual and the authority of the castes. Like Hinduism, Buddhism tolerates many local variations, including belief in local deities, not insisting on a single view. Buddhism today is a major influence in several states in the Far East, including Thailand, Burma, Sri Lanka, China, Japan and Korea.

Confucianism was the basis of the culture of the ruling groups in traditional China. 'Confucius' (the latinized form of the name K'ung Fu-tzu), lived in the sixth century BC, the same period as Buddha. Like Lao-tzu, the founder of Taoism, Confucius was a teacher, not a religious prophet in the manner of the Middle Eastern religious leaders. Confucius is not seen by his followers as a god, but as 'the wisest of wise men'. Confucianism seeks to adjust human life to the inner harmony of nature, emphasizing the veneration of ancestors. *Taoism* shares similar principles, stressing meditation and non-violence as means to the higher life. Although some elements survive in the beliefs and practices of many Chinese, Confucianism and Taoism have lost much of their influence in China as a result of determined opposition from the government.

THEORIES OF RELIGION

Sociological approaches to religion are still strongly influenced by the ideas of the three 'classical' sociological theorists: Marx, Durkheim and Weber. None of the three was himself religious, and all thought that the significance of religion would decrease in modern times. Each believed that religion is in a fundamental sense an illusion. The advocates of different faiths may be wholly persuaded of the validity of the beliefs they hold and the rituals in which they participate, yet the very diversity of religions and their obvious connection to different types of society, the three thinkers held, make these claims inherently implausible. An individual born into an Australian society of hunters and gatherers would plainly have different religious beliefs from someone born into the caste system of India or the Catholic church of medieval Europe.

Marx and religion

In spite of his influence on the subject, Karl Marx never studied religion in any detail. His ideas mostly derived from the writings of several early nineteenth-century theological and philosophical authors. One of these was Ludwig Feuerbach, who wrote a famous work called *The Essence of Christianity* (Feuerbach 1957; originally published 1841). According to Feuerbach, religion consists of ideas and values produced by human beings in the course of their cultural development, but mistakenly projected onto divine forces or gods. Because human beings do not fully understand their own history, they tend to attribute socially created values and norms to the activities of gods. Thus the story of the ten commandments given to Moses by God is a mythical version of the origin of the moral precepts which govern the lives of Jewish and Christian believers.

So long as we do not understand the nature of the religious symbols we ourselves have created, Feuerbach argues, we are condemned to be prisoners of forces of history we cannot control. Feuerbach uses the term **alienation** to refer to the establishing of gods or divine forces distinct from human beings. Humanly created values and ideas come to be seen as the product of *alien* or separate beings – religious forces and gods. While the effects of alienation have in the past been negative, the understanding of religion as alienation, according to Feuerbach, promises great hope for the future. Once human beings realize that the values projected on to religion are really their own, those values become capable of realization on this earth, rather than being deferred to an after-life. The powers believed to be possessed by God in Christianity can be appropriated by human beings themselves. Christians believe that while God is all-powerful and all-loving, human beings themselves are imperfect and flawed. However, the potential for love and goodness and the power to control our own lives, Feuerbach believed, are present in human social institutions and can be brought to fruition once we understand their true nature.

Marx accepts the view that religion represents human self-alienation. It is often believed that Marx was dismissive of religion, but this is far from true. Religion, he writes, is the 'heart of a heartless world' – a haven from the harshness of daily reality. In Marx's view, religion in its traditional form will, and should, disappear; yet this is because the positive values embodied in religion can become guiding ideals for improving the lot of humanity on this earth, *not* because ideals and values themselves are mistaken. We should not fear the gods we ourselves have created, and we should cease endowing them with values we ourselves can realize.

Marx declared, in a famous phrase, that religion has been the 'opium of the people'. Religion defers happiness and rewards to the after-life, teaching the resigned acceptance of existing conditions in this life. Attention is thus diverted away from inequalities and injustices in this world by the promise of what is to come in the next. Religion has a strong ideological element: religious beliefs and values often provide justifications of inequalities of wealth and power. For example, the teaching that 'the meek shall inherit the earth' suggests attitudes of humility and non-resistance to oppression.

Durkheim and religious ritual

In contrast to Marx, Émile Durkheim spent a good part of his intellectual career studying religion, concentrating particularly on religion in small-scale, traditional societies. Durkheim's work, *The Elementary Forms of the Religious Life*, first published in 1912, is perhaps the single most influential study in the sociology of religion (Durkheim 1976). Durkheim does not connect religion primarily with social inequalities or power, but with the overall nature of the institutions of a society. He bases his work on a study of totemism as practised by Australian aboriginal societies, and he argues that totemism represents religion in its most 'elementary' or simple form – hence the title of his book.

A totem, as has been mentioned, was originally an animal or plant taken as having particular symbolic significance for a group. It is a *sacred* object, regarded with veneration and surrounded by various ritual activities. Durkheim defines religion in terms of a distinction between the **sacred** and the **profane**. Sacred objects and symbols, he holds, are treated as *apart* from the routine aspects of existence – the realm of the profane. Eating the totemic animal or plant, except on special ceremonial occasions, is usually forbidden, and as a sacred object the totem is believed to have divine properties which separate it completely from other animals that might be hunted, or crops gathered and consumed.

Why is the totem sacred? According to Durkheim, it is because it is the symbol of the group itself; it stands for the values central to the group or community. The reverence which people feel for the totem actually derives from the respect they hold for central social values. In religion, the object of worship is actually society itself.

Durkheim strongly emphasizes the fact that religions are never just a matter of belief. All religion involves regular ceremonial and ritual activities, in which a group of believers meets together. In collective ceremonials, a sense of group solidarity is affirmed and heightened. Ceremonials take individuals away from the concerns of profane social life into an elevated sphere, in which they feel in contact with higher forces. These higher forces, attributed to totems, divine influences or gods, are really the expression of the influence of the collectivity over the individual.

Ceremony and ritual, in Durkheim's view, are essential to binding the members of groups together. This is why they are found not only in regular situations of worship, but in the various life crises at which major social transitions are experienced, for example birth, marriage and death. In virtually all societies, ritual and ceremonial procedures are observed on such occasions. Durkheim reasons that collective ceremonials reaffirm group solidarity at a time when people are forced to adjust to major changes in their lives. Funeral rituals demonstrate that the values of the group outlive the passing of particular individuals, and so provide a means for bereaved people to adjust to their altered circumstances. Mourning is not the spontaneous expression of grief – or, at least, it is only so for those personally affected by the death. Mourning is a duty imposed by the group.

In small traditional cultures, Durkheim argues, almost all aspects of life are permeated by religion. Religious ceremonials both originate new ideas and categories of thought, and reaffirm existing values. Religion is not just a series of sentiments and activities; it actually conditions the *modes of thinking* of individuals in traditional cultures. Even the most basic categories of thought, including how time and space are thought of, were first framed in religious terms. The concept of 'time', for instance, was originally derived from counting the intervals involved in religious ceremonials.

Durkheim's expectations of religious change

With the development of modern societies, Durkheim believes, the influence of religion wanes. Scientific thinking increasingly replaces religious explanation, and ceremonial and ritual activities come to occupy only a small part of individuals' lives. Durkheim agrees with Marx that traditional religion – that is, religion involving divine forces or gods – is on the verge of disappearing. 'The old gods', Durkheim writes, 'are dead.' Yet he says that there is a sense in which religion, in altered form, is likely to continue. Even modern societies depend for their cohesion on rituals that reaffirm their values; new ceremonial activities can thus be expected to emerge to replace the old. Durkheim is vague about what these might be, but it seems that he has in mind the celebration of humanist and political values such as freedom, equality and social cooperation.

It could be argued that most industrialized states have in fact fostered **civil religions** (Bellah 1970). In Britain, symbols such as the flag, songs like *Land of Hope and Glory* and rituals such as coronations all act to reaffirm the 'British way of life'. Whether we can really justify speaking of 'religion' in these contexts is debatable; these symbols and practices coexist with traditional religions. Yet it is difficult to deny that civil symbols and rituals draw on similar social mechanisms to those found in traditional forms of religion.

Weber and the world religions

Durkheim bases his arguments on a very small range of examples, even though he claims his ideas apply to religion in general. Max Weber, by contrast, embarked on a massive study of religions worldwide. No scholar before or since has undertaken a task of such scope. Most of his attention was concentrated on what he called the *world religions* – those that have attracted large numbers of believers and decisively affected the course of global history. He made detailed studies of Hinduism, Buddhism, Taoism and ancient Judaism (Weber 1951, 1952, 1958, 1963), and in *The Protestant Ethic and the Spirit of Capitalism* (1976; originally published 1904–5) and elsewhere he wrote extensively about the impact of Christianity on the history of the West. He did not, however, complete his projected study of Islam.

Weber's writings on religion differ from those of Durkheim in concentrating on the connection between religion and social change, something to which Durkheim gave little attention. They contrast with the work of Marx because Weber argues that religion is not necessarily a conservative force; on the contrary, religiously inspired movements have often produced dramatic social transformations. Thus Protestantism – particularly Puritanism – was the source of the capitalistic outlook found in the modern West. The early entrepreneurs were mostly Calvinists. Their drive to succeed, which helped initiate Western economic development, was originally prompted by a desire to serve God. Material success was for them a sign of divine favour.

Weber saw his research on the world religions as a single project. His discussion of the impact of Protestantism on the development of the West is part of a comprehensive attempt to understand the influence of religion on social and economic life in varying cultures. Analysing the eastern religions, Weber concludes that they provided insuperable barriers to the development of industrial capitalism, such as took place in the West. This is not because the non-Western civilizations are backward; they simply have accepted values different from those which came to predominate in Europe.

In traditional China and India, Weber points out, there was at certain periods a significant development of commerce, manufacture and urbanism, but these did not generate the radical patterns of social change involved in the rise of industrial capitalism in the West. Religion was a major influence in inhibiting such change. For example, Hinduism is what Weber calls an 'other-worldly' religion. That is to say, its highest values stress escape from the toils of the material world to a higher plane of spiritual existence. The religious feelings and motivations produced by Hinduism do not focus on controlling or shaping the material world. On the contrary, Hinduism sees material reality as a veil hiding the true concerns to which humankind should be oriented. Confucianism also acted to direct effort away from economic development, as this came to be understood in the West, emphasizing harmony with the world rather than promoting active mastery of it. Although China was for a long while the most powerful and culturally most developed civilization in the world, its dominant religious values acted as a brake on a strong commitment to economic development for its own sake.

Weber regards Christianity as a *salvation religion*, involving the belief that human beings can be 'saved' if they adopt the beliefs of the religion and follow its moral tenets. The notions of sin and of being rescued from sinfulness by God's grace are important here. They generate a tension and an emotional dynamism essentially absent from the eastern religions. Salvation religions have a 'revolutionary' aspect. While the religions of the East cultivate an attitude of passivity towards the existing order within the believer, Christianity involves a constant struggle against sin, and hence can stimulate revolt against the existing order of things. Religious leaders – like Jesus – arise, who reinterpret existing doctrines in such a way as to challenge the existing power structure.

Assessment

Marx, Durkheim and Weber each identify some important general characteristics of religion, and in some ways their views complement one another. Marx is right to claim that religion often has ideological implications, serving to justify the interests of ruling groups at the expense of others: there are innumerable instances of this in history. Take as an example the influence of Christianity on the European colonialists' efforts to subject other cultures to their rule. The missionaries who sought to convert 'heathen' peoples to Christian beliefs were no doubt sincere, yet the effect of their teachings was to reinforce the destruction of traditional cultures and the imposition of white domination. The various Christian denominations almost all tolerated, or

445

endorsed, slavery in the United States and other parts of the world up to the nineteenth century. Doctrines were developed claiming slavery to be based on divine law, disobedient slaves being guilty of an offence against God as well as their masters.

Yet Weber is certainly correct to emphasize the unsettling, and often revolutionary, impact of religious ideals on pre-established social orders. Despite the churches' early support for slavery in the United States, many church leaders later played a key role in the fight to abolish it. Religious beliefs have prompted many social movements seeking to overthrow unjust systems of authority, for instance playing a prominent part in the civil rights movements of the 1960s in the US. Religion has also influenced social change – often provoking much bloodshed – through the armed clashes and wars fought for religious motives.

These divisive influences of religion, so prominent in history, find little mention in Durkheim's work. Durkheim emphasizes above all the role of religion in promoting social cohesion. Yet it is not difficult to redirect his ideas towards explaining religious division, conflict and change as well as solidarity. After all, much of the strength of feeling which may be generated *against* other religious groups derives from the commitment to religious values generated *within* each community of believers.

Among the most valuable aspects of Durkheim's writings is his stress on ritual and ceremonial. All religions involve regular assemblies of believers, at which ritual prescriptions are observed. As he rightly points out, ritual activities also mark the major transitions of life – birth, entry to adulthood (rituals associated with puberty are found in many cultures), marriage and death (van Gennep 1977).

In the rest of this chapter we shall make use of ideas developed by all three authors. First, we shall look at different types of religious organization, and consider the issue of religion and gender. Then we'll go on to discuss religious movements which set out to challenge the existing social order – the *millenarian* movements of medieval Europe and some non-European cultures in the twentieth century. We will then discuss one of the most important instances of religious revival in current times, the rise of Islamic fundamentalism, before discussing religion in Western societies today.

TYPES OF RELIGIOUS ORGANIZATION

Weber and Troeltsch: churches and sects

All religions involve communities of believers, but there are many different ways in which such communities are organized. One mode of classifying religious organizations was first put forward by Max Weber and his colleague, the religious historian Ernst Troeltsch (Troeltsch 1981). Weber and Troeltsch distinguished between **churches** and **sects**. A church is a large, well-established religious body – like the Catholic Church or the Church of England. A sect is a smaller, less highly organized grouping of committed believers, usually setting itself up in protest against a church – as Calvinists or Methodists have done.

Robert Wuthnow: the sociologist as religious believer

Many sociologists who study religion are members of a church or temple. In their hearts, they may believe that some religious views come closer to divine truth than others. How do sociologists balance their professional obligations to be objective with their personal beliefs?

One answer comes from Robert Wuthnow, whose book *Christianity in the Twenty-first Century: Reflections on the Challenges Ahead* (1993) deals with the future prospects of Christianity. Although he is a social scientist, Wuthnow made it clear that he came to his research agenda as both a Christian and a sociologist. As a Christian, Wuthnow was concerned with maintaining the vitality of the church into the next century. As a sociologist, he was trying to understand how social change affects the church and its members.

Wuthnow's research method was to interview church members. These discussions led him to conclude that the Christian identity is becoming increasingly global. Denominational boundaries are breaking down. 'In the past, people were Baptists or Presbyterians as much as they were Christians,' but now, 'Christians are realizing their kinship with fellow Christians around the world.' With the impact of globalization, what will be the role of the denominational church?

Wuthnow believes that church members want to 'think globally and act locally.' That is, they look for the common identity of other believers around the world, but seek fellowship with like believers nearby. Thus, if Lily and Sam are Presbyterian, it's not because of loyalty to the denomination at large, but rather because 'they like the pastor, they feel comfortable with the people, the building fits their architectural tastes, the church is not too far away.' Wuthnow argues that the only way the church can remain vibrant is to 'provide people with a strong sense of community—communities of support, service, and residence'.

Although Wuthnow is a Christian, his concerns are sociological and his style of analysis is objective. His subjects regarded him more as a university professor than as a fellow Christian. It appears Wuthnow's concerns as a Christian did not bias his collection of data.

As you think about sociological issues such as secularization or fundamentalism, do you find it difficult to prevent your own views about religion from clouding your analysis?

Churches normally have a formal, bureaucratic structure, with a hierarchy of religious officials, and tend to represent the conservative face of religion, since they are integrated within the existing institutional order. Most of their adherents are like their parents in being church members.

Sects are comparatively small; they usually aim at discovering and following 'the true way', and tend to withdraw from the surrounding society into communities of their own. The members of sects regard established churches as corrupt. Most have few or no officials, all members being regarded as equal participants. A small proportion of people are born into sects, but most actively join them in order to further their beliefs.

Becker: denominations and cults

Other authors have further developed the church/sect typology as originally set out by Weber and Troeltsch. An example is the work of Howard Becker, who added two further types: the **denomination** and the **cult** (Becker 1950). A denomination is a sect which has 'cooled down' and become an institutionalized body rather than an active protest group. Sects which survive over any period of time inevitably become denominations. Thus Calvinism and Methodism were sects during their early formation, when they generated great fervour among their members; but over the years they have become more 'respectable'. Denominations are recognized as more or less legitimate by churches and exist alongside them, quite often cooperating harmoniously with them.

Cults resemble sects, but have different emphases. They are the most loosely knit and transient of all religious organizations, being composed of individuals who reject what they see as the values of the outside society. Their focus is on individual experience, bringing like-minded individuals together. People do not formally *join* a cult, but rather follow particular theories or prescribed ways of behaviour. Members are usually allowed to maintain other religious connections. Like sects, cults quite often form around an inspirational leader. Instances of cults in the West today would include groups of believers in spiritualism, astrology or transcendental meditation.

Evaluation

The four concepts just discussed are useful for analysing aspects of religious organization, but have to be applied with caution, partly because they reflect specifically Christian traditions. As the case of Islam indicates, there is not always a distinct *church* separate from other institutions in non-Christian religions, and other established religions do not have a developed bureaucratic hierarchy. Hinduism, for example, is such an internally heterogeneous religion that it is hard to find within it features of bureaucratic organization. Nor would it make much sense to call the various subdivisions of Hinduism 'denominations'.

The concepts of sect and cult perhaps have broad application, but here again a degree of caution is necessary. Sect-like groupings have often existed within the major world religions. They show most of the characteristics – commitment, exclusiveness, divergence from orthodoxy – characteristic of Western sects. However, many of these groups, for instance in Hinduism, are more like traditional ethnic communities than they are like Christian sects (B. Wilson 1982). Many such groups lack the fervour of 'true believers' commonly found in Christianity, because in the 'ethical religions' of the East there is more tolerance of diverse outlooks. A group may 'go its own way' without necessarily meeting opposition from other more established organizations. The term 'cult' has wide usage, and can be applied, for instance, to some kinds of millenarian movement, yet these are often more similar to sects than to the types of cult Becker had in mind in formulating the concept.

The concepts of church, sect and denomination may be somewhat culture-bound, but they do help us to analyse the tension which all religions tend to generate between revivalism and institutionalization. Religious organizations which have been in existence for some while tend to become bureaucratic and inflexible. Yet religious symbols have extraordinary emotive power for believers and resist becoming reduced to the level of the routine. New sects and cults are constantly arising. We can find a use here for Durkheim's distinction between the sacred and the profane. The more religious activities become standardized, a matter for unthinking re-enactment, the more the element of sacredness is lost and religious ritual and belief become like mundane parts of the everyday world. On the other hand, ceremonials can help revitalize a sense of the distinct qualities of religious experience, and lead to inspirational experiences that may diverge from established orthodoxy. Groups might break away from the main community, mobilize protest or separatist movements, or otherwise differ from patterns of established ritual and belief.

GENDER AND RELIGION

Churches and denominations, the preceding discussion has indicated, are religious organizations with defined systems of authority. In these hierarchies, as in other areas of social life, women are mostly excluded from power. This is very clear in Christianity, but is also characteristic of all the major religions.

Religious images

The Christian religion is a resolutely male affair in its symbolism as well as its hierarchy. While Mary, the mother of Jesus, may sometimes be treated as if she had divine qualities, God is *the Father*, a male figure, and Jesus took the human shape of a man. Woman is portrayed as created from a rib taken from man. There are many female characters in the biblical texts, and some are portrayed as acting charitably or bravely, but the prime parts are reserved for males. There is no female equivalent to Moses, for example, and in the New Testament all the apostles are men.

These facts have not gone unnoticed by those involved in women's movements. In 1895, Elizabeth Cady Stanton published a series of commentaries on the scriptures, entitled *The Woman's Bible* (Stanton 1985). In her view, the deity had created women and men as beings of equal value, and the Bible should fully reflect this fact. Its masculine character, she believed, reflected not the authentic view of God, but the fact that it was written by men. In 1870, the Church of England had established a committee to do what had been done many times before – revise and update the biblical texts. As she pointed out, the committee contained not a single woman. She asserted that there is no reason to suppose that God is male, since it was clear in the scriptures that *all* human beings were fashioned in the image of God. When one of her colleagues opened a women's rights conference with a prayer to 'God, our Mother', there was virulent reaction from church authorities, yet Stanton pressed ahead in organizing a Women's Revising Committee of twenty-three women to advise her in preparing *The Woman's Bible*. In her introduction she summed up her position:

The canon and civil law; church and state; priests and legislators; all political parties and religious denominations have alike taught that woman was made after man, of man, and for man, an inferior being, subject to man. The fashions, forms, ceremonies and customs of society, church ordinances and discipline all grow out of this idea. . . . Those who have the divine insight to translate, transpose and transfigure this mournful object of pity into an exalted, dignified personage, worthy of our worship as the mother of the race, are to be congratulated as having a share of the occult mystical power of the eastern Mahatmas. (Stanton 1985, pp. 7–8; see also Gage 1980, originally published 1893)

Female deities are quite often found in religions across the world. These are sometimes thought of as 'womanly', gentle and loving; in other instances, goddesses appear as fearful destroyers. Women warrior-gods, for example, are found fairly often, even though in actual social life women are only very occasionally military leaders. No wide-ranging study of the symbolic and material involvement of women in different religions has yet been undertaken. But there seem to be few, if any, religions in which females are the dominant figures, either symbolically or as religious authorities (Bynum et al. 1986).

Take Buddhism as an example. Females appear as important figures in the teachings of some Buddhist orders. In one branch of the religion especially, Mahayana Buddhism, women are represented in a particularly favourable light. But as a prominent scholar writing on the issue has remarked, on the whole Buddhism – like Christianity – is 'an overwhelmingly male-created institution dominated by a patriarchal power structure', in which the feminine is mostly 'associated with the secular, powerless, profane and imperfect' (Paul 1985, p. xix). Contrasting pictures of women appear in the Buddhist texts, mirroring no doubt the ambivalent attitudes of men towards women in the secular world. On the one hand, females appear as wise, maternal and gentle; on the other, as mysterious, polluting and destructive, threatening evil.

It is not surprising that religions have stressed masculine images if one accepts Feuerbach's view that religion expresses the deeply held values of society.

Women in religious organizations

In Buddhism, women have traditionally been allowed a role as nuns, which has also been the main avenue for the direct expression of female religious conviction within Christianity. The monastic life derives from the practices of very early Christian groups, who lived a life of extreme poverty given over to meditation. These individuals (many of whom were hermits) and groups sometimes had few connections with the established church, but by the early Middle Ages the church had managed to gain control of most of the orders they had founded. Monasteries became fixed buildings, with their inmates bound to the authority system of the Catholic church. Some of the most influential male monastic orders, such as the Cistercians and Augustinians, were founded in the twelfth and thirteenth centuries – the same era as the Crusades. The majority of women's orders were not established until some two centuries later. Their membership remained relatively small, however, until the nineteenth century. Many women at this time became nuns partly because of the careers which were thereby opened up to them in teaching and nursing, since these occupations were controlled by the religious orders. As the professions became separated from the church, the proportion of women in the orders fell.

Although the rituals and observances of different orders vary, all nuns are regarded as 'brides of Christ'. Until changes were made in some of the orders in the 1950s and 1960s, sometimes elaborate 'marriage' ceremonies were carried out, during the course of which the novice would cut her hair, receive a religious name and be given a wedding ring. A novice is free to leave, or can be dismissed. After several years, however, vows of perpetual membership are taken.

Women's orders today show a considerable diversity in their beliefs and modes of life. In some convents, sisters dress in full traditional habit and keep to established routines. Other communities, by contrast, are not only housed in modern buildings, but have dropped many of the old regulations, the sisters wearing ordinary dress. Restrictions on talking to others at certain periods of the day have been relaxed, together with rules about the position of the body, such as walking with the hands folded and hidden under the habit. These changes were made possible by edicts from the church authorities in the 1960s.

Those in monastic orders usually wield little or no authority within the church hierarchy, even though they are subject to it. The existence of women's orders has never given women any direct power in the wider religious organizations, which in the Catholic and Anglican churches remain almost exclusively dominated by men, although they are now under strong pressure from women's organizations. In 1977 the Sacred Congregation for the Doctrine of the Faith, in Rome, declared formally that women were not admissible to the Catholic priesthood. The reason given was that Jesus did not call a woman to be one of his disciples (Noel 1980). The year 1987 was officially designated by the Catholic church as the 'Year of the Madonna', in which women were advised to recall their traditional roles as wives and mothers.

In a letter published in May 1994, Pope John Paul II reaffirmed the Roman Catholic church's ban on the ordination of women. The letter stated: 'Wherefore, in order that all doubt may be removed regarding a matter of great importance . . . I declare that the Church has no authority to confer priestly ordination on women and that this judgement is to be definitively held by all the Church's faithful.'

In the Church of England up to 1992, women were permitted to be deaconesses, but not priests. They were officially part of the laity, and were not allowed to conduct some basic religious rituals, like pronouncing blessings or solemnizing marriages. On the other hand, at the direction of a minister, a deaconess was able to administer certain sacraments and conduct baptisms, among other duties. A report was issued by the standing committee of the General Synod, the Church of England's governing body, in 1986 to examine the legislation which would be needed were women to be admitted to the priesthood. The group consisted of ten men and two women. Their task was to consider the 'safeguards' necessary to meet the objections of 'those within the Church of

England who are unable to accept, for one reason or another, the ordination of women as priests' (quoted in Aldridge 1987, p. 377). The feelings and aspirations of women themselves received little mention.

The Christian religion was born of what was in a fundamental sense a revolutionary movement; but in their attitudes towards women, some of the major Christian churches are among the most conservative organizations in modern societies. Women ministers have long been accepted in some sects and denominations, but the Catholic and Anglican churches persisted in formally supporting inequalities of gender. The Anglican Bishop of London, Graham Leonard, was asked on a radio programme in August 1987 whether he thought the Christian notion of God would be affected by seeing a woman regularly up at the altar. He replied: 'I think it would. My instinct when faced with her would be to take her in my arms . . .' The possibility of sexual attraction between a woman priest and members of the congregation, he claimed, was a reason why women should not be admitted as full members of the priesthood. In religion as elsewhere, 'it is the male who takes the initiative and the female who receives' (Jenkins 1987).

In 1992 the Church of England voted to make the priesthood at last open to women. Many groups opposed the decision, including the organization Women Against the Ordination of Women, formed by Mrs Margaret Brown. According to her, as well as some male Anglican groups, the full acceptance of women is a blasphemous deviation from revealed biblical truth. Some groups withdrew from the church as a result of the decision. Along with others, Graham Leonard announced his decision to leave the Church of England and enter the Catholic church.

MILLENARIAN MOVEMENTS

The existence and number of **millenarian** movements show very clearly that religion frequently inspires activism and social change. A millenarian group is one that anticipates immediate, collective salvation for believers, either because of some cataclysmic change in the present, or through a recovery of a golden age supposed to have existed in the past. (The term 'millenarian' actually derives from the thousand-year reign of Christ, the *millennium* prophesied in the Bible.) Millenarian movements are deeply entwined with the history of Christianity, and they have arisen in two major contexts – among the Western poor in the past and among colonized peoples in other parts of the world more recently.

The followers of Joachim

One European medieval millenarian movement was known as Joachimism, and flourished in the thirteenth century (Cohn 1970a, 1970b). At this period, Europe's economic prosperity was increasing rapidly and the dominant Catholic church was becoming richer. Many abbots converted their monasteries into luxurious castles, bishops built palaces where they lived as magnificently as secular feudal lords, and the popes maintained splendid courts. Joachimism developed in protest against these tendencies in the official church.

In the mid-thirteenth century, a number of Franciscan friars (whose order stressed denial of material pleasure and wealth) began to protest against the indulgent habits of church officials. They based their movement on the prophetic writings of the abbot Joachim of Fiore, who had died about fifty years earlier. Joachim's writings were interpreted to foretell that in 1260 the 'Spirituals', as they called themselves, would inaugurate the Third and Last Age of Christendom. This would lead to the millennium, in which all human beings, regardless of their previous religious affiliation, would unite in a life of Christian devotion and voluntary poverty. It was prophesied that the existing church would be disbanded and that the clergy would be massacred by the German emperor.

When the year 1260 passed without the occurrence of this cataclysm, the date of the millennium was postponed – and put off again and again. The fervour of the followers of Joachim did not diminish. Condemned by the religious authorities, the Joachimite Spirituals came to see the official church as the Whore of Babylon, and the Pope as the Antichrist and the Beast of the Apocalypse. They expected a saviour to emerge from their own ranks, to ascend the papal throne as the 'Angelic Pope', chosen by God to convert the whole world to a life of voluntary poverty. Among the groups within the movement was one led by Fra Dolcino; with more than a thousand armed men, he waged war against the armies of the Pope in northern Italy until eventually his force was defeated and massacred. Dolcino was burned to death at the stake as a heretic, but for many years afterwards other groups arose claiming to draw inspiration from him.

The Ghost Dance

A quite different example of a millenarian movement is the Ghost Dance cult that arose among the Plains Indians of North America in the late nineteenth century. Prophets preached that a general catastrophe would occur, heralding the millennium, in which storms, earthquakes, whirlwinds and floods would destroy all the white intruders. The Indians would survive to see again the prairies covered with herds of buffalo and other game. After the catastrophe all ethnic divisions would be dissolved, and any whites who came to the land would live amicably with the Indians. The Ghost Dance ritual spread from community to community in the area, just as religious cults have spread more recently from village to village in New Guinea. The rituals of the Ghost Dance, which included singing, chanting and the attainment of trance-like states, were based partly on ideas derived from contact with Christianity and partly on the traditional Sun Dance which the Indians used to perform before the arrival of the whites. The Ghost Dance died out after the massacre at Wounded Knee, in which 370 Indian men, women and children were slaughtered by white soldiers.

The nature of millenarian movements

Why do millenarian movements occur? A number of common elements which most or all share can be identified. Virtually all seem to involve the activities of *prophets* ('inspired' leaders or teachers), who draw on established religious ideas and proclaim the need to revitalize them. They successfully develop a following if they manage to put into words what others only vaguely feel, and if they tap emotions that stir people to action. Prophecy has always been strongly associated with salvation religions, especially Christianity, and most of those who have led millenarian movements in colonized areas have been familiar with Christian practices and beliefs. Many have in fact been mission teachers, who have turned their adopted religion against those who schooled them in it.

Millenarian movements often arise where there is either radical cultural change or a sudden increase in poverty (Worsley 1970). They tend to attract people who have a strong sense of deprivation as a result of such changes, which leads them to abandon their earlier acceptance of the *status quo*. In medieval Europe, millenarian movements were frequently the last, desperate resort of those who found themselves suddenly impoverished. Peasants in times of famine, for example, were drawn to follow prophets who offered a vision of a 'world turned upside down', in which the poor would finally inherit the earth. Millenarian movements among colonized peoples tend to develop when a traditional culture is being destroyed by the impact of Western colonizers, as was the case with the Ghost Dance.

Millenarianism has sometimes been interpreted as essentially a rebellion of the poor against the privileged (Lantenari 1963) or the oppressed against the powerful, and this is obviously a factor in many cases. But it is too simplistic: some millenarian movements, such as that of the Joachimite Spirituals, are forged through influences and sentiments that initially have little to do with material deprivation.

CURRENT DEVELOPMENTS IN RELIGION: THE ISLAMIC REVOLUTION

One view that Marx, Durkheim and Weber all shared was that traditional religion was becoming more and more marginal to the modern world – that *secularization* was an inevitable process. Of the three, probably only Weber would have suspected that a traditional religious system like Islam could undergo a major revival and become the basis of important political developments in the late twentieth century; yet this is exactly what occurred in the 1980s in Iran. In recent years, Islamic **fundamentalism** (an emphasis on a literal interpretation of scriptural texts) has also had a significant impact on other countries, including Egypt, Syria, Lebanon and Algeria. What explains this large-scale renewal of Islam?

The development of the Islamic faith

To understand the phenomenon, we have to look both to aspects of Islam as a traditional religion and to secular changes that have affected modern states within which its influence is pervasive. Islam, like Christianity, is a religion that has continually stimulated activism: the Qur'ān – the Islamic holy scripture – is full of instructions to believers to 'struggle in the way of God'. This struggle is against both unbelievers and those who introduce corruption within the Muslim community. Over the centuries there have been successive generations of Muslim reformers, and Islam has become as internally divided as Christianity. *Kharigism* and *Shi'ism* split from the main body of orthodox Islam early in its history. The Kharigites were the first distinct sect to develop within Islam. They held strongly egalitarian beliefs, rejecting all forms of material privilege, and proclaimed that those guilty of serious sins should no longer be regarded as Muslims. They did not last long as a sect, but they were in some respects forerunners of all subsequent fundamentalist Muslim revival movements – that is, movements claiming to return to the 'essentials' of Islam.

The other major sect, the Shi'ites, has remained influential. Shi'ism is today the official religion of Iran (earlier known as Persia) and was the source of the ideas behind the Iranian revolution. The Shi'ites trace their beginnings to Imam Ali, a seventh-century religious and political leader who is believed to have shown qualities of personal devotion to God and virtue outstanding among the worldly rulers of the time. Ali's descendants came to be seen as the rightful leaders of Islam, since they were held to belong to the prophet Muhammad's family, unlike the dynasties actually in power. The Shi'ites believed that the rule of Muhammad's rightful heir would eventually be instituted, doing away with the tyrannies and injustices associated with existing regimes. Muhammad's heir would be a leader directly guided by God, governing in accordance with the Qur'ān.

Shi'ism has been the official religion of Iran since the sixteenth century. There are large Shi'ite populations in other Middle Eastern countries, including Iraq, Turkey and Saudi Arabia – and in India and Pakistan. Islamic leadership in these countries, however, is in the hands of the majority, the Sunnis. The Sunni Muslims follow the 'Beaten Path', a series of traditions deriving from the Qur'ān which tolerate considerable diversity of opinion, in contrast to the more rigidly defined views of the Shi'ites. Sunni doctrines have themselves changed considerably, particularly since the expansion of Western power over the last two or three centuries.

Islam and the West

During the Middle Ages, there was a more or less constant struggle between Christian Europe and the Muslim states, which controlled large sections of what became Spain, Greece, Yugoslavia, Bulgaria and Romania. Most of the lands conquered by the Muslims were reclaimed by the Europeans, and many of their possessions in North Africa were in fact colonized as Western power grew in the eighteenth and nineteenth centuries. These reverses were catastrophic for Muslim religion and civilization, which Islamic believers held to be the highest and most advanced possible, transcending all others. In the late nineteenth century, the inability of the Muslim world effectively to resist the spread of Western culture led to reform movements seeking to restore Islam to its original purity and strength. A key idea was that Islam should respond to the Western challenge by affirming the identity of its own beliefs and practices.

This idea has been developed in various ways in the twentieth century, and formed a backdrop to the 'Islamic revolution' in Iran of 1978–9. The revolution was fuelled initially by internal opposition to the Shah, Mohammed Reza, who had accepted and tried to promote forms of modernization modelled on the West – for example, land reform, extending the vote to women, and developing secular education. The movement that overthrew the Shah brought together people of diverse interests, by no means all of whom were attached to Islamic fundamentalism, but a dominant figure was the Ayatollah Khomeini, who provided a radical reinterpretation of Shi'ite ideas.

Khomeini established a government organized according to traditional Islamic law, calling that government the 'Representative of Ali'. The Islamic revolution made religion, as specified in the Qur'ān, the direct basis of all political and economic life. Under the revived Islamic law, men and women are kept rigorously segregated, women are obliged to cover their bodies and heads in public, practising homosexuals are sent to the firing squad, and adulterers are stoned to death. The strict code is accompanied by a very nationalistic outlook, which sets itself especially against Western influences. Although the ideas underlying the revolution are supposed to unite the whole of the Islamic world against the West, governments of countries where the Shi'ites are in a minority have not aligned themselves closely with the Islamic revolution in Iran. Yet Islamic fundamentalism has achieved significant popularity in most of these states, and various forms of Islamic revivalism elsewhere have been stimulated by it.

The aim of the Islamic Republic in Iran was to Islamicize the state – to organize government and society so that Islamic teachings become dominant in all spheres. The process has by no means been completed, however, and there are forces acting against it. Zubaida (1996) has distinguished three sets of groups engaged in struggle with one another. The *radicals* want to carry on with and deepen the Islamic revolution. They also believe that the revolution should be actively exported to other Islamic countries.

The *conservatives* are made up mostly of religious functionaries, who think that the revolution has proceeded far enough. It has given them a position of power in society which they wish to hold on to. The *pragmatists* favour market reforms and the opening up of the economy to foreign investment and trade. They oppose the strict imposition of Islamic codes on women, the family and the legal system. This group is most active in conflicts with the radicals.

Zubaida shows that the Islamic revolution has left more untouched from the previous, 'Westernized', regime than is usually supposed. For example, the Islamic government has maintained most provisions of family law coming from that regime. Women also have a much more active public role in Iran than in some other Islamic countries – such as Saudi Arabia.

The spread of Islamic revivalism

Islamic revivalism plainly cannot be understood wholly in religious terms; it represents in part a reaction against the impact of the West and is a movement of national or cultural assertion. It is doubtful whether Islamic revivalism, even in its most fundamentalist forms, should be seen only as a renewal of traditionally held ideas. What has occurred is something more complex. Traditional practices and modes of life have been revived, but have been combined with concerns that relate specifically to modern times.

Islamic fundamentalist movements have gained influence in many countries in North Africa, the Middle East and South Asia over the past ten to fifteen years (see figure 16.1). Algeria is a case in point. In December 1991, the Islamic Salvation Front gained a comfortable victory in the first-round elections to the National Assembly. Its programme was to turn Algeria into an Islamic state along the lines of Iran. However, the army intervened and suspended the elections (Pilkington 1992).

A clash of civilizations?

Many worry that the Islamic world is heading for a confrontation with those parts of the world which do not share its beliefs. The Islamic countries seem resistant to the waves of democratization sweeping across much of the world. Of thirty-nine countries in which Islam is the dominant form of religion, only a handful could be thought to be liberal democracies. Turkey is one example, although it experienced several attempts at military rule in the period between 1960 and 1980.

In some other countries which for a time were reasonably democratic, such as Algeria, democracy has been suspended or destroyed. The Algerian government permitted free elections in 1991, but refused to take them to a second round when it became clear that the Islamic Party, strongly influenced by religious fundamentalism, was heading for victory. The military took control and ever since there has been something close to civil war in the country between the government and Islamic guerrillas.

If the Islamic movement comes into power in Algeria, other countries close by may also follow suit. Egypt, with 55 million people, has its own Islamic rebels, who wish to establish a religious state there. So, too, do many Muslims in Morocco and Libya.

The political scientist Samuel Huntington (1993) has argued that struggles between Western and Islamic views might become part of a worldwide 'clash of civilizations' with the ending of the Cold War and with

Islam's heartland*

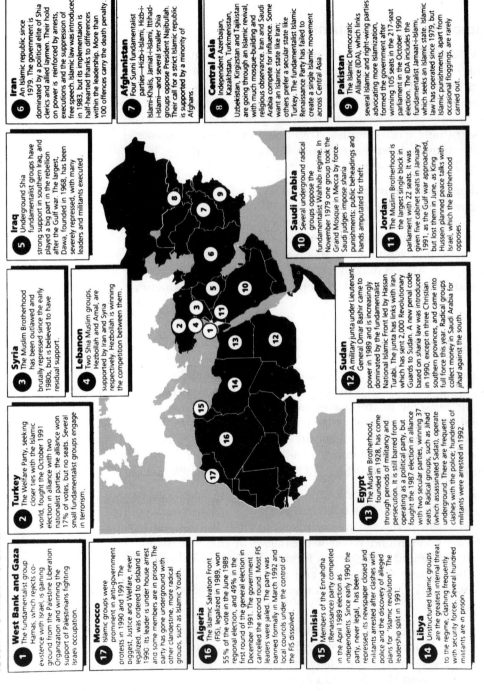

1 West Bank and Gaza
The fundamentalist group Hamas, which rejects co-existence with Israel, is gaining ground from the Palestine Liberation Organization and winning the support of Palestinians fighting Israeli occupation.

2 Turkey
The Welfare Party, seeking closer ties with the Islamic world, fought the October 1991 election in alliance with two nationalist parties; the alliance won 17% of votes, but no seats. Several small fundamentalist groups engage in terrorism.

3 Syria
The Muslim Brotherhood has been outlawed and brutally repressed since the early 1980s, but is believed to have residual support.

4 Lebanon
Two Shia Muslim groups, Hezbollah and Amal, are supported by Iran and Syria respectively. Hezbollah is winning the competition between them.

5 Iraq
Underground Shia fundamentalist groups have strong support in southern Iraq, and played a big part in the rebellion after the Gulf war. The largest, Dawa, founded in 1968, has been severely repressed, with many leaders and militants executed.

6 Iran
An Islamic republic since 1979. The government is dominated by a political elite of Shia clerics and allied laymen. Their hold on power is reinforced by arrests, executions and the suppression of free speech. Islamic law was introduced in 1983, but its implementation is half-hearted thanks to differences within the leadership. More than 100 offences carry the death penalty.

7 Afghanistan
Four Sunni fundamentalist parties—Hizb-i-Islami, Hizbi-Islami-Khalis, Jamiat-i-Islami, Ittihad-i-Islami—and several smaller Shia groups oppose President Najibullah. Their call for a strict Islamic republic is supported by a minority of Afghans.

8 Central Asia
Independent Azerbaijan, Kazakhstan, Turkmenistan, Uzbekistan, Kirgizstan and Tajikistan are going through an Islamic revival, with much mosque-building and religious observance. Iran and Saudi Arabia compete for influence. Some want an Islamic state like Iran; others prefer a secular state like Turkey. The fundamentalist Islamic Renaissance Party has failed to create a single Islamic movement across Central Asia.

9 Pakistan
The Islamic Democratic Alliance (IDA), which links several Islamic and right-wing parties advocating more Islamization, formed the government after winning 105 seats in the 217-seat parliament in the October 1990 election. The IDA includes the fundamentalist Jamaat-i-Islami, which seeks an Islamic state. Islamic law has operated since 1979, but Islamic punishments, apart from occasional floggings, are rarely carried out.

10 Saudi Arabia
Several underground radical groups oppose the fundamentalist Wahhabi regime. In November 1979 one group took the Grand Mosque in Mecca by force. Saudi judges impose sharia punishments: public beheadings and hands amputated for theft.

11 Jordan
The Muslim Brotherhood is the largest single block in parliament with 22 seats. It was given five cabinet seats in January 1991, but lost them in June, as King Hussein planned peace talks with Israel, which the Brotherhood opposes.

12 Sudan
A military junta under Lieutenant-General Omar Bashir came to power in 1989 and is increasingly dominated by the fundamentalist National Islamic Front led by Hassan Turabi. The junta has links with Iran, which has sent 2,000 Revolutionary Guards to Sudan. A new penal code based on sharia law was introduced in 1990, except in three Christian southern provinces, and came into full force this year. Radical groups collect money in Saudi Arabia for jihad against the south.

13 Egypt
The Muslim Brotherhood, founded in 1928, has come through periods of militancy and persecution. It is still barred from operating as a political party, but fought the 1987 election in alliance with two secular parties, winning 37 seats. Radical groups, such as jihad (which assassinated Sadat), operate underground. There are frequent clashes with the police; hundreds of militants were arrested in 1992.

14 Libya
Unstructured Islamic groups are the greatest internal threat to the regime, clashing frequently with security forces. Several hundred militants are in prison.

15 Tunisia
Members of the Ennahdha (Renaissance) party competed in the April 1989 election as independents. Since early 1990 the party, never legal, has been repressed, its newspaper closed and militants arrested after clashes with police and the discovery of alleged plans for 'Islamic revolution'. The leadership split in 1991.

16 Algeria
The Islamic Salvation Front (FIS), legalized in 1989, won 55% of the vote in the June 1989 regional election, and 49% in the first round of the general election in December 1991. The government cancelled the second round. Most FIS leaders were jailed. The party was banned formally in March 1992 and local councils under the control of the FIS dissolved.

17 Morocco
Islamic groups were prominent in anti-government protests in 1990 and 1991. The biggest, Justice and Welfare, never legalized, was ordered to disband in 1990. Its leader is under house arrest and some members are in prison. The party has gone underground with other clandestine, more radical groups, such as Islamic Youth.

Fig. 16.1 Islam's heartland, 1992 (countries and black areas have a Muslim majority; Bangladesh, Indonesia, Malaysia omitted)

Source: The Economist, 4 April 1992, p. 73.

increasing globalization. The nation-state is no longer the main influence in international relations; rivalries and conflicts will therefore occur between larger cultures or civilizations. It is just such a conflict which was enacted in Bosnia, in ex-Yugoslavia, where the Bosnian Muslims fought against the Serbs, who represent a Christian culture.

Islam and Christianity are each religions which lay claim to certainty, to special access to the word of God. Christianity has learned to live along with capitalism and democracy, and if Max Weber was right might even have inspired their early development. To many Islamic believers such an accommodation appears much more difficult. Capitalist enterprise and liberal democracy for them represent the impact of Western culture. Moreover, Islam refuses to draw a distinction between the private life of the believer and public issues.

Yet, as 'civilizations', Christianity and Islam – as the opening quotations in the chapter showed – have more in common with one another than they have differences, originating as they do from overlapping sources. Each has inspired hundreds of bloody wars over the centuries. However, each also contains very strong traditions of tolerance and moderation. We must hope that these allow the two cultures increasingly to live peacefully alongside one another.

Let us now turn to look at the recent development of religion in the West, concentrating particularly on Britain and the United States.

EVANGELISTS INVADE THE STATES OF THE FORMER SOVIET UNION

The collapse of communism opened the former USSR to a wave of religious missionaries. The main church of Russia, the Eastern Orthodox Church, has expressed concern about the number of new religious movements, such as the Hare Krishnas, and the many evangelical and fundamentalist Christian groups entering the country. This concern is shared by all the established mainstream churches, such as the Roman Catholics and the Baptists.

More than 300 US missionary groups are now active in Russia alone, and one of them is sending more than 2,000 missionaries a year into the Commonwealth of Independent States (CIS) and E Europe. These groups bring with them a very different creed from that taught and practised by the older churches of the country. For many such missionary groups, the older churches are not valid Christian churches anyway and part of the missionary zeal comes from a conviction that these older churches are either apostate or even the work of the Devil.

Many of the groups bring the assumption that the American way of life is the fullest expression of true Christian living. This is proving very tempting to people who long to have the consumer lifestyle of the West. However, leaders of the mainstream churches fear that these values will not only force increased division in the expression of Christianity in the CIS, but also undermine core traditional religious values of community and solidarity that have survived the communist persecution only to run the risk now of falling to US evangelical consumerism.

Source: Hutchinson Gallup, *INFO* 1995, (Helicon 1994), p. 183.

RELIGION IN THE UNITED KINGDOM

According to the 1851 census of religion, about 40 per cent of adults in England and Wales attended church each Sunday; by 1900 this had dropped to 35 per cent, by 1950 to 20 per cent and today the total is nearer to 10 per cent. The main British denominations lost an average 5 per cent of churchgoers during the 1980s, with the most substantial decline (of 8 per cent) among Roman Catholics (HMSO 1992).

The pattern, however, is somewhat uneven. A difference exists, for example between Trinitarian and non-Trinitarian churches. Trinitarian churches, which include Anglicans, Catholics, Methodists and Presbyterians, among others, are those which believe in the unity of the Trinity in one God. Membership of Trinitarian churches fell from 8.8 million in 1970 to 6.5 million in 1994. However, there was an increase in the membership of some non-Trinitarian churches, such as the Mormons and the Jehovah's Witnesses, over the same period (see table 16.2).

Most of the adult population of Britain in fact regard themselves as belonging to a religious organization. In a survey, only about 5 per cent of Britons stated they had no religious affiliation at all. Almost 70 per cent of the total population saw themselves as belonging to the Church of England, even though most may not have actually attended church more than a few times in their lives, if at all. In addition to the Church of England, the Presbyterian Church of Scotland and the Catholic Church, the range of other religious groups in Britain includes Jews, Mormons, Muslims, Sikhs and Hindus. Smaller sects include the Plymouth Brethren, the Rastafarians and the Divine Light Mission.

A number of new religious movements have also emerged in Western countries, including the UK. These derive from many religious traditions, some of which were almost unknown in the West until recently. A few, such as the Aestherius Society and the Emin Foundation, already existed at an earlier period in Britain, while others came from different European countries. The majority, however, originated in the US or the East. Membership mostly consists of converts rather than individuals brought up in a particular faith. Members more often than not are well educated and from middle-class backgrounds.

Most of the new religious movements place far more demands on their members, in terms of time and commitment, than older established religions. Some groups have been known to use the technique of 'love bombing' to gain the individual's total adherence. A potential convert is overwhelmed by attention and constant displays of instant affection until he or she is drawn emotionally into the group. Some new movements, in fact, have been accused of 'brainwashing' their adherents – seeking to control their minds in such a way as to rob them of the capacity for independent decision-making. 'Moonies' (see below) have been accused of such practices. On the whole, however, research indicates that such an interpretation is far-fetched; the movements rarely seek, or achieve, this degree of dominance over their members, and

Table 16.2 Church membership in the United Kingdom (millions)				
	1970	**1980**	**1992**	**1994**
Trinitarian churches				
Roman Catholic	2.7	2.4	2.1	2.0
(attendance at mass)				
Anglican	2.6	2.2	1.8	1.8
Presbyterian	1.8	1.4	1.2	1.1
Methodist	0.7	0.5	0.4	0.4
Baptist	0.3	0.2	0.2	0.2
Other free churches	0.5	0.5	0.6	0.7
Orthodox	0.2	0.2	0.3	0.3
All Trinitarian churches	8.8	7.4	6.6	6.5
Non-Trinitarian churches				
Mormons	0.1	0.1	0.2	0.2
Jehovah's Witnesses	0.1	0.1	0.1	0.1
Other Non-Trinitarian	0.1	0.2	0.2	0.2
All Non-Trinitarian churches	0.3	0.4	0.5	0.5
Other religions				
Muslims	0.1	0.3	0.5	0.6
Sikhs	0.1	0.2	0.3	0.3
Hindus	0.1	0.1	0.1	0.1
Jews	0.1	0.1	0.1	0.1
Others	0.0	0.1	0.1	0.1
All other religions	0.4	0.8	1.1	1.2

Source: Christian Research. From *Social Trends*, 1996.

most potential members are well able to decline the movements' overtures if they so wish.

There is a discernible pattern to religion in the UK in terms of age, sex, class and geography. Generally, older people are more religious than those in younger age groups. Churchgoing among young people reaches a peak at the age of fifteen, after which average levels of attendance slump until people reach their thirties and forties and enthusiasm returns; churchgoing thereafter rises with increasing age. Women are more likely to be involved in organized religion than men. In Anglican churches this is only marginally the case, but in Christian Science churches, for example, women outnumber men by four to one.

In general, church attendance and professed religious belief are higher among more affluent than among poorer groups. The Church of England has been called 'the Conservative Party at prayer', and there is still some truth in this. Catholics are more likely to be working class. This class orientation shows itself in voting patterns: Anglicans tend to vote Conservative and Catholics to vote Labour, as do many Methodists, Methodism having originally been closely connected with the rise of the Labour Party. Religious participation also varies widely according to where people live: 35 per cent of adults in Merseyside and 32 per cent in Lancashire are church members, compared with only 9 per cent in Humberside and 11 per cent in Nottinghamshire. One reason for this is immigration – Liverpool has a large population of Irish Catholics, just as North London has its Jews, and Bradford its Muslims and Sikhs.

In terms of their consequences for day-to-day behaviour, religious differences are much more marked in Northern Ireland than anywhere else in Britain. The clashes between Protestants and Catholics which occur there involve only a minority from either faith, but are often acute and violent. The influence of religion in Northern Ireland is not easy to disentangle from other factors involved in the antagonisms; the belief there in a 'united Ireland', in which Eire and Northern Ireland would become one state, is generally held among Catholics and rejected by Protestants. But political considerations and ideas of nationalism play an important role alongside religious beliefs.

RELIGION IN THE UNITED STATES

Diversity

The position of religious organizations in the United States is unusual in several respects. Freedom of religious expression was made an article of the American constitution long before tolerance of varied religious beliefs and practices was widespread in any other Western society. The early settlers were refugees from religious oppression by political authorities, and insisted upon the separation of state and church. The US doesn't have an 'official' church, like the Anglican church in England.

The United States also contains a far greater diversity of religious groups than any other industrialized country. In most Western societies the majority of the population are formally affiliated to a single church, such as the Anglican church in Britain or the Roman Catholic church in Italy. Some 90 per cent of the American population are Christian, but belong to a diversity of churches and denominations. Many groups number only hundreds, but more than ninety religious organizations claim memberships of more than fifty thousand, and twenty-two of these report memberships of over a million. The largest body by far in the United States is the Catholic church, which has some fifty million members. However, it makes up only about 27 per cent of total membership of religious organizations. About 60 per cent of the population are Protestant, divided among numerous denominations. The Southern Baptist Convention is the largest, with over thirteen million members, followed by the United Methodist church, the National Baptist Convention, the Lutheran and Episcopal churches. Among non-Christian groups, the largest are the Jewish congregations, numbering about six million members.

Some 40 per cent of the American population attend a church service each week. Almost 70 per cent belong to churches, synagogues or other religious organizations, and the majority of these claim to be active within their congregations.

Captain Scott O'Grady, of the US Air Force, was shot down over Bosnia in 1995. He spent six perilous days avoiding capture by the Serbian forces, before being picked up and taken to safety. 'Right off the bat,' he said to the world's media, 'the first thing I want to do is to thank God. If it wasn't for God's love for me and my love for God, I wouldn't have got through it. He's the one that delivered me here, and I know that in my heart.' Had a British or French pilot said the same thing in the situation there would have been some mild surprise. Coming from an American, the words seem quite normal. America has a much higher level of religiosity than that found in most European societies. 'In God we trust' appears on every piece of American money, a reminder of the power of religion in the United States.

Survey results show that 95 per cent of Americans say they believe in God, 80 per cent believe in miracles and in life after death, 72 per cent believe in angels and 65 per cent in the devil (Stark and Bainbridge 1985). A World Values Survey published in 1994 showed that 82 per cent of respondents considered themselves 'a religious person', compared to 55 per cent in Britain, 54 per cent in Western Germany and 48 per cent in France. The same poll showed that 44 per cent of Americans said they went to church at least once a week, compared to 14 per cent in the UK, 10 per cent in France and a mere 4 per cent in Sweden (see figure 16.2 and *The Economist*, 8 July 1995, p. 20).

Since World War Two, the US has witnessed a far greater proliferation of religious movements than at any previous time in its history, including an unprecedented series of mergers and divisions between denominations. Most have been short-lived, but a few have achieved remarkable followings. An example is the Unification Church, founded by the Korean Sun Myung Moon. The sect was introduced into the United States at the beginning of the 1960s, displaying all the characteristics of a millenarian movement. Moon's followers accepted his prediction that the world would come to an end in 1967, but the fact that the world carried on in much the same way after that year did not spell the end of the sect. As many previous leaders of millenarian movements have done, Moon readjusted his ideas in the light of his failed prediction. His new doctrines in fact gained even more adherents than before, a claimed membership now of forty thousand people. The beliefs of the Unification Church mix eastern teachings with aspects of fundamentalist Christianity and anti-communism, and new members undergo strict religious training.

Christian fundamentalism

The growth of Christian fundamentalist religious organizations in the United States is one of the most notable features of the past twenty-five or so years. Fundamentalists believe that 'the Bible, quite bluntly, is a workable guidebook for politics, government, business, families, and all of the affairs of mankind' (Capps 1990). Fundamentalism is a reaction against liberal theology and against attendance at church by people who do not take much active interest in religion. The most influential fundamentalist groups in the United States are the Southern

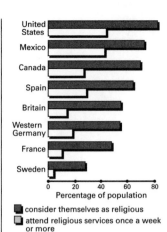

Fig. 16.2 Commitment to religion by country, 1990–1993

Source: World Values Study Group, Inter-University Consortium for Political and Social Research. From *The Economist*, 8 July 1995, p. 20.

Baptist Convention, the Assemblies of God, and the Seventh-Day Adventists.

The 'electronic church'

The electronic media (television and radio) have been centrally involved in changes affecting religion in the United States since the 1960s. The Reverend Billy Graham was the first to preach regularly across the airwaves, and through effective use of the media this Baptist preacher amassed a large following. Increasingly over the last twenty years, we have seen even more sophisticated and systematic use of the media for spreading religious messages and raising money for ministries. The 'electronic church' – religious organizations that operate primarily through the media rather than local congregation meetings – has come into being. Through satellite communications, religious programmes can now be beamed across the world into Third World countries (for example, in Africa and Asia) as well as to other industrialized societies.

Fundamentalist and other groups seeking to convert non-believers have been the main pioneers of the electronic church. One reason for this is the 'star system', inspirational preachers who draw followers to themselves on the basis of their personal appeal. Some such preachers are ideally suited to the electronic media, by means of which their charismatic qualities can be projected to an audience of thousands or even millions of people. Besides Billy Graham, other 'electronic preachers' in the US such as Oral Roberts, Jerry Falwell, Jimmy Swaggart, Pat Robertson, and Jim Bakker and his ex-wife Tammy Faye have made the media their main preoccupation, relying almost wholly on broadcasting to gain a following.

Some religious broadcasters, including Jim and Tammy Bakker and Jimmy Swaggart, were caught up in sexual or financial scandals that seriously damaged their reputations. Because the standing of such individuals has suffered, some have suggested that the peak of the influence of the electronic church has passed. It may be true that revivalist and fundamentalist groups are losing their dominant position, but the broader connections between religious organizations and the electronic media are unlikely to come to an end. As chapter 14 shows, TV, radio and other forms of electronic communication constitute a prime influence in the modern world, and this is bound to continue to stimulate religious programming.

Pat Robertson, a prominent tele-evangelist failed in an attempt to gain nomination as presidential candidate for the Republican Party in 1988. Following this abortive enterprise, he founded the Christian Coalition, a religiously oriented political movement which has achieved some considerable influence. The Coalition has 1.6 million members and large financial resources, enabling it to pour money into lobbying and advertising. In 1995 the Coalition presented a 'contract with the American family', involving a crackdown on abortion, and promotion of family tax relief, prison discipline and the control of pornography.

In response, liberal church leaders drew up a 'Cry for renewal'. They accepted the argument of the Christian Coalition that there is a need to bring moral values into political debates, but insisted that these values should be those of tolerance and humanity, not the conservative values of the Republican Right.

The electronic preaching of religion has become particularly prevalent in Latin America, where North American programmes are shown. As a result, Protestant movements, most of them of the Pentecostal kind, have made a dramatic impact on such countries as Chile and Brazil, which are predominantly Catholic.

CONCLUSION: RELIGION, SECULARIZATION AND SOCIAL CHANGE

When questioned in surveys, some 70 per cent of Britons say they believe in a deity of some sort, and in the US, as we have seen, many sects and cults thrive alongside the established churches. In Iran and other areas of the Middle East, Africa and India, a vital and dynamic Islamic fundamentalism challenges Westernization. In Northern Ireland, Protestants and Catholics keep alive a set of divided religious loyalties established for centuries, while the more activist members of each denomination engage in open warfare against one another. The Pope tours South America, and millions of Catholics there enthusiastically follow his progress. In the face of all this, it might appear strange to suggest that the influence of religion in the modern world is declining.

However, sociologists generally agree that such a decline has taken place, considered as a long-term trend. SECULARIZATION describes the process whereby religion loses its influence over the various spheres of social life. Secularization has a number of aspects or dimensions. One concerns the *level of membership* of religious organizations – how many people belong to a church or other religious body and are active in attending services or other ceremonies. With the exception of the US, the industrialized countries have all experienced considerable secularization when indexed in this way. The pattern of religious decline seen in Britain is found in most of Western Europe, including Catholic countries such as France or Italy. More Italians than French attend church regularly, and participate in the major rituals (such as Easter communion), but the overall pattern of declining religious observance is similar in both cases.

A second dimension of secularization concerns how far churches and other religious organizations *maintain their social influence, wealth and prestige*. In earlier times, religious organizations could wield considerable influence over governments and social agencies, and commanded high respect in the community. How far is this still the case? The answer to the question is clear. Even if we confine ourselves to the present century, we see that religious organizations have progressively lost much of the social and political influence they previously had, and the trend is worldwide, although there are some exceptions. Church leaders can no longer automatically expect to be influential with the powerful. While some established churches remain very wealthy by any standards, and new religious movements may rapidly build up fortunes, the material circumstances of many long-standing religious organizations are insecure. Churches and temples have to be sold off, or are in a state of disrepair.

The third dimension of secularization concerns beliefs and values. We can call this the dimension of *religiosity*. Levels of churchgoing and the degree of social influence of churches are obviously not necessarily a direct expression of the beliefs or ideals held. Many who have religious beliefs do not regularly attend services or take part in public ceremonies; regularity of such attendance or participation, on the other hand, does not always imply the holding of strong religious views – people may attend out of habit or because it is expected of them in their community.

As in the other dimensions of secularization, we need an accurate understanding of the past to see how far religiosity has declined today. In many traditional societies, including medieval Europe, commitment to religious belief was less strong and less important in day-to-day life than might be supposed. Research into English history, for example, shows that lukewarm commitment to religious beliefs was common among the ordinary people. Religious sceptics seem to have been found in most cultures, particularly in the larger traditional societies (Ginzburg 1980).

Yet there can be no doubt at all that the hold of religious ideas today is less than was generally the case in the traditional world – particularly if we include under the term 'religion' the whole range of the supernatural in which people believed. Most of us simply do not any longer experience our environment as permeated by divine or spiritual entities. Some of the major tensions in the world today – like those which afflict Israel and neighbouring Islamic states – derive primarily, or in some part, from religious differences. But the majority of conflicts and wars are now mainly secular in nature – concerned with divergent political creeds or material interests.

The influence of religion has diminished along each of the three dimensions of secularization. Should we conclude that the nineteenth-century authors were correct after all? Perhaps the death-throes of religion have merely been more long-drawn-out than they anticipated? Such a conclusion would be questionable. The appeal of religion, in its traditional and novel forms, is likely to be long-lasting. Modern rationalist thought and a religious outlook exist in an uneasy state of tension. A rationalist perspective has conquered many aspects of our existence, and its hold seems unlikely to be weakened in the foreseeable future. Nevertheless, there are bound to be reactions against rationalism, leading to periods of religious revival. There are probably few people on the face of the earth who have never been touched by religious sentiments, and science and rationalist thought remain silent on such fundamental questions as the meaning and purpose of life – matters which have always been at the core of religion.

SUMMARY

1 Religion exists in all known societies, although religious beliefs and practices vary from culture to culture. All religions involve a set of symbols, involving feelings of reverence, linked to rituals practised by a community of believers.

2 Totemism and animism are common types of religion in smaller cultures. In totemism, a species of animal or plant is perceived as possessing supernatural powers. Animism means a belief in spirits or ghosts, populating the same world as human beings, sometimes possessing them.

3 The three most influential monotheistic religions (religions in which there is only one God) in world history are Judaism, Christianity and Islam. Polytheism (belief in several or many gods) is common in other religions. In some religions, like Confucianism, there are no gods or supernatural beings.

4 Sociological approaches to religion have been most influenced by the ideas of the three 'classical' thinkers: Marx, Durkheim and Weber. All held that religion is in a fundamental sense an illusion. They believed that the 'other' world which religion creates is our world, distorted through the lens of religious symbolism.

To Marx, religion contains a strong ideological element: religion provides justification for the inequalities of wealth and power found in society.

To Durkheim, religion is important because of the cohesive functions it serves, especially in ensuring that people meet regularly to affirm common beliefs and values.

To Weber, religion is important because of the role it plays in social change, particularly the development of Western capitalism.

5 There are four main types of religious organizations. Churches are large and established religious bodies, normally with a formal bureaucratic structure and a hierarchy of religious officials. Sects are smaller, less formal groups of believers, usually set up to revive an established church. If a sect survives over a period of time and becomes institutionalized it is called a denomination. Cults resemble sects, but rather than trying to revive an established church, cults seek to form a new religion.

6 Religious organizations are generally dominated by men. In most religions, particularly Christianity, the images and symbols are mostly masculine; however, female deities are also common in some religions.

7 A millenarian movement is one that anticipates immediate, collective salvation – either because of some fundamental change in the present, or a recovery of a long-lost golden age. Virtually all such movements involve the activities of prophets – professional or 'inspired' interpreters of established religious ideas.

8 Fundamentalism has become common among some believers in different religious groups across the world. 'Fundamentalists' are called this because they believe in returning to the fundamentals of their religious doctrines. Islamic fundamentalism was the prime source of the revolution in Iran which set up a religiously inspired government in that country.

9 Rates of regular church attendance in the UK and most other European countries are low. In the United States, by contrast, a much higher proportion of the population goes regularly to church. Far more people in the UK, Europe and the US say they believe in God than attend church regularly.

10 Secularization refers to the declining influence of religion. Measuring the level of secularization is complicated, because several dimensions of change are involved. Although the influence of religion has definitely declined, religion is certainly not on the verge of disappearing, and continues to unite as well as to divide people in the modern world. Religions can act as both conservative and revolutionary forces in society.

FURTHER READING

Eileen Barker, *New Religious Movements* (London: HMSO, 1991). A survey of the impact of new religious movements in the United Kingdom.

Peter B. Clarke and **Peter Byrne**, *Religion Defined and Explained* (Basingstoke: Macmillan, 1993). A useful primer on the nature of religion.

Sir James George Frazer, *The Golden Bough: A Study in Magic and Religion* (London: Macmillan, 1995). The classic study of mythology, magic, superstition and religion.

Ernest Gellner, *Postmodernism, Reason and Religion* (London:

Routledge, 1992). A provocative discussion of the resurgence and significance of religion in current times.

Gilles Kepel, *The Revenge of God* (Cambridge: Polity Press, 1994). A study of fundamentalism.

Joseph M. Kitagaura (ed.), *The History of Religions: Retrospect and Prospect* (London: Macmillan, 1985). A collection of articles representative of different perspectives on religion.

Josh McDowell and **Don Stewart**, *Concise Guide to Today's Religions* (Amersham-on-the-Hill: Scripture Press, 1988). Comprehensive overview of the topics in religion.

IMPORTANT TERMS

- *monotheism*
- *magic*
- *shaman*
- *totemism*
- *animism*
- *polytheism*
- *prophets*
- *ethical religions*
- *alienation*

- *sacred*
- *profane*
- *civil religion*
- *church*
- *sect*
- *denomination*
- *cult*
- *millenarianism*
- *fundamentalism*

CITIES AND THE DEVELOPMENT OF MODERN URBANISM

➲

BASIC CONCEPT
● *urbanism*

THE TRADITIONAL CITY

Cities in traditional societies were mostly very small by modern standards. Babylon, for example, one of the largest ancient cities of the Middle East, extended over an area of only 3.2 square miles – and probably at its height had a population of no more than fifteen or twenty thousand people. The world's first cities appeared in about 3500 BC, in the river valleys of the Nile in Egypt, the Tigris–Euphrates in what is now Iraq, and the Indus in what is today Pakistan. Rome under Emperor Augustus was easily the largest ancient city outside China, having some 300,000 inhabitants.

Certain common features have been found in most cities of the ancient world, despite the variety of their civilizations. Cities were usually walled; the walls, primarily for military defence, emphasized the separation of the urban community from the countryside. The central area, often including a large public space, was sometimes enclosed within a second, inner wall. Although it usually contained a market, the centre was quite different from the business districts found at the core of modern cities. The main buildings were nearly always religious or political, such as temples and palaces or courts. The dwellings of the ruling class or elite tended to be concentrated in or near the centre, while the less privileged lived towards the edges of the city, with some living outside the walls but able quickly to get within them if they came under attack.

Different ethnic and religious groups were often allocated to separate neighbourhoods, where their members would both live and work. Sometimes these neighbourhoods were also surrounded by walls. The central square, where ceremonial gatherings took place, was usually too small to hold more than a minority of the citizens, and communication between the city-dwellers was usually erratic; public pronouncements might be made by officials shouting at the tops of their voices. Although a few traditional cities had large thoroughfares, in most there were few 'streets' in the modern sense; paths were usually strips of land on which no one had yet built. For most people, the home and workshop were part of the same building, sometimes even the same room. The 'journey to work' was more or less unknown.

In a few traditional states, sophisticated road systems linked the cities, but these existed mainly for military purposes, and communication for the most part was slow and limited in nature. Travel was largely a specialized affair, merchants and soldiers being the only people who regularly travelled any distance. Cities were the main focus of science, the arts and cosmopolitan culture in traditional states, but their level of influence over the rural areas was always relatively low. No more than a tiny proportion of the population lived in the cities, and the division between cities and countryside was pronounced. By far the majority of people lived in small rural communities, rarely if ever coming into contact with more than the odd state official or merchant from the towns.

In studying modern cities in this chapter, we shall be analysing some of the most basic changes which separate our world from the traditional one. For in all industrialized countries most of the population lives in urban areas. Moreover, modern urban life affects everyone, not only those who live in cities themselves. We shall first study the vast growth in the number of city-dwellers that has occurred over the past century and analyse some of the main theories of urbanism, before going on to compare different patterns of **urbanization**, contrasting Britain, the United States and Third World cities.

FEATURES OF MODERN URBANISM

All modern industrial societies are very heavily urbanized. The largest cities in the industrialized countries include up to twenty million inhabitants, and **conurbations** – clusters of cities making large built-up areas – may include much larger numbers. The most extreme form of urban life today is represented by what some have called the **megalopolis**, the 'city of cities'. The term was originally coined in ancient Greece to refer to a city-state that was planned to be the envy of all civilizations, but in current usage it bears little relation to that dream. It was first used in modern times to refer to the north-eastern seaboard of the United States, a conurbation covering some 450 miles from north of Boston to below Washington DC. In this region about forty million people live at a density of over 700 persons per square mile. An urban population almost as large and dense is concentrated in the Great Lakes area of the United States and Canada.

Britain, the first society to undergo industrialization, was also the earliest to move from being a rural to a predominantly urban country. In 1800 well under 20 per cent of the population lived in towns or cities of more than 10,000 inhabitants. By 1900 this proportion had become 74 per cent. The capital city, London, was home to about 1.1 million people in 1800; it increased in size to a population of over 7 million by the start of the twentieth century. London was then by far the largest city ever seen in the world, a vast manufacturing, commercial and financial centre at the heart of a still-expanding British empire.

The urbanization of most other European countries and the United States took place somewhat later – but in some cases, once under way, accelerated even faster. In 1800 the United States was a more rural society than the leading European countries at the same date. Less than 10 per cent of the population lived in communities with populations of more than 2,500 people. Today well over three-quarters of Americans do so. Between 1800 and 1900 the population of New York leapt from 60,000 people to 4.8 million!

Urbanization in the twentieth century is a global process, into which the Third World is increasingly being drawn (see figure 17.1). Before

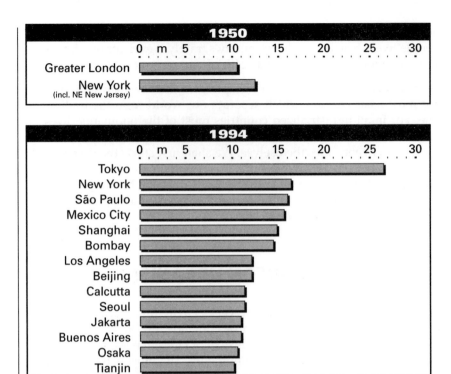

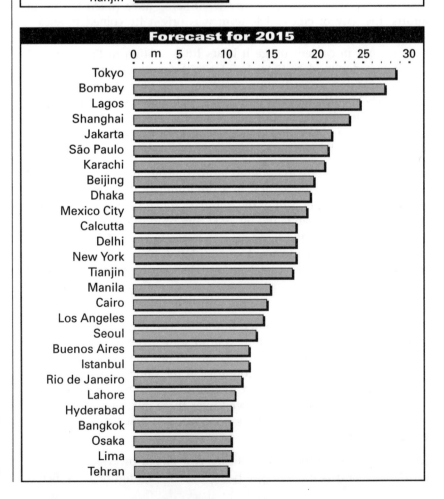

Fig. 17.1 A world of cities: urban areas with populations above 10 million in 1950, 1994 and expected in 2015

Source: World Bank. From *The Economist*, 29 July 1995, p. 5.

1900 nearly all the growth in cities was in the West: there was some expansion in Third World cities over the following fifty years, but the main period of their growth has been over the last forty years or so. Between 1960 and 1992 the number of city-dwellers worldwide rose by 1.4 billion. It is set to rise by 1 billion more over the next fifteen years. In Third World countries the number of people living in cities is increasing by the equivalent of the population of Spain every year.

Urban populations are growing much faster than the world's overall population: 39 per cent of the world's population lived in urban localities in 1975; the figure is predicted to be 50 per cent in 2000 and 63 per cent in 2025, according to United Nations estimates. East and South Asia will contain about half of the world's population in 2025, and by that date the urban populations of Africa and South America will each exceed that of Europe.

The development of modern cities: consciousness and culture

Only at the turn of the twentieth century did statisticians and social observers begin to distinguish between the town and the city. Cities with large populations were recognized to be usually more cosmopolitan than smaller centres, with their influence extending beyond the national society of which they were a part.

The expansion of cities came about as a result of population increase, plus the migration of outsiders from farms, villages and small towns. This migration was often international, with people moving from peasant backgrounds directly into cities in the countries to which they came. The immigration of very large numbers of Europeans from poor, farming backgrounds to the United States is the most obvious example.

Cross-national immigration into cities was also widespread between countries in Europe itself. Peasants and villagers migrated to the towns (as they are doing on a massive scale in Third World countries today) because of lack of opportunities in the rural areas, coupled with the apparent advantages and attractions of cities, where the streets were 'paved with gold' (jobs, wealth, a wide range of goods and services). Cities, moreover, became concentrated centres of financial and industrial power, entrepreneurs sometimes creating new urban areas almost from scratch. Chicago grew to a population of well over two million by 1900, in an area which was almost completely uninhabited until the 1830s.

The development of modern cities has had an enormous impact, not only on habits and modes of behaviour, but on patterns of thought and feeling. From the beginning of large urban agglomerations, in the eighteenth century, views about the effects of cities on social life have been polarized – and remain so today. Some saw cities as representing 'civilized virtue', the fount of dynamism and cultural creativity. For these authors, cities maximize opportunities for economic and cultural development, and provide the means of living a comfortable and satisfying existence. James Boswell frequently praised the virtues of London, which he compared to a 'museum, a garden, to endless musical combinations' (Byrd 1978, p. 92). Others branded the city as a smoking inferno thronged with aggressive and mutually distrustful crowds, riddled with crime, violence and corruption.

Interpretations of city life

During the nineteenth and early twentieth centuries, as cities mushroomed in size, these contrasting views found new forms of expression. Critics found easy targets for their attacks, as the living conditions of the poor in the most rapidly developing urban areas were frequently appalling. George Gissing, an English novelist and social analyst, personally experienced extreme poverty in both London and Chicago in the 1870s. His descriptions of the East End of London, the poorest sections of the city, convey a grim picture. Gissing portrayed the area as:

> a region of malodorous market streets, of factories, timberyards, grimy warehouses, of alleys swarming with small trades and crafts, of filthy courts and passages leading into pestilential gloom; everywhere toil in its most degrading forms; the thoroughfares thundering with high-laden waggons, the pavements trodden by working folk of the coarsest type, the corners and lurking-holes showing destitution at its ugliest. (Gissing 1973, pp. 25–6)

At this time, poverty in American cities received less attention than European poverty. Towards the end of the century, however, reformers began increasingly to condemn the squalor of large parts of New York, Boston, Chicago and other major cities. A Danish immigrant, Jacob Riis, who became a reporter for the *New York Tribune*, travelled extensively across the United States, documenting conditions of poverty and lecturing about needed reforms. Riis's book, *How the Other Half Lives*, which appeared in 1890, reached a wide audience (Riis 1957; Lane 1974). Others added their voices to his. As one poet put it, speaking of the Boston poor:

> In a great, Christian city, died friendless, of hunger!
> Starved to death, where there's many a bright banquet hall!
> In a city of hospitals, died in a prison!
> Homeless, died in a land that boasts free homes for all!
> In a city of millionaires, died without money!
>
> (Quoted in Lees 1985, pp. 128–9)

The extent of urban poverty and the vast differences between city neighbourhoods were among the main factors prompting early sociological analyses of urban life. Unsurprisingly, the first major sociological studies of, and theories about, modern urban conditions originated in Chicago – a city marked by a phenomenal rate of development and by very pronounced inequalities.

THEORIES OF URBANISM

The Chicago School

A number of writers associated with the University of Chicago from the 1920s to the 1940s, especially Robert Park, Ernest Burgess and Louis Wirth, developed ideas which were for many years the chief basis of theory and research in urban sociology. Two concepts developed by the 'Chicago School' are worthy of special attention. One is the so-called **ecological approach** to urban analysis; the other the characterization of URBANISM as a *way of life*, developed by Wirth (Park 1952; Wirth 1938).

Urban ecology

Ecology is a term taken from a physical science: the study of the adaptation of plant and animal organisms to their environment. (This is the sense in which 'ecology' is used in the context of problems of the environment in general, see chapter 19.) In the natural world, organisms tend to be distributed in systematic ways over the terrain, such that a balance or equilibrium between different species is achieved. The Chicago School believed that the siting of major urban settlements and the distribution of different types of neighbourhoods within them can be understood in terms of similar principles. Cities do not grow up at random, but in response to advantageous features of the environment. For example, large urban areas in modern societies tend to develop along the shores of rivers, in fertile plains or at the intersection of trading routes or railways.

'Once set up,' in Park's words, 'a city is, it seems, a great sorting mechanism which . . . infallibly selects out of the population as a whole the individuals best suited to live in a particular region or a particular milieu' (Park 1952, p. 79). Cities become ordered into 'natural areas', through processes of competition, invasion and succession – all of which occur in biological ecology. If we look at the ecology of a lake in the natural environment, we find that competition between various species of fish, insects and other organisms operates to reach a fairly stable distribution between them. This balance is disturbed if new species 'invade' – try to make the lake their home. Some of the organisms which used to proliferate in the central area of the lake are driven out to suffer a more precarious existence around its fringes. The invading species are their successors in the central sections.

Patterns of location, movement and relocation in cities, according to the ecological view, have a similar form. Different neighbourhoods develop through the adjustments made by inhabitants as they struggle to gain their livelihoods. A city can be pictured as a map of areas with distinct and contrasting social characteristics. In the initial stages of the growth of modern cities, industries congregate at sites suitable for the raw materials they need, close to supply lines. Population clusters around these workplaces, which come to be more and more diversified, as the number of the city's inhabitants grows. The amenities thus developed become correspondingly more attractive, and greater competition develops for their acquisition. Land values and property taxes rise, making it difficult for families to carry on living in the central neighbourhood, except in cramped conditions or in decaying housing in which rents are low. The centre becomes dominated by businesses and entertainment, with the more affluent private residents moving out to newly forming suburbs around the perimeter. This process follows transport routes, since these minimize the time taken in travelling to work; the areas between these routes develop more slowly.

Cities can be seen as formed in concentric rings, broken up into segments. In the centre are the **inner city** areas, a mixture of big business prosperity and decaying private houses. Beyond these are older-established neighbourhoods, housing workers employed in stable manual occupations. Further out still are the suburbs in which higher-income groups tend to live. Processes of invasion and succession occur within the segments of the concentric rings. Thus as property decays in a central or near-central area, ethnic minority groups might start to move into it. As they do so, more of the pre-existing population start to leave, precipitating a wholesale flight to neighbourhoods elsewhere in the city or out to the suburbs.

Although for a period the **urban ecology** approach fell into disrepute, it was later revived and elaborated in the writings of a number of authors, particularly Amos Hawley (Hawley 1950, 1968). Rather than concentrating on competition for scarce resources, as his predecessors did, Hawley emphasized the *interdependence* of different city areas. *Differentiation* – the specialization of groups and occupational roles – is the main way in which human beings adapt to their environment. Groups on which many others depend will have a dominant role, often reflected in their central geographical position. Business groups, for example, like large banks or insurance companies, provide key services for many in a community, and hence are usually to be found in the central areas of settlements. But the zones which develop in urban areas, Hawley points out, arise from relationships not just of space, but of time. Business dominance, for example, is expressed not only in patterns of land use, but in the rhythm of activities in daily life – an illustration being the rush hour. The ordering in time of people's daily lives reflects the hierarchy of neighbourhoods in the city.

The ecological approach has been as important for the amount of empirical research it has helped to promote as for its value as a theoretical perspective. Many studies of cities as a whole, and of particular neighbourhoods, have been prompted by ecological thinking – concerned, for example, with the processes of 'invasion' and 'succession' just mentioned. However, various criticisms can justifiably be made. The ecological perspective tends to underemphasize the importance of conscious design and planning in city organization, regarding urban development as a 'natural' process. The models of spatial organization developed by Park, Burgess and their colleagues were drawn from American experience, and fit only some types of city in the United States, let alone cities in Europe, Japan or the Third World.

Urbanism as a way of life

Wirth's thesis of urbanism as a *way of life* is concerned less with the internal differentiation of cities than with what urbanism *is* as a form of social existence. Wirth observes:

> the degree to which the contemporary world may be said to be 'urban' is not fully or accurately measured by the proportion of the total population living in cities. The influences which cities exert on the social life of man are greater than the ratio of the urban population would indicate; for the city is not only increasingly the dwelling-place and the workshop of modern man, but it is the initiating and controlling centre of economic, political

and cultural life that has drawn the most remote communities of the world into its orbit and woven diverse areas, peoples and activities into a cosmos. (Wirth 1938, p. 342)

In cities, Wirth points out, large numbers of people live in close proximity to one another, without knowing most others personally – a fundamental contrast to small, traditional villages. Most contacts between city-dwellers are fleeting and partial, and are means to other ends, rather than being satisfying relationships in themselves. Interactions with sales clerks in shops, cashiers in banks, passengers or ticket collectors on trains are passing encounters, entered into not for their own sake but as means to other aims.

Since those who live in urban areas tend to be highly mobile, there are relatively weak bonds between them. People are involved in many different activities and situations each day – the 'pace of life' is faster than in rural areas. Competition prevails over cooperation. Wirth accepts that the density of social life in cities leads to the formation of neighbourhoods having distinct characteristics, some of which may preserve the characteristics of small communities. In immigrant areas, for example, traditional types of connections between families are found, with most people knowing most others on a personal basis. The more such areas are absorbed into wider patterns of city life, however, the less these characteristics survive.

Wirth's ideas have deservedly enjoyed wide currency. The impersonality of many day-to-day contacts in modern cities is undeniable – and to some degree this is true of social life in general in modern societies. Wirth's theory is important for its recognition that urbanism is not just *part* of a society, but expresses and influences the nature of the wider social system. Aspects of the urban way of life are characteristic of social life in modern societies as a whole, not just the activities of those who happen to live in big cities. Yet Wirth's ideas also have marked limitations. Like the ecological perspective, with which it has much in common, Wirth's theory is based mainly on observations of American cities, yet generalized to urbanism everywhere. Urbanism is not the same at all times and places. As has been mentioned, for example, ancient cities were in many respects quite different from those found in modern societies. Life for most people in the early cities was not much more anonymous or impersonal than for those living in village communities.

Wirth also exaggerates the impersonality of modern cities. Communities involving close friendship or kinship links are more persistent within modern urban communities than he supposed. Everett Hughes, a colleague of Wirth's at the University of Chicago, wrote of his associate: 'Louis used to say all those things about how the city is impersonal – while living with a whole clan of kin and friends on a very personal basis' (quoted in Kasarda and Janowitz 1974). Groups such as those Herbert Gans calls 'the urban villagers' are common in modern cities (Gans 1962). His 'urban villagers' are Italian Americans living in an inner-city Boston neighbourhood. Such 'white ethnic' areas are probably becoming less significant in American cities than was once the case, but they are being replaced by inner-city communities involving newer immigrants.

More importantly, neighbourhoods involving close kinship and personal ties seem often to be actively *created* by city life; they are not just remnants of a pre-existing way of life which survive for a period within the city. Claude Fischer has put forward an interpretation of why large-scale urbanism tends actually to promote diverse subcultures, rather than swamp everyone within an anonymous mass. Those who live in cities, he points out, are able to collaborate with others of like background or interests to develop local connections; and they can join distinctive religious, ethnic, political and other subcultural groups. A small town or village does not allow the development of such subcultural diversity (Fischer 1984). Those who form ethnic communities within cities, for instance, might have little or no knowledge of one another in their land of origin. When they arrive, they gravitate to areas where others from a similar linguistic and cultural background are living, and new subcommunity structures are formed. An artist might find few others in a village or small town with whom to associate, but in a large city, on the other hand, he or she might become part of a significant artistic and intellectual subculture.

A large city is a 'world of strangers', yet it supports and creates personal relationships. This is not paradoxical. We have to separate urban experience into the public sphere of encounters with strangers and the more private world of family, friends and work colleagues. It may be difficult to 'meet people' when one first moves to a large city. But anyone moving to a small, established rural community may find the friendliness of the inhabitants largely a matter of public politeness – it may take years to become 'accepted'. This is not the case in the city. As Edward Krupat has commented:

> The urban egg . . . has a harder shell to crack. Lacking the occasion and circumstances for making an entrée, many persons who see each other day after day at a bus or railroad station, in a cafeteria or passing in the hallways at work, never become anything more than 'familiar strangers'. Also, some people may remain totally on the outside because they lack social skills or initiative. Yet the overwhelming evidence is that because of the diversity of strangers – each one is a *potential friend* – and the wide range of lifestyles and interests in the city, people do move from the outside in. And once they are on the inside of one group or network, the possibilities for expanding their connections multiply greatly. As a result, the evidence indicates that the positive opportunities in the city often seem to outweigh the constraining forces, allowing people to develop and maintain satisfying relationships. (Krupat 1985, p. 36)

Wirth's ideas retain some validity, but in the light of subsequent contributions it is clear that they are overgeneralized. Modern cities frequently involve impersonal, anonymous social relationships, but they are also sources of diversity – and, sometimes, intimacy.

Urbanism and the created environment

More recent theories of urbanism have stressed that urbanism is not an autonomous process, but has to be analysed in relation to major patterns of political and economic change. The two leading writers in urban analysis, David Harvey and Manuel Castells, have both been strongly influenced by Marx (Harvey 1973, 1982, 1985; Castells 1977, 1983).

Harvey: the restructuring of space

Urbanism, Harvey emphasizes, is one aspect of **the created environment** brought about by the spread of industrial capitalism. In traditional societies, city and countryside were clearly differentiated. In the modern world, industry blurs the division between city and countryside. Agriculture becomes mechanized and is run simply according to considerations of price and profit, just like industrial work, and this process lessens the differences in modes of social life between urban and rural people.

In modern urbanism, Harvey points out, space is continually *restructured*. The process is determined by where large firms choose to place their factories, research and development centres and so forth; the controls which governments operate over both land and industrial production; and the activities of private investors, buying and selling houses and land. Business firms, for example, are constantly weighing up the relative advantages of new locations against existing ones. As production becomes cheaper in one area than another, or as the firm moves from one product to another, offices and factories will be closed down in one place and opened up elsewhere. Thus at one period, when there are considerable profits to be made, there may be a spate of office-block building in the centre of large cities. Once the offices have been built, and the central area 'redeveloped', investors look for potential for further speculative building elsewhere. Often what is profitable in one period will not be so in another, when the financial climate changes.

The activities of private home-buyers are strongly influenced by how far, and where, business interests buy up land, as well as by rates of loans and taxes fixed by local and central government. After World War Two, for instance, there was vast expansion of suburban development in major cities in the United States. This was partly due to ethnic discrimination and the tendency of whites to move away from inner-city areas. However, it was only made possible, Harvey argues, because of government decisions to provide tax concessions to home buyers and construction firms, and by the setting up of special credit arrangements by financial organizations. These provided the basis for the building and buying of new homes on the peripheries of cities, and at the same time promoted demand for industrial products such as the motor car. The growth in size and prosperity of towns and cities in the south of England since the 1960s is directly connected to the decline of older industries in the north, and the consequent movement of investment to new industrial opportunities.

Castells: urbanism and social movements

Like Harvey, Castells stresses that the spatial form of a society is closely linked to the overall mechanisms of its development. To understand cities, we have to grasp the processes whereby spatial forms are created and transformed. The lay-out and architectural features of cities and neighbourhoods express struggles and conflicts between different groups in society. In other words, urban environments represent symbolic and spatial manifestations of broader social forces. For example, skyscrapers may be built because they are expected to provide profit, but the giant buildings also 'symbolise the power of money over the city through technology and self-confidence and are the cathedrals of the period of rising corporate capitalism' (Castells 1983, p. 103).

In contrast to the Chicago sociologists, Castells sees the city not only as a distinct *location* – the urban area – but as an integral part of processes of **collective consumption**, which in turn are an inherent aspect of industrial capitalism. Homes, schools, transport services and leisure amenities are ways in which people 'consume' the products of modern industry. The taxation system influences who is able to buy or rent where, and who builds where. Large corporations, banks and insurance companies, which provide capital for building projects, have a great deal of power over these processes. But government agencies also directly affect many aspects of city life, by building roads and public housing, planning green belts and so forth. The physical shape of cities is thus a product of both market forces and the power of government.

But the nature of the created environment is not just the result of the activities of wealthy and powerful people. Castells stresses the importance of the struggles of underprivileged groups to alter their living conditions. Urban problems stimulate a range of social movements, concerned with improving housing conditions, protesting against air pollution, defending parks and green belts, and combating building development that changes the nature of an area. For example, Castells has studied the gay movement in San Francisco, which succeeded in restructuring neighbourhoods around its own cultural values – allowing many gay organizations, clubs and bars to flourish – and gained a prominent position in local politics.

Cities, Harvey and Castells both emphasize, are almost wholly artificial environments, constructed by ourselves. Even most rural areas do not escape the influence of human intervention and modern technology, for human activity has reshaped and reordered the world of nature. Food is not produced for local inhabitants, but for national and international markets, and in mechanized farming, land is rigorously subdivided and specialized in its use, ordered into physical patterns which have little relationship to natural features of the environment. Those who live on farms and in isolated rural areas are economically, politically and culturally tied to the larger society, however different some of their modes of behaviour may be from those of city-dwellers.

Evaluation

The views of Harvey and Castells have been widely debated, and their work has been important in redirecting urban analysis. In contrast to the ecologists' approach, it places emphasis not on 'natural' spatial processes, but on how land and the created environment reflect social and economic systems of power. This marks a significant shift of emphasis. Yet the ideas of Harvey and Castells are often stated in a highly abstract way, and have not stimulated such a large variety of research studies as did the work of the Chicago School.

In some ways, the views set out by Harvey and Castells and those of the Chicago School usefully complement each other, and can be combined to give a comprehensive picture of urban processes. The contrasts between city areas described in urban ecology do exist, as does the overall impersonality of city life. But these are more variable than the members of the Chicago School believed, and are primarily governed by the social and economic influences analysed by Harvey and Castells. John Logan and Harvey Molotch have suggested an approach that directly connects the perspectives of authors like Harvey and Castells with some features of the ecological standpoint (Logan and Molotch 1987). They agree with Harvey and Castells that broad features of economic development, stretching nationally and internationally, affect urban life in a quite direct way. But these wide-ranging economic factors, they argue, are focused through local organizations, including neighbourhood businesses, banks and government agencies, together with the activities of individual house buyers.

Places – land and buildings – are bought and sold, according to Logan and Molotch, just like other goods in modern societies, but the markets which structure city environments are influenced by how different groups of people want to *use* the property they buy and sell. Many tensions and conflicts arise as a result of this process – and these are the key factors structuring city neighbourhoods. For instance, an apartment block is seen as a 'home' by its residents, but as a 'source of rent' by its landlord. Businesses are most interested in buying and selling property in an area to obtain the best production sites or to make profits in land speculation. Their interests and concerns are quite different from those of residents, for whom the neighbourhood is a 'place to live'.

In modern cities, Logan and Molotch point out, large financial and business firms continually try to intensify land use in specific areas. The more they can do so, the more there are opportunities for land speculation and for the profitable construction of new buildings. These companies have little concern with the social and physical effects of their activities on a given neighbourhood – with whether or not, for example, attractive older residences are destroyed to make room for large new office blocks. The growth processes fostered by big firms involved in property development often go against the interests of local businesses or residents, who may attempt actively to resist them. People come together in neighbourhood groups in order to defend their interests as residents. Such local associations may campaign for the extension of zoning restrictions, block new building in green belt areas or on parkland, or press for more favourable rent regulations.

POSTWAR PATTERNS OF WESTERN URBAN DEVELOPMENT

Far more research on urban processes has been carried out in the United States than in Britain, but generally patterns of urban development in the UK in the postwar period have mirrored those that occurred somewhat earlier in the US. We shall therefore look at the

American experience before discussing urban problems and issues in the UK.

Urbanism in the United States

Suburbanization

One of the clearest developments in US cities since the war has been the expansion of *suburbia*. The word 'suburb' has its origins in the Latin term *sub urbe*, meaning 'under city control'. Throughout most of the history of urbanism, this meaning of the term was an appropriate one. Suburbs were small pockets of dwellings dependent on urban centres for their amenities and livelihood. In current times, the word has come to be used to refer to any built-up area adjoining a large city.

In the United States, the process of **suburbanization** reached its peak in the 1950s and 1960s. Central cities during those decades had a 10 per cent growth rate, while that of the suburban areas was 48 per cent. Most of the movement to the suburbs involved white families. The enforcement of racial mixing in schools contributed to the decamping of whites from inner-city areas, many of whom wished to put their children in all-white schools. Of course, there were other reasons too. People moved to escape the pollution, congestion and higher crime rates of the central city areas; they were also attracted by lower property taxes and the prospect of more spacious houses, or having homes with gardens rather than apartments. At the same time, an extensive road-building programme made previously far-flung areas more accessible to places of work, and led to the establishment of industries and services in suburban areas themselves. Many suburban areas became themselves essentially separate cities, connected by rapid highways to others around them. From the 1960s onwards the proportion of those commuting between suburbs increased faster than those commuting to cities (a pattern found today in the UK).

While suburbia in the United States is white-dominated, more and more members of racial and ethnic minorities are moving there. From 1980 to 1990 the suburban population of blacks grew by 34.4 per cent, of Latinos by 69.3 per cent, and of Asians by 125.9 per cent. In contrast, the suburban white population grew by only 9.2 per cent. Members of minority groups move to the suburbs for reasons similar to those who preceded them: better housing, schools and amenities. Like the people who began the exodus to suburbia in the 1950s, they are mostly middle-class professionals. According to the chairman of the Chicago Housing Authority, 'Suburbanization isn't about race now; it's about class. Nobody wants to be around poor people because of all the problems that go along with poor people: poor schools, unsafe streets, gangs' (quoted in DeWitt 1994).

The suburbs nevertheless remain mostly white. Minority groups constituted only 18 per cent of the total suburban population in 1990. Three out of every four African Americans continue to live in the inner cities, compared with one in every four whites. Most black suburban residents live in black-majority neighbourhoods in towns bordering the city.

Inner-city decay

The inner-city decay which has marked all large American cities over the past few decades is a direct consequence of the growth of the suburbs. The movement of high-income groups away from the city means a loss of their local tax revenues. Since those that remain, or replace them, include many living in poverty, there is little scope for replacing that lost income. If rates are raised in the central city, wealthier groups and businesses tend to move further out.

This situation is worsened by the fact that the building stock in central cities becomes more run-down than in the suburbs, crime rates rise and there is higher unemployment. More therefore must be spent on welfare services, schools, the upkeep of buildings and police and fire services. A cycle of deterioration develops in which the more suburbia expands, the greater become the problems of the city centres. In many American urban areas, the effect has been horrifying – particularly in the older cities, such as New York, Boston or Washington DC. In some neighbourhoods in these cities, the deterioration of property is probably worse than in large urban areas anywhere else in the industrialized world. Decaying tenement blocks and boarded-up and burnt-out buildings alternate with empty areas of land covered in rubble.

Urban decay and urban conflict

Riots flared in Los Angeles in the spring of 1992. Henry Cisneros, secretary of the Department of Housing and Urban Development, flew out to the city to investigate at first hand what was going on:

> What I saw was a city in which smoke was everywhere. It smelled of burning wire and plastic. The smoke was so thick that it obscured the lights of a helicopter circling directly overhead. Sirens screamed every few seconds, as strike teams of fire engines escorted by California highway patrol cars – literally convoys of twenty vehicles, the patrol cars to protect the firefighters – raced from one fire to the next. . . . Los Angeles that Thursday night was truly the urban apocalypse in a kind of smoky orange, an assault on all of the senses, people wide-eyed, all-out panic just one loud sound away. (Cisneros 1993)

Los Angeles, you might think, is different. Perhaps it is more violent, living more on its nerves, than most cities. Also, it sits upon a spider's web of geological fault lines; in February 1994, a major earthquake produced scenes not dissimilar from those described above. Yet Los Angeles shares a great deal with most other major US cities – and with large cities in Britain and other parts of the world as well. The city is a concentrated and intensified expression of social problems that afflict American society as a whole.

One such problem is poverty; another is ethnic division and antagonism, particularly between whites and blacks; a third is crime; a fourth is simply insecurity. Insecurities and uncertainties arise from the first three factors, whether individuals are directly affected by them or not.

As in the UK, poverty in the US became more widespread over the 1980s. The proportion of the population living below the official poverty line in the mid-1990s is the highest it has been for more than a quarter-century. Particularly when it creates deprived underclasses,

LOS ANGELES: ETHNIC CONFLICT AND ECONOMIC RESTRUCTURING

The three ethnic groups – blacks, Latinos, and Koreans – have found themselves in conflict and competition with one another over jobs, housing, and scarce public resources.

Part of this conflict stems from the fact that the Los Angeles economy has undergone a fairly drastic restructuring over the last two decades. This restructuring includes, on the one hand, the decline of traditional, highly unionized, high-wage manufacturing employment, and on the other, the growth of employment in the high-technology-manufacturing, the craft-speciality, and the advanced-service sectors of the economy. South Central Los Angeles – the traditional industrial core of the city – bore the brunt of the decline in manufacturing employment, losing 70,000 high-wage, stable jobs between 1978 and 1982.

At the same time as these well-paying and stable jobs were disappearing from South Central Los Angeles, local employers were seeking alternative sites for their manufacturing activities. As a consequence of these seemingly routine decisions, new employment growth nodes of 'technopoles' emerged in the San Fernando Valley, in the San Gabriel Valley, and in El Segundo near the airport in Los Angeles County, as well as in nearby Orange County. In addition, a number of Los Angeles-based firms, including Hughes Aircraft, Northrop, and Rockwell, as well as a host of smaller firms, participated in this deconcentra-tion process. Such capital flight, in conjunction with the plant closings, has essentially closed off to the residents of South Central Los Angeles access to what were formerly well-paying, unionized jobs.

It is important to note that, while new industrial spaces were being established elsewhere in Los Angeles County (and in nearby Orange County as well as along the US–Mexico border), new employment opportunities were emerging within or near the traditional industrial core in South Central Los Angeles. But, unlike the manufacturing jobs that disappeared from this area, the new jobs are in competitive sector industries, which rely primarily on undocumented labour and pay, at best, minimum wage.

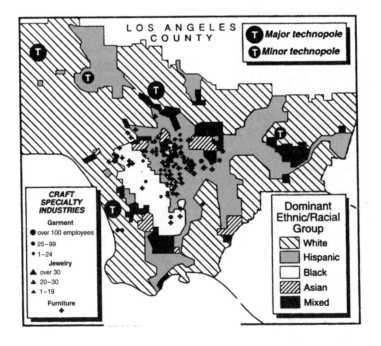

Source: Maya Blum, Kathryn Carlson, Exteln J. Morales, Ross Nussbaum and Patricia J. Wilson, 'Black Male Joblessness, Spatial Mismatch, and Employer Preferences: A Case Study of Los Angeles', unpublished paper, Center for the Study of Urban Poverty, University of California, Los Angeles, May 1993. Map, Chase Langford.

poverty separates large segments of the population from the wider society; many of the poorest groups are concentrated in disintegrating inner-city areas or slums.

Ethnic divisions and class divisions overlap. During the 1980s more immigrants came to the United States than in any other decade since the 1920s. They mostly settled in the major cities, swelling the non-white populations already living there. Atlanta, Washington DC, Baltimore, Chicago, Detroit, New Orleans and Oakland all contain 'minority populations' – now really a misnomer! – of more than 60 per cent. Detroit has an almost 80 per cent 'minority', the most segregated of all American cities. Most of the former white population have deserted the city over the last fifty years, leaving behind them a great deal of distrust and resentment.

Crimes of violence in the cities have reached epidemic proportions. A higher proportion of the American population is in prison than in any other country. Each day, ten young people are shot and killed in US cities, and thirty are wounded. Meanwhile, affordable housing in inner-city neighbourhoods is in such short supply that many of the urban poor must devote two-thirds of their income to paying for lodging.

'All of this hardship and tragic violence', as Cisneros says,

> is not just taking place in Los Angeles – it's everywhere. In the slow burn of hundreds of communities, we're reaping a harvest of inattention, of withdrawal, of an unwillingness or an incapacity to invest in all our people . . . Even if we do not spend much time within city limits, urban vitality is essential for the entire country to generate the productivity, create the opportunity, and achieve the promise of a better future. (1993)

Urbanism in Britain

Suburbanization and inner-city decay

Most of the main patterns of urban change found in postwar America also appear in Britain. Over the past thirty years, the population of all the major central city areas in the UK has declined, largely through movement to outlying suburbs and *dormitory towns* (towns outside the city boundaries lived in mainly by people who work in the city) or villages. The population of Greater London dropped by about half a million over the period 1970–85, while that of many smaller cities and towns has grown over that time – for example, Cambridge, Ipswich, Norwich, Oxford and Leicester. The inner cities have experienced a rapid loss of manufacturing industry, especially in the North.

With some exceptions, the 'flight to the suburbs' has not been as pronounced as in the US, and the resulting central city decay has been less marked. Yet some inner-city areas – for instance, in Liverpool – are as dilapidated as many neighbourhoods in American cities. The Church of England report of 1985, *Faith in the City*, described the inner-city areas in bleak terms: 'Grey walls, littered streets, boarded-up windows, graffiti, demolition and debris are the drearily standard features of the districts and parishes with which we are concerned . . . the dwellings in the inner cities are older than elsewhere. Roughly one-quarter of England's houses were built before 1919, but the proportion in the inner areas ranged from 40 to 60 per cent' (Church of England 1985, p. 18).

As in the United States, new industry is largely being established away from the inner-city areas, either around the outer rim of the cities, or in

smaller towns. This process has in some part been deliberately reinforced by the creation of planned *new towns*, like Milton Keynes in
Buckinghamshire. A range of national schemes – involving, for example, grants for the rehabilitation of houses by their owners or tax incentives to attract business – has been introduced to try to revive the
fortunes of the inner cities, but for the most part these have met with
little success. The Scarman Report of 1982, the result of an official
enquiry into the Brixton riots in London a year earlier, noted that there
was no coordinated approach to inner-city problems (Scarman 1982).
Rioting occurred in several areas again in 1985 (including in Brixton
once more and at the Broadwater Farm estate at Tottenham, North
London, where a policeman was murdered). Further urban riots
occurred in 1990 and 1991, in Oxford, Bristol and other cities. Rioting
happened also in Brixton in 1995.

Paul Harrison, describing Hackney, one of the poorest of London boroughs, reported an atmosphere of despair:

> The police force face the virtually impossible task of keeping the lid on the
> explosive mixture of ingredients that the dynamics of British society have
> assembled in the inner city. This mixture, heated by recession and high
> unemployment, inevitably generates a high level of crime. This necessi-
> tates, in turn, a far more numerous and ubiquitous police presence than in
> other kinds of area, far more frequent unpleasant contact with the public as
> potential suspects, and far greater opportunities for police misjudgement
> or abuse. (Harrison 1983, p. 369)

A vicious circle results. The most deprived are not only the victims of
more crime than other groups, they also have to put up with a much
stronger police presence. In turn, more of them take up criminal pursuits than would otherwise be the case. In areas like Hackney, Harrison
warned, there is coming into being 'a society of barricaded self-
defence', marked also by 'a steady erosion of civil liberties'.

Unemployment in 1995 in some London neighbourhoods is more than
40 per cent among men under twenty-five, and among young blacks it
is sometimes as high as 60 per cent. Homelessness has become probably as great a problem in London as in New York: in London, the
numbers of homeless people rose by a factor of four or five times over
the period from the early 1980s to the beginning of the 1990s. A government commission which reported on inner London in 1987 concluded
that poor urban management – especially lack of public services – had
contributed to the problems of New York, and that London was tread-
ing a similar path.

The government's *Action for Cities* programme of 1988, however, looked
more to private investment and free market forces to generate improvement than to state intervention. Nevertheless, Michael Heseltine, the
minister concerned, did call for 'partnership', a combination of private
initiative and public inducements. By 1990, according to the government, some £900 million of private redevelopment money had been
lured into needy areas as a result of grants and assistance provided
from public funds. However, the response from business was much
weaker than had been anticipated.

Studies indicate that, apart from the odd showpiece project, providing incentives and expecting private enterprise to do the job is ineffective as a way of tackling the fundamental social problems generated by the central cities. So many oppressive circumstances come together in the inner city that reversing processes of decay once they have got under way is in any case exceedingly difficult. Without major public expenditure, however – which is unlikely to be forthcoming from government – the prospects for radical improvement are slender indeed (Macgregor and Pimlott 1991).

Financial crises in British cities

Financial crises have affected many inner-city areas in Britain. The Local Government Act of 1972 set up six new 'metropolitan counties' – Merseyside, Greater Manchester, South Yorkshire, West Midlands, West Yorkshire, and Tyne and Wear. The county councils of these areas were given responsibility for the overall planning of the urban regions, with smaller district councils providing education, some social services, housing and other amenities. London had a different system. For a period of twenty-one years, it was administered by the Greater London Council (GLC), established in 1965. About half the income on which the metropolitan counties depend, as in the case of the GLC prior to its abolition in 1985, comes from central government sources.

From the late 1970s onwards, very strong pressure was put on the local authorities to limit their budgets and to cut local services, even in inner-city areas most subject to decay. A bill passed through parliament in 1980 introduced penalties for authorities which exceeded expenditure levels set by the national government. Some of the councils running the most distressed inner-city areas were not able to meet their set budget levels, and this led to intense conflicts between the government and a number of metropolitan councils, especially those controlled by the Labour Party – such as in Liverpool or Sheffield. Some initially refused to accept the limits drawn up in Whitehall, eighty councillors in Liverpool and Lambeth being personally fined in March 1986 for their lack of cooperation.

Towards the end of the 1980s, local government finances were affected by the introduction of the Poll Tax (officially called the 'community charge'). It was intended to make sure that everyone who might vote for, or benefit from, higher local government expenditure would become aware of its cost implications by having to contribute through a tax levied on each individual – rich or poor – rather than through rates, which was a property tax. In spite of modifications, the new tax proved difficult to collect, and although it was eventually scrapped, its effects were significant. Many city councils found themselves with less revenue than before and were compelled to cut back on what were regarded by everyone as essential services. The proportion of people refusing to pay the tax was far higher in inner-city areas than elsewhere, and in trying to avoid payment, many people in the poorest groups disappeared from the electoral register, losing their right to vote.

Public into private housing

An Act passed in 1980 gave people living in council housing – rented accommodation provided by local government – the right to buy their homes at discounts of up to 60 per cent, depending on the length of time they had lived in them. The policy proved very popular, and large numbers of people took advantage of the opportunity offered. Some 85 per cent of the properties sold were houses rather than flats, indicating that most such purchases were outside the central city areas. By 1988 there were 1.3 million fewer rented houses in the country than eight years previously.

This situation has come about partly because there was no equivalent replacement for the council dwellings sold off, and partly as a result of a decline in the rented property market. The private rented sector has been shrinking for decades, but previously this was offset by the building of new public rented accommodation. A Housing Act passed in 1988 deregulated the rented property market, dropping some of the rent controls that had existed hitherto. Yet the amount of available rented property has only marginally increased.

The council house stock, inevitably, has been largely bought up by the better-off tenants. Thus for the most part the more attractive properties have been disposed of. The danger is that the remaining council housing will become degraded, places where people live when they have nowhere else at all to go. In many of the council homes which remain, processes of deterioration have set in, to some degree because of the financial constraints to which many councils have become subject (Raynsford 1991).

Against a backdrop of prolonged recession in the UK in the late 1980s and early 1990s, the value of housing fell sharply. Many people, including some who had purchased their council dwellings, had taken out large mortgages at a time when it looked as if the value of houses would rise indefinitely, promising them large capital gains when they sold on. The bonanza they had looked for did not materialize, and the number of repossessions from those who could not keep up their mortgate payments multiplied. The UK has a far higher number of owner-occupiers than any other country, and the majority of people prefer to owe money to a building society and own their own home, rather than live in rented dwellings. Yet the sale of council houses has to some extent rebounded against those who stood to gain most from it.

Gentrification or 'urban recycling'

Urban recycling – the refurbishing of old buildings to put them to new uses – has become fairly common in large cities. Occasionally this has been attempted as part of planning programmes, but more often it is the result of the renovation of buildings in dilapidated city neighbourhoods for use by those in higher-income groups, plus the provision of amenities like shops and restaurants to serve them.

The prime example is the renovation of the Docklands area in London. A unique success story in urban regeneration, or a more or less complete disaster? Each view has its advocates, although everyone accepts that, once the economy went into recession, the level of progress in rejuvenating Docklands was lower than its supporters had counted on. The Docklands area occupies some eight and half square miles of territory in East London adjoining the Thames – left economically functionless by dock closures and industrial decline. It was called 'the largest redevelopment area in Western Europe' and 'the greatest opportunity since the Fire of London'.

Docklands is close to the financial district of the City of London, but also adjoins poor, working-class areas on the other side. From the 1960s onwards there were intense battles – which continue today – about what should happen to the area. Many living in or close to Docklands favoured redevelopment by means of community development projects, which would protect the interests of poorer residents. In the event, with the setting up of the Docklands Development Corporation in 1981, the region became a central part of the strategy of encouraging private enterprise to play the prime part in urban regeneration.

The area today is visibly and strikingly different from the impoverished neighbourhoods which border it. Modern buildings, often adventurous in design, abound. Warehouses have been converted into luxury flats, and new blocks constructed alongside them. A very large office development, with a central building visible from many other parts of London, has been constructed at Canary Wharf. Yet amid the glitter there are dilapidated buildings and empty stretches of wasteland. Office space quite often lies empty, as do some of the new dwellings which have proved unsaleable at the prices they were originally projected to fetch. The boroughs of the Docklands have some of the poorest housing in the country, but the people living in such housing have benefited little from the construction that has gone on around them. A good deal of 'affordable' housing was provided; however, only a small proportion of local residents were either able or willing to buy. In 1991, Canary Wharf entered a state of severe financial crisis, and for a long time most of the buildings remained empty.

Docklands is riven between the haves and have-nots to a degree that has few parallels elsewhere. Although it has produced a great deal of renovation and new building, it has certainly not produced an integrated neighbourhood. 'Sunday desert given over to making money,' it has been called, 'with no real soul and without the saving grace of classical architecture, good transport or public spaces' (Brownhill 1990, p. 177).

Arguing against developments such as Docklands in his book about the history of the city, *The Conscience of the Eye* (1993), Richard Sennett has argued that attempts should be made by urban planners to preserve, or to return to, what he calls 'the humane city'. The large, impersonal buildings in many cities turn people inward, away from one another. But cities can turn people outward, putting them into contact with a variety of cultures and ways of life. We should look to create city streets that are not only unthreatening but 'full of life', in a way that 'traffic arteries, for all their rushing vehicular motion, are not'. The suburban shopping mall with its standardized walkways and stores is just as remote from 'the humane city' as the traffic highway. We should instead draw our inspiration from older city areas, such as are found in many Italian city centres, which are on a human scale and mix diversity with elegance of design.

URBANISM AND INTERNATIONAL INFLUENCES

In urban analysis today – as in many areas of sociology – we must be prepared to link global and local issues. Some of the factors influencing the inner cities originate in changes happening well beyond the borders of Britain. For example, the problems suffered by Liverpool, or Teesside, originate largely in the decline of some of the major industries previously centred there, in the face of international competition.

Discussing the ways in which urban areas are increasingly tied to an international system of economic relations, Logan and Molotch have distinguished five emerging forms of city (Logan and Molotch 1987, chapter 7). One is the **headquarters city**. Cities of this type are the centres where the large, transnational corporations house their key activities, and are oriented to global concerns. London, for example, has become one of the world's leading headquarters cities – the centre of financial and industrial transactions, as well as of networks of communication and transportation which stretch worldwide.

A second type of city is the **innovation centre**. This is an urban area where research and development industries become concentrated, developing the technical and scientific processes used to make goods produced elsewhere. Cambridge is an example, where the university has connections with a large 'science park'. The most influential world centre is the Silicon Valley area of northern California. Innovation centres in the United States, and to a lesser degree in Britain, are often directly connected to military production needs. The research and development budget of the Defense Department makes up about a third of all research and development expenditure in the United States; where major contracts are placed strongly influences the level of prosperity of innovation centres.

Silicon Valley is an assortment of towns sprawling over many square miles. Much the same thing can happen in some other industries too. The Po valley, in northern Italy, for example, is where the Italian fashion industry congregates. The valley involves people working in a range of interdependent occupations – as designers, stitchers, weavers and dyers. It consists of a string of small towns, such as Prats or Biella, which together produce 80 per cent of the country's output of wool textiles.

The third type of city is the **module production place**. In the complex international division of labour that now exists, goods are made and assembled in regions distant from one another across the world. Some urban areas become the sites for production processes for parts of products, final assembly being carried out in other regions or countries. A number of transnational companies, for example, have set up plants in Belfast, making parts utilized in final production elsewhere.

A fourth form is the **Third World entrepôt**, related even more directly than the other types to international influences. Cities of this kind are border centres, with substantial new immigrant populations drawn from Third World countries. An example would be Marseilles, a major point of entry for North Africans coming into France. In the United States, the clearest examples are the cities linked to the South American societies, like Miami with its large Cuban population and Los Angeles with its ever-growing Mexican areas.

Finally, there are cities developing as **retirement centres**. Retired people now move in considerable numbers to places with good climates. This is partly internal migration; for example, in England people go to live in resorts on the south coast like Bournemouth or Worthing. Retirement areas also have a strongly international flavour: British people who have holiday houses in Spain may move to these when they retire.

The global city

The leading headquarters cities are examples of what Saskia Sassen (1991) calls the **global city**. She bases her work on the study of three such cities: New York, London and Tokyo. The contemporary development of the world economy, she argues, has created a novel strategic role for major cities. Most such cities have long been centres of international trade, but they now have four new traits:

1 They have developed into 'command posts' – centres of direction and policy-making – for the global economy.
2 Such cities are the key locations for financial and specialized service firms, which have become more important in influencing economic development than is manufacturing.
3 They are the sites of production and innovation in these newly expanded industries.
4 These cities are markets on which the 'products' of financial and service industries are bought, sold or otherwise disposed of.

New York, London and Tokyo have very different histories, yet we can trace out comparable changes in their nature over the past two or three decades. Within the highly dispersed world economy of today, cities like these provide for central control of crucial operations. The more globalized economic life becomes, Sassen claims, the more its management becomes concentrated in a few leading centres. Global cities are much more than simply places of coordination, however; they are contexts of production. What is important here is not the production of material goods, but the production of the specialized services required by business organizations for administering offices and factories scattered across the world, and the production of financial innovations and markets. Services and financial goods are the 'things' the global city makes.

The downtown areas of global cities provide concentrated sites within which whole clusters of 'producers' can work in close interaction, often including personal contact, with one another. In the global city, local firms mingle with national and multinational organizations, including a multiplicity of foreign companies. Thus 350 foreign banks have offices in New York City, plus 2,500 other foreign financial corporations; one out of every four bank employees in the city works for a foreign bank. Global cities compete with one another, but they also constitute an interdependent system, partly separate from the nations in which they are located.

The global city has its downside. Those who work in finance and global services receive high salaries, and the areas where they live become gentrified. At the same time, orthodox manufacturing jobs are lost, and the very process of gentrification creates a vast supply of low-wage jobs – in restaurants, hotels and boutiques. Alongside resplendent affluence there is poverty: the self-same contradiction, one might say, expressed in the sharply contrasting landscapes of London's Docklands.

THIRD WORLD URBANIZATION

The urban areas now developing rapidly in Third World countries differ dramatically from cities in the industrialized countries. People are drawn to cities in the Third World either because their traditional systems of rural production have disintegrated, or because the urban areas offer superior job opportunities. They may intend to migrate to the city only for a relatively short time, aiming to return to their villages once they have earned enough money. Some actually do return, but most find themselves forced to stay, having for one reason or another lost their position in their previous communities. Migrants crowd into squatters' zones mushrooming around the edges of cities. In urban areas in the West, newcomers are most likely to settle close to the central parts of the city, but the reverse tends to happen in Third World countries, where migrants populate what has been called the 'septic fringe' of the urban areas. Many live in conditions which are almost unbelievable to someone accustomed to Western conditions of life, even in slum neighbourhoods.

As illustrations we can take cities in India and Latin America. The Indian population is still growing very rapidly, and the increasing numbers cannot be accommodated within the traditional economy of the rural areas. The rate of migration to cities, even by Third World standards, is exceptionally high. Delhi, the capital, has been the fastest growing of all, but Calcutta, Bombay and Madras all have several million inhabitants. These cities are massively congested. In many areas, large numbers of individuals wander the streets during the day and sleep on the streets at night. They have no homes of any kind.

Others exist in shanty dwellings made of hessian or cardboard, set up around the edges of the city wherever there is a little space. Even if

The new Asian cities owe nothing to the European ideal of picture-postcard Tuscan hill towns, or even the boulevards of Paris. They are dense, raw, chaotic, and they are vast. They have shopping malls and skyscrapers, airports and business parks. But all of these apparently familiar landmarks have been subverted into something very different from their Western originals. Architects here have a weakness for glossy white tiles, mirror glass and chrome. Public spaces, grand plans, picturesque skylines are all but non-existent.

Europe has forgotten what it is like to live in a city in which the population doubles and redoubles in a single lifetime, where a surveyor's grid laid out with pegs and string in open fields can mushroom into a skyline of skyscrapers with an urgency that suggests time-lapse photography. But that is exactly what is happening around the Pacific Rim, in a building boom not seen since London and Paris turned themselves into the largest cities in the world during the nineteenth century. By comparison, Europe's present worries about green belts and inner-city decay look trivial.

As in many Third World cities, in Jakarta in Indonesia, plush new buildings adjoin the shanty town areas.

some of the immigrants do find jobs, the rate of urban immigration is much too high for the provision of permanent housing. The shanty dwellers in Indian cities have virtually no personal possessions, but there are often strongly developed forms of community and self-help organizations.

Delhi

To show how patterns of neighbourhood organization differ from those of Western cities, we shall look at the example of Delhi, the capital city of India. The Delhi urban area incorporates an ancient 'old city' and New Delhi, a section built much later, where government buildings are concentrated. As in other large Indian cities, some areas have an extremely high population density in relatively small neighbourhoods, with quite low density population in other areas. The old city is a convoluted maze of small streets, while some adjoining neighbourhoods have broad avenues. Most of the population move about on foot or by bicycle, rather than by motorized transport.

There is no distinct business district on the model of Western cities; banks and offices are mostly out of the centre. In the old city, there are innumerable small businesses, mainly devoted to commerce, many of the shops being no more than a few feet wide. It is common to find the manufacture and sale of articles combined in these establishments. There are large numbers of streetsellers and hawkers. The New Delhi sections of the city are relatively open and quiet. Those who work in them tend to live in comparatively affluent suburbs situated several miles away towards the edge of the urban area. Makeshift squatter housing surrounds the outer edges of the city, however, and is found along many access routes. Squatter housing tends to spring up in any cleared or undeveloped area, including public parks, and sometimes in neighbourhoods which in the past have been affluent. Squatter dwellings are sometimes found in small clumps or, more often, in clusters of many thousands. The city authorities periodically clear some of the squatter areas, only to see the makeshift huts reappear elsewhere.

Mexico City

The major Latin American cities are similarly surrounded by large-scale shanty neighbourhoods, whose occupants include both recent migrants and families displaced from other sections by urban renewal and highway construction. In Mexico City, over a third of the population live in dwellings or neighbourhoods without running water, and nearly a quarter of these buildings lack sewerage. The city contains an old centre, business and entertainment districts, and affluent housing areas (which are all most tourists see). Almost all the outer perimeter, however, is occupied by shanty or slum dwellings. There is a large amount of state-subsidized housing, but this demands a level of income that no more than 40 per cent of the city's population can afford. Only about 10 per cent of the inhabitants are able to buy or rent on the private housing market. The majority of the city's population, therefore, are excluded from access to available housing. Most housing is provided by the occupants themselves, who have cleared the land and built their own homes. The majority of these housing settlements are in fact illegal, but tolerated by the city authorities.

Three types of 'popular housing' areas are found in Mexico City. The *colonias proletarias* are composed of self-constructed shanty dwellings, mainly put up illegally, on the edges of the city. Over half the population of the metropolitan area of Mexico City lives in such housing. Most of these areas were not spontaneously colonized by squatters, but were organized with the connivance of local authorities and illegal private developers. The developers have their local network of organizers, to whom regular payments have to be made by those living there. Most of the land occupied by the *colonias* was in fact originally public or communal, supposedly protected by the Mexican constitution from being sold or transferred.

A second type of housing is the *vecindadas* or slums. These are mostly in the older sections of the city, and are characterized by the multifamily occupation of dilapidated rental units. Two million people live in such slums, in conditions which are at least as deprived as those in the squatters' areas. The third type is the *ciudades perdidas*, or shanty towns. These are similar to the *colonias proletarias*, but put up in the middle of the city rather than on the periphery. Some of these settlements have been demolished by city authorities in recent years, and their inhabitants have moved to the outer areas.

Ninety-four per cent of the federal district of Mexico City consists of built-up areas, with only 6 per cent of land being open space. The level of 'green spaces' – parks and open stretches of green land – is far below that found in even the most densely populated North American or European cities. Pollution is a major problem, coming mostly from the cars, buses and trucks which pack the inadequate roads of the city, the rest deriving from industrial pollutants. It has been estimated that living in Mexico City is equivalent to smoking forty cigarettes a day. In March 1992, pollution reached its highest level ever. Whereas an ozone level of just under 100 points was deemed 'satisfactory' for health, in that month the level climbed to 398 points. The government had to order factories to close down for a period, schools were shut and 40 per cent of cars were banned from the streets on any one day. One observer described the city at the time in the following way: 'Seen from the air . . . its outlines barely visible beneath a dense grey-brown murk, Mexico City looked as though it was suffering a torrential rainstorm. Down on the ground, the city was bone dry and dusty – but bathed in "ozone"' (Reid 1992).

Yet only some thirty years previously Carlos Fuentes could call his novel about Mexico City *La Region Mas Transparente* – 'Where the Air is so Clear'.

Cities and overpopulation

The largest Third World cities are teeming with people, partly because of population growth and partly as a result of people seeking a job or at least trying to avoid the extreme poverty in the regions from which they came. In the cities, they aren't necessarily any better off; but having made their move, the majority stay on anyway.

Those of us who live in industrialized countries might feel Third World population growth is not our problem, and that those societies should deal with their swelling populations as best they can. There are two reasons why such a view cannot be justified, apart from the immorality of taking a detached stand on the fate of three-quarters of the world's human beings.

One reason is that population growth in the Third World is largely due to factors deriving from Western influence. Some of these are intrinsically beneficial, particularly improvements in hygiene and health care. But others, such as dependence on international trade, have broken down traditional ways of life. If it continues at the present rate, world population growth carries the risk of global catastrophe. The pressure placed on the world's limited resources may lead to global conflict, which could end in major wars.

Virtually all the industrialized countries today have low birth and death rates compared with their past history. Then why has the world population increased so dramatically? In the majority of Third World countries, because of the relatively sudden introduction of modern medicine and methods of hygiene, there has been a rapid drop in mortality. But birth-rates remain high. This combination has produced a completely different age structure in Third World countries compared with the industrialized ones. In Mexico City, for example, 45 per cent of the population is under fifteen years old. In the industrialized countries, only about a quarter of the population is in this age group. The unbalanced age distribution in the non-industrialized countries adds to their social and economic difficulties. A youthful population needs support and education, and during that time its members would not be economically productive. But many Third World countries lack the resources to provide universal education and, as a result, children must either work full-time or scratch a living as street children, begging for whatever they can. When the street children mature, most become unemployed, homeless, or both.

Prospects for change

Fertility remains high in Third World societies because traditional attitudes to family size have been maintained. Having large numbers of children is often still regarded as desirable, providing a source of labour on family-run farms. Some religions are either opposed to birth control or affirm the desirability of having many children. Contraception is opposed by Islamic leaders in several countries and by the Catholic church, whose influence is especially marked in South and Central America. The motivation to reduce fertility has not always been forthcoming even from political authorities. In 1974 contraceptives were banned in Argentina as part of a programme to double the population of the country as fast as possible; this was seen as a means of developing its economic and military strength.

Yet a decline in fertility levels has at last occurred in some large Third

World countries. An example is China, which currently has a population of over 1 billion people – almost a quarter of the world's population as a whole. The Chinese government established one of the most extensive programmes of population control that any country has undertaken, with the object of stabilizing the country's numbers at close to their current level. The government instituted incentives (such as better housing and free health care and education) to promote single-child families, while families who have more than one child face special hardships (wages are cut for those who have a third child). As a response to this government programme, some families went to the extreme of killing their female infants. There is evidence that China's anti-natal policies, harsh as they are, have had a substantial impact on its population. Yet there is also much resistance within the country. People are reluctant to regard parents with one child as a proper family.

China's programme demands a degree of centralized government control that is either unacceptable or unavailable in most other developing countries. In India, for instance, many schemes for promoting family planning and the use of contraceptives have been tried, but with only relatively small success. India in 1988 had a population of 789 million. Its average annual growth of population from 1975 to 1985 was 2.3 per cent; this is projected to decline to 1.8 per cent over the twenty years from 1980 to 2000. But by the latter year, the population will be 1 billion. Even if its population growth rate does diminish, the increase in population will remain extremely large.

Technological advances in agriculture and industry are unpredictable, so no one can be sure how large a population the world might eventually be able to support. Yet even at current population levels, global resources may already be well below those required to create living standards in the Third World comparable to those of the industrialized countries. The consumption of energy, raw materials and other goods is vastly higher in the Western countries than in other areas of the world. Each person in the United States consumes 32 times as much energy as an individual in countries like China or India. These consumption levels partly depend, moreover, on resources transferred from Third World regions. Unless there are major changes in patterns of world energy consumption – such as expanding the use of solar energy and wind power – there seems little possibility of extending this Western level of energy consumption to everyone in the world. There are probably not enough known energy resources to go round.

CONCLUSION

What does the future hold for cities and city-dwellers, considered in relation to population growth? The patterns analysed in this chapter form a complicated mosaic, with no single overall trend emerging. In the industrial countries, the expansion of cities has come more or less to a halt. Improved systems of communication allow people to live farther from their places of work than before. At the same time, their places of work are coming to them, as new industries are located away from city centres. Some older cities, particularly those based on the older manufacturing industries, will continue to decline in population as people are drawn away to other areas. Yet these same circumstances will stimulate further gentrification. The more dilapidated central cities become, in fact, the more opportunities there are for gentrification; property becomes so cheap that renovation can be undertaken at reasonable cost.

While cities in the industrial countries remain stable or diminish in population, those in developing societies will continue to expand. Conditions of life in Third World cities seem likely to decline even further, at least for the urban poor. The problems that exist in the industrialized countries, important as they are, pale almost into insignificance when compared with those faced in the Third World.

SUMMARY

1 Traditional cities differed in many ways from modern urban areas. They were mostly very small by modern standards, were surrounded by walls, and dominated in the centre by religious buildings and palaces.

2 In traditional societies, only a small minority of the population lived in urban areas. In the industrialized countries today, between 60 and 90 per cent do so. Urbanism is developing very rapidly in Third World societies too.

3 Early approaches to urban sociology were dominated by the work of the Chicago School, whose members saw urban processes in terms of ecological models derived from biology. Louis Wirth developed the concept of urbanism as a way of life, arguing that city life breeds impersonality and social distance. These approaches have been challenged, without being discarded altogether. Critics have pointed out that city life isn't always impersonal: many close, personal ties can be sustained in urban neighbourhoods.

4 The more recent work of David Harvey and Manuel Castells connects patterns of urbanism to the wider society, rather than treating urban processes as self-contained. The modes of life people develop in cities, as well as the physical lay-out of different neighbourhoods, express broad features of the development of industrial capitalism.

5 The expansion of suburbs and dormitory towns has contributed to inner-city decay. Wealthier groups and businesses tend to move out of the central city to take advantage of lower local tax rates. A cycle of deterioration is set under way, so that the more suburbia expands, the greater are the problems faced by those living in the central cities. Urban recycling – the refurbishing of old buildings to put them to new uses – has become common in many large cities, but there currently seems little sign of reversing the trend towards inner-city decay.

6 Urban analysis today must be prepared to link global and local issues. Factors which influence urban development locally are sometimes part of much more far-reaching processes. The structure of local neighbourhoods, and their patterns of growth and decline, often reflect changes in industrial production internationally.

7 Like many areas of sociology urbanism is subject to the influence of globalization. A new model of classification has identified five city types: headquarters cities, innovation centres, module production places, Third World entrepôts and retirement centres.

8 Massive processes of urban development are occurring in Third World countries. Cities in these societies differ in major respects from those of the West, and are often dominated by makeshift illegal housing, where conditions of life are extremely impoverished.

FURTHER READING

Jim Kemeny, *Housing and Social Theory* (London: Routledge, 1991). A study which connects housing with wider debates in science and sociology.

Anthony D. King, *Global Cities* (London: Routledge, 1991). Argues for a global approach to the understanding of the modern city.

Paul Lawless, *Britain's Inner Cities* (London: Chapman, 1989). Discusses the development of the inner city and what policies could be developed to try to counter its problems.

Suzanne Macgregor and **Ben Pimlott**, *Tackling the Inner Cities* (Oxford: Clarendon Press, 1991). Discusses the plight of the inner cities in Britain today.

Richard Sennett, *The Conscience of the Eye: The Design and Social Life of Cities* (London: Faber and Faber, 1993). An imaginative interpretation of the nature of urban life, considered historically.

Philip J. Waller, *Town, City and Nation: England 1850–1914* (Oxford: Clarendon Press, 1991). An analysis of social conditions of urbanization in the nineteenth to the twentieth centuries.

IMPORTANT TERMS

- *urbanization*
- *conurbation*
- *megalopolis*
- *ecological approach*
- *inner city*
- *urban ecology*
- *the created environment*
- *collective consumption*
- *suburbanization*
- *urban recycling*
- *headquarters city*
- *innovation centre*
- *module production place*
- *Third World entrepôt*
- *retirement centre*
- *global city*

18

REVOLUTIONS AND SOCIAL MOVEMENTS

In 1989, the Berlin Wall, which separated West Berlin from what was then communist East Germany, was opened by the East German authorities. Thousands of East Germans who had never been able to visit the western part of the divided city came pouring through. The occasion was one of great celebration. People on both sides of the wall who hadn't seen their relatives for some twenty years were reunited with their loved ones.

The fall of the Berlin Wall symbolized a major transition in modern world history: the ending of the Cold War. It was part of a tremendous sequence of changes described earlier (chapter 13), which led to the disappearance of Eastern European communism and to the eventual breaking up of what was then the Soviet Union. Mass unrest was the main social force that brought these changes about. The same year saw thousands of people in the major countries of Eastern Europe – including, besides East Germany, Poland, Czechoslovakia, Bulgaria and Romania – taking to the streets to protest against the domination of their countries by the Soviet Union and to claim political and economic freedoms that, under communism, they had been denied. Their actions led to the eventual collapse of the communist governments in these countries and their replacement by forms of government modelled on those of Western Europe and the United States.

The year 1989 has been described as the 'year of revolutions'; and indeed, the transformations that took place in Eastern Europe and the Soviet Union then and after were quite extraordinary. But what is a revolution? What are the social conditions that lead to revolutionary change? How should we best analyse movements of protest or rebellion? These are the questions we shall address in this chapter.

One revolution has affected world history more than any other in the twentieth century: the Russian revolution of 1917. It led to the formation of the Soviet Union and to the spread of communist societies in Eastern Europe. These were the very societies brought down by the revolutions of 1989.

Let us first of all, however, see what the term 'revolution' actually means.

DEFINING REVOLUTION

We need to define the concept of REVOLUTION as precisely as possible. There are several necessary characteristics:

- A revolution is a *mass social movement*. This serves to exclude instances in which either a party comes to power through electoral processes or a small group, such as army leaders, seize power.

● A revolution leads to *major processes of reform or change* (Skocpol 1979). John Dunn has pointed out that this means that those who take power must genuinely be more capable of governing the society over which they assume control than those who have been overthrown; the leadership must be capable of achieving at least some of its targets (Dunn 1972). A society in which a movement succeeds in gaining the formal trappings of power but is then unable to rule effectively cannot be said to have experienced a revolution; it is likely rather to be a society in chaos or threatened with disintegration.

● Revolution involves the *threat or use of violence* on the part of those participating. Revolutions are political changes brought about in the face of opposition from the pre-existing authorities who cannot be persuaded to relinquish their power without the threatened or actual use of violent means.

Combining these three criteria, we can define a revolution as the seizure, often involving the use of VIOLENCE, of political power by the leaders of a mass movement, where that power is subsequently used to initiate major processes of social reform. In these terms, the events of 1989 in Eastern Europe were definitely revolutions. Mass social movements were involved. Violence was threatened and sometimes (in Romania, for example) used against the government authorities. And the events certainly led to major processes of social reform.

The revolutions of 1989, however, are only the most recent in a history of revolutionary change in modern societies that goes as far back as the eighteenth century. The American and French revolutions, of 1776 and 1789 respectively, were the most important examples during the eighteenth century. The ideals of freedom, citizenship and equality, in the name of which those revolutions were fought, have become fundamental political values. Indeed, these were the values that guided the movements of 1989 in Eastern Europe. Eighteenth-century revolutions in fact played a major role in establishing the political systems of most Western societies, not just the United States and France. But most of the revolutions occurring across the world in the twentieth century, up to the events of 1989, took place in developing societies such as Russia, China, Mexico, Turkey, Egypt, Vietnam, Cuba and other Third World countries.

In the sections that follow, we shall look at the origins and consequences of the Russian Revolution, using this as an example to investigate why revolutions happen. We shall then move on to consider in a more general way one of the influences most important to revolutions – social movements. All revolutions involve social movements, but social movements range well beyond situations of revolutionary change. They come in different shapes and sizes, and have a very strong influence in modern society.

THE RUSSIAN REVOLUTION

Before 1917, Russia was an economically backward society ruled in an autocratic way by the tsars (emperors or kings). Most of the population lived in rural poverty, and the tsarist regime was for the most part a dictatorial one, which employed secret police and informers to keep dissidents powerless. Serfdom (or slavery) was not abolished in Russia until after 1860. The decision of the government to free the serfs was part of an attempt to modernize a society no longer able to compete militarily with the leading European powers. Russia was the loser in the Crimean War of 1854–5, and again in a war with the Japanese, fought in 1904–5. Largely in response to these defeats, programmes of investment in industrial development, including the building of new roads and railways, were instituted. While some economic success was achieved, the tsarist government was too traditionalist to permit the thorough social reforms that were taking place in the European countries.

Russia by 1905 was already a society under considerable strain. The beginnings of rapid industrialization had produced a developing class of industrial workers, whose conditions of life were sometimes as miserable as those of most of the peasantry. Prevented from organizing effective trade unions and completely excluded from political influence, the workers became increasingly hostile to the government. (For a far longer period, there had been growing hostility to the tsars among some of the peasantry.) During the Russo-Japanese war of 1904–5, factory workers and members of the armed forces disillusioned with the progress of the war led an uprising. It was only quelled because the government rapidly signed a peace treaty with the Japanese, disciplining the dissident troops and forcing them to crush the rebel workers. Tsar Nicholas II introduced a few reforms, such as the establishing of a representative parliament, but retracted them all once he felt his power was again secure.

Between 1905 and 1917, there was considerable discontent among industrial workers and peasants, expressed in numerous strikes. Some of these were led by the Bolsheviks, a party professing allegiance to **socialism** and Marxism. The influence of such parties increased during the early years of World War One (1914–18), in which Russia again fared badly – with much more serious consequences than in earlier wars, because of the huge numbers of people involved. Russia had 15 million men in its armies but could not afford to equip them well enough to defeat the Germans. Several million were killed, wounded or taken prisoner.

Shortages of food and fuel caused considerable suffering among civilians, as most resources were devoted to the war effort. The wealthier groups, as well as the poor, started to turn decisively against the government. Tsar Nicholas II, maintaining his right to absolute rule and guided by his strange adviser Rasputin, became more and more isolated. In March 1917 workers and soldiers in Petrograd initiated a series of strikes and riots that rapidly spread throughout western Russia. The Tsar was forced to abdicate, and a new provisional government was set up.

The army, meanwhile, had more or less disintegrated, and most of the soldiers returned to their homes. Peasants began forcibly to take over land from the major landowners, and the provisional government was unable to contain continuing unrest and violence among workers and demobilized soldiers. Lenin, the leader of the Bolsheviks, determined to seize power, using as his slogan 'Factories – to workers; land – to peasants; peace – to soldiers' – an appeal to the impoverished masses. In October 1917 the Bolsheviks forcibly dismissed the provisional government. After reorganizing and remobilizing the armed forces in the new Red Army and successfully emerging from a period of bitter civil war, the new Soviet government set about implementing fundamental social changes, and thus laid the basis for what became the second most mighty industrial and military power in the world.

The Russian Revolution was unusual in certain ways. The uprisings that initially undermined the tsarist regime were more spontaneous and occurred on a larger scale than in most other revolutions in this century. At the beginning of 1917, not even the Bolsheviks anticipated that a revolution would succeed within such a short time. Yet the Russian experience teaches us a good deal about modern revolutions in general. First, we see that revolutions are likely to take place against the background of a war – although that was not the case with those of 1989. Prolonged war puts strain on accepted institutions and may result in a sharply declining level of support for the government. Disaffection within the armed forces removes a regime's major means of suppressing those who oppose it. Second, peasants – rural farmworkers – may play an important role. Before the Russian Revolution, many people (including Lenin) believed peasants to be a conservative force, wedded to traditional ways of life and unlikely to join any movement for radical social change. This assumption was shown to be false.

THEORIES OF REVOLUTION

Since revolutions have been so important in world history over the past two centuries, it is not surprising that a diversity of theories exists to try to account for them. Some theories were formulated early in the history of the social sciences; the most important was that of Karl Marx. Marx, who lived well before any of the revolutions undertaken in the name of his ideas took place, intended his views to be taken not just as an analysis of the conditions of revolutionary change, but as a means of furthering such change. Whatever their intrinsic validity, Marx's ideas have had an immense practical impact on twentieth-century social change.

We shall look at three frameworks for the study of revolution: Marx's view, the account of revolution and rising economic expectations put forward by James Davies, and the interpretation of collective protest proposed by the historical sociologist Charles Tilly.

Marx's theory

Marx's view of revolution is based on his interpretation of human history in general (see chapter 1). According to Marx, the development of societies is marked by periodic **class conflicts** that, when they become acute, tend to end in a process of revolutionary change. Class struggles derive from the **contradictions** – unresolvable tensions – in societies. The main sources of contradiction can be traced to economic changes, or changes in the forces of production. In any stable society, there is a balance between the economic structure, social relationships and the political system. As the forces of production alter, contradiction is intensified, leading to open clashes between classes – and ultimately to revolution.

Marx applied this model both to the past development of feudalism and to what he saw as the probable future evolution of industrial capitalism. The traditional, feudal societies of Europe were based on peasant production; the producers were serfs ruled by a class of landed aristocrats and gentry. Economic changes within these societies gave rise to towns and cities, where trade and manufacture developed. This new economic system, created *within* feudal society, threatened its very basis. Rather than being founded on the traditional lord–serf relationship, the emerging economic order encouraged industrialists to produce goods for sale in open markets. The contradictions between the old feudal economy and the newly emerging capitalist one eventually became acute, taking the form of violent conflicts between the rising capitalist class and the feudal landowners. Revolution was the outcome of this process, the most important example being the French Revolution of 1789. Through such revolutions and revolutionary changes occurring in other European societies, Marx argued, the capitalist class managed to achieve dominance.

But the coming of industrial capitalism, according to Marx, set up new contradictions, which would eventually lead to a further series of revolutions prompted by ideals of *communism*. Marx meant by **communism** the ownership of industry by society as a whole, rather than by individuals. Industrial capitalism, an economic order based on the private pursuit of profit and on competition between firms to sell their products, creates a gulf between a rich minority who control the industrial resources and an impoverished majority of wage workers. Workers and capitalists come into more and more intense conflict with one another. Labour movements and political parties representing the mass of the working population eventually mount a challenge to the rule of the capitalist class and overthrow the existing political system. When the position of a dominant class is particularly entrenched, Marx believed, violence is necessary to bring about the required transition. In other circumstances, this process might happen peacefully through parliamentary action; a revolution (in the sense defined above) would not be necessary.

James Davies: why do revolutions occur?

Criticizing Marx, sociologist James Davies pointed out that there are many periods of history when people have lived in dire poverty but have not risen up in protest. Constant poverty or deprivation does not make people into revolutionaries; rather, they usually endure such conditions with resignation or mute despair. Social protest, and ultimately revolution, is more likely to occur, Davies argued, when there is an *improvement* in people's living conditions. Once standards of living have started to rise, people's levels of expectation also go up. If improvement in actual conditions subsequently slows down, propensities to revolt are created because rising expectations are frustrated (Davies 1962).

Thus, it is not absolute deprivation that leads to protest but *relative deprivation* – the discrepancy between the lives people are forced to lead and what they think could realistically be achieved. Davies's theory is useful in understanding the connections between revolution and modern social and economic development. The influence of ideals of progress, together with expectations of economic growth, tend to induce rising expectations, which, if then frustrated, spark protest. Such protest gains further strength from the spread of ideas of equality and democratic political participation.

As Charles Tilly has pointed out, however, Davies's theory does not show how and why different groups *mobilize* to seek revolutionary change. Protest might well often occur against a backdrop of rising expectations; to understand how it is transformed into revolutionary action, we need to identify how groups become collectively organized to make effective political challenges.

Charles Tilly's theory of protest

In *From Mobilization to Revolution*, Charles Tilly analysed processes of revolutionary change in the context of broader forms of protest and violence (Tilly 1978). He distinguished four main components of COLLECTIVE ACTION, action taken to contest or overthrow an existing social order:

1 The *organization* of the group or groups involved. Protest movements are organized in many ways, varying from the spontaneous formation of crowds to tightly disciplined revolutionary groups. The movement Lenin led in Russia, for example, began as a small group of activists.

2 *Mobilization*, the ways in which a group acquires sufficient resources to make collective action possible. Such resources may include supplies of material goods, political support and weaponry. Lenin was able to acquire material and moral support from a sympathetic peasantry, together with many townspeople.

3 The *common interests* of those engaging in collective action, what they see as the gains and losses likely to be achieved by their policies. Some common goals always underlie mobilization to collective action. Lenin managed to weld together a broad coalition of support because many people had a common interest in removing the existing government.

4 *Opportunity*. Chance events may occur that provide opportunities to pursue revolutionary aims. Numerous forms of collective action, including revolution, are greatly influenced by such incidental events. There was no inevitability to Lenin's success, which depended on a number of contingent factors – including success in battle. If Lenin had been killed, would there have been a revolution?

Collective action itself can simply be defined as people acting together in pursuit of interests they share – for example, gathering to demonstrate in support of their cause. Some of these people may be intensely involved, others may lend more passive or irregular support. Effective collective action, such as action that culminates in revolution, usually moves through stages 1 to 4.

The resumption of French nuclear testing at Muraroa atoll in 1995 produced mass anger and demonstrations in the Asia/Pacific region.

Social movements, in Tilly's view, tend to develop as means of **mobilizing** group resources either when people have no institutionalized means of making their voices heard or when their needs are directly repressed by the state authorities. Although collective action at some point involves open confrontation with the political authorities – 'taking to the streets' – only when such activity is backed by groups who are systematically organized is confrontation likely to have much impact on established patterns of power.

Typical models of collective action and protest vary with historical and cultural circumstances. In Britain today, for example, most people are familiar with forms of demonstration such as mass marches, large assemblies and street riots, whether or not they have participated in such activities. Other types of collective protest, however, have become less common or have disappeared altogether in most modern societies (such as fights between villages, machine breaking or lynching). Protesters can also build on examples taken from other countries: for instance, **guerrilla movements** proliferated in various parts of the world once disaffected groups learned how successful guerrilla actions can be against regular armies.

When and why does collective action become violent? After studying a large number of incidents that have occurred in Western Europe since 1800, Tilly concludes that most collective violence develops from action that is not itself initially violent. Whether violence occurs depends not so much on the nature of the activity as on other factors – in particular, how the authorities respond. A good instance is the street demonstration. The vast majority of such demonstrations take place without damage either to people or to property. A minority lead to violence, and are then labelled as riots. Sometimes the authorities step in when violence has already occurred; more often, the historical record shows, they are the originators of violence. In Tilly's words, 'In the modern European experience repressive forces are themselves the most consistent initiators and performers of collective violence' (1978). Moreover, when violent confrontations do occur, the agents of authority are responsible for the largest share of deaths and injuries. This is not surprising given their special access to arms and military discipline. The groups they are attempting to control, conversely, do greater damage to objects or property.

Revolutionary movements, according to Tilly, are a type of collective action that occurs in situations of what he calls **multiple sovereignty** – these occur when a government for some reason lacks full control over the areas it is supposed to administer. Multiple sovereignty can arise as a result of external war, internal political clashes, or the two combined. Whether a revolutionary takeover of power is accomplished depends on how far the ruling authorities maintain control over the armed forces, the extent of conflicts within ruling groups and the level of organization of the protest movements trying to seize power.

Tilly's work represents one of the most sophisticated attempts to analyse collective violence and revolutionary struggles. The concepts he develops seem to have wide application, and his use of them is sensitive to the variabilities of historical time and place. How social movements are organized, the resources they are able to mobilize, the common interests of groups contending for power, and chance opportunities are all important aspects of revolutionary transformation.

Tilly says little, however, about the circumstances that lead to multiple sovereignty. This is such a fundamental part of explaining revolution that it represents a serious omission. According to Theda Skocpol, Tilly assumes that revolutionary movements are guided by the conscious and deliberate pursuit of interests, and successful processes of revolutionary change occur when people manage to realize these interests. Skocpol, by contrast, sees revolutionary movements as more ambiguous and indecisive in their objectives. Revolutions, she emphasizes, largely emerge as unintended consequences of more partial aims:

> In fact, in historical revolutions, differently situated and motivated groups have become participants in complex unfoldings of multiple conflicts. These conflicts have been powerfully shaped and limited by existing social, economic and international conditions. And they have proceeded in different ways depending upon how each revolutionary situation emerged in the first place. (1979)

CROWDS, RIOTS AND OTHER FORMS OF COLLECTIVE ACTION

All revolutions involve collective action. But, as Tilly's theory indicates, collective action is found in other circumstances besides those of revolutionary change, and can occur whenever there is the chance of large numbers of people gathering together. From the first development of cities, the 'urban rabble' constituted a potential danger to political authorities. In urban neighbourhoods, in contrast to rural areas, many people live in close proximity to one another and can relatively easily take to the streets to demonstrate support for causes or express grievances.

The actions of urban groups are one example of **crowd activities**. A crowd is any sizeable collection of people who are in direct interaction with one another in a public place. Crowds are an everyday part of urban life in one sense. We speak of a crowded shopping street or a crowded theatre or amusement park, for instance, meaning that many people are jostling together in a physically confined space. These are individuals in circumstances of unfocused interaction (see chapter 4): they are physically present in the same setting and aware of one another's presence, but they are pursuing, in small groups or as individuals, their own aims, going their separate ways. However, when there is a **riot**, demonstration or panic, everyone's actions become bound up with the others'. The situation suddenly becomes one of focused interaction; however temporarily, the crowd starts acting as a single unit. Crowd action in this sense has stimulated the interest of sociologists and historians for years – in fact, ever since the French Revolution of 1789.

Mob action and rioting, as Tilly emphasized, characteristically express the frustrations of people who cannot gain access to orthodox channels to express grievances or press for reforms they think necessary. Ruling authorities of all types have always feared mob activity, not just because of the direct threat it poses, but because it gives a public and tangible form to felt social injustices. But even riots that seem negative, giving rise to wanton destruction and loss of life, may stimulate change and produce at least some desired benefits.

SOCIAL MOVEMENTS

A wide variety of social movements besides those leading to revolution, some enduring, some transient, have existed in modern societies. Social movements are as evident a feature of the contemporary world as are the formal, bureaucratic organizations they often oppose. The study of their nature and impact forms an area of major interest in sociology.

A SOCIAL MOVEMENT may be defined as *a collective attempt to further a common interest or secure a common goal, through collective action outside the sphere of established institutions*. The definition has to be a broad one, precisely because of the variations between different types of movements. Some social movements are very small, numbering no more than a few dozen members; others may include thousands or even millions of people. Some movements carry on their activities within the laws of the society in which they exist, while others operate as illegal or underground groups. Often, laws are altered as a result of the action of social movements. For example, it used to be that groups of workers that called their members out on strike were engaging in illegal activity, punished with varying degrees of severity in different countries. Eventually, however, the laws were amended, making the strike a permissible tactic of industrial conflict. Other modes of economic protest, such as sit-ins in factories or workplaces, still remain outside the law in most countries.

The dividing line between a social movement and a formal organization is sometimes blurred, because movements that become well established usually take on bureaucratic characteristics. The Salvation Army, for example, began as a social movement, but has now taken on most of the characteristics of a more permanent organization. Less frequently, an organization may devolve into a social movement, as when, for instance, a political party is banned and forced to go underground, perhaps becoming a guerrilla movement.

Classifying social movements

Various ways of classifying social movements have been proposed. Perhaps the neatest and most comprehensive classification is that developed by David Aberle, who distinguishes four types of movement (Aberle 1966). **Transformative movements** aim at far-reaching, cataclysmic and often violent change in the society of which they are a part. Examples are revolutionary movements and some radical religious movements; many millenarian movements, as well, have foreseen a

GREEN MOVEMENT: CHRONOLOGY

1798	Thomas Malthus's *An Essay on the Principle of Population* published, setting out the idea that humans are also bound by ecological constraints.
1865	Commons Preservation Society founded, raising the issue of public access to the countryside, taken further by the mass trespasses of the 1930s.
1893	National Trust founded in the UK to buy land in order to preserve places of natural beauty and cultural landmarks.
1930	Chlorofluorocarbons (CFCs) invented; they were hailed as a boon for humanity as they were not only cheap and nonflammable but also thought not to be harmful to the environment.
1934	Drought exacerbated soil erosion, causing the 'Dust Bowl Storm' in the Great Plains region of North America, during which some 350 million tons of topsoil were blown away.
1948	United Nations created special environmental agency, the International Union for the Conservation of Nature.
1952	Air pollution caused massive smog in London, killing some 4,000 people and leading to Clean Air legislation.
1968	Garret Hardin's essay *The Tragedy of the Commons* challenges individuals to recognize their personal responsibility for environmental degradation as a result of lifestyle choices.
1969	Friends of the Earth launched in USA as a more dynamic breakaway group from increasingly conservative Sierra Club; there was an upsurge of more radical active groups within the environmental movement over the following years.
1974	First scientific warning of serious depletion of protective ozone layer in upper atmosphere by CFCs.
1980	US President Jimmy Carter commissions *Global 2000* report, reflecting entry of environmental concerns into mainstream of political issues.
1983	German Greens (*Die Grünen*) win 5% of vote, giving them 27 seats in the Bundestag.
1985	Greenpeace boat Rainbow Warrior sunk by French intelligence agents while in a New Zealand harbour during a protest against French nuclear testing in the South Pacific. One crew member was killed.
1989	European elections put green issues firmly on political agenda as Green parties across Europe attracted unprecedented support; especially in the UK, where the Greens received some 15% of votes cast (though not of seats).
1992	United Nations Earth Summit in Rio de Janeiro aroused great media interest but achieved little progress in tackling difficult global environmental issues as many nations feared possible effects on trade.
1994	Anti-road protests in the UK reached new height with 'Battle of Wanstonia' as green activists occupied buildings and trees in Wanstead, East London, in attempt to halt construction of M11 motorway.

Source: 1994 Hutchinson Gallup, *INFO 1995*, Helicon, p. 514.

more or less complete restructuring of society when the era of salvation arrives. **Reformative movements** aspire to alter only some aspects of the existing social order. They concern themselves with specific kinds of inequality or injustice. A case in point would be Life and other anti-abortion groups.

Transformative and reformative movements are both concerned primarily with securing changes in society. Aberle's other two types are mainly aimed at changing the habits or outlook of individuals. **Redemptive movements** seek to rescue people from ways of life seen as corrupting. Many religious movements belong in this category, in so far as they concentrate on personal salvation. Examples are the Pentecostal sects, which believe that individuals' spiritual development is the true indication of their worth. The somewhat clumsily titled

alterative movements aim at securing partial change in individuals. They do not seek to achieve a complete alteration in people's habits, but are concerned with changing certain specific traits. An illustration is Alcoholics Anonymous.

Feminist movements

Theories of revolution inevitably tend to overlap with those of social movements. Charles Tilly's emphasis on resource mobilization, for example, has been applied to social movements such as the feminist movement – to which we now turn. **Feminist movements** have not been separate from other forms of social movement. Feminism has been strongly influenced by revolutions – including the American and French revolutions of the eighteenth century.

The first groups actively organized to promote women's rights date from the period immediately following the two revolutions. In the 1790s, inspired by the ideals of freedom and equality for which the French Revolution had been fought, several women's clubs were formed in Paris and major provincial cities. The clubs provided meeting places for women, but also petitioned for equal rights in education, employment and government. Marie Gouze, a leader of one of the clubs, drew up a statement entitled 'Declaration of the Rights of Women', based on the 'Declaration of the Rights of Man and Citizen', the main constitutional document of the revolution. How could true equality be achieved, she argued, when half the population were excluded from the privileges that men share?

The response from the male revolutionary leaders was less than sympathetic – Marie Gouze was executed in 1793, charged with 'having forgotten the virtues which belong to her sex'. The women's clubs were subsequently dissolved by government decree. Feminist groups and women's movements have been formed repeatedly in Western countries since that date, almost always encountering hostility, and sometimes provoking violence, from the established authorities. Marie Gouze was by no means the only feminist to give her life to the cause of achieving equal rights for her sex.

In the nineteenth century, feminism became more advanced in the United States than elsewhere, and most leaders of women's movements in other countries looked to the struggles of American women as a model. In the 1840s and 1850s, American feminists were closely involved with groups devoted to the abolition of slavery. Yet, having no formal political rights (the Constitution did not give women the right to vote), women were excluded from the political lobbying through which reformers could pursue their objectives. No women were allowed to participate in a world anti-slavery convention held in London in 1840. This fact led the women's groups to turn more directly to considering gender inequalities. In 1848, just as their French counterparts had done a half century before, women leaders in the United States met to approve a 'Declaration of Sentiments', modelled on the Declaration of Independence. 'We hold these truths to be self-evident,' it began, 'that all men and women are created equal.' The declaration set out a long list of the injustices to which women were subject. However, few real gains in improving the social or political position of women were made during this period. When slavery ended, Congress ruled that only freed *male* slaves should be given the vote.

Some African-American women played a part in the early development of the women's movement in the United States, although they often had to contend with hostility from their white sisters. One, Sojourner Truth, spoke out against both slavery and the disenfranchisement of women, linking the two issues closely. When she forcefully and passionately addressed an anti-slavery rally in Indiana in the 1850s and a white man yelled at her, 'I don't believe you really are a woman', she publicly bared her breasts to prove him wrong. Although Truth played a prominent part in women's struggles of the period (hooks 1981), other black women who tried to participate became disillusioned with the prejudice they encountered; African-American feminists as a result were few in number.

One of the most important events in the early development of feminist movements in Europe was the presentation of a petition, signed by 1,500 women, to the British Parliament in 1866, demanding that the electoral reforms then being discussed include full voting rights for women. The petition was ignored; in response, its organizers set up the National Society for Women's Suffrage the following year. The members of the society became known as suffragists, and throughout the remainder of the nineteenth century they continued to petition Parliament to extend voting rights to women. By the early twentieth century, the world influence of British feminism rivalled that of feminists in the United States. Frequent marches and street demonstrations were organized in both countries. An open-air meeting held in London in June 1908 attracted a crowd of half a million people. During this period, women's movements mushroomed in all the major European countries, together with Australia and New Zealand.

By 1920, women had attained the right to vote in many Western countries. After achieving that right, though, most feminist movements fell into decline. Radical women tended to be absorbed into other movements, such as those combating fascism, a political doctrine of the extreme right gaining ground in Germany, Italy and elsewhere in the 1930s. Little was left of feminism as a distinct movement combating male-dominated institutions. The achievement of equal political rights did little to extend equality to other spheres of women's lives.

The resurgence of feminism

In the late 1960s, women's movements again burst back to prominence. Over the decades since then, feminism has become a major influence in countries throughout the world, including many in the Third World. The resurgence began in the United States, influenced by the civil rights movement and by the student activism of the period. From there it spread to other parts of the world. Women who were active in these causes often found themselves relegated by male activists to a traditionally subordinate role. Civil rights leaders were resistant to women's rights being included in their manifestos of equality. So women's groups began to establish independent organizations concerned primarily with feminist issues.

Women's movements today have addressed a much wider range of issues than their predecessors. They have pressed for economic equality, the availability of abortion and alterations in laws concerning divorce. In addition to significant practical achievements, feminists have made an intellectual impact far beyond anything previously achieved. Throughout the social sciences, for example, feminist authors have forced a rethinking of established notions and theories. A great deal of the research carried out in recent years into historical and cultural factors affecting the position of women, and into gender relations more generally, has been prompted by the influence of modern feminism.

Feminist movements: an interpretation

The rise of women's movements over the past century can easily be interpreted in terms of the concepts set out by Charles Tilly. Social movements arise, Tilly argues, when people have no chance of making themselves heard or when they lack outlets for their aspirations. In the first phase of development of feminist movements, in the nineteenth and early twentieth centuries, feminist leaders sought above all to *gain a voice* for women in the political process – in other words, to obtain the right to vote. In the second phase, women's movements sought to extend the gains they had achieved, fighting for economic as well as political equality for women.

In both phases, the leaders of women's movements were able to *mobilize collective resources* to place effective pressure on the governing authorities. During the early period, the chief resource of women activists was mass marches and demonstrations. Later on, organizations were able to fight for women's rights in a more consistent and organized way. The *common interests* to which women's group leaders have been able to appeal include the concern that women should have a role in political decision-making, be able to engage in paid work if they wish, and have equal rights in divorce proceedings.

Finally, the *opportunity* of feminist activists to influence social change has been affected by a variety of factors. The outbreak of World War One, for example, helped in the aim of securing the vote: governments fighting the war needed the support and active involvement of women in the war effort. In the second phase of the development of feminism, the civil rights movement was the spark that ignited a new wave of activism.

SOCIAL MOVEMENTS AND SOCIOLOGY

Social movements hold a double interest for the sociologist. They provide subject matter for study, but more than this, they help to shift the ways in which sociologists look at certain areas of behaviour. The women's movement, for instance, is not just relevant to sociology because it provides material for research. It has identified weaknesses in established frameworks of sociological thought and developed concepts (such as that of patriarchy) that help us to understand issues of gender and power. There is a continuing dialogue not only between social movements and the organizations they confront, but between social movements and sociology itself.

SUMMARY

1 Revolutions have occurred in most areas of the world over the past two centuries. The American Revolution of 1776 and the French Revolution of 1789 introduced ideals and aspirations which have come to be very widespread in political life.

2 Revolution is a slippery concept to define. To count as a revolution, a process of political change must involve the influence of a mass social movement which is prepared to use violence to achieve its ends and able both to seize power and subsequently to initiate reform.

3 Various different theories of revolution have been advanced. Marx's interpretation of revolution is particularly significant, not just because of its intellectual contribution – which can be questioned in various ways – but because it has served in some part to shape actual processes of revolution in the current century.

4 Since revolution is such a complex phenomenon, generalizing about the conditions leading to revolutionary change is difficult. Most revolutions occur in circumstances where governmental power has become fragmented (for instance, as a result of war), and where an oppressed group is able to create and sustain a mass movement. Revolutions are usually unintended consequences of more partial aims towards which such movements initially strive.

5 Crowd activities occur not only in revolutions, but in many other circumstances of less dramatic social change – as in urban riots. The actions of rioting mobs might seem wholly destructive and haphazard, but often serve definite purposes for those involved.

6 Many types of social movement are found in modern societies. Social movements involve a collective attempt to further common interests through collaborative action outside the sphere of established institutions. Sociology not only studies such movements but also responds to the issues they raise.

7 One major type of modern social movement is that associated with feminism. The first significant feminist movements developed in the mid-nineteenth century, concentrating their attention particularly on obtaining the vote for women. Although falling into decline after the 1920s, in the 1960s feminism again burst into prominence, and since has had an impact in many spheres of social life and intellectual activity.

FURTHER READING

Zbigniew Brzezinski, *The Grand Failure* (London: McDonald, 1989). A study of the rise and fall of communism in the twentieth century, arguing that communism represents 'a historical tragedy'.

John Dunn, *'Understanding Revolutions'* in his *Rethinking Modern Political Theory* (Cambridge: Cambridge University Press, 1985). A discussion of the problems of understanding modern revolutions.

Ron Eyerman and **Andrew Jamison**, *Social Movements* (Cambridge: Polity Press, 1991). A useful survey and analysis of current theoretical thinking about the nature of social movements, giving particular attention to the newer social movements.

Chester Hartman and **Pedro Vilanova**, *Paradigms Lost: The Post-Cold War Era* (London: Pluto, 1991). A discussion of the state of the world following the collapse of communism in the Soviet Union and Eastern Europe.

Max Weber, *The Russian Revolutions* (Cambridge: Polity Press, 1995). Weber's view of the revolutionary events in Russia.

IMPORTANT TERMS

- *socialism*
- *class conflict*
- *contradiction*
- *communism*
- *mobilization*
- *guerrilla movement*
- *multiple sovereignty*
- *crowd activity*
- *riot*
- *transformative movement*
- *reformative movement*
- *redemptive movement*
- *alterative movement*
- *feminist movement*

19

GLOBAL CHANGE AND ECOLOGICAL CRISIS

➡

Human beings have existed on earth for about half a million years. Agriculture, the necessary basis of fixed settlements, is only about twelve thousand years old. Civilizations date back no more than six thousand years or so. If we were to think of the entire span of human existence thus far as a day, agriculture would have come into existence at 11.56 p.m. and civilizations at 11.57. The development of modern societies would get under way only at 11.59 and 30 seconds! Yet perhaps as much change has taken place in the last 30 seconds of this human day as in all the time leading up to it.

The pace of change in the modern era is easily demonstrated if we look at rates of technological development. As the economic historian David Landes has observed in a celebrated study:

> Modern technology produces not only more and faster; it turns out objects that could not have been produced under any circumstances by the craft methods of yesterday. The best Indian handspinner could not turn out yarn so fine and regular as that of the mule; all the forges in eighteenth-century Christendom could not have produced steel sheets so large, smooth and homogeneous as those of a modern strip mill. Most important, modern technology has created things that could scarcely have been conceived in the pre-industrial era; the camera, the motor car, the aeroplane, the whole array of electronic devices from the radio to the high-speed computer, the nuclear power plant, and so on almost ad infinitum . . . The result has been an enormous increase in the output and variety of goods and services and this alone has changed man's way of life more than anything since the discovery of fire: the Englishman [and, we might add, the Englishwoman] of 1750 was closer in material things to Caesar's legionnaires than to his own great-grandchildren. (Landes 1969)

The modes of life and social institutions characteristic of the modern world are radically different from those of even the recent past. During a period of only two or three centuries – a minute sliver of time in the context of human history – human social life has been wrenched away from the types of social order in which people lived for thousands of years.

Far more than any generation before us, we face an uncertain future. To be sure, conditions of life for previous generations were always insecure: people were at the mercy of natural disasters, plagues and famines. But though we are largely immune from plague and famine in the industrialized countries today, we must deal now with the social forces we ourselves have unleashed. These forces bring social change into our lives in a continuous way.

DEFINING CHANGE

How should we define SOCIAL CHANGE? There is a sense in which everything changes, all of the time. Every day is a new day; every moment is a new instant in time. The Greek philosopher Heraclitus pointed out that a person cannot step into the same river twice. On the second occasion, the river is different, since water has flowed along it and the person has changed in subtle ways too. While this observation is in a sense correct, we *do* of course normally want to say that it is the same river and the same person stepping into it on two occasions. There is sufficient continuity in the shape or form of the river and in the physique and personality of the person with wet feet to say that each remains 'the same' through the changes that occur.

Identifying significant change involves showing how far there are alterations in the *underlying structure* of an object or situation over a period of time. In the case of human societies, to decide how far and in what ways a system is in a process of change, we have to show to what degree there is any modification of *basic institutions* during a specific period. All accounts of change also involve showing what remains stable, as a baseline against which to measure alterations. Even in the rapidly moving world of today there are continuities with the distant past. Major religious systems, for example, such as Christianity or Islam, retain their ties with ideas and practices initiated some two thousand years ago. Yet most institutions in modern societies clearly change much more rapidly than did institutions of the traditional world.

In this chapter, we shall look at attempts to interpret patterns of change affecting human history as a whole; we shall then consider why the modern period should be associated with such especially profound and rapid social change. Much change today is *global* – it is either happening simultaneously in many parts of the world, or is affecting the future of the planet as a whole.

INFLUENCES ON SOCIAL CHANGE

Social theorists have tried for the past two centuries to develop a grand theory that explains the nature of social change. But no single-factor theory has a chance of accounting for the diversity of human social development from hunting and gathering and pastoral societies to traditional civilizations and finally to the highly complex social systems of today. We can, however, identify the three main factors that have consistently influenced social change: the *physical environment*, *political organization* and *cultural factors*.

The physical environment

The physical environment often has an effect on the development of human social organization. This is clearest in more extreme environmental conditions, where people must organize their ways of life in relation to weather conditions. Inhabitants of polar regions necessarily develop habits and practices different from those living in subtropical areas. People who live in Alaska, where the winters are long and cold, tend to follow different patterns of social life from people who live in the much warmer Mediterranean countries. Alaskans spend more of their lives indoors and, except for the short period of the summer, plan outdoor activities very carefully, given the inhospitable environment in which they live.

Less extreme physical conditions can also affect society. The native population of Australia has never stopped being hunters and gatherers, since the continent contained hardly any indigenous plants suitable for regular cultivation, or animals that could be domesticated to develop pastoral production. The world's early civilizations mostly originated in areas that contained rich agricultural land – for instance, in river deltas. The ease of communications across land and the availability of sea routes are also important: societies cut off from others by mountain ranges, impassable jungles or deserts often remain relatively unchanged over long periods of time.

Yet the direct influence of the environment on social change is not very great. People are often able to develop considerable productive wealth in relatively inhospitable areas. This is true, for example, of Alaskans, who have been able to develop oil and mineral resources in spite of the harsh nature of their environment. Conversely, hunting and gathering cultures have frequently lived in highly fertile regions without becoming involved in pastoral or agricultural production. For example, the Kwakiutl Indians of Vancouver Island, whose way of life survived largely intact until about half a century ago, lived in an environment rich in fish, fruit and edible plants. They were content with a hunting and gathering way of life in such favourable conditions and never sought to convert to settled agriculture.

There is little direct relation between the environment and the systems of production that develop. The emphasis of evolutionists on adaptation to the environment is thus less illuminating than Marx's ideas in explaining social development. For Marx stressed that human beings rarely just adapt to their surrounding circumstances as animals do. Humans always seek to master the world around them rather than take it as given. Moreover, there is no doubt that types of production strongly influence the level and nature of social change, although they do not have the overriding impact Marx attributed to them.

Political organization

A second factor strongly influencing social change is the type of political organization. In hunting and gathering societies, this influence is at a minimum, since there are no political authorities capable of mobilizing the community. In all other types of society, however, the existence of distinct political agencies – chiefs, lords, kings and governments – strongly affects the course of development a society takes. Political systems are not, as Marx believed, direct expressions of underlying economic organization; quite different types of political order may exist in societies that have similar production systems. For instance, some societies based on industrial capitalism have had authoritarian political systems (examples are Nazi Germany and South Africa under apartheid), while others are much more democratic (for example, the United States, Britain or Sweden).

Military power played a fundamental part in the establishment of most traditional states; it influenced their subsequent survival or expansion in an equally basic way. But the connections between the level of production and military strength are again indirect. A ruler may choose to channel resources into building up the military, for example, even when this impoverishes most of the rest of the population – as has happened in Iraq under the rule of Saddam Hussein.

Cultural factors

The third main influence on social change consists of cultural factors, which include the effects of religion, communication systems and leadership. As we have seen in chapter 16, religion may be either a conservative or an innovative force in social life. Some forms of religious belief and practice have acted as a brake on change, emphasizing above all the need to adhere to traditional values and rituals. Yet, as Max Weber emphasized, religious convictions frequently play a mobilizing role in pressures for social change.

A particularly important cultural influence that affects the character and pace of change is the nature of communication systems. The invention of writing, for instance, allowed for the keeping of records, making possible increased control of material resources and the development of large-scale organizations. In addition, writing altered people's perception of the relation between past, present and future. Societies that write keep a record of past events and know themselves to have a history. Understanding history can develop a sense of the overall movement or line of development a society is following, which people can then actively seek to promote further.

Under the general heading of cultural factors we should also place *leadership*. Individual leaders have had an enormous influence in world history. We have only to think of great religious figures (like Jesus), political and military leaders (like Julius Caesar), or innovators in science and philosophy (like Isaac Newton) to see that this is the case. A leader capable of pursuing dynamic policies and generating a mass following or radically altering pre-existing modes of thought can overturn a previously established order.

However, individuals can only reach positions of leadership and become effective if favourable social conditions exist. Adolf Hitler was able to seize power in Germany in the 1930s, for instance, partly as a result of the tensions and crises that beset the country at that time. If those circumstances had not existed, he would probably have remained an obscure figure within a minor political faction. The same was true at a later date of Mahatma Gandhi, the famous pacifist leader in India during the period after World War Two. Gandhi was able to be effective in securing his country's independence from Britain because the war and other events had unsettled the existing colonial institutions in India.

CHANGE IN THE MODERN PERIOD

What explains why the last two hundred years, the period of modernity, have seen such a tremendous acceleration in the speed of social change? This is a complex issue, but it is not difficult to pinpoint some of the factors involved. Not surprisingly, we can categorize them along lines similar to factors that have influenced social change throughout history, except that we shall subsume the impact of the physical environment within the overall importance of economic factors.

Economic influences

Of economic influences, the most far-reaching is the impact of industrial capitalism. Capitalism differs in a fundamental way from pre-existing production systems, because it involves the constant expansion of production and ever-increasing accumulation of wealth. In traditional production systems, levels of production were fairly static since they were geared to habitual, customary needs. Capitalism promotes the constant revision of the technology of production, a process into which science is increasingly drawn. The rate of technological innovation fostered in modern industry is vastly greater than in any previous type of economic order.

The impact of science and technology on how we live may be largely driven by economic factors, but it also stretches beyond the economic sphere. Science and technology both influence and are influenced by political and cultural factors. Scientific and technological development, for example, helped to create modern forms of communication such as radio and television. As we have seen, such electronic forms of communication have produced changes in politics in recent years. Radio, television and the other electronic media have also come to shape how we think and feel about the world.

Political influences

The second major type of influence on change in the modern period consists of political developments. The struggle between nations to expand their power, develop their wealth and triumph militarily over their competitors has been an energizing source of change over the past two or three centuries. Political change in traditional civilizations was normally confined to elites. One aristocratic family, for example, would replace another as rulers, while for the majority of the population life would go on relatively unchanged. This is not true of modern political systems, in which the activities of political leaders and government officials constantly affect the lives of the mass of the population. Both externally and internally, political decision-making promotes and directs social change far more than in previous times.

Political development in the last two or three centuries has certainly influenced economic change as much as economic change has influenced politics. Governments now play a major role in stimulating (and sometimes retarding) rates of economic growth, and in all industrial societies there is a high level of state intervention in production, the government being far and away the largest employer.

Military power and war have also been of far-reaching importance. The military strength of the Western nations from the seventeenth century onwards allowed them to influence all quarters of the world – and provided an essential backing to the global spread of Western lifestyles. In the twentieth century, the effects of the two world wars have been profound – the devastation of many countries, which led to processes of rebuilding that brought about major institutional changes, for example in Germany and Japan after World War Two. Even those states which were the victors – like the UK – experienced major internal changes as a result of the impact of the war on the economy.

Cultural influences

Among the cultural factors affecting processes of social change in modern times, the development of science and the secularization of thought have each contributed to the *critical* and *innovative* character of the modern outlook. We no longer assume that customs or habits are acceptable merely because they have the age-old authority of tradition.

On the contrary, our ways of life increasingly require a 'rational' basis. For instance, a design for a hospital would not be based mainly on traditional tastes, but would consider its capability for serving the purpose of a hospital – effectively caring for the sick.

In addition to *how* we think, the *content* of ideas has also changed. Ideals of self-betterment, freedom, equality and democratic participation are largely creations of the past two or three centuries. Such ideals have served to mobilize processes of social and political change, including revolutions. These ideas cannot be tied to tradition, but rather suggest the constant revision of ways of life in the pursuit of human betterment. Although they were initially developed in the West, such ideals have become genuinely universal and global in their application, promoting change in most regions of the world.

CURRENT CHANGE AND FUTURE PROSPECTS

Where is social change leading us today? What are the main trends of development likely to affect our lives as the twenty-first century opens? Social theorists do not agree on the answers to these questions, which obviously involve a great deal of speculation. We shall look at three different perspectives: the notion that we are now living in a postindustrial society; the idea that we have reached a postmodern period; and the theory that we have reached the 'end of history'.

Towards a postindustrial society?

Some observers have suggested that what is occurring today is a transition to a new society no longer primarily based on industrialism. We are entering, they claim, a phase of development beyond the industrial era altogether. A variety of terms have been coined to describe this new social order, such as the **information society**, *service society* and *knowledge society*. The term that has come into most common usage, however

– first employed by Daniel Bell in the United States and Alain Touraine in France – is POSTINDUSTRIAL SOCIETY (Bell 1973; Touraine 1974), the 'post' (meaning 'after') referring to the sense that we are moving beyond the old forms of industrial development.

The diversity of names is one indication of the myriad of ideas put forward to interpret current social changes. But one theme that appears consistently is the significance of *information* or *knowledge* in the society of the future. Our way of life, based on the manufacture of material goods, centred on the power machine and the factory, is being displaced by one in which information is the basis of the productive system.

The clearest and most comprehensive portrayal of the postindustrial society was provided by Daniel Bell in *The Coming of the Post-Industrial Society* (1973). The postindustrial order, Bell argues, is distinguished by a growth of service occupations at the expense of jobs that produce material goods. The blue-collar worker, employed in a factory or workshop, is no longer the most essential type of employee. White-collar (clerical and professional) workers outnumber blue-collar, with professional and technical occupations growing fastest of all.

People working in higher-level white-collar occupations specialize in the production of information and knowledge. The production and control of what Bell calls **codified knowledge** – systematic, coordinated information – is society's main strategic resource. Those who create and distribute this knowledge – scientists, computer specialists, economists, engineers and professionals of all kinds – increasingly become the leading social groups, replacing the industrialists and entrepreneurs of the old system. On the level of culture, there is a shift away from the 'work ethic' characteristic of industrialism; people are freer to innovate and enjoy themselves in both their work and their domestic lives.

How valid is the view that the old industrial order is being replaced by a postindustrial society? While the thesis has been widely accepted, the empirical assertions on which it depends are suspect in several ways.

1   The trend towards service occupations, accompanied by a decline in employment in other production sectors, dates back almost to the beginning of industrialism itself; it is not simply a recent phenomenon. From the early 1800s manufacture and services both expanded at the expense of agriculture, with the service sector consistently showing a faster rate of increase than manufacture. The blue-collar worker never really was the most common type of employee; a higher proportion of paid employees has *always* worked in agriculture and services, with the service sector increasing proportionally as the numbers in agriculture dwindled. Easily the most important change has not been from industrial to service work but from farm employment to all other types of occupation.

2   The service sector is very heterogeneous. Service occupations cannot simply be treated as identical to white-collar jobs; many service jobs (such as that of petrol station attendant) are blue-collar, in the sense that they are manual. Most white-collar positions involve little specialized knowledge and have become substantially mechanized. This is true of most lower-level office work.

3   Many service jobs contribute to a process that in the end produces material goods, and therefore should really be counted as part of manufacture. Thus a computer programmer working for an industrial firm, designing and monitoring the operation of machine tools, is directly involved in a process of making material goods.

4   No one can be sure what the long-term impact of the spreading use of microprocessing and electronic communications systems will be. At the moment, these are integrated within manufacturing production, rather than displacing it. It seems certain that such technologies will continue to show high rates of innovation and will permeate more areas of social life. But how far we yet live in a society in which codified knowledge is the main resource is unclear.

5   The postindustrial society thesis tends to exaggerate the importance of economic factors in producing social change. Such a society is

described as the outcome of developments in the economy that lead to changes in other institutions. Most of those advancing the post-industrial hypothesis have been little influenced by, or are directly critical of, Marx; but their position is a quasi-Marxist one in the sense that economic factors are held to dominate social change.

Some of the developments cited by the postindustrial theorists are important features of the current era, but it is not obvious that the concept of the postindustrial society is the best way to come to terms with them. Moreover, the forces behind the changes going on today are political and cultural as well as economic.

Postmodernity and the end of history

Some authors have recently gone as far as saying that the developments now occurring are even more profound than signalling the end of the era of industrialism. What is happening is nothing short of a movement beyond modernity – the attitudes and ways of life associated with modern societies, such as our belief in progress, the benefits of science and our capability to control the modern world. A *postmodern* era is arriving, or has already arrived.

The advocates of the idea of postmodernity claim that modern societies took their inspiration from the idea that history has a shape – it 'goes somewhere' and leads to progress – and that now this notion has collapsed. There are no longer any 'grand narratives' – overall conceptions of history – that make any sense (Lyotard 1985). Not only is there no general notion of progress that can be defended, there is no such thing as history. The postmodern world is thus a highly pluralistic and diverse one. In countless films, videos and TV programmes, images circulate around the world. We come into contact with many ideas and values, but these have little connection with the history of the areas in which we live, or indeed with our own personal histories. Everything seems constantly in flux. As one group of authors expressed things:

> Our world is being remade. Mass production, the mass consumer, the big city, big-brother state, the sprawling housing estate, and the nation-state are in decline: flexibility, diversity, differentiation, and mobility, communication, decentralization and internationalization are in the ascendant. In the process our own identities, our sense of self, our own subjectivities are being transformed. We are in transition to a new era. (S. Hall et al. 1988)

History ends alongside modernity, it is said, because there is no longer any way of describing in general terms the pluralistic universe that has come into being.

Fukuyama and the end of history

The writer whose name has come to be synonymous with the phrase 'end of history' is Francis Fukuyama. Fukuyama's conception of the end of history at first sight seems completely contrary to the ideas advanced by the theorists of postmodernity. His views are based not on the collapse of modernity but on its worldwide triumph, in the shape of capitalism and liberal democracy.

In the wake of the 1989 revolutions in Eastern Europe, the dissolution of the Soviet Union and a movement towards multiparty democracy in other regions, Fukuyama argues, the ideological battles of earlier eras are over. The **end of history** is the end of alternatives. No one any longer defends monarchism, and fascism is a phenomenon of the past. So is communism, for so long the major rival of Western democracy. Capitalism has won in its long struggle with socialism, contrary to Marx's prediction, and liberal democracy now stands unchallenged. We have reached, Fukuyama asserts, 'the end point of mankind's ideological evolution and [the] universalization of Western democracy as the final form of human government' (1989).

The two versions of the end of history, however, are not as far apart as may appear. Liberal democracy is a framework for the expression of diverse views and interests. It does not specify how we should behave, apart from insisting that we should respect the views of others; hence it is compatible with a pluralism of attitudes and ways of life.

Assessment

It seems very doubtful that history has come to a stop in the sense that we have exhausted all alternatives open to us. Who can say what new forms of economic, political or cultural order may emerge in the future? Just as the thinkers of medieval times had no inkling of the industrial society that was to emerge with the decline of feudalism, so we can't at the moment anticipate how the world will change over the coming century.

We should have reservations, therefore, about the idea of the end of history, and also about the idea of postmodernity. The postmodern theorists stress diversity and fragmentation too much, at the expense of new forms of global integration. Pluralism is important, but humanity today faces common problems, problems that require for their solutions general initiatives. One-sided capitalistic expansion cannot continue indefinitely; the world has only finite resources. As collective humanity, we need to take steps to overcome the economic divisions that separate the rich and poor countries, as well as such divisions within societies. We need to do so while also protecting the resources on which we all depend. On the level of the political order, liberal democracy is indeed not enough. As a framework confined to the nation-state, it does not resolve the issue of how a global pluralistic order, free from violence, can be created.

THREATS TO THE GLOBAL ENVIRONMENT

One problem we all face in common concerns **environmental ecology**. Irreparable damage to the environment may already have been done by the spread of industrial production. Ecological questions concern not only how we can best cope with and contain environmental damage – and recurrent industrial disasters – but the very ways of life within industrialized societies. If the goal of continuous economic growth

CONSUMPTION AND THE ENVIRONMENT

The world is undergoing a consumption revolution. Since the 1950s, the rate at which we consume energy, meat, copper, steel, and timber has doubled. Car ownership has quadrupled, while plastic use has quintupled and air travel has multiplied by a staggering 33 times.

Use of resources is not evenly spread. A fifth of the world's population are listed among the 'consumer class', but consumption at the level enjoyed by most Western middle classes is confined to a much smaller subgroup. Only a tenth of people in the USA ever fly in an aeroplane, for example. Yet this tiny group of high consumers has an impact on the environment out of all proportion with its size.

Rapid use of nonrenewable or limited resources puts ecosystems at risk. Cocoa is grown in developing countries, but eaten mainly in the North. Africa only consumes 3% of the cocoa it produces, for example. Yet natural ecosystems are being destroyed to produce chocolate.

Increased pollution is also damaging forests, freshwaters, and oceans. A German study calculated that, over ten years, the average car is responsible for 2,040 million cu m/72,040 million cu ft of polluted air, 26.5 tonnes/26.9 tons of rubbish, three dead trees and 30 'sick' trees through its contribution to acid rain, and 200 sq m/2,200 sq ft of tarmac and concrete.

Consumption is putting extra pressures on agricultural land and fisheries. Tuna fishing in Mexico kills 50–100,000 dolphins a year. Synthetic gill nets catch 60 seabird species around the world and the jackass penguin is directly threatened.

Despite much talk about 'overpopulation' in the South, many pressures on the world's resources come instead from the rich countries. It would be impossible for the whole of the world's population to consume at the Northern level. Tackling these problems will not be easy. Conservation, recycling, and longer-life products can all help. The sensitive issue of reducing consumption among the rich has scarcely begun to be addressed and is likely to become increasingly important in the future.

Source: 1994 Hutchinson Gallup, *INFO 1995*, Helicon, p. 527.

---

must be abandoned, new social institutions will probably be pioneered. Technological progress is unpredictable, and it may be that the earth will in fact yield sufficient resources for processes of industrialization. At the moment, however, this does not seem feasible, and if the Third World countries are to achieve living standards comparable to those currently enjoyed in the West, global readjustments will be necessary.

Since the beginning of the practice of agriculture thousands of years ago, human beings have left an imprint on nature. Hunting and gathering societies mainly lived *from* nature; they existed on what the natural environment provided and made little attempt to change the world around them. With the coming of agriculture, this situation was altered. To grow crops, land must be cleared, trees cut down and encroaching weeds and wild foliage kept at bay. Even primitive farming methods can lead to soil erosion. Once natural forests are cut down and clearings made, the wind may blow away the topsoil. The farming community then clears some fresh plots of land, and so the process goes on. Some landscapes that we today think of as natural, such as the rocky areas and scrubland in south-western Greece, are actually the result of soil erosion created by farmers five thousand years ago.

Yet before the development of modern industry, nature dominated human life far more than the other way round. Today the human onslaught on the natural environment is so intense that there are few natural processes uninfluenced by human activity. Nearly all cultivable land is under agricultural production. What used to be almost inaccessible wildernesses are often now nature reserves, visited routinely by thousands of tourists. Even the world's climate, as we shall see, has probably been affected by the global development of industry.

'Green' movements and parties (like Friends of the Earth or

Greenpeace), which are themselves sometimes global organizations, have developed in response to the new environmental hazards. While there are varied green philosophies, a common thread is the concern to take action to protect the world's environment, conserve rather than exhaust its resources and protect the remaining animal species. Hundreds of animal species have become extinct even over the past fifty years, and at the moment this process is a continuing one.

Some environmental problems are particularly concentrated in specific areas. In the formerly communist societies of Eastern Europe and the Soviet Union, rivers, forests and the air are highly polluted by industrial wastes. The consequences of such pollution if it goes on unchecked are potentially worldwide. As we have learned, the societies of the earth have become much more interdependent than ever before. As travellers on 'spaceship earth', no matter where we live, we are all menaced by corrosion of the environment. The German sociologist Ulrich Beck has spoken of this situation as producing a global **risk society** (Beck 1992). We live now in a global order where we face risks to our security, including ecological risks, which previous generations did not experience.

Sources of threat

Global environmental threats are of several basic sorts: pollution, the creation of waste that cannot be disposed of in the short term or recycled, and the depletion of resources that cannot be replenished. The amount of domestic waste – what goes into our rubbish bins – produced each day in the industrialized societies is staggering; these countries have sometimes been called the 'throw-away societies' because the volume of items discarded as a matter of course is so large. For instance, food is mostly bought in packages that are thrown away at the

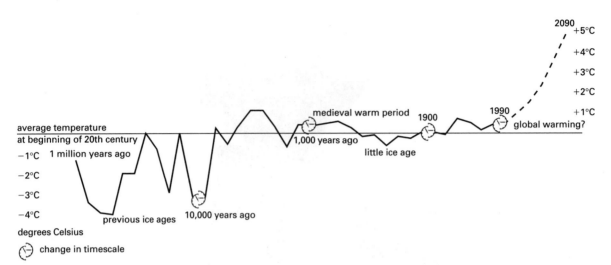

Fig. 19.1 Past and future global temperatures compared with average temperature at the beginning of the twentieth century

Source: IPCC. From Michael Kidron and Ronald Segal, *The State of the World Atlas*, 5th edn, 1995.

end of the day. Some of these can be reprocessed and reused, but most cannot. Some kinds of widely employed plastic simply become unusable waste; there is no way of recycling them, and they have to be buried in refuse tips.

When environmental analysts speak of waste materials, however, they mean not only goods that are thrown away, but also gaseous wastes pumped into the atmosphere. Examples are the carbon dioxide released into the atmosphere by the burning of fuels like oil and coal in cars and power stations, and gases released into the air by the use of aerosol cans, material for insulation and air-conditioning units. Carbon dioxide is the main influence on the process of global warming that many scientists believe is occurring (see figure 19.1), while the other gases attack the ozone layer around the earth.

Global warming is thought to happen in the following way. The build-up of carbon dioxide in the earth's atmosphere functions like the glass of a greenhouse. It allows the sun's rays to pass through, but acts as a barrier to prevent them from passing back. The effect is to heat up the earth; global warming is sometimes termed the 'greenhouse effect' for this reason. If global warming is indeed taking place, the consequences are likely to be devastating. Among other things, sea levels will rise as the polar ice caps melt and the oceans warm and expand. Cities that lie near the coasts or in low-lying areas will be flooded and become uninhabitable. Large tracts of fertile land will become desert.

The ozone layer, which is high in the earth's atmosphere, forms a shield that protects against ultraviolet radiation. The gases used in aerosols and refrigerators produce particles that react with the ozone layer in such a way as to weaken it. It is thought that these chemicals have produced detectable holes in the ozone layer at both poles, and thinning elsewhere. The radiation that as a result is let into the earth's atmosphere produces a variety of potentially harmful effects, including an increase in cataracts of the eyes (which can cause blindness) and in levels of skin cancer.

Modern industry, still expanding worldwide, has led to steeply climbing demands for sources of energy and raw materials. Yet the world's supply of such energy sources and raw materials is limited. Even at current rates of use, for example, the known oil resources of the world will be completely consumed by the year 2050. New reserves of oil may be discovered, or alternative sources of cheap energy invented, but there plainly is a point at which some key resources will run out if global consumption is not limited.

THE ENVIRONMENT: A SOCIOLOGICAL ISSUE?

Why should the environment be a concern for sociologists? Aren't we talking of issues that are the province purely of scientists or technologists? Isn't the impact of human beings on nature a physical one, created by modern technologies of industrial production? Yes, but modern industry and technology have come into being in relation to distinctive social institutions. The origins of our impact on the environment are social, and so are many of its consequences.

Rescuing the global environment will thus mean social as well as technological change. Given the vast global inequalities that exist, there is little chance that the poor Third World countries will sacrifice their own economic growth because of environmental problems created largely by the rich ones. Yet the earth doesn't seem to possess sufficient resources for everyone on the planet to live at the standard of living most people in the industrialized societies take for granted. Hence, if the impoverished sectors of the world are to catch up with the richer ones, the latter are likely to have to revise their expectations about constant economic growth. Some 'green' authors argue that people in the rich countries must react against consumerism and return to more simple ways of life if global ecological disaster is to be avoided.

GLOBAL CHANGE: LOOKING INTO THE FUTURE

As we peer over the edge of our century into the next, we cannot foresee whether the coming hundred years will be marked by peaceful social and economic development or by a multiplication of global problems – perhaps beyond humanity's ability to solve. Unlike the sociologists writing two hundred years ago, we see clearly that modern industry, technology and science are by no means wholly beneficial in their consequences. Our world is much more populous and wealthy than ever before; we see the possibility of controlling our destiny and shaping our lives for the better, unimaginable to previous generations, yet the world hovers close to economic and ecological disaster. To say this is not to encourage an attitude of resigned despair. If there is one thing sociology offers us, it is a profound consciousness of the human

'A NEW SPECIES OF RISK'

In the industrialized countries we may be largely immune from the insecurities associated with plagues, famines and other natural disasters, but our own uncertainties are of equal scale. They derive from the impact of technology, one of the primary influences on social change we have unleashed upon ourselves.

Among the most frightening of these uncertainties is the prospect of radiation and other kinds of toxic contamination. Disasters have occurred in areas like Three Mile Island in Pennsylvania, Bhopal in India and Chernobyl in Ukraine. While the disaster itself may be local, the consequences reach across far distances, reminding us that life around the world is increasingly interconnected. The magnitude of danger is such that more than any other generation before us, we face an uncertain fate of our own making.

In *A New Species of Trouble* (1994), Kai Erikson, a sociologist at Yale University, observes that these humanly created catastrophes are unlike the natural disasters that wreaked havoc on earlier societies, because 'toxic poisons affect human beings in new and special ways.' Erikson has spent much time travelling to the sites of natural and human disasters and interviewing the victims. As a sociologist, he has used the data from these interviews in his scholarship, but he has also repeatedly testified in lawsuits involving the victims of such catastrophes, bringing his scholarly expertise to bear on the issues involved.

As a pioneer in the study of community disasters, Erikson argues that while natural disasters like hurricanes and famines are tangible and observable, most forms of toxic poison 'cannot be detected by the usual human senses'. Human beings often have no way of knowing if they are being affected. A second difference between natural and manmade catastrophes is that a natural disaster has a distinguishable beginning and end, while the results of a human disaster 'have no duration, no natural term; and as a result victims remain in a permanent state of alarm and anxiety'. As one victim of a gas leak explained to Erikson,

I think that the source of most of my frustration is that we feel like this has gone on and on and on, and it's never going to end. It's such a helpless feeling to be in the middle of a situation like this and to want to make other plans for what to do with your life. And you can't do it because you're tied up with not knowing whether or not you can sell the house, whether or not you can move. Do you need to be in town? Can you leave? If this was a disaster that was over and done with – tornado or an earthquake – we would know where we stand and we could go ahead and get on with our life.

authorship of social institutions. Our understanding of the dark side of modern social change need not prevent us from sustaining a realistic and hopeful outlook towards the future.

SUMMARY

1 The modern period – from about the eighteenth century to the present day – has seen an extraordinary acceleration in processes of change. Probably more profound changes have occurred in this period, which is a tiny segment of time in human history, than in the whole previous existence of humankind.

2 No 'single factor' theory can explain all social change. A number of major influences on change can be distinguished, of which adaptation to the material environment is one. Others include the physical environment, political organization and cultural factors.

3 Among the important factors in modern social change are the expansion of industrial capitalism; the development of centralized nation-states; the industrialization of war; and the emergence of science and 'rational' or critical modes of thought.

4 Some now speak of the arrival of a 'postindustrial' society. In this view, the old industrial order is being left behind in the development of a new social order based on knowledge and information. These ideas underestimate the extent to which service work is embedded within manufacture, and also give too much emphasis to economic factors.

5 Others have suggested that we have reached the end of modernity – that we have moved into a 'postmodern' world. Fukuyama has suggested that we should speak of the 'end of history'. By this he doesn't mean that historical change has come to an end, but that there are no future alternatives to capitalism and liberal democracy, which have triumphed globally over all rival systems.

6 Traditional debates between the advocates of free market capitalism and socialism are becoming outdated. New, global, issues are coming to the fore which cannot easily be grasped or responded to within the framework of established positions in sociological theory.

7 Environmental threats have emerged as among the greatest dangers which humanity has to face in the near future. Most such threats are genuinely global – they endanger the fabric of the earth as a whole. The three main types of environmental threat are the production of waste materials, pollution and the depletion of mineral resources. Concern about the environment is a social issue, not just a technological one; the human onslaught on the environment comes from the development and global spread of Western social institutions, with the importance these give to continuous economic growth.

FURTHER READING

Martin Albrow, *The Global Age* (Cambridge: Polity Press, 1996). A critical discussion of both modernist and postmodernist visions of the idea of globalization.

Daniel Bell, *The Coming of Post-industrial Society* (London: Heinemann, 1974). One of the first and most influential books about the idea of an emerging postindustrial order.

Francis Fukuyama, *The End of History and the Last Man* (London: Hamish Hamilton, 1992). A much-discussed work which argues that we have now run out of historical alternatives to capitalism and liberal democracy.

Margaret A. Rose, *The Post-modern and Post-industrial: A Critical Analysis* (Cambridge: Cambridge University Press, 1991). A historical and critical guide to the debates about postmodernity and the postindustrial society.

Danilo Zolo, *Cosmopolis: Prospects for World Government* (Cambridge: Polity Press, 1996). A challenging critique of the idea of Cosmopolis – that is, the idea of world or 'global' government.

IMPORTANT TERMS

- *information society*
- *codified knowledge*
- *end of history*
- *environmental ecology*
- *risk society*

20

SOCIOLOGICAL RESEARCH METHODS

BASIC CONCEPT

● *research methods*

The issues with which sociologists are concerned, in their theorizing and their research, are often similar to those which worry many other people. What are the circumstances in which minority groups live? How can mass starvation exist in a world that is far wealthier than it has ever been before? What effects will the increasing use of information technology have on our lives? Is the family beginning to disintegrate as an institution? Sociologists try to provide answers to these and many other problems. Their findings are by no means conclusive. Nevertheless, it is always the aim of sociological theorizing and research to break away from the speculative manner in which the ordinary person usually considers such questions. Good sociological work tries to make the questions as precise as possible and seeks to gather factual evidence before coming to conclusions. To achieve these aims, we must know the most useful RESEARCH METHODS to apply in a given study and how to best analyse the results.

Some of the questions sociologists ask in their research studies are largely **factual**, or empirical. For example, many aspects of crime and justice need direct and systematic sociological investigation. Thus we might ask: What forms of crime are most common? What proportion of people who engage in criminal behaviour are caught by the police? How many of these are in the end found guilty and imprisoned? Factual questions such as these often need much research before they can be answered; official statistics on crime, for example, are of dubious value in indicating the real level of criminal activity. Researchers who have studied crime levels have found that only about half of all serious crimes are reported to the police.

Factual information about one society, of course, will not always tell us whether we are dealing with an unusual case or a very general set of influences. Sociologists often want to ask **comparative questions**, relating one social context within a society to another, or contrasting examples drawn from different societies. There are significant differences, for example, between the social and legal systems of Britain and the United States. A typical comparative question might be: How do patterns of criminal behaviour and law enforcement vary between the two countries? (Some important differences are in fact found between them.)

In sociology we need to look not only at existing societies in relation to one another, but also to compare their present and past. The questions sociologists ask here are **developmental**. To understand the nature of the modern world, we have to look at previous forms of society and analyse the main direction that processes of change have taken. Thus we can investigate, for example, how the first prisons originated and what they are like today.

Factual – or what sociologists usually prefer to call **empirical** – investigations concern *how* things occur. Yet sociology does not consist of just collecting facts, however important and interesting they may be. We always need to interpret what facts mean, and to do so we must learn to pose **theoretical questions**. Many sociologists work primarily on empirical questions, but unless they are guided in research by some knowledge of theory, their work is unlikely to be illuminating. This is true even of research carried out with strictly practical objectives.

In this chapter, we shall start out by considering some key elements involved in sociological research. We shall then move on to discuss the different forms of research methods which sociologists use in their work. We shall also analyse some actual investigations – for there are often contrasts between the ways in which research ideally should be carried out and real-life studies.

THE RESEARCH PROCESS

Let us look first at the stages normally involved in research work. The research process takes in a number of distinct steps, leading from when the investigation is begun to the time its findings are published or made available in written form.

The research problem

All research starts from a research problem. This is sometimes an area of factual ignorance: we may simply wish to improve our knowledge about certain institutions, social processes or cultures. A researcher might set out to answer questions like: What proportion of the population holds strong religious beliefs? Are people today really disaffected with 'big government'? How far does the economic position of women lag behind that of men?

The best sociological research, however, begins with problems that are also puzzles. A puzzle is not just a lack of information, but a gap in our understanding. Much of the skill in producing worthwhile sociological research consists in correctly identifying puzzles. Rather than simply answering the question 'What is going on here?', puzzle-solving research tries to contribute to our understanding of why events happen as they do. Thus we might ask: Why are patterns of religious belief changing? What accounts for the change in the proportions of the population voting in elections in recent years? Why are women poorly represented in high-status jobs?

No piece of research stands alone. Research problems emerge as part of ongoing work; one research project may easily lead to another because it raises issues the researcher had not previously considered. A sociologist may discover puzzles by reading the work of other researchers in books and professional journals or by being aware of specific trends in society. For example, over recent years, there have been an increasing number of programmes that seek to treat the mentally ill in the community rather than confine them in psychiatric hospitals.

Sociologists might be prompted to ask: What has given rise to this shift in attitude towards the mentally ill? What are the likely consequences both for the patients themselves and for the rest of the community?

Reviewing the evidence

Once the problem is identified, the next step taken in the research process is usually to review the available evidence in the field; it might be that previous research has already satisfactorily clarified the problem. If not, the researcher will need to sift through whatever related research does exist to see how useful it is. Have previous researchers spotted the same puzzle? How have they tried to resolve it? What aspects of the problem has their research left unanalysed? Drawing on others' ideas helps the sociologist to clarify the issues that might be raised and the methods that might be used in the research.

Making the problem precise

A third stage involves working out a clear formulation of the research problem. If relevant literature already exists, the researcher might return from the library with a good notion of how the problem should be approached. Hunches about the nature of the problem can sometimes be turned into definite **hypotheses** – educated guesses about what is going on – at this stage. If the research is to be effective, a hypothesis must be formulated in such a way that the factual material gathered will provide evidence either supporting or disproving it.

Working out a design

The researcher must then decide just how the research materials are to be collected. A range of different research methods exists, and which one is chosen depends on the overall objectives of the study as well as the aspects of behaviour to be analysed. For some purposes, a survey (in which questionnaires are normally used) might be suitable. In other circumstances, interviews or an observational study might be appropriate. We shall learn more about various research methods later.

Carrying out the research

At the point of actually proceeding with the research, unforeseen practical difficulties can easily crop up. It might prove impossible to contact some of those to whom questionnaires are to be sent or whom the researcher wishes to interview. A business firm or government agency may be unwilling to let the individual carry out the work planned. For example, if the researcher is studying how business corporations have complied with equal opportunities programmes for women, then companies that have not complied might not want to be studied. The findings could be biased as a result.

Interpreting the results

Once the material to be analysed has been gathered, the researcher's troubles are not over – they may be just beginning! Working out the implications of the data collected and relating these back to the research problem are rarely easy. While it may be possible to reach a clear answer to the initial questions, many investigations are in the end less than fully conclusive.

Reporting the findings

The research report, usually published as a journal article or a book, provides an account of the nature of the research and seeks to justify whatever conclusions are drawn. This is a final stage only in terms of the individual research project. Most reports indicate questions that

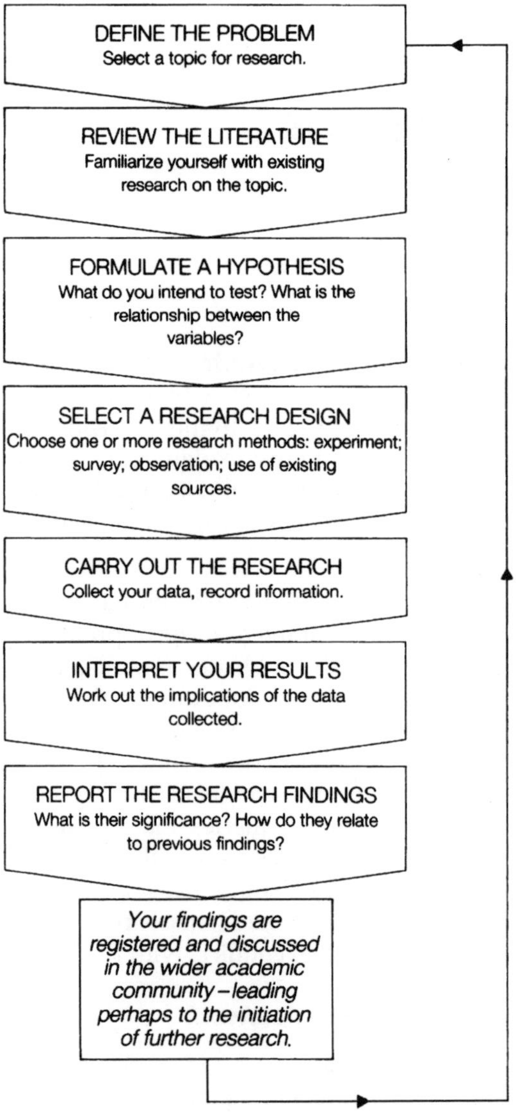

Fig. 20.1 Steps in the research process

remain unanswered and suggest further research that might profitably be done in the future. All individual research investigations are part of the continuing process of research taking place within the sociological community.

Reality intrudes!

The preceding sequence of steps is a simplified version of what happens in actual research projects. In real sociological research, these stages rarely succeed each other so neatly, and there is almost always a certain amount of sheer 'muddling through'. The difference is a bit like that between the recipes outlined in a cookbook and the actual process of preparing a meal. People who are experienced cooks often don't work from recipes at all, yet they might cook better than those who do. Following fixed schemes can be unduly restricting; most outstanding sociological research could not in fact be fitted rigidly into this sequence, although some of the steps would be there.

RESEARCH METHODS

Let's now move on to look at the various research methods sociologists commonly employ in their work.

Fieldwork

In fieldwork, or **participant observation** (the words are often used interchangeably), the investigator lives with a group or community and perhaps takes a direct part in their activities. A fieldworker cannot just be present in a community, but must explain and justify his or her presence to its members. The researcher must gain the cooperation of the community and sustain it over a period of time if any worthwhile results are to be achieved.

For a long while, it was usual for research based on participant observation to exclude any account of the hazards or problems that had to be overcome, but more recently the published reminiscences and diaries of fieldworkers have been more open about these. Frequently, feelings of loneliness must be coped with – it isn't easy to fit into a social context or community where you don't really belong. The researcher may be constantly frustrated because the members of the group refuse to talk frankly about themselves; direct queries may be welcomed in some contexts, but meet with a chilly silence in others. Some types of fieldwork may even be physically dangerous; for instance, a researcher studying a delinquent gang might be seen as a police informer or might become unwittingly embroiled in conflicts with rival gangs.

Advantages and limitations of fieldwork

Where it is successful, fieldwork provides richer information about social life than most other research methods. Once we see how things

'Anthropologists! Anthropologists!'
Cartoon by Gary Larson © *San Francisco Chronicle*, reprinted by permission.

look from the inside of a given group, we are likely to have a better understanding of why members act as they do.

Fieldwork also gives the investigator more flexibility than most other research methods. The researcher is able to adjust to novel or unexpected circumstances and follow up any leads that might develop. Fieldwork is probably more likely to turn up unexpected results than most other methods of investigation, as the investigator may discover with a jolt that preconceived ideas about the group were completely wrong.

But fieldwork also has major limitations. Only fairly small groups or communities can be studied. Much depends on the skill of the researcher in gaining the confidence of the individuals involved. Without this skill, the research is unlikely to get off the ground at all. The reverse is also possible. A researcher could begin to identify so closely with the group that she or he becomes too much of an 'insider' and loses the perspective of an outside observer.

Surveys

Interpreting field studies usually involves problems of generalization. Since only a small number of people are concerned, we cannot be sure that what is found in one context will apply in other situations as well, or even that two different researchers would come to the same conclusions when studying the same group. This is usually less of a problem in *survey* research. In a **survey**, questionnaires are either sent or given directly in interviews to a selected group of people – sometimes as many as several thousand. Fieldwork is best suited for in-depth studies of small slices of social life; survey research tends to produce information that is less detailed but that can usually be applied over a broad area.

Standardized and open-ended questionnaires

Two sorts of questionnaires are used in surveys. Some contain a **standardized**, or fixed-choice, set of questions, to which only a fixed range of responses is possible – for instance, 'Yes/No/Don't know' or 'Very likely/Likely/Unlikely/Very unlikely'. Such surveys have the advantage that responses are easy to compare and count up, since only a small number of categories are involved. On the other hand, because they do not allow for subtleties of opinion or verbal expression, the information they yield is likely to be restricted in scope.

Other questionnaires are **open-ended**. Respondents have more opportunity to express their views in their own words; they are not limited to making fixed-choice responses. Open-ended questionnaires typically provide more detailed information than standardized ones. The researcher can follow up answers to probe more deeply into what the respondent thinks. On the other hand, the lack of standardization means that responses may be more difficult to compare statistically.

Questionnaire items are normally organized so that a team of interviewers can ask the questions and record responses in the same predetermined order. All the items must be readily understandable to interviewer and interviewees alike. In the large national surveys undertaken regularly by government agencies and research organizations, interviews are carried out more or less simultaneously across the whole country. Those who conduct the interviews and those who analyse the results could not do their work effectively if they constantly had to be checking with each other about ambiguities in the questions or answers.

Questionnaires should also take into consideration the characteristics of respondents. Will they see the point the researcher has in mind in asking a particular question? Have they enough information to answer usefully? Will they answer at all? The terms of a questionnaire might be unfamiliar to the respondents. For instance, the question 'What is your marital status?' might baffle some people. It would be more appropriate to ask, 'Are you single, married, separated or divorced?' Most surveys are preceded by *pilot studies* in order to pick up problems not anticipated by the investigator. A pilot study is a trial run in which a questionnaire is completed by just a few people. Any difficulties can then be ironed out before the main survey is done.

Sampling

Often sociologists are interested in the characteristics of large numbers of individuals – for example, the political attitudes of the British population as a whole. It would be impossible to study all these people directly, so in such situations research studies concentrate on **sampling**, or taking a small proportion of the overall group. One can usually be confident that results from a population sample, as long as it is properly chosen, can be generalized to the total population. Studies of only two to three thousand voters, for instance, can give a very accurate indication of the attitudes and voting intentions of the population as a whole. But to achieve such accuracy, a sample must be **representative**: the group of individuals studied must be typical of the population as a whole. Sampling is more complex than it might seem, and statisticians have developed rules for working out the correct size and nature of samples.

A particularly important procedure used to ensure that a sample is representative is **random sampling**, in which a sample is chosen so that every member of the population has the same probability of being included. The most sophisticated way of obtaining a random sample is to give each member of the population a number and then use a computer to generate a random list, from which the sample is derived – for instance, by picking every tenth number in the random series.

'The people's choice?'

One of the most famous early examples of survey research was 'The people's choice?', a study carried out by Paul Lazarsfeld and a number of colleagues about half a century ago (Lazarsfeld et al. 1948). This study, which investigated the voting intentions of residents of Erie County, Ohio, during the 1940 campaign for the US presidency, pioneered several of the main techniques of survey research in use to this day. In order to probe a little more deeply than a single questionnaire would do, the investigators interviewed each member of a sample of voters on seven separate occasions. The aim was to trace, and understand the reasons for, changes in voting attitudes.

The research was set up with a number of definite hypotheses in view. One was that relationships and events close to voters in a community influence voting intentions more than distant world affairs, and the findings on the whole confirmed this. The researchers developed sophisticated measurement techniques for analysing political attitudes; yet their work also made significant contributions to theoretical thinking. Among the concepts they helped to introduce were those of 'opinion leaders' and the 'two-step flow of communication'. The study showed that some individuals – opinion leaders – tend to shape the political opinions of those around them. People's views are not formed in a direct fashion, but in a two-step process. In the first step, opinion leaders react to political events; in the second step, those leaders influence others – relations, friends and colleagues.

Advantages and disadvantages of surveys

Surveys are widely used in sociological research for several reasons. Questionnaire responses can be more easily quantified and analysed than material generated by most other research methods; large numbers of people can be studied; and given sufficient funds, researchers can employ an agency specializing in survey work to collect the responses.

Many sociologists are critical, however, of the survey method. They argue that an appearance of precision can be given to findings whose accuracy may be dubious, given the relatively shallow nature of most survey responses. Levels of non-response are sometimes high, especially when questionnaires are sent and returned by post. It is not uncommon for studies to be published based on results derived from little over half of those in a sample – although normally an effort is made to recontact non-respondents or to substitute other people. Little is known about those who choose not to respond to surveys or refuse to be interviewed.

Experiments

An **experiment** can be defined as an attempt to test a hypothesis under highly controlled conditions established by an investigator. Experiments are often used in the natural sciences, as they offer major advantages over other research procedures. In an experimental situation the researcher directly controls the circumstances being studied. As compared with the natural sciences, the scope for experimentation in sociology is quite restricted. We can bring only small groups of individuals into a laboratory setting, and in such experiments people know that they are being studied and may behave unnaturally.

Nevertheless, experimental methods can occasionally be applied in a helpful way in sociology. An example is the ingenious experiment carried out by Philip Zimbardo, who set up a make-believe jail, assigning some student volunteers to the role of guards and other volunteers to the role of prisoners (Zimbardo 1972). His aim was to see how far playing these different parts led to changes in attitude and behaviour. The results shocked the investigators. Students who played at being guards quickly assumed an authoritarian manner; they displayed real hostility towards the prisoners, ordering them around and verbally abusing and bullying them. The prisoners, by contrast, showed a mixture of apathy and rebelliousness often noted among inmates in real prisons. These effects were so marked and the level of tension so high that the experiment had to be called off at an early stage. The results, however, were important. Zimbardo concluded that behaviour in prisons is more influenced by the nature of the prison situation itself than by the individual characteristics of those involved.

Life histories

In contrast to experiments, **life histories** belong purely to sociology and the other social sciences; they have no place in natural science. Life histories consist of biographical material assembled about particular individuals – usually as recalled by the individuals themselves. Other procedures of research don't usually yield as much information as the life-history method about the development of beliefs and attitudes over time. Life-historical studies rarely rely wholly on people's memories, however. Normally sources such as letters, contemporary reports and newspaper descriptions are used to expand on and check the validity of the information individuals provide. Sociologists' views differ on the value of life histories: some feel they are too unreliable to provide useful information, but others believe they offer sources of insight that few other research methods can match.

Life histories have been successfully employed in studies of major importance. A celebrated early study was *The Polish Peasant in Europe and America*, by W. I. Thomas and Florian Znaniecki, the five volumes of which were first published between 1918 and 1920 (Thomas and Znaniecki 1966).

Historical analysis

A historical outlook is often essential in sociological research. For we frequently need a *time perspective* to make sense of the material we collect about a particular problem.

Sociologists often want to investigate past events directly. Some periods of history can be studied in a direct way, when there are still survivors of the time around – as in the case of the Holocaust in Europe during World War Two. Research in oral history means interviewing people about events they witnessed at some point earlier in their lives. This kind of research work, obviously, can only stretch at the most some sixty or seventy years back in time. For historical research on an earlier period, sociologists are dependent on the use of documents and written records, often contained in the special collections of libraries or the national archives.

An interesting example of **documentary research** in a historical context is sociologist Anthony Ashworth's study of trench warfare during World War One (Ashworth 1980). Ashworth was concerned with analysing what life was like for men who had to endure being under constant fire, crammed in close proximity for weeks on end. He drew on a diversity of documentary sources: official histories of the war, including those written about different military divisions and battalions, official publications of the time, the notes and records kept informally by individual soldiers, and personal accounts of war experiences. By drawing on such a variety of materials, Ashworth was able to develop a rich and detailed description of life in the trenches. He discovered that most soldiers formed their own ideas about how often they intended to engage in combat with the enemy, and often effectively ignored the commands of their officers. For example, on Christmas Day, German and Allied soldiers suspended hostilities, and in one place the two sides even staged an informal soccer match.

Combining comparative and historical research

Ashworth's research concentrated on a relatively short time period. As an example of a study that investigated a much longer one, and that also applied **comparative analysis** in a historical context, we can take Theda Skocpol's *States and Social Revolutions* (1979), one of the best-known studies of social change. Skocpol set herself an ambitious task: to produce a theory of the origins and nature of revolution grounded in detailed empirical study. She looked at processes of revolution in three different historical contexts: the 1789 revolution in France, the 1917

Four of the main methods used in sociological research

Research method	Strengths	Limitations
Fieldwork	Usually generates richer and more in-depth information than other methods.	Can only be used to study relatively small groups or communities.
	Provides flexibility for the researcher to alter strategies and follow up new leads.	Findings might apply only to the groups or communities studied; it is not easy to generalize on the basis of a single fieldwork study.
Surveys	Make possible the efficient collection of data on large numbers of individuals.	The material gathered may be superficial; where a questionnaire is highly standardized, important differences between respondents' viewpoints may be glossed over.
	Allow for precise comparisons to be made between the answers of respondents.	
		Responses may be what people profess to believe rather than what they actually believe.
Documentary research	Can provide sources of in-depth materials as well as data on large numbers, according to the type of documents studied.	The researcher is dependent on the sources that exist, which may be partial.
	Is often essential when a study is either wholly historical or has a defined historical dimension.	The sources may be difficult to interpret in terms of how far they represent real tendencies — as in the case of some official statistics.
Experiments	The influence of specific variables can be controlled by the investigator.	Many aspects of social life cannot be brought into the laboratory.
	Are usually easier for subsequent researchers to repeat.	The responses of those studied may be affected by their experimental situation.

revolution in Russia (which brought the communists to power and established the Soviet Union, dissolved again in 1989) and the revolution of 1949 in China (creating Communist China).

By analysing a variety of documentary sources, Skocpol was able to develop a powerful explanation of revolutionary change, one that emphasized the underlying social structural conditions. She showed that social revolutions are largely the consequences of unintended results. Before the Russian Revolution, for instance, various political groups were trying to overthrow the existing regime, but none of these – including the Bolsheviks, who eventually came to power – anticipated the revolution that occurred. A series of clashes and confrontations gave rise to a process of social transformation much more radical than anyone had foreseen.

RESEARCH IN THE REAL WORLD: METHODS, PROBLEMS, PITFALLS

All research methods, as was stressed earlier, have their advantages and limitations. Hence it is common to combine several methods in a single piece of research, using each to supplement and check on the others. We can see the value of combining methods – and, more generally, the problems and pitfalls of real sociological research – by looking at an influential study in the sociology of religion: Roy Wallis's investigation of the movement known as Scientology.

Roy Wallis and Scientology

The founder of Scientology, L. Ron Hubbard, developed religious doctrines that came to form the basis of a church. According to Scientology, we are all spiritual beings – Thetans – but we have neglected our spiritual nature. We can recover forgotten supernatural powers through training that makes us aware of our real spiritual capacities. Wallis was first drawn to the research because of the 'exotic' nature of Scientology. The movement was very controversial but had attracted a large following. Why had this particular movement, one of many new religious groups, become so prominent?

Initiating the research presented problems. Wallis knew that the leaders of the movement were likely to be unwilling to cooperate in sociological research because they had already been investigated by various government agencies. While reading about the movement's history, he came across a book by one of its former members. He contacted the author and was eventually put in touch with a number of his acquaintances who had also mostly severed their ties with Scientology. Many of these people agreed to be interviewed. These early interviewees provided Wallis with a range of documents and literature, including the mailing list of a Scientology organization. Wallis drew up and sent off a questionnaire to a sample of the names on the list. But the list proved so out of date that many among the sample had moved from the addresses given; others had been placed on the list merely because they had bought a single book on Scientology and had no real connections with the movement.

The survey thus proved of limited value as a sample of Scientologists in general. Yet it provided Wallis with further contacts. Some respondents to the questionnaire indicated that they would be willing to be interviewed. Wallis therefore travelled around Britain and the United States conducting interviews and collecting more documentary information at the same time. He began with a fixed set of questions but found it more profitable to adopt a more flexible style, allowing respondents to talk at length on matters they regarded as important. Some people were willing to be tape-recorded; others were not.

Wallis soon came to believe that he needed to understand more about the particular doctrines of Scientology, so he signed up for an introductory 'communications' course taught by a Scientology group. He thus began participant observation, but he did not reveal his identity as a researcher. Staying at the Scientology house during the course, Wallis found the role of covert participant observer difficult to sustain. Conversation with other members required a display of commitment to ideas he did not share. Expressing disagreement with these views led to such difficulties that it became clear he couldn't continue without publicly assenting to some of the main principles of Scientology, which he wasn't willing to do. He therefore slipped away quietly without finishing the course.

Later Wallis wrote to the leaders of the movement, explaining that he was a sociologist engaged in research into Scientology. Pointing out that the movement had been under much attack, he suggested that his own research would provide a more balanced view. He subsequently visited the headquarters of the sect in Britain and spoke to one of the officials there. This person was concerned about his having dropped out of the communications course; he also knew about the questionnaires sent to the list of Scientologists. None the less, he gave Wallis permission to interview some staff members and students and supplied addresses of people to be contacted in the United States. Eventually Wallis managed to gather enough material to complete his work (see Wallis 1976, 1987). He concluded that Scientology drew its appeal less from the ideas it advocated than from its energetic attempts to attract new members – and from the pressures towards conformity placed on them once they had become involved.

Ethical problems of research: the respondents answer back

All research concerned with human beings can pose ethical dilemmas. Wallis was less than truthful to those whose behaviour he studied, because he didn't reveal his identity as a sociologist when registering for the Scientology course. He tried to avoid any direct lies, but he did not give the real reason for his participation. Was this behaviour ethical? The answer is that on balance, it probably was. Had Wallis been completely frank at every stage, the research might not have got as far as it did, and it could be argued that it is in society's interest to know what goes on inside secretive organizations. On these grounds, we might consider his strategy justified.

Problems in publication: Wallis's experience

Ethical issues are also often posed by the potential consequences of the publication of research findings. Before publishing his book, Wallis sent his manuscript to the Scientology headquarters. Although he made alterations to meet some of their objections, the Scientologists in turn sent the manuscript to a lawyer experienced in libel cases. On his advice, further deletions were made. A commentary on the book, highly critical of Wallis's research methods and conclusions, was prepared by a sociologist who was also a practising Scientologist, and was eventually incorporated into the published work as an appendix. The Scientologists also published an article analysing Wallis's research in one of their own periodicals. In their discussion, they quoted the Panel on Privacy and Behavioral Research set up by the US president's Office of Science and Technology, which had stressed that 'informed consent should be obtained by researchers engaged in work on human subjects'. Informed consent, the Scientologists emphasized, had not been secured, and they added that Wallis's published work was based on information gained from only a small circle of people, mostly hostile to the Church of Scientology.

Wallis was dealing with a powerful and articulate group, who were able to persuade him to modify early versions of his research reports. Other individuals or groups studied by sociologists do not have similar influence. In studying people who are vulnerable or relatively power-less, such as psychiatric patients or prisoners, the researcher has a par-ticular obligation to weigh the ethical implications of her or his research. For the ability of such people to answer back in a direct way is likely to be limited.

The subjects of a study may find its published results offensive, either because they are portrayed in a light they find unappealing – the reac-tion of the Scientologists – or because attitudes and behaviour they would prefer to keep private are made public. In most settings of social life, people engage in practices they wouldn't want to become public knowledge. Some people working in factories and offices regularly pil-fer materials; hospital nurses sometimes wrap terminally ill patients in mortuary sheets before they die and give them little care; prison guards may accept bribes from inmates and recognize certain prisoners as 'trusties', allowing them to perform tasks they should take care of themselves.

THE INFLUENCE OF SOCIOLOGY

Sociological research is rarely of interest only to the intellectual community of sociologists. Its results are often disseminated more widely. This was the case with Wallis's work, which so concerned the Scientologists. Sociology, it must be emphasized, is not just the *study* of modern societies; it is a significant element *in the continuing life* of those societies. Take as an example the transformations taking place affecting marriage, sexuality and the family. Few people living in a modern soci-ety do not have some knowledge of these changes, as a result of the fil-tering down of sociological research. Our thinking and behaviour are affected by sociological knowledge in complex and often subtle ways, thus reshaping the very field of sociological investigation. A way of describing this phenomenon, using the technical concepts of sociology, is to say that sociology stands in a reflexive relation to the human beings whose behaviour is studied. 'Reflexive' describes the inter-change between sociological research and human behaviour. We should not be surprised that sociological findings often correlate closely with **commonsense beliefs**. The reason is not simply that sociology comes up with findings we knew already; it is rather that sociological research continually influences what our commonsense knowledge of society actually *is*.

APPENDIX 1: STATISTICAL TERMS

Research in sociology often makes use of statistical techniques in the analysis of findings. Some are highly sophisticated and complex, but those used most often are easy to understand. The most common are *measures of central tendency* (ways of calculating averages) and *correlation coefficients* (measures of the degree to which one variable relates consistently to another).

There are three methods of calculating averages, each of which has certain advantages and shortcomings. Take as an example the amount of personal wealth (including all assets such as houses, cars, bank accounts and investments) owned by thirteen individuals. Suppose the thirteen own the following amounts:

1	£000(zero)	8	£80,000
2	£5,000	9	£100,000
3	£10,000	10	£150,000
4	£20,000	11	£200,000
5	£40,000	12	£400,000
6	£40,000	13	£10,000,000
7	£40,000		

The *mean* corresponds to the average, arrived at by adding together the personal wealth of all thirteen people and dividing the result by 13. The total is £11,085,000; dividing this by 13, we reach a mean of £852,692.31. This mean is often a useful calculation because it is based on the whole range of data provided. However, it can be misleading where one or a small number of cases are very different from the majority. In the above example, the mean is not in fact an appropriate measure of central tendency, because the presence of one very large figure, £10,000,000, skews all the rest. One might get the impression that most of the people own far more than they actually do.

In such instances, one of two other measures may be used. The *mode* is the figure that occurs most frequently in a given set of data. In our example, it is £40,000. The problem with the mode is that it doesn't take into account the *overall distribution* of the data, that is the range of figures covered. The most frequently occurring case in a set of figures is not necessarily representative of their distribution as a whole, and thus may not be a useful average. In this case, £40,000 is too close to the lower end of the figures.

The third measure is the *median*, which is the middle of any set of figures; here, this would be the seventh figure, £40,000. Our example gives an odd number of figures, 13. If there had been an even number – for instance, 12 – the median would be calculated by taking the mean of the two middle cases, figures 6 and 7. Like the mode, the median gives no idea of the actual *range* of the data measured.

Sometimes a researcher will use more than one measure of central tendency to avoid giving a deceptive picture of the average. More often, he or she will calculate the *standard deviation* for the data in question. This is a way of calculating the *degree of dispersal*, or the range, of a set of figures – which in this case goes from zero to £10,000,000.

Correlation coefficients offer a useful way of expressing how closely connected two (or more) variables are. Where two variables correlate completely, we can speak of a perfect positive *correlation*, expressed as 1.0. Where no relation is found between two variables – they have no consistent connection at all – the coefficient is zero. A perfect negative correlation, expressed as −1.0, exists when two variables are in a completely inverse relation to one another. Perfect correlations are never found in the social sciences. Correlations of the order of 0.6 or more, whether positive or negative, are usually regarded as indicating a strong degree of connection between whatever variables are being analysed. Positive correlations on this level might be found between, say, social class background and voting behaviour.

APPENDIX 2: READING A TABLE

SAMPLE TABLE
Car ownership: international comparisons of several selected countries

Number of cars per 1,000 of the adult population[a]				
	1971	1981	1984	1989	1993 or latest
Brazil	12	78	84	98	–
Chile	19	45	56	67	–
Eire	141	202	226	228	–
France	261	348	360	475	420
Greece	30	94	116	150	–
Italy	210	322	359	424	500
Japan	100	209	207	286	300
Sweden	291	348	445	445	410
UK	224	317	343	366	360
US	448	536	540	607	570
West Germany	247	385	312	479	470[b]

[a]Includes all licensed cars
[b]Germany as a whole in 1993
Sources: International Road Federation, *United Nations Annual Bulletin of Transport Statistics*, reported in *Social Trends* (London: HMSO, 1987), p. 68; Statistical Office of the European Community, *Basic Statistics of the Community* (Luxembourg: European Union, 1991); data for 1993 or latest from *The Economist*, *Pocket World in Figures*, 1996.

Several interesting trends can be seen in the figures in our table. First, the level of car ownership varies considerably between different countries: the number of cars per 1,000 people is nearly ten times greater in the US than in Chile.

Second, there is a clear connection between car ownership and the level of affluence of a country. In fact, we could probably use car ownership ratios as a rough indicator of differential prosperity.

Third, in nearly all countries represented, the level of car ownership has increased between 1971 and 1993, but in some the rate of increase is higher than in others – probably indicating differences in the degree to which countries have successfully generated economic growth or are catching up.

Fourth, these data should be viewed in a wider political perspective. For example, some decrease of car ownership in 1993 in Germany will reflect the process of unification of West and East Germany.

Fifth, sources of data must be taken into account. For example, the lower numbers for 1993 in comparison with 1989 for the UK, France, Sweden and the US can be partly explained by the difference in sources. Work with data requires caution and, ideally, cross-checking of statistics.

You will often come across tables in reading sociological literature. They sometimes look complex, but are easy to decipher if you follow a few basic steps, listed below; with practice, these will become automatic. Do not succumb to the temptation to skip over tables; they contain information in concentrated form, which can be read more quickly than would be possible if the same material were expressed in words. By becoming skilled in the interpretation of tables, you will also be able to check how far the conclusions a writer draws actually seem justified.

1 Read the title in full. Tables frequently have longish titles, which represent an attempt by the researcher to state accurately the nature of the information conveyed. The title of the sample table gives first the subject of the data, second the fact that the table provides material for comparison and third the fact that data are given only for a limited number of countries.

2 Look for explanatory comments or notes about the data. A note at the foot of the sample table linked to the main column heading indicates that the data cover all licensed cars. This is important, because in some countries the proportion of vehicles properly licensed may be less than in others. Notes may say how the material was collected, or why it is displayed in a particular way. If the data have not been gathered by the researcher but are based on findings originally reported elsewhere, a source will be included. The source sometimes gives you some insight into how reliable the information is likely to be, as well as showing where to find the original data. In our table, the source note makes clear that the data have been taken from more than one source.

3 Read the headings along the top and left-hand side of the table. (Sometimes tables are arranged with 'headings' at the foot rather than the top.) These tell you what type of information is contained in each row and column. In reading the table, keep in mind each set of headings as you scan the figures. In our example, the headings on the left give the countries involved, while those at the top refer to the levels of car ownership and the years for which they are given.

4 Identify the units used; the figures in the body of the table may represent cases, percentages, averages or other measures. Sometimes it may be useful to convert the figures to a form more useful to you: if percentages are not provided, for example, it may be worth calculating them.

5 Consider the conclusions that might be reached from the information in the table. Most tables are discussed by the author, and what he or she has to say should of course be borne in mind. But you should also ask what further issues or questions could be suggested by the data.

APPENDIX 3: HOW TO USE LIBRARIES

Libraries, especially large ones, can seem daunting places. Many people feel rather lost when confronted with the apparently innumerable sources of information which libraries contain. They may therefore end up using only a small proportion of what they have to offer, perhaps with damaging effects on their academic work. It is a good idea to get to know – at the beginning of your course – the range of resources libraries have. If you do this early on, the 'lost' feeling won't last long!

All the information available in the library is stored and catalogued in a systematic way, in order to make finding things easy. Most smaller libraries operate with *open stacks* – the books can be visibly inspected on the shelves, and the user can select whichever volume he or she wants directly. Most larger collections keep only a proportion of their books on open shelves, and store others in vaults where less space is required to keep them. In these libraries anyone who wishes to use or borrow a book must ask for it or fill in a request slip. Some libraries have some books in each system.

If you are looking for a particular book, you'll be able to look it up under author or title in the index or catalogue. This may be a computerized list, drawerfuls of index cards, or a microfiche – or all three! Once you find its catalogue number, you can then either order it from library staff, quoting that number, or find it on the open shelves, which are always arranged by catalogue numbers. All – or most – sociology books will be in one area. Any librarian will be able to explain how the cataloguing system works.

Finding books on a particular topic when you don't know any names or titles involves using a subject index (again, this may be computerized or on cards). A subject index lists books by topics – such as 'class', 'bureaucracy', etc.

Many of the larger libraries today have computer-trace systems, which are very easy to operate and are normally available to all library users. You simply key in the area or areas about which you require bibliographical information and the computer will display a list of titles relevant to them.

Most libraries provide very similar services, but different libraries do have their own ways of doing things, and there are variations in cataloguing systems. Never be afraid to ask the librarian or assistants for their help if there is any aspect of library procedure which puzzles you or about which you need guidance. You should not be worried about bothering them; librarians are trained professionals, committed to making sure that the library resources are available to everyone who wants to make use of them. They are usually highly knowledgeable about the range of material the library contains, and only too willing to provide guidance if asked.

Sources of general information in sociology

If you are beginning the study of a particular topic in sociology and want to find some general information about it, there are a number of useful sources. Several dictionaries of sociology are available. These provide brief discussions of the major concepts in the subject and also accounts of the ideas of some of the leading contributors to the discipline. The major encyclopaedias – like the *Encyclopaedia Britannica* – contain many entries relevant to sociological topics. The entries in dictionaries and encyclopaedias virtually always provide short lists of books or articles as a guide to further reading.

There are various other ways in which books and articles relevant to a given problem or issue can be traced. The *International Bibliography of the Social Sciences*, published annually by UNESCO, offers a comprehensive listing of works that have appeared in different social science subjects over the course of any year. Thus, for example, you can look up the heading 'sociology of education' and find a range of up-to-date materials in that field. An equally useful source is *Sociological Abstracts*, which not only lists books and articles in the different areas of sociology, but gives a short description of the contents of each of them.

Sociological journals

It is worth familiarizing yourself with the main journals in sociology. Journals usually appear three or four times a year. The information and debates they contain are often more up-to-date than those in books, which take longer to write and publish. Journal articles are sometimes quite technical, and a person fairly new to sociology may well not find them readily understandable. But all the leading journals regularly publish articles of general interest, accessible to those with only limited knowledge of the subject.

The most important journals include *Sociology* (the official journal of the British Sociological Association), the *British Journal of Sociology*, the *Sociological Review* and the *American Journal of Sociology*.

Research for dissertations or for longer periods

On some occasions you may wish to use the library to pursue a particular research project, perhaps in the course of writing a dissertation. Such a task may involve carrying out a more 'in-depth' search of relevant sources than is required for normal study.

If you require statistical information concerning Britain, a good place to start is *Social Trends*, a book published each year by the government (HMSO). *Social Trends* contains selected statistical information on many aspects of British social life. Further information is contained in the *General Household Survey*, and more detailed statistical information is contained in the *Annual Abstract of Statistics*, both of these also being government publications.

Newspaper articles provide a mine of valuable information for the sociological researcher. A few newspapers are what are sometimes called 'journals of record'. That is to say, they not only carry news stories, but also record sections from parliamentary speeches, government reports and other official sources. *The Times, Guardian* and *Independent* are the most important examples in Britain, and each produces an index of topics and names that have appeared in its pages.

Looking further

Once you start using a library regularly, you are likely to find that it is more common to feel overwhelmed by the number of works available in a particular area than to experience difficulty in tracing relevant literature. One way of dealing with this problem, of course, is to base your selection of books or articles on reading lists provided by lecturers and tutors. Where such lists are not available or you want to look further, the best procedure to follow is to define the information you require as precisely as possible. This will allow you to narrow the range of choice to feasible limits. If your library is an open-stack one, it is worth looking through a number of potentially relevant books or articles before selecting those you decide to work with. If you have a book you trust, you might use its bibliography as a guide. In making the decision, apart from considerations of the subject matter, bear in mind *when* the book was written. New developments are constantly taking place in sociology and in the other social sciences, and obviously older books won't cover these.

SUMMARY

1 All research begins with a research problem which worries or puzzles the investigator. Research problems may be suggested by gaps in the existing literature, or by theoretical debates or practical issues in the social world. A number of clear steps can be distinguished in the development of research strategies – although these are rarely followed precisely in actual research.

2 Sound sociological research involves the use of a reliable approach for analysing a particular social phenomenon. Research methods concern how research is carried out. In fieldwork, or participant observation, the researcher spends lengthy periods of time with the group or community being studied. A second method, survey research, involves sending or administering questionnaires to sample groups from larger populations. Other methods include experiments, the use of life histories and diaries, and documentary research.

3 Each of the various methods of research has its limitations. For this reason, researchers will often combine two or more methods in their work, each being used to check or supplement the material obtained from the others. The best examples of sociological work combine both historical and comparative perspectives.

4 Sociological research often presents the investigator with ethical dilemmas. These may arise either where the subjects of the research are deceived by the researcher, or where the publication of research findings might adversely affect the feelings or lives of those studied. There is no entirely satisfactory way to deal with these issues, but all researchers have to be sensitive to the dilemmas they pose.

5 Various statistical techniques are used in the analysis of research that generates quantitative data. The most important are measures of central tendency and correlation coefficients. Measures of central tendency are ways of calculating averages from a given set of figures; correlation coefficients measure the degree to which one variable consistently relates to another.

FURTHER READING

Margaret Fonow and **Judith A. Cook**, *Beyond Methodology: Feminist Scholarship as Lived Research* (Bloomington: Indiana University Press, 1991). A collection of essays examining the implications of feminism for research methods in the social sciences.

Lee Harvey, Morag MacDonald and **Anne Devany**, *Doing Sociology* (London: Macmillan, 1992). A project-based approach to methodology written for students new to sociology.

Catherine Marsh, *Exploring Data* (Cambridge: Polity Press, 1988). An excellent introduction to data analysis, concentrating on the study of real issues to illustrate statistical techniques.

Ken Plummer, *Documents of Life* (London: Routledge, 1990). An introduction to qualitative study in the social sciences.

Lynne Williams and **Audrey Dunsmuir**, *How to do Social Research* (London: HarperCollins, 1990). A practically oriented introduction to social research covering most aspects of the basic research methods in sociology.

IMPORTANT TERMS

- *factual questions*
- *comparative questions*
- *developmental questions*
- *empirical investigation*
- *theoretical questions*
- *hypothesis*
- *participant observation*
- *survey*
- *standardized questionnaires*
- *open-ended questionnaires*
- *sampling*
- *representative sample*
- *random sampling*
- *experiment*
- *life histories*
- *documentary research*
- *comparative analysis*
- *commonsense beliefs*
- *correlation*

21

SOCIOLOGICAL THEORY

➡️

BASIC CONCEPTS

- *consensus* • *conflict* • *social structure*
- *theoretical approach* • *theory*

In this chapter, we shall analyse the development of the major theoretical approaches in sociology, identifying the dilemmas to which they point. We shall also consider some main theoretical transformations in the present day.

THEORETICAL APPROACHES

The origins of sociology – in the work of Marx, Durkheim and Weber – were mainly European. However, in this century the subject has become firmly established worldwide, and some of the most important developments have taken place in the United States. The work of George Herbert Mead (1863–1931), a philosopher teaching at the University of Chicago, has had an important influence on the development of sociological theory. Mead emphasized the centrality of language and of symbols as a whole in human social life. The perspective he developed later came to be called *symbolic interactionism*. Mead gave more attention to analysing small-scale social processes than to the study of overall societies. Although its beginnings go further back, symbolic interactionism only became widely influential fairly late on. We shall therefore discuss it after functionalism and structuralism.

Talcott Parsons (1902–1979) was the most prominent American sociological theorist of the postwar period. He was a prolific author who wrote on many empirical areas of sociology as well as on theory. He made contributions to the study of the family, bureaucracy, the professions and the study of politics, among other areas. He was one of the main contributors to the development of *functionalism*, a theoretical approach originally pioneered by Durkheim and Comte. According to the functionalist viewpoint, in studying any given society, we should look at how its various 'parts', or institutions, combine to give that society continuity over time.

Yet European thinkers continue to be prominent in the latter-day development of sociological theory. An approach which has achieved particular prominence is *structuralism*, which links sociological analysis closely to the study of language. Structuralist thought was originally pioneered in linguistics, and was then imported into the social sciences by the anthropologist Claude Lévi-Strauss (1908–). Its origins can also be traced back to Durkheim and Marx.

Marx's thought continued to be discussed and developed for more than a century after his death. The work of Marx's followers is categorized as *Marxism*.

Functionalism

Functionalist thought, as was pointed out, was originally pioneered by Durkheim, who regarded functional analysis as a key part of his formulation of the tasks of sociological theorizing and research. The development of **functionalism** in its modern guise, however, was strongly influenced by the work of anthropologists. Until early this century, anthropology was based mainly on reports and documents produced by colonial administrators, missionaries and travellers. Nineteenth-century anthropology therefore used to be rather speculative and inadequately documented. Writers would produce books collecting examples from all over the world, without bothering too much about either how authentic they were or the particular cultural context from which they came. For instance, religion would be analysed by comparing numerous examples of belief and practice drawn from the most diverse cultures.

Modern **anthropology** dates from the time when researchers became dissatisfied with this approach, and started to spend long periods of field study in different cultures around the world. Two of the originators of anthropological fieldwork were a British author strongly influenced by Durkheim, A. R. Radcliffe-Brown (1881–1955), and Bronislaw Malinowski (1884–1942), a Pole who spent much of his career in Britain. Malinowski produced some of the most celebrated anthropological studies ever written, as a result of spending a lengthy period in the Trobriand Islands in the Pacific. Radcliffe-Brown studied the Andaman Islanders, who lived on an archipelago just off the coast of Burma.

Radcliffe-Brown and Malinowski both assert that we must study a society or a culture as a whole if we are to understand its major institutions and explain why its members behave as they do. We can analyse the religious beliefs and customs of a society, for example, only by showing how they relate to other institutions within it, for the different parts of a society develop in close relation to one another.

To study the *function* of a social practice or institution is to analyse the contribution which that practice or institution makes to the continuation of the society as a whole. The best way to understand this is by analogy to the human body, a comparison which Comte, Durkheim and many subsequent functionalist authors make. To study a bodily organ like the heart, we need to show how it relates to other parts of the body. By pumping blood around the body, the heart plays a vital role in the continuation of the life of the organism. Similarly, analysing the function of a social item means showing the part it plays in the continued existence of a society. According to Durkheim, for instance, religion reaffirms people's adherence to core social values, thereby contributing to the maintenance of social cohesion.

Merton's version of functionalism

Functionalism 'moved back' into sociology through the writings of Talcott Parsons (1952, 1966) and Robert K. Merton, each of whom saw functionalist analysis as providing the key to the development of sociological theory and research. Merton's version of functionalism has been particularly influential, serving to focus the work of a whole generation of American sociologists in particular, but also being widely used elsewhere. Merton produced a more sophisticated account of functionalist analysis than was offered by either Radcliffe-Brown or Malinowski. At the same time, he readapted it to the study of industrialized societies, which differ in certain basic ways from the simpler cultures studied by anthropologists.

Merton distinguishes between **manifest** and **latent functions**. Manifest functions are those known to, and intended by, the participants in a specific type of social activity. Latent functions are consequences of that activity of which participants are unaware (Merton 1957). To illustrate this distinction, Merton uses the example of a rain dance performed by the Hopi Indians of New Mexico. The Hopi believe that the ceremonial will bring the rain they need for their crops (manifest function). This is the reason why they organize and participate in it. But the rain dance, Merton argues, using Durkheim's theory of religion, also has the effect of promoting the cohesion of the society (latent function). A major part of sociological explanation, according to Merton, consists in uncovering the latent functions of social activities and institutions.

Merton also distinguishes between functions and *dysfunctions*. The small cultures anthropologists study, he points out, tend to be more integrated and solidary than the large-scale, industrialized societies which are the main concern of sociology. Radcliffe-Brown and Malinowski could concentrate solely on identifying functions, because the cultures they analysed were stable and integrated. In studying the modern world, however, we must be aware of disintegrative tendencies. **Dysfunctions** refer to aspects of social activity which tend to produce change because they *threaten* social cohesion.

To look for the dysfunctional aspects of social behaviour means focusing on features of social life which challenge the existing order of things. For example, it is mistaken to suppose that religion is always functional – that it contributes only to social cohesion. When two groups support different religions or even different versions of the same religion, the result can be major social conflicts, causing widespread social disruption. Thus wars have often been fought between religious communities – as in the struggles between Protestants and Catholics in European history.

Recent developments

For a long while functionalist thought was probably the leading theoretical tradition in sociology, particularly in the United States. In recent years its popularity has begun to wane, as its limitations have become apparent – although it still has articulate defenders (Alexander 1985). While this was not true of Merton, many functionalist thinkers (Talcott Parsons was an example) unduly stress factors leading to social cohesion, at the expense of those producing division and conflict. In addition, it has seemed to many critics that functional analysis gives societies qualities they do not have. Functionalists often write as though societies have 'needs' and 'purposes', even though these concepts make sense only when applied to individual human beings. Take, for instance, Merton's analysis of the Hopi rain dance. Merton writes as though, if we can show that the ceremonial helps integrate Hopi culture, we have explained why it 'really' exists – because, after all, we know that the dance does not actually bring rain. This is not so, unless we imagine that somehow Hopi society 'propels' its members to act in ways which it 'needs' to hold it together. But this cannot be the case, for societies are not endowed with will-power or purposes; only human individuals have these.

Structuralism

Like functionalism, **structuralism** has been influenced by Durkheim's writings, although the main impetus to its development lies in linguistics. The work of the Swiss linguist Ferdinand de Saussure (1857–1913) was the most important early source of structuralist ideas. Although Saussure only wrote about language, the views he developed were subsequently incorporated into numerous disciplines in the social sciences as well as the humanities.

Before Saussure's work, the study of language was concerned mainly with tracing detailed changes in the way words were used. According to Saussure, this procedure omits the central feature of language. We can never identify the basic characteristics – or *structures* – of language if we look only at the words people use when they speak (Saussure 1974). Language consists of rules of grammar and meaning that 'lie behind' the words, but are not stated in them. To take a simple example: in English we usually add '-ed' to a verb when we want to signal that we are referring to an event in the past. This is one grammatical rule among thousands of others which every speaker of the language knows, and which is used to *construct* what we say. According to Saussure, analysing the structures of language means looking for the rules which underlie our speech. Most of these rules are known to us only implicitly: we could not easily state what they are. The task of linguistics, in fact, is to uncover what we implicitly *know*, but know only on the level of being able to use language in practice.

Language and meaning

Saussure argues that the meaning of words derives from the structures of language, not the objects to which the words refer. We might naively imagine that the meaning of the word 'tree' is the leafy object to which the term refers. According to Saussure, however, this is not so. We can see this by the fact that there are plenty of words in language which do not refer to anything – like 'and', 'but' or 'nevertheless'. Moreover, there are perfectly meaningful words which refer to mythical objects and have no existence in reality at all – like 'unicorn'. If the meaning of a word does not derive from the object to which it refers, where does it come from? Saussure's answer is that meaning is created by the *differences* between related concepts which the rules of a language recognize. The meaning of the word 'tree' comes from the fact that we distinguish 'tree' from 'bush', 'shrub', 'forest' and a host of words which have similar – but distinct – meanings. Meanings are created internally within language, not by the objects in the world which we refer to by means of them.

Structuralism and semiotics

To this analysis, Saussure adds the important observation that it is not only sounds (speaking) or marks on paper (writing) that can create meaning. Any objects which we can systematically distinguish can be used to *make meanings*. An example is a traffic light. We use the contrast between green and red to mean 'go' and 'stop' (yellow means 'get ready to start' or 'get ready to stop'). Notice that it is the *difference* that creates the meaning, not the actual colours themselves. It would not matter if we used green to mean 'stop' and red to mean 'go' – so long as we were consistent in recognizing the difference. Saussure calls the study of non-linguistic meanings *semiology*, but the term most often used today is **semiotics**.

Semiotic studies can be made of many different aspects of human culture. One example is clothing and fashion. What makes a certain style of clothing fashionable at a given time? It is certainly not the actual clothes that are worn, for short skirts may be fashionable one year and unfashionable the next. What makes something fashionable is again the *difference* between what is worn by those who are 'in the know' and those who lag behind. Another example from the sphere of clothing is the wearing of mourning dress. In our culture, we show we are in mourning by wearing black. In some other cultures, on the other hand, people who are in mourning wear white. What matters is not the colour itself, but the fact that people in mourning dress differently from their normal style.

The structuralist approach has been used more widely in anthropology than in sociology, particularly in the United States. Following the lead of Lévi-Strauss – who popularized the term *structuralism* – structuralist analysis has been employed in the study of kinship, myth, religion and other areas. However, many writers on sociological theory have been influenced by notions drawn from structuralism. Although he didn't like being called a structuralist, Michel Foucault, whose works are touched on in several chapters, employed several key notions from structuralist thought. Structuralist concepts have been applied to the study of the media (newspapers, magazines, television), ideology and culture in general.

Structuralist thought has weaknesses which limit its appeal as a general theoretical framework in sociology. Structuralism originated in the study of language, and has proved more relevant to analysing certain aspects of human behaviour than others. It is useful for exploring communication and culture, but has less application to more practical concerns of social life, such as economic or political activity.

Symbolic interactionism

Symbolic interactionism gives more weight to the active, creative individual than either of the other theoretical approaches. Since Mead's time it has been further developed by many other writers, and in the United States has been the principal rival to the functionalist standpoint. As in the case of structuralism, symbolic interactionism springs from a concern with language; but Mead develops this in a different direction.

Symbols

Mead claims that language allows us to become self-conscious beings – aware of our own individuality, and the key element in this process is the **symbol**. A symbol is something which *stands for* something else. Pursuing the example used by Saussure, the word 'tree' is a symbol by means of which we represent the object, tree. Once we have mastered such a concept, Mead argues, we can think of a tree even if none is visible. We have learned to think of the object symbolically. Symbolic thought frees us from being limited in our experience to what we actually see, hear or feel.

Unlike the lower animals, human beings live in a richly symbolic universe. This applies to our very sense of self. (Animals do not have a sense of self as human beings do.) Each of us is a self-conscious being, because we learn to be able to 'look at' ourselves as if from the outside – seeing ourselves as others see us. When a child begins to use 'I' to refer to that object (himself or herself) which others call 'you', he or she is exhibiting the beginnings of self-consciousness.

Virtually all interaction between human individuals, symbolic interactionists reason, involves an exchange of symbols. When we interact with others, we constantly look for 'clues' about what type of behaviour is appropriate in the context and about how to interpret what others intend. Symbolic interactionism directs our attention to the detail of interpersonal interaction, and how that detail is used to make sense of what others say and do. For instance, suppose a man and a woman are out on a date for the first time. Each is likely to spend a good part of the evening sizing the other up and assessing how the relationship is likely to develop – if at all. Neither wishes to be seen doing this too openly, although each recognizes that it is going on. Both individuals are careful about their own behaviour, being anxious to present themselves in a favourable light; but, knowing this, each is likely to be looking for aspects of the other's behaviour which would reveal their true opinions. A complex and subtle process of symbolic interpretation shapes the interaction between the two.

Sociologists influenced by symbolic interactionism usually focus on face-to-face interaction in the contexts of everyday life. Erving Goffman, whose work is discussed in chapter 4 ('Social interaction and everyday life'), has made particularly illuminating contributions to this type of study, introducing wit and verve into what in the hands of Mead was a drier, abstract theoretical approach. In the hands of Goffman and others, symbolic interactionism yields many insights into the nature of our actions in the course of day-to-day social life. But symbolic interactionism is open to the criticism that it concentrates too much on the small-scale. Symbolic interactionists have always found difficulty in dealing with more large-scale structures and processes –

the very phenomena which the other two traditions most strongly emphasize.

Marxism

Functionalism, structuralism and symbolic interactionism are not the only theoretical traditions of any importance in sociology, nor is this threefold division the only way in which we can classify theoretical approaches. One influential type of approach which straddles this division is **Marxism**. Marxists, of course, all trace their views back in some way to the writings of Marx, but numerous interpretations of Marx's major ideas are possible and there are today schools of Marxist thought which take very different theoretical positions.

Broadly speaking, Marxism can be subdivided along lines that correspond to the boundaries between the three theoretical traditions previously described. Many Marxists have implicitly or openly adopted a functionalist approach to historical materialism. Their version of Marxism is quite different from that of Marxists influenced by structuralism, the most well-known writer developing such a standpoint being the French author Louis Althusser (Althusser 1969). Both these types of Marxist thought differ from that of Marxists who have laid stress on the active, creative character of human behaviour. Few such writers have been directly influenced by symbolic interactionism, but they have adopted a perspective quite close to it. An example is Jürgen Habermas whose work has been discussed in chapter 1 and elsewhere (see also Habermas 1987).

In all of its versions, Marxism differs from non-Marxist traditions of sociology. Most Marxist authors see Marxism as part of a 'package' of sociological analysis and political reform. Marxism is supposed to generate a programme of radical political change. Moreover, Marxists put more emphasis on class divisions, conflict, power and ideology than many non-Marxist sociologists, especially most of those influenced by functionalism. It is best to see Marxism not as a type of approach within sociology, but as a body of writing existing alongside sociology, each overlapping and quite frequently being influenced by the other. Non-Marxist sociology and Marxism have always existed in a relationship of mutual influence and opposition.

THEORETICAL DILEMMAS

How should we assess the relative value of these four theoretical approaches? Although each has its committed advocates, there are obvious respects in which they are complementary to one another. Functionalism and most versions of Marxism concentrate on the more large-scale properties of social groups or societies. They are principally concerned with the 'grand questions' like 'How do societies hold together?' or 'What are the main conditions producing social change?' Symbolic interactionism, by contrast, concentrates more on face-to-face

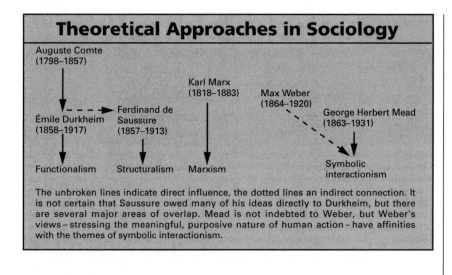

Theoretical Approaches in Sociology

The unbroken lines indicate direct influence, the dotted lines an indirect connection. It is not certain that Saussure owed many of his ideas directly to Durkheim, but there are several major areas of overlap. Mead is not indebted to Weber, but Weber's views – stressing the meaningful, purposive nature of human action – have affinities with the themes of symbolic interactionism.

contexts of social life. Structuralism differs from the other approaches by being focused mainly on cultural features of social activity.

To some extent, therefore, we can draw selectively on all the theories in discussing specific sociological problems; but in certain respects they clearly do clash. There are several basic **theoretical dilemmas** – matters of continuing controversy or dispute – which these clashes of viewpoint bring to our attention, some of which concern very general matters to do with how we should interpret human activities and social institutions. We shall discuss four such dilemmas here.

1 One dilemma concerns *human action* and *social structure*. The issue is the following: How far are we creative human actors, actively controlling the conditions of our own lives? Or is most of what we do the result of general social forces outside our control? This issue has always divided, and continues to divide, sociologists. Symbolic interactionism stresses the active, creative components of human behaviour. The other three approaches (with the exception of some variants of Marxism) emphasize the constraining nature of social influences on our actions.

2 A second theoretical issue concerns *consensus* and *conflict* in society. Some standpoints in sociology – including many linked to functionalism – emphasize the inherent order and harmony of human societies. Those taking this view – such as Talcott Parsons – regard continuity and CONSENSUS as the most evident characteristics of societies, however much they may change over time. Other sociologists, on the other hand – particularly those strongly influenced by Marx or Weber – accentuate the pervasiveness of social CONFLICT. They see societies as plagued with divisions, tensions and struggles. To them, it is illusory to claim that people tend to live amicably with one another most of the time; even when there are no open confrontations, they say, there remain deep divisions of interest which at some point are liable to break out into active conflicts.

3 There is a third basic dilemma of theory which hardly figures at all in orthodox traditions of sociology, but which can no longer be

ignored. This is the problem of how we are to incorporate a satisfactory understanding of *gender* within sociological analysis. All the major figures in the past development of sociological theory were men, and in their writings they gave virtually no attention to the fact that human beings are gendered (Sydie 1987). In their works, human individuals appear as if they were 'neuter' – they are abstract 'actors', rather than differentiated women and men. Since we have very little to build on in relating issues of gender to the more established forms of theoretical thinking in sociology, this is perhaps at the current time the most acutely difficult problem of the four to grapple with.

One of the main theoretical dilemmas associated with gender is the following. Shall we build 'gender' as a general category into our sociological thinking? Or, alternatively, do we need to analyse gender issues by breaking them down into more specific influences affecting the behaviour of women and men in different contexts? Put in another way: Are there characteristics that separate men and women, in terms of their identities and social behaviour, in all cultures? Or are gender differences always to be explained mainly in terms of other differences which divide societies (such as class divisions)?

4 A fourth problem concerns not so much the general characteristics of human behaviour or of societies as a whole, but rather features of *modern social development*. It is to do with the determining influences affecting the origins and nature of modern societies, and derives from the differences between non-Marxist and Marxist approaches. This dilemma centres on the following issue: How far has the modern world been shaped by the economic factors which Marx singled out – in particular, the mechanisms of capitalist economic enterprise? How far, alternatively, have other influences (such as social, political or cultural factors) shaped social development in the modern era?

We shall look at each of these dilemmas in turn.

Dilemma I: Structure and action

A major theme pursued by Durkheim and by many other sociological authors since is that the societies of which we are members exert **social constraint** over our actions. Durkheim argued that society has primacy over the individual person. Society is far more than the sum of individual acts; when we analyse SOCIAL STRUCTURE, we are studying characteristics that have a 'firmness' or 'solidity' comparable to structures in the material environment. Think of a person standing in a room with several doors. The structure of the room constrains the range of her or his possible activities. The siting of the walls and the doors, for example, defines the routes of exit and entry. Social structure, according to Durkheim, constrains our activities in a parallel way, setting limits to what we can do as individuals. It is 'external' to us, just as the walls of the room are.

This point of view is expressed by Durkheim in a famous statement:

> When I perform my duties as a brother, a husband or a citizen and carry out the commitments I have entered into, I fulfil obligations which are defined in law and custom and which are external to myself and my actions . . . Similarly, the believer has discovered from birth, ready fashioned, the beliefs and practices of his religious life; if they existed before he did, it follows that they exist outside him. The system of signs that I employ to express my thoughts, the monetary system I use to pay my debts, the credit instruments I utilise in my commercial relationships, the practices I follow in my profession, etc. – all function independently of the use I make of them. Considering in turn each member of society, the following remarks could be made for each single one of them. (Durkheim 1982, pp. 50–1)

Although the type of view Durkheim expresses has many adherents, it has also met with sharp criticism. What is 'society', the critics ask, if it is not the composite of many individual actions? If we study a group, we do not see a collective entity, only individuals interacting with one another in various ways. 'Society' is only many individuals behaving in regular ways in relation to each other. According to the critics (who include most sociologists influenced by symbolic interactionism), as human beings we have reasons for what we do, and we inhabit a social world permeated by cultural meanings. Social phenomena, according to them, are precisely *not* like 'things', but depend on the symbolic meanings with which we invest what we do. We are not the *creatures* of society, but its *creators*.

Assessment

It is unlikely that this controversy will ever be fully resolved, since it has existed since modern thinkers first started systematically to try to explain human behaviour. Moreover, it is a debate which is not just confined to sociology, but preoccupies scholars in all fields of the social sciences. You must decide, in the light of your reading of this book, which position you think more nearly correct.

Yet the differences between the two views can be exaggerated. While both cannot be wholly right, we can fairly easily see connections between them. Durkheim's view is clearly in some respects valid. Social institutions do precede the existence of any given individual; it is also evident that they exert constraint over us. Thus, for example, I did not invent the monetary system which exists in Britain. Nor do I have a choice about whether I want to use it or not if I wish to have the goods and services which money can buy. The system of money, like all other established institutions, does exist independently of any individual member of society, and constrains that individual's activities.

On the other hand, it is obviously mistaken to suppose that society is 'external' to us in the same way as the physical world is. For the physical world would go on existing whether or not any human beings were alive, whereas it would plainly be nonsensical to say this of society. While society is external to each individual taken singly, by definition it cannot be external to *all* individuals taken together.

Moreover, although what Durkheim calls 'social facts' might constrain what we do, they do not *determine* what we do. I could choose to live without using money, should I be firmly resolved to do so, even if it might prove very difficult to eke out an existence from day to day. As human beings, we do make choices, and we do not simply respond passively to events around us. The way forward in bridging the gap between 'structural' and 'action' approaches is to recognize that we *actively make and remake* social structure during the course of our every-day activities. For example, the fact that I use the monetary system contributes in a minor, yet necessary, way to the very existence of that system. If everyone, or even the majority of people, at some point decided to avoid using money, the monetary system would dissolve.

Dilemma II: Consensus and conflict

It is also useful to begin with Durkheim when contrasting the *consensus* and *conflict* viewpoints. Durkheim sees society as a set of interdependent parts. For most functionalist thinkers, in fact, society is treated as an *integrated whole*, composed of structures which mesh closely with one another. This is very much in accord with Durkheim's emphasis on the constraining, 'external' character of 'social facts'. However, the analogy here is not with the walls of a building, but with the physiology of the body.

A body consists of various specialized parts (such as the brain, heart, lungs, liver and so forth), each of which contributes to sustaining the continuing life of the organism. These necessarily work in harmony with one another; if they do not, the life of the organism is under threat. So it is, according to Durkheim (and Parsons), with society. For a society to have a continuing existence over time, its specialized institutions (such as the political system, religion, the family and the educational system) must work in harmony with one another. The continuation of a society thus depends on cooperation, which in turn presumes a general consensus, or agreement, among its members over basic values.

Those who focus mainly on conflict have a very different outlook. Their guiding assumptions can easily be outlined using Marx's account of class conflict as an example. According to Marx, societies are divided into classes with unequal resources. Since such marked inequalities exist, there are divisions of interest which are 'built into' the social system. These conflicts of interest at some point break out into active struggle between classes – which can generate processes of radical change. Not all of those influenced by this viewpoint concentrate on classes to the degree which Marx did; other divisions are regarded as important in promoting conflict – for example, divisions between racial groups or political factions. Whatever the conflict groups on which most emphasis is put, society is seen as essentially *full of tension* – even the most stable social system represents an uneasy balance of antagonistic groupings.

Assessment

As with the case of structure or action, it is not likely that this theoretical debate can be completely brought to a close. Yet, once more, the difference between the consensus and conflict standpoints seems wider than it is. The two positions are by no means wholly incompatible. All societies probably involve some kind of general agreement over values, and all certainly involve conflict.

Moreover, as a general rule of sociological analysis we have always to examine the connections *between* consensus and conflict within social systems. The values different groups hold and the goals their members pursue often reflect a mixture of common and opposed interests. For instance, even in Marx's portrayal of class conflict, different classes share some common interests as well as being pitted against one another. Thus capitalists depend on a labour force to work in their enterprises, just as workers depend on capitalists to provide their wages. Open conflict is not continuous in such circumstances; rather, sometimes what both sides have in common tends to override their differences, while in other situations the reverse is the case.

A useful concept which helps analyse the interrelations of conflict and consensus is that of *ideology* – values and beliefs which help secure the position of more powerful groups at the expense of less powerful ones. Power, ideology and conflict are always closely connected. Many conflicts are *about* power, because of the rewards it can bring. Those who hold most power may depend mainly on the influence of ideology to retain their dominance, but are usually able also to use force if necessary. For instance, in feudal times aristocratic rule was supported by the idea that a minority of people were 'born to govern', but aristocratic rulers often resorted to the use of violence against those who dared to oppose their power.

Dilemma III: The problem of gender

Issues of gender are scarcely central in the writings of the major figures who established the framework of modern sociology. The few passages in which they did touch on gender questions, however, allow us at least to specify the outlines of a basic theoretical dilemma – even if there is little in their works to help us try to resolve it. We can best describe this dilemma by contrasting a theme which occasionally occurs in Durkheim's writings with one that appears in those of Marx. Durkheim notes at one point, in the course of his discussion of suicide, that man is 'almost entirely the product of society', while woman is 'to a far greater extent the product of nature'. Expanding on these observations, he says of man: 'his tastes, aspirations and humour have in large part a collective origin, while his companion's are more directly influenced by her organism. His needs, therefore, are quite different from hers . . .' (Durkheim 1952, p. 385). In other words, women and men have different identities, tastes and inclinations because women are less socialized and are 'closer to nature' than men.

No one today would accept a view stated in quite this manner. Female identity is as much shaped by socialization as that of males. Yet, when modified somewhat, Durkheim's claim does represent one possible view of the formation and nature of gender. This is that gender differences rest fundamentally on biologically given distinctions between men and women. Such a view does not necessarily mean believing that gender differences are mostly inborn. Rather, it presumes that women's social position and identity are mainly shaped (as Chodorow suggests; see chapter 5, 'Gender and sexuality') by their involvement in reproduction and child-rearing. If this view is correct, differences of gender are deeply embedded in all societies. The discrepancies in power between women and men reflect the fact that women bear children and are their primary caretakers, whereas men are active in the 'public' spheres of politics, work and war.

Marx's view is substantially at odds with this. For Marx, gender differences in power and status between men and women mainly reflect other divisions – in his eyes, especially class divisions. According to him, in the earliest forms of human society neither gender nor class divisions were present. The power of men over women only came about as class divisions appeared. Women came to be a form of 'private property' owned by men, through the institution of marriage. Women will be freed from their situation of bondage when class divisions are overcome. Again, few if any would accept this analysis today, but we can make it a much more plausible view by generalizing it further. Class is not the only factor shaping social divisions which affect the behaviour of men and women. Other factors include ethnicity and cultural background. For instance, it might be argued that women in a minority group (say, blacks in the United States) have more in common with men in that minority group than they do with women in the majority (that is, white women). Or it may be the case that women from a particular culture (like a small hunting and gathering culture) share more common characteristics with the males of that culture than they do with women in an industrial society.

Evaluation

The issues involved in this third dilemma are highly important, and bear directly on the challenge which feminist authors have thrown down to sociology. No one can seriously dispute that a great deal of sociological analysis in the past has either ignored women, or has operated with interpretations of female identity and behaviour that are drastically inadequate. In spite of all the new research on women carried out in sociology over the past twenty years, there still are many areas in which the distinctive activities and concerns of women have been insufficiently studied. But 'bringing the study of women into sociology' is not in and of itself the same as coping with problems of gender, because gender concerns the relations between the identities and behaviour of women *and* men. For the moment it has to be left as an open question how far gender differences can be illuminated by means of other sociological concepts (class, ethnicity, cultural background and so forth), or how far, on the contrary, other social divisions need to be explained in terms of gender. Certainly some of the major explanatory tasks of sociology in the future will depend on tackling this dilemma effectively.

Dilemma IV: The shaping of the modern world

The Marxist perspective

Marx's writings throw down a powerful challenge to sociological analysis, one which has not been ignored. From his own time to the present day, many sociological debates have centred on Marx's ideas about the development of modern societies (Marx and Engels 1968). As was mentioned earlier, Marx sees modern societies as *capitalistic*. The driving impulse behind social change in the modern era is the pressure towards constant economic transformation which is an integral part of capitalist production. Capitalism is a vastly more dynamic economic system than any preceding one. Capitalists compete with one another to sell their goods to consumers, and, to survive in a competitive market, firms have to produce their wares as cheaply and efficiently as possible. This leads to constant technological innovation, because increasing the effectiveness of the technology used in a particular production process is one way in which companies can secure an edge over their rivals.

There are also strong incentives to seek out new markets in which to sell goods, acquire cheap raw materials and make use of cheap labour power. Capitalism, therefore, according to Marx, is a restlessly expanding system, pushing outwards across the world. This is how Marx explains the spread of Western industry globally.

Marx's interpretation of the influence of capitalism has found many supporters, and subsequent authors have considerably refined Marx's own portrayal. On the other hand, numerous critics have set out to rebut Marx's view, offering alternative analyses of the influences shaping the modern world. Virtually everyone accepts that capitalism *has* played a major part in creating the world we live in today. But other sociologists have argued both that Marx exaggerated the impact of purely *economic* factors in producing change, and that capitalism is *less central* to modern social development than he claimed. Most of these writers have also been sceptical of Marx's belief that a socialist system would eventually replace capitalism. It would seem that their scepticism has been borne out by the events of 1989 and after in Eastern Europe.

Weber's view

One of Marx's earliest, and most acute, critics was Max Weber. Weber's writings, in fact, have been described as involving a lifelong struggle with 'the ghost of Marx' – with the intellectual legacy that Marx left. The alternative position which Weber worked out remains important today. According to him, non-economic factors have played a key role in modern social development. Weber's celebrated and much discussed work *The Protestant Ethic and the Spirit of Capitalism* argues that religious values – especially those associated with Puritanism – were of fundamental importance in creating a capitalistic outlook. This outlook did not emerge, as Marx supposed, from economic changes as such.

Weber's understanding of the nature of modern societies and the reasons for the spread of Western modes of life across the world contrasts substantially with that of Marx. According to Weber, capitalism – a distinct way of organizing economic enterprise – is one among other major factors shaping social development in the modern period. Underlying capitalistic economic mechanisms, and in some ways more fundamental than them, is the impact of *science* and *bureaucracy*. Science has shaped modern technology – and will presumably continue to do so in any future socialist society. Bureaucracy is the only way of organizing large numbers of people effectively, and therefore inevitably expands with economic and political growth. The development of science, modern technology and bureaucracy Weber refers to collectively as **rationalization**. Rationalization means the organization of social and economic life according to principles of efficiency, on the basis of technical knowledge.

Evaluation

Which type of interpretation of modern societies, that deriving from Marx or that coming from Weber, is correct? Again, scholars are divided on the issue. The box lists some of these differences. (It must be remembered that within each camp there are variations, so not every theorist will agree with all the points.)

The contrasts between Marxist and Weberian standpoints inform many areas of sociology. They influence not only how we analyse the nature of the industrialized societies, but our view of less developed societies

---

MARX AND WEBER COMPARED

Broadly Marxist Ideas	Broadly Weberian Ideas
The main dynamic of modern development is the expansion of capitalistic economic mechanisms.	The main dynamic of modern development is the rationalization of production.
Modern societies are riven with class inequalities, which are basic to their very nature.	Class is one type of inequality among many – such as inequalities between men and women – in modern societies.
Major divisions of power, like those affecting the differential position of men and women, derive ultimately from economic inequalities.	Power in the economic system is separable from other sources. For instance, male–female inequalities cannot be explained in economic terms.
Modern societies as we know them today (capitalist societies) are of a transitional type – we may expect them to become radically reorganized in the future. Socialism, of one type or another, will eventually replace capitalism.	Rationalization is bound to progress further in the future, in all spheres of social life. All modern societies are dependent on the same basic modes of social and economic organization.
The spread of Western influence across the world is mainly a result of the expansionist tendencies of capitalist enterprise.	The global impact of the West comes from its command over industrial resources, together with superior military power.

also. In addition, the two perspectives are linked to differing political positions, authors on the left on the whole adopting views on the first side, liberals and conservatives those on the second side. Yet the factors with which this particular dilemma is concerned are of a more directly empirical nature than those involved in the other dilemmas. Factual studies of the paths of development of modern societies and Third World countries help us assess how far patterns of change conform to one side or the other.

THEORIES

We can draw a distinction between THEORETICAL APPROACHES and THEORIES. So far in this chapter we have been concerned with theoretical approaches, which are broad overall orientations to the subject matter of sociology. Theories are more narrowly focused and represent attempts to explain particular sets of social conditions or types of occurrence. They are usually formed as part of the process of research, and in turn suggest problems to which research investigations should be devoted. An example would be Durkheim's theory of suicide.

Innumerable theories have been developed in the many different areas of research in which sociologists work. Some are very precisely set out, and even occasionally expressed in mathematical form – although this is more common in other social sciences (especially economics) than in sociology.

Some types of theory attempt to explain much more than others, and opinions vary about how far it is desirable or useful for sociologists to concern themselves with very wide-ranging theoretical efforts. Robert Merton, for example, argues forcefully that sociologists should concentrate their attention on what he calls *theories of the middle range* (Merton 1957). Rather than attempting to create grand theoretical schemes (in the manner of Parsons, for instance), we should be more modest.

Middle-range theories are specific enough to be able to be directly tested by empirical research, yet sufficiently general to cover a range of different phenomena. A case in point is the theory of **relative deprivation**. This theory holds that how people evaluate their circumstances depends on whom they compare themselves to. Thus feelings of deprivation do not relate directly to the level of material poverty individuals experience. A family living in a small home in a poor area, where everyone is in more or less similar circumstances, is likely to feel less deprived than one living in a similar house in a neighbourhood where the majority of homes are much larger and more affluent.

It is indeed true that the more wide-ranging and ambitious a theory is, the more difficult it is to test it empirically. Yet there seems no obvious reason why theoretical thinking in sociology should be confined to the 'middle range'. To see why this is so, let us take as an example the theory that Weber advances in *The Protestant Ethic and the Spirit of Capitalism*.

An example: the Protestant ethic

In *The Protestant Ethic* (1976; originally published 1904–5), Weber sets out to tackle a fundamental problem: why capitalism developed in the West and nowhere else. For some thirteen centuries after the fall of ancient Rome, other civilizations were much more prominent in world history than the West. Europe in fact was a rather insignificant area of the globe, while China, India and the Ottoman empire in the Near East were all major powers. The Chinese in particular were a long way ahead of the West in terms of their level of technological and economic development. What happened to bring about a surge in economic development in Europe from the seventeenth century onwards?

To answer this question, Weber reasons, we must show what separates modern industry from earlier types of economic activity. We find the desire to accumulate wealth in many different civilizations, and this is not difficult to explain: people have valued wealth for the comforts, security, power and enjoyment it can bring. They wish to be free of want, and, having accumulated wealth, they use it to make themselves comfortable.

If we look at the economic development of the West, Weber argues, we find something quite different: an attitude towards the accumulation of wealth found nowhere else in history. This attitude is what Weber calls the *spirit of capitalism* – a set of beliefs and values held by the first capitalist merchants and industrialists. These people had a strong drive to accumulate personal wealth. Yet, quite unlike the wealthy elsewhere, they did not seek to use their accumulated riches to follow a luxurious lifestyle. Their way of life was in fact self-denying and frugal; they lived soberly and quietly, shunning the ordinary manifestations of affluence. This very unusual combination of characteristics, Weber tries to show, was vital to early Western economic development. For unlike the wealthy in previous ages and in other cultures, these groups did not dissipate their wealth. Instead, they reinvested it to promote the further expansion of the enterprises they headed.

The core of Weber's theory is that the attitudes involved in the spirit of capitalism derived from religion. Christianity in general played a part in fostering such an outlook, but the essential motive force was provided by the impact of Protestantism – and especially one variety of Protestantism, *Puritanism*. The early capitalists were mostly Puritans, and many subscribed to Calvinist views. Weber argues that certain Calvinistic doctrines were the direct source of the spirit of capitalism. One was the idea that human beings are God's instruments on earth, required by the Almighty to work in a *vocation* – an occupation – for the greater glory of God.

A second important aspect of Calvinism was the notion of *predestination*, according to which only certain predestined individuals are to be among the 'elect' – to enter heaven in the after-life. In Calvin's original doctrine, nothing a person does on this earth can alter whether he or she happens to be one of the elect; this is predetermined by God. However, this belief caused such anxiety among his followers that it was modified to allow believers to recognize certain signs of election.

Success in working in a vocation, indicated by material prosperity, became the main sign that a person was truly one of the elect. A tremendous impetus towards economic success was created among groups influenced by these ideas. Yet this was accompanied by the believer's need to live a sober and frugal life. The Puritans believed luxury to be an evil, so the drive to accumulate wealth became joined to a severe and unadorned lifestyle.

The early entrepreneurs had little awareness that they were helping to produce momentous changes in society; they were impelled above all by religious motives. The ascetic – that is, self-denying – lifestyle of the Puritans has subsequently become an intrinsic part of modern civilization. As Weber says:

> The Puritan wanted to work in a calling; we are forced to do so. For when asceticism was carried out of the monastic cells into everyday life, and began to dominate worldly morality, it did its part in building the tremendous cosmos of the modern economic order. . . . Since asceticism undertook to remodel the world and to work out its ideals in the world, material goods have gained an increasingly and finally an inexorable power over the lives of men as at no previous period in history. . . . The idea of duty in one's calling prowls about in our lives like the ghost of dead religious beliefs. Where the fulfilment of the calling cannot directly be related to the highest spiritual and cultural values, or when, on the other hand, it need not be felt simply as economic compulsion, the individual generally abandons the attempt to justify it at all. In the field of its highest development, in the United States, the pursuit of wealth, stripped of its religious and ethical meaning, tends to become associated with purely mundane passions . . . (Weber 1976, pp. 181–2)

Weber's theory has been criticized from many angles. Some have argued, for example, that the outlook he called 'the spirit of capitalism' can be discerned in the early Italian merchant cities long before Calvinism was ever heard of. Others have claimed that the key notion of 'working in a vocation', which Weber associated with Protestantism, already existed in Catholic beliefs. Yet the essentials of Weber's account are still accepted by many, and the thesis he advanced remains as bold and illuminating as it did when first formulated. If Weber's thesis is valid, modern economic and social development has been decisively influenced by something that seems at first sight utterly distant from it – a set of religious ideals.

Weber's theory meets several criteria important in theoretical thinking in sociology.

1 It is **counterintuitive** – it suggests an interpretation that breaks with what common sense would suggest. The theory thus develops a fresh perspective on the issues it covers. Most authors before Weber gave little thought to the possibility that religious ideals could have played a fundamental role in the origins of capitalism.
2 The theory is neither a purely 'structural' nor a purely 'individual' account. The early development of capitalism was an unintended consequence of what the Puritan businessmen aspired to – to live virtuously according to God's will.
3 The theory makes sense of something that is otherwise puzzling:

why individuals would want to live frugally while making great efforts to accumulate wealth.

4 The theory is capable of illuminating circumstances beyond those it was originally developed to understand. Weber emphasized that he was trying to understand only the early origins of modern capitalism. None the less, it seems reasonable to suppose that parallel values to those instilled by Puritanism might be involved in other situations of successful capitalist development.

5 A good theory is not just one that happens to be valid. It is also one that is *fruitful* in terms of how far it generates new ideas and stimulates further research work. Weber's theory has certainly been highly successful in these respects, providing the springboard for a vast amount of subsequent research and theory.

THEORETICAL THINKING IN SOCIOLOGY

Assessing theories, and especially theoretical approaches, in sociology is a challenging and formidable task. Theoretical debates are by definition more abstract than controversies of a more empirical kind. The fact that there is not a single theoretical approach which dominates the whole of sociology might seem to be a sign of weakness in the subject. But this is not so. On the contrary, the jostling of rival theoretical approaches and theories is an expression of the vitality of the sociological enterprise. In studying human beings – ourselves – theoretical variety rescues us from dogma. Human behaviour is complicated and many-sided, and it is very unlikely that a single theoretical perspective could cover all its aspects. Diversity in theoretical thinking provides a rich source of ideas that can be drawn on in research, and stimulates the imaginative capacities so essential to progress in sociological work.

SUMMARY

1 A diversity of theoretical approaches is found in sociology (and also in the other social sciences). The reason for this is not particularly puzzling: theoretical disputes are difficult to resolve even in the natural sciences, and in sociology we face special difficulties because of the complex problems involved in subjecting our own behaviour to study.

2 The main theoretical approaches in sociology are functionalism, structuralism, symbolic interactionism and Marxism. To some extent, these approaches are complementary to one another. However, there are also major contrasts between them which influence the ways in which theoretical issues are handled by authors adopting different approaches.

3 One main theoretical dilemma in sociology concerns how we should relate human action to social structure. Are we the creators of society, or created by it? The choice between these alternatives is not as stark as may initially appear, and the real problem is how to relate the two aspects of social life to one another.

4 A second dilemma concerns whether societies should be pictured as harmonious and orderly, or whether they should be seen as marked by persistent conflict. Again, the two views are not completely opposed, and we need to show how consensus and conflict interrelate. The concepts of ideology and power are useful in undertaking this task.

5 A third dilemma concerns how we should cope with issues of gender in sociological analysis. Feminists have thrown down a challenge to sociology which is slowly being met on the level of empirical research: far more studies of the concerns and outlooks of women are being carried out than before. But these do not in and of themselves resolve the question of how we should best analyse gender in relation to the existing approaches and concepts of sociological theory.

6 A fourth focus of continuing debate in sociology is to do with the analysis of modern social development. Are processes of change in the modern world mainly shaped by capitalist economic development or by other factors, including non-economic ones? Positions taken in this debate to some extent are influenced by the political beliefs and attitudes held by different sociologists.

7 Weber's thesis about the influence of Puritanism on modern economic development provides a useful example in thinking about what makes a theory valuable. Weber's ideas remain controversial, but in several respects his theory broke new ground, stimulating much subsequent research.

FURTHER READING

Roslyn W. Bologh, *Love or Greatness: Max Weber and Feminist Thinking – a Feminist Enquiry* (London: Unwin Hyman, 1990). A feminist critique of Max Weber.

Anthony Giddens, *Capitalism and Modern Social Theory*, revised edn (Cambridge: Cambridge University Press, 1992). A discussion of the writings of Marx, Durkheim and Weber.

Charles Wright Mills, *The Sociological Imagination*

(Harmondsworth: Penguin, 1979). A classic analysis of the themes which should inform theoretical thinking in sociology.

The Polity Reader in Social Theory (Cambridge: Polity Press, 1994).

Quentin Skinner (ed.), *The Return of Grand Theory* (Cambridge: Cambridge University Press, 1986). A collection of articles dealing with leading traditions of theory.

IMPORTANT TERMS

- *functionalism*
- *anthropology*
- *manifest functions*
- *latent functions*
- *dysfunctions*
- *structuralism*
- *semiotics*
- *symbolic interactionism*

- *symbol*
- *Marxism*
- *theoretical dilemma*
- *social constraint*
- *rationalization*
- *relative deprivation*
- *counterintuitive thinking*

GLOSSARY OF BASIC CONCEPTS

AUTHORITY The legitimate power which one person or a group holds over another. The element of legitimacy is vital to the notion of authority and is the main means by which authority is distinguished from the more general concept of power. Power can be exerted by the use of force or violence. Authority, by contrast, depends on the acceptance by subordinates of the right of those above them to give them orders or directives.

BUREAUCRACY An organization of a hierarchical sort, which takes the form of a pyramid of authority. The term 'bureaucracy' was popularized by Max Weber. According to Weber, bureaucracy is the most efficient type of large-scale human organization. As organizations grow in size, Weber argued, they inevitably tend to become more and more bureaucratized.

CLASS Although it is one of the most frequently used concepts in sociology, there is no clear agreement about how the notion should best be defined. However, most sociologists use the term to refer to socioeconomic differences between groups of individuals which create differences in their material prosperity and power.

CLASS STRUCTURE The distribution of classes in a society. Classes are mainly based on economic inequalities, and such inequalities are never random. Most societies have a limited number of classes. In modern societies, for example, some of the main class groups are the upper class, middle class, working class and underclass.

COLLECTIVE ACTION Action undertaken in a relatively spontaneous way by a large number of people assembled together in a particular place or area. One of the most important forms of collective action is crowd behaviour. In crowds, individuals can seek to achieve objectives which in ordinary circumstances are denied to them.

COMMUNICATION The transmission of information from one individual or group to another. Communication is the necessary basis of all social interaction. In face-to-face contexts, communication is carried on by the use of language, but also by many bodily cues which individuals interpret in understanding what others say and do. With the development of writing and of electronic media like radio, television, or computer transmission systems, communication becomes in some part detached from immediate contexts of face-to-face social relationships.

CONFLICT Antagonism between individuals or groups in society. Conflict may take two forms. One occurs where there is a clash of interests between two or more individuals or groups; the other happens where people or collectivities engage in active struggle with one another. Interest conflict does not always lead to open struggle, while active conflicts may sometimes occur between parties who mistakenly believe their interests are opposed.

CONFORMITY Behaviour which follows the established norms of a group or society. People do not always conform to social norms because they accept the values that underlie them. They may behave in the approved ways simply because it is expedient to do so, or because of sanctions.

CONSENSUS Agreement over basic social values by the members of a group, community or society. Some thinkers in sociology strongly emphasize the importance of consensus as a basis for social stability. These writers believe that all societies which endure over any substantial period of time involve a 'common value system' of consensual beliefs held by the majority of the population.

CRIME Any action which contravenes the laws established by a political authority. Although we may tend to think of 'criminals' as a distinct subsection of the population, there are few people who have not broken the law in one way or another during the course of their lives. While laws are formulated by state authorities, it is by no means unknown for those authorities to engage in criminal behaviour in certain contexts.

CULTURAL REPRODUCTION The transmission of cultural values and norms from generation to generation. Cultural reproduction refers to the mechanisms by which continuity of cultural experience is sustained across time. The processes of schooling in modern societies are among the main mechanisms of cultural reproduction, and do not operate solely through what is taught in courses of formal instruction. Cultural reproduction occurs in a more profound way through the hidden curriculum – aspects of behaviour which individuals learn in an informal way while at school.

CULTURE   The values, norms and material goods characteristic of a given group. Like the concept of society, the notion of culture is very widely used in sociology, as well as in the other social sciences (particularly anthropology). Culture is one of the most distinctive properties of human social association.

DEMOCRACY   A political system that allows the citizens to participate in political decision-making, or to elect representatives to government bodies.

DEVIANCE   Modes of action which do not conform to the norms or values held by most of the members of a group or society. What is regarded as 'deviant' is as widely variable as the norms and values that distinguish different cultures and subcultures from one another. Many forms of behaviour which are highly esteemed in one context, or by one group, are regarded negatively by others.

DISCRIMINATION   Activities that deny to the members of a particular group resources or rewards which can be obtained by others. Discrimination has to be distinguished from prejudice, although the two are usually quite closely associated. It can be the case that individuals who are prejudiced against others do not engage in discriminatory practices against them; conversely, people may act in a discriminatory fashion even though they are not prejudiced against those subject to such discrimination.

DIVISION OF LABOUR   The division of a production system into specialized work tasks or occupations, creating economic interdependence. All societies have at least some rudimentary form of division of labour, especially between the tasks allocated to men and those performed by women. With the development of industrialism, however, the division of labour becomes vastly more complex than in any prior type of production system. In the modern world, it is international in scope.

THE ECONOMY   The system of production and exchange which provides for the material needs of individuals living in a given society. Economic institutions are of key importance in all social orders. What goes on in the economy usually influences many other aspects of social life. Modern economies differ very substantially from traditional ones, because the majority of the population is no longer engaged in agricultural production.

EDUCATION   The transmission of knowledge from one generation to another by means of direct instruction. Although educational processes exist in all societies, it is only in the modern period that mass education takes the form of schooling – that is, instruction in specialized educational environments in which individuals spend several years of their lives.

ENCOUNTER   A meeting between two or more individuals in a situation of face-to-face interaction. Our day-to-day lives can be seen as a series of different encounters strung out across the course of the day. In modern societies, many of the encounters we have with others involve strangers rather than people we know well.

ETHNICITY   Cultural values and norms which distinguish the members of a given group from others. An ethnic group is one whose members share a distinct awareness of a common cultural identity, separating them from other groups around them. In virtually all societies ethnic differences are associated with variations in power and material wealth. Where ethnic differences are also racial, such divisions are sometimes especially pronounced.

FAMILY   A group of individuals related to one another by blood ties, marriage or adoption, who form an economic unit, the adult members of which are responsible for the upbringing of children. All known societies involve some form of family system, although the nature of family relationships is widely variable. While in modern societies the main family form is the nuclear family, a variety of extended family relationships are also often found.

FORMAL RELATIONS   Relations which exist in groups and organizations laid down by the norms or rules of the 'official' system of authority.

GENDER   Social expectations about behaviour regarded as appropriate for the members of each sex. Gender does not refer to the physical attributes in terms of which men and women differ, but to socially formed traits of masculinity and femininity. The study of gender relations has become one of the most important areas of sociology in recent years, although for a long time they received little attention.

GLOBALIZATION   Growing interdependence between different peoples, regions and countries in the world.

GOVERNMENT   The process of the enacting of policies and decisions on the part of officials within a political apparatus. We can speak of 'government' as a process, or *the* government to refer to the officialdom responsible for the taking of binding political decisions. While in the past virtually all governments were headed by monarchs or emperors, in most modern societies governments are run by officials, who do not inherit their positions of power, but are elected or appointed on the basis of expertise and qualifications.

IDENTITY   The distinctive characteristics of a person's character or the character of a group. Both individual and group identity are largely provided by social markers. Thus one of the most important markers of an individual's identity is his or her name. The name is an important part of the person's individuality. Naming is also important for group identity. For instance, national identity is governed by whether one is 'English', 'French', 'American' and so forth.

IDEOLOGY   Shared ideas or beliefs which serve to justify the interests of dominant groups. Ideologies are found in all societies in which there are systematic and ingrained inequalities between groups. The concept of ideology connects closely with that of power, since ideological systems serve to legitimize the differential power which groups hold.

INDUSTRIALIZATION   The development of modern forms of industry – factories, machines and large-scale production processes. Industrialization has been one of the main sets of processes influencing the social world over the past two centuries. Those societies which are industrialized have characteristics quite different from those of the less developed countries. For instance, with the advance of industrialization only a tiny proportion of the population works in agriculture – a major contrast with preindustrial countries.

INDUSTRIALIZATION OF WAR   The application of modes of industrial production to weaponry, coupled with the organization of fighting forces as 'military machines'. The industrialization of war is as fundamental an aspect of the development of modern societies as is industry evolved for peaceful purposes. It is closely associated with the emergence of total war in the twentieth century – warfare involving hundreds of thousands or millions of soldiers, plus the overall mobilizing of the economy for war-related needs.

INDUSTRIAL SOCIETIES   Societies in which the vast majority of the labour force works in industrial production.

INFORMAL RELATIONS   Relations which exist in groups and organizations developed on the basis of personal connections; ways of doing things that depart from formally recognized modes of procedure.

KINSHIP   A relation which links individuals through blood ties, marriage or adoption. Kinship relations are by definition involved in marriage and the family, but extend much more broadly than these institutions. While in most modern societies few social obligations are involved in kinship relations extending beyond the immediate family, in many other cultures kinship is of vital importance for most aspects of social life.

MARRIAGE   A socially approved sexual relationship between two individuals. Marriage almost always involves two persons of opposite sexes, but in some cultures types of homosexual marriage are tolerated. Marriage normally forms the basis of a family of procreation – that is, it is expected that the married couple will produce and bring up children. Many societies permit polygamy, in which an individual may have several spouses at the same time.

MASS MEDIA   Forms of communication, such as newspapers, magazines, radio and television, designed to reach mass audiences.

NATION-STATE   A particular type of state, characteristic of the modern world, in which a government has sovereign power within a defined territorial area, and the mass of the population are citizens who know themselves to be part of a single nation. Nation-states are closely associated with the rise of nationalism, although nationalist loyalties do not always conform to the boundaries of specific states that exist today. Nation-states developed as part of an emerging nation-state system, which originated in Europe, but in current times spans the whole globe.

NATURE   Physical characteristics either of the external world, or of the body, which are uninfluenced by human intervention. An event or situation is 'natural' if it exists or happens independently of human control. Much of the external environment in which we live is no longer part of nature, because human beings intervene in so many aspects of it. Global warming is an example of this process: it is not a natural state, but is caused by pollution produced by human beings. Much of what happens to our bodies, however, is also no longer natural. For instance, as a result of new forms of reproductive technology, such as modern contraception or genetic engineering, our bodies are less and less governed by natural processes.

NORMS   Rules of conduct which specify appropriate behaviour in a given range of social contexts. A norm either prescribes a given type of behaviour, or forbids it. All human groups follow definite types of norm, which are always backed by sanctions of one kind or another – varying from informal disapproval to physical punishment or execution.

ORGANIZATION   A large group of individuals, involving a definite set of authority relations. Many types of organization exist in industrial societies, influencing most aspects of our lives. While not all organizations are bureaucratic in its formal sense, there are quite close links between the development of organizations and bureaucratic tendencies.

POLITICS   The means by which power is employed to influence the nature and content of governmental activities. The sphere of the 'political' includes the activities of those in government, but also the actions of many other groups and individuals. There are many ways in which people outside the governmental apparatus seek to influence it.

POPULAR CULTURE Entertainment created for large audiences, such as popular films, shows, music, videos and TV programmes. Popular culture is often contrasted to 'high' or 'elite' culture, which refers to the tastes of educated minorities. Classical music, opera and painting are examples of high culture.

POSTINDUSTRIAL SOCIETY A notion advocated by those who believe that processes of social change are taking us beyond the industrialized order. A postindustrial society is one based on the production of information, rather than on the production of material goods. According to those who favour this concept, we are currently experiencing a series of social changes as profound as those which initiated the industrial era some two hundred years ago.

POWER The ability of individuals, or the members of a group, to achieve aims or further the interests they hold. Power is a pervasive aspect of all human relationships. Many conflicts in society are struggles over power, because how much power an individual or group is able to achieve governs how far they are able to put their wishes into practice at the expense of those of others.

PREJUDICE The holding of preconceived ideas about an individual or group, ideas that are resistant to change even in the face of new information. Prejudice may be either positive or negative.

RACISM The attributing of characteristics of superiority or inferiority to a population sharing certain physically inherited characteristics. Racism is one specific form of prejudice, focusing on physical variations between people. Racist attitudes became entrenched during the period of colonial expansion by the West, but seem also to rest on mechanisms of prejudice and discrimination found in very many contexts of human societies.

RELIGION A set of beliefs adhered to by the members of a community, involving symbols regarded with a sense of awe or wonder, together with ritual practices in which members of the community engage. Religions do not universally involve a belief in supernatural entities. Although distinctions between religion and magic are difficult to draw, it is often held that magic is primarily practised by individuals rather than being the focus of community ritual.

RESEARCH METHODS The diverse methods of investigation used to gather empirical (factual) material. Numerous different research methods exist in sociology, but perhaps the most commonly used are fieldwork (or participant observation) and survey methods. For many purposes it is useful to combine two or more methods within a single research project.

REVOLUTION A process of political change, involving the mobilizing of a mass social movement, which by the use of violence successfully overthrows an existing regime and forms a new government. A revolution is distinguished from a *coup d'état* because it involves a mass movement and the occurrence of major change in the political system as a whole. A *coup d'état* refers to the seizure of power through the use of arms by individuals who then replace the existing political leaders, but without otherwise radically transforming the governmental system. Revolutions can also be distinguished from rebellions, which involve challenges to the existing political authorities, but again aim at the replacement of personnel rather than the transformation of the political structure as such.

RITUAL Formalized modes of behaviour in which the members of a group or community regularly engage. Religion represents one of the main contexts in which rituals are practised, but the scope of ritual behaviour extends well beyond this particular sphere. Most groups have ritual practices of some kind or another.

SCIENCE In the sense of physical science, the systematic study of the physical world. Science involves the disciplined marshalling of empirical data, combined with the construction of theoretical approaches and theories which illuminate or explain those data. Scientific activity combines the creation of boldly new modes of thought with the careful testing of hypotheses and ideas. One major feature which helps distinguish science from other types of idea system (such as that involved in religion) is the assumption that *all* scientific ideas are open to mutual criticism and revision on the part of the members of the scientific community.

SECULARIZATION A process of decline in the influence of religion. Although modern societies have become increasingly secularized, tracing the extent of secularization is a complex matter. Secularization can refer to levels of involvement with religious organizations (such as rates of church attendance), the social and material influence wielded by religious organizations, and the degree to which people hold religious beliefs.

SELF-CONSCIOUSNESS Awareness of one's distinct social identity, as a person separate from others. Human beings are not born with self-consciousness, but acquire an awareness of self as a result of early socialization. The learning of language is of vital importance to the processes by which the child learns to become a self-conscious being.

SEX The anatomical differences which separate men from women. Sociologists often contrast sex with gender. Sex refers to the physical characteristics of the body; gender concerns socially learned forms of behaviour. Sex and gender divisions are not the same. A transvestite, for example, is someone who is physically a man but sometimes assumes the gender of a woman.

SOCIAL CHANGE   Alteration in basic structures of a social group or society. Social change is an ever-present phenomenon in social life, but has become especially intense in the modern era. The origins of modern sociology can be traced to attempts to understand the dramatic changes shattering the traditional world and promoting new forms of social order.

SOCIAL GROUPS   Collections of individuals who interact in systematic ways with one another. Groups may range from very small associations to large-scale organizations or societies. Whatever their size, it is a defining feature of a group that its members have an awareness of a common identity. Most of our lives are spent in group contact; in modern societies, most people belong to groups of many different types.

SOCIAL INTERACTION   Any form of social encounter between individuals. Most of our lives are made up of social interaction of one type or another. Social interaction refers to both formal and informal situations in which people meet one another. An illustration of a formal situation of social interaction is a school classroom; an example of informal interaction is two people meeting in the street or at a party.

SOCIALIZATION   The social processes through which children develop an awareness of social norms and values, and achieve a distinct sense of self. Although socialization processes are particularly significant in infancy and childhood, they continue to some degree throughout life. No human individuals are immune from the reactions of others around them, which influence and modify their behaviour at all phases of the life cycle.

SOCIAL MOBILITY   Movement of individuals or groups between different social positions. Vertical mobility refers to movement up or down a hierarchy in a stratification system. Lateral mobility is physical movement of individuals or groups from one region to another. When analysing vertical mobility, sociologists distinguish between how far an individual is mobile in the course of his or her own career, and how far the position which the person reaches differs from that of his or her parents.

SOCIAL MOVEMENT   A large grouping of people who have become involved in seeking to accomplish, or to block, a process of social change. Social movements normally exist in relations of conflict with organizations whose objectives and outlook they frequently oppose. However,

movements which successfully challenge for power, once they become institutionalized, can develop into organizations.

SOCIAL POSITION   The social identity an individual has in a given group or society. Social positions may be very general in nature (such as those associated with gender roles) or may be much more specific (as in the case of occupational positions).

SOCIAL ROLE   The expected behaviour of an individual occupying a particular social position. The idea of social role originally comes from the theatre, referring to the parts which actors play in a stage production. In every society individuals play a number of different social roles, according to the varying contexts of their activities.

SOCIAL STRATIFICATION   The existence of structured inequalities between groups in society, in terms of their access to material or symbolic rewards. While all societies involve some forms of stratification, only with the development of state-based systems do wide differences in wealth and power arise. The most distinctive form of stratification in modern societies involves class divisions.

SOCIAL STRUCTURE   Patterns of interaction between individuals or groups. Social life does not happen in a random fashion. Most of our activities are structured: they are organized in a regular and repetitive way. Although the comparison can be misleading, it is handy to think of the social structure of a society as rather like the girders which underpin a building and hold it together.

SOCIETY   The concept of society is one of the most important of all sociological notions. A society is a group of people who live in a particular territory, are subject to a common system of political authority, and are aware of having a distinct identity from other groups around them. Some societies, like those of hunters and gatherers, are very small, numbering no more than a few dozen people. Others are very large, involving many millions – modern Chinese society, for instance, has a population of more than a billion individuals.

SOCIOLOGY   The study of human groups and societies, giving particular emphasis to the analysis of the industrialized world. Sociology is one of a group of social sciences, which includes also anthropology, economics, political science and human geography. The divisions between the various social sciences are not clear-cut, and all share a certain range of common interests, concepts and methods.

SOCIOLOGY OF THE BODY   The study of social influences on our physical make-up.

THE STATE   A political apparatus (government institutions, plus civil service officials) ruling over a given territorial order, whose authority is backed by law and the ability to use force. Not all societies are characterized by the existence of a state. Hunting and gathering cultures, and smaller agrarian societies, lack state institutions. The emergence of the state marks a distinctive transition in human history, because the centralization of political power involved in state formation introduces new dynamics into processes of social change.

STATUS The social honour or prestige which a particular group is accorded by other members of a society. Status groups normally involve distinct styles of life – patterns of behaviour which the members of a group follow. Status privilege may be positive or negative. 'Pariah' status groups are regarded with disdain, or treated as outcasts, by the majority of the population.

THEORETICAL APPROACH A perspective on social life derived from a particular theoretical tradition. Some of the major theoretical traditions in sociology include functionalism, structuralism, symbolic interactionism and Marxism. Theoretical approaches supply overall 'perspectives' within which sociologists work, and influence the areas of their research as well as the modes in which research problems are identified and tackled.

THEORY An attempt to identify general properties which explain regularly observed events. The construction of theories forms an essential element of all sociological work. While theories tend to be linked to broader theoretical approaches, they are also strongly influenced by the research results they help generate.

THE UNCONSCIOUS Motives and ideas unavailable to the conscious mind of the individual. A key psychological mechanism involved in the unconscious is repression – parts of the mind are 'blocked off' from an individual's direct awareness. According to Freud's theory, unconscious wishes and impulses established in childhood continue to play a major part in the life of the adult.

UNEMPLOYMENT A situation in which an individual wishes to get a paid job but is unable to do so. Unemployment is a more complicated notion than might appear at first sight. A person who is 'out of work' is not necessarily unemployed in the sense of having nothing to do. Housewives, for instance, don't receive any pay, but they usually work very hard.

URBANISM A term used by Louis Wirth to denote distinctive characteristics of urban social life, such as its impersonality.

VALUES Ideas held by human individuals or groups about what is desirable, proper, good or bad. Differing values represent key aspects of variations in human culture. What individuals value is strongly influenced by the specific culture in which they happen to live.

VIOLENCE The use, or threat, of physical force on the part of one individual or group towards another. Warfare is the most extreme form of violence. Violence, however, is commonplace in many more informal settings of social life. For instance, many marriages are characterized by a history of violence on the part of one spouse towards the other.

WORK The activity by which human beings produce from the natural world and so ensure their survival. Work should not be thought of exclusively as paid employment. In traditional cultures, there was only a rudimentary monetary system, and very few people worked for money payments. In modern societies, there remain many types of work which do not involve direct payment of wages or salary (such as housework).

GLOSSARY OF IMPORTANT TERMS

ABSENT FATHER   A father who, as a result of divorce or for other reasons, has little or no contact with his children.

ABSOLUTE POVERTY   Poverty as defined in terms of the minimal requirements necessary to sustain a healthy existence.

ADDICTION   A process whereby someone becomes dependent on a substance or a fixed pattern of behaviour, which it is difficult to alter. An alcoholic is an addict; so is a 'workaholic'.

AFFECTIVE INDIVIDUALISM   The belief in romantic attachment as a basis for contracting marriage ties.

AGEISM   Discrimination or prejudice against a person on the grounds of age.

AGRARIAN SOCIETIES   Societies whose means of subsistence is based on agricultural production (crop-growing).

AIDS   A disease that attacks the auto-immune system of the body.

ALIENATION   The sense that our own abilities, as human beings, are taken over by other entities. The term was originally used by Marx to refer to the projection of human powers onto gods. Subsequently he employed the term to refer to the loss of control on the part of workers over the nature of the labour task, and over the products of their labour.

ALTERATIVE MOVEMENT   A movement concerned to alter individuals' behaviour or consciousness.

ANIMISM   A belief that events in the world are mobilized by the activities of spirits.

ANOMIE   A concept first brought into wide usage in sociology by Durkheim, referring to a situation in which social norms lose their hold over individual behaviour.

ANOREXIA   The so-called 'slimmer's disease', where individuals deliberately starve themselves of food.

ANTHROPOLOGY   A social science, closely linked to sociology, which concentrates on the study of traditional cultures and on the evolution of the human species.

APARTHEID   The system of racial segregation established in South Africa, today mostly dismantled.

ARMS TRADE   The selling of armaments for profit, whether carried on by governments or by private contractors.

ASSIMILATION   The acceptance of a minority group by a majority population, in which the group takes over the values and norms of the dominant culture.

AUTHORITARIAN PERSONALITY   A set of specific personality characteristics, involving a rigid and intolerant outlook and an inability to accept ambiguity.

AUTOMATION   Production processes monitored and controlled by machines with only minimal supervision from human beings.

BACK REGION   An area away from 'front region' performances, as specified by Erving Goffman, in which individuals are able to relax and behave in an informal way.

BULIMIA   An eating disorder in which individuals over-eat, but do not properly digest the food. A bulimic person, for example, may eat and then deliberately force him- or herself to vomit before the food is digested.

CAPITALISM   A system of economic enterprise based on market exchange. 'Capital' refers to wealth or money used to invest in a market with the hope of achieving a profit. Nearly all industrial societies today are capitalist in orientation – their economic systems are based on free enterprise and on economic competition.

CAPITALISTS   Those who own companies, land or stocks and shares, using these to generate economic returns.

CASTE   A form of stratification in which an individual's social position is fixed at birth and cannot be changed. There is virtually no intermarriage between the members of different caste groups.

CHURCH   A large body of people belonging to an established religious organization. The term is also used to refer to a place where religious ceremonials are carried on.

CITIZEN   A member of a political community, having both rights and duties associated with that membership.

CIVIL INATTENTION   The process whereby individuals who are in the same physical setting of interaction demonstrate to one another that they are aware of each other's presence, without being either threatening or over-friendly.

CIVIL RELIGION   Forms of ritual and belief similar to those involved in religion, but concerning secular activities – such as political parades or ceremonials.

CLASS CONFLICT   Struggles between different classes in society. Karl Marx believed class conflict to be at the source of many other divisions and antagonisms in society.

CLASSROOM WITHOUT WALLS   Education carried on by means of electronic media.

CLOCK TIME   Time as measured by the clock – that is, assessed in terms of hours, minutes or seconds. Before the invention of clocks, time-reckoning was based on events in the natural world, such as the rising and setting of the sun.

CODIFIED KNOWLEDGE   A concept associated with the sociologist Daniel Bell. It refers to systematic forms of knowledge, such as those produced by modern science. Bell believes the production of such knowledge to be the most dynamic force shaping modern society.

COGNITION   Human thought processes involving perception, reasoning and remembering.

COHABITATION   Two people living together in a sexual relationship of some permanence, without being married to each other.

COLD WAR   The situation of conflict between the United States and the Soviet Union, together with their allies, which existed from the late 1940s until 1990. It was a 'Cold War' because the two sides never actually engaged in military confrontation with each other.

COLLECTIVE CONSUMPTION   A concept used by Manuel Castells to refer to processes of urban consumption – such as the buying and selling of property.

COLONIALISM   The process whereby Western nations established their rule in parts of the world away from their home territories.

COMMONSENSE BELIEFS   Widely shared beliefs about the social or natural worlds held by lay (non-specialist) members of society.

COMMUNISM   A set of political ideas associated with Marx, as developed particularly by Lenin, and institutionalized in China and, until 1990, in the Soviet Union and Eastern Europe.

COMPARATIVE ANALYSIS   Analysis based on comparison between different societies or cultures.

COMPARATIVE QUESTIONS   Questions concerned with the drawing of comparisons between different human societies for the purposes of sociological theory or research.

CONCRETE OPERATIONAL STAGE   A stage of cognitive development, as formulated by Piaget, in which the child's thinking is based primarily on physical perception of the world. In this phase, the child is not yet capable of dealing with abstract concepts or hypothetical situations.

CONSTITUTIONAL MONARCH   A king or queen who is largely a 'figurehead', real power resting in the hands of other political leaders.

CONTRADICTION   A term used by Marx to refer to mutually antagonistic tendencies in a society.

CONTRADICTORY CLASS LOCATIONS   Positions in the class structure, particularly involving routine white-collar and lower managerial jobs, which share characteristics of the class positions both above and below them.

CONURBATION   An agglomeration of towns or cities into an unbroken urban environment.

CONVERSATION   Verbal communication between two or more individuals.

CORRELATION   The regular relationship between two dimensions or variables, often expressed in statistical terms. Correlations may be positive or negative. A positive correlation between two variables exists where a high rank on one variable is associated with a high rank on the other. A negative correlation is where a high rank on one variable is associated with a low rank on the other.

COUNTERINTUITIVE THINKING   Thinking which suggests ideas contrary to commonsense assumptions.

THE CREATED ENVIRONMENT   Those aspects of the physical world which derive from the use of humanly created technology. The created environment refers to constructions established by human beings to serve their needs – including, for example, roads, railways, factories, offices, private homes and other buildings.

CRIMES OF THE POWERFUL   Criminal activity carried out by those in positions of power.

CROWD ACTIVITY   Actions carried on by individuals when associated together as a crowd.

CULT   A fragmentary religious grouping, to which individuals are loosely affiliated, but which lacks any permanent structure.

CULTURAL PLURALISM   The coexistence of several subcultures within a given society on equal terms.

CYBERSPACE   Electronic networks of interaction between individuals at different computer terminals.

DENOMINATION   A religious sect which has lost its revivalist dynamism, and has become an institutionalized body, commanding the adherence of significant numbers of people.

DEVELOPMENTAL QUESTIONS Questions which sociologists pose when looking at the origins and path of development of social institutions from the past to the present.

DEVIANT SUBCULTURE A subculture whose members have values which differ substantially from those of the majority in a society.

DIFFERENTIAL ASSOCIATION An interpretation of the development of criminal behaviour proposed by Edwin H. Sutherland. According to him, criminal behaviour is learnt through association with others who regularly engage in crime.

DISPLACEMENT The transferring of ideas or emotions from their true source to another object.

DOCUMENTARY RESEARCH Research based on evidence drawn from the study of documents, such as archives or official statistics.

DOMESTIC VIOLENCE Violent behaviour directed by one member of a household against another. Most serious domestic violence is carried out by males against females.

DOWNWARD MOBILITY Social mobility in which individuals find themselves in worse jobs than, or inferior economic circumstances to, those they once had or their parents had.

DRAMATURGICAL MODEL An approach to the study of social interaction based on the use of metaphors derived from the theatre.

DYSFUNCTIONS Social influences which tend to be disruptive or disintegrative.

ECOLOGICAL APPROACH A perspective on urban analysis emphasizing the 'natural' distribution of city neighbourhoods into areas having contrasting characteristics.

ECONOMIC INTERDEPENDENCE Refers to the fact that, in the division of labour, individuals depend on others to produce many or most of the goods they need to sustain their lives.

ECONOMIC SYSTEM The system of production and distribution of economic goods in a society.

EDUCATIONAL SYSTEM The system of educational provision operating within a given society.

EGOCENTRISM The characteristic outlook of a child, according to Piaget, during the early years of its life. Egocentric thinking involves understanding objects and events in the environment solely in terms of the child's own position.

ELABORATED CODE A form of speech involving the deliberate and constructed use of words to designate precise meanings.

EMOTIONAL INTELLIGENCE How capable an individual is of being in tune with his or her own emotions and the emotions of others.

EMPIRICAL INVESTIGATION Factual enquiry carried out in any given area of sociological study.

END OF HISTORY An idea associated with the American author Francis Fukuyama. With the fall of communism, Fukuyama argues, history has come to an end because we can see no form of society which might supplant Western-style capitalism.

ENVIRONMENTAL ECOLOGY A concern with preserving the integrity of the physical environment in the face of the impact of modern industry and technology.

ESTATE A form of stratification involving inequalities between groups of individuals established by law.

ETHICAL RELIGIONS Religions which depend on the ethical appeal of a 'great teacher' (like Buddha or Confucius), rather than on a belief in supernatural beings.

ETHNIC ANTAGONISM Hostilities or conflicts between different ethnic groups or communities.

ETHNOCENTRIC TRANSNATIONALS Transnational companies largely run directly from the headquarters of the parent company.

ETHNOCENTRISM Understanding the ideas or practices of another culture in terms of those of one's own culture. Ethnocentric judgements fail to recognize the true qualities of other cultures. An ethnocentric individual is someone who is unable, or unwilling, to look at other cultures in their own terms.

ETHNOMETHODOLOGY The study of how people make sense of what others say and do in the course of day-to-day social interaction. Ethnomethodology is concerned with the 'ethnomethods' by means of which human beings sustain meaningful interchanges with one another.

EUROPEAN UNION An association of Western European nations, who have joined together to develop common economic, political and cultural interests. Fifteen nations are currently members of the European Union, but others also wish to join.

EVOLUTION The development of biological organisms by means of the adaptation of species to the demands of the physical environment.

EXPERIMENT A research method in which variables can be analysed in a controlled and systematic way, either in an artificial situation constructed by the researcher, or in naturally occurring settings.

EXTENDED FAMILY A family group consisting of more than two generations of relatives living either within the same household or very close to one another.

FACE-TO-FACE INTERACTION   Interaction between individuals who are physically present in the same context with one another.

FACTUAL QUESTIONS   Questions which raise issues concerning matters of fact (rather than theoretical or moral issues).

FEMININITY   The characteristic forms of behaviour expected of women in any given culture.

FEMINIST MOVEMENT   A movement concerned with promoting the rights and interests of women in society.

FIRST WORLD   The group of nation-states that possesses mature industrialized economies, based on capitalistic production.

FLEXIBLE PRODUCTION   A system of production in industry in which production processes can be easily altered at any time. Flexible production is believed by many to be supplanting the more rigid production systems which dominated in the era of Taylorism and Fordism.

FOCUSED INTERACTION   Interaction between individuals engaged in a common activity or a direct conversation with one another.

FORDISM   The system of production pioneered by Henry Ford, involving the introduction of the assembly line.

FORMAL OPERATIONAL PERIOD   A stage of cognitive development, according to Piaget's theory, at which the growing child becomes capable of handling abstract concepts and hypothetical situations.

FRONT REGION   A setting of social activity in which individuals seek to put on a definite 'performance' for others.

FUNCTIONALISM   A theoretical perspective based on the notion that social events can best be explained in terms of the functions they perform – that is, the contributions they make to the continuity of a society.

FUNDAMENTALISM   A belief in returning to the literal meanings of scriptural texts.

GANG   An informal group of individuals meeting regularly to engage in common activities, which may be outside the framework of the law.

GAY-PARENT FAMILIES   Families in which children are brought up either by lesbian partners or by two male homosexuals living together.

GENDER SOCIALIZATION   How individuals develop different gender characteristics in the course of socialization processes.

GENERALIZED OTHER   A concept in the theory of G. H. Mead, according to which the individual takes over the general values of a given group or society during the socialization process.

GENRE   A concept applied in media studies to refer to a distinct type of media product or cultural item. In the world of television, for example, different genres include soap opera, comedy, news programmes, sport and drama.

GEOCENTRIC TRANSNATIONALS   Transnational companies whose administrative structure is global, rather than organized from any particular country.

GLOBAL CITY   A city, such as London, New York or Tokyo, which has become an organizing centre of the new global economy.

GLOBAL CORPORATIONS   Business firms which operate on a global scale.

GLOBAL VILLAGE   A notion associated with the Canadian writer Marshall McLuhan. Particularly as a result of the spread of electronic communication, McLuhan believed, the world becomes like a small community. For instance, people in many different parts of the world follow the same news events through television programming.

GROUP CLOSURE   The means whereby a group establishes a clear boundary for itself and thereby separates itself from other groups.

GUERRILLA MOVEMENT   A non-governmental military organization.

HEADQUARTERS CITY   A city which has a coordinating role in the international division of labour – a headquarters of world finance or commerce.

HETEROSEXUALITY   An orientation in sexual activity or feelings towards people of the opposite sex.

HIDDEN CURRICULUM   Traits of behaviour or attitudes that are learned at school, but which are not included within the formal curriculum. The hidden curriculum is the 'unstated agenda' involved in schooling – conveying, for example, aspects of gender differences.

HIGHER EDUCATION   Education beyond school level, in colleges or universities.

HIGH-TRUST SYSTEMS   Organizations, or work settings, in which individuals are permitted a great deal of autonomy and control over the work task.

HOMOSEXUALITY   An orientation of sexual activities or feelings towards others of the same sex.

HOUSEWORK (DOMESTIC LABOUR)   Unpaid work carried on, usually by women, in the home, concerned with day-to-day domestic chores such as cooking, cleaning and shopping.

HUNTING AND GATHERING SOCIETIES   Societies whose mode of subsistence is gained from hunting animals, fishing and gathering edible plants.

HYPERREALITY An idea associated with the French author Jean Baudrillard. Baudrillard argues that, as a result of the spread of electronic communication, there is no longer a separate 'reality' to which TV programmes and other cultural products refer. Instead, what we take to be 'reality' is structured by such communication itself. For instance, the items reported on the news are not just about a separate series of events, but actually themselves define and construct what those events are.

HYPOTHESIS An idea, or a guess, about a given state of affairs, put forward as a basis for empirical testing.

IDEAL TYPE A 'pure type', constructed by emphasizing certain traits of a given social item which do not necessarily exist anywhere in reality. The traits are defining, not necessarily desirable ones. An example is Max Weber's ideal type of bureaucratic organization.

IMPRESSION MANAGEMENT An idea associated with the American sociologist, Erving Goffman. People 'manage' or control the impressions others have of them by choosing what to conceal and what to reveal when they meet with other people.

INCARCERATION The placing of individuals within physically closed organizations, such as prisons or asylums.

INCEST Sexual relations between close relatives, such as fathers and daughters or brothers and sisters. All societies have incest prohibitions of one sort or another.

INCOME Payment, usually derived from wages, salaries or investments.

THE INFORMAL ECONOMY Economic transactions carried on outside the sphere of orthodox paid employment.

INFORMATION POVERTY The 'information poor' are people who have little or no access to information technology, such as computers.

INFORMATION SOCIETY A society no longer based primarily on the production of material goods but on the production of knowledge. The notion of the information society is closely bound up with the rise of 'information technology' – computers and electronic communications systems.

INFORMATION SUPERHIGHWAY A vision for the future in which most people's homes and workplaces will be wired for a diversity of forms of electronic communication, all carried along a single cable.

INNER CITY The areas composing the central neighbourhoods of a city, which normally have characteristics distinct from the suburbs. In many

modern urban settings in the First World, inner-city areas are subject to dilapidation and decay, the more affluent residents having moved to outlying areas.

INNOVATION CENTRE A city or town whose prosperity depends on being a centre of technological innovation or creativity.

INSTINCT A fixed pattern of behaviour which has genetic origins and which appears in all normal animals within a given species.

INTELLIGENCE Level of intellectual ability, particularly as measured by IQ (Intelligence Quotient) tests.

INTERESTS In a political context, the concerns or motives which individuals or groups have.

INTERGENERATIONAL MOBILITY Movement up or down a social stratification hierarchy from one generation to another.

INTERNATIONAL DIVISION OF LABOUR A phrase referring to the interdependence of countries or regions which trade on global markets.

INTERNET A global system of connections between computers.

INTRAGENERATIONAL MOBILITY Movement up or down a social stratification hierarchy within the course of a personal career.

IQ (INTELLIGENCE QUOTIENT) A score attained on tests of symbolic or reasoning abilities.

KIBBUTZIM Communities established in Israel in which production is carried on cooperatively, and inequalities of wealth and income are kept to a minimum.

LABELLING THEORY An approach to the study of deviance which suggests that people become 'deviant' because certain labels are attached to their behaviour by political authorities and others.

LATENT FUNCTIONS Functional consequences which are not intended or recognized by the members of a social system in which they occur.

LATERAL MOBILITY Movement of individuals from one region of a country to another, or across countries.

LAW A rule of behaviour established by a political authority and backed by state power.

LEGITIMACY The belief that a particular political order is just and valid.

LESBIANISM Homosexual activities or attachment between women.

LIBERAL DEMOCRACY A system of democracy based on parliamentary institutions, coupled to the free market system in the area of economic production.

LIFE COURSE The different stages in an individual's life from birth through to adolescence, adulthood and death.

LIFE EXPECTANCY The number of further years which people at any given age can on average expect to live.

LIFE HISTORIES Studies of the overall lives of individuals, often based both on self-reporting and on documents such as letters.

LIMITED WAR Warfare involving relatively small numbers of the population, and fought principally by soldiers.

LITERACY The ability of individuals to read and write.

LONE-PARENT HOUSEHOLD A household in which only one parent, whether female or male, is bringing up the children.

LOW-TRUST SYSTEMS An organizational or work setting in which individuals are allowed little responsibility for, or control over, the work task.

MACROSEGREGATION Segregation between very large numbers of the members of different racial groups, separated territorially.

MACROSOCIOLOGY The study of large-scale groups, organizations or social systems.

MAGIC Rites which attempt to influence spirits or supernatural beings in order to achieve human aims. In most societies, magic exists in a relation of some tension with religion. In contrast to religion, magic tends to be more of an 'individual' activity, practised by a sorcerer or shaman.

MALE INEXPRESSIVENESS The difficulties men have in expressing, or talking about, their feelings to others.

MANIFEST FUNCTIONS The functions of an aspect or type of social activity which are known to, and intended by, the individuals involved in a given situation of social life.

MARXISM A body of thought deriving its main elements from Marx's ideas.

MASCULINITY The characteristic forms of behaviour expected of men in any given culture.

MATERIALIST CONCEPTION OF HISTORY The view developed by Marx, according to which 'material' or economic factors have a prime role in determining historical change.

MATRILINEAL INHERITANCE The inheritance of property or titles through the female line.

MEANS OF PRODUCTION The means whereby the production of material goods is carried on in a society, including not just technology but the social relations between producers.

MEDIA REGULATION The use of legal means to control media ownership and the content of media communications.

MEDIATED INTERACTION Interaction between individuals who are not physically in one another's presence – for example a telephone conversation.

MEDIATED QUASI-INTERACTION A notion associated with the British writer John Thompson. The term refers to interaction which is one-sided and partial, as where a person is watching a television programme.

MEGALOPOLIS The 'city of all cities' in ancient Greece – used in modern times to refer to very large conurbations.

MELTING POT The idea that ethnic differences can be combined to create new patterns of behaviour drawing on diverse cultural sources.

MEZZOSEGREGATION Segregation between racial groups in terms of areas of neighbourhood residence.

MICROSEGREGATION Segregation between racial groups enforced in the details of daily life – for example separate waiting rooms in bus or railway stations.

MICROSOCIOLOGY The study of human behaviour in contexts of face-to-face interaction.

MIDDLE CLASS A social class composed broadly of those working in white-collar and lower managerial occupations.

MILITARY POWER Power coming from control of the armed forces and of weaponry.

MILLENARIANISM Beliefs held by the members of certain types of religious movement, according to which cataclysmic changes will occur in the near future, heralding the arrival of a new epoch.

MINORITY GROUP (OR ETHNIC MINORITY) A group of people in a minority in a given society who, because of their distinct physical or cultural characteristics, find themselves in situations of inequality within that society.

MOBILIZATION The 'gearing up' of groups for collective action.

MODULE PRODUCTION PLACE An urban area in which parts are made for products whose final assembly is carried out elsewhere.

MONOGAMY A form of marriage in which each married partner is allowed only one spouse at any given time.

MONOTHEISM Belief in a single god.

MULTIMEDIA The combination of what used to be different media requiring different technologies (for instance, visuals and sound) on a single medium, such as a CD-ROM which can be played on a computer.

MULTIPLE SOVEREIGNTY A situation in which there is no single sovereign power in a society.

MUTATION A process of random genetic change introducing an alteration in the physical characteristics of an animal or plant. The vast majority of mutations lead 'nowhere' in the course of evolution – that is, the mutant organisms fail to survive. In a tiny proportion of cases, however, mutation produces characteristics which allow new species to flourish.

NATIONALISM A set of beliefs and symbols expressing identification with a given national community.

NATION-STATE A particular type of state, characteristic of the modern world, in which a government has sovereign power within a defined territorial area, and the mass of the population are citizens who know themselves to be part of a single nation. Nation-states are closely associated with the rise of nationalism, although nationalist loyalties do not always conform to the boundaries of specific states that exist today. Nation-states developed as part of an emerging nation-state system, originating in Europe, but in current times spanning the whole globe.

NATURAL SELECTION An idea associated with the founder of modern evolutionary biology, Charles Darwin. Animal species survive and prosper according to how well they are adapted to their environment; those which are less adaptive are 'weeded out' while the better adapted species replace them.

NEW LABOUR The reforms introduced by Tony Blair when he assumed leadership of the British Labour Party, and by means of which he sought to move the party in new directions.

NEWLY INDUSTRIALIZING COUNTRIES Third World countries which over the past two or three decades have begun to develop a strong industrial base, such as Singapore and Hong Kong.

NON-VERBAL COMMUNICATION Communication between individuals based on facial expression or bodily gesture, rather than on the use of language.

NUCLEAR FAMILY A family group consisting of mother, father (or one of these) and dependent children.

NUCLEAR PROLIFERATION The spread of nuclear weapons across the world.

OCCUPATION Any form of paid employment in which an individual works in a regular way.

OCCUPATIONAL SYSTEM The division of labour between occupations in a society.

OEDIPUS COMPLEX A phase of early human psychological development, according to Freud, in which the child experiences intense feelings of love for the mother, together with hatred for the father. The overcoming of the Oedipus complex marks a key transition, in Freud's view, in the development of the child as an autonomous being. Freud took the term 'Oedipus' from the classical story of Oedipus, who according to myth, without knowing who they were, married his mother and killed his father.

OFFICIALS Individuals who occupy formal positions in large-scale organizations.

OLIGARCHY Rule by a small minority within an organization or society.

OPEN-ENDED QUESTIONNAIRES Questionnaires, as used in survey research, which allow scope for individuals to give shorter or longer responses as they wish.

ORGANIZED CRIME Criminal activities carried out by organizations established as businesses.

PARIAH GROUPS Groups who suffer from negative status or discrimination – in other words, are 'looked down on' by most other members of society. The Jews have been a pariah group throughout much of European history.

PARTICIPANT OBSERVATION (FIELDWORK) A method of research widely used in sociology and anthropology, in which the researcher takes part in the activities of a group or community being studied.

PARTICIPATORY DEMOCRACY A system of democracy in which all members of a group or community participate collectively in the taking of major decisions.

PASTORAL SOCIETIES Societies whose subsistence derives from the rearing of domesticated animals.

PATRILINEAL INHERITANCE The inheritance of property or titles through the male line.

PEASANTS People who produce food from the land, using traditional farming methods.

PERSONAL SPACE The physical space individuals maintain between themselves and others when they know them on a personal basis.

POLITICAL PARTY An organization established with the aim of achieving governmental power and using that power to pursue a specific programme.

POLYANDRY A form of marriage in which a woman may simultaneously have two or more husbands.

POLYCENTRIC TRANSNATIONALS Transnational corporations run from two or several main administrative centres in different countries.

POLYGAMY A form of marriage in which a person may have two or more spouses simultaneously.

POLYGYNY A form of marriage in which a man may have more than one wife at the same time.

POLYTHEISM   Belief in two or more gods.

PORTFOLIO WORKER   A worker who possesses a diversity of skills or qualifications and is therefore able to move easily from job to job.

PRE-OPERATIONAL STAGE   A stage of cognitive development, in Piaget's theory, in which the child has advanced sufficiently to master basic modes of logical thought.

PRESTIGE   The respect accorded to an individual or group by virtue of their status.

PRIVATE HEALTH CARE   Health-care services available only to those who pay the full cost of them.

PROFANE   That which belongs to the mundane, everyday world.

PROJECTION   The attributing to others of feelings that one actually has oneself.

PROPHETS   Religious leaders who mobilize followers through their interpretation of sacred texts.

PROSTITUTION   The sale of sexual favours.

PSYCHOANALYSIS   The technique of psychotherapy invented by Sigmund Freud. The word 'psychoanalysis' has also come to be used for the intellectual system of psychological theory that Freud constructed.

PSYCHOPATH   A specific personality type. Such individuals lack the moral sense and concern for others held by most normal people.

PUBLIC DISTANCE   The physical space individuals maintain between themselves and others when engaged in a public performance, such as giving a lecture.

PUBLIC HEALTH CARE   Health-care services available to all members of the population, supported by government funding.

PUBLIC OPINION   The views which members of the public hold on issues of the day.

PUBLIC SPHERE   An idea associated with the German sociologist Jürgen Habermas. The public sphere refers to an arena of public debate and discussion in modern societies.

RACE   Differences in human physical stock regarded as categorizing large numbers of individuals together.

RANDOM SAMPLING   A method of social research which tries to ensure that a group studied is representative of a larger population by choosing individuals to be included at random.

RAPE   The threat, or use, of force to compel one individual to engage in a sexual act with another.

RATIONALIZATION   A concept used by Weber to refer to the process by which modes of precise calculation and organization, involving abstract rules and procedures, increasingly come to dominate the social world.

RECIDIVISM   Reoffending by individuals previously found guilty of a crime.

REDEMPTIVE MOVEMENT   A social movement aiming to produce a return to a past state of affairs believed to be superior to the current one.

REFORMATIVE MOVEMENT   A social movement concerned to implement a practical, but limited, programme of social change.

REGIONALIZATION   The division of social life into different regional settings or zones.

RELATIVE DEPRIVATION   Feelings of deprivation relative to a group with which an individual compares himself or herself.

RELATIVE POVERTY   Poverty defined by reference to the living standards of the majority in any given society.

REPRESENTATIVE SAMPLE   A means of social research which tries to match a group studied to a wider population whose qualities it matches.

REPRODUCTIVE TECHNOLOGIES   Technologies which affect the process of human reproduction, such as contraception or *in vitro* fertilization.

RESOURCE ALLOCATION   How different social and material resources are employed by social groups or social movements.

RESPONSE CRIES   Seemingly involuntary exclamations individuals make when, for example, being taken by surprise, dropping something inadvertently, or expressing pleasure.

RESTRICTED CODE   A mode of speech which rests on strongly developed cultural understandings, such that many ideas do not need to be put into words.

RETIREMENT CENTRE   A city or town, normally having a favourable climate, to which many people move when they retire.

RIOT   An outbreak of illegal violence, directed against persons, property or both.

RISK SOCIETY   A notion associated with the German sociologist Ulrich Beck. Beck argues that industrial society has created many new dangers of risks unknown in previous ages. The risks associated with global warming are one example.

SACRED   That which inspires attitudes of awe or reverence among believers in a given set of religious ideas.

SAMPLING   Taking a proportion of individuals or cases from a larger population, studied as representative of that population as a whole.

SANCTION   A mode of reward or punishment that reinforces socially expected forms of behaviour.

SCAPEGOATING   Blaming an individual or group for wrongs that were not of their doing.

SECONDARY DEVIANCE   An idea associated with the American criminologist Edwin Lemert. Primary deviance refers to an initial act which contravenes a norm or law – for instance, stealing an item from a shop. Secondary deviance is where a label becomes attached to the individual who carried out the act, as where the person stealing from the shop becomes labelled a 'shoplifter'.

SECOND WORLD   The industrialized, formerly communist societies of Eastern Europe and the Soviet Union.

SECT   A religious movement which breaks away from orthodoxy.

SELF-ENLIGHTENMENT   The increased understanding of the conditions of their lives which people may achieve through social investigation – possibly allowing them to take action to alter those conditions.

SEMIOTICS   The study of the ways in which non-linguistic phenomena can generate meaning – as in the example of a traffic light.

SENSORIMOTOR STAGE   A stage of human cognitive development, according to Piaget, in which the child's awareness of its environment is dominated by perception and touch.

SERIAL MONOGAMY   The practice of a person contracting several marriages in succession, but not having more than one spouse at any one time.

SEXUAL ABUSE OF CHILDREN   The sexual exploitation of children by adults.

SEXUAL HARASSMENT   The making of unwanted sexual advances by one individual towards another, in which the first individual persists even though it is made clear that the other party is resistant.

SEXUALITY   A broad term which refers to the sexual characteristics, and sexual behaviour, of human beings.

SHAMAN   An individual believed to have special magical powers; a sorcerer or witch doctor.

SHARED UNDERSTANDINGS   The common assumptions which people hold and which allow them to interact in a systematic way with one another.

SIMULACRUM   A notion used by the French author Jean Baudrillard. A simulacrum is a copy of an item for which there is no original. For example, a 'mock Tudor' house looks nothing like original Tudor buildings.

SLAVERY   A form of social stratification in which some individuals are literally owned by others as their property.

SLIPS OF THE TONGUE   The mispronunciation of words, as when someone means to say 'six' and instead says 'sex'. Freud believed that slips of the tongue conceal hidden anxieties or emotions.

SOCIAL CLOSURE   Practices by which groups separate themselves off from other groups.

SOCIAL CONSTRAINT   A term referring to the fact that the groups and societies of which we are a part exert a conditioning influence on our behaviour. Social constraint was regarded by Durkheim as one of the distinctive properties of 'social facts'.

SOCIAL DISTANCE   The level of spatial separation maintained when individuals interact with others whom they do not know well.

SOCIALISM   A set of political ideas emphasizing the cooperative nature of modern industrial production and stressing the need to achieve an egalitarian social community.

SOCIALIZATION OF NATURE   The impact of social and technological forces on the natural world.

SOCIAL REPRODUCTION   The processes which sustain or perpetuate characteristics of social structure over periods of time.

SOCIAL SELF   The basis of self-consciousness in human individuals, according to the theory of G. H. Mead. The social self is the identity conferred on an individual by the reactions of others. A person achieves self-consciousness by becoming aware of this social identity.

SOCIAL TRANSFORMATION   Processes of change in 'societies' or social systems.

SOCIOBIOLOGY   An approach which attempts to explain the behaviour of both animals and human beings in terms of biological principles.

THE SOCIOLOGICAL IMAGINATION   The application of imaginative thought to the asking and answering of sociological questions. The sociological imagination involves one in 'thinking oneself away' from the familiar routines of day-to-day life.

SOVEREIGNTY   The undisputed political rule of a state over a given territorial area.

STANDARDIZED QUESTIONNAIRES   Questionnaires, as used in survey research, which involve fixed categories, so that respondents have only a limited number of choices in terms of which to give their answers.

STEP-FAMILIES   Families in which at least one partner has children from a previous marriage, either living in the home or nearby.

STEREOTYPICAL THINKING   Thought processes involving rigid and inflexible categories.

STIGMA   Any physical or social characteristic believed to be demeaning.

STREAMING The separation of pupils in schools into different ability groups.

STRIKE A temporary stoppage of work by a group of employees in order to express a grievance or enforce a demand.

STRUCTURALISM A theoretical approach, derived originally from the study of language, concerned with the identification of structures in social or cultural systems.

SUBCULTURE Values and norms distinct from those of the majority, held by a group within a wider society.

SUBURBANIZATION The development of suburbia, areas of housing outside inner cities.

SURPLUS VALUE The value of an individual's labour power, in Marxist theory, which is 'left over' when an employer has repaid the cost involved in hiring a worker.

SURVEILLANCE The supervising of the activities of some individuals or groups by others in order to ensure compliant behaviour.

SURVEILLANCE SOCIETY A society in which individuals are regularly watched and their activities documented. The spread of video cameras on motorways, in streets and shopping centres is one aspect of the expansion of surveillance.

SURVEY A method of sociological research involving the administration of questionnaires to a population being studied.

SYMBOL One item used to stand for or represent another – as in the case of a flag which symbolizes a nation.

SYMBOLIC INTERACTIONISM A theoretical approach in sociology developed by Mead, which places strong emphasis on the role of symbols and language as core elements of all human interaction.

SYMBOLIC POWER Power exercised by means of symbols rather than by direct control. Those who run the culture industry, for instance, have a great deal of symbolic power over the audiences who watch their TV programmes or read their newspapers.

TALK The carrying on of conversations or verbal exchanges in the course of day-to-day social life.

TAYLORISM A set of ideas, also referred to as 'scientific management', developed by Frederick Winslow Taylor, involving simple, coordinated operations in industry.

TECHNOLOGY The application of knowledge to production from the material world. Technology involves the creation of material instruments (such as machines) used in human interaction with nature.

THATCHERISM The doctrines associated with the former British prime minister Margaret Thatcher. These doctrines emphasize the importance of the economic enterprise coupled to strong national government.

THEORETICAL DILEMMA A basic theoretical problem that forms the focus of long-standing debates in sociology.

THEORETICAL QUESTIONS Questions posed by the sociologist when seeking to explain a particular range of observed events. The asking of theoretical questions is crucial to allowing us to generalize about the nature of social life.

THIRD WORLD The less developed societies, in which industrial production is either virtually non-existent or only developed to a limited degree. The majority of the world's population live in Third World countries.

THIRD WORLD ENTREPÔT A city serving as an entry point for migration from less developed countries to a more developed one.

TIME–SPACE CONVERGENCE The process whereby distances become 'shortened in time', as the speed of modes of transportation increases.

TOTAL WAR Warfare in which large numbers of the population are involved, directly or indirectly, and in which hundreds of thousands or millions of soldiers are deployed.

TOTEMISM A system of religious belief which attributes divine properties to a particular type of animal or plant.

TRADE UNION A body of people set up to represent workers' interests in an industrial setting.

TRADITIONAL STATES State-based societies in which the main basis of production is agriculture or pastoralism. Traditional states are also often referred to as 'early civilizations'.

TRANSFORMATIVE MOVEMENT A social movement aiming to produce major processes of social change.

TRANSITIONAL CLASSES A term used by Marx to refer to classes belonging to a declining type of society which linger on in a new one – such as peasants or large landowners in a system which has become capitalist.

TRANSNATIONAL COMPANIES Business corporations located in two or more countries.

UNDERCLASS A class of individuals situated right at the bottom of the class system, normally composed of people from ethnic minority backgrounds.

UNFOCUSED INTERACTION Interaction occurring among people present in a particular setting, but where they are not engaged in direct face-to-face communication.

UNINTENDED CONSEQUENCES Consequences which result from behaviour initiated for other purposes. Many of the major features of social activity are unintended by those who participate in it.

UNIVERSAL CONSCRIPTION A system of national service, under which all individuals of a certain age (or, more commonly, all males of a certain age) have to undergo a period of military training.

UNIVERSITY OF THE THIRD AGE The 'third age' refers to individuals living in retirement. The 'university of the third age' provides study programmes for such individuals.

UPPER CLASS A social class broadly composed of the more affluent members of society, especially those who have inherited wealth, own businesses or hold large numbers of stocks and shares.

URBAN ECOLOGY An approach to the study of urban life based on an analogy with the adjustment of plants and organisms to the physical environment. According to ecological theorists, the various neighbourhoods and zones within cities are formed as a result of natural processes of adjustment on the part of urban populations as they compete for resources.

URBANIZATION The development of towns and cities.

URBAN RECYCLING The process of renovating deteriorating neighbourhoods by encouraging the renewal of old buildings and the construction of new ones.

VERTICAL MOBILITY Movement up or down a hierarchy of positions in a social stratification system.

VOLUNTARY WORK Work undertaken without payment and without economic compulsion – for instance, unpaid charity work.

VOTING BEHAVIOUR Patterns of voting in political elections.

WEALTH Money and material possessions held by an individual or group.

WELFARE DEPENDENCY A situation where people on welfare, such as those receiving unemployment benefit, treat this as a 'way of life' rather than attempt to secure a paid job.

WHITE-COLLAR CRIME Criminal activities carried out by those in white-collar or professional jobs.

WORKING CLASS A social class broadly composed of people involved in blue-collar or manual occupations.

WORLD INFORMATION ORDER A global system of communications, operating through satellite links, radio and TV transmission, telephone and computer links.

ACKNOWLEDGEMENTS

The author and publishers wish to thank the following for permission to use copyright material:

Aldine de Gruyter for Fig. 3.1 from Richard B. Lee and Irven de Vore, eds. *Man the Hunter*, frontispiece. Copyright © 1968 by the Wenner Gren Foundation for Anthropological Research, Inc; Philip Allan Publishers for Fig. 7.3 and Table 8.2 and material from various issues of *Sociology Review*; American Anthropological Association for material from Horace Miner, 'Body ritual among the Nacirema', *American Anthropologist*, 58:3, 1956, pp. 503–4; Blackwell Publishers for Fig. 12.2 from Peter Sinclair, *Unemployment: Economic Theory and Evidence*, 1987, Fig. 1.1, p. 2; Butterworth-Heinemann for Fig. 11.1 from Shaun Gregson and Frank Livesey, *Organizations and Management Behaviour*, 1993; Cambridge University Press for material from Laing, *Popular Music*, 1993; Centre for Research in Ethnic Relations, University of Warwick, for Table 9.1 from D. Owen, *Ethnic Minorities in Britain: Settlement Patterns*, 1991 Census Statistical Paper No. 1; and Table 9.2 from D. Owen, *Ethnic Minorities in Britain: Economic Characteristics*, 1991 Census Statistical Paper No. 3. Crown Copyright; The Economist for Fig. 16.1 from *The Economist*, 4.4.92, p. 73. Copyright 1992 The Economist; Fig 17.1 from *The Economist*, 29.7.95, p. 5. Copyright © 1995 The Economist; Fig. 14.2 from *The Economist*, 1.7.95, p. 5. Copyright © 1995 The Economist; Fig. 16.2 from *The Economist*, 8.7.95, p. 20. Copyright © 1995 The Economist; Fig. 7.1 from *The Economist*, 28.5.94, p. 77. Copyright © 1994 The Economist; Fig. 12.3 from *The Economist*, 22.7.95, p. 92. Copyright © 1995 The Economist; and Fig. 11.3 from *The Economist*, 24.6.95, p. 19. Copyright © 1995 by The Economist; Food and Agriculture Organization of the United Nations for Fig. 3.2 from Nikos Alexandratos, ed. *World Agriculture: Towards 2010*, FOA, 1995, Table A.1; Guardian News Service Ltd for material from David Brindle, 'Blacks and Asians still at social disadvantage', *Guardian*, 8.8.96: Fig. 8.5, 'Getting older', *Guardian*, 19.1.96, p. 1; 'Transsexuals' (text), *Guardian*, 1.2.96, p. 96; 'The vicious street cycle', *Guardian*, 5.3.96; 'New Job: Househusband' and 'Old Job: Housewife', *Guardian*, 6.3.96; and 'Legality and illegality: drugs and the law in modern Britain', *Guardian*, 12.11.91; Harvard University Press for Table 7.2 from Sara McLanahan and Gary Sandefur, *Growing Up With a Single Parent: What Hurts, What Helps.* Copyright © 1994 by the President and Fellows of Harvard College; Helicon for 'Green movement: chronology', 'Consumption and the environment', and 'Evangelists invade the states of the former Soviet Union' and Fig. 13.1 from Hutchinson Gallup, *Info 1995*, 1994, pp. 514, 527, 183, 176; The Controller of HMSO and the Office for National Statistics for Figs. 7.2, 8.1, 8.2, 8.4, 10.2, 12.1, 15.1 and Tables 6.2, 7.1, 10.1, 10.3, 12.1, 14.1, 16.2 from *Social Trends*, 1995/6. Crown copyright material; The Independent for Fig. 10.1, 'Rising inequality 1979–95', *Independent on Sunday*, 21.7.96; W. W. Norton & Company, Inc. for Fig. 3.4 from Philip Lee Ralph et al., *World Civilizations*, Eighth Edition, Vol. 2. p. 385. Copyright © 1991, 1986, 1982, 1974, 1969, 1964, 1958 by W. W. Norton & Company, Inc.; The Open University for Fig 9.1 from Ben Crow and Mary Thorpe, *Survival and Change in the Third World*, 1988, p. 15; Open University Press for Fig. 8.3 from A. K. Bottomley and K. Pease, *Crime and Punishment: Interpreting the Data*, 1986, Fig. 1.1, p. 9; Oxford University Press for Figs. 11.2, 13.2, 14.1 from *Commission on Global Governance: Our Global Neighbourhood*, 1995, pp. 25, 13, 174; Profile Books Ltd for Tables 6.1, 8.1, 15.1 from *The Economist Pocket World in Figures: 1996 Edition*. Copyright © 1996 The Economist Newspaper Ltd; Routledge for material from Selma Fraiberg, *The Magic Years: Understanding and Handling the Problems of Early Childhood*, 1959, Methuen & Co., pp. 49–50; Sage Publications Ltd for Table 6.3 from Arber & Ginn, *Gender and Later Life*, 1991, Table 1.3, p. 8; John Wiley & Sons, Inc. for material from S. Katz and S. A. Mazur, *Understanding the Rape Victim*, 1979, p. 307.

Every effort has been made to trace the copyright holders but if any have been inadvertently overlooked the publishers will be pleased to make the necessary arrangement at the first opportunity.

PICTURE CREDITS

BIBLIOGRAPHY

Abercrombie, Nick 1966: *Television and Society* (Cambridge: Polity Press)

Aberle, David 1966: *The Peyote Religion Among the Navaho* (Chicago: Aldine Press)

Adorno, Theodor W. et al. 1950: *The Authoritarian Personality* (New York: Harper and Row)

Ainsworth, M. D. S. 1977: *Infancy in Uganda* (Baltimore: Johns Hopkins University Press)

Albert, Michel 1993: *Capitalism vs Capitalism: How America's Obsession with Individual Achievement and Short-term Profit has Led it to the Brink of Collapse* (New York: Four Walls Eight Windows)

Aldridge, Alan 1987: 'In the absence of the minister: structures of subordination in the role of deaconess in the Church of England', *Sociology*, 21

Alexander, Jeffrey C. (ed.) 1985: *Neofunctionalism* (London: Sage)

Alexandratos, Nikos (ed.) 1995: *World Agriculture: Towards 2010: An FAO Study* (Chichester: FAO and John Wiley)

Allmän/månad statistik 1987: *Sveriges Officiella Statistik* (Stockholm: Statistika Central-byrån)

Althusser, Louis 1969: *For Marx* (London: Allen Lane)

Altman, Dennis 1986: *AIDS and the New Puritanism* (London: Pluto Press)

Amato, P. R. 1993: 'Children's adjustment to divorce: theories, hypotheses and empirical support', *Marriage and the Family*, 55

Anderson, Elijah 1990: *Streetwise: Race, Class, and Change in an Urban Community* (Chicago: University of Chicago Press)

Anderson, F. S. 1977: 'TV violence and viewer aggression: accumulation of study results 1956–1976', *Public Opinion Quarterly*, 41

Angier, Natalie 1994: 'Feminists and Darwin: scientists try closing the gap', *New York Times*, 21 June

Arber, Sara and Jay Ginn 1991: *Gender and Later Life: A Sociological Analysis of Resources and Constraints* (London: Sage)

Ariès, Philippe 1973: *Centuries of Childhood* (Harmondsworth: Penguin)

Aschenbrenner, Joyce 1983: *Lifelines: Black Families in Chicago* (Prospect Heights, Ill.: Waveland Press)

Ashworth, A. E. 1980: *Trench Warfare, 1914–1918* (London: Macmillan)

Atholl, Justin 1954: *Shadow of the Gallows* (London: Hutchinson)

Ayres, Robert and Steven Miller 1985: 'Industrial robots on the line', in Tom Forrester (ed.), *The Information Technology Revolution* (Oxford: Blackwell)

Bahrami, Homa and Stuart Evans 1995: 'Flexible recycling and high-technology entrepreneurship', *California Management Review*, 22

Baldwin-Evans, Martin and Martin Schain 1995: *The Politics of Immigration in Western Europe* (London: Cass)

Barnaby, Frank 1992: 'Nuclear countdown', *New Statesman and Society*, 5 (187), January

Beck, Ulrich 1992: *Risk Society* (London: Sage)

Becker, Howard 1950: *Through Values to Social Interpretation* (Durham, NC: Duke University Press)

Bell, Daniel 1973: *The Coming of Post-industrial Society: A Venture in Social Forecasting* (London: Heinemann)

Bellah, Robert N. 1970: *Beyond Belief* (New York: Harper and Row)

Bennetto, Jason 1995: 'Caution: you are about to enter gangland Britain', *Independent*, 21 August

Bernstein, Basil 1975: *Class, Codes and Control* (3 vols, London: Routledge and Kegan Paul)

Bertelson, David 1986: *Snowflakes and Snowdrifts: Individualism and Sexuality in America* (Lanham: University Press of America)

Blackburn, Clare 1991: *Poverty and Health: Working with Families* (Milton Keynes: Oxford University Press)

Blackburn, Joseph C. 1990: *Time Based Competition: The Next Battleground in American Manufacturing* (Burr Ridge, Ill.: Irwin)

Blankenhorn, David 1995: *Fatherless America* (New York: Basic Books)

Blau, Peter M. 1963: *The Dynamics of Bureaucracy* (Chicago: University of Chicago Press)

Blau, Peter M. and Otis Dudley Duncan 1967: *The American Occupational Structure* (New York: Wiley)

Blumler, J. 1986: *Television in the United States: Funding Sources and Programming Consequences* (London: HMSO)

Blyton, Paul 1985: *Changes in Working Time: An International Review* (London: Croom Helm)

Boden, Deirdre and Harvey Molotch 1994: 'The compulsion of proximity', in Deirdre Boden and Roger Friedland (eds), *Nowhere: Space, Time, and Modernity* (Berkeley: University of California Press)

Bogdanor, V. 1990: *Women at the Top* (London: Hansard)

Bonney, Norman 1992: 'Theories of social class and gender', *Sociology Review*, 1

Booth, Charles 1889: *Labour and Life of the People*. Vol. I of *Life and Labour of the People in London* (London: Williams and Norgate)

Booth, William 1970: *In Darkest England and the Way Out* (London: Macmillan. First pub. 1890)

Boswell, John 1995: *The Marriage of Likeness: Same-sex Unions in Pre-modern Europe* (London: Fontana)

Bottomley, A. K. and K. Pease 1986: *Crime and Punishment: Interpreting the Data* (Milton Keynes: Open University Press)

Bourdieu, Pierre 1986: *Distinction: A Social Critique of Judgements of Taste* (London: Routledge and Kegan Paul)

Bourdieu, Pierre 1988: *Language and Symbolic Power* (Cambridge: Polity Press)

Bourdieu, Pierre 1990: *The Logic of Practice* (Cambridge: Polity Press)

Bourdieu, Pierre and Jean-Claude Passeron 1977: *Reproduction: In Education, Society and Culture* (London: Sage)

Bowles, Samuel and Herbert Gintis 1976: *Schooling in Capitalist America* (London: Routledge and Kegan Paul)

Braverman, Harry 1974: *Labour and Monopoly Capital: The Degradation of Work in the Twentieth Century* (New York: Monthly Review Press)

Brennan, Teresa 1988: 'Controversial discussions and

feminist debate', in Naomi Segal and Edward Timms, *The Origins and Evolution of Psychoanalysis* (New Haven, Conn.: Yale University Press)

Brown, Catrina and Karin Jasper (eds) 1993: *Consuming Passions: Feminist Approaches to Eating Disorders and Weight Preoccupations* (Toronto: Second Story Press)

Brownhill, Sue 1990: *Developing London's Docklands: Another Great Planning Disaster?* (London: Chapman)

Brownmiller, Susan 1975: *Against Our Will: Men, Women and Rape* (London: Secker and Warburg)

Buckle, Abigail and David P. Farrington 1984: 'An observational study of shoplifting', *British Journal of Criminology*, 24

Bull, Peter 1983: *Body Movement and Interpersonal Communication* (New York: Wiley)

Burns, E. M. and P. L. Ralph 1974: *World Civilizations* (New York: Norton)

Burt, Martha R. 1992: *Over the Edge: The Growth of Homelessness in the 1980s* (New York: Russell Sage)

Butler, David and Donald Stokes 1974: *Political Change in Britain* (London: Macmillan)

Bynum, Caroline Walker, Steven Harrell and Paula Richman (eds) 1986: *Gender and Religion: On the Complexity of Symbols* (Boston, Mass.: Beacon Press)

Byrd, Max 1978: *London Transformed: Images of the City in the Eighteenth Century* (New Haven, Conn.: Yale University Press)

Campbell, Anne 1986a: *The Girls in the Gang* (Oxford: Blackwell)

Campbell, Anne 1986b: 'Self-reporting of fighting by females', *British Journal of Criminology*, 26

Campbell, Anne and John T. Gibbs (eds) 1986: *Violent Transactions* (Oxford: Blackwell)

Campbell, Beatrix 1993: *Goliath: Britain's Dangerous Places* (London: Methuen)

Capps, Walter H. 1990: *The New Religious Right: Piety, Patriotism, and Politics* (Columbia: University of South Carolina Press)

Carlen, Pat et al. 1985: *Criminal Women: Autobiographical Accounts* (Cambridge: Polity Press)

Carswell, John 1985: *Government and the Universities in Britain: Progress and Performance 1960–1980* (Cambridge: Cambridge University Press)

Castells, Manuel 1977: *The Urban Question: A Marxist Approach* (London: Edward Arnold)

Castells, Manuel 1983: *The City and the Grass Roots: A Cross-cultural Theory of Urban Social Movements* (London: Edward Arnold)

Chapman, Karen 1986: *The Sociology of Schools* (London: Tavistock)

Chigwada, Ruth 1991: 'The policing of black women', in Ellis Cashmore and Eugene McLaughlin, *Out of Order? Policing Black People* (London: Routledge)

Chitty, Clyde 1993: 'The education system transformed', *Sociology Review*, February

Chodorow, Nancy 1978: *The Reproduction of Mothering* (Berkeley: University of California Press)

Chodorow, Nancy 1988: *Psychoanalytic Theory and Feminism* (Cambridge: Polity Press)

Church of England 1985: *Faith in the City: The Report of the Archbishop of Canterbury's Commission on Urban Priority Areas* (London: Christian Action)

CIBA Foundation 1984: *Child Sexual Abuse within the Family* (London: Tavistock)

Cisneros, Henry G. (ed.) 1993: *Interwoven Destinies: Cities and the Nation* (New York: Norton)

Claessen, Henri J. M. and Peter Skalnik 1978: *The Early State* (The Hague: Mouton)

Clark, David and Douglas Haldane 1990: *Wedlocked?*

Intervention and Research in Marriage (Cambridge: Polity)

Clinard, Marshall 1978: *Cities with Little Crime: The Case of Switzerland* (Cambridge: Cambridge University Press)

Cloward, R. and L. Ohlin 1960: *Delinquency and Opportunity* (New York: Free Press)

Cockburn, Cynthia 1991: *In the Way of Women* (London: Macmillan)

Cohn, Norman 1970a: *The Pursuit of the Millennium* (London: Paladin)

Cohn, Norman 1970b: 'Mediaeval millenarianism', in Sylvia L. Thrupp (ed.), *Millennial Dreams in Action: Studies in Revolutionary Religious Movements* (New York: Schocken Books)

Coleman, James S. 1987: 'Families and schools', *Educational Researcher*, 16.6

Coleman, James S., Thomas Hoffer and Sally Kilgore 1981: *Public and Private Schools* (Chicago: National Opinion Research Centre)

Coleman, James S. et al. 1966: *Equality of Educational Opportunity* (Washington DC: US Government Printing Office)

Collins, James and Jerry Porras 1994: *Built to Last* (New York: Century)

Commission on Global Governance 1995: *Our Global Neighbourhood* (Oxford: Oxford University Press)

Coward, Rosalind 1984: *Female Desire: Women's Sexuality Today* (London: Paladin)

Crewe, Ivor 1983: 'The electorate: partisan dealignment ten years on', *Western European Politics*, 6

Crompton, Rosemary and Gareth Jones 1984: *White Collar Proletariat* (London: Macmillan)

Crow, Ben and Mary Thorpe 1988: *Survival and Change in the Third World* (The Open University)

Crow, Graham and Michael Hardey 1992: 'Diversity and ambiguity among lone-parent households in modern Britain', in Catherine Marsh and Sara Arber, *Families and Households: Divisions and Change* (London: Macmillan)

Currell, Melville E. 1974: *Political Woman* (London: Croom Helm)

Davenport, W. 1965: 'Sexual patterns and their regulation in a society of the South West Pacific', in F. Beach (ed.), *Sex and Behaviour* (New York: Wiley)

Davies, Bronwyn 1991: *Frogs and Snails and Feminist Tales* (Sydney: Allen and Unwin)

Davies, James C. 1962: 'Towards a theory of revolution', *American Sociological Review*, 27

Davis, Stanley M. 1988: *2001 Management: Managing the Future Now* (London: Simon and Schuster)

Dertouzos, Michael L. 1989: *Made in America: Regaining the Productive Edge* (Cambridge: MIT Press)

De Witt, Karen 1994: 'Wave of suburban growth is being fed by minorities', *New York Times*, 15 August

Dicken, Peter 1992: *Global Shift*, revised 2nd edn (London: Paul Chapman)

Donaldson, Margaret 1979: *Children's Minds* (New York: Norton)

Dore, Ronald 1973: *British Factory, Japanese Factory: the Origins of National Diversity in Industrial Relations* (London: Allen and Unwin)

Dunn, John 1972: *Modern Revolutions: An Introduction to the Analysis of a Political Phenomenon* (Cambridge: Cambridge University Press)

Durkheim, Émile 1952: *Suicide: A Study in Sociology* (London: Routledge and Kegan Paul. First pub. 1897)

Durkheim, Émile 1976: *The Elementary Forms of the Religious Life* (London: Allen and Unwin. First pub. 1912)

Durkheim, Émile 1982: *The Rules of Sociological Method* (London: Macmillan. First pub. 1895)

Dworkin, Ronald M. 1993: *Life's Dominion: An Argument*

about Abortion, Euthanasia, and Individual Freedom (New York: Knopf)

The Economist 1996: The Pocket World in Figures (London: Economist Publications)

Eibl-Eibesfeldt, I. 1973: 'The expressive behaviour of the deaf-and-blind born', in M. von Cranach and I. Vine (eds), Social Communication and Movement (New York: Academic Press)

Eisenstadt, S. N. 1963: The Political System of Empires (Glencoe: Free Press)

Ekman, Paul and W. V. Friesen 1978: Facial Action Coding System (New York: Consulting Psychologists Press)

Eldridge, John 1993 (ed.), Getting the Message: News, Truth and Power (London: Routledge)

Elliot, Dorinda and Melinda Liu 1995: 'Hostile takeover', Newsweek, 2 October

Elshtain, Jean Bethke 1987: Women and War (New York: Basic Books)

Engbersen, Godfried et al. 1993: Cultures of Unemployment: A Comparative Look at Long-Term Unemployment and Urban Poverty (Boulder, Colo.: Westview)

Ennew, Judith 1986: The Sexual Exploitation of Children (Cambridge: Polity Press)

Erikson, Kai 1994: A New Species of Trouble: Explorations in Disaster, Trauma, and Community (New York: Norton)

Erikson, Robert and John Goldthorpe 1993: The Constant Flux: A Study of Class Mobility in Industrial Societies (Oxford: Clarendon Press)

Estrich, Susan 1987: Real Rape (Cambridge, Mass.: Harvard University Press)

Evans, David J. 1992: 'Left realism and the spatial study of crime', in David J. Evans et al., Crime, Policing and Place: Essays in Environment Criminology (London: Routledge)

Evans-Pritchard, E. E. 1940: The Nuer: A Description of the Modes of Livelihood and Political Institutions of a Nilotic People (Oxford: Clarendon Press)

Evans-Pritchard, E. E. 1956: Nuer Religion (Oxford: Oxford University Press)

Fagan, Jeffrey A., Douglas K. Stewart and Karen V. Hansen 1983: 'Violent men or violent husbands? Background factors and situational correlates', in David Finkelhor et al., The Dark Side of Families: Current Family Violence Research (Beverly Hills, Ca.: Sage)

Feuerbach, Ludwig 1957: The Essence of Christianity (New York: Harper and Row. First pub. 1841)

Field, Frank 1989: Losing Out: The Emergence of Britain's Underclass (Oxford: Blackwell)

Fielding, A. J. 1995: 'Migration and middle class formation in England and Wales 1981–1991', in T. Butler and M. Savage (eds), Social Change and the Middle Classes (London: UCL Press)

Finkelhor, David 1984: Child Sexual Abuse: New Theory and Research (New York: Free Press)

Finkelhor, David and K.Yllo 1982: 'Forced sex in marriage: a preliminary report', Crime and Delinquency, 28

Finley, Moses I. (ed.) 1968: Slavery in Classical Antiquity (Cambridge: Heffer)

Finley, Moses I. 1980: Ancient Slavery and Modern Ideology (London: Chatto and Windus)

Firestone, Shulamith 1971: The Dialectic of Sex (London: Paladin)

Fischer, Claude S. 1984: The Urban Experience (2nd edn, New York: Harcourt Brace Jovanovich)

Flowers, Ronald Barri 1987: Women and Criminality: The Woman as Victim, Offender and Practitioner (New York: Greenwood Press)

Ford, Clellan S. and Frank A. Beach 1951: Patterns of Sexual Behaviour (New York: Harper and Row)

Foucault, Michel 1970: The Order of Things: An Archaeology of the Human Sciences (London: Tavistock)

Foucault, Michel 1978: The History of Sexuality (London: Penguin)

Foucault, Michel 1979: Discipline and Punish (Harmondsworth: Penguin)

Foucault, Michel 1988: 'Technologies of the self', in Luther H. Martin, Huck Gutman and Patrick H. Hutton (eds), Technologies of the Self : A Seminar with Michel Foucault (Amherst: University of Massachusetts Press)

Fraiberg, Selma 1959: The Magic Years: Understanding and Handling the Problems of Early Childhood (New York: Scribner's)

Fraser, Steven (ed.) 1995: The Bell Curve Wars: Race, Intelligence and the Future of America (New York: Basic Books)

Freud, Sigmund 1975: The Psychopathology of Everyday Life (Harmondsworth: Penguin)

Friedlander, Daniel and Gary Burtless 1994: Five Years After: The Long-Term Effects of Welfare-to-Work Programs (New York: Russell Sage)

Fryer, David and Stephen McKenna 1987: 'The laying off of hands – unemployment and the experience of time', in Stephen Fineman (ed.), Unemployment: Personal and Social Consequences (London: Tavistock)

Fryer, Peter 1984: Staying Power: The History of Black People in Britain (London: Pluto Press)

Fukuyama, Francis 1989: 'The end of history?', The National Interest, 16

Fukuyama, Francis 1994: Trust: The Social Virtues and the Creation of Prosperity (London: Hamish Hamilton)

Fussell, Sam W. 1991: Muscle: Confessions of an Unlikely Bodybuilder (New York: Poseidon Press)

Gage, Matilda Joslyn 1980: Women, Church and State (Watertown, Mass.: Persephone Press. First pub. 1893)

Gans, Herbert J. 1962: The Urban Villagers: Group and Class in the Life of Italian-Americans (2nd edn, New York: Free Press)

Gardner, Howard 1993: Multiple Intelligences: The Theory in Practice (New York: Basic Books)

Garfinkel, Harold 1963: 'A conception of, and experiments with, "trust" as a condition of stable concerted actions', in O. J. Harvey (ed.), Motivation and Social Interaction (New York: Ronald Press)

Garfinkel, Harold 1984: Studies in Ethnomethodology (Oxford: Blackwell)

Geary, Dick 1982: European Labour Protest, 1848–1939 (London: Croom Helm)

Gelis, Jacques 1991: History of Childbirth: Fertility, Pregnancy, and Birth in Early Modern Europe (Boston: Northeastern University Press)

Gerbner, George et al. 1979: 'The demonstration of power: violence profile no. 10', Journal of Communication, 29

Gerbner, George et al. 1980: 'The "mainstreaming" of America: violence profile no. 11', Journal of Communication, 30

Gershuny, J. I. and I. D. Miles 1983: The New Service Economy: The Transformation of Employment in Industrial Societies (London: Frances Pinter)

Gibbons, John H. 1990: Trading Around the Clock: Global Securities Markets and Information Technology (Washington D.C.: US Congress)

Giddens, Anthony 1984: The Constitution of Society (Cambridge: Polity Press)

Ginzburg, Carlo 1980: The Cheese and the Worms (London: Routledge and Kegan Paul)

Gissing, George 1973: Demos (Brighton: Harvester. First pub. 1892)

Glasgow Media Group 1976: Bad News (London: Routledge)

Glass, David (ed.) 1954: Social Mobility in Britain (London: Routledge and Kegan Paul)

Glueck, Sheldon W. and Eleanor Glueck 1956: *Physique and Delinquency* (New York: Harper and Row)

Goffman, Erving 1969: *The Presentation of Self in Everyday Life* (Harmondsworth: Penguin)

Goffman, Erving 1971: *Relations in Public: Microstudies of the Public Order* (London: Allen Lane)

Goffman, Erving 1974: *Frame Analysis* (New York: Harper and Row)

Goffman, Erving 1981: *Forms of Talk* (Philadelphia: University of Pennsylvania Press)

Goldsmith, Edward 1988: 'Foreword', in Edward Goldsmith and Nicholas Hilyard, *The Earth Report: Monitoring the Battle for our Environment* (London: Mitchell Beazley)

Goldstein, Paul J. 1979: *Prostitution and Drugs* (Lexington, Mass.: D. C. Heath)

Goldthorpe, John H. 1983: 'Women and class analysis: in defence of the conventional view', *Sociology*, 17

Goldthorpe, John H. and C. Payne 1986: 'Trends in intergenerational class mobility in England and Wales 1972–1983', *Sociology*, 20

Goldthorpe, John H., C. Llewellyn and C. Payne 1980, 1988: *Social Mobility and Class Structure in Modern Britain*, 1st and 2nd edns (Oxford: Oxford University Press)

Goldthorpe, John H. et al. 1968–9: *The Affluent Worker in the Class Structure* (3 vols, Cambridge: Cambridge University Press)

Goleman, Daniel 1996: *Emotional Intelligence: Why It Can Matter More than IQ* (London: Bloomsbury)

Goode, William J. 1963: *World Revolution in Family Patterns* (New York: Free Press)

Goodhardt, G. J., A. S. C. Ehrenberg and M. A. Collins 1987: *The Television Audience: Patterns of Voting* (2nd edn, London: Gower)

Gordon, P. 1986: *Racial Violence and Harassment* (London: Runnymede Trust)

Gorz, André 1982: *Farewell to the Working Class* (London: Pluto)

Gould, Stephen Jay 1995: 'Curveball', in Steven Fraser (ed.), *The Bell Curve Wars: Race, Intelligence and the Future of America* (New York: Basic Books)

Graef, Roger 1989: *Talking Blues* (London: Collins)

Greenblat, Cathy Stein 1983: 'A hit is a hit . . . or is it? Approval and tolerance of the use of physical force by spouses', in David Finkelhor et al., *The Dark Side of Families: Current Family Violence Research* (Beverly Hills, Ca.: Sage)

Gregson, Shaun and Frank Livesey 1993: *Organizations and Management Behaviour* (Oxford: Made Simple Books)

Griffin, Susan 1978: *Rape: The Power of Consciousness* (New York: Harper and Row)

Grint, Keith 1991: *The Sociology of Work* (Cambridge: Polity Press)

Grusky, David B. and Robert M. Hauser 1984: 'Comparative social mobility revisited: models of convergence and divergence in 16 countries', *American Sociological Review*, 49

Gunter, Barrie 1985: *Dimensions of Television Violence* (London: Gower)

Habermas, Jürgen 1987: *Theory of Communicative Action*, 2 vols (Cambridge: Polity Press)

Habermas, Jürgen 1989: *The Structural Transformation of the Public Sphere: An Inquiry into a Category of Bourgeois Society* (Cambridge: Polity Press)

Hagen, John 1988: *Structural Criminology* (Cambridge: Polity Press)

Hall, Edward T. 1959: *The Silent Language* (New York: Doubleday)

Hall, Edward T. 1966: *The Hidden Dimension* (New York: Doubleday)

Hall, Ross Hume 1990: *Health and the Global Environment* (Cambridge: Polity Press)

Hall, Ruth 1985: *Ask Any Woman: A London Enquiry into Rape and Sexual Assault* (Bristol: Falling Wall Press)

Hall, Ruth, Selma James and Judith Kertesz 1984: *The Rapist who Pays the Rent* (2nd edn, Bristol: Falling Wall Press)

Hall, Stuart et al. 1988: 'New times', *Marxism Today*, October

Hammer, Michael and James Champy 1993: *Reengineering the Corporation: A Manifesto for Business Revolution* (London: Nicholas Brealey)

Hamnett, Chris et al. 1990: *Restructuring Britain: The Changing Social Structure* (London: Sage)

Handy, Charles 1994: *The Empty Raincoat: Making Sense of the Future* (London: Hutchinson)

Harding, Vincent 1980: *The Other American Revolution* (Los Angeles: University of California Center for Afro-American Studies, Culture and Society Monograph Series, vol. 4)

Hardyment, Christina 1987: *Labour Saved?* (Cambridge: Polity Press)

Harrison, Martin 1985: *TV News: Whose Bias?* (Hermitage: Policy Journals)

Harrison, Paul 1983: *Inside the Inner City: Life under the Cutting Edge* (Harmondsworth: Penguin)

Hartley, E. 1946: *Problems in Prejudice* (New York: Kings Crown Press)

Harvey, David 1973: *Social Justice and the City* (Oxford: Blackwell)

Harvey, David 1982: *The Limits to Capital* (Oxford: Blackwell)

Harvey, David 1985: *Consciousness and the Urban Experience: Studies in the History and Theory of Capitalist Urbanization* (Oxford: Blackwell)

Hawley, Amos H. 1950: *Human Ecology: A Theory of Community Structure* (New York: Ronald Press)

Hawley, Amos 1968: 'Human ecology', *International Encyclopaedia of Social Science*, vol. 4 (Glencoe: Free Press)

Heath, Anthony 1981: *Social Mobility* (London: Fontana)

Heath, Anthony et al. 1986: *How Britain Votes* (Oxford: Pergamon Press)

Held, David 1987: *Models of Democracy* (Cambridge: Polity Press)

Henslin, James M. and Mae A. Briggs 1971: 'Dramaturgical desexualization: the sociology of the vaginal examination', in Henslin (ed.), *Studies in the Sociology of Sex* (New York: Appleton-Century-Crofts)

Heritage, John 1984: *Garfinkel and Ethnomethodology* (Cambridge: Polity Press)

Herrnstein, Richard J. and Charles Murray 1994: *The Bell Curve: Intelligence and Class Structure in American Life* (New York: Free Press)

Hindelang, Michael J. et al. 1978: *Violence of Personal Crime* (Cambridge: Ballinger)

HMSO (Her Majesty's Stationery Office) 1992: *Social Trends* 22 (London: HMSO)

HMSO (Her Majesty's Stationery Office) 1996: *Social Trends* 26 (London: HMSO)

Hodge, Robert and David Tripp 1986: *Children and Television: A Semiotic Approach* (Cambridge: Polity Press)

Homans, Hilary 1987: 'Man-made myth: the reality of being a woman scientist in the NHS', in Anne Spencer and David Podmore (eds), *In a Man's World: Essays on Women in Male-Dominated Professions* (London: Tavistock)

hooks, bell 1981: *Ain't I a Woman: Black Women and Feminism* (London: Pluto Press)

Hughes, Gordon 1991: 'Taking crime seriously? A critical analysis of New Left Realism', *Sociology Review, 1*

Hugill, Barry 1996: 'Death of the comprehensives', *Observer*, 7 January

Huntington, Samuel 1990: 'Democratisation and security in Eastern Europe', in P. Volten, *Uncertain Futures: Eastern Europe and Democracy* (New York: Institute for East–West Security Studies)

Huntington, Samuel 1993: 'One clash of civilizations?', *Foreign Affairs*, 72.3

Hutchinson Gallup 1994: *INFO 1995* (Oxford: Helicon)

Hyman, Richard 1984: *Strikes* (2nd edn, London: Fontana)

Illich, Ivan D. 1973: *Deschooling Society* (Harmondsworth: Penguin)

Innis, Harold A. 1950: *Empire and Communications* (Oxford: Oxford University Press)

Innis, Harold A. 1951: *The Bias of Communication* (Toronto: Toronto University Press)

Iyer, Pico 1989: *Video Nights in Katmandu* (New York: Vintage)

James, William 1890: *Principles of Psychology* (New York: Holt, Rinehart and Winston)

Janus, S. S. and D. H. Heid Bracey 1980: 'Runaways: pornography and prostitution' (New York: mimeo)

Jencks, Christopher 1994: *The Homeless* (Cambridge, Mass.: Harvard University Press)

Jencks, Christopher et al. 1972: *Inequality: A Reassessment of the Effects of Family and School in America* (New York: Basic Books)

Jenkins, Simon 1987: 'Eve versus the Adams of the Church', *Sunday Times*, 6 September

Jensen, Arthur 1967: 'How much can we boost IQ and scholastic achievement?', *Harvard Educational Review*, 29

Jensen, Arthur 1979: *Bias in Mental Testing* (New York: Free Press)

Johnson, Richard 1991: 'A new road to serfdom? A critical history of the 1988 Act', in Education Group II, *Education Limited: Schooling, Training and the New Right in England since 1979* (London: Unwin Hyman)

Jones, Trevor 1993: *Britain's Ethnic Minorities* (London: Policy Studies Institute)

Jopke, Christian 1995: 'Multiculturalism and immigration: a comparison of the United States, Germany and Great Britain', mimeo

Jordan, Winthrop 1968: *White Over Black* (Chapel Hill: University of North Carolina Press)

Kamin, Leon J. 1977: *The Science and Politics of IQ* (Harmondsworth: Penguin)

Kasarda, John D. and Morris Janowitz 1974: 'Community attachment in mass society', *American Sociological Review*, 39

Katz, Sedelle and Mary Ann Mazur 1979: *Understanding the Rape Victim: A Synthesis of Research Findings* (London: Wiley)

Kautsky, John J. 1982: *The Politics of Aristocratic Empires* (Chapel Hill: University of North Carolina Press)

Kavanagh, Dennis A. 1987: *Thatcherism and British Politics* (Oxford: Oxford University Press)

Keane, Fergal 1995: *The Bondage of Fear: A Journey through the Last White Empire* (London: Penguin)

Kellner, Peter 1992: 'Does sex matter in the polling booth?', *Independent*, 18 March

Kelly, Kevin 1996: 'Off the desktop on to the Web', in *The Economist: The World in 1996* (London: The Economist)

Kelly, Liz 1988: *Surviving Sexual Violence* (Cambridge: Polity Press)

Kelsey, Tim 1996: 'I want to live for ever', *Sunday Times News Review*, 7 January

Kenway, Jane et al. 1995: 'Pulp fictions? Education, markets and the information superhighway' (revised version of Kenway, 'Reality bytes: education, markets and the information superhighway', *Australian Educational Reasearcher*, 22

Kesselman, Mark et al. 1987: *European Politics in Transition* (Lexington, Mass.: D. C. Heath)

Kidron, Michael and Ronald Segal 1995: *The State of the World Atlas*, 5th edn (London: Penguin)

Kingdom, John 1991: *Government and Politics in Britain* (Cambridge: Polity Press)

Kinsey, Alfred C. et al. 1948: *Sexual Behaviour in the Human Male* (Philadelphia: W. B. Saunders)

Kinsey, Alfred C. et al. 1953: *Sexual Behaviour in the Human Female* (Philadelphia: W. B. Saunders)

Knorr-Cetina, Karen and Aaron V. Cicourel (eds) 1981: *Advances in Social Theory and Methodology: Towards an Interpretation of Micro- and Macro-Sociologies* (London: Routledge and Kegan Paul)

Koenigsburger, H. G. 1987: *Mediaeval Europe, 400–1500* (London: Longman)

Kogan, Maurice, with David Kogan 1988: *The Attack on Higher Education* (London: Kogan Page)

Krupat, Edward 1985: *People in Cities: The Urban Environment and its Effects* (Cambridge: Cambridge University Press)

Kübler-Ross, Elisabeth 1987: *Living with Death and Dying* (London: Souvenir Press)

Kumar, Uinod 1993: *Poverty and Inequality in the UK and the Effects on Children* (London: National Children's Bureau)

La Fontaine, Jean 1990: *Child Sexual Abuse* (Cambridge: Polity Press)

Laing, Dave and Phil Hardy 1990: *The Faber Companion to Twentieth Century Popular Music* (London: Faber and Faber)

Landes, David S. 1969: *The Unbound Prometheus* (Cambridge: Cambridge University Press)

Lane, Harlan 1976: *The Wild Boy of Aveyron* (Cambridge, Mass.: Harvard University Press)

Lane, James B. 1974: *Jacob A. Riis and the American City* (London: Kennikat Press)

Lantenari, Vittorio 1963: *The Religions of the Oppressed: A Study of Modern Messianic Cults* (New York: Knopf)

Laumann, Edward O. et al. 1994: *The Social Organization of Sexuality: Sexual Practices in the United States* (Chicago: University of Chicago Press)

Lazarsfeld, Paul F., Bernard Berelson and Hazel Gaudet 1948: *The People's Choice* (New York: Columbia University Press)

Le Grand, Julian 1994: 'Evaluating the NHS reforms', London School of Economics, mimeo

Leadbetter, Charles and Edward Helmore 1995: 'This man is twice as big as Murdoch', *Independent*, 3 August.

Lee, Laurie 1965: *Cider with Rosie* (London: Hogarth Press)

Lee, R. B. 1968: 'What hunters do for a living or, how to make out on scarce resources', in R. B. Lee and I. de Vore (eds), *Man the Hunter* (Chicago: Aldine)

Lee, R. B. 1969: '!Kung Bushman subsistence: an input–output analysis', in A. P. Vayda (ed.), *Environment and Cultural Behaviour* (New York: Natural History Press)

Lee, R. B. and I. de Vore (eds) 1968: *Man the Hunter* (Chicago: Aldine)

Lees, Andrew 1985: *Cities Perceived: Urban Society in European and American Thought, 1820–1940* (New York: Columbia University Press)

Leiuffsrud, Hakon and Alison Woodward 1987: 'Women at class crossroads: repudiating conventional theories of family class', *Sociology*, 21

Lemert, Edwin 1972: *Human Deviance, Social Problems and Social Control* (Englewood Cliffs, NJ: Prentice-Hall)

Leventhal, Paul and Sharon Tanzer 1991: 'Fear and folly in a deadly trade', *Guardian*, 4 October

Lewontin, Richard 1982: *Human Diversity* (London: W. H. Freeman)

Lewontin, Richard C. 'Sex, lies and social science', *New York Review of Books*, 20 April

Lie, Suzanne S. and Virginia E. O'Leary 1990: *Storming the Tower: Women in the Academic World* (London: Kogan Page)

Liebert, Robert M., Joyce N. Sprafkin and M. A. S. Davidson 1982: *The Early Window: Effects of Television on Children and Youth* (London: Pergamon Press)

Lipset, Seymour Martin and Reinhard Bendix 1959: *Social Mobility in Industrial Society* (Berkeley: University of California Press)

Logan, John R. and Harvey L. Molotch 1987: *Urban Fortunes: The Political Economy of Place* (Berkeley: University of California Press)

Lorber, Judith 1994: *Paradoxes of Gender* (New Haven: Yale University Press)

Lull, James 1995: *Media, Communication, Culture* (Cambridge: Polity Press)

Lyon, Christina and Peter de Cruz 1993: *Child Abuse* (London: Family Law)

Lyon, David 1994: *The Electronic Eye: The Rise of Surveillance Society* (Cambridge: Polity Press)

Lyotard, Jean-François 1985: *The Postmodern Condition* (Minneapolis: University Minnesota Press)

Macgregor, Susanne and Ben Pimlott 1991: 'Action and inaction in the cities', in Macgregor and Pimlott, *Tackling the Inner Cities: The 1980s Reviewed, Prospects for the 1990s* (Oxford: Clarendon Press)

MccGwire, Michael 1996: 'Why do we need to eliminate nuclear weapons?', paper presented to the Canberra Commission, Canberra

McLanahan, Sara and Gary Sandefur 1994: *Growing up with a Single Parent: What Hurts, What Helps* (Cambridge: Harvard University Press)

McLuhan, Marshall 1964: *Understanding Media* (London: Routledge and Kegan Paul)

McNeill, William H. 1983: *The Pursuit of Power: Technology, Armed Force and Society since AD 1000* (Oxford: Blackwell)

MacPike, Loralee 1989: *There's Something I've Been Meaning to Tell You* (Tallahassee: Naiad)

Malinowski, Bronislaw 1982: '*Magic, Science and Religion', and Other Essays* (London: Souvenir Press)

Mann, Michael 1986: *The Sources of Social Power*. Vol. I: *A History of Power from the Beginning to 1760* (Cambridge: Cambridge University Press)

Marable, Manning 1991: *Race, Reform and Rebellion: The Second Reconstruction in Black America, 1945–1990* (London: Macmillan)

Marshall, Gordon et al. 1988: *Social Class in Modern Britain* (London: Hutchinson)

Marx, Karl 1970: *Capital*, vol. I (London: Lawrence and Wishart. First pub. 1864)

Marx, Karl and Friedrich Engels 1968: *Selected Works in One Volume* (London: Lawrence and Wishart)

Mead, George Herbert 1934: *Mind, Self and Society* (Chicago: University of Chicago Press)

Merton, Robert K. 1957: *Social Theory and Social Structure* (revised edn, Glencoe: Free Press)

Michels, Roberto 1967: *Political Parties* (New York: Free Press. First pub. 1911)

Mills, C. Wright 1970: *The Sociological Imagination* (Harmondsworth: Penguin)

Miner, Horace 1956: 'Body ritual among the Nacirema', *American Anthropologist*, 58

Mitchell, Juliet 1973: *Psychoanalysis and Feminism* (London: Allen Lane)

Mohan, John 1991: 'Privatisation in the British health sector: a challenge to the NHS?', in Jonathan Gabe et al., *The Sociology of the Health Service* (London: Routledge)

Molotch, Harvey and Deirdre Boden 1985: 'Talking social structure: discourse, dominance and the Watergate hearings', *American Sociological Review*, 50

Money, John and Anke A. Ehrhardt 1972: *Man and Woman/Boy and Girl* (Baltimore, Md.: Johns Hopkins University Press)

Morris, Jan 1974: *Conundrum* (Oxford: Oxford University Press)

Morris, Lydia 1993: *Dangerous Classes: The Underclass and Social Citizenship* (London: Routledge)

Moynihan, Daniel P. 1965: *The Negro Family: A Case for National Action* (Washington DC: US Government Printing Office)

Mumford, Lewis 1973: *Interpretations and Forecasts* (London: Secker and Warburg)

Murdoch, Rupert 1994: 'The century of networking', *Eleventh Annual John Bonython Lecture*, Centre for Independent Studies, Australia

Murdock, George 1949: *Social Structure* (New York: Macmillan)

Murray, Charles A. 1984: *Losing Ground: American Social Policy, 1950–1980* (New York: Basic Books)

Murray, Charles 1990: *The Emerging British Underclass* (London: Institute of Economic Affairs)

Naisbitt, John 1995: *Global Paradox* (London: Breadley)

Najman, Jake M. 1993: 'Health and poverty: past, present, and prospects for the future', *Social Science and Medicine*, 36.2

Negroponte, Nicholas 1995: *Being Digital* (London: Hodder and Stoughton)

Neuberger, Julia 1991: *Whatever's Happening to Women? Promises, Practices and Pay Offs* (London: Kyle Cathie)

Newman, Philip L. 1965: *Knowing the Gururumba* (New York: Holt, Rinehart and Winston)

Nicoll, Ruaridh 1995: 'Gang babes love to kill', *Observer*, 12 November

Noel, Gerard 1980: *The Anatomy of the Catholic Church* (London: Hodder and Stoughton)

Oakes, Jeannie 1985: *Keeping Track: How Schools Structure Inequality* (New Haven, Conn.: Yale University Press)

Oakes, Jeanne 1990: *Multiplying Inequalities: The Effects of Race, Social Class, and Tracking on Opportunities to Learn Mathematics and Science* (Santa Monica: Rand)

Oakley, Ann 1974: *The Sociology of Housework* (Oxford: Martin Robertson)

Ouchi, William G. 1979: 'A conceptual framework for the design of organizational control mechanisms', *Management Science*, 25

Ouchi, William G. 1981: *Theory Z: How American Business Can Meet the Japanese Challenge* (Reading, Mass.: Addison-Wesley)

Owen, D. 1992: *Ethnic Minorities in Britain: Settlement Patterns*, 1991 Census Statistical Paper no. 1, National Ethnic Minority Data Archive

Owen, D. 1993: *Ethnic Minorities in Britain: Economic Characteristics*, 1991 Census Statistical Paper no. 3, National Ethnic Minority Data Archive

Pahl, R. E. 1984: *Divisions of Labour* (Oxford: Blackwell)

Park, Robert E. 1952: *Human Communities: The City and Human Ecology* (New York: Free Press)

Parkin, Frank 1971: *Class Inequality and Political Order* (London: McGibbon and Kee)

Parsons, Talcott 1952: *The Social System* (London: Tavistock)

Parsons, Talcott 1966: *Societies: Evolutionary and Comparative Perspectives* (Englewood Cliffs, NJ: Prentice-Hall)

Parten, Mildred 1932: 'Social play among preschool children', *Journal of Abnormal and Social Psychology*, 27

Paul, Diana Y. 1985: *Women in Buddhism: Images of the Feminine in the Mahayana Tradition* (Berkeley: University of California Press)

Perlmutter, H. V. 1972: 'The development of nations, unions and firms as worldwide institutions', in H. Gunter (ed.), *Transnational Industrial Relations* (New York: St Martin's Press)

Philo, Greg 1991: 'Seeing is believing', *Social Studies Review*, May

Pilkington, Edward 1992: 'Hapless democratic experiment', *Guardian*, 28 January

Player, E. 1991: 'Women and crime in the city', in David Downes, *Crime in the City* (London: Routledge)

Plummer, John 1979: 'Racism: built into immigration control', *Searchlight*, no. 45

Plummer, Kenneth 1975: *Sexual Stigma: An Interactive Account* (London: Routledge and Kegan Paul)

President's Commission on Organized Crime 1985 and 1986: *Records of Hearings, March 14, 1984 and June 24–26, 1985* (Washington DC: US Government Printing Office)

Provenzo, Eugene 1991: *Video Kids: Making Sense of Nintendo* (Cambridge, Mass.: Harvard University Press)

Purnell, James and Richard Collins 1995: 'An evaluation of UK ownership rules', Institute of Public Policy Research mimeo

Ralph, Philip Lee et al. 1991: *World Civilizations*, 8th edn, vol. 2 (New York: Norton)

Rapoport, Robert and Rhona Rapoport 1982: 'British families in transition', in R. N. Rapoport et al., *Families in Britain* (London: Routledge and Kegan Paul)

Raynsford, Nick 1991: 'Housing conditions, problems and policies', in Susanne Macgregor and Ben Pimlott, *Tackling the Inner Cities: The 1980s Reviewed, Prospects for the 1990's* (Oxford: Clarendon Press)

Reid, Ivan et al. 1991: 'The education of the elite', in G. Walford, *Private Schooling: Tradition, Change and Diversity* (Oxford: Chapman)

Reid, Mike 1992: 'Mexico's vale of tears', *Guardian*, 27 March

Richards, Martin 1995: 'The interests of children at divorce', Centre for Family Research, University of Cambridge, mimeo

Richards, Martin and Paul Light (eds) 1986: *Children of Social Worlds* (Cambridge: Polity Press)

Riddell, Peter 1985: *The Thatcher Government* (Oxford: Blackwell)

Riis, Jacob A. 1957: *How the Other Half Lives: Studies among the Tenements of New York* (New York: Dover. First pub. 1890)

Ross, Arthur M. 1954: 'The natural history of the strike', in Arthur Kornhauser, Robert Dubin and Arthur M. Ross, *Industrial Conflict* (New York: McGraw-Hill)

Ross, Arthur M. and P. T. Hartman 1960: *Changing Patterns of Industrial Conflict* (New York: Wiley)

Rossides, Daniel W. 1990: *Social Stratification: The American Class System in Comparative Perspective* (Englewood Cliffs: Prentice Hall)

Rubin, Lillian 1990: *Erotic Wars: What Happened to the Sexual Revolution?* (New York: Farrar)

Rubin, Lillian B. 1994: *Families on the Fault Line* (New York: HarperCollins)

Rubinstein, W. D. 1986: *Wealth and Inequality in Britain* (London: Faber and Faber)

Russell, Diana 1984: *Sexual Exploitation: Rape, Child Abuse and Sexual Harassment* (Beverly Hills, Ca.: Sage)

Ryan, Tom 1985: 'The roots of masculinity', in Andy Metcalf and Martin Humphries (eds), *Sexuality of Men* (London: Pluto)

Sabel, Charles F. 1982: *Work and Politics: The Division of Labour in Industry* (Cambridge: Cambridge University Press)

Sahlins, Marshall 1972: *Stone Age Economics* (Chicago: Aldine)

Sassen, Saskia 1991: *The Global City: New York, London, Tokyo* (Princeton: Princeton University Press)

Saussure, Ferdinand de 1974: *Course in General Linguistics* (London: Fontana)

Sayers, Janet 1986: *Sexual Contradiction: Psychology, Psychoanalysis and Feminism* (London: Tavistock)

Scarman, Leslie George 1982: *The Scarman Report* (Harmondsworth: Penguin)

Schiller, Herbert I. 1989: *Culture Inc.: The Corporate Takeover of Public Expression* (New York: Oxford University Press)

Schiller, Herbert I. 1991: 'Not yet the post-imperialist era', *Critical Studies in Mass Communications*, 8

Schmitter, Philippe C. 1991: 'The European Community as an emergent and novel form of political domination', Working Paper of the Centre for Advanced Studies in the Social Sciences, Madrid

Scott, John 1991: *Who Rules Britain?* (Cambridge: Polity Press)

Scriven, Jeannie 1984: 'Women at work in Sweden', in Marilyn J. Davidson and Cary L. Cooper (eds), *Working Women: An International Survey* (New York: Wiley)

Segura, Denise A. and Jennifer L, Pierce 1993: 'Chicana/o family structure and gender personality: Chodorow, familism, and psychoanalytic sociology revisited', *Signs*, 19

Sennett, Richard 1993: *The Conscience of the Eye: The Design and Social Life of Cities* (London: Faber and Faber)

Shattuck, Roger 1980: *The Forbidden Experiment: The Story of the Wild Boy of Aveyron* (New York: Farrar, Straus and Giroux)

Sheldon, William A. 1949: *Varieties of Delinquent Youth* (New York: Harper)

Shepherd, Gill 1987: 'Rank, gender and homosexuality: Mombasa as a key to understanding sexual options', in Pat Caplan (ed.), *The Social Construction of Sexuality* (London: Tavistock)

Sinclair, Peter 1987: *Unemployment: Economic Theory and Evidence* (Oxford: Blackwell)

Skocpol, Theda 1979: *States and Social Revolutions: A Comparative Analysis of France, Russia and China* (Cambridge: Cambridge University Press)

Smeeding, Timothy M. 1990: *Poverty, Inequality, and Income Distribution in Comparative Perspective* (New York: Harvester)

Smith, David J. and Stephen Small 1983: *A Group of Young Black People*, vol. 2 of *Police and People in London* (London: Policy Studies Institute)

Smith, Donna 1990: *Stepmothering* (London: Harvester)

Solomos, John and Tim Rackett 1991: 'Policing and urban unrest: rotten constitution and policy response', in Ellis Cashmore and Eugene McLaughlin, *Out of Order? Policing Black People* (London: Routledge)

Sorokin, Pitirim A. 1927: *Social Mobility* (New York: Harper)

Sreberny-Mohammadi, Annabelle 1992: 'Media integration in the Third World', in B. Gronbeck et al., *Media, Consciousness and Culture* (London: Sage)

Stanton, Elizabeth Cady 1985: *The Woman's Bible: The Original Feminist Attack on the Bible* (Edinburgh: Polygon Books. First pub. 1895)

Stanworth, Michelle 1984: 'Women and class analysis: a reply to John Goldthorpe', *Sociology*, 18

Stark, Rodney and William Sims Bainbridge 1985: *The Future of Religion: Secularization, Revival and Cult Formation* (Berkeley: University of California Press)

Statham, June 1986: *Daughters and Sons: Experiences of Non-sexist Childraising* (Oxford: Blackwell)

Stone, Lawrence 1977: *The Family, Sex and Marriage in England, 1500–1800* (London: Weidenfeld and Nicolson)

Sullivan, Andrew 1995: *Virtually Normal: An Argument about Homosexuality* (London: Picador)

Suransky, Valerie P. 1982: *The Erosion of Childhood* (Chicago: University of Chicago Press)

Sutherland, Edwin H. 1949: *Principles of Criminology* (Chicago: Lippincott)

Swann Committee 1985: *Education for All: Report of the Committee into the Education of Ethnic Minority Children* (London: HMSO)

Swartz, S. 1985: *Sugar Plantations in the Formation of Brazilian Society: Bahia, 1550–1835* (Cambridge: Cambridge University Press)

Sydie, R. A. 1987: *Natural Women, Cultured Men: A Feminist Perspective on Sociological Theory* (New York: Methuen)

Taylor, Steve 1992: 'Measuring child abuse', *Sociology Review*, 1

Thomas, W. I. and Florian Znaniecki 1966: *The Polish Peasant in Europe and America* (New York: Dover. First pub. in 5 vols 1918–20)

Thompson, John B. 1990: *Ideology and Modern Culture* (Cambridge: Polity Press)

Thompson, John B. 1995: *The Media and Modernity: A Social Theory of the Media* (Cambridge: Polity Press)

Thurow, Lester 1993: *Head to Head: The Coming Economic Battle among Japan, Europe, and America* (New York: Morrow)

Tilly, Charles 1978: *From Mobilization to Revolution* (Reading, Mass.: Addison-Wesley)

Tinbergen, Niko 1974: *The Study of Instinct* (Oxford: Oxford University Press)

Tizard, Barbara and Martin Hughes 1984: *Young Children Learning, Talking and Thinking at Home and at School* (London: Fontana)

Tough, Joan 1976: *Listening to Children Talking* (London: Ward Lock Educational)

Touraine, Alain 1974: *The Post-industrial Society* (London: Wildwood)

Troeltsch, Ernst 1981: *The Social Teaching of the Christian Churches* (2 vols, Chicago: University of Chicago Press)

Trowler, Paul 1994: *Investigating the Media* (London: Unwin Hyman)

Turnbull, Colin 1983: *The Mbuti Pygmies: Change and Adaptation* (New York: Holt, Rinehart and Winston)

Turner, Ted 1994: 'The mission thing', *Index on Censorship*, 23

Tuttle, Lisa 1986: *Encyclopedia of Feminism* (London: Longman)

UNICEF 1987: *The State of the World's Children* (Oxford: Oxford University Press)

van den Berghe, Pierre L. 1970: *Race and Ethnicity: Essays in Comparative Sociology* (New York: Basic Books)

van Gennep, Arnold 1977: *The Rites of Passage* (London: Routledge and Kegan Paul. First pub. 1908.

Vass, Anthony A. 1990: *Alternatives to Prison: Punishment, Custody and the Community* (London: Sage)

Vaughan, Diane 1986: *Uncoupling: Turning Points in Intimate Relationships* (Oxford: Oxford University Press)

Verney, Tim 1992: 'Women still face work inequality', *Cambridge Evening News*, 20 March

Viorst, Judith 1987: 'And the prince knelt down and tried to put the glass slipper on Cinderella's foot', in Jack Zipes, *Don't Bet on the Prince: Contemporary Feminist Fairy Tales in North America and England* (London: Methuen)

Vischer, Emily B. and John S. Vischer 1979: *A Guide to Working with Step-parents and Step-children* (Secaucus, NJ: Citadel Press)

Waitzkin, Howard 1986: *The Second Sickness: Contradictions of Capitalist Health Care* (Chicago: University of Chicago Press)

Walby, Sylvia A. 1986: 'Gender, class and stratification: toward a new approach', in Rosemary Crompton and

Michael Mann (eds), *Gender and Stratification* (Oxford: Blackwell)

Walford, Geoffrey 1993: 'Education and private schools', *Sociology Review*, November

Walker, Carol 1994: 'Managing poverty', *Sociology Review*, April

Walker, Martin 1994: 'Meat on the table', *Guardian*, 21 July

Walker, Nick 1995: 'Could you be a fitness junkie?', *Independent*, 4 December

Wallerstein, Judith S. and Sandra Blakeslee 1989: *Second Chances: Men, Women, and Children a Decade after Divorce* (New York: Ticknor and Fields)

Wallerstein, Judith S. and Joan Berlin Kelly 1980: *Surviving the Break-Up: How Children and Parents Cope with Divorce* (New York: Basic Books)

Wallis, Roy 1976: *The Road to Total Freedom: A Sociological Analysis of Scientology* (London: Heinemann)

Wallis, Roy 1987: 'My secret life: dilemmas of integrity in the conduct of field research', in Ragnhild Kristensen and Ole Riis, *Religiose Minoriteter* (Aarhus: Aarhus Universitetsfarlag)

Watson, Peggy 1992: 'Eastern Europe's silent revolution: gender' (Cambridge: mimeo)

Webb, Rob and Hal Westergaard 1991: 'Social stratification, culture and education', *Sociology Review*, 1

Weber, Max 1951: *The Religion of China* (New York: Free Press)

Weber, Max 1952: *Ancient Judaism* (New York: Free Press)

Weber, Max 1958: *The Religion of India* (New York: Free Press)

Weber, Max 1963: *The Sociology of Religion* (Boston, Mass.: Beacon)

Weber, Max 1976: *The Protestant Ethic and the Spirit of Capitalism* (London: Allen and Unwin. First pub. 1904–5)

Weeks, Jeffrey 1986: *Sexuality* (London: Methuen)

Weitzman, Lenore et al. 1972: 'Sexual socialization in picture books for preschool children', *American Journal of Sociology*, 77

Wells, John 1995: *Crime and Unemployment* (London: Employment Policy Institute)

West, Candace and Don Zimmerman 1987: 'Doing gender', *Gender and Society*, 1 (June)

White, Michael and Malcolm Trevor 1983: *Under Japanese Management: The Experience of British Workers* (London: Heinemann)

Widom, Cathy Spatz and Joseph P. Newman 1985: 'Characteristics of non-institutionalized psychopaths', in David P. Farrington and John Gunn, *Aggression and Dangerousness* (Chichester: Wiley)

Wilkinson, Helen 1994: *No Turning Back* (London: Demos)

Wilkinson, Helen and Geoff Mulgan 1995: *Freedom's Children: Work, Relationships and Politics for 18–34 year olds in Britain Today* (London: Demos)

Will, J., P. Self and N. Datan 1976: 'Maternal behaviour and perceived sex of infant', *American Journal of Orthopsychiatry*, 46

Willis, Paul 1977: *Learning to Labour: How Working Class Kids Get Working Class Jobs* (London: Saxon House)

Wilson, Bryan 1982: *Religion in Sociological Perspective* (Oxford: Oxford University Press)

Wilson, Edward O. 1975: *Sociobiology: The New Synthesis* (Cambridge, Mass.: Harvard University Press)

Wilson, Edward O. 1978: *On Human Nature* (Cambridge, Mass.: Harvard University Press)

Wilson, William Julius 1978: *The Declining Significance of Race: Blacks and Changing American Institutions* (Chicago: University of Chicago Press)

Winn, Marie 1983: *Children Without Childhood* (New York: Pantheon)

Wirth, Louis 1938: 'Urbanism as a way of life', *American Journal of Sociology*, 44

Wolfgang, Marvin 1958: *Patterns of Homicide* (Philadelphia: University of Pennsylvania Press)

World Bank 1994: *World Development Report* (Oxford: Oxford University Press)

Worrall, Anne 1990: *Offending Women: Female Lawbreakers and the Criminal Justice System* (London: Routledge)

Worsley, Peter 1970: *The Trumpet Shall Sound: A Study of 'Cargo Cults' in Melanesia* (London: Paladin)

Worsley, Peter 1984: *The Three Worlds: Culture and World Development* (London: Weidenfeld and Nicolson)

Wright, Erik Olin 1978: *Class, Crisis and the State* (London: New Left Books)

Wright, Erik Olin 1985: *Classes* (London: Verso)

Wuthnow, Robert 1993: *Christianity in the Twenty-First Century: Reflections on the Challenges Ahead* (New York: Oxford University Press)

Young, Jock 1988: 'Recent developments in criminology', in Michael Haralambos, *Developments in Sociology*, vol. 4

Young, Michael and Tom Schuller 1991: *Life After Work: The Arrival of the Ageless Society* (London: Harper Collins)

Zammuner, Vanda Lucia 1987: 'Children's sex-role stereotypes: a cross-cultural analysis', in Phillip Shaver and Clyde Hendrick, *Sex and Gender* (London: Sage)

Zeitlin, Irving 1984: *Ancient Judaism: Biblical Criticism from Max Weber to the Present* (Cambridge: Polity Press)

Zeitlin, Irving 1988: *The Historical Jesus* (Cambridge: Polity Press)

Zerubavel, Eviatar 1979: *Patterns of Time in Hospital Life* (Chicago: University of Chicago Press)

Zerubavel, Eviatar 1982: 'The standardization of time: a sociohistorical perspective', *American Journal of Sociology*, 88

Zimbardo, Philip 1972: 'Pathology of imprisonment', *Society*, 9

Zubaida, Sami 1996: 'How successful is the Islamic Republic in Islamizing Iran?', in J. Beinin and J. Stork (eds), *Political Islam: Essays from the Middle East Report* (Berkeley: University of California Press)

INDEX